# The Exim SMTP Mail Server

# The Exim SMTP Mail Server

## Official guide for Release 4

**Philip Hazel**

**UIT Cambridge**

**Cambridge, England**

Published by UIT Cambridge, PO Box 145, Cambridge CB4 1GQ, England.

Printed and bound in the UK by Biddles Ltd of Guildford and King's Lynn.

10 9 8 7 6 5 4 3 2 1

ISBN 0-9544529-0-9

# Contents

# Preface

In 1995, the central servers at the University of Cambridge were running a variety of mail transfer agents, including Sendmail, Smail 3, and PP. Some years before, I had converted the systems whose mail I managed from Sendmail to Smail, to make it easier to handle the special requirements of the early 1990s in UK academic networking during the transition from a private X.25-based network to the Internet. By 1995, the transition was complete, and it was time to move on.

Up to that time, the Internet had been a pretty friendly place, and there was little need to take many precautions against hostile acts. Most sites ran open mail relays, for example. It was clear, however, that this situation was changing and that new requirements were arising. I had done some modifications to the code of Smail, but by then it was eight-year-old code, written in prestandard C, and originally designed for use in a very different environment that involved a lot of support for UUCP. I therefore decided to see if I could build a new MTA from scratch, taking the basic philosophy of Smail and extending it, but leaving out the UUCP support, which was not needed in our environment. Because I wasn't exactly sure what the outcome would be, I called it *EXperimental Internet Mailer* (Exim).

One of my colleagues in Computer Science got wind of what I was doing, begged for an evaluation copy, and promptly put it into service, even before I was running it on my hosts. He started telling others about it, so I began putting releases on an FTP site and answering email about it. The early releases were never "announced"; they just spread by word of mouth. After some time, a UK ISP volunteered to run a web site and mailing list, and it has continued to grow from there. There has been a continuous stream of comments and suggestions, and there are far more facilities in current releases than I ever planned at the start.

Although I make a point of maintaining a comprehensive reference manual, one thing that was lacking for some time was introductory and tutorial material. I kept hoping that somebody else would write something, but in the end I was asked to write a book myself. This first book described Exim 3, and was published by O'Reilly.

With the advent of Exim 4, extensive revision was required because Exim 4 differs from Exim 3 in a number of fundamental ways, and the result is this new book. I have not attempted to cover both versions in a single book; there are too many differences, and it would make for a very long book which would be especially confusing to newcomers. If you are still using Exim 3, you need a copy of the earlier book.

# Who should read this book

In these days of frequent network abuse and high volumes of junk mail, anybody who is administering a mail server needs to have a basic understanding of how Internet mail works, and how their server processes it. This applies as much to small personal hosts as it does to large server farms.

If you are running, or thinking about running, an Exim server of any size, this book will give you a grounding in the way Exim works. In addition, it contains many examples of particular ways in which Exim can be configured to support specific mail processing requirements.

I hope this book will make life easier for those who find the reference manual difficult to work with on its own.

# Organization of the book

After a short overview chapter, this book continues with a general introduction to Internet email, because this is a subject that does not seem to be well covered elsewhere. The rest of the book is devoted to explaining how Exim works, and how you can use its configuration to control what it does. Here is a detailed breakdown of the chapters:

Chapter 1   *Introduction*

   This chapter is a short "executive" summary.

Chapter 2   *How Internet mail works*

   This chapter is a general introduction to the way email is handled on Internet systems.

Chapter 3   *Exim overview*

   This chapter contains a general overview of the way Exim works, and introduces you to the way it is configured, in particular in regard to the way messages are delivered.

Chapter 4   *Exim operations overview*

   This chapter continues with more overview material, mostly about topics other than the delivery of messages.

Chapter 5   *Extending the delivery configuration*

   In this chapter, we return to the subject of message delivery, and show how the configuration can be extended to support additional functionality.

**Chapter 6    *Generic options that apply to all routers***

This chapter discusses the generic options that are common to all routers, which are the components of Exim that determine how a message is to be delivered.

**Chapter 7    *The routers***

This chapter describes each of the routers in detail.

**Chapter 8    *Generic options that apply to all transports***

This chapter discusses the generic options that are common to all transports, which are the components of Exim that actually transport messages.

**Chapter 9    *The transports***

This chapter discusses each of the transports in detail.

**Chapter 10    *Message filtering***

This chapter describes the filtering language that is used both by users' filter files and the system filter.

**Chapter 11    *Shared data and Exim processes***

This chapter describes the various different kinds of Exim process, and the data that they share.

**Chapter 12    *Delivery errors and retrying***

This chapter is concerned with temporary delivery errors, and how Exim handles them.

**Chapter 13    *Encryption, authentication, and other SMTP processing***

This chapter covers a number of topics that are concerned with the transmission and reception of messages using SMTP, including authentication and encryption.

**Chapter 14    *Message reception and policy controls***

This chapter describes the facilities that are available for controlling the reception of incoming messages.

**Chapter 15    *Rewriting addresses***

This chapter covers the facilities for rewriting addresses in messages as they pass through Exim.

**Chapter 16    *File and database lookups***

This is the first of three chapters that go into detail about the three main facilities that provide flexibility in Exim's configuration. They are all introduced in earlier chapters, but full details begin here.

Chapter 17 *String expansion*

This chapter covers details about Exim's string expansion mechanism.

Chapter 18 *Domain, host, and address lists*

This chapter gives more details about the several kinds of list that can appear in Exim configurations.

Chapter 19 *Miscellany*

This chapter collects together a number of items that do not fit naturally into the other chapters, but which are too small to warrant individual chapters of their own.

Chapter 20 *Command-line interface to Exim*

This chapter describes the options and arguments that are used to control what a call to Exim actually does.

Chapter 21 *Administering Exim*

This chapter discusses a number of topics concerned with administration, and describes the utility programs that are available to help with this, including the Exim monitor, which is an application for displaying information about Exim's activities in an X window.

Chapter 22 *Building and installing Exim*

This chapter describes how to build and install Exim from the source distribution.

Appendix A *Summary of string expansion*

This appendix is a summary of string expansion items.

Appendix B *Regular expressions*

This appendix is a reference description of the regular expressions that are supported by Exim.

## Conventions used in this book

The following is a list of the typographical conventions used in this book:

*Italic*

Used for file and directory names, program and command names, host and domain names, email addresses, mail headers, URLs, and new terms.

**Bold**

Used for the names of Exim routers, transports, and authenticators.

*Slanted*

Used for the names of Exim variables.

`Constant Width`

Used in examples to show the contents of files or the output from commands, and in the text to mark Exim options or other strings that appear literally in configuration files.

`<Constant Italic>`

Used to indicate variable options, keywords, or text that the user is to replace with an actual value.

`Constant Bold`

Used in examples to show commands or other text that should be typed literally by the user.

Cross-references within the book are by section number, and they are often shown in parentheses like this: (☞ 7.2).

## Suggestions and comments on this book

The author and publisher welcome feedback from all readers. If you have any comments on this book, would like to make a suggestion, or have noticed an error, please email us on the appropriate address:

> *comments@exim-book.com*
> *suggestions@exim-book.com*
> *errors@exim-book.com*

## Acknowledgments

I could not have produced Exim without the support and assistance of many people and organizations. There are too many to acknowledge individually, even if I had been organized enough to keep a full list, which, to my regret, I have not done. I hope that I have not made any major omissions in what follows.

For Exim itself, I must first acknowledge my colleagues in the Computing Service at the University of Cambridge. The management allowed me to write Exim, and once it appeared, the Computing Service has supported its use around the University and elsewhere. Since the first Exim release, many people have sent suggestions for improvements or new features, and fixes for problems, and this continues unabated.

Piete Brooks was brave enough to put the first version into service, to handle mail for the Cambridge computer scientists, and he also implemented the scheme for compiling on multiple operating systems. Piete suggested that an integral filter would be a good thing. Alan Barratt provided the initial code for relay checking. Nigel Metheringham persuaded his employers at that time, Planet Online Ltd, to provide support for an Exim web site and mailing list. Although he no longer works for them, he still manages the site and the mailing lists, and Planet (now called Energis) still provides hardware and network resources. Nigel also provided code for interfacing to the Berkeley DB library, for supporting cdb files, and for delivering to mailboxes in maildir format. Yann Golanski provided the code for the numerical hash function. Steve Clarke did experiments to determine the most efficient way of finding the load average in Linux. Philip Blundell implemented the first support for IPv6 while he was a student at Cambridge. Jason Gunthorpe provided additional IPv6 code for Linux. Stuart Lynne provided the first code for LDAP support; subsequent modifications came from Michael Haardt, Brian Candler, Barry Pederson, and Peter Savitch. Steve Haslam provided some preliminary code for supporting TLS/SSL, and continues to provide many ideas. Malcolm Beattie wrote the interface for calling an embedded Perl interpreter. Paul Kelly wrote the original code for calling MySQL, and Petr Čech did the same for PostgreSQL. Marc Prud'hommeaux repackaged some code from the Samba project for client SPA authentication. Alexander Sabourenkov did a similar job for authentication using the *pwcheck* daemon from the Cyrus SASL library. Ian Kirk provided code for Radius support. Stuart Levy contributed a replacement for a broken *inet_ntoa()* function on IRIX. Matthew Byng-Maddick suggested the `dsearch` lookup type and provided a preliminary implementation. Robert Wal provided an implementation of the `whoson` lookup type. Pierre Humblet got Exim to work under Cygwin. Steve Campbell took over maintenance of the *eximstats* utility and greatly extended it.

Finally, for Exim itself, I must acknowledge my debt to Smail 3, written by Ron Karr, on which I based the first versions of Exim. Though Exim has now changed almost out of all recognition, its parentage is still visible.

The Exim reference manual has been improved as a result of many useful comments that I have received. Jeff Goldberg pointed out that I was using the word "fail" in two different senses in the Exim documentation, and suggested "decline" for one of them. John Horne reads every edition of the reference manual, and picks up my typos and other mistakes.

While writing both versions of this book, I have continued to enjoy the support of my colleagues and the Exim community. My wife Judith was not only generally supportive, but also read both an early draft and the latest version as a professional copy editor, and found many places where I was unclear or inconsistent. Ken Bailey made some useful comments about some of the early chapters. John Horne read an early draft and made suggestions that helped me to put the material into a more accessible order, and then read the first book again in a late draft, providing further useful feedback. John also read and commented on the entirely new chapter on access control for the second book. Michael Shappe read the early chapters of the second book and provided me with yet more useful technical and editorial feedback.

My editor at O'Reilly for the first book was Andy Oram. His comments and guidance had a great effect on the form and shape of the finished book, and much of what he did has carried over into this new book.

I am grateful to a number of organizations who have sponsored the production of this book. You can read about them in the pages that follow the index.

Last but by no means least, I must thank Niall Mansfield, of UIT Cambridge, who came to my rescue when I needed a new publisher.

# 1

# Introduction

Exim is a *mail transfer agent* (MTA)[1] that can be run as an alternative to Sendmail on most Unix and Unix-like systems.[2] Exim is open-source software that is distributed under the GNU General Public License (GPL).[3] A number of operating system distributions include Exim as their default MTA.

I wrote Exim for use on medium-sized servers with permanent Internet connections in a university environment, but it is now used in a wide variety of different situations, from single-user machines on dial-up connections to clusters of servers supporting millions of customers. The code is small (between 500 KB and 1.2 MB on most hardware, depending on the compiler and which optional modules are included), and its performance scales well.

The job of a mail transfer agent is to receive messages from different sources and to deliver them to their destinations, potentially in a number of different ways. Exim can accept messages from remote hosts using SMTP[4] over TCP/IP, as well as from local processes. It handles local deliveries to mailbox files or to pipes attached to commands, as well as remote deliveries via SMTP to other hosts. Exim contains support for the new IPv6 protocol, as well as for the current IPv4 protocol. It does not directly support UUCP, though it can be interfaced to other software which does, provided that UUCP "bang path" addressing is not required, because Exim supports only Internet-style, domain-based addressing.

Exim's configuration is flexible and can be set up to deal with a wide variety of requirements, including virtual domains and the expansion of mailing lists. Once you have grasped the general principles of how Exim works, you will find that the runtime configuration is straightforward and simple to set up. The configuration consists of a single file that is divided into a number of sections. Entries in each section are keyword/value pairs. Regular expressions, compatible with Perl 5, are available for use in a number of options.

The configuration file can reference data from other files, in linear and indexed formats, and from NIS, NIS+, LDAP, MySQL, Oracle, and PostgreSQL databases. By this means, you can make much of Exim's operation table-driven. For example,

---

[1] The terms mail transfer agent and mail transport agent are synonymous, and are used interchangeably.

[2] Exim can also be run in the Cygwin environment; however, this book does not cover that case.

[3] See *http://www.gnu.org/copyleft/gpl.html*.

[4] If you are not familiar with SMTP or some of the other acronyms used here, do not be put off. The next chapter contains a description of how Internet mail works.

you can arrange to do local deliveries on a machine on which the users do not have accounts. The ultimate flexibility can be obtained (at a price) by running a Perl interpreter while processing certain option strings.

The maximum size of messages can be specified, and you can use *access control lists* (ACLs) for checking and controlling incoming messages. A number of tests can be applied to a message and its recipients before it is accepted. These include checking the sending host or network and the sender's identity. You can block hosts explicitly, and use online lists such as the *Realtime Blackhole List* (RBL).[1] You can control which hosts are permitted to use the Exim host as a relay for onward transmission of mail. The SMTP AUTH mechanism can be used to authenticate client hosts for this purpose.

End users are not normally concerned with which MTA is delivering into their mailboxes, but when Exim is in use, its filtering facility, which extends the power of the traditional *.forward* file, can be made available to them. A filter file can test various characteristics of a message, including the contents of the header lines and the start of the body, and then direct delivery to specified addresses, files, or pipes according to what it finds. The filtering feature can also be used by the system administrator to inspect each message before delivery.

Like many MTAs, Exim has adopted the Sendmail command line interface so that it can be installed as a replacement for */usr/sbin/sendmail* or */usr/lib/sendmail*. All the relevant Sendmail options are implemented. There are also some additional options that are compatible with Smail 3, and some further options that are specific to Exim.

Messages on the queue can be controlled by certain privileged command-line options. There is also an optional monitor program called *eximon*, which displays current information in an X window, and contains interfaces to the command-line options.

Exim is not designed for storing mail for dial-up hosts. When the volume of such mail is large, it is better to "deliver" the messages into files (that is, off Exim's queue), and subsequently pass them on by other means.

There are some things that Exim does not do: it does not support any form of delivery status notification (as described in RFC 1891),[2] and it has no built-in facilities for modifying the bodies of messages. In particular, it never translates message bodies from one form of encoding to another, although you could use a filter, combined with an external program, to handle this requirement.

The aim of this book is to explain how Exim works, and to give background and tutorial information on the core facilities that the majority of administrators will need

---

[1]  See *http://mail-abuse.org/rbl/*.

[2]  RFCs are the documents that lay down the standards by which the Internet operates. You can find them online at *http://www.ietf.org* (and numerous other places). We say a bit about those that relate to mail in the next chapter.

to know about. Some options that are required only in special circumstances are not covered. In any case, a book can never keep up with developing software; if you want to know exactly what is available in any given release, you should consult the reference manual and other documentation that is included in the distribution for that release.

Exim is still being developed in the light of experience, changing requirements, and feedback from users. The first book, published in 2001, covered all the major features of the 3.2*x* releases. The text was extensively revised for this new book, to bring it up-to-date with the 4.10 release. For Exim 4, major changes were made to the way addresses are routed, and to the way policy controls are specified for incoming messages. Several other features were revised and simplified.

By the time this book is published, the current release is likely to be 4.14. This contains a number of extensions to the 4.10 release. Some of the more important post-4.10 changes have been included in the book at a late stage of preparation, but for full details you will need to read the manual.

The Exim reference manual and an FAQ are online at the Exim web site, at *http://www.exim.org* and its mirrors. Here you will also find the latest release of Exim, as a source distribution. In addition to the plain text version that is included in the distribution, the manual can be downloaded in HTML (for faster browser access), in PostScript or PDF (for printing), and in Texinfo format for the *info* command.

Some versions of GNU/Linux are distributed with binary versions of Exim included. For this reason, I have left the material on building Exim from source until the end of the book, and concentrated on the runtime aspects first. If you are working with a binary distribution, make sure you have a copy of the text version of the reference manual that comes with the source distribution. It provides full coverage of every configuration option, and can easily be searched.

The next chapter is a general discussion of the way email on the Internet works; Exim is hardly mentioned. This material has been included for the benefit of the many people who find themselves having to run a mail server without this essential background knowledge. You can skip to chapter 3 if you already know about RFC 2822 message format, SMTP, mail routing, and DNS usage.

# 2

# How Internet mail works

The programs that people use to send and receive mail (often just called "mailers") are formally called *mail user agents* (MUAs). They are concerned with providing a convenient mail interface for users. They display incoming mail that is in users' mailboxes, assist the user in constructing messages for sending, and provide facilities for managing folders of saved messages. They are the "front end" of the mail system. Many different user agents can be installed, and can be simultaneously operational on a single computer, thereby providing a choice of different user interfaces. However, when an MUA sends a message, it does not take on the work of actually delivering it to the recipients. Instead, it sends it to a *mail transfer agent* (MTA), which may be running on the same host or on some local server.

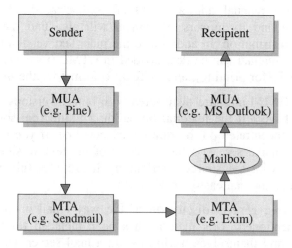

*Figure 2-1: Message data flow*

Mail transfer agents transfer messages from one host to another. When a message reaches its destination host, the MTA delivers it to a user mailbox or to a process that is managing user mailboxes. This job is complicated, and it would not be sensible for every MUA to contain all the necessary apparatus. The flow of data from a message's sender to its recipient is as shown in figure 2-1. However, when an application program or script needs to send a mail message as part of some automatic activity, it normally calls the MTA directly without involving an MUA.

Only one MTA can be fully operational on a host at once, because only one program can be designated to receive incoming messages from other hosts. On Unix-like systems, the MTA has to be a privileged program in order to listen for incoming SMTP connections on TCP port 25 (the standard SMTP port) and to be able to write to users' mailboxes. The choice of which MTA to run is made by the system administrator, whereas the choice of which MUA to run is made by the end user.

An MTA must be capable of handling many messages simultaneously. If it cannot deliver a message, it must send an error report back to the sender. An MTA must be able to cope with messages that cannot be immediately delivered, storing such messages on its local disk, and retrying periodically until it succeeds in delivering them or some configurable timeout expires. The most common causes of such delays are network connectivity problems and hosts that are down.

From an MTA's point of view, there are two sources of incoming messages: local processes and other hosts. There are three types of destination: local files, local processes via pipes, and other hosts, as indicated in figure 2-2.

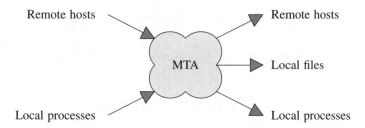

*Figure 2-2: The job of an MTA*

The division of labour between MUAs and MTAs also means that an MUA need not be running on the same host as its MTA; figure 2-3 illustrates the relationship between MUAs and MTAs in two common configurations.

In the top part of the figure, the MUA, MTA, and the disk storage are all part of a single system, indicated by the dashed line. The users access the system by logging on and authenticating themselves by a password or some other means. The MUA is started by a user command as a process on the system, and when it passes a message to the MTA for delivery, it is communicating with another process on the same system. Consequently, both the MUA and the MTA know the authenticated identity of the message's sender, and the MTA can ensure that this identity is included in the outgoing message. As specified in RFC 2822, if the contents of the *From:* header line do not match the actual sender, the MTA should normally add a *Sender:* line containing the authenticated identity.

Messages are held by the MTA in its spool area while awaiting delivery. The word "spool", as applied to disk storage, has two different meanings. In this book, we use it to mean the disk storage that an MTA uses for messages in transit. You will

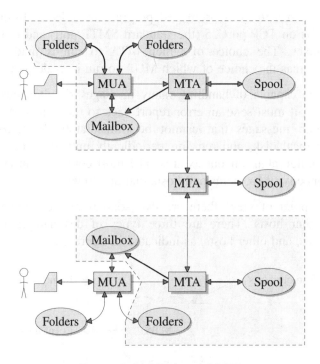

*Figure 2-3: MUAs and MTAs*

sometimes see "spool" used for the disk area in which users' mailboxes are kept, but this is not the sense in which it is used here.

Messages that are destined for other hosts are transmitted over the Internet to other MTAs using the *Simple Mail Transfer Protocol* (SMTP). When the originating host and the final host are both directly connected to the Internet, the message can be delivered directly to the final host, but sometimes it has to travel via an intermediate MTA. Large organizations often arrange for all their incoming mail to be routed via a central *mail hub*, which then delivers it to other hosts within the organization's local network. These may be behind a firewall and therefore inaccessible to the Internet at large. When a message reaches its destination host, the MTA delivers it into the mailbox of the recipient, who can then access it with the MUA of their choice.

Another case where an intermediate MTA is involved is when the final destination or its network connection is down. Using the *Domain Name Service* (DNS, ☞ 2.7), or some private method, a backup host may be designated for a domain. Incoming mail accumulates on this host until the main one starts working again, at which point the backlog is transferred. The advantage of this is that the accumulated mail can be stored close to the final destination, and can eventually be transferred quickly and in a controlled manner. In contrast, when a busy host without a backup restarts, it is liable to receive a very large number of simultaneous incoming SMTP connections from all over the Internet, which may cause performance problems.

The bottom part of figure 2-3 illustrates another popular configuration, in which the MUA is not running on the same system as the MTA. Instead it runs on a user's workstation. Receiving and sending messages in this configuration are entirely separate operations. When a user reads mail, the MUA uses either the POP (RFC 1939) or IMAP (RFC 2060) protocol to access the mailbox and remote folders on the server system. In order to do so, the user has to be authenticated in some way; commonly a username and password are used to gain access to the mailbox and remote mail folders. However, neither the POP nor IMAP protocols contain any facilities for sending messages. MUAs of this type have therefore traditionally used the SMTP protocol to pass messages to an MTA in a server system. Thus a protocol that was originally designed for passing messages between MTAs is subverted for the purpose of submitting new messages to an MTA, which is really a different kind of operation. This usage leads to a number of problems:

- The MTA cannot distinguish between a new message submission from an MUA and a message being passed on from another MTA. It may be able to make a guess, based on the IP address of local hosts it knows not to be running MTAs, but this is not always easy to arrange. This means that it cannot treat submissions specially, as it does when messages originate on the local host.

- The sender of the message is not authenticated; the MTA may be able to verify that the domain of the sender exists, but often it cannot check the local part of the address. MUAs of this type require the user to specify a username when starting; a typo made while doing this may go undetected, leading to incorrect sender addresses in outgoing messages. Furthermore, it is easy for a user to deliberately forge the sender address, as spammers often do.

- The MUA is not constrained to sending outgoing mail to the server that it is using for reading mail. It may sometimes be desirable to use different servers, but because of the existence of this flexibility, it is possible to direct MUA software to send mail to any host on the Internet. This makes it easy for unscrupulous persons to attempt to dump unsolicited mail on arbitrary servers for relaying. The fact that this has happened on numerous occasions has led to the tightening up of relaying servers, and the creation of databases such as the MAPS *Dial-up User List*.[1]

There are some moves afoot to remedy this situation by defining a new submission protocol (RFC 2476). This is effectively the same as SMTP, but it uses a different port number. However, at the time of writing, this technology is not yet in common use.

---

[1]  See *http://mail-abuse.org/dul/*.

# 2.1 Different types of MTA

The framework for mail delivery just described is very general, and in practice there are many different kinds of MTA configuration that operate within it. At the simplest level, there are single hosts running in small offices or homes, each handling a few mailboxes in one domain, receiving incoming external messages from one ISP's mail server only, and sending all outgoing messages to the ISP for onward delivery. Many such hosts are not permanently connected to the Internet, but instead dial up from time to time to exchange mail with the server. In such an environment, the MTA does not have to be capable of full mail routing or complicated queue management.

Hosts that are permanently connected need not send everything via the same server. Instead, they can use the DNS to discover how to send outgoing messages directly to their final destinations. A single outgoing message may have several recipients, thus requiring copies to be sent to more than one remote server. This means that the MTA has to cope with messages where some of the addresses cannot be immediately delivered, and it must implement suitable retrying mechanisms for use with multiple servers. For incoming mail, the domain can be configured so that mail comes direct from anywhere on the Internet, without having to pass through an intermediate server.

An organization may not want to have all its local mailboxes on the same host. Even a small organization with just one domain may have users running their own desktop systems who want their mail delivered to them. The host running the "corporate" MTA has now become a *hub*, receiving mail from the world, and distributing it by user within its local network. It is common in such configurations for all outgoing mail from the network to pass through the hub. For security reasons, it is also common to configure the network router so that direct SMTP connections between the world and the workstations are not permitted.

Single organizations may support more than one domain, but the MTAs that support very large numbers of domains are usually those run by ISPs, and there are two common ways in which these are handled:

- For personal clients, the ISP normally provides a mailbox for each account, from which the mail is collected by some means when the client connects. As far as the MTA is concerned, it is doing a local delivery into a mailbox on the ISP's server.

- For corporate clients, ISPs are more likely to transfer mail to the clients' MTAs based purely on the domains in the addresses, with the ISP's MTA acting as a standard intermediate MTA between unrelated systems.

# 2.2 Internet message standards

Electronic mail messages on the Internet are formatted according to RFC 2822, which defines the format of a message as it is transferred between hosts, but not the protocol that is used for the exchange. The Simple Mail Transfer Protocol (SMTP) is used to transfer messages between hosts (☞ 2.2.3). This is defined in RFC 2821.

The original Internet mail RFCs (821 and 822) were published in 1982, and subsequently other RFCs that describe extensions were published. RFCs 2821 and 2822 are recent revisions, consolidating the material from the earlier RFCs, and incorporating current Internet practice. At the time of writing the formal status of these new RFCs is still "draft", but in practice, they are the documents that implementors are now using.

The SMTP address syntax is more restrictive than that of RFC 2822, and requires that components of domain names consist only of letters, digits, and hyphens. Since any message may need to be transported using SMTP if its destination is not on the originating host, the formats of all addresses are normally restricted to what RFC 2821 permits.

## 2.2.1 RFC 2822 message format

A message consists of lines of text, and when it is in transit between hosts, each line is terminated by the character *carriage return* (ASCII code 13) immediately followed by *linefeed* (ASCII code 10), a sequence that is commonly written as CRLF. Within a host, messages are normally stored for convenience in RFC 2822 format. Many applications use the local operating system's convention for line termination when doing this, but some use CRLF. The normal Unix convention is to terminate lines with a single linefeed character, without a preceding carriage return.

A message consists of a *header* and a *body*. The header contains a number of lines that are structured in specific ways as defined by RFC 2822. The following examples are the header lines that are commonly shown to someone who is composing a message, and will be familiar to any email user:

```
From: Philip Hazel <ph10@exim.example>
To: My Readers <all@exim.book.example>,
    My Loyal Fans <fans@exim.example>
Cc: My Personal Assistant <cwbaft@exim.example>
Subject: How electronic mail works
```

An individual header line can be continued over several actual lines by starting the continuations with whitespace. The entire header section is terminated by a blank line. The body of the message then follows. In its simplest form, the body is unstructured text, but other RFCs (MIME, RFC 1521) define additional header lines that allow the body to be split up into several different parts. Each part can be in a different encoding, and there are standard ways of translating binary data into print-

able characters so that it can be transmitted using SMTP. This is the mechanism that
is used for message "attachments".

RFC 2822 permits many variations for addresses that appear in message header lines.
For example:

```
To: caesar@rome.example.com
To: Julius Caesar <caesar@rome.example.com>
To: caesar@rome.example.com (Julius Caesar)
```

Text in parentheses anywhere in the line is a comment. This applies to all header
lines whose structure is constrained by the RFC, not just those header lines that
contain addresses. For example, in the following:

```
Date: Tue, 7 Jan 2003 14:20:24 -0500 (EST)
```

the time zone abbreviation is a comment as far as RFC 2822 formatting is concerned.
Along with the generally available parenthetical comments, headers that contain
addresses may contain a sequence of words before an actual address in angle
brackets; these are normally used for descriptive text such as the recipient's full
name. When a header line contains more than one address, a comma must be used to
terminate all but the last of them.[1]

The terms *local part* and *domain* are used to refer to the parts of a mail address that
precede and follow the @ sign, respectively. In the email address *caesar@*
*rome.example.com*, the local part is *caesar* and the domain is *rome.example.com*. The
local part is often a username, but because it can also be an abstraction such as the
name of a mailing list or an address in some other mail domain in a message that is
being sent to a gateway, the more general term is used here, as it is in the Exim
reference documentation.

## 2.2.2 The message "on the wire"

A message that is transmitted between MTAs has several things added to it over and
above what the composing user sees. In addition to the header section and the body,
another piece of data called the *envelope* is transmitted immediately before the RFC
2822 data, using the SMTP commands MAIL and RCPT. The envelope contains the
sender address and one or more recipient addresses. These addresses are of the form
*<user@domain>* without the additional textual information, such as the user's full
name, that may appear in message header lines.

The deliveries done by the receiving MTA (either to local mailboxes or by passing
the message on to other hosts) are based on the recipients listed in the envelope, not
on the *To:* or *Cc:* header lines in the message. If any delivery fails, it is to the

---

[1] Some MUAs allow lists of recipients to be entered using whitespace, semicolons, or other characters
as separators; they may also use these characters when displaying addresses. However, when such
lists are used to construct *To:*, *Cc:*, or *Bcc:* header lines for transmission over the Internet, the
separators are changed to commas.

envelope sender address that the failure report is sent, not the address in the *From:* or *Reply-To:* header line.

The need for a separate envelope becomes obvious when considering a message with multiple recipients. In this case, the mailboxes to which the message is delivered may be on several different hosts. The RFC 2822 header lines normally list all the recipients, but in order to be delivered, the message has to be cloned into separate copies, one for each receiving host, and in each copy the envelope contains just those recipients whose mailboxes are on that host.

As well as adding an envelope, both the MUA and the MTA add extra header lines before a message is transmitted to another host. Here is an example of a message "in transit", where the envelope lists only two of the three recipients. This example shows just the SMTP commands and data that the client sends, without the responses from the server:

```
MAIL FROM:<ph10@exim.example>
RCPT TO:<fans@exim.example>
RCPT TO:<cwbaft@exim.example>
DATA
Received: from ph10 by draco.exim.example with local (Exim 4.01)
          id 14Tli0-000501-00;
          Fri, 15 Feb 2002 14:18:05 +0000
From: Philip Hazel <ph10@exim.example>
To: My Readers <all@exim.book.example>,
    My Loyal Fans <fans@exim.example>
Cc: My Personal Assistant <cwbaft@exim.example>
Subject: How electronic mail works
Date: Fri, 15 Feb 2002 14:18:05 +0000
Message-ID: <Pine.SOL.3.96.990117111343.19032A-100000@
  draco.exim.example>
MIME-Version: 1.0
Content-Type: TEXT/PLAIN; charset=US-ASCII

Hello,
   If you want to know about Internet mail, look at chapter 2.
.
```

The first three lines are the envelope; the message itself follows the DATA command, and is terminated by a line containing only a dot. Notice that lines have been added at both the start and the end of the header section.

Before passing a message to an MTA, an MUA normally adds *Date:* (required by RFC 2822) and *Message-ID:*. The MUA may also add header lines such as *MIME-Version:* and *Content-Type:* if the body of the message is structured according to the MIME definitions. Each MTA through which a message passes adds a *Received:* header line at the front, as required by RFC 2821. The routing history of a message can therefore be obtained by reading these header lines in reverse order.

Because there may be quite a number of "behind-the-scenes" header lines by the time a message is delivered, most MUAs normally show only a subset when displaying a message to a user (typically the lines containing addresses, the subject, and the date). However, there is usually some way to configure the MUA to show all the header lines.

A recipient address that appears in the envelope need not appear in any header line in the message itself. This is usually the case after a message has passed through a mailing list expander, and is also the means by which "blind carbon copies" are implemented. When a user sends a message, either the MUA or the first MTA creates the envelope, taking the recipients from the *To:*, *Cc:*, and *Bcc:* data, and removing any *Bcc:* header line, unless there are no other recipients, in which case an empty *Bcc:* header line is retained.[1] An alternative permitted implementation is to retain the *Bcc:* header line only in those copies of the message that are transmitted to *Bcc:* recipients.

When a message is delivered into a user's mailbox, some MTAs, including Exim (as normally configured), add an *Envelope-to:* header line giving the envelope recipient address that was received with the message. This can be helpful if the final envelope recipient does not appear in the header lines. For example, consider a message sent from a mailing list to an address such as *postmaster@xyz.example*, which is handled by an alias. Messages from mailing lists do not normally contain the recipient in any of the header lines. Instead, there is likely to be a line such as:

```
To: some-list@listdomain.example
```

The address *postmaster@xyz.example* appears only in the envelope. Suppose that aliasing causes this message to be delivered into the mailbox of the user called *pat*, who is the local postmaster. Without the addition of *Envelope-to:*, there is nothing in the message itself that indicates why it ended up in Pat's mailbox.

The envelope sender is also known as the *return path*, because of its use for returning delivery failure reports. In most personal messages, it is identical to the address in the *From:* header, but it need not be. There are two common cases where it differs:

- When a message is sent to a mailing list, the original envelope sender that was received with the message is normally replaced with the address of the list manager before the message is sent out to the subscribers. This means that any delivery failures are reported to the list manager, who can take appropriate action, rather than to the original sender, who cannot.

- Delivery failure reports (often called "bounce messages") that are generated by MTAs are sent out with empty envelope sender addresses. These often appear in listings as < >. This convention is used to identify such messages as bounces, so that if they in turn fail to be delivered, no subsequent failure report is generated.

---

[1]  RFC 2822 does not permit empty *To:* or *Cc:* header lines; if there are no relevant addresses, these lines must be omitted. Only *Bcc:* may appear with no addresses. RFC 822 required at least one of *To:*, *Cc:*, or *Bcc:* to be present; this restriction is relaxed in RFC 2822.

This avoids the possibility of mail bounce loops, where bounce messages that cannot be delivered give rise to further bounce messages that cannot be delivered, and so on *ad infinitum.*

When a message is delivered into a user's mailbox, Exim (as normally configured) adds a *Return-path:* header line, in which it records the envelope sender.

## 2.2.3 Summary of the SMTP protocol

SMTP is a simple, text-based, command-reply protocol. The client host sends a command to the server, and then waits for a reply before proceeding to the next command.[1] Replies always start with a three-digit decimal number, for example:

```
250 Message accepted
```

The text is usually information intended for human interpretation, though there are some exceptions. The number encodes the type of response; the first digit is the most important, and is always one of those shown in table 2-1.

*Table 2-1: SMTP response codes*

| Code | Meaning |
| --- | --- |
| $2xx$ | The command was successful |
| $3xx$ | Additional data is required for the command |
| $4xx$ | The command suffered a temporary error |
| $5xx$ | The command suffered a permanent error |

The second and third digits give additional information about the response, but an MTA need not pay any attention to them. Exim, for example, operates entirely on the first digit of SMTP response codes. Replies may consist of several lines of text. For all but the last of them, the code is followed by a hyphen; in the last line it is followed by whitespace. For example:

```
550-Host is not on relay list
550 Relaying prohibited by administrator
```

When a client connects to a server's SMTP port, it must wait for an initial success response before proceeding. Some servers include the identity of the software they are running (and maybe other information) in the response, but none of this is actually required. Others send a minimal response such as:

```
220 ESMTP Ready
```

---

[1]  There is an optional optimization called "pipelining", which allows batches of commands to be sent, and batches of replies to be received, but this is purely to improve performance. The overall behaviour remains the same, and we describe only the simple case here.

The client initializes the session by sending an EHLO (extended hello) command, which gives its own name.[1] For example:

```
EHLO client.example.com
```

Unfortunately, there are many MTAs in use that are misconfigured, either accidentally or deliberately, such that they do not give their correct name in the EHLO command. This means that the data obtained from this command is not of much use. The server's response to EHLO gives the server's name in the first line, optionally followed by other information text, and lists the extended SMTP features that the server supports in subsequent lines. For example, the following:

```
250-server.example.com Hello client.example.com
250 SIZE 10485760
```

indicates that the server supports the SIZE option, with a maximum message size of 10 485 760 characters.

Once an EHLO command has been accepted, the client may attempt to send any number of messages to the host. Each message is begun by a MAIL command, which contains the envelope sender address. If the SIZE option is supported by the server, the size of the message may also be given. For example:

```
MAIL FROM:<caesar@rome.example> SIZE=12345
```

After this has been accepted, each relevant recipient address is transmitted in a separate RCPT command such as:

```
RCPT TO:<brutus@rome.example>
```

The recipient addresses are taken from the message's envelope, not from the header lines. The client waits for a response to each RCPT command before sending the next one. The server may accept some recipients and reject others, either permanently or temporarily. After a permanent error, the client should not attempt to resend the message to that address. The most common reasons for permanent rejection are:

- The address contains a domain that is local to the server, but the local part is not recognized.

- The address contains a domain that is not local to the server, and the client is not authorized to relay through the server to that domain.

Temporary errors are caused by problems that are expected to be resolved in due course, such as the inability to check an incoming address because a database is down, or a lack of disk space. After a temporary error, a client is expected to try the address again in a new SMTP connection, after a suitable delay. This is normally at

---

[1]   The original SMTP protocol used HELO (sic) as the initializing command, and servers are still obliged to recognize this. The difference is that the response to EHLO includes a list of the optional SMTP extensions that the server supports.

least 10 or 15 minutes after the first failure; if the temporary error condition persists, the time between retries is usually increased.

After the client has transmitted all the recipients in RCPT commands, and at least one recipient has been accepted, the client sends:

```
DATA
```

and the server responds with a 354 code, requesting further data (the message itself). The client transmits the message, without waiting for any further responses, and ends it with a line containing only a single dot character. If the message contains any lines that begin with a dot, an extra dot is inserted to guard against premature termination. The server strips a leading dot from any lines that contain more text. If the server returns a success response after the data has been sent, it assumes responsibility for subsequent handling of the message, and the client may discard its copy. Once it has sent all its messages, a client ends the SMTP session by sending a QUIT command.

Because SMTP transmits the envelope separately from the message itself, servers can reject envelope addresses individually, before much data has been sent. However, if a server is unhappy with the contents of a message, it cannot send a rejection until the entire message has been received.[1] Unfortunately, some client software (in violation of RFC 2821) treats any error response to DATA or following the data itself as a temporary error, and continues to try to deliver the message at successive intervals.

## 2.3 Forgery

It is trivial to forge unencrypted mail. In general, MTAs are "strangers" to each other, so there is no way a receiving MTA can authenticate the contents of the envelope or the message itself. All it can do is log the IP address of the sending host, and include it in the *Received:* line that it adds to the message.

Unsolicited junk mail (spam) usually contains some forged header lines. You need to be aware of this if you ever have to investigate the origin of such mail. If a message contains a header line such as:

```
Received: from foobar.com.example ([10.9.8.7])
        by podunk.edu.example (8.9.1/8.9.1) with SMTP id DAA00447;
        Tue, 6 Mar 2001 03:21:43 -0500 (EST)
```

it does not mean that the FooBar company or the University of Podunk are necessarily involved at all; the header may simply have been inserted by the spam perpetrator, in order to mislead. The only *Received:* headers you can count on are those at the top of the message that were added by MTAs running on hosts whose administrators you trust. Once you pass these *Received:* headers, those below them,

---

[1]  For example, the message may be too big, or the server may be configured to check the syntax of addresses in header lines.

even if they appear to relate to a reputable organization such as an ISP, may be forged.

# 2.4 Authentication and encryption

The original SMTP protocol had no facilities for authenticating clients or for encrypting messages as they were transmitted between hosts. As the Internet expanded, it became clear that these features were required, and the protocol has been extended to allow for them. However, the vast majority of Internet mail is still transmitted between unauthenticated hosts, over unencrypted connections. For this reason, we will not go into any details in this introductory chapter; there is some discussion in chapter 13 about the way Exim handles these features.

# 2.5 Routing a message

The most fundamental part of any MTA is the apparatus for deciding where to send a message. There may be many recipients, both local and remote. This means that a number of different copies may need to be made and sent to different destinations. Some domains may be known to the local host and processed specially; the others normally cause copies of the message to be sent to remote hosts. These may either be the final destinations or intermediate hosts.

There are two distinct types of address: those for which the local part is used when deciding how to deliver the message, and those for which only the domain is relevant. Typically, when a domain refers to a remote host, the local part of the address plays no part in the routing process, but if the domain is the name of the local host, the local part is all-important. The steps that an MTA has to perform in order to handle a message are as follows, though they are not necessarily done in exactly this order:

- First, the MTA has to decide what deliveries are required for each recipient address. In order to do this, it must:

  - Process addresses that contain domains for which this host is the ultimate destination. These are often called "local addresses". Processing may involve expanding aliases into lists of replacement addresses, handling users' *.forward* files, dealing with mailing lists, and checking that the remaining local parts refer to existing local user mailboxes.

  - Process the non-local addresses for which there is local routing knowledge (for example, domains for which the host is a mail hub or firewall) to determine which of its client hosts these addresses should be sent to.

- For the remaining addresses, those for which there is no local knowledge, look up destination hosts in the DNS (☞ 2.8). Successful routing produces a list of one or more remote hosts for each address.

- After sorting out what deliveries need to be done, the MTA must carry out the local deliveries, that is, deliveries to pipes or files on the local host.

- For each remote delivery, it must try to send to each host in turn, until one succeeds or gives a hard failure. If several addresses are routed to the same set of hosts, the RFCs recommend sending a single copy with multiple recipients in the envelope.

- If all hosts give temporary failures, the MTA must try the corresponding addresses again later. Many MTAs send a warning message to the sender if delivery is delayed by more than a few hours. If the delay goes on long enough (normally a few days), the MTA gives up trying to deliver the message. Instead, it sends it back to the sender as part of a bounce message. Unlike some other MTAs, Exim measures timeouts for common failures (such the inability to contact a host) from when the host first fails, not from the arrival of the message (☞ 12.2).

## 2.6 Checking incoming mail

There are a number of checks that are commonly applied to incoming messages from other hosts.

### 2.6.1 Checking recipient addresses

Some MTAs check the validity of local addresses during the SMTP transaction. If an incoming message has an incorrect local part, the RCPT command that transfers that part of the envelope is rejected by giving an error response. This means that the sending MTA retains control of the message for that recipient, and is the one that generates the bounce message that goes back to the sender. This checking stops undeliverable messages from being accepted by the local host. However, receiving a bounce message from an MTA that is not at the site they were mailing to confuses some users, and makes them think that something is broken. "How can the local mailer daemon know that this is an invalid address at the remote site?" they ask.

The alternative approach that is adopted by some MTAs is to accept messages without checking the recipient addresses, and do the checking later. This has the benefit of minimizing the duration of the SMTP transaction, and for invalid addresses, the bounce messages are what the users intuitively expect. In addition, they can be made to contain helpful information about finding correct mail addresses. The disadvantage is that undeliverable messages whose envelope senders are also invalid give rise to undeliverable bounce messages that have to be sorted out by the postmaster. Many unsolicited junk messages ("spam") are of this type, and the volume of these messages is such that more and more administrators configuring their MTAs to implement the former behaviour.

Another abuse that achieves a kind of unwanted relaying has been used against the second type of MTA. The perpetrator deliberately sends a message with an invalid recipient, but with the envelope sender set to the victim's address. If the MTA accepts the message and deals with the recipients later, the bounce message (which normally contains a copy of the original message) is sent to the victim.

Exim can be configured to behave in either of these ways, and the behaviour can be made conditional on the domain of the sender address. For example, all addresses from within a local environment can be accepted, and unknown ones passed to a program that sends back a helpful message, while unknown addresses from the outside can be rejected in the SMTP protocol. However, because of the high level of abuse, Exim's default configuration checks all recipient addresses at SMTP time.

## 2.6.2 Checking sender addresses

Not all MTAs check the validity of envelope sender addresses. These can be invalid for a number of reasons, such as:

*   Misconfigured MUAs or MTAs. For an MUA running on a workstation, the user has to supply the sender address, and an MTA's configuration contains a default domain that it adds to local usernames to create sender addresses. In either case, a typo can render the address invalid. Errors can also arise in gateways that are converting messages from some other protocol regime.

*   Use of domains not registered in the DNS.

*   Misconfigured DNS name servers, for example, a typo in a zone file.

*   Forgery.

In general, the checking of sender addresses is normally confined to verifying that the domain is registered in the DNS. Exim does contain a facility for making a "callout" to verify that an incoming sender address is acceptable as a recipient to a host that handles its domain, but this is a costly approach that is not always suitable for use on busy servers.

## 2.6.3 Other policy controls

The enormous increase in the amount of unsolicited mail being transmitted over the Internet has caused MTA implementors to add facilities for blocking certain types of message as a matter of policy. Typical features include the following:

*   Checking local lists of known miscreant hosts and sender addresses.

- Checking one or more of the public "black lists", such as the Realtime Blackhole List (*http://mail-abuse.org*), and either refusing messages from black-listed hosts, or annotating them by adding an informational header line.

- Blocking third-party relaying through the local host. That is, preventing arbitrary hosts from sending mail to the local host for onward transmission to some other destination. MTAs that do not block such mail are called "open relays" and are a favourite target of spammers.

- Refusing messages with malformed header lines.

- Recognizing junk mail by scanning the content, and either discarding it or annotating it to inform the recipient, who then has the choice of discarding it by means of a filter file.

- Checking for certain types of attachment in order to block viruses.

## 2.7 Overview of the DNS

The DNS is a worldwide, distributed database that holds various kinds of data indexed by keys that are called *domain names*. Here is a very brief summary of the facilities that are relevant to mail handling.[1] The data is held in units called *records*, each containing a number of fields, of which the domain name, record type, and data specific to the record type are relevant to applications that use the DNS.[2] For example, for the record:

```
www.web.example.  A  192.168.6.4
```

the domain name is *www.web.example*, the record type is "A" (for "address"), and the data is 192.168.6.4. Address records like this are used for finding the IP addresses of hosts from their names, and are probably the most common type of DNS record.

The present Internet addressing scheme, which uses 32-bit addresses and is known as IPv4, is being supplemented by a new scheme called IPv6, which uses 128-bit addresses. Support for IPv6 is becoming common in operating systems and application software, and IPv6 is already being widely deployed in some parts of the world where there are shortages of IPv4 addresses. Some people believe that IPv6 will ultimately replace IPv4 completely, though the timescale of this change is unclear.

---

[1]  For a full discussion, see *DNS and BIND* by Paul Albitz and Cricket Liu (O'Reilly). The primary DNS RFCs are 1034 and 1035.

[2]  The other fields are concerned with the internal management of the DNS itself.

In the world of the DNS, a complete, fully qualified domain name is always shown with a terminating dot, as in the previous example. Incomplete domain names, without the trailing dot, are relative to some superior domain. Unfortunately, there is confusion because some applications that interact with the DNS do not show or require the trailing dot. In particular, domains in email addresses must *not* include it, because that is contrary to RFC 2821/2822 syntax.

IPv6 addresses are normally written in hexadecimal, using colon separators between each pair of octets. In the DNS, the AAAA record, which is a direct analogue to the A record, is used to record them. For example:

```
ipv6.example.   AAAA   3ffe:ffff:836f:0a00:000a:0800:200a:c031
```

A second record type, A6, has also been defined for holding IPv6 addresses (see RFC 2874). This provides a more flexible scheme, in which prefix portions of IPv6 addresses can be held separately. A6 was at first expected to supersede the AAAA type, but it was not universally liked, and so was reduced to experimental status.

If a host has more than one IP interface, each appears in a separate address record with the same domain name. The case of letters in DNS domain names is not significant, and the individual components of a name may contain a wide range of characters. For example, a record in the DNS could have the domain name *abc_xyz#2.example.com*. However, the characters that are used for host names are restricted by RFC 952 to letters, digits, and hyphens, and the same restrictions apply to domains that are used in email addresses.

It is not possible to send mail to an address such as *user@abc_xyz#2.example.com* using SMTP, because of the characters in the domain that are invalid according to RFC 2821. For this reason, all MX domain names (which are described shortly) and host names use only the restricted character set. This constraint is often misunderstood to be an internal DNS restriction, which it is not.[1]

The servers that implement the DNS are called *name servers*, and are distributed throughout the Internet. The hierarchical name space is broken up into *zones*, each of which is managed by its own administrator, and stored on its own master server. Division into zones that are stored on independent servers is what makes the management of such a large set of data practicable.[2]

---

[1]  See also RFC 2181, *Clarifications to the DNS Specification*.

[2]  Before the DNS, the list of Internet hosts was kept in a single file that had to be copied in its entirety to all of them.

The breakpoints between zones are always between components of a domain name, but not necessarily at every boundary. For example, there is a *uk* zone, and *ac.uk* and *cam.ac.uk* zones, but there is no separate *csx.cam.ac.uk* zone, although there are domain names ending with those components. The data for those names is held within the *cam.ac.uk* zone. This does not prevent there being other different zones below *cam.ac.uk*. This example is illustrated in figure 2-4, using dashed ellipses to represent the zones.

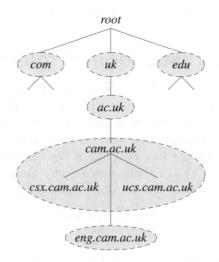

*Figure 2-4: DNS domains and zones*

There is usually one master name server for a zone, and several slaves that copy their data from the master. A single name server may be a master for some zones and a slave for others. Any name server (master or slave) that has its own complete copy of a zone file is said to be *authoritative* for that zone. You will sometimes see that word used in output from commands such as *host*, which interrogate the DNS. Data that a name server has obtained from some other name server without transferring the entire zone is non-authoritative.

It is preferable for the slaves to be at least on different LANs to the master, and best if some of them are at entirely different locations in order to maximize the availability of the zone for queries. ISPs commonly provide name server slaving facilities for their customers. A name server for a zone that has subzones knows the location of the servers for those zones. At the base of the hierarchy are the *root* name servers at "well-known" locations on the Internet.

Caching is extensively used in DNS software to improve performance. Each record contains a time-to-live field, and name servers are entitled to remember and reuse the data for that length of time. A typical time-to-live is around one day. Data is looked up by passing the domain name and type to a nearby name server; if there has been a recent request for the same data, it will be in the server's cache and the request can be answered immediately. Otherwise, if the server happens to have cached the identity of the name servers for the required zone, it can query them directly, but if it has no relevant information, it starts by querying one of the root name servers and works its way down the zone hierarchy. For example, if a query for *www.cam.ac.uk* is received by a root name server, it responds with the list of name servers for the *uk* zone. Querying one of them produces a list of name servers for the *ac.uk* zone, and so on, until a name server that contains the actual data is reached.

# 2.8 DNS records used for mail routing

The domain in a mail address need not correspond to a host name. For example, an organization might use the domain *plc.example.com* for all its email, but handle it with hosts called *mail-1.plc.example.com* and *mail-2.plc.example.com*. This kind of flexibility is obtained by making use of *mail exchange* (MX) records in the DNS. An MX record maps a mail domain to a host that is registered as handling mail for that domain, with a preference value. There may be any number of MX records for a domain, and when a name server is queried, it returns all of them. For example:

```
hermes.example.com.   MX  5   green.csi.example.com.
hermes.example.com.   MX  7   sw3.example.com.
hermes.example.com.   MX  7   sw4.example.com.
```

shows three hosts that handle mail for *hermes.example.com*. The preference values can be thought of as distances from the target; the smaller the value, the more preferable the corresponding host, so in this example, *green.csi.example.com* is the most preferred. An MTA that is delivering mail for *hermes.example.com* first tries to deliver to *green.csi.example.com*; if that fails, it tries the less preferred hosts in order of their preference values. It is only the numerical order of the preferences that is used; the absolute values do not matter. When there are MX records with identical preference values (as in this example), they are ordered randomly before they are used.

Before an MTA can make use of the list of hosts it has obtained from MX records, it first has to find the IP addresses for the hosts. It does this by looking up the corresponding address records (A records for IPv4, and AAAA records for IPv6). For example, there might be the following address records:

```
green.csi.example.com.   A  192.168.8.57
sw3.example.com.         A  192.168.8.38
sw4.example.com.         A  192.168.8.44
```

In practice, if a name server already has an address record for any host in an MX list that it is returning, it sends the address record along with the MX records. In many cases, this saves an additional DNS query.

In the early days of the DNS there were no MX records, and mail domains corresponded to host names. For backward compatibility to that time, if there are no MX records for a domain, an MTA is entitled to look for an address record and treat it as if it were obtained from an MX record with a preference value of zero (most preferred). However, if it cannot determine whether or not there are any MX records (because, for example, the relevant name servers are unreachable), it must not do this.

MX records were originally invented for use by gateways to other mail systems, but nowadays they are heavily used to implement "corporate" mail domains that do not necessarily correspond to any one specific host.

## 2.9 Related DNS records

Two other kinds of DNS record are useful in connection with mail. PTR ("pointer") records map IP addresses to names via special zones called *in-addr.arpa* for IPv4 addresses, and *ip6.arpa* for IPv6 addresses.[1] PTR records allow the reverse of a normal host lookup: given an IP address, PTR records allow you to find out the corresponding host name. The name of a PTR record consists of the IP address followed by one of the special domains. However, for the *in-addr.arpa* and *ip6.arpa* domains, the components of the address are reversed to allow for DNS delegation of parts of an IP network. For the address 192.168.8.57, the PTR record would be as follows:

```
57.8.168.192.in-addr.arpa.   PTR   green.csi.example.com.
```

This registers that the name of the host that has the IP address 192.168.8.57 is *green.csi.example.com*. For IPv6 addresses in the *ip6.arpa* domain, the components that are reversed are the hexadecimal digits. For the address:

```
3ffe:ffff:836f:0a00:000a:0800:200a:c031
```

the name of the PTR record is as follows:

```
1.3.0.c.a.0.0.2.0.0.8.0.a.0.0.0.0.0.a.0.f.6.3.8.f.f.f.f.e.f.f.3.ip6.arpa.
```

PTR records do not have to match the corresponding address record. In the example in the previous section, the address record:

```
sw4.example.com.   A   192.168.8.44
```

is shown. If you use the address 192.168.8.44 to look up the host name via a PTR record, you might find the name *sw4.example.com*, or you might find something completely different, for example:

---

[1] The top-level domain name *arpa* is rooted in history. It refers to the original wide-area network called the Arpanet, but has now been redesignated as an acronym for *Address and Routing Parameter Area*.

```
44.8.168.192.in-addr.arpa.  PTR  lilac.csi.example.com.
```

This record gives the name *lilac.csi.example.com* for the address 192.168.8.44, despite the fact that the address was given for the name *sw4.example.com*. This kind of arrangement is often found where the name of some kind of service is widely published, with an address record to point to a host that is currently providing the service. The host itself, however, has a different primary name, which is what the PTR record contains.

For example, the name we have been using, *sw4.example.com*, might be the name of a mail switching service that currently is provided by the host *lilac.csi.example.com*. Moving the service to another host just requires the DNS to be updated; no host has to change its name. If more than one host is providing the service, several address records may exist for the same domain. Modern name servers return these in a different order each time they are queried, which provides a form of load-sharing.

There is no enforced connection between address records and PTR records, and for any given host, one may exist without the other. The main use of these records in connection with mail is for finding the name of the remote host that is sending a message, because all that is initially known about the host at the far end of an incoming TCP/IP connection is its IP address. The host name may be required for checking against policy rules controlling what types of message remote hosts may send.

CNAME ("canonical name") records provide another kind of aliasing facility. For example:

```
pelican.example.com.  CNAME  redshank.csx.example.com.
```

states that the canonical name (real or main name) for the host that can be accessed as *pelican.example.com* is actually *redshank.csx.example.com*. There can be no other DNS records with the same name as that of a CNAME record. CNAME records should not normally be used in connection with mail routing. MX records provide sufficient redirection capabilities, and excessive aliasing just slows things down.

# 2.10 Common DNS errors

A number of mistakes commonly made by DNS administrators (who are usually known as "hostmasters") are shown in the following list. All except the first prevent mail from being delivered.

- MX records point to aliases instead of canonical names. That is, the domains on the right-hand side of MX records are the names of CNAME records instead of A or AAAA records. This should not prevent mail from working, but it is inefficient, and not strictly correct.

- MX records point to non-existent hosts, that is, to names that have no corresponding A or AAAA record.

- MX records contain IP addresses on the right-hand side instead of host names. This error is unfortunately becoming more widespread, abetted by some MTAs, which, in violation of RFC 1034, support the usage. Exim does not do so by default, but does have an option to enable this unrecommended, non-standard behaviour.

- MX records do not contain preference values.

Some broken name servers give a server error when asked for a non-existent MX record. This prevents mail from being delivered because an MTA is permitted to search for an address record only if it is sure there are no MX records. In the case of a server error, the MTA does not know this. Similar server errors have been seen in cases where a preference value has been omitted from an MX record. More robust name servers check records when loading their zones, and generate an error if any zones contain bad data.

Occasionally, the DNS appears to be giving different answers to identical queries. In the context of mail, this causes some messages to be rejected with "unknown domain" errors, whereas other messages to the same domain are delivered normally. The most common cause of this kind of behaviour is that the name servers for the zone are out of step. If you suspect this, you can check by directing a DNS query to a specific name server.

The first step is to find the relevant name servers by looking for the zone's NS records. To find the name servers for the zone *ioe.example.com*, for example, you can use the command:

```
$ nslookup -type=ns ioe.example.com
```

which might give these lines as the relevant parts of its answer:[1]

```
ioe.example.com    nameserver = mentor.ioe.example.com
ioe.example.com    nameserver = ns0.example.net
```

Once you know the name servers, you can query each one in turn for the domain in question; if the *nslookup* command is given a second argument, it is the name of a specific name server to which the query is to be sent. This sequence of commands and responses (where the commands are shown in boldface) indicates that there is a problem because the different name servers are giving conflicting answers:

---

[1] *nslookup* is one of the applications that omits the trailing dots when it displays domain names.

```
$ nslookup saturn.example.com mentor.ioe.example.com
Server:   mentor.ioe.example.com
Address:  192.168.34.22

Name:     saturn.example.com
Address:  192.168.5.4
$ nslookup saturn.example.com ns0.example.net
Server:   ns0.example.net
Address:  192.168.255.249

*** ns0.example.net can't find saturn.example.com:
    Non-existent host/domain
```

The problem may, however, be temporary. When a master name server is updated, it can take some hours before the data reaches the slaves, during which time this behaviour may be seen. However, if the discrepancy persists for any length of time, it is indicative of some kind of DNS error.

# 2.11 Role of the postmaster

*Postmaster* is the name given to the person who is in charge of administering an MTA. He or she should be familiar with the software and its configuration, and should regularly monitor its behaviour. If there are local users of the system, they should be able to contact the postmaster about any mail problems. If the MTA sends or receives mail to or from the Internet at large, people on other hosts must also be able to contact the postmaster.

The traditional way that this is done is by maintaining an alias address *postmaster@your.domain*, which redirects to the person who is currently performing the postmaster role. Indeed, the RFCs state that *postmaster* must always be supported as a case-insensitive local name.

# 3

# Exim overview

In the previous chapter, the job of an MTA is described in general terms. In this chapter, we explain how Exim is organized to do this job, and the overall way in which it operates. Then in the next chapter, we cover the basics of Exim administration before launching into more details about its configuration.

## 3.1 Exim philosophy

Exim is designed for use on a network where most messages can be delivered at the first attempt. This is usually true for most of the Internet. Measurements taken in the author's environment (a British university) indicate that well over 90% of messages are delivered almost immediately under normal conditions. This means that there is no need for an elaborate centralized queuing mechanism through which all messages pass. When a message arrives, an immediate delivery attempt is likely to be successful; only for a small number of messages is it necessary to implement a store and forward mechanism.

Therefore, although it is possible to configure Exim otherwise, the normal action is to try an immediate delivery as soon as a message has been received. In many cases this is successful, and nothing more is needed to process the message. Nevertheless, some precautions must be taken to avoid system overload in times of stress. For example, if the system load rises above some threshold, or if there are a large number of simultaneous incoming SMTP connections, immediate delivery may be temporarily disabled. In these events, incoming messages wait on Exim's queue and are delivered later.

All operations are performed by a single Exim binary, which operates in different ways that depend on the arguments with which it is called. Although receiving and delivering messages are treated as entirely separate operations, the code for determining how to deliver to a specific address is required in both cases, because during message reception, addresses are verified by checking whether it would be possible to deliver to them. For example, Exim verifies a remote sender address by looking up the domain in the DNS in exactly the same way as when setting up a delivery to that address.

On a system where Exim is fully installed as a replacement for Sendmail, one or both of the paths */usr/lib/sendmail* or */usr/sbin/sendmail* is a symbolic link to the

Exim binary. Therefore, any MUA, program, or script that attempts to send a message by calling Sendmail actually calls Exim.[1]

## 3.2 Exim's queue

The word *queue* is used for the set of messages that Exim has under its control at any one time, because this word is common in the context of mail transfer. However, Exim's queue is normally treated as a collection of messages with no implied ordering, more like a "pool" than a "queue". Furthermore, Exim does not maintain separate queues for different domains or different remote hosts. There is just a single, unordered collection of messages awaiting delivery, each of which may have several recipients. If you are an Exim administrator, you can list the messages on the queue by running the command:

```
exim -bp
```

assuming that your path is set up to contain the directory where the Exim binary is located. Exim administrators are referred to as "admin users" (☞ 19.3.2).

Messages that are not delivered immediately on arrival are picked up later by *queue runner* processes that scan the entire queue and start a delivery process for each message in turn. A queue runner process waits for each delivery process to complete before starting the next one.

## 3.3 Receiving and delivering messages

Message reception and message delivery are two entirely separate operations in Exim, and their only connection is that Exim normally tries to deliver a message as soon as it has received it. Receiving a message consists of writing it to local spool files ("putting it on the queue") and checking that the files have been successfully written before acknowledging receipt to the sending host or local process. There is only one copy of each message, however many recipients it has, and the collection of spool files *is* the queue; there are no additional files or in-memory lists of messages.

All the data about the state of a message is kept in its spool files. Each attempt at delivery causes every undelivered recipient address to be processed afresh. Exim does alias, forwarding, and mailing list expansion for local addresses (where configured) and domain lookups for remote addresses every time it handles a message. It does not normally retain previous alias, forwarding, or mailing list expansions from one delivery attempt to another.

---

[1]  Linux and BSD-based systems tend to use */usr/sbin/sendmail*, whereas Solaris uses */usr/lib/sendmail*. Different MUAs have different defaults, so some administrators set both paths to be on the safe side.

However, there is one exception to this: if the `one_time` option is set for a mailing list, the list's addresses are added to the original list of recipients at the first delivery attempt, and no re-expansion occurs at subsequent attempts (☞ 5.3.3).

# 3.4 Exim processes

Parallelism is obtained by the use of multiple processes, but one important aspect of Exim's design is that there is no central process that has overall responsibility for coordinating Exim's actions. Therefore, there is no concept of starting or stopping Exim as a whole. Exim processes can be started at any time by other processes. For example, user agents are always able to start Exim processes in order to send messages. Such processes perform a single task and then exit. Most processes are therefore short-lived, but Exim does make use of long-running daemon processes for two purposes:

(1)   To listen on the SMTP port for incoming TCP/IP connections. On receiving such a connection, the listener forks a new process to deal with it. An upper limit to the number of simultaneously active SMTP reception processes can be set. When the limit is reached, additional SMTP connections are refused.

(2)   To start up queue runner processes at fixed intervals. These scan the pool of waiting messages (by default in an arbitrary order) and initiate fresh delivery attempts. A message may be on the queue because a previous delivery attempt failed, or because no delivery attempt was initiated when the message was received. Each delivery attempt processes a single message and runs in its own process, and the queue runner waits for it to complete before moving on to the next message. A limit may be set for the number of simultaneously active queue runner processes run by a daemon.

A single daemon process can be used to perform both these functions, and this is the most common configuration. However, it is possible to run Exim without using a daemon at all; *inetd* can be used to accept incoming SMTP connections and start up an Exim process for each one, and queue runner processes can be started by *cron* or some other means. However, in these cases Exim has no control over how many such processes are run, so if you are worried about system overload, you must control the number of processes yourself.[1]

# 3.5 Coordination between processes

Processes for receiving and delivering messages are for the most part entirely independent. The small amount of coordination that is necessary is achieved by sharing files. Minimizing synchronization and serialization requirements between processes

---

[1]   *xinetd* (*www.xinetd.org*) is a replacement for *inetd* that includes additional control facilities.

helps Exim to scale well. Apart from the messages themselves, the shared data consists of a number of files containing "hints" about mail delivery. For example, if a remote host cannot be contacted, the time of the failure and the suggested next time to try that host are recorded. Any delivery process that has a message for that host will read the hint and refrain from trying the delivery if the retry time has not been reached. This does not affect delivery of the same message to other hosts when there is more than one recipient address.

Because the coordinating data is treated as a collection of hints, it is not a major disaster if any or all of it is lost; there may be a period of less optimal mail delivery, but that is all. Consequently, the code that maintains the hints can be simple, because it does not have to be made robust against unusual circumstances.

## 3.6 How Exim is configured

Configuration information, supplied by the administrator, is used at two different times: one configuration file is used when building the Exim binary, and another is read whenever the binary is run. Most options can be specified in only one of these files. That is, they either control how the binary is built, or they modify its behaviour at runtime. However, there are a few build-time options that set defaults for runtime behaviour. The sources of Exim's configuration information are shown in figure 3-1.

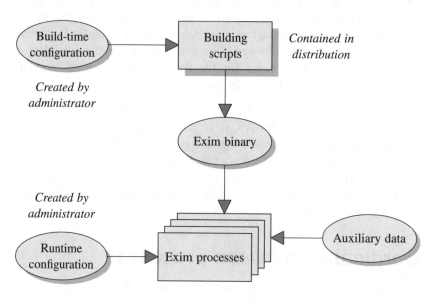

*Figure 3-1: Exim configuration*

The build-time options are of three kinds:

- Those that specify the inclusion of optional code, for example, to support specific database lookups such as LDAP, or to support IPv6.

- Those that specify fixed values that cannot be changed at runtime, for example, the mode (permissions) of message files in Exim's spool directory.

- Those that specify default values for certain runtime options, for example, the location of Exim's log files.

The process of building Exim from source is described in chapter 22. Here, we consider the runtime configuration. This is controlled by a single text file, often called something like */usr/exim/configure* or */etc/exim.conf*. You can find out the actual name by running the following command:

```
exim -bP configure_file
```

Whenever Exim is executed, it starts by reading its runtime configuration file. A large number of settings can be present, but for any one installation only a few are normally used. The data from the file is held in main memory while an Exim process is running. For this reason, if you change the file, you have to tell the Exim daemon to reload it. This is done by sending the daemon a SIGHUP signal. All other Exim processes are short-lived, so as new ones start up after the change, they pick up the new configuration automatically.

For very simple installations, it may be possible to include all the configuration data within the runtime configuration file. A configuration of this type is shown in the next chapter (☞ 4.3.2). Normally, however, the runtime configuration refers to auxiliary data, which can be in ordinary files, or in databases such as NIS or LDAP. Common examples are the system alias file (usually called */etc/aliases*) and users' *.forward* files. Files or databases can also be used for lists of hosts, domains, or addresses that are to be handled in some special way and that are too long to conveniently include within the configuration file itself. Data from such sources is read afresh every time it is needed, so updates take immediate effect and there is no need to send a SIGHUP signal to the daemon.

The simplest item that is found in the runtime configuration file is an option set to a fixed string. For example, the following line:

```
qualify_domain = example.com
```

specifies that addresses containing only a local part and no domain are to be turned into complete addresses ("qualified") by appending @*example.com*.[1] Each such setting appears on a line by itself. For many option settings, fixed data suffices, but Exim also provides ways for you to supply data that is re-evaluated and modified

---

[1]  Unqualified addresses are accepted only from local processes, or from certain remote hosts that you explicitly designate.

every time it is used. Examples and explanations of this feature are introduced later in this chapter.

# 3.7 How Exim delivers messages

Exim's configuration determines how it processes addresses; this processing involves finding information about the destinations of a message and how to transport it to those destinations. In this and the following sections, we discuss how the configuration that you set up controls what happens.

There are many different ways an address can be processed. For example, looking up a domain in the DNS involves a completely different way of processing from looking up a local part in an alias file, and delivering a message using SMTP over TCP/IP has very little in common with appending it to a mailbox file. There are separate blocks of code in Exim for doing the different kinds of processing, and each is separately and independently configurable. The word *driver* is used as the general term for one of these code blocks. In many cases, when you specify that a particular driver is to be used, you need only give one or two parameters for it. However, most drivers have a number of other options whose defaults can be changed to vary their behaviour.

There are three different kinds of driver. Two of them are concerned with handling addresses and delivering messages, and are called *routers* and *transports*. The job of routers is to process addresses and decide what deliveries are to take place. Transports, on the other hand, are the components of Exim that actually deliver messages by writing them to files, or to pipes, or over SMTP connections. The third kind of driver handles SMTP authentication and is described in chapter 13.

Before going into more detail, we take a brief look at the way drivers are used as a message makes its way through the system. Exim has to decide whether each address is to be delivered on the local host or to a remote one. Then it has to choose the correct form of transport for each address (appending to a user's mailbox, for instance, or connecting to another host via SMTP), and finally it has to invoke those transports. For example, in a typical configuration, a message addressed to *bug_reports@exim.example*, where *exim.example* is a local domain, might be handled like this:

(1)   The first router in the configuration is a **dnslookup** router that handles addresses that are not in a local domain by looking up MX records in the DNS. As the address we are considering is in a local domain, this router is skipped.

(2)   The next router handles system aliases; this tells Exim to check the */etc/aliases* file. Here it finds that the local part *bug_reports* is indeed an alias, and that it resolves to two other addresses: the local address *brutus@exim.example*, and the remote address *julia@helpersys.org.example*. Exim adds these two new

addresses to the list of recipients that it is routing. It has now finished with the original address.

(3)    The two new addresses are considered in turn. For the first of them, *brutus@exim.example*, the first router is again skipped because the domain is local. This time, the second router does not find an alias for *brutus*, so the address is passed on to the following routers. One of them is a router that recognizes local users such as *brutus*, and it arranges for Exim to run a transport called **appendfile**, which adds a copy of the message to Brutus' mailbox. The actual delivery does not take place until after Exim has worked out how to handle all the addresses.

(4)    For the other recipient, because the domain *helpersys.org.example* is not local, the first router is run. It looks up the domain in the DNS, and finds the IP address of the remote host to which the message should be sent. It then arranges for Exim to run the **smtp** transport to carry out the delivery.

This example has introduced several of the most commonly used drivers. Later in this chapter, we work through a similar example in much more detail. The individual drivers are described in their own sections in later chapters; here is an alphabetical list of them:

**accept**

A router that accepts any address that is passed to it. Normally, it is constrained by one or more preconditions, as described in the next section. For example, **accept** is used with the `check_local_user` option to accept messages for local users. Without any preconditions, **accept** can be used as a "catchall" router.

**appendfile**

A transport that writes messages to local files. It can be configured either to append to a single file that holds multiple messages, or to write a new file for each message.

**autoreply**

A transport that generates automatic replies to messages.

**dnslookup**

A router that looks up domains in the DNS and does MX processing.

**ipliteral**

A router that handles "IP literal" addresses such as *user@[192.168.5.6]*. These are relics of the early Internet that are no longer in common use.

**lmtp**

A transport that delivers messages to external processes using the LMTP protocol (RFC 2033), which is a variation of SMTP that is designed for passing messages between local processes.

**manualroute**

A router that routes domains using locally supplied information such as a list of domains and corresponding hosts.

**pipe**

A transport that passes messages to external processes via pipes.

**queryprogram**

A router that runs an external program in order to route an address.

**redirect**

A router that handles several different kinds of redirection, including alias files, users' *.forward* files, and Exim filter files. It can also explicitly force failure of an address.

**smtp**

A transport that writes messages to other hosts over TCP/IP connections, using either SMTP or LMTP.

The configuration may refer to the same driver code more than once, but with different options, thus allowing for multiple instances of the same driver type. Each driver instance is given an identifying name in the configuration file, for use in logging and for reference from other drivers.

# 3.8 Processing an address

When routing an address, Exim offers it to each configured router in turn, until one of them is able to deal with it. The order in which routers are defined in the configuration file is therefore important. However, before running a router, Exim first checks a number of preconditions. If any of them are not met, the router is skipped. For example, a router can be configured to apply only to certain domains or local parts. A wide range of conditions can be tested; as an extreme example, you can even restrict routers to certain times of day if you wish. The process of routing an address is illustrated in figure 3-2.

A router that successfully handles an address may add that address to a queue for a particular transport. Alternatively, a router may generate one or more "child" addresses that are added to the message's address list and processed in their own

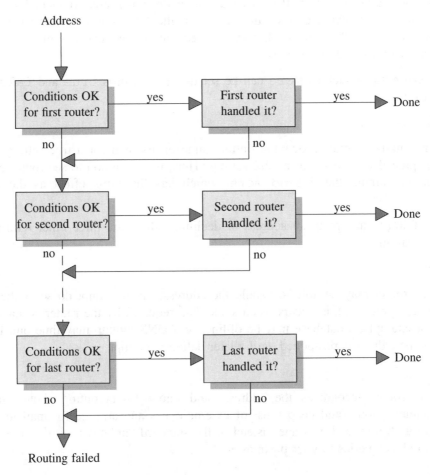

*Figure 3-2: Routing an address*

right, with the original address no longer playing any part. This is what happens when a local part matches an entry in an alias list, or when a user's *.forward* file is activated.

When a router cannot handle an address, it is said to *decline*. When this happens, the address is by default passed to the next router. If every router declines or is skipped, the address cannot be handled at all, and delivery fails. However, you can cut the routing process short by setting the more option on a router to be false. In this case, addresses that cause the router to decline are not passed on. Instead, routing fails immediately. For example, the first router in a configuration is often a **dnslookup** router that has a precondition for checking that the domain is not local, together with the more option set false. For a local domain, the router is skipped and the following routers are used, because the precondition is not met. For a non-local domain, the router does a DNS lookup. If it succeeds, the address is routed to a suitable transport; if it fails, the router declines, but because of the false setting of more, no further routers are run. This means that the subsequent routers can assume that they are dealing with local domains only.

Boolean options such as more can be set using the words true and false, as in this example:

```
more = false
```

An alternative syntax allows the option name on its own for a true setting, and the name preceded by no_ for a false setting. Thus, it is common to see router configurations containing the line no_more, which has the same effect as the example above.

In addition to accepting an address or declining, there are three other returns that a router can give:

*defer*

The router may be able to handle the address, but it cannot do so at the present time. Typically, this occurs when some data required by the router is inaccessible. For example, a database may be offline, or a DNS lookup may time out. Delivery to the address is postponed until a later delivery attempt.

*fail*

The router recognizes the address, and knows that routing should fail. For example, you could keep a list of ex-employees and arrange for mail to them to fail with a special message instead of the standard "unknown user", in an attempt to reduce queries to your postmaster.

*pass*

The router recognizes the address, but cannot handle it itself. It requests that the address be passed to a later router, overriding a false setting of more.

Figure 3-3 illustrates these outcomes for an individual router. However, most routers are restricted to just a few of these possibilities.

# 3.9 A simple example in detail

To help clarify the mechanisms just described, and to introduce some details of the runtime configuration file, a complete example of a message delivery is presented here. The scenario is a host called *simple.example*, where the host name is the only local mail domain. The host is using a simple Exim configuration file that supports aliases, users' forward files, delivery to local users' mailboxes, and remote SMTP

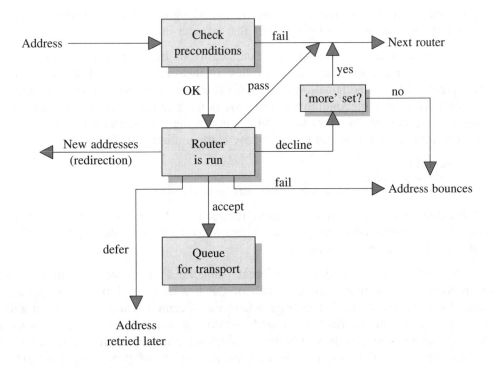

*Figure 3-3: An individual router*

delivery. Suppose a user of this host has sent a message addressed to one local and one remote recipient:

```
postmaster@simple.example
friend@another.example
```

At the start of delivery, Exim's list of addresses to process is initialized with the two original recipients, and its first job is to work through this list, deciding what to do for each address. We suppose that it starts by routing *postmaster@simple.example*. The first router in the configuration is this:

```
notlocal:
  driver = dnslookup
  domains = ! simple.example
  transport = remote_smtp
  no_more
```

The first line, terminated by a colon, is the name for this particular router instance, chosen by the system administrator. Each driver instance of a particular type (router or transport) must have a distinct name. The second configuration line specifies which kind of router this is (or, to put it another way, it chooses which block of router code to run), and the remaining lines are options for the router. Options specify both preconditions and parameters that a router uses.

The only precondition on this router is the setting of the `domains` option, which specifies the domains that the router handles. In this case, there is just one domain listed, preceded by an exclamation mark. This is a sign of negation in Exim configuration lists. Thus, this precondition means "the domain must not be *simple.example*". Consequently, this router is skipped when processing *postmaster@simple.example*, and Exim moves on to the next router, whose configuration is as follows:

```
system_aliases:
  driver = redirect
  data = ${lookup{$local_part}lsearch{/etc/aliases}}
```

The **redirect** router implements address redirection of various kinds, and in this instance it is configured to search the system aliases file (*/etc/aliases*) to see if the local part of the address is an alias.

The value of the `data` option is different from the settings we have met so far, which have all been fixed values. Much of the flexibility of Exim's configuration comes from the use of option settings where the specified strings contain variables and other special items. Each time such a string is used, it undergoes a process known as *string expansion* in which the variables are replaced by their current values and the other special items are replaced by the results of processing the text in various ways. String expansion is used in many examples throughout this book. A complete description of all the expansion features is given in chapter 17. Here, we will just give a brief description of this particular example.

The embedded dollar characters in the string trigger the expansion mechanism. The first of them introduces a lookup item, which is replaced by data that is looked up in a file. The second dollar introduces a variable substitution; in this case, the value of the *$local_part* variable is being used as the key for the lookup. As you might guess, *$local_part* contains the local part of the address being processed, which in this case is *postmaster*.

The remainder of the lookup item specifies the file, and the way in which it is to be searched. In this case, the file is */etc/aliases*, and a linear search ("lsearch") is required. This expects each line of the file to contain an alias name, optionally terminated by a colon, followed by the list of replacement addresses for the alias, which may be continued onto subsequent lines by starting them with whitespace. A comma is used to separate addresses in the list. For example:

```
root:       postmaster@simple.example,
            herb@simple.example
postmaster: simon@simple.example
```

Notice that the first line specifies that *root* is an alias for *postmaster*, which itself is an alias. This is a common practice, and works exactly as you might expect, though care must be taken to avoid routing loops (☞ 3.10.3). Exim reads through the file, and finds the entry for *postmaster* with its associated data. The result of the expansion of the `data` option is the string:

```
simon@simple.example
```

The **redirect** router adds this new address to the list of addresses to be routed, and returns a code that indicates success. This means that *postmaster@simple.example* has been completely processed. The list of pending addresses now contains the following:

```
simon@simple.example
friend@another.example
```

Suppose Exim tackles *simon@simple.example* next. This is another local address, so again the **notlocal** router is skipped, and the address is offered to the **system_aliases** router. This time, however, there is no match for *simon* in */etc/aliases*, so the result of expanding the `data` option is empty. The router returns a code indicating "decline", which causes Exim to offer the address to the next router, whose configuration is as follows:

```
userforward:
  driver = redirect
  check_local_user
  file = $home/.forward
```

This is another instance of the **redirect** router. This time there is one precondition: the `check_local_user` option. This checks that the local part of the address corresponds to a user login name on the local host. If there is no matching user, the router is skipped. However, we suppose that *simon* is a valid user, so the router is run. The `data` option is not set for this instance of **redirect**; instead there is a setting of the `file` option. The value of the option is expanded (with *$home* replaced by *simon*'s home directory), but instead of being a list of redirection addresses (as `data` was for the previous router), the expanded string is interpreted as a file name. The router now checks to see if the file exists.

If *simon* has a *.forward* file in his home directory, its contents are a list of forwarding addresses and other types of item (☞ 7.6.7). The addresses are added to the list of addresses to be routed, and the **userforward** router returns a code indicating success. The new addresses are eventually processed independently, in the same way that the new address from the **system_aliases** router was handled.

If *simon* does not have a *.forward* file, the router declines, and *simon@simple.example* is offered to the next router in the configuration:

```
localuser:
  driver = accept
  check_local_user
  transport = local_delivery
```

This has the same precondition (`check_local_user`) as the previous router. Exim keeps a cache of the most recently looked-up username to avoid wasteful repetition, so it already knows that this precondition is met. If *simon* were not a local user, the router would decline, and as there are no more routers in this configuration, the address would fail. It would be placed on a list of failed addresses and used to generate a bounce message at the end of the delivery attempt.

The **accept** router imposes no conditions of its own. If its preconditions are met, it accepts the address and places it on a queue for the transport that is specified by the `transport` option (in this case, **local_delivery**). The uid, gid, and home directory that were looked up for *simon* are attached to the address, so that they can be used by the transport.

That is all that happens at this stage; no actual delivery takes place until later. The processing of *postmaster@simple.example* is illustrated in figure 3-4, where the ellipses represent sources of information, and the rectangles represent routers. The **notlocal** router, which is skipped for this address, is not shown.

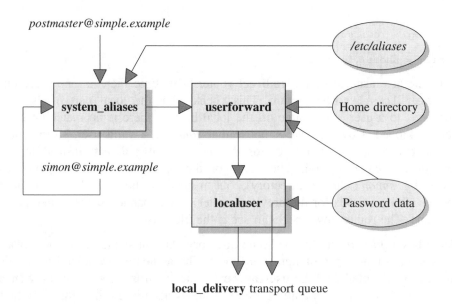

*Figure 3-4: Routing postmaster@simple.example*

There is still one address to process: *friend@another.example*. Exim offers it to the first router:

```
notlocal:
  driver = dnslookup
  domains = ! simple.example
  transport = remote_smtp
  no_more
```

This time, the precondition is met because the domain is not *simple.example*, and so the router is run. The job of **dnslookup** is to obtain a list of remote hosts by looking up the domain in the DNS, using MX and address records (☞ 2.8). If it fails to find the domain in the DNS, the router declines. In this configuration, we have the more option set false (by virtue of the no_more line), which means that no further routers are run. In other words, if the domain is not found in the DNS, the address is bounced.

When **dnslookup** is successful, it ends up with an ordered list of hosts and their IP addresses. It puts the mail address on a queue for the **remote_smtp** transport, attaching the host list. In our example, if the MX and address records were the following:

```
another.example.         MX   6    mail-2.another.example.
another.example.         MX   4    mail-1.another.example.
mail-1.another.example.  A         192.168.34.67
mail-2.another.example.  A         192.168.88.32
```

then the list of hosts to be passed with the address to **remote_smtp** would be:

```
mail-1.another.example   192.168.34.67
mail-2.another.example   192.168.88.32
```

Any hosts that have the same MX preference value are sorted into a random order. The processing of *friend@another.example* is illustrated in figure 3-5.

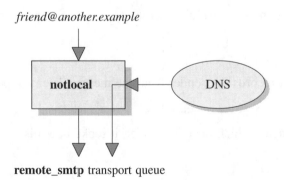

*Figure 3-5: Routing friend@another.example*

There are now no more unprocessed addresses, so the routing phase of the delivery process is complete. Exim moves on to carry out the actual deliveries by running the transports that have been set up. Local transports are run first; in our example, one local delivery is set up for the address *simon@simple.example*, using the **local_delivery** transport. This was specified by the **localuser** router that handled the address. The transport is configured thus:

```
local_delivery:
  driver = appendfile
  file = /var/mail/$local_part
  delivery_date_add
  envelope_to_add
  return_path_add
```

This specifies an **appendfile** transport (☞ 9.4), which adds a copy of the message to the end of a mailbox file in conventional Unix format when configured in this way. The name of the file is given by the `file` option, which is an expanded string. Exim replaces the substring `$local_part` by the local part of the address that is being delivered, so the file that is actually used is */var/mail/simon*. The remaining three options request the addition of three generally useful header lines as the message is written:

*Delivery-date:*

A header line that records the date and time of delivery, for example:

```
Delivery-date: Fri, 31 Dec 1999 23:59:59 +0000
```

*Envelope-to:*

A header line that records the original recipient address (the "envelope to" address) that caused the delivery; in this example it would be:

```
Envelope-to: postmaster@simple.example
```

Preserving this address is useful in case it does not appear in the *To:* or *Cc:* header lines.

*Return-path:*

A header line that records the sender from the message's envelope. For example:

```
Return-path: <user@simple.example>
```

For bounce messages, which have no sender, it looks like this:

```
Return-path: <>
```

Local deliveries are run sequentially in separate processes that change their user identity to an appropriate value in each case (☞ 19.1). In this case, the user ID (uid) and group ID (gid) of the local user were passed to the transport by the **localuser** router, so these are used. The delivery subprocess is therefore running "as the user" when it accesses the mailbox.

When the subprocess has finished, there are no more local deliveries, so Exim proceeds to the remote ones. These are also run in separate processes, in this case using Exim's own uid and gid. Exim can be configured to run a number of remote deliveries in parallel when there is more than one remote delivery to be done, but in our example there is only one remote delivery. This was set up for *friend@ another.example* by the **notlocal** router, which routed it to the **remote_smtp** transport:

```
remote_smtp:
  driver = smtp
```

There are no option settings here beyond the one that selects the type of transport, because the list of hosts was obtained by the **notlocal** router and passed to the transport along with the address. The parameters of the outgoing SMTP connection (for example, the timeouts) can be changed by other options, but in this case we accept all the defaults. The **smtp** transport tries to make an SMTP connection to each host in turn. If all goes well, a connection is made to one of them, and the message is transferred.

There are now no more deliveries to be done, and all the recipients have been successfully handled, so at this point Exim can delete the message files on its spool and log the fact that this message has been delivered. The delivery process then exits.

# 3.10 Complications while routing

Things do not always go as smoothly as described in the simple example. Some of the more common complications that can be encountered when routing an address are given below.

## 3.10.1 Duplicate addresses

Duplicate addresses are a complication that Exim may have to handle, either because the sender of the message specified the same address more than once, or because aliasing or forwarding duplicated an existing recipient address. For any given address, only a single delivery takes place, except when the duplicates are pipe commands. If one user is forwarding to another, and a message is sent to both of them, only a single copy is delivered. If, on the other hand, two different users set up their *.forward* files to pipe to */usr/bin/vacation* (for example), a message that is sent to both of them runs the vacation program twice, once as each user.

## 3.10.2 Missing data

Sometimes, a router is unable to determine whether it can handle an address. For example, if the administrator has misspelled the name of an alias file, or if it has been accidentally deleted, a **redirect** router cannot operate. Timeouts can occur when a router queries the DNS, and routers can refer to databases that may at times be offline. In these situations, the router returns a code indicating "defer" to the main part of Exim, and the address is neither delivered nor failed, but left on the spool for another delivery attempt at a later time. The control of retry times is described in chapter 12. If the error condition is felt to be sufficiently serious, the message is "frozen", which means that queue runner processes will not try to deliver it. Because frozen messages are highlighted in queue listings, this also serves to bring them to the administrator's attention.

### 3.10.3 Routing loops

When a **redirect** router handles an address, the new addresses that it generates are each processed afresh, just like the original recipient addresses.[1] This means that one alias can refer to another, as in the example we showed earlier:

```
root:        postmaster@simple.example
postmaster:  simon@simple.example
```

However, this opens up the possibility of routing loops. To prevent this, Exim automatically skips a router if the address it is handling has a "parent" address that was processed by that router. Consider the following broken alias file:

```
chicken:     egg@simple.example
egg:         chicken@simple.example
```

This router turns the address *chicken@simple.example* into *egg@simple.example*, and then turns it back into *chicken@simple.example* the next time through. However, on the third pass, Exim notices that the address was previously processed by the router, so it is skipped and the next router is called. The chances are that the resulting delivery or bounce are not what was intended, but at least the loop is broken.

### 3.10.4 Remote address routing to the local host

After Exim has routed an address to a list of remote hosts, it checks to see whether the first host on the list is the local host. Usually, this indicates some kind of configuration error, and by default Exim treats it as such. However, there are types of configuration where this is legitimate, and for these cases, the `self` option can be used to specify what is to be done (☞ 6.5).

## 3.11 Complications during delivery

A successful routing process for a remote address discovers a list of hosts to which it can be sent, but it cannot check the local part of the address. The most common permanent error during a remote delivery is "unknown user" in response to an SMTP

---

[1] This is the normal practice; there are occasions when it is not wanted, and there is an option, `redirect_router`, that can be used to disable it.

RCPT command. Responsibility for the message remains with the sending host, which must return a bounce message to the sender.

There are other reasons a remote host might permanently refuse a message, and in addition, there are many common temporary errors, such as the inability to contact a host. These cause a message to remain on the spool for later delivery.

In contrast, routers for local addresses normally check local parts, so any "unknown user" errors happen at routing time. The only problems a local transport is likely to encounter are errors in the actual copying of the message. The most common is a full mailbox; Exim respects system quotas and can also be configured to impose its own quotas (☞ 9.4.6). A quota failure leaves the message on the spool for later delivery.

The runtime configuration contains a set of retry rules (see chapter 12) that specify how often, and for how long, Exim is to go on trying to deliver messages that are suffering temporary failures. The rules can specify different behaviours for different kinds of error.

## 3.12 Complications after delivery

When all delivery attempts for a message are complete, a delivery process has two final tasks. If any deliveries suffered temporary errors, or if any deliveries succeeded after previous temporary errors, the delivery process has to update the retry hints database. This work is saved up for the end of delivery so that the process opens the hints database for updating only once at most, and for as short a time as possible. If the updating should fail, the new hint information is lost, but previous hint information remains. In practice, except in exceptional circumstances such as a power loss, hint information is rarely lost.

Finally, unsuccessful delivery may cause a message to be sent to the sender. If any addresses failed, a single bounce message is generated, containing information about all of them. If any addresses were deferred, and have been delayed for more than a certain time (☞ 19.8.3), a warning message may be sent.

Exim sends such messages by calling itself in a subprocess. Failure to create a bounce message causes Exim to write to its panic log and immediately exit. This has the effect of leaving the message on the spool so that there will be another delivery attempt, and presumably another attempt at sending the bounce message when the delivery fails again. Failure to create a warning message, on the other hand, is not treated as serious. Another attempt to send it is made when the original message is processed again.

# 3.13 Use of transports by routers

In the simple example we have been considering, the **localuser** and **notlocal** routers both include the `transport` option (referring to the **local_delivery** and **remote_smtp** transports, respectively), whereas the other routers do not have any transport settings. A transport is required for any router that actually sets up a message delivery, in order to determine how the delivery should be carried out. When a router is just changing the delivery address by aliasing or forwarding, a transport is not required because no delivery is being set up at that stage.

The **redirect** router has additional options for some special-purpose transports. This router can deliver a message to a specific file, or to a pipe associated with a given command. For example, a line in an alias file of the form:

```
majordomo:  |/usr/mail/majordomo ...
```

specifies that a message addressed to the local part *majordomo* is to be passed via a pipe to a process running the command:

```
/usr/mail/majordomo ...
```

The other entries in the alias file may just be changing delivery addresses, and may therefore not require a transport. However, this line is setting up a delivery, and so a transport is required. We can add the following line to the **system_aliases** router configuration:

```
pipe_transport = alias_pipe
```

This tells Exim which transport to run when a pipe is specified in the alias file. The transport itself is very simple:

```
alias_pipe:
  transport = pipe
  ignore_status
  return_output
```

A **pipe** transport runs a given command in a new process, and passes the message to it using a pipe for its standard input. In this example, the command is provided by the alias file, so the transport does not need to define it.[1] Setting `ignore_status` tells Exim to ignore the status returned by the command; without this, any value other than zero is treated as an error, causing the delivery to fail and a bounce message to be returned to the sender.

Setting `return_output` changes what happens if the command produces output on its standard output or standard error streams. By default, such output is discarded, but if `return_output` is set, the production of such output is treated as an error, and the output itself is returned to the sender in the bounce message.

---

[1] If the **pipe** transport is run directly from a router, the command to be run is defined using its `command` option.

There is one piece of information that the **alias_pipe** transport needs that we have not yet given, and that is the uid and gid under which it should run the command. When a pipe is triggered by an entry in a user's *.forward* file, the user's identity is assumed by default, but when an alias file is used, as it is here, there is no default. The `user` (and, optionally, `group`) option can appear in either the router or the transport's configuration, so the transport could become:[1]

```
alias_pipe:
  transport = pipe
  ignore_status
  return_output
  user = majordom
```

In addition to delivery to pipes, alias files and forward files may also specify files into which messages are to be delivered. For example, if user *caesar* has a *.forward* containing:

```
caesar@another.domain.example, /home/caesar/mail-archive
```

it requests delivery to another mail address, and also into the named file, which is a delivery that needs a transport. To support this feature, the **userforward** router could contain:

```
file_transport = address_file
```

This tells Exim which transport to run when a filename is specified instead of an address in a forward file. The transport itself is even more simple than the **alias_pipe** transport:

```
address_file:
  driver = appendfile
```

The filename comes from the forward file, and all other options are defaulted.

An alias or forward file may contain both these kinds of entry, thus requiring both `pipe_transport` and `file_transport` to be given on a single router. These options are used for these very specific purposes only, and should not be confused with the generic `transport` option that can be set for any router instance.

---

[1]  This assumes that all the pipes specified in the alias file are to be run under the same uid. If there are several instances that require different user identities, an expansion string can be used to select the correct uid, but that is too advanced for the discussion here.

# 4

# Exim operations overview

The previous chapter used some fragments from a simple configuration file to show how Exim goes about delivering a message. Later chapters go into more detail about the various options that can be used to set up configurations for handling many different circumstances. However, if you have just installed Exim, or if you have inherited responsibility for an Exim system from somebody else, you probably want to know a little about the basic operational aspects. This chapter is an overview; the features that are described reappear later in more detailed discussions. In particular, chapter 21 covers Exim administration in detail.

## 4.1 How Exim identifies messages

Each message that Exim handles is given a unique *message ID* when it is received. The ID is 16 characters long, and consists of three parts separated by hyphens, for example, 11uNWX-0004fP-00. Each part is actually a number, encoded in base 62, with decimal digits, upper-case letters, and lower-case letters used to represent values in the range 0–61.[1] The first part of the ID is the conventional Unix representation of the time that the message started to be received, that is, the number of seconds since the epoch (1 January 1970). The second part is the ID of the process (the pid) that received the message. The third part is used to distinguish between messages that are received by the same process in the same second.

For most installations, uniqueness of message ID is required only within a single host. However, in some cluster configurations, it is useful to ensure that message IDs are unique within the cluster. For example, suppose two hosts are providing identical gateway or hubbing services for some domain, and one of the processors has a catastrophic failure. If its disk can be attached to the other processor, and the message IDs are unique across both systems, spooled message files can simply be moved into the survivor's spool directory.

Uniqueness across several hosts can be ensured by assigning each host a number in the range 0–16, and specifying it in each Exim configuration. For example:

```
localhost_number = 4
```

When this option is set, the host number is incorporated into the third part of message IDs.

---

[1] When Exim is run on an operating system where file names are case-insensitive, base 36 has to be used instead of base 62, because message IDs are used to form spool file names.

# 4.2 Watching Exim at work

As a new administrator of an MTA, the first questions you should ask are:

- How do I find out what messages are on the queue?

- How do I find out what the MTA has been doing?

Exim can display the status of its queue in a number of ways (☞ 20.7). The most basic is the -bp command-line option. This option is compatible with Sendmail, though the output is specific to Exim:[1]

```
$ exim -bp
25m  2.9K  0t5C6f-0000c8-00 <caesar@rome.example>
             brutus@rome.example
```

This shows that there is just one message, from *caesar@rome.example* to *brutus@rome.example*, which is 2.9 KB in size, and which has been on the queue for 25 minutes. Exim also outputs the same information if it is called under the name *mailq*, which is a fairly common convention.[2]

Exim logs every action it takes in its main log file (☞ 21.1). A log line is written whenever a message arrives and whenever a delivery succeeds or fails. The name of the log file depends on the configuration, with two common choices being */var/spool/exim/log/mainlog* and */var/log/exim_mainlog*.[3] If you have access to an X Window server, you can run the *eximon* utility (☞ 21.7), which displays a "tail" of the main log in a window.

Exim uses two additional log files that are in the same directory as the main log. One is called *rejectlog*; it records details of messages that have been rejected for reasons of policy. The other is called *paniclog*; this is used when Exim encounters some disaster that it cannot handle. The panic log should normally be empty; it is a good idea to set up some automatic monitoring to let you know if something has been written to it, because that usually indicates an incident that warrants investigation.

# 4.3 The runtime configuration file

Exim's runtime configuration is held in a single text file that you can modify with your favourite text editor. If you make a change, newly started Exim processes will immediately pick up the new file, but the daemon process will not. You have to tell the daemon to reread its configuration, and this is done in the traditional Unix way, by sending it a SIGHUP signal. The process number of the daemon is stored in

---

[1]  In examples of commands that are run from the shell, the input is shown in boldface type.

[2]  Many operating systems are set up with the *mailq* command as a symbolic link to *sendmail*; if this in turn has been linked to *exim*, the *mailq* command will "just work".

[3]  It is possible to configure Exim to use *syslog* instead, but this has several disadvantages.

Exim's spool directory, so that you can do this by running (as *root* or *exim*) the
following command:

```
kill -HUP `cat /var/spool/exim/exim-daemon.pid`
```

On receiving a SIGHUP signal, the daemon closes down and then restarts itself,
thereby picking up the new configuration.

Lines in the configuration file that begin with a # character are comments, which are
ignored by Exim.

---

 # is a comment character only when it occurs at the start of a line. It is
not treated specially elsewhere because it may legitimately appear as
part of a file name or an email address. However, in files that contain
one-per-line lists (see chapter 18), # can be used to add comments at
the ends of lines.

---

Throughout the runtime configuration, any non-comment line can be continued by
ending it with a backslash. For example:

```
hold_domains = dom1.example.com : \
               dom2.example.com : \
               dom3.example.com
```

Trailing whitespace after the backslash and leading whitespace at the start of the next
line is ignored. Comment lines may appear in the middle of a sequence of continuation lines.

## 4.3.1 Layout of the configuration file

The runtime configuration file is divided into the following seven sections:

*Main section*

General option settings and overall input controls

*ACL section*

Access control lists

*Routers section*

Configuration for the routers

*Transports section*

Configuration for the transports

*Retry section*

   Rules for specifying how often Exim is to retry temporarily failing addresses

*Rewrite section*

   Global address rewriting rules

*Authenticator section*

   Configuration for the SMTP authenticators

The main configuration must always appear at the start of the file. Except when we are discussing a specific driver, unqualified references to options always refer to the options in the main configuration section. Each of the other sections is introduced by a line that starts with the word begin, followed by the name of the section. For example:

```
begin routers
```

These sections can appear in any order, and any that are not needed can be omitted. This means that a completely empty file is, in fact, a valid configuration file, but it would not be much use because no way to deliver messages is defined.

The ACL, retry, and rewrite configuration sections each contain lines in a format that is unique to the section, and we discuss these in later chapters. The remaining sections contain option settings in the form *<name>=<value>*, one per line.

## 4.3.2 A minimal configuration file

The simplest complete configuration that is capable of delivering both local and remote mail is as follows:

```
# Main configuration: no policy checks

acl_smtp_rcpt = accept

# Routers: standard DNS routing and local users

begin routers

lookuphost:
  driver = dnslookup
  domains = ! localdomain.example
  transport = remote_smtp

localuser:
  driver = accept
  check_local_user
  transport = local_delivery
```

```
# Transports: SMTP and local mailboxes

begin transports

remote_smtp:
  driver = smtp

local_delivery:
  driver = appendfile
  file = /var/mail/$local_part
```

This example is even simpler in its handling of the local domain than the case we considered in the previous chapter; it does not support aliasing or forwarding. Because there are no retry rules in this configuration, messages that suffer temporary delivery failures will be returned to their senders without any retries. Furthermore, there are no policy checks on incoming SMTP mail, which means that this is an "open relay" configuration. It would not be a sensible example to use for real.

## 4.3.3 Option setting syntax

We have already seen a number of examples of option settings. Each one is on a line by itself, and they can always be in the form *<name>=<value>*. For those that are on/off switches (Boolean options), other forms are also permitted. The name on its own turns the option on, whereas the name preceded by no_ or not_ turns it off. These settings are all equivalent:

```
split_spool_directory
split_spool_directory = true
split_spool_directory = yes
```

So are these:

```
no_split_spool_directory
not_split_spool_directory
split_spool_directory = false
split_spool_directory = no
```

You do not have to use quotes for option values that are text strings, but if you do, any backslashes in the strings are interpreted specially. Exim recognizes only double-quote characters for this purpose. For example, the sequence \n in a quoted string is converted into a linefeed character. This feature is not needed very often.

Some options specify a time interval such as the timeout period for an SMTP connection. A time interval is specified as a number followed by one of the letters w (week), d (day), h (hour), m (minute), or s (second). You can combine several of these to make up one value. For example, the following:

```
connect_timeout = 4m30s
```

specifies a time interval of 4 minutes and 30 seconds. Exim makes no check on the values used in these combinations.

## 4.3.4 Including other files in the configuration

If you want to, you can keep parts of the configuration in other files, and include them in the main configuration by using one or more lines of the following form:

```
.include <filename>
```

For example, suppose you are running Exim on a number of different hosts with almost identical configurations. You can have the same master configuration file on all the hosts, and use `.include` to incorporate the host-specific parts.

## 4.3.5 Macros in the configuration file

For more complicated configuration files, it may be helpful to make use of the simple macro facility. If a line in the main part of the configuration (that is, before the first `begin` line) begins with an upper-case letter, it is taken as a macro definition, of the form:

```
<name> = <rest of line>
```

The name must consist of letters, digits, and underscores, and need not all be in upper case, though that is recommended. The rest of the logical line is the replacement text, and has leading and trailing whitespace removed. Quotes are not removed.

Once a macro is defined, all subsequent lines in the file are scanned for the macro name; if there are several macros, the line is scanned for each in turn, in the order in which the macros are defined. The replacement text is not rescanned for the current macro, though it will be for subsequently defined macros. For this reason, a macro name may not contain the name of a previously defined macro as a substring. You could, for example, define the following:

```
ABCD_XYZ = <something>
ABCD = <something>
```

but putting those definitions in the opposite order would provoke a configuration error.

As an example of macro usage, suppose you are using one of the SQL databases to store additional aliases. If the alias is not found in */etc/aliases*, you want Exim to try looking it up in the database. The text of an SQL query is quite long and can clutter up a router configuration if included inline; you can keep things neater by defining the query as a macro, such as this:

```
ALIAS_QUERY = select replacement from aliases where alias = \
              '${quote_pgsql:$local_part}'
```

The router for handling aliases can then be as follows:

```
db_aliases:
  driver = redirect
  data = ${lookup{$local_part}lsearch{/etc/aliases}{$value}\
        {${lookup pgsql{ALIAS_QUERY}}}
```

The expansion of the `data` option first looks in the file, and then queries the
database. We will go into the gory details of lookup syntax later, but you can see that
this setting would be harder to understand if the macro were replaced by the full
SQL statement.

In earlier versions of Exim, macros were also useful for abstracting lists of domains
or hosts. In Exim 4, however, it is better to use the "named list" facility (☞ 4.4).

The values of macros can be overridden by the `-D` command-line option (☞ 20.6).

## 4.3.6 Hiding configuration data

The command-line option `-bP` asks Exim to output the value of one or more
configuration options. This can be used by any caller of Exim, but some configurations may contain data that should not be generally accessible. For example, a
configuration that references an SQL database or an LDAP server may contain
passwords for controlling such access. If any option setting is preceded by the word
`hide`, only an admin user is permitted to see its value. For example, if the configuration contains:

```
hide mysql_servers = localhost/usertable/admin/secret
```

an unprivileged user sees this response:

```
$ exim -bP mysql_servers
mysql_servers = <value not displayable>
```

## 4.3.7 String expansions

We have already seen several examples of string expansions such as the following
setting for an **appendfile** transport:

```
file = /var/mail/$local_part
```

Expansions are a powerful feature in configuration files. We explain some more of
their abilities in examples in subsequent chapters. If you want to know everything
they can do, skip ahead to chapter 17, which has the full story. Meanwhile, remember
that whenever you see a `$` character in a configuration setting, it means that the
string will change in some way whenever it is expanded for use.

Incorrect syntax in a string expansion is a serious error, and usually causes Exim to
give up what it is trying to do; for example, an attempt to deliver a message is
deferred if Exim cannot expand a relevant string. However, there are some operations
during an expansion that deliberately provoke a special kind of error, called a *forced*

*expansion failure.* In a number of such cases these failures just cause Exim to abandon the activity that uses the string, but otherwise to carry on. For example, a forced expansion failure during an attempt to rewrite an address just abandons the rewriting. Whenever a forced expansion failure has a special effect like this, we will mention it.

## 4.3.8 File and database lookups

The ability to use data from databases and files in a variety of formats is another powerful feature of Exim's configuration. Earlier, we showed this router for handling traditional alias files:

```
aliasfile:
   driver = redirect
   data = ${lookup{$local_part}lsearch{/etc/aliases}}
```

This looks up data in */etc/aliases* by means of a linear search, but it could equally use an indexed file format such as DBM:

```
aliasfile:
   driver = redirect
   data = ${lookup{$local_part}dbm{/etc/aliases.db}}
```

or, the aliasing data could be held in a database:

```
aliasfile:
   driver = redirect
   data = ${lookup mysql{select addresses from aliases \
        where name='${quote_mysql:$local_part}'}}
```

Each different lookup type is implemented in a different module. Exim's build-time configuration specifies which ones are included in the Exim binary. As far as the main part of Exim is concerned, there is a fixed internal interface (API) to these lookups, and it is unaware of the details of the actual lookup mechanism. However, it does distinguish between two different kinds of lookup:

*Single-key*

Use a single key string to extract data from a file. The key and the file have to be specified. Linear search and DBM lookups are of this type.

*Query-style*

Access a database using a query written in the query language of the database package. Exim has support for NIS+, LDAP, and several SQL databases.

As well as being used to replace part of an expansion string with data that comes from a file or database, lookups can also be used as a mechanism for managing lists of domains, hosts, or addresses. We encounter examples of these uses throughout the book. Full details of all the lookup types and how they operate are given in chapter 16.

## 4.3.9 Domain, host, and address lists

The list mechanism is the third facility that, together with string expansion and lookups, is the main building block of Exim configurations. Earlier, when discussing continuation lines, we showed the example:

```
hold_domains = dom1.example.com : \
               dom2.example.com : \
               dom3.example.com
```

This example shows a colon-separated list of three domains that are specified as being "held" (that is, deliveries to them are suspended). Similar list facilities are used for recognizing specific hosts and email addresses for particular purposes. The full description of lists is in chapter 18, but we come across plenty of examples before then.

If a colon is actually needed as part of an item in a list, it must be entered as two colons. Leading and trailing whitespace on each item in a list is ignored. This makes it possible to include items that start with a colon, and in particular, certain forms of IPv6 address. For example:

```
local_interfaces = 127.0.0.1 : ::::1
```

defines the IPv4 address `127.0.0.1` followed by the IPv6 address `::1`. Because the requirement to double colons is particularly unfortunate in the case of IPv6 addresses, there is a way of changing the separator.[1] If a list starts with a left angle bracket followed by any punctuation character, that character becomes the list separator. The previous example could be rewritten as:

```
local_interfaces = <; 127.0.0.1 ; ::1
```

where the separator is changed to a semicolon.

# 4.4 Named lists

In the first part of the runtime configuration, lists of domains, hosts, email addresses, or local parts can be given names. These can then be used to refer to the lists elsewhere in the configuration. This is particularly convenient if the same list is required in several different places. Also, giving lists meaningful names can improve the readability of the configuration. For example, it is conventional to define a domain list called *local_domains* for all the domains that are handled locally on a host, by a configuration line such as this:

```
domainlist local_domains = localhost:my.dom.example
```

---

[1]  This applies to all lists, with the exception of `log_file_path`.

Named lists are referenced by giving their name preceded by a plus sign. For example, the first router in the default configuration, which is configured to handle non-local domains, is as follows:

```
notlocal:
  driver = dnslookup
  domains = ! +local_domains
  transport = remote_smtp
  no_more
```

At first sight, a named list might seem to be no different from a macro. However, macros are just textual substitutions, so if you write this:

```
ALIST = host1 : host2
auth_advertise_hosts = !ALIST
```

it probably will not do what you want, because that is exactly the same as this setting:

```
auth_advertise_hosts = !host1 : host2
```

Notice that the second host name is not negated. However, if you use a host list, and instead write this:

```
hostlist alist = host1 : host2
auth_advertise_hosts = ! +alist
```

then the negation applies to the whole list. Another advantage of using named lists is that Exim understands what they are, and can do some optimization. For example, when an address is being routed, the result of matching the domain against a named list is remembered. If the same named list is used in another router, the test does not have to be repeated.

## 4.5 The default qualification domain

In a locally submitted message, if an unqualified address (that is, a local part without a domain) is found in the envelope or any of the header lines that contain addresses, it is qualified using the domain defined by `qualify_domain` (for senders) or `qualify_recipient` (for recipients) at the time the message is received. User agents normally use fully qualified addresses, but there are exceptions.

The default value for both these options is the name of the local host. If `qualify_domain` is set, its value is used as the default for `qualify_recipient`. It is common to use these options for setting a generic domain. For example, the Acme Widget Corporation might have two hosts handling its mail, *mail1.awc.example.com* and *mail2.awc.example.com*, but would probably require messages created on these hosts to use just *awc.example.com* as the default domain, rather than the individual host names. This can be done by the following setting:

```
qualify_domain = awc.example.com
```

The value of `qualify_domain` is also used when Exim creates an envelope sender address for a locally submitted message from an unprivileged user.

# 4.6 Handling frozen bounce messages

When a message on Exim's queue is marked as *frozen*, queue runner processes skip over it and do not attempt to deliver it. One reason why a message might be frozen is a problem with Exim's configuration (☞ 3.10.2). However, by far the most common reason for a message becoming frozen is that it is a bounce message that cannot be delivered. Such messages are often the result of incoming junk mail that is addressed to an unknown local user, but which contains an invalid sender address that causes the resulting bounce message to fail.

It is recommended that you let Exim verify the sender and recipients before a message is accepted (☞ 14.8.16, 14.8.17), as implemented in the default configuration. This can dramatically cut down the number of frozen messages.

In order to avoid mail loops, Exim does not let a failing bounce message give rise to another bounce message. Instead, Exim freezes the message to bring it to the postmaster's attention. Some administrators do not have the human resources to inspect each frozen message in order to determine what the problem is, and their policy may be to discard such failures. Exim can be configured to do this by setting `ignore_bounce_errors_after`. This option allows such failures to be kept for a given time before being discarded. If you set the following:

```
ignore_bounce_errors_after = 0s
```

bounce messages that fail are discarded immediately, whereas with this setting:

```
ignore_bounce_errors_after = 12h
```

Exim retains failing bounce messages for 12 hours. After the first failure, the message is frozen as in the default case, but after it has been on the queue for the specified time, it is automatically unfrozen at the next queue run. If delivery fails again, the message is discarded. This gives the postmaster time to inspect the message.

# 4.7 Reducing activity at high load

In the main section of the configuration file, there are several options that allow you to limit or reduce Exim's activities when a large quantity of mail arrives at once, or when the system load is too high. "System load" in this sense is the average number of processes in the operating system's run queue over the last minute, a figure that can be obtained by running the *uptime* command to obtain output like this:

```
4:15pm  up 1 day(s), 22:23,  75 users, load average: 0.09, 0.15, 0.22
```

The first of the "load average" figures is the one-minute average. On an unloaded system, it is a small number, usually well under 10. When it is high, everything slows down; reducing the load created by mail reception and delivery can alleviate the impact of this.

## 4.7.1 Delaying or suspending delivery when the load is high

By default, Exim starts a delivery process for each new message, and uses its queue for messages that cannot be delivered immediately. You can use various configuration options to modify Exim's behaviour when system load is sufficiently high.

If the system load is higher than the value of `queue_only_load`, automatic delivery of incoming messages does not occur; instead, they wait on Exim's queue until the next queue runner process finds them. The effect of this is to serialize their delivery because a queue runner delivers just one message at a time. This reduces the number of simultaneously running Exim processes without significantly affecting mail delivery, as long as queue runners are started fairly frequently. For example, a setting of:

```
queue_only_load = 8
```

is a useful insurance against an overload caused by the simultaneous arrival of a large number of messages. Another threshold can be specified for deliveries in queue runs by setting `deliver_queue_load_max`. For example this setting:

```
deliver_queue_load_max = 14
```

means that deliveries are suppressed in queue runs when the load is above 14.

Deliveries that are forced with the `-M` or `-qf` command-line options override these load checks.

## 4.7.2 Suspending incoming mail when the load is high

There is no option for stopping incoming messages from local processes when the load is high, but mail from other hosts can be stopped or restricted to certain hosts. If `smtp_load_reserve` is set, and the system load exceeds its value, incoming SMTP connections over TCP/IP are accepted only from those hosts that match an entry in `smtp_reserve_hosts`. If this is unset, all connections from remote hosts are rejected with a temporary error code. For example, with the following:

```
smtp_load_reserve = 5
smtp_reserve_hosts = 192.168.24.0/24
```

only hosts in the 192.168.24.0/24 network can send mail to the local host when its load is greater than 5. The host list in `smtp_reserve_hosts` is also used by the `smtp_accept_reserve` option, which is described in the next section.

If you are running user agents that submit messages by making TCP/IP calls to the loopback interface, you should probably add 127.0.0.1 (or ::1 in an IPv6 system) to `smtp_reserve_hosts`, to allow these submissions to proceed even at high load.

## 4.7.3 Controlling the number of incoming SMTP connections

It is a good idea to set a limit on the number of simultaneous incoming SMTP connections, because each one uses the resources required for a separate process. Exim has the `smtp_accept_max` option for this purpose. The default setting is 20, which is reasonable for small to medium-sized systems, but if you are running a large system, increase this to 100 or 200.

You can reserve some of these incoming SMTP slots for specific hosts by setting `smtp_accept_reserve`. Its value is the number of slots that are reserved for the hosts listed in `smtp_reserve_hosts`. This feature is typically used to reserve slots for hosts on the local LAN so that external connections can never take up all the slots. For example, if you set:

```
smtp_accept_max = 200
smtp_accept_reserve = 40
smtp_reserve_hosts = 192.168.24.0/24
```

then once 160 connections are active, new connections are accepted only from hosts in the 192.168.24.0/24 network.

 The `smtp_accept_reserve` option does not impose a limit on the number of connections from the listed hosts. It just reserves a number of slots that only they may use. It does not prevent them from using other slots as well.

You can also set `smtp_accept_queue`; if the number of simultaneous incoming SMTP connections exceeds its value, automatic delivery of incoming SMTP messages is suspended; they are placed on the queue and left there for the next queue runner, thus limiting the number of simultaneously active delivery processes. The default for this option is unset, so that all messages are delivered immediately.

If new SMTP connections arrive while the daemon is busy setting up a process to handle a previous connection, they are held in a queue by the operating system, waiting for the daemon to request the next connection. The size of this queue is set by the `smtp_connect_backlog` option, which has a default value of 20. On large systems, this should be increased, say to 50 or more.

### 4.7.4 Checking for free disk space

You can arrange for Exim to refuse incoming messages temporarily if the amount of free space in the disk partition that holds its spool directory falls below a given threshold. For example:

```
check_spool_space = 50M
```

specifies that no mail can be received unless there is at least 50 MB of free space in which to store it.[1] The check is not a complete guarantee because of the possibility of several messages arriving simultaneously.

## 4.8 Limiting message sizes

It is a good idea to set a limit on the size of message your host will process. You can set, for example:

```
message_size_limit = 20M
```

to apply a limit of 20 MB per message. The default limit is 50 MB. It is also possible to set a limit for individual transports (☞ 8.4).

## 4.9 Parallel remote delivery

If a message has a number of recipients that route to different remote hosts, Exim carries out several of these deliveries at once (each in its own process). The amount of parallelism is controlled by the `remote_max_parallel` option, whose default value is two. On systems that are handling mostly personal mail, where messages typically have at most two or three recipients, this is not an important issue. However, on systems that are handling mailing lists, where a single message may end up being delivered to hundreds or even thousands of addresses, parallel delivery can make a noticeable improvement to performance. For example:

```
remote_max_parallel = 12
```

allows Exim to create up to 12 simultaneous remote delivery processes for a message with multiple recipients.

---

[1]  Digits in a numerical option setting can always be followed by K or M, which cause multiplication by 1024 and 1024×1024, respectively.

The `remote_max_parallel` option applies only to the parallel delivery of individual messages; it is not an overall limit on the number of Exim delivery processes.

## 4.10 Controlling the number of delivery processes

In a conventional configuration, where Exim attempts to deliver each message as soon as it receives it, there is no control over the number of delivery processes that may be running simultaneously. On a host where processing mail is just one activity among many, this is not usually a problem. However, on a heavily loaded host that is entirely devoted to delivering mail, it may be desirable to have such control. It can be achieved by suppressing immediate delivery (which means that all deliveries take place in queue runs) and limiting the number of queue runner processes. For example, you could put these settings in the configuration file:

```
queue_only
queue_run_max = 15
```

Setting `queue_only` disables immediate delivery, and `queue_run_max` specifies the maximum number of simultaneously active queue runners. The maximum number of simultaneous delivery processes is then the value of `queue_run_max` multiplied by the value of `remote_max_parallel`.

With this kind of configuration, you should arrange to start queue runner processes frequently (up to the maximum number) so as to minimize any delivery delay. This can be done by starting a daemon with an option such as -q1m, which starts a new queue runner every minute (☞ 11.7).

## 4.11 Large message queues

In chapter 3, we explained that Exim is designed for an environment in which most messages can be delivered almost instantaneously. Consequently, the queue of messages awaiting delivery is expected to be short. In some situations, nevertheless, large queues of messages occur, resulting in a large number (thousands) of files in a single directory (usually called */var/spool/exim/input*). This can affect performance significantly. To reduce this degradation, you can set:

```
split_spool_directory
```

When this is done, the input directory is split into 62 subdirectories, with names consisting of a single letter or digit. Incoming messages are distributed between them according to the sixth character of the message ID, which changes every second. This requires Exim to do more work when it is scanning the queue, but the directory access performance is much improved when there are many messages.

# 4.12 Large installations

One of the advantages of Exim's decentralized design is that it scales fairly well, and can handle substantial numbers of mailboxes and messages on a single host. However, when the numbers become really large, a conventional configuration may not be able to cope. In this section, a number of general observations are made that are relevant to large installations.

## 4.12.1 Linear password files

Above a thousand or so users, the use of a linear password file is extremely inefficient, and can slow down local mail delivery substantially. Some operating systems (for example, FreeBSD) automatically make use of an indexed password file, or can be configured to do so, which is one easy way around this problem if you happen to be using such a system. The alternative is to make use of NIS or some other database for the password information, provided that it operates quickly.

Even if you do not have any login accounts on your mail server, you still need some kind of list of local users, and it is important to make the searching of this list as efficient as possible.

It is not only mail delivery that provokes password file lookups. If you are running a POP daemon, a password check happens every time a POP client connects; in environments where users remain connected and leave their POP MUAs running, these checks happen every few minutes for each user, whenever the POP client checks for the arrival of new mail.[1] IMAP is much less expensive than POP in this regard, because it establishes a session that remains active, so there is a password check only at the start.

## 4.12.2 Mailbox directories

Performance will be poor if you have too many mailboxes in a single directory. What constitutes too many depends on your operating system. It has been said that the default GNU/Linux filing system starts to degrade at about one thousand files in a single directory, whereas for Solaris the number is around ten thousand. However, I have not been able to find references to back up these claims. The degradation applies whether you are using individual files as multimessage mailboxes, or delivering messages as separate files in a directory.

---

[1] Users have been known to configure their MUAs to check as often as every 20 or 30 seconds; such usage will eat up your machine and should be strongly discouraged.

The solution to this is to use multiple directory levels. For example, instead of storing *jimbo*'s mailbox in */var/mail/jimbo*, you could use */var/mail/j/jimbo*. Splitting on the initial character(s) of the local part is easy to implement, but it is not as good as using some kind of hashing function. Exim's string expansion facilities can be used to implement either a substring-based or hash-based split. Of course, you will have to ensure that all the programs that read the mailboxes use the same algorithm.

For a very large number of mailboxes, a two-level split is recommended, using Exim's numeric hash function, as in this example:

```
file = /var/mail/${nhash_8_512:$local_part}/$local_part
```

The hashing expansion generates two numbers separated by a slash, in this case using the local part as the data and ensuring that the numbers are in the ranges 0–7 and 0–511. This example places *jimbo*'s mailbox in */var/mail/6/71/jimbo*. The initial split could be between different disks or file servers, and the second one could be between directories on the same disk.

## 4.12.3 Simultaneous message delivery

If two messages for the same mailbox arrive simultaneously, they cannot both be delivered at once if the mailbox is just a single file. One delivery process has to wait for the other, thus tying up resources. The default way that Exim does this (in the **appendfile** transport) is by sleeping for a bit, and then starting the process of locking the mailbox from scratch. This is the safest approach, and the only way to operate when lock files are in use.

Attempts to lock a mailbox continue for a limited time. If a process cannot gain access to a mailbox within that time, it defers delivery with the error message:

```
failed to lock mailbox
```

and Exim will try the delivery again later. If you see many such messages in the main log file, it is an indication that there is a problem with contention for the mailbox.

If you are in an environment in which only *fcntl()* locks are used, and no separate lock files, you can configure the **appendfile** transport to use blocking calls, instead of sleeping and retrying. This gives better performance because a waiting process is released as soon as the lock is available instead of waiting out its sleep time. In this environment, this single change can make a big performance difference.

The whole problem of locking can be bypassed if you use mailboxes in which each message is stored in a separate file.[1] One example of this type of message storage, called *maildir* format (☞ 9.4.5), is now quite popular, and has support in a number

---

[1] There is still some locking, of course, between processes that are updating the mailbox directory, but it is handled internally in the file system and is no longer Exim's responsibility.

If the mailbox files are NFS-mounted, and more than one host can access them, you *must not* disable the use of lock files. If you do, you are likely to end up with mangled mailboxes.

of MUAs and other programs that handle mailboxes. Because each message is entirely independent, no locking is required, several messages can be delivered simultaneously, and old messages can even be deleted while new ones are arriving.

## 4.12.4 Minimizing name server delays

A busy mail server makes a large number of calls to the DNS. For this reason, you should arrange for it to run its own name server, or make sure that there is a name server running on a nearby host with a high-speed connection, typically on the mail server's LAN. Ensure that the name server has plenty of memory so that it can build up a large cache of DNS data.

## 4.12.5 Storing messages for dial-up hosts

You should not plan to store large numbers of messages for intermittently connected clients in Exim's spool. It is much better to have them delivered into local files, for onward transmission by some other means (☞ 12.12).

## 4.12.6 Hardware configuration

If you keep increasing the workload of an Exim installation, disk I/O capacity is what runs out first. Each message that is handled requires the creation and deletion of at least four files, though this can be reduced to three by setting the message_logs option false to suppress the use of individual message logs (☞ 21.1). Large installations should therefore use disks with as high a performance as possible. Also, it does not make sense to keep on increasing the performance of the processor if the disks cannot keep up.

Better overall performance can be obtained by splitting up the work between a number of different hosts, each with its own set of disks. For example, separate hosts can be used for incoming and outgoing mail. A general form of scalable configuration that is used by some very large installations is shown in figure 4-1.

This configuration has separate servers for incoming and outgoing messages, and can be expanded "sideways" by the addition of more servers (indicated by the dashed lines) as necessary. Incoming mail is delivered to one or more file servers, which hold local mailboxes in a split directory structure, as described earlier, as well as messages that are waiting for dial-up hosts. The mailboxes are accessed from POP

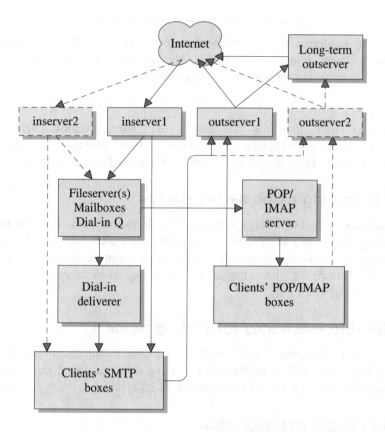

*Figure 4-1: Large system configuration*

and IMAP servers, and the dial-up hosts use yet another server to access their stored mail.

The outgoing servers send messages that they cannot deliver in a short time to a long-term outgoing server, so as not to impact their performance with very long message queues. This can be implemented using `fallback_hosts` on appropriate drivers on the main servers, or using the *$message_age* variable to move messages after some fixed time.

# 5

# Extending the delivery configuration

In chapter 3, we described the basics of how Exim delivers messages, and worked through a simple, straightforward example. The chapters that follow this one cover all the different drivers and their options, but before we descend into such detail, we will look at some further examples of fairly common delivery requirements and discuss ways of configuring Exim to support them. In many cases, the suggested solution is not necessarily the only possible approach; there are often several ways of achieving the same result. The main intent of this chapter is to show you some more of the many ways in which the driver options can be used.

## 5.1 Multiple local domains

In the earlier introductory configuration example we assumed that Exim was handling only one local domain, and we put its name (*simple.example*) into the **notlocal** router:

```
notlocal:
  driver = dnslookup
  domains = ! simple.example
  transport = remote_smtp
  no_more
```

Later, we introduced named domain lists, and showed this example with two domains:

```
domainlist local_domains = localhost:my.dom.example
```

By changing the router to read as follows:

```
notlocal:
  driver = dnslookup
  domains = ! +local_domains
  transport = remote_smtp
  no_more
```

we arranged for both domains to be treated as local. This is the most convenient approach to use for multiple local domains. So far, we have used only complete domain names, but there are other possibilities (☞ 18.5). For example:

```
domainlist local_domains = simple.example : *.simple.example
```

The second item in this list is a wildcard item, matching any domain that ends in *.simple.example*. An asterisk can be used only at the start of an item. If you want to match more complicated patterns, you can use a regular expression.

If there are many local domains, it is cumbersome to include the list in the configuration file, and it is better to refer to a file instead. A setting such as:

```
domainlist local_domains = /etc/local.domains
```

can be used with a file containing lines such as:

```
simple.example
*.simple.example
unsimple.example
...
```

The file can contain any type of item that may appear in a domain list, except for another filename. It is read each time it is needed, and so can be updated independently of Exim's configuration file. However, it is still scanned linearly, just like an in-memory list, and this can be slow when the number of items in the list is large. If the list contains only fixed names (that is, no wildcarded items of any kind), it can be converted into an indexed file that can be searched more quickly. A utility program called *exim_dbmbuild* is supplied to do the conversion. You can refer to the indexed file by a setting such as:

```
domainlist local_domains = dbm;/etc/local.domains.db
```

This form of list entry specifies a lookup type (that is, a way of looking something up) as well as additional data required by the lookup, separated by a semicolon. In this example, the lookup type is dbm and the additional data is a filename.

There are several different software libraries that support indexed files; *DBM* is a generic term that refers to this kind of file access method.[1] Most modern operating systems have a suitable library installed as standard. As a user of Exim, all you really need to know is that an indexed file gives quicker access to specific data, just as an index in a book allows you to find something more quickly than reading through. The details of how the index is implemented inside the DBM library are not important.

Although DBM libraries support the addition and removal of individual entries in a DBM file, the usual approach for applications that are just using the file as a fast way of accessing fixed data is to rebuild the file from scratch whenever the data changes. This is how *exim_dbmbuild* works.

When Exim is testing a domain list that contains a DBM lookup item, if an entry with a matching key is found in the file, the domain matches the list. The data that

---

[1] DBM probably once stood for "database management", but nobody ever spells it out in full any more.

was looked up is not itself used in this case; Exim is interested only in whether or not the key exists in the file.

You do not have to put every local domain into a single lookup, because a lookup is just one item in the list that is searched. For example, you could have some domains inline, and some in one or more lookups:

```
domainlist local_domains = maindomain.example : \
                           dbm;/etc/otherdomains.db
```

Exim processes lists from left to right, so it makes sense to put the most commonly expected domains first.

DBM is only one of several lookup types supported by Exim; they are described in chapter 16. Whenever a lookup is permitted, any of the available types may be used. For example, a list of local domains could be held in a MySQL database, and checked by a setting such as:

```
domainlist local_domains = mysql;\
  select * from domainlist where domain='$domain'
```

When processing lists of this sort, the domain that is being tested is put into the variable *$domain* so that it can be included in database queries. If you do choose to put a list of local domains into a database, remember that the performance is likely to be slower than an indexed file on a local disk. Also, if the database server becomes unavailable, no mail can be delivered.

## 5.1.1 Differentiating between multiple domains

If you define a set of local domains using the `local_domains` list, and make no other changes to the default configuration, Exim treats all of them as synonymous, with the same local part at any one of them being handled in the same way. In order to distinguish between different domains, the routers that follow the **notlocal** router have to be made to act differently for different domains. The usual way this is done is to set the `domains` option on one or more routers. This option provides a list of domains for which the router is to operate. Here is a simple example with two local domains, each with its own alias file:

```
domainlist local_domains = a.local.domain : b.local.domain

begin routers

notlocal:
  driver = dnslookup
  domains = ! +local_domains
  transport = remote_smtp
  no_more
```

```
a_aliases:
  driver = redirect
  domains = a.local.domain
  data = ${lookup{$local_part}lsearch{/etc/a.aliases}}

b_aliases:
  driver = redirect
  domains = b.local.domain
  data = ${lookup{$local_part}lsearch{/etc/b.aliases}}

. . .
```

Addresses of the form *user@a.local.domain* are processed by the first **redirect** router, but not the second, whereas *user@b.local.domain* is processed by the second and not the first. If there are a number of domains whose alias filenames follow a regular pattern, there is no need to have a separate router for each one, because the filename can be varied depending on the domain, and a single router can be used:

```
aliases:
  driver = redirect
  data = ${lookup{$local_part}lsearch{/etc/$domain.aliases}}
```

In this example, all domains are processed, but because the filename contains the expansion variable *$domain*, a different file is used for each domain. Using the string expansion features of Exim, much more complicated transformations of the domain name are possible, including, for example, looking up the name of a domain's alias file in a file or database.

# 5.2 Virtual domains

The term *virtual domain* is used to refer to a domain in which all the valid local parts are aliases for other addresses. There are no real mailboxes associated with a virtual domain. Because each address that is generated by an aliasing operation is independently processed, the result of handling an address in a virtual domain can be the address of a local mailbox, or a remote address that causes the message to be sent to another host.

The aliasing scheme just described can be used to handle virtual domains with a separate alias file for each domain. This makes it easy to have a separate maintainer for each file. However, it is important to consider what happens when a local part does not match any item in an alias file. Exim would normally offer the address to the next router. However, for a virtual domain, no further routers should be run, and instead the address should fail.

One way of doing this is for all subsequent routers to have a setting of `domains` that excludes the virtual domains, but it is usually easier to set `more` false, as we do for remote domains. Here is an extract from a configuration file that handles a mixture of real and virtual domains:

```
domainlist local_domains = realdom.example : cdb;/etc/virtuals

begin routers

notlocal:
  driver = dnslookup
  domains = ! +local_domains
  transport = remote_smtp
  no_more

virtuals:
  driver = redirect
  domains = cdb;/etc/virtuals
  data = ${lookup{$local_part}lsearch{/etc/$domain.aliases}}
  no_more

system_aliases:
  driver = redirect
  data = ${lookup{$local_part}lsearch{/etc/aliases}}

...
```

The list of virtual domains in this example is kept in an indexed file in *cdb* format. This is a format that is optimized for files that are never updated after they have been created, and it performs better than conventional DBM, which allows for both reading and writing (☞ 16.1).

The virtual domains are handled by the second router; the real domain is handled by the remaining routers (of which only the first is shown here). The lookup in the */etc/virtuals* file happens twice in principle (once to establish that the domain is local, and again to check before running the **virtuals** router), but Exim caches the results of the last lookup on a per-file basis, so the file is read only once in practice.

For more complicated requirements (for example, when some virtual domains are synonymous, and therefore use the same alias file), multiple routers can be used, or the name of the alias file for each domain can be looked up by a setting such as:

```
data = ${lookup{$local_part}lsearch\
       {${lookup{$domain}cdb{/etc/virtuals}}}}
```

We know that the inner lookup is going to succeed, because it is the same lookup that was used by domains to control the running of the router.[1] The data that is used to create the *cdb* file for this example could contain lines like this, where the first two domains use the same alias file:

```
virt10.example:    /etc/virt1.aliases
virt11.example:    /etc/virt1.aliases
virt20.example:    /etc/virt2.aliases
```

Another approach to virtual domains that is sometimes used when the alias lists are not too large and are managed by a single person is to keep a single list for all of them, containing entries like this:

---

[1]   In fact, because there is lookup caching, the lookup is not repeated; the cached result is reused.

```
jan@virt1.example:     J.Smith@dom1.example
jim@virt1.example:     J.Smith@dom2.example
jan@virt2.example:     J.Jones@dom1.example
jim@virt2.example:     J.Joyce@dom3.example
```

Note that this differs from a "traditional" alias file in that the aliases are listed with domains attached, instead of just being local parts. The router might look like this:

```
virtuals:
  driver = redirect
  domains = cdb;/etc/virtuals
  data = ${lookup{$local_part@$domain}cdb{/etc/virtual.aliases}}
  no_more
```

There is scope for confusion if local parts without domains are used in alias files. Consider the following:

```
jac@virt2.example:    J.Hawkins
```

What domain should be added to *J.Hawkins* to make it a fully qualified address? Does it refer to a user on the local host, or should it retain the incoming domain *virt2.example*? Unless you tell it otherwise, Exim assumes that unqualified local parts are local, and it uses the value of qualify_recipient (a main configuration option) to create a complete address. If you want the other behaviour, you must set qualify_preserve_domain on the **virtuals** router.

## 5.2.1 Defaults in virtual domains

When you configure a virtual domain, you may want to trap unknown local parts and forward them to a designated address such as the postmaster. Adding an asterisk to the search type causes Exim to look for a single asterisk entry if it cannot find the original address, so a configuration such as:

```
virtuals:
  driver = redirect
  domains = cdb;/etc/virtuals
  data = ${lookup{$local_part}lsearch*{/etc/$domain.aliases}}
  no_more
```

would allow a separate default to be specified for each domain in its alias file. For example, in the file */etc/virt3.example.aliases*, you could have:

```
*:           postmaster@virt3.example
postmaster:  pat@dom5.example
jill:        jkr@dom4.example
```

When Exim looks up a local part other than *postmaster* or *jill* in this file, it fails. Because of the asterisk in the search type, it then does a second lookup for the key string *, which finds the default entry that redirects all other local parts to the postmaster.

Putting the default entry first in a file that is linearly searched is a good idea, because it is then found quickly. This may look like a wildcard that would match any keystring, including *postmaster* and *jill*, but this is not the case. The asterisk is just being used as a special key that means "default".

If lookup defaulting is used when domains are included as part of lookup keys, it provides a single default for all the domains. You can give each domain its own default by adding *@ (instead of just *) to the search type. For example:

```
virtuals:
  driver = aliasfile
  domains = cdb;/etc/virtuals
  data = ${lookup{$local_part@$domain}lsearch*@\
        {/etc/virtual.aliases}}
  no_more
```

Then you can include data such as:

```
*@virt4.example:  virt4-admin@dom6.example
```

in the combined virtual domain file. If an initial lookup fails, the local part is replaced with an asterisk for the second attempt, and only if that also fails is the plain asterisk tried as a key.

## 5.2.2 Postmasters in virtual domains

If each virtual domain has its own postmaster, these can be included in the alias data and there is no problem. Sometimes, however, there is a requirement for a single address to receive postmaster mail for a number of domains, and there is an easier approach than maintaining the same entry in all the alias files. If this applies to all local domains, an extra **redirect** router, placed before the others, can be used:

```
postmaster:
  driver = redirect
  local_parts = postmaster
  data = postmaster@your.domain.example
```

The effect of setting `local_parts` is analogous to setting `domains`. It causes the router to be run only for those local parts that it matches. In this case, the router runs only when the local part is *postmaster*. As there is no `domains` setting, the post-master address for all the local domains is redirected to the same fixed address.

The new address is reprocessed in its own right; if *your.domain.example* is a local domain, it is processed again by this router, but on the third occasion, the antilooping rule takes effect, and the router is skipped. The unnecessary second pass through the router can be avoided in one of two ways:

- You can arrange to skip this router when the domain is already correct, by adding:

  ```
  domains = ! your.domain.example
  ```

  to its configuration.

- Alternatively, you can arrange to process the new address by starting at a specific router, instead of at the first one. This is done by setting redirect_router to the name of the router at which to start:

  ```
  postmaster:
    driver = redirect
    local_parts = postmaster
    data = postmaster@your.domain.example
    redirect_router = system_aliases
  ```

  This goes straight to the **system_aliases** router.

If some of the virtual domains do have their own postmasters, but you want to pick up postmaster mail for the others, you can extend the domains setting to exclude the unwanted domains (or include the wanted ones, if that is easier). Another possibility, if defaults are not being used, is to place the **redirect** router for *postmaster* after those that handle the virtual domains.

# 5.3 Mailing lists

Exim can be used on its own to run simple mailing lists that are maintained by hand, but for large or complicated requirements, the use of additional specialized mailing list software is strongly recommended (☞ 5.3.5).

Lists of just a few addresses can be managed as aliases, but when larger lists are involved, it is usually more convenient to keep each list in a separate file. Also, this allows each list to be managed by its own manager, who does not need to have access to other Exim configuration files.

A **redirect** router can be used to "explode" such mailing lists, and the domains option can be used if it is required to run these lists in a separate domain from normal mail. For example, if your domain is *simple.example*, you might want to use *lists.simple.example* for addresses that refer to mailing lists, in order to keep them entirely separate from normal mail. This router does just that:

```
lists:
  driver = redirect
  domains = lists.simple.example
  more = false
  file = /usr/lists/$local_part
  errors_to = $local_part-request@$domain
  forbid_pipe
  forbid_file
```

On the other hand, if you use list names that are distinct from any of your local usernames, you can have them in your normal domain. The domains and more settings are then not needed.

This instance of the **redirect** router is different from those we used earlier, because it has a setting of file instead of data. These are mutually exclusive options that define the list of replacement addresses in two different ways:

- When data is used, its expanded value is the list. If the value is empty, the router declines.

- When file is used, its expanded value is the name of a file that contains the list. If the file does not exist, the router declines.

In the example above, the local part is used to construct the file name, so each list's subscribers are held in a separate file. A message that is sent to a list's managers has -request added to the local part, so another file, whose name ends in *-request* is also required. This file contains the managers' addresses.

The errors_to option specifies that any delivery errors caused by addresses taken from a mailing list are to be sent to the given address rather than the original sender of the message. In other words, it changes the envelope sender of the message as it passes through. However, before acting on errors_to, Exim verifies the error address. If verification fails, the envelope sender is not changed. In this example, verification succeeds if the -request file that corresponds to the mailing list exists.

The forbid_pipe and forbid_file options prevent a local part from being expanded into a filename or a pipe delivery, which is not normally appropriate for a mailing list.

Using this scheme, you can create a list by creating the main file containing the members, and the -request file containing the managers. For example, as soon as a file called */usr/lists/exim-users* is created, mail to *exim-users@lists.simple.example* is accepted, and sent to all the addresses in that file. As soon as */usr/lists/exim-users-request* is created, verification of the address *exim-users-request@lists.simple.example* succeeds, allowing the envelope sender address of messages to *exim-users@ lists.simple.example* to be changed when they are forwarded.

An alternative to handling both the list address and the manager address with the same router is to set up an earlier router to handle the manager address (☞ 5.3.4).

## 5.3.1 Syntax errors in mailing lists

If an address in a file of redirections contains a syntax error, Exim normally defers all deliveries for the original address. This may not be appropriate when the list is being maintained automatically from address texts supplied by users, because a single bad address shuts down the entire list.

If `skip_syntax_errors` is set on an instance of the **redirect** router, the router just skips entries that fail to parse, noting the incident in the log. Valid addresses are recognized and used. If in addition `syntax_errors_to` is set to a verifiable address, messages about skipped addresses are sent to it. It is usually appropriate to set this to the same value as `errors_to`.

## 5.3.2 NFS-mounted mailing lists

It is not advisable to have list files that are NFS-mounted, because the absence of the mount cannot be distinguished from a non-existent file. Thus, Exim would behave as if a list did not exist when the NFS server was down. One way around this problem is to access the list indirectly. If an item in a redirection list is `:include:` followed by a filename, the contents of the file are included at that point in the list. This means that you can set up a file on a local disk containing a list of lists in the following form:

```
exim-users:      :include:/usr/lists/exim-users
exim-announce:   :include:/usr/lists/exim-announce
```

and then use it in the following router:

```
lists:
  driver = redirect
  data = ${lookup{$local_part}lsearch{/etc/listoflists}}
  forbid_pipe
  forbid_file
  errors_to = $local_part-request@$domain
```

For an existing mailing list, the lookup succeeds, so the existence of the list can be determined without reference to the NFS file. However, if Exim is unable to open the included file, delivery is deferred, because `:include:` is expected to name an accessible file.

This is a bit more complicated to maintain, because in addition to creating the files, the aliases have to be updated in order to set up a new list.

## 5.3.3 Re-expansion of mailing lists

In order to avoid duplicate deliveries, Exim remembers every individual address to which a message has been delivered, but it normally stores only the original recipient addresses with a message. If all the deliveries to a mailing list cannot be done at the first attempt, the mailing list is re-expanded when the delivery is next tried. This means that alterations to the list are taken into account at each delivery attempt, and as a consequence, addresses that have been added to the list since the message arrived will receive a copy of the message, even though it predates their subscription.

If this behaviour is felt to be undesirable, the one_time option can be set on the relevant **redirect** router. When this is done, any addresses generated by the router that fail to deliver at the first attempt are added to the message as "top level" addresses, and the address that generated them is marked "delivered". As a result, expansion of the mailing list does not happen again at subsequent delivery attempts. The disadvantage of this is that if any of the failing addresses are incorrect, changing them in the file has no effect on pre-existing messages.

## 5.3.4 Closed mailing lists

The examples so far have assumed open mailing lists, to which anybody may send mail. It is also possible to set up closed lists, where mail is accepted from specified senders only. This is done by making use of the senders option that restricts the running of a router to messages that have specific senders.

The following example uses one file for each list, both as a list of recipients and as a list of permitted senders, but different or multiple sender lists could, of course, be used. For instance, a list for announcements could restrict senders to those people who are permitted to make the announcements.

First, it is necessary to set up a separate router to handle the -request address, to which anybody may send mail:

```
lists_request:
  driver = redirect
  domains = lists.simple.example
  local_part_suffix = -request
  file = /usr/lists/$local_part-request
  no_more
```

Here we see a new option, local_part_suffix, which we have not met before. This is a precondition option that has the effect of testing the local part for the given suffix, and skipping the router if it does not match. This router, therefore, is run only for local parts that end with -request.

The router runs with *$local_part* stripped of the suffix, which is placed in *$local_part_suffix* (though that variable is not used in this example). There is an analagous option called local_part_prefix, which operates by testing the other end of the local part. You would use this if your mailing lists used the form *owner-xxx* for list management instead of *xxx-request*.

The next router handles the closed list itself:

```
lists:
  driver = redirect
  domains = lists.simple.example
  senders = ${if exists {/usr/lists/$local_part}\
             {lsearch;/usr/lists/$local_part}{*}}
  file = /usr/lists/$local_part
  forbid_pipe
  forbid_file
  one_time
  skip_syntax_errors
  errors_to = $local_part-request@lists.simple.example
  no_more
```

The senders option is a precondition that tests the envelope sender of the message. For an existing mailing list, we want to search the list of subscribers. However, if we just used this setting:

```
senders = lsearch;/usr/lists/$local_part
```

there would be a problem for unknown lists, because a non-existent file in an address list item such as this causes Exim to defer delivery. Instead, we use a conditional expansion item to test for the file's existence. An expansion item that starts with $if{ tests a condition, and expands one substring if the condition is met, and another if it is not (☞ 17.7). In this case, if the file does not exist, the expansion yields *, which matches all senders. Thus, in this case, the precondition is always met, which means that the router runs, discovers for itself that the file does not exist, and so declines. The no_more setting ensures that no other routers are run; the address is therefore failed.

Suppose that a mailing list called *exim-users* exists, with a list of subscribers in */usr/lists/exim-users*. When a message is received for that list, the test for file existence succeeds, and so the expansion of the value of the senders option yields lsearch;/usr/lists/exim-users. This causes Exim to search the file for the sender address. If it is found, the router is run and the message is delivered to the list. However, if the file does not contain the sender address, the router is skipped and the address is offered to the next router, because senders is a precondition that is not affected by no_more. Consequently, we must add a third router to catch this case. This enables us to specify a customized error message, as follows:

```
closed_reject:
  driver = redirect
  domains = lists.simple.example
  allow_fail
  data = :fail: $local_part@$domain is a closed mailing list
```

A :fail: item in a redirection list causes the recipient address to be bounced. Its use has to be enabled by setting allow_fail.

## 5.3.5 External mailing list software

The use of specialized mailing list software such as Majordomo, SmartList, or Mailman is recommended if you are running large or numerous mailing lists.[1] Messages addressed to a mailing list are handed off to an external program, which ultimately resubmits them to Exim for delivery to the subscribers. This can be done either by providing a recipient list with each resubmitted message, or by using Exim's aliasing or forwarding mechanisms to pick up lists of addresses from files. This approach helps you to deal with the following issues:

- Although Exim is capable of delivering a single message to thousands of recipients, having one large forwarding list is not the best way of handling a mailing list with thousands of subscribers. Remember that Exim routes every address in a message before it does any deliveries. Routing is done serially, so if there are many recipients, a long time may elapse between the arrival of a message and the first delivery. To avoid this delay, mailing list software should normally be configured to send multiple copies of messages, with a maximum of around a hundred recipients in each copy. This introduces some parallelism into the routing process. If the addresses can be sorted, it is advantageous if all those in the same domain can be kept together.

  Public mailing lists often contain many subscribers from large ISP domains such as *aol.com* and *hotmail.com*. Unless you are using VERP (☞ 8.7), making sure the addresses are sorted minimizes the number of copies sent to such domains.

- An external program makes it easier to check and possibly modify the contents of messages posted to your lists. For example, some lists prohibit the use of attachments; others require modification of header lines or the addition of standard texts to messages.

- The common practice of sending an email message for automatic subscription and unsubscription from lists can be supported only by using an external mailing list agent.

Different mailing list software packages provide different facilities. For example, automatic subscription might be supported without the ability to generate multiple copies of the message when there are large numbers of recipients. You should investigate several packages to see which one best fits your needs.

When external mailing list software is in use, Exim has to recognize certain local parts and pipe the messages to appropriate programs. Occasionally, there is also a requirement to recognize messages that have come back from the mailing list software, and process their addresses in some special way. Exim is usually configured to

---

[1] For information on Majordomo, see *http://www.greatcircle.com/majordomo*; for SmartList see *http://www.procmail.org* (sic); for Mailman see *http://www.gnu.org/software/mailman/mailman.html*.

run as a specific mailing list user when delivering incoming messages through a pipe. For example, if you are using Majordomo and keeping all the mailing list information in a single alias file, you could use this router:

```
majordomo_aliases:
  driver = redirect
  data = ${lookup{$local_part}lsearch\
         {/usr/local/majordomo/lists/majordomo.aliases}}
  pipe_transport = address_pipe
  user = majordom
  group = majordom
```

This ensures that any pipes that are run as a result of that particular alias file do so as the user *majordom*.

When an ordinary user submits a message to Exim from a process running on the same host, an envelope sender address is created from the user's login name and the domain in `qualify_domain` (which defaults to the host name). There is a command-line option `-f` that can override this, but Exim ignores it unless the caller is *trusted* (☞ 19.3). The idea is that trusted users are allowed to forge sender addresses and other message data. If you are using Majordomo, for example, you should have the following:

```
trusted_users = majordom
```

in your Exim configuration, so that the `-f` option is honoured for messages coming from Majordomo, thus allowing it to specify an appropriate envelope sender for each mailing list.

Using aliases as the means of routing messages to list management software is not the only possibility. Another approach is to use specialized routers and transports. For example, the following transport could be used to pipe messages to SmartList:

```
list_transport:
  driver = pipe
  command = /usr/slist/.bin/flist $local_part$local_part_suffix
  current_directory = /usr/slist
  home_directory = /usr/slist
  user = slist
  group = slist
```

The transport is activated from a router like this:

```
list_router:
  driver = accept
  local_part_suffix = -request
  local_part_suffix_optional
  local_parts = !.bin:!.etc
  require_files = /usr/slist/$local_part/rc.init
  transport = list_transport
```

The require_files option is a precondition that tests for the existence of one or more files. In this case, it ensures that the router runs only when the local part is the name of an existing list. That is, the existence of a file whose name includes the list name is used as the trigger for passing the message to SmartList. Note the use of the local_parts option to avoid treating */usr/slist/.bin* and */usr/slist/.etc* as mailing lists.

# 5.4 Using an external local delivery agent

An alternative to using the **appendfile** transport for writing to local mailboxes is to use an external program for this purpose. This could be for all local deliveries, or only for certain local parts. The **pipe** transport can be used to pass messages to a separate local delivery agent such as *procmail*.[1] We use *procmail* as an example of a local delivery agent in what follows, but a similar approach could be used for any local delivery agent.

Individual users can arrange for their mail to be delivered using *procmail* by calling it from their *.forward* files, provided that the Exim configuration permits the use of pipes from *.forward* files. In some installations, however, there may be a requirement always to use *procmail* for local deliveries, or to allow users to choose to use it without letting them run pipe commands from their *.forward* files. One way to handle these cases is to set up a separate transport just for the use of *procmail*.

When doing this, care must be taken to ensure that the pipe is run under an appropriate uid and gid. In some configurations, one wants this to be a uid that is trusted by the delivery agent to supply the correct sender of the message. It may be necessary to recompile or reconfigure the delivery agent so that it trusts an appropriate user. The following is an example of a transport that delivers using *procmail*:

```
procmail_pipe:
   driver = pipe
   command = /usr/local/bin/procmail -d $local_part
   return_path_add
   delivery_date_add
   envelope_to_add
   check_string = "From "
   escape_string = ">From "
   user = $local_part
   group = mail
```

This runs *procmail* with the user's uid, but with the group set to mail. The settings of check_string and escape_string ensure that any lines beginning with "From " are escaped. This is the default for the **appendfile** transport, but not for **pipe**.

---

[1]  See *http://www.procmail.org*. Many, but not all, of the things *procmail* can do can also be done using an Exim filter. See chapter 10 for a discussion of the differences.

The command specified for the transport does *not* begin with the following:

```
IFS=" "
```

as shown in some *procmail* documentation. This setting arose on systems where the MTA runs pipe commands via a shell; it ensures that the separator character between the arguments of a shell command is a space. Exim does not by default use a shell to run pipe commands, so if this shell construct is present, it is not recognized. Instead of using a shell, Exim splits up the command into separate arguments itself, before string expansion. This means that any shell metacharacters that occur in substituted values (for example, in *$local_part*) cannot affect the parsing of the command. Exim then runs the command directly. This approach not only avoids problems with shell metacharacters, but also saves the overhead of starting another process.

The **procmail_pipe** transport could be used by a router that checks for the user's *.procmailrc* file:

```
procmail:
  driver = accept
  check_local_user
  require_files = $home/.procmailrc
  transport = procmail_pipe
```

If there is no *.procmailrc* file in the user's home directory, this router declines to handle the address. The following router could be a conventional **accept** router that routes to an **appendfile** transport in the usual way. Thus, all a user needs to do to change from Exim's normal delivery to delivery via *procmail* is to create *.procmailrc*. No *.forward* file is required.

The next example shows a transport for a system where local deliveries are handled by the Cyrus IMAP server:

```
local_delivery_cyrus:
  driver = pipe
  command = /usr/cyrus/bin/deliver \
            -m ${substr_1:$local_part_suffix} \
            -- $local_part
  user = cyrus
  group = mail
  return_output
  log_output
  message_prefix =
  message_suffix =
```

If any text is written by Cyrus, `return_output` ensures that it is returned to the sender, and `log_output` causes the first line of it to be logged. The settings of `message_prefix` and `message_suffix` disable the addition of a separator line containing the return path that is added at the beginning of a message by default, and a blank line at the end, respectively. This transport could be activated by a router such as this:

```
local_user_cyrus:
  driver = accept
  check_local_user
  transport = local_delivery_cyrus
```

# 5.5 Multiple user addresses

A single user normally has a single email address and a single mailbox. For example, the user *caesar* on the host *simple.example* has the following address:

```
caesar@simple.example
```

and mail to that address is commonly delivered into */var/mail/caesar*. Users with high volumes of incoming mail often like to use some method of automatically sorting it into categories to make it more convenient to handle. One way of doing this is to make use of Exim's filtering capability or to run an external local delivery agent such as *procmail*. These methods rely on analysing the header lines or message content.

Another approach is to allow the use of prefixes or suffixes on usernames in the local parts of incoming mail. For example, additional addresses such as the following:

```
caesar-rome@simple.example
casear-gaul@simple.example
```

are recognized as belonging to the user *caesar*. The user can then make use of forwarding or filtering files to inspect the suffix. Fixed suffixes could be specified, but usually the wildcard facility is used so that users can choose their own suffixes. For example, the router shown in the following example:

```
userforward:
  driver = redirect
  check_local_user
  file = $home/.forward
  local_part_suffix = -*
  local_part_suffix_optional
  filter
```

runs a user's *.forward* file (usually this would be an Exim filter file) for all local parts that start with a valid username, optionally followed by a hyphen and then arbitrary text. Within a filter file, the user can distinguish different cases by testing the variable *$local_part_suffix*. For example:

```
if $local_part_suffix contains -special then
  save /home/$local_part/Mail/special
endif
```

If the filter file does not exist or does not deal with such addresses, they are offered to subsequent routers, and assuming no subsequent use of the `local_part_` `suffix` option is made, those with suffixes presumably fail. Thus, users have control over which suffixes are valid.

An alternative way of differentiating between suffixes in local parts is to arrange for a suffix to trigger the use of a different *.forward* file. This has the advantage that the user does not need to learn about Exim filter files. For example:

```
userforward:
  driver = redirect
  check_local_user
  file = $home/.forward$local_part_suffix
  local_part_suffix = -*
  local_part_suffix_optional
  filter
```

If there is no suffix, *.forward* is used; if the suffix is `-special`, for example, *.forward-special* is used. Once again, if the appropriate file does not exist, or does not deal with the address, it is offered to subsequent routers. Whether the address is delivered or bounced depends on how they are configured. The user controls which suffixes are valid by creating appropriate files, which may forward messages to other addresses or redirect them to specific files or pipe commands using traditional *.forward* features or Exim filter commands.

# 5.6 Mixed local/remote domains

Consider a corporate mail gateway that delivers some local parts into local mailboxes, and sends others on to personal workstations. To simplify the discussion, we will assume there is only one domain involved, so we need not specify the `domains` option on any routers except the initial one, which handles remote domains. This will be the standard **notlocal** router that we have shown several times, so we will not repeat it again.

To implement our mixed domain, a mapping from local parts to workstation names is required. For example:

```
ceo:      bigcheese.plc.co.example
alice:    castor.plc.co.example
bob:      pollux.plc.co.example
```

means that mail addressed to the local part *ceo* is to be sent on to the host *bigcheese.plc.co.example*, and so on. We will show two different ways of using this table (which we will assume is in the file */etc/wsusers*), because they introduce different new features of Exim. In both cases, a single router is used for the local parts that are to be delivered to other hosts. Other local parts are passed on to subsequent routers, which can deliver them to mailboxes on the local host in the usual way.

## 5.6.1 Using a manualroute router

The **manualroute** router is Exim's main way of routing addresses to remote hosts using local routing data. It enables you to set up routing rules of the form "send mail for these addresses to that host". In our example, this router picks off the local parts that are to be delivered to workstations:

```
workstation_people:
  driver = manualroute
  local_parts = lsearch;/etc/wsusers
  route_list = *  $local_part_data
  transport = remote_smtp
```

The `local_parts` precondition restricts this router to those local parts that are found in the file. The routing rule is specified by the `route_list` option, which has two parts:

- The asterisk means "for all domains". In this example, we are handling only one domain, but in general a **manualroute** router can handle more than one, with different rules for different domains (☞ 7.4).

- The second part of the rule is the name of the host to which the message should be sent. The value of *$local_part_data* is the result of the lookup that was done to match the local part. If the local part is *ceo*, *$local_part_data* contains *bigcheese.plc.example*.

Because the router is defining the host to which the message is to be sent, the standard **remote_smtp** transport can be used.

## 5.6.2 Using an accept router and a special transport

In earlier examples, the **accept** router was used to set up local deliveries to pipe or files. In this alternative solution for a mixed domain, we use it to send some addresses to remote hosts. However, the router itself cannot specify host names. Its configuration is as follows:

```
workstation_people:
  driver = accept
  local_parts = lsearch;/etc/wsusers
  transport = local_smtp
```

Once again we use `local_parts` to select the relevant local parts; this time we route them to a special transport called **local_smtp**. Its configuration is this:

```
local_smtp:
  driver = smtp
  hosts = $local_part_data
```

Earlier examples of the **smtp** transport do not use the `hosts` option, because they are referenced from routers that supply a list of hosts. In this case, however, the transport is referenced from a router that cannot pass a host list, so the list must appear on the transport itself. The variable *$local_part_data* contains the data from the lookup in the `local_parts` router option, which is the relevant host name.

# 5.7 Delivering to UUCP

Exim contains no special UUCP features, and in particular, it does not support UUCP's "bang path" method of addressing.[1] However, if you stick to using Internet domain addresses, mail can easily be routed to UUCP. First of all, you must set up a mapping from domain names to UUCP host names. This could be a file containing data such as:

```
darksite.plc.example:  darksite
bluesite.plc.example:  indigo
```

Then you need a router that uses this data:

```
uucphost:
  driver = manualroute
  route_data = ${lookup{$domain}lsearch{/usr/local/uucpdomains}}
  transport = uucp
```

This is a **manualroute** router that searches the file */usr/local/uucpdomains* for routing information. If it finds the domain, it routes the address to the **uucp** transport:

```
uucp:
  driver = pipe
  command = /usr/local/bin/uux -r - $host!rmail $local_part
  user = nobody
  return_fail_output = true
```

Because **pipe** is a local transport, the **manualroute** router cannot pass a host list for delivery (as it did for the **smtp** transport in an example in the previous section). Instead, the router places the host name in the *$host* variable. Using this configuration, a message addressed to:

```
postmaster@bluesite.plc.example
```

would end up being piped to the command:

```
/usr/local/bin/uux -r - indigo!rmail postmaster
```

---

[1]  A UUCP "bang path" is an address of the form *host1!host2!host3...!user*.

which is run as the user *nobody*. The `return_fail_output` setting ensures that, if the command fails, any output it produces is returned in the bounce message.

# 5.8 Ignoring the local part in local deliveries

Local deliveries are not required to make use of the local part of an address. One common example is a small company that has only one person reading incoming email. Rather than setting up fixed local parts such as *sales*, *info*, *enquiries*, and so on, they want all mail delivered into a single mailbox, whatever the local part. Assuming the chosen recipient is *postmaster*, all you need is the following router:

```
catchall:
  driver = redirect
  data = postmaster
```

This should be placed last in the list of routers, so that it picks up all unknown local parts and redirects them to *postmaster*.

Some ISPs allocate a domain name to each small account, and then deliver all messages addressed to that domain into a single mailbox, ignoring local parts. For Exim running on such an ISP's mail server, there are two issues to consider:

*   How to find the mailbox from the domain name

*   How to enable the owner of the mailbox to distinguish between different recipients

Suppose that the ISP allocates the domain name *diego.isp.example* to a customer whose username is *diego* and whose mailbox is */var/mail/diego* on the ISP's mail host. The Exim configuration on the mail host could use a single **accept** router to pick up these addresses and route them to a special transport:

```
onebox_customers:
  driver = accept
  domains = *.isp.example
  address_data = ${if match{$domain}{^([^.]+)}{$1}}
  transport = onebox
```

The `address_data` option is something new. When it appears on a router, its value is expanded just before the router is run, and the result is saved in the variable *$address_data*. This can be used in the router's options, or in a subsequent transport. It is most often used to remember data that is looked up from a file or database. In this example, however, we use it to save repeating a slightly complicated expansion string in the transport.

The conditional expansion item in the `address_data` setting extracts the first component of the domain by matching the contents of *$domain* (that is, `diego.isp.example` in our example) against a regular expression. The regular expression `^([^.]+)` matches a string that begins with a sequence of non-dot characters, and saves that sequence in *$1*. Since the domain has already been checked by the `domains` option, we know that the regular expression will always match. In our example, the value of *$1* will be `diego`. This is then substituted in the final set of braces, giving `diego` as the result of the whole `if` expansion item.

The transport makes use of this value to deliver to the mailbox file while running as the correct user:

```
onebox:
   driver = appendfile
   file = /var/mail/$address_data
   user = $address_data
   envelope_to_add
   return_path_add
```

Setting `envelope_to_add` and `return_path_add` has the effect of preserving the envelope addresses in header lines, so it is possible for the owner of the mailbox to distinguish between messages to different local parts, even if the recipient addresses do not appear in the *To:* header lines.

In practice, the technique of delivering all local parts into a single mailbox is no longer as useful as it once was, because of the increasing volume of junk mail that is sent out to randomly generated addresses. These days, most sites prefer to check incoming local parts during the SMTP dialogue, and reject those that are not recognized.

## 5.9 Handling case-sensitive local parts

RFC 2822 states that the case of letters in the local parts of addresses must be assumed to be significant. In contrast, the case of letters in domain names is never significant. Exim preserves the case of both parts of addresses, and transmits them exactly as they were received. However, on most Unix-like systems, usernames are in lower case, and local parts in email addresses are expected to be handled without regard to case, so that messages addressed to:

```
icarus@knossos.example
Icarus@knossos.example
ICARUS@knossos.example
iCaRuS@knossos.example
```

are all delivered to the local user *icarus*. For this reason, whenever it is routing an address, Exim by default uses a copy in which both the local part and the domain are lower-cased. In a conventional configuration, the fact that the local part is lower-cased while routing remote addresses is not a problem, because the local part is not normally used when routing remote addresses.

If you want a particular router to handle local parts in a case-sensitive way, you can change the default value of the `caseful_local_part` option:

```
caseful_local_part = true
```

This applies only to the router on which it is set. The four addresses in the previous example would be treated as having different local parts by such a router, and if the router sends an address to a transport, the value of *$local_part* when the transport is run retains the original case. In contrast, *$domain* is always entirely in lower case.

Sites that use mixed-case usernames do not usually have accounts that differ only in the case of their letters. They generally still want to have case-insensitive treatment of local parts in email. That is, they still want to recognize local parts without regard to the case of their letters, but deliver them to case-sensitive mailboxes.

Setting `caseful_local_part` on all the relevant routers is therefore not sufficient; you also have to arrange to convert incoming local parts to the correct case. One way of doing this is to set up the first router for the local domain as a **redirect** router that does the conversion by a file lookup such as:

```
adjust_case:
  driver = redirect
  data = ${lookup{$local_part}cdb{/etc/usercased.cdb}{$value}fail}\
      @$domain
```

This router does *not* have `caseful_local_part` set, so the value of *$local_part* is lower-cased. It is used as the key for a lookup in (in this example) a *cdb* file, whose data might contain entries such as:

```
icarus:    Icarus
j.caesar: J.Caesar
```

The redirected address is completed by adding the domain. Thus, all four addresses previously listed would be turned into *Icarus@knossos.example*. The new address has the correct case, and can therefore be successfully handled by subsequent routers that do have `caseful_local_part` set. If the local part is not found in the file, the `fail` in the lookup causes a forced expansion failure, in which case the router declines, and the address is processed using its original case.

For maximum efficiency, a router such as this should contain a setting of the `redirect_router` option. Without it, the new address is processed afresh, and if it is different from the original address, it passes through the **adjust_case** router for a second time, though this just regenerates the same new address. The next time around, the router is skipped because it has already processed that address. Setting `redirect_router` to point to the next router, as shown in this example:

```
redirect_router = system_aliases
```

avoids the second pass through **adjust_case**.

# 5.10 Scanning messages for viruses

There are a number of programs that will scan an email message to determine whether it contains any viruses as attachments. Some of these run on Unix systems, but others are available only for other operating systems. The general technique for using such a program from Exim is the same in both cases: incoming messages are delivered to the scanner, which has a secure means of passing those that are "clean" back to Exim for final delivery. This process causes an additional *Received:* header to be added to the message, but that is not usually a problem.

Messages can be diverted to the scanner program directly from a router, or a system filter can be used in some cases. We have not discussed Exim's filtering facilities yet (details are in chapter 10), but, in brief, a system filter allows a message to be inspected before it is delivered, and various actions can be taken, depending on what the filter finds. In the context of virus scanning, this can save some resources by doing some initial testing before calling an external scanner. However, using a system filter introduces some complications that can be avoided if a filter is not used.

As an example of how a filter might be used, consider checking a message for the existence of attachments. MIME messages that have attachments must contain a header line such as:

```
Content-Type: multipart/mixed;
   boundary="------------9D6D28528332819A908698F9"
```

A "boundary" has to be defined for there to be any attachments. You could test for this in a system filter by this command:

```
if $h_Content-Type: contains "boundary" then ...
```

and pass the message to an external scanner only if the condition was met.

 Attachments are not the only way that viruses can be transmitted. In practice, you would need some additional tests, such as checking for the absence of "uuencoded" material, before skipping the full virus check.

## 5.10.1 Virus checking on the local host

If your virus scanner runs on the local host, Exim can deliver a message to it via a pipe, and it can be returned by running a new Exim reception process and passing the message back through another pipe. It is important to preserve the original sender address. This can be done by making use of the -f command-line option when returning the message, or by transferring the message in batch SMTP format. In both cases, the process that returns the message to Exim must be running as a trusted user, because only trusted users are permitted to specify sender addresses.

The normal way of identifying messages that have come back from the scanner is to make use of the -oMr command-line option. This defines the protocol by which the message is received. Normally, it is set to values such as smtp or local, but trusted callers can set it to an arbitrary string. The value is recorded in the log and is available in the *$received_protocol* variable, but it is not otherwise used by Exim.

In order to make this work, therefore, you need to decide which uid is to be used to run the scanner, and to set it up as an Exim trusted user. It is a good idea to reserve a special uid just for this purpose. Suppose you have set up a user called *vircheck*. Adding the following to your Exim configuration:

```
trusted_users = vircheck
```

makes it trusted. This means that any process running under the uid of *vircheck* can supply arbitrary sender addresses and protocol values for messages it submits.

Next, you need to set up a transport to pipe the message to the scanner. The following example uses batch SMTP (BSMTP):

```
pipe_to_scanner:
  driver = pipe
  command = /path/to/scanner/command
  user = vircheck
  use_bsmtp
  batch_max = 100
```

Setting use_bsmtp causes the message to be delivered in BSMTP format, which includes the envelope in the form of SMTP commands. The value of batch_max ensures that only a single copy of the message is sent for up to 100 recipients. (The default for local transports is one copy per recipient.)

Using BSMTP makes it easy for the scanner to return the message with the sender and recipients unchanged. If the special protocol value is scanned-ok, for instance, the scanner can run a command of the form:

```
exim -oMr scanned-ok -bS
```

and copy the message it received to the standard input of this command, without modification. For example, the following Perl script is a dummy scanner that does not actually do any checking, but simply resubmits the message:

```
#!/usr/bin/perl
open(OUT, "|exim -oMr scanned-ok -bS")
   || die "Failed to set up Exim process\n";
print OUT while (<STDIN>);
close(OUT);
```

You now have to arrange for new messages to be routed to the transport that passes them to the scanner. You can do this by inserting a new router at the beginning of the router configuration:

```
send_to_scanner:
  driver = accept
  transport = pipe_to_scanner
  condition = ${if eq {$received_protocol}{scanned-ok}{no}{yes}}
```

By putting this router first, you ensure that all unchecked messages are sent to the scanner, whether their recipients are local or remote. If you want to check only those messages that have a local recipient, you can place this router after those that handle remote addresses – in a typical configuration such as we have previously discussed, this would be after the **nonlocal** router.

We have previously encountered options such as domains and local_parts that apply preconditions to the running of routers. These options exist independently because they implement commonly required tests. To cope with less common requirements, the condition option exists. Its value is a string that is expanded. If the result is 0, no, or false, the router is skipped. For any other values, the router is run (assuming other preconditions are met, of course). This facility allows customized preconditions to be applied, using any of the features available in string expansions.

The condition option in this example checks the value of *$received_protocol* and skips the router if its value is scanned-ok. Without this check, messages would loop forever between Exim and the scanner. For messages not received from the scanner, all addresses are routed to the **pipe_to_scanner** transport. Unless there are more than 100 recipients, the transport batches them into a single delivery to the scanner program because of the setting of batch_max.

This configuration sends all messages, both incoming and outgoing, to the scanner. If you want to restrict it to incoming messages only, you can do so by means of a suitable domains setting on the router, to exclude non-local domains.

## 5.10.2 Virus checking using a system filter

An alternative way of arranging for messages to be passed to a scanner program is to make use of a system filter (see chapter 10), which will apply whether the recipients are local or remote. However, in several ways this is more complicated. The filter would contain a command such as this:

```
if $received_protocol is not scanned-ok then
  pipe "/the/scanner/command $sender_address '$recipients'"
endif
```

When a system filter sets up a delivery in this way, it is considered to have handled the delivery arrangements for the message, so normal delivery to the regular recipient addresses is bypassed, and the only delivery is to the scanner. In this example, the sender address is passed to the command as the first argument, and the list of recipients (which are separated by a comma and a space) is the second argument, created by expanding *$recipients*.[1] To return a clean message for delivery, the scanner should call Exim with the equivalent of this command line:

```
exim -oi -oMr scanned-ok -f '$sender_address' '$recipients'
```

and write the message to the standard input. Although no additional router is required, you still have to define a transport. It should not have a `command` setting, because the command is specified by the filter. So all that is needed is:

```
pipe_to_scanner:
  driver = pipe
  user = vircheck
  message_prefix =
```

Unsetting `message_prefix` is necessary because, when BSMTP is not in use, it defaults to a message separator line. Having defined the transport, you must set:

```
system_filter_pipe_transport = pipe_to_scanner
```

in the main configuration, to tell Exim which transport to run when it encounters a `pipe` command in a system filter. Batch SMTP cannot be used in this case, because this is a special kind of one-off delivery for the whole message, independent of the normal recipients.

## 5.10.3 Virus checking on an external host

If your virus checker runs on an external host, all that is needed is a configuration that sends messages to the checking host, unless they arrived from there. Suppose the checker is running on IP address 192.168.13.13; a transport to deliver messages there is:

```
smtp_to_scanner:
  driver = smtp
  hosts = 192.168.13.13
```

The router to send unchecked messages to the scanner is now:

```
send_to_scanner:
  driver = accept
  transport = smtp_to_scanner
  condition = ${if eq {$sender_host_address}{192.168.13.13}\
              {no}{yes}}
```

If you have more than one host running a virus checker, you can specify the transport as:

```
smtp_to_scanner:
  driver = smtp
  hosts = 192.168.13.13 : 192.168.14.14 : ...
  hosts_randomize
```

---

[1] The *$recipients* variable is available only in system filters. For privacy reasons, it is not available in user filters.

The `hosts_randomize` option makes Exim put the hosts in a random order before trying them, each time the transport is run. The condition in the router is now more complicated:

```
send_to_scanner:
  driver = accept
  transport = smtp_to_scanner
  condition = ${if or {\
                  {eq {$sender_host_address}{192.168.13.13}}\
                  {eq {$sender_host_address}{192.168.14.14}}\
                  ...
               }{no}{yes}}
```

It is not straightforward to use a system filter directly when an external checker is in use because of the complication of preserving the message's recipients. A system filter could, however, add a header line that is used by routers to determine whether to send a message to the checker.

# 5.11 Modifying message bodies

There have been many questions on the Exim mailing list about modifying the bodies of messages as they pass through the MTA. There are three specific things that people want to do:

- Lawyers want to add standard disclaimers.

- Marketroids want to add advertisements.

- The paranoid want to remove attachments.

There are legal and ethical issues that arise in this connection which will not be discussed here,[1] but there are also serious technical problems. Since the advent of MIME (RFC 2025), message bodies are no longer (in general) just strings of text characters. Just adding extra characters on the end of a message is likely to break the syntax of the message, causing it to become unreadable by standard MUAs.[2] Furthermore, if the message is digitally signed, making any change to the body invalidates the signature. Digital signatures are becoming more widely used now that they are legally binding in some countries.

Finally, it is not the job of an MTA to modify the bodies of messages. If such modification is to be undertaken, the program that does it needs specialist knowledge about body formats, which is inappropriate to include in an MTA.

---

[1]  See *http://www.goldmark.org/jeff/stupid-disclaimers* for a discussion of the silliness of some disclaimers.

[2]  One such client (now obsolete) crashes on encountering a message that has been tampered with in this way.

If, despite all these considerations, you find yourself wanting to do this kind of thing using Exim, you can make use of a transport filter (☞ 8.8). A transport filter lets you pass outgoing messages through a program or script of your choice. It is the job of this script to make any changes to the message that you require. By this means, you have full control over what changes are made, and Exim does not need to know anything about message bodies. However, using a transport filter requires additional resources, and may slow down mail delivery.

For example, suppose you want to do this for messages from addresses in your domain that are being delivered to a remote host. Instead of the normal setting:

```
transport = remote_smtp
```

for the router that handles remote addresses, you could have this:

```
transport = ${if eq {$sender_address_domain}{your.domain}\
            {remote_smtp_filter}{remote_smtp}}
```

The expansion of the `transport` option tests the contents of the variable *$sender_address_domain*, which contains the domain of the sender of the message. If it is *your.domain*, the address is routed to the **remote_smtp_filter** transport instead of **remote_smtp**. The new transport is defined thus:

```
remote_smtp_filter:
  driver = smtp
  transport_filter = /your/filter/command
```

The entire message is passed to your filter command on its standard input. It must write the modified version to the standard output, taking care not to break the RFC 2822 syntax. As this is a remote transport, the command is run as the Exim user.

# 6

# Generic options that apply to all routers

Earlier chapters introduce a number of general options that can be set for any router, to show how some common configuration requirements can be met. This chapter recaps those options, and also includes the remaining options that are common to all routers. These are usually called *generic* options. In addition, each router has some options that are specific to its operation; these are described in the following chapter in the sections on the individual routers.

As the earlier examples show, one generic option that is always set is driver. This determines which particular router is to be used. Another generic option that has already been discussed is transport. When a router decides to accept an address and queue it for a transport, the value of transport is expanded, and must yield the name of an available transport. If it does not, delivery is deferred.

A generic option that appears in many earlier examples is more. When a router declines to handle an address, setting more false stops Exim from passing the address to any more routers, thereby causing routing to fail. Because more is a Boolean option, the following two settings are synonymous, and are used interchangeably:

```
more = false
no_more
```

Another generic option, caseful_local_part, for handling local parts in a case-sensitive manner, was discussed in the previous chapter (☞ 5.9).

The remaining generic options can be divided into the following types:

- Those that set conditions for the running of the router

- Those that change what happens when a router is successful, that is, when it accepts an address

- Those that add data to an address accepted by the router, for use when that address is delivered

- Those that modify Exim's behaviour in error circumstances such as a DNS timeout or a remote domain that routes to the local host

- Those that provide debugging information

The options for a router may be given in any order in the configuration file, except that those specific to the individual router must follow the setting of `driver`. For this reason, `driver` is normally given first.

# 6.1 Conditional running of routers

As we have seen in several examples, Exim offers an address to all the defined routers in turn, until one is found that can handle it, or until all have been tried. However, before any particular router is run, Exim checks a number of preconditions. These tests are applied in the order in which they are described in the rest of this section; the order in which they appear in the configuration is immaterial.

## 6.1.1 Local part prefixes and suffixes

There are a number of common situations in which it is helpful to be able to recognize a prefix or a suffix on a local part, and to handle the affix and the remainder of the local part independently. The `local_part_prefix` and `local_part_suffix` options that provide this facility were introduced earlier (☞ 5.3.4). They can be set to colon-separated lists of strings. If either is set, the router is skipped unless the local part starts with, or ends with (respectively), one of the given strings. When the router is run, the value of the affix is stripped from the local part and placed in *$local_part_prefix* or *$local_part_suffix*, as appropriate.

---

 Processing of `local_part_prefix` and `local_part_suffix` happens before checking the `local_parts` condition. Therefore, the local part that is checked against `local_parts` is not the full local part, because any prefix or suffix is removed beforehand.

---

Another example of the use of a prefix is to provide a way of bypassing users' *.forward* files. For example, you can do this by putting the following router before the one that handles *.forward* files:

```
real_users:
    driver = accept
    check_local_user
    local_part_prefix = real-
    transport = local_delivery
```

If a local part begins with *real-*, this router is run, and if the rest of the local part is a login name, the address is accepted and routed to the **local_delivery** transport. Local parts that do not start with the prefix are not handled by this router, and are therefore passed on.

The use of a prefix or suffix can be made optional by setting `local_part_prefix_optional` or `local_part_suffix_optional`, as appropriate. In these cases, the router is run whether or not the affix matches, but if there is an affix, it is removed while running the router. The values of *$local_part_prefix* and *$local_part_suffix* can be used to determine whether or not there was an affix in the original local part.

A limited form of wildcard is available for prefixes and suffixes. If a prefix begins with an asterisk, it matches the longest possible sequence of arbitrary characters at the start of the local part. Similarly, if a suffix ends with an asterisk, it matches the longest possible sequence at the end. There is an earlier example of this (☞ 5.5) that uses the following option:

```
local_part_suffix = -*
```

If you use this kind of wildcard, you must choose a character that never appears in non-affixed local parts as a separator, such as the hyphen in the previous example.

If both `local_part_prefix` and `local_part_suffix` are set for a router, both conditions must be met if they are not optional. Care must be taken if wildcards are used in both a prefix and a suffix on the same router. Different separator characters must be used to avoid ambiguity.

## 6.1.2 Use of routers while verifying

Exim draws a distinction between processing an address in order to deliver a message to it, and *verifying* an address to check that it is valid. Verification is mostly used to check the validity of addresses during incoming SMTP connections, at the point when the message's envelope is received. It can also be requested explicitly by the SMTP command VRFY. Exim uses an ACL to decide if a client host is permitted to use VRFY, with the default being to deny it (☞ 14.8.2).

Verification consists of running the address though the routers, as if it were being processed for delivery. An address verifies successfully if one of the routers accepts it. Verification is discussed in detail in chapter 14.

Sometimes you want routing to behave differently when verifying an address, as opposed to processing it for delivery. For example, while verifying that a local part refers to a user mailbox, there is no point wasting time checking the user's *forward* file. Setting:

```
verify = false
```

on a router causes it to be skipped during verification. In fact, this is just a short-hand for:

```
verify_sender = false
verify_recipient = false
```

which suppress the router during verification of senders and recipients independently.

As an example of where this could be useful, suppose you are using a **accept** router with no preconditions to pass all unrecognized local parts to a script that tries to generate helpful error messages, or to a different host that might be able to handle these addresses. This means that no local part that is passed to the routers will ever cause a failure during message delivery. However, if verification of senders at SMTP time is configured, you do not want arbitrary local parts in your domain to be accepted as valid incoming senders. The solution is to set `no_verify_sender` on the special **accept** router, so that it is not run when verifying senders.

There may be occasional circumstances where it is helpful to run a router only during verification and not during delivery. This can be configured by setting:

```
verify_only
```

in its configuration. If you really want to, by making use of `verify_only` and `no_verify`, you can partition the routers into a set that is used only for delivery and another set that is used only for verification.

## 6.1.3 Control of EXPN

The SMTP `EXPN` command is not used for mail delivery, but instead requests the expansion of an address, to show the result of aliasing or forwarding. EXPN has fallen out of favour recently, and many sites consider it to be a privacy exposure. For this reason, Exim uses an ACL to decide if a client host is permitted to use EXPN, with the default being to deny it.

When EXPN is permitted, the given address is passed to the routers for expansion. However, if the `expn` option is set false for any router, it is skipped when expanding an address as a result of processing an EXPN command. If you permit EXPN at all, you might, for example, want to turn the option off on a router for users' *.forward* files, while leaving it on for the system alias file.

## 6.1.4 Restricting routers to specific domains

The `domains` option is used to specify that a particular router is to run only when the address contains certain domains, as in the virtual domains example from the previous chapter:

```
virtuals:
  driver = redirect
  domains = cdb;/etc/virtuals
  data = ${lookup{$local_part}lsearch{/etc/$domain.aliases}}
  no_more
```

## 6.1.5 Restricting routers to specific local parts

Just as the `domains` option restricts a router to specific domains, the `local_parts` option restricts a router to specific local parts. We showed an example of this when redirecting postmaster mail for a group of local domains to the same address:

```
postmaster:
  driver = redirect
  local_parts = postmaster
  data = postmaster@your.domain.example
```

As mentioned earlier, processing of `local_part_prefix` and `local_part_suffix` happens before the `local_parts` test.

## 6.1.6 Checking for local user accounts

Several earlier examples show the `check_local_user` option, which is a precondition that ensures that the local part is a valid username on the local host before running the router. The check is done by calling the system function *getpwnam()* rather than looking at */etc/passwd* directly, so that users defined by other means (such as NIS) are recognized.

## 6.1.7 Restricting routers to specific senders

The `senders` option restricts a router to messages with certain senders only. We saw an example of how it could be used to implement a closed mailing list in the previous chapter (☞ 5.3.4). It is the envelope sender that is tested, not the contents of the *From:* header line.

## 6.1.8 Restricting routers by file existence

The `require_files` option causes the existence (or non-existence) of certain files to determine whether a router is run, and there are examples of its use in the previous chapter. Here is the router that was shown as an example of how to call SmartList:

```
list_router:
  driver = accept
  local_part_suffix = -request
  local_part_suffix_optional
  local_parts = !.bin:!.etc
  require_files = /usr/slist/$local_part/rc.init
  transport = list_transport
```

Before running a router, Exim works its way through the `require_files` list, expanding each item separately. If an expansion is forced to fail, or if any expanded string is empty, the item is ignored. Other expansion failures cause delivery to be deferred. Otherwise, except as described here, each expanded string must be a fully qualified file path, optionally preceded by an exclamation mark (indicating negation).

If the `require_files` option is used on a router that has `check_local_user` set, the expansion variable *$home* may be used to refer to the home directory of the user whose name is that of the local part of the address.

The router is skipped if any required path does not exist, or if any path preceded by ! does exist. If Exim cannot determine whether or not a file exists, delivery of the message is deferred. This can happen when NFS-mounted filesystems are unavailable.

 You cannot use `require_files` to check for a file in which to look up a domain, local part, or sender address, because the `domains`, `local_parts`, and `senders` options are checked first. Instead, you must use an `exists` expansion condition within these other options. The earlier discussion of closed mailing lists showed this example:

```
senders = ${if exists {/usr/lists/$local_part}\
          {lsearch;/usr/lists/$local_part}{*}}
```

The `require_files` option is intended for checking files that the router may use internally, or which are needed by a transport (for example, a user's *.procmailrc* file).

When Exim is routing an address as part of a message delivery, the `require_files` check is run as *root*, but there is a facility for checking the accessibility of a file by another user. If an item in a `require_files` list does not contain any forward slash characters, it is taken to be the username (and optional group name, separated by a comma) to be checked for subsequent files in the list. For example:

```
require_files = $local_part:$home/.procmailrc
```

If no group is specified but the user is specified symbolically, the user's primary group is used. If a user or group name in a `require_files` list does not exist, the precondition fails.

Exim performs this check by scanning along the components of the file path and checking the access for the given user and group. It checks for "execute" access on directories and "read" access on the final file name.[1]

When Exim is verifying an address as part of the policy checks on an incoming SMTP message, the routers are run as *exim*, and not as *root*. This may affect the result of a `require_files` test and lead to a "Permission denied" error because

---

[1]   This means that file access control lists, if the operating system has them, are ignored.

the Exim user cannot access one of the directories on the file's path. The default action is to treat this as a configuration error; a temporary verification failure occurs.

In many cases you can get round this by setting `no_verify` on the router. For example, checking whether a user has a *.procmailrc* file is not usually relevant for verification. However, in some circumstances it may be desirable to treat this condition as if the file did not exist. If the filename (or the exclamation mark that precedes the filename for non-existence) is preceded by a plus sign, the "Permission denied" error is treated as if the file did not exist. For example:

```
require_files = +/some/file
```

## 6.1.9 Restricting routers by other conditions

The `domains`, `local_parts`, `senders`, and other options just described exist because these are common preconditions that are often needed. For less common cases, there is an option called `condition`. Its value is expanded, and if the result is a forced failure, an empty string, or one of the strings 0, `no`, or `false`, the router is not run. There are some examples of this in the discussion of virus scanning in the previous chapter. Because of the flexibility of the string expansion mechanism, a wide range of conditions can be tested. However, like all options, `condition` can be set only once on a given router, though the condition can be arbitrarily complex.

For example, suppose you are prepared to deliver small messages directly over the Internet, but want to send large ones to some other host (which might, for example, send them out overnight). The **notlocal** router could be modified like this:

```
notlocal:
  driver = dnslookup
  domains = ! +local_domains
  transport = remote_smtp
  condition = ${if < {$message_size}{500K}{yes}{no}}
```

The expansion string is using a numeric comparison (specified by a "less than" sign) on the variable *$message_size*, which contains the size of the message. If the message is less than 500 KB in size, the string expands to `yes`. Otherwise it expands to `no`. Thus, this router handles messages that are smaller than 500 KB only. You would, of course, also need a subsequent router to deal with the large messages. A **manualroute** router could be used for this.

# 6.2 Changing a router's successful outcome

The generic options described in this section allow you to change what happens in some cases when a router successfully handles an address.

## 6.2.1 Processing redirected addresses

When a router redirects an address and generates one or more child addresses, each of the children is routed independently, normally starting from the first router. However, you can specify that child addresses should start at a different router by setting the `redirect_router` option. For example, if you have an aliasing router that turns real names into login names, it is a waste of resources to reprocess the login names with the same router because it will always decline. You can save resources by configuring the aliasing router as follows:

```
real_names:
  driver = redirect
  data = ${lookup{$local_part}lsearch{/etc/real-to-login}}
  redirect_router = system_aliases

system_aliases:
  ...
```

The router specified by `redirect_router` can be earlier or later in the configuration.

## 6.2.2 Setting up multiple deliveries

When a router successfully handles an address, that address does not normally require further action, and so it is not passed to any more routers. Suppose, however, that you want to save copies of messages addressed to certain recipients.[1] Using a router to set up deliveries of the required copies is a convenient way to handle this requirement, but of course the messages must go on to be delivered normally as well. The `unseen` option is provided for just this purpose. It is the complement of `no_more`; `unseen` causes routing to continue when it would otherwise cease. Thus, the router below sends a copy of every message addressed to *ceo@plc.example* to *secretary@plc.example*, without disturbing the normal delivery:

```
copy_ceo:
  driver = redirect
  local_parts = ceo
  domains = plc.example
  data = secretary@plc.example
  unseen
```

For this to work, this router must precede the router that sets up the normal delivery. The `domains` setting is necessary only if the routers are handling different domains in different ways.

---

[1] If you want to save copies of messages independently of the recipients, it is best to use a system filter (see chapter 10) because it can arrange for a single copy, however many recipients the message has.

## 6.2.3 Forcing failure for address verification

Sometimes, when verifying addresses, you may want to force a specific address to fail. If a router has `fail_verify` set and succeeds in handling an address that is being verified, verification fails instead of succeeding. Actually, `fail_verify` is just a shorthand for:

```
fail_verify_sender
fail_verify_recipient
```

These options control the forced failure mechanism independently for sender and recipient addresses. They make it possible to fail verification for a set of addresses that is defined by what a specific router matches. These options apply only during verification, and are ignored when processing an address for delivery. Here is an example of a real case where this is used.

When an account is cancelled on one of the central systems at the University of Cambridge, it is not immediately removed from the password data; instead the password is reset and the home directory is set to */home/CANCELLED*. This makes it easy to reinstate an account. Only after some time has passed is it completely removed. Mail for these cancelled accounts must not be accepted, and therefore verification of their addresses must fail, so that incoming SMTP mail for them is rejected. Action is needed to achieve this, because the usernames are still in the password data. The simplest thing to do would be to add:

```
condition = ${if eq{$home}{/home/CANCELLED}{no}{yes}}
```

to the normal **localuser** router, so that accounts that do not have a normal home directory are not recognized. This achieves two things:

• Incoming SMTP messages for cancelled users are rejected because the recipient address fails to verify.

• If a message addressed to a cancelled user is received from a local process (where recipient verification does not happen), it is bounced because routing the address fails.

The problem with this is that the error given in bounce messages is "unknown user", which often causes the senders to pester the postmaster with questions as to what has happened to the account "that worked yesterday". Therefore, we use a different strategy. The following additional router is inserted before those that handle local users:

```
cancelled_users:
  driver = accept
  check_local_user
  condition = ${if eq{$home}{/home/CANCELLED}{yes}{no}}
  fail_verify
  transport = cancelleduser_pipe
```

This router checks for a local user whose home directory is */home/CANCELLED*; other local parts are passed on to the next router. When delivering, the message is passed to a **cancelleduser_pipe** transport in order to generate a bounce message that explains what has happened. Setting `fail_verify` ensures that when addresses are being verified, any that are matched cause a verification error.

## 6.2.4 Ignoring erroneous IP addresses

There are certain IP addresses (for example, 127.0.0.1) that should never be found in the DNS as the targets for mail deliveries. Unfortunately, some DNS administrators (either through ignorance or malice) do set these up. If Exim encounters 127.0.0.1 as the IP address of a supposedly remote host, it normally freezes the message (☞ 6.5). This makes work for the local administrator.

The `ignore_target_hosts` option makes it possible to specify that certain IP addresses are to be completely ignored. Exim behaves as if the relevant DNS record (or other source of information) does not exist. For example, in Exim's default configuration file, the **dnslookup** router that handles remote domains contains this setting:

```
ignore_target_hosts = 0.0.0.0 : 127.0.0.0/8
```

This ignores 0.0.0.0[1] as well as any IP address that starts with 127. Any domains that resolve to these addresses are treated in the same way as domains that cannot be looked up.

# 6.3 Adding data for use by transports

When a router accepts an address, it can attach data to it for use when the address is finally transported. Some items are relevant only when the router passes the address directly to the transport; others accumulate as the address passes through several routers (for example, multiple instances of aliasing or forwarding).

## 6.3.1 Remembering arbitrary data

On a system where all the information about local users is kept in a database, it is desirable to minimize the number of database lookups that are done. During the course of routing and delivering a message, different Exim options may need to refer to different fields in the same database record.

You could set up the configuration with a separate database lookup for each field every time it is used. It is more efficient, however, to specify a single lookup to retrieve all the fields just once. The `address_data` option makes this possible.

---

[1]  Many TCP/IP stacks interpret 0.0.0.0 as "the local host", but in other situations (for example, firewall tables) it can mean "any host".

Just before a router is run, its value is expanded and associated with the address. The result can be accessed via the *$address_data* variable in the router's private options, and in the options of the transport to which the address is routed.

If the router generates child addresses, the value of *$address_data* propagates to them. If the router declines, *$address_data* remains set, and can be used in subsequent routers. However, if another router uses the `address_data` option, it overwrites the previous value.

If the expansion of `address_data` is forced to fail, the router declines, leaving *$address_data* empty. Any other expansion failure causes delivery of the address to be deferred.

Consider a host where user information is kept in a MySQL database. The first router that handles local users could be as follows:

```
userforward:
  driver = redirect
  address_data = ${lookup mysql{\
        select uid,gid,mailbox,home,forward from users\
        where name='${mysql_quote:$local_part}'}{$value}fail}
  data = ${extract{home}{$address_data}\
        /${extract{forward}{$address_data}}
```

The router has no preconditions, so it always attempts to expand `address_data`, causing a lookup for the local part in the database. If the lookup fails (that is, the user does not exist), the expansion is forced to fail, and the router declines. Otherwise, because the MySQL statement selects several fields, the value of *$address_data* might be set to something like this for a user whose login name is *adc*:

```
uid=1234 gid=5678 mailbox=/var/mail/adc home=/home/adc forward=.forward
```

The router runs, and expands the `data` option, which uses two `extract` expansion items to obtain the name of the home directory and the forward file within it from the string in *$address_data*. If this file exists, it is processed; if not, the router declines, leaving the value of *$address_data* set for the next router:

```
localuser:
  driver = accept
  condition = ${if def:address_data{no}{yes}}
  transport = local_delivery
```

This router checks for a valid user by seeing if *$address_data* is set to anything other than an empty string. It then routes the address to this transport:

```
local_delivery:
  driver = appendfile
  file = ${extract{mailbox}{$address_data}}
  user = ${extract{uid}{$address_data}}
  group = ${extract{gid}{$address_data}}
```

The transport uses *$address_data* to obtain the name of the mailbox and the user and group under which to run the delivery.

The `address_data` option can also be useful in cases where lookups are not involved at all. You can use it as a general means of passing data between routers and transports. We showed a use of `address_data` that did not involve a lookup earlier (☞ 5.8).

---

 Because the `address_data` option is not expanded until after a router's preconditions have been tested, you cannot use the value of *$address_data* in the preconditions of the same router. However, it can be used in the preconditions of subsequent routers.

---

## 6.3.2 Adding or removing header lines

The header section of a message can be modified by adding or removing individual header lines at the time it is transported. Such modifications naturally apply only to the copy of the message that the transport delivers. This is not a very common requirement, but some installations find it useful.

Header line additions and removals can be specified on routers (as well as on transports) by setting `headers_add` and `headers_remove`, respectively. Note, however, that addresses with different `headers_add` or `headers_remove` settings cannot be transported as multiple envelope recipients on a single copy of the message. This may reduce performance.

Each of these options sets a string that is expanded at routing time, and retained for use at transport time. If the expansion is forced to fail, the option has no effect. For `headers_remove`, the expanded string must consist of a colon-separated list of header names, not including their terminating colons. The comparison is not case-sensitive. For example:

```
headers_remove = return-receipt-to:acknowledge-to
```

For `headers_add`, the expanded string must be in the form of one or more RFC 2822 header lines, separated by newlines (coded as \n inside a quoted string). For example:

```
headers_add = "X-added-header: added by $primary_hostname\n\
               X-another: added at time $tod_full"
```

Exim does not check the syntax of these added header lines, except that a newline is supplied at the end if one is not present. If an address passes through several routers as a result of aliasing or forwarding operations, any `headers_add` or `headers_remove` specifications are cumulative and are all retained for use by the transport. This makes it possible to add header lines that record aliasing and forwarding operations on the address. For example, you could add:

```
headers_add = X-Delivered-To: $local_part@$domain
```

to the configuration of every **redirect** router. A message addressed to *postmaster@example.com* that was aliased to *p.master@example.com* and then forwarded to *pat@example.com* would end up with these added header lines:

```
X-Delivered-To: postmaster@example.com
X-Delivered-To: p.master@example.com
```

This provides a complete record of the way the address was handled.

Because the addition of header lines does not actually happen until the message is transported, the added lines are not accessible to subsequent routers that may handle an address. For example, the expansion of `$header_X-Delivered-To:` would be an empty string in the example just discussed.

At transport time, removal applies only to the original header lines that arrived with the message, plus any that were added by a system filter. It is not possible to remove header lines that are added by a router. For each address, all the original header lines listed in `headers_remove` are removed, and those specified by `headers_add` are added in the order in which they were attached to the address. Then any additional header lines specified by the transport are added.

---

 If you are making use of the `unseen` option to take copies of messages, header lines that are added by routers that have `unseen` set are not present in the other deliveries of the message.

---

## 6.3.3 Changing the return path

When an address is redirected, it is sometimes desirable to change the address to which subsequent bounce messages will be sent. This is variously known as the *return path*, *error address*, or *envelope sender*.

The most common case is when a mailing list is being "exploded". Bounce messages should return to the manager of the list, not the poster of the message. The generic option `errors_to` can be used on any router to change the envelope sender for deliveries of any addresses it handles or generates. If the address subsequently passes through other routers that have their own `errors_to` settings, these override any earlier settings. The value of the option is expanded, and checked for validity by verifying it. It is not used if verification fails. The router that we used for mailing lists in the previous chapter is the following:

```
lists:
  driver = redirect
  domains = lists.simple.example
  no_more
  file = /usr/lists/$local_part
  forbid_pipe
  forbid_file
  errors_to = $local_part-request@$domain
```

It shows a very typical use of `errors_to`.

## 6.3.4 Controlling the environment for local deliveries

If a router queues an address for a local transport, the `user` and `group` options can be used to specify the uid and gid under which to run the local delivery process. One common case where the `user` option is needed is when an alias file sets up a delivery to a pipe or a file. For example, if */etc/aliases* contains this line:

```
majordomo:   |/usr/mail/majordomo ...
```

then either the **system_aliases** router or the transport to which it sends such deliveries must define the uid and gid under which the pipe command is to be run. The router's configuration could contain, for example:

```
user = majordom
```

The `user` and `group` options are strings that are expanded at the time the router is run, and must yield either a digit string or a name that can be looked up from the system's password data.[1] By this means, different values can be specified for different circumstances.

Suppose you are running another program via a pipe from an alias file, in addition to Majordomo. Perhaps it is an automated way of obtaining help, so that your aliases are:

```
majordomo:   |/usr/mail/majordomo ...
autohelp:    |/usr/etc/autohelp ...
```

Each pipe must run under its own uid, so a fixed value such as the one just shown is no longer possible. An expanded string can be used to select the correct user like this:

```
user = ${if eq {$local_part}{majordomo}{majordom}{autohelp}}
```

This expansion string checks the local part for the value `majordomo` and expands to `majordom` if it matches. Otherwise it expands to `autohelp`.

---

[1]  Exim uses the operating system's functions for looking up users and groups. These may consult */etc/passwd* and */etc/group*, but in larger systems the password data is usually kept elsewhere, such as in NIS or NIS+ databases.

If user is given without group, the group associated with the user is used as a default. The default for these options is unset unless check_local_user is set, in which case the defaults are taken from the password data.

The uid and gid set by a router can be overridden by options on the transport. If neither the router nor the transport specifies a uid or gid, the delivery runs as the Exim user or group, respectively.

Another way to handle the previous example is to put the setting of user on the transport instead of the **system_aliases** router. If you do this, however, you would probably want to set up a dedicated transport for all the pipe commands generated by this router, so that other pipe commands (for example, from users' *.forward* files) do not use a transport with this user setting. You can use pipe_transport on the **system_aliases** router to specify which transport is used for the pipe commands generated within that router.

A user may be a member of many groups, but (at least on some operating systems) it is quite an expensive operation to find them and set them all up when changing a uid, so Exim does not do this by default. If you want this to be done, then in addition to setting user you must set initgroups, which is a Boolean option that takes no data. For example:

```
user = majordom
initgroups
```

Two other options, transport_current_directory and transport_home_directory, are available for setting a current and a home directory, respectively, for use by local transports. Their values are expanded at the time the transport is run, but can be overridden by settings on the transport itself. When check_local_user is set, the default for the home directory is the user's home directory.

## 6.3.5 Specifying fallback hosts

The final option that sets up data to be passed to a transport is fallback_hosts. This option provides a "use a smart host only if delivery fails" facility. It applies only to remote transports, and its value must be a colon-separated list of host names or IP addresses. It is not string expanded. If the transport is unable to deliver to any of the normal hosts, and the errors are not permanent rejections, the addresses are put on a separate transport queue with their host lists replaced by the fallback hosts.

For example, you might want to set up a host that attempts remote deliveries according to the normal MX routing, but sends to a smart host any messages that cannot immediately be delivered. You could use this router:

```
notlocal:
  driver = dnslookup
  domains = ! +local_domains
  transport = remote_smtp
  fallback_hosts = smart.host.example
```

When a message is being delivered, Exim first tries the hosts that are found by the router from the MX records. If all of them give temporary errors, the address, instead of being deferred, is put onto a queue of addresses that are awaiting fallback processing.

Once normal delivery attempts are complete, the fallback queue is processed by rerunning the same transports with the new host lists. It is done this way (instead of trying the fallback hosts as soon as the ordinary hosts fail) so that if several failing addresses have the same fallback hosts (and `max_rcpt` permits it), a single copy of the message, with multiple recipients, is sent.

The **smtp** transport also has a `fallback_hosts` option. However, a setting of `fallback_hosts` on a router overrides any setting on the transport.

There is one situation in which fallback hosts are not used. For any address that is routed using MX records, if the current host is in the MX list (that is, it is an MX backup for the address), fallback hosts are not used for that address for the following reason. Suppose a host is using a configuration such as this, and is a secondary MX for some domain. When the primary MX host for that domain is down, mail for the domain arrives at the secondary host. It cannot deliver it to the primary MX host (because it is down), but it must not send it to its fallback host, because that host is likely to send it straight back, causing a mail loop.

## 6.4 Handling DNS timeouts

We have described many cases where routers decline (for example, when a local part is not found in an alias file, or when a *.forward* file does not exist). There is another return value, called "pass", that a router may give when it cannot handle an address. It means that the router has recognized the address in some way, and knows that it should be passed on to another router. A router passes only when explicitly configured to do so, never by default. The two most common cases where "pass" is useful are for handling DNS timeouts and domains that route to the local host.

There are two differences between the way "decline" and "pass" are handled:

- The value of the `more` option affects what happens when a router declines. If it is set false, no further routers are run. When a router passes, the value of `more` is ignored.

- The value of the `pass_router` option is relevant when a router passes. It names the router to which the address should be passed. This must be a router that is later in the configuration (to avoid routing loops). If `pass_router` is unset, the address is passed to the next router. When a router declines, `pass_router` is ignored.

If a router times out while trying to look up an MX record or an IP address for a host, it normally causes delivery of the address to be deferred. However, if `pass_on_timeout` is set, the router passes. This may be helpful for systems that are intermittently connected to the Internet, or those that want to pass to a smart host any messages that cannot be delivered immediately, as in this example:

```
notlocal_direct:
  driver = dnslookup
  domains = ! +local_domains
  transport = remote_smtp
  pass_on_timeout
  no_more

notlocal_smarthost:
  driver = manualroute
  transport = remote_smtp
  route_list = ! +local_domains smart.host.example
```

The first router looks up the domain in the DNS; if it is not found, the router declines, but because of `no_more`, no further routers are tried and the address fails. However, if the DNS lookup times out, the address is passed to the next router, which sends it to a smart host.

A timeout is just one example of a temporary error that can occur while doing DNS lookups. All such errors are treated in the same way as a timeout, and `pass_on_timeout` applies to all of them.

# 6.5 Domains that route to the local host

Normally, the **dnslookup** router considers it to be an error if the local host appears in the MX list with the lowest preference. Similarly, the **manualroute** router considers it to be an error if the first host in a list that it generates is the local host.[1]

This situation can arise as a result of a mistake in Exim's configuration (for example, the domain is a local one that should not be processed by this router), or it may be an error in the DNS (for example, the lowest numbered MX record should not point to this host). In a simple configuration, sending the message would cause a mail loop. Exim's default action is therefore to defer delivery and freeze the message to bring it to the administrator's attention.

---

[1] If the local host appears other than at the start of the list, it is discarded, along with any less preferred hosts. The test for the local host involves checking the IP address(es) of the supposedly remote host against the interfaces on the local host. If `local_interfaces` is set, only the interfaces it lists are tested.

In more complicated situations, a different action may be required. What Exim does when a domain routes to the local host is controlled by the value of the generic `self` option. This can be set to one of a number of descriptive words, the default being `freeze`.

## 6.5.1 Deferring domains routed to self without freezing

If the `self` option is set to `defer`, delivery of the address is deferred, but the message is not frozen, so delivery will be retried at intervals. If this goes on long enough, the address will time out and be bounced.

## 6.5.2 Passing domains routed to self to another router

If `self` is set to `pass`, the router returns "pass", which means that the address is passed to the following router, or the router named in the `pass_router` option (☞ 6.4). The variable *$self_hostname* is set to the name of the host that was first in the list (that is, the name that resolved to the local host).

Because "pass" overrides `no_more`, the combination of:

```
self = pass
no_more
```

ensures that only those addresses that routed to the local host are passed on. Without `no_more`, an address that was declined because the domain did not exist would also be offered to the next router. A corporate mail gateway might have this as its first router:

```
notlocal:
   driver = dnslookup
   transport = remote_smtp
   self = pass
   no_more
```

Domains that resolve to remote hosts are routed to the **remote_smtp** transport in the normal way. Domains that are unrecognized are bounced, because `no_more` prevents them being offered to any subsequent routers, but domains that resolve to the local host are passed on because of the setting of `self`. Subsequent routers can then assume they are dealing with the set of domains whose DNS entries point to the local host.

This approach is an alternative to using an explicit list in a `domains` option, as shown in earlier examples of routers for non-local domains. If the number of domains is small, checking an explicit list is more efficient than doing a DNS lookup. However, if the number of domains is large, and especially if it changes frequently, keeping just one list (in the DNS) may make maintenance easier.

You should be aware that there is nothing to stop any hostmaster from pointing an arbitrary domain at your host. If you use a "pass" router like this with further routers that relay to other hosts, you must check the domains you relay. For example, you could use a single wildcard to check that they are all within your corporate domain. Without such a check, a rogue hostmaster can turn your host into an open relay.

### 6.5.3 Rerouting domains routed to self

If `self` is set to `reroute:` followed by a domain name, the domain is changed to the given domain, and the address is passed back to be reprocessed by the routers. This is another form of address redirection. For example:

```
self = reroute: newdom.example.com
```

changes the domain to *newdom.example.com* and reprocesses the address from scratch. No rewriting of header lines takes place, but there is an alternative form that does cause header rewriting:

```
self = reroute: rewrite: newdom.example.com
```

In this case, any addresses in the header lines that contain the old domain are rewritten with the new one.

### 6.5.4 Failing domains routed to self

If the `self` option is set to `fail`, the router declines, but the address is not passed to any following routers. Consequently, delivery fails and an error report is generated.

### 6.5.5 Transporting domains routed to self

Finally, if the `self` option is set to `send`, the routing anomaly is ignored and the address is passed to the transport in the usual way. This setting should be used with extreme caution because of the danger of looping. For remote deliveries, it makes sense only in cases where the program that is listening on the TCP/IP port of the local host is not this version of Exim. That is, it must be some other MTA, or Exim with a different configuration file that handles the domain in another way.

# 6.6 Debugging routers

There is a generic option called `debug_print` whose sole purpose is to help debug Exim configurations. When Exim is run with debugging turned on (☞ 20.10), the value of `debug_print` is expanded and added to the debugging output that is written to the standard error stream (*stderr*). This happens before checking `senders`, `require_files`, and `condition`, but after the other precondition checks. This facility can be used to check that the values of certain variables are what you think they should be.

For example, if a `condition` option appears not to be working, `debug_print` can be used to output the values it references. In the previous chapter (☞ 5.10), we used this router for sending messages to a virus scanner program:

```
send_to_scanner:
  driver = accept
  transport = pipe_to_scanner
  condition = ${if eq {$received_protocol}{scanned-ok}{no}{yes}}
```

This router should be skipped if *$received_protocol* has the value `scanned-ok`. Suppose that this configuration is not working, and you are trying to find out why. One obvious approach is to check the value of *$received_protocol* at the time the router is run. You can do this by adding:

```
debug_print = received_protocol=$received_protocol
```

to the router, running a delivery with debugging turned on, and examining the standard error output.

# 6.7 Summary of generic router options

The generic options that are applicable to all routers are summarized in this section:

`address_data` (string, default = unset)
  The string is expanded just before the router is run, and the value is retained with the address. It can be accessed using the variable *$address_data* in the router's private options, in any subsequent routers that the address passes through, and in the final transport.

`caseful_local_part` (Boolean, default = false)
  If this option is set true, local parts of addresses are handled in a case-sensitive manner by the router.

`check_local_user` (Boolean, default = false)
  If this option is set true, the router is skipped unless the local part of the address is the login name of a local user.

`condition` (string, default = unset)
  This option specifies a general precondition that has to succeed for the router to be called. The string is expanded. If the result is a forced failure, an empty string, or one of the strings `0`, `no`, or `false` (checked without regard to the case of the letters), the router is not run.

`debug_print` (string, default = unset)

    If this option is set and debugging is enabled, the string is expanded and included in the debugging output.

`domains` (domain list, default = unset)

    This option restricts a router to specific mail domains. The router is skipped unless the current domain matches an item in the list. If the match is achieved by means of a file lookup, the data that the lookup returned for the domain is placed in the *$domain_data* variable for use in string expansions of the router's private options, and in the options of any transport that the router sets up.

`driver` (string, default = unset)

    This option must always be set. It specifies which of the available router drivers is to be used.

`errors_to` (string, default = unset)

    Delivery errors for any addresses handled or generated by the router are sent to the address that results from expanding this string, provided that it verifies as a valid address.

`expn` (Boolean, default = true)

    If this option is set false, the router is skipped when testing an address as a result of processing an SMTP EXPN command.

`fail_verify` (Boolean, default = false)

    Setting this option has the effect of setting both `fail_verify_sender` and `fail_verify_recipient` to the specified value.

`fail_verify_recipient` (Boolean, default = false)

    If this option is true when the router successfully verifies a recipient address, verification fails instead of succeeding.

`fail_verify_sender` (Boolean, default = false)

    If this option is true when the router successfully verifies a sender address, verification fails instead of succeeding.

`fallback_hosts` (string list, default = unset)

    If a router queues an address for a remote transport, this host list is associated with the address and used instead of the transport's fallback host list. String expansion is not applied to this option. The argument must be a colon-separated list of host names or IP addresses.

`group` (string, default = see description)

    If a router queues an address for a transport, and the transport does not specify a group, the group given here is used when running the delivery process. The default is unset, unless `check_local_user` is set, in which case the default is taken from the password data.

headers_add (string, default = unset)
This option specifies a string of text that is expanded at routing time, and associated with any addresses that are processed by the router. At transport time, the string is added to the message's header. If the expanded string is empty, or if the expansion is forced to fail, the option has no effect. Other expansion failures are treated as configuration errors.

headers_remove (string, default = unset)
The string is expanded at routing time and is then associated with any addresses that are processed by the router. If the expansion is forced to fail, the option has no effect. Other expansion failures are treated as configuration errors. After expansion, the string must consist of a colon-separated list of header names. At transport time, these header lines are omitted from the message.

ignore_target_hosts (host list, default = unset)
Although this option is a host list, it should normally contain IP addresses rather than names. If any host that is looked up by a router has an IP address that matches an item in this list, Exim behaves as if that IP address did not exist.

initgroups (Boolean, default = false)
If the router queues an address for a transport, and this option is true, and the uid supplied by the router is not overridden by the transport, the *initgroups()* function is called when running the transport to ensure that any additional groups associated with the uid are added to the secondary groups list.

local_part_prefix (string list, default = unset)
If this option is set, the router is skipped unless the local part starts with one of the given strings, or local_part_prefix_optional is true. If a prefix begins with an asterisk, this matches the longest possible sequence of arbitrary characters at the start of the local part. The prefix is stripped from the local part and placed in *$local_part_prefix* while the router is running.

local_part_prefix_optional (Boolean, default = false)
See local_part_prefix.

local_part_suffix (string list, default = unset)
If this option is set, the router is skipped unless the local part ends with one of the given strings, or local_part_suffix_optional is true. If a suffix ends with an asterisk, this matches the longest possible sequence of arbitrary characters at the end of the local part. The suffix is stripped from the local part and placed in *$local_part_suffix* while the router is running.

local_part_suffix_optional (Boolean, default = false)
See local_part_suffix.

`local_parts` (string list, default = unset)

This option restricts a router to specific local parts. The router is run only if the local part of the address matches the list. If the match is achieved by a lookup, the data that the lookup returned for the local part is placed in the variable *$local_part_data* for use in expansions of the router's private options, and in the options of any transport that the router sets up.

`more` (Boolean, default = true)

If this option is set false and the router runs but declines to handle an address, no further routers are tried.

`pass_on_timeout` (Boolean, default = false)

If this option is set, a router that encounters a timeout while doing a DNS lookup passes the address to the next router (or the router specified by `pass_router`) instead of deferring delivery.

`pass_router` (string, default = unset)

When a router returns "pass", the address is normally handed to the next router. This can be changed by setting `pass_router` to the name of a different router. However, the new router must be later in the configuration.

`redirect_router` (string, default = unset)

When a router generates child addresses, they are independently processed, starting with the first router by default, but otherwise with the router that is named by this option. Unlike `pass_router`, the named router may be anywhere in the configuration.

`require_files` (string list, default = unset)

This option checks for the existence or non-existence of specified files or directories. If any string is empty, it is ignored.

`self` (string, default = freeze)

This option specifies what happens when a router that generates a list of hosts discovers that the first host in the list is the local host. The allowed values are `defer`, `reroute:` *<domain name>*, `pass`, `fail`, and `send`.

`senders` (address list, default = unset)

This option restricts a router to messages that have specific sender addresses.

`transport` (string, default = unset)

Some routers require a transport to be supplied, except when `verify_only` is set, where it is not relevant. The string must be the name of a configured transport after expansion. This allows transports to be dynamically selected.

`transport_current_directory` (string, default = unset)
  If the router sets up a local delivery for an address, the value of this option is passed to the transport, where it is expanded and used to set the current directory during delivery, unless overridden by a setting on the transport. If there is no setting on either the router or the transport, the home directory is used; if there is no home directory setting, the root directory / is used.

`transport_home_directory` (string, default = see description)
  If the router sets up a local delivery for an address, the value of this option is passed to the transport, where it is expanded and used to set the home directory during delivery, unless overridden by a setting on the transport. The default is unset unless `check_local_user` is set for the router, in which case the default is the user's home directory.

`unseen` (Boolean, default = false)
  Setting this option has a similar effect to the `unseen` command qualifier in filter files. It causes a copy of the incoming address to be passed on to subsequent routers, even when the current one succeeds in handling it.

`user` (string, default = see description)
  If the router queues an address for a transport, and the transport does not specify a user, the user given here is used when running the delivery process. This user is also used by the **redirect** router when running a filter file. The default is unset, except when `check_local_user` is set, in which case the default is taken from the password data.

`verify` (Boolean, default = true)
  Setting this option has the effect of setting both `verify_sender` and `verify_recipient` to the specified value.

`verify_only` (Boolean, default = false)
  If this option is set, the router is used only when verifying an address or testing with the -bv option, not when actually doing a delivery, testing with the -bt option, or running the SMTP EXPN command. The router can be further restricted to verifying only senders or recipients by means of `verify_sender` and `verify_recipient`.

`verify_recipient` (Boolean, default = true)
  If this option is false, this router is skipped when verifying recipient addresses.

`verify_sender` (Boolean, default = true)
  If this option is false, this router is skipped when verifying sender addresses.

# 7

# The routers

In this chapter, we discuss each of the router drivers in detail. Routers are the components of Exim that make decisions about message deliveries. The actual deliveries are carried out by transports, which are discussed in the following two chapters. Some routers are able to attach a list of hosts to an address for the transport to use, but there are no constraints between routers and transports; any router can route an address to any transport. The available routers are as follows:

**accept**

A router that accepts any address that is passed to it. It is used with the `check_local_user` option to accept messages for local users. Without any preconditions, it can be used as a "catchall" router to handle addresses that the other routers have declined.

**dnslookup**

A router that looks up domains in the DNS and does MX processing.

**ipliteral**

A router that handles "IP literal" addresses such as *user@[192.168.5.6]*. These are relics of the early Internet that are no longer in common use.

**manualroute**

A router that routes domains using locally supplied information such as a list of domains and corresponding hosts.

**queryprogram**

A router that runs an external program in order to route an address.

**redirect**

A router that handles several different kinds of redirection, including alias files, users' *.forward* files, and Exim filter files. It can also explicitly force failure of an address.

## 7.1 The accept router

The **accept** router is the simplest of Exim's routers. It has no conditions of its own. It always accepts the address and sets up a delivery by putting the address on a queue for a transport. Of course, the router may not always run if there are preconditions

defined in its configuration. A common precondition that is used with **accept** is
`check_local_user`, as seen in earlier examples such as the following:

```
local_users:
  driver = accept
  check_local_user
  transport = local_delivery
```

This defines a router for accepting local parts that match local user names. Another
use for **accept** is for picking up addresses that other routers are unable to handle, by
placing an **accept** router at the end of the router configuration. This can be unconditional, or subject to any of the generic preconditions, so that it could be used for all
addresses in certain domains, all local parts with certain prefixes or suffixes, specific
local parts, or any other generic condition.

### 7.1.1 Transports for accept

The `transport` option must always be specified for **accept**, unless the `verify_`
`only` option is set, in which case the router is used only for checking addresses. The
transport does not have to be a local transport; any transport can be used. For
example, suppose that all local users have accounts on a central mail system, but
have their mail delivered by SMTP to their individual workstations. On the central
server, an **accept** router such as this:

```
checklocals:
  driver = accept
  check_local_user
  transport = workstations
```

could be used with a remote transport such as this:

```
workstations:
  driver = smtp
  hosts = ${lookup{$local_part}cdb{/etc/workstations}{$value}fail}
```

where the file */etc/workstations* contains a mapping from username to workstation
name.

## 7.2 The dnslookup router

The **dnslookup** router uses the DNS to find the hosts that handle mail for the domain
of the address. A transport must always be set for this router, unless `verify_only`
is set. We have previously shown a straightforward configuration of **dnslookup** as:

```
notlocal:
  driver = dnslookup
  domains = ! +local_domains
  transport = remote_smtp
```

The **dnslookup** router uses the DNS according to the standard mail routing rules: it first looks for MX records for the domain; if found, they provide a list of hosts. If there are no MX records, the router looks up address records for a host whose name is the same as the domain.

If the router cannot find out whether the domain does or does not have any MX records (because of a timeout or other DNS failure), it cannot proceed because it is not allowed to carry on looking for address records in these circumstances. When this happens, delivery is deferred unless the generic `pass_on_timeout` option is set (this is described in chapter 6).

The **dnslookup** router does have some private options (described in what follows), but they are unlikely to be needed in the majority of installations.

## 7.2.1 Optimizing repeat routing

Addresses with the same domains are normally routed by the **dnslookup** router to the same list of hosts. However, this cannot be presumed, because the router's options and preconditions may refer to the local part of an address. For this reason, Exim routes every address in a message independently, even if it comes across an address that has the same domain as a previous one.

DNS servers run caches, so repeated DNS lookups of the same domain are not normally expensive, and in any case, personal messages rarely have more than a few recipients. However, if you are running mailing lists with many subscribers in the same domain, and you are using a **dnslookup** router that is independent of the local parts of addresses, you can set `same_domain_copy_routing` to bypass repeated DNS lookups when possible.[1] In this configuration, when **dnslookup** routes an address to a remote transport, any other unrouted addresses in the message that have the same domain are automatically given the same routing without processing them independently. This may give some performance improvement.

## 7.2.2 Controlling DNS lookups

There are two options that control the way DNS lookups are done. The resolver option `RES_DEFNAMES` is set by default. This causes the resolver to qualify domains that consist of a single component (that is, contain no dots) with a default domain. This is normally the name of the local host minus its leading component. So, for example, on a host called *dictionary.book.example*, the effect of looking up the domain *thesaurus* would be to look for *thesaurus.book.example*. This is usually a useful behaviour for groups of hosts in the same superior domain, which is why it happens by default. However, it can be disabled if necessary by setting `qualify_single` to false.

---

[1] It is not possible if `headers_add` or `headers_remove` is set, or if the router "widens" the domain.

The resolver option RES_DNSRCH is not set by default, but can be requested by setting search_parents. In this case, if the initial lookup fails, the resolver searches the default domain and its parent domains. Continuing the previous example, the effect of looking up *animal.farm* with this option is first to look it up as given, and if that fails, to look up *animal.farm.book.example*. The option is turned off by default because it causes problems in domains that have wildcard MX records.[1] Suppose the following record:

```
*.example.  MX  6  mail.example.
```

exists and there is a host called *a.book.example* that has no MX records of its own. What happens when a user on some other host in the *book.example* domain mails to *someone@a.book*? On failing to find an MX record for *a.book*, if search_ parents is set, the resolver goes on to try *a.book.book.example*, which matches the wildcard MX record but is likely to be totally inappropriate.

## 7.2.3 Conditions for MX records

Two other **dnslookup** options affect what is done after MX records have been looked up in the DNS. If check_secondary_mx is set, the router declines unless the local host is found in the list of hosts obtained from an MX lookup.[2] This identifies domains for which the local host is an MX backup, and can therefore be used to process these domains in some special way. It differs from the generic self option, which applies only when the *lowest* numbered MX record points to the local host.

The other option, mx_domains, can be used to prevent Exim from looking up DNS address records for certain domains when no MX records are found.

One of the problems of the proliferation of personal computers on the Internet is that many of them do not run MTAs, yet if their DNS-registered domain names appear in email addresses, sending MTAs are obliged to try to deliver to them using their DNS address records. A sending MTA normally tries for several days before giving up. This can easily happen if an MUA on a workstation is incorrectly configured so that it sends out mail containing its own domain name in return addresses, instead of using the domain that refers to its email server.

The RFCs still mandate the use of address records when MX records do not exist, and there are still hosts on the Internet that rely on this behaviour. In general, therefore, you cannot do anything about this problem. However, if you know that there are MX records for all your own email domains, you can avoid the problem within your own local network, by setting, for example:

```
mx_domains = *.your.domain
```

---

[1]  Wildcard MXs are useful mostly for domains at non-IP-connected sites. Because their effects are often not what is really wanted, they are rarely encountered.

[2]  The local host, and any with greater or equal MX preference values, are then removed from the list, in accordance with the usual MX processing rules.

on a **dnslookup** router. For any domain that matches mx_domains, Exim looks only for MX records. It does not go on to look for address records when there are no MX records. This means that domains without MX records are immediately bounced instead of being retried.

## 7.2.4 Explicit lookup widening

When a host lookup fails, **dnslookup** can be configured to try adding specific strings onto the end of the domain name, using the widen_domains option. This provides a more controlled extension mechanism than search_parents, because instead of searching every enclosing domain, only those extensions that you specify are used. Furthermore, because it operates only after both an MX and an address record lookup have failed, it avoids the problem with wildcard MX records mentioned earlier. For example, suppose we have:

```
widen_domains = cam.ac.example : ac.example
```

on a host called *users.mail.cam.ac.example*, and a user on that host sends mail to the domain *semreh.cam*. First, **dnslookup** looks for MX and address records for *semreh.cam*, and because search_parents is not set, the resolver does no widening of its own. As there is no top-level domain called *cam*, the lookup fails, so **dnslookup** goes on to try *semreh.cam.cam.ac.example* and then *semreh.cam.ac.example* as a result of the setting of widen_domains, but no other widening is done.

## 7.2.5 Header rewriting

When an abbreviated name is expanded to its full form, either as part of lookup processing, or as a result of the widen_domains option, all occurrences of the abbreviated name in the header lines of the message are rewritten with the full name.[1] This can be suppressed by setting rewrite_headers to false, but this option should be turned off only when it is known that no message is ever going to be sent outside an environment where the abbreviation makes sense.

## 7.2.6 Summary of dnslookup options

The options that are specific to **dnslookup** are summarized in this section:

check_secondary_mx  (Boolean, default = false)
    If this option is set, the router declines unless the local host is found in the list of hosts obtained by MX lookup.

---

[1] When an MX record is looked up in the DNS and matches a wildcard record, name servers normally return a record containing the name that has been looked up, making it impossible to detect whether a wildcard is present or not. However, some name servers have recently been seen to return the wildcard entry itself. If the name returned by a DNS lookup begins with an asterisk, Exim does not use it for header rewriting.

`mx_domains` (domain list, default = unset)

A domain that matches `mx_domains` is required to have an MX record in order to be recognized.

`qualify_single` (Boolean, default = true)

The resolver option that causes it to qualify single-component names with the default domain (`RES_DEFNAMES`) is set if this option is true.

`rewrite_headers` (Boolean, default = true)

An abbreviated name may be expanded to its full form when it is looked up, or as a result of the `widen_domains` option. If this option is true, all occurrences of the abbreviated name in the headers of the message are rewritten with the full name.

`same_domain_copy_routing` (Boolean, default = false)

When this option is set, only one routing operation is carried out for those addresses in a message that have the same domain. You must not set it if the configuration for the router refers to the local part of an address.

`search_parents` (Boolean, default = false)

The resolver option that causes it to search parent domains (`RES_DNSRCH`) is set if this option is true. This is different from the `qualify_single` option in that it applies to domains containing dots.

`widen_domains` (string list, default = unset)

If a lookup fails and this option is set, each of its strings in turn is added onto the end of the domain and the lookup is tried again. Note that the `qualify_single` and `search_parents` options cause some widening to be undertaken inside the DNS resolver.

## 7.3 The ipliteral router

In the early days of the Internet, before the general deployment of the DNS, domain names were not always available. For this reason, RFCs 2821 and 2822 allow for the use of an *IP domain literal* instead of a domain name in an email address. For example:

```
A.User@[192.168.3.4]
```

The intention is that such an address causes the message to be delivered to the host with that IP address. These days, allowing end users to address messages to individual machines is not something many administrators are prepared to permit, and the increasing use of firewalls often makes it impossible. However, since the facility is still current in the RFCs, Exim supports it, though the options that set it up are commented out in the default configuration file.

The **ipliteral** router has no options of its own. It simply checks whether the domain in an address has the format of a domain literal, and if so, routes the address to a transport specified by the generic `transport` option, passing the IP address to which the message should be sent. If a domain literal turns out to refer to the local host, the generic `self` option determines what happens.

# 7.4 The manualroute router

Sometimes, you know exactly how you want to route a particular non-local domain. For instance, a client host on a dial-up connection normally sends all outgoing mail to a single host (often called a *smart host*) for onward transmission. A less trivial example is the case of a gateway that is handling all incoming mail to a local network. In this case you will know that certain domains should be routed to specific hosts on your network. The MX records for these domains point to the gateway, so another means of routing onwards from the gateway is required.

The **manualroute** router exists in order to handle this kind of routing. It is configured with a list of domains that it is to handle, together with information as to what to do with them. There are in fact two ways of doing this: the rules can be given inline in the configuration file, or they can be stored in a file and looked up on a per-domain basis.

## 7.4.1 Inline routing rules

Inline rules are given by the `route_list` option. Each rule has up to three parts, separated by whitespace:

(1)   A pattern that matches the domains to be handled by the rule.

(2)   A host list. This is an expanded item, which means that it might contain internal whitespace. If this is the case, you must enclose the host list in quotes. If there is a forced failure when a host list is expanded, the router declines.

(3)   An option that specifies how the IP addresses for the hosts are looked up.

The domain pattern is the only mandatory item in the rule. (You do not, for example, need a host list if the router is sending addresses to a local transport.) The pattern is in the same format as one item in a domain list, which means that it is expanded before use. It may be a domain that starts with a wildcard, a regular expression, or a file or database lookup (☞ 18.5).

If the pattern at the start of a rule is a lookup item, the data that was looked up is available in the variable *$value* during the expansion of the host list. For example, this rule:

```
route_list = dbm;/etc/rdomains $value:backup.example
```

matches domains by a DBM lookup; the data from the lookup is used in the host list, with an additional backup host name.

If the pattern at the start of a rule in `route_list` is a regular expression, the numeric variables *$1*, *$2*, and so on hold any captured substrings during the expansion of the host list. A setting such as:

```
route_list = \N^(ab\d\d)\.example\N  $1.mail.example
```

routes mail for the domain *ab01.example* to the host *ab01.mail.example* (for example).

The simplest use of **manualroute** is found on client hosts that send all non-local addresses to a single *smart host* for onward delivery. Such a configuration has a single router for non-local domains:

```
smarthost:
  driver = manualroute
  domains = !+local_domains
  transport = remote_smtp
  route_list = *  smarthost.example.com
```

A single asterisk as a domain pattern matches all domains, so this router causes all messages containing remote addresses to be sent to the host *smarthost.example.com*. An alternative way of achieving the same result is to use this router:

```
smarthost:
  driver = manualroute
  transport = remote_smtp
  route_list = !+local_domains  smarthost.example.com
```

As they stand, these two configurations operate in exactly the same way. However, there is a potential difference between testing domains using a `domains` precondition and testing domains with `route_list`. In the former case, the router is skipped when the domain does not match, and the next router is always run. In the latter case, the router declines when the domain does not match, so if `more` is set false, no more routers are run.

You can specify how the **manualroute** router finds IP addresses by including one of the options `bydns` or `byname` after the host list, as in the following example:

```
route_list = !+local_domains  smarthost.example.com  byname
```

For `bydns`, Exim does its own DNS lookup; for `byname`, it calls the system function for looking up host names.[1] This normally consults local files such as */etc/hosts* and may also do a DNS lookup. Exactly what it does is specified by local configuration.

---

[1] When IPv6 is supported, *getipnodebyname()* is used; otherwise the function is *gethostbyname()*.

If you do not specify either of these options, Exim first does a DNS lookup. If that gives a "host not found" error, Exim then tries the system lookup function.

If a host is found not to exist, delivery is deferred and the message is frozen, on the grounds that this is most probably a configuration error. However, a different action can be requested by setting the `host_find_failed` option. The values it can take are as follows:

`decline`

   The router declines, and the address is passed to the next router unless `more` is set false.

`defer`

   Delivery is deferred, but the message is not frozen.

`fail`

   The router declines, but no more routers are tried, so the address fails.

`freeze`

   Delivery is deferred, and the message is frozen. This is the default action.

`pass`

   The router passes the address to the next router, or the router defined by the generic `pass_router` option. This setting overrides a false setting of the `more` option.

The `host_find_failed` option applies only to a definite "does not exist" state. If a host lookup has a temporary error, delivery is deferred unless the generic `pass_on_timeout` option is set.

## 7.4.2 Randomizing the order of hosts

When a host list in a routing rule contains more than one host, they are normally tried in the order in which they are listed. However, if you set the option `hosts_randomize`, the order is changed randomly every time the router is used. The **smtp** transport has an option of the same name that does the same thing at transport time.

## 7.4.3 Multiple inline routing rules

So far we have been discussing a single inline routing rule, but `route_list` can contain any number of such rules. Exim scans them in order until it finds one that matches the domain of the address it is handling. If none of them match, the router declines. When there is more than one rule, they are separated by semicolons, because a colon is used as the separator in the host lists. Here is an example that uses a setting of `route_list` containing several rules:

```
private_routes:
  driver = manualroute
  transport = remote_smtp
  route_list = domain1.example    host1.example; \
               *.domain2.example  host2.example: \
                                  host3.example  bydns; \
               domain3.example    192.168.45.56
```

This router operates as follows:

- The domain *domain1.example* is routed to the host *host1.example*, whose IP address is looked up using the system host lookup function.

- The domains that match *\*.domain2.example* are routed to the two hosts *host2.example* and *host3.example*, whose IP addresses are obtained directly from DNS address records.

- The domain *domain3.example* is routed to the host whose IP address is 192.168.45.56.

- For all other domains, the router declines, so the address is passed to the next router.

## 7.4.4 Looked-up routing rules

Sometimes is it more convenient to keep manual routing information in a file or database rather than include it inline in the configuration file. If you want to do this, you can set the `route_data` option instead of `route_list`. This is a string that is expanded; most commonly the expansion involves a lookup using the domain as a key. For example:

```
private_routes:
  driver = manualroute
  transport = remote_smtp
  route_data = ${lookup{$domain}cdb{/etc/routes.cdb}}
```

This specifies that the routing data is to be obtained by looking up the domain in */etc/routes.cdb* using a *cdb* lookup. Partial single-key lookups (☞ 16.5) may be used to cause a set of domains all to use the same routing data.

If the expansion is forced to fail, or yields an empty string, the router declines. Otherwise, the routing data returned from a successful lookup must be a string containing a host list and options, separated by whitespace. These are used in exactly the same way as described earlier for inline routing rules. The final example in the previous section, if reorganized to use a file lookup, would be configured like this:

```
private_routes:
  driver = manualroute
  transport = remote_smtp
  route_data = ${lookup{$domain}partial-lsearch{/etc/routes}}
```

with the file */etc/routes* containing:

```
domain1.example:      host1.example
*.domain2.example:    host2.example:host3.example  bydns
domain3.example:      192.168.45.56
```

## 7.4.5 Routing to a local transport

An instance of **manualroute** that is configured to route addresses to a local transport is often used for handling messages for dial-up hosts. Rather than leaving them on Exim's queue, where they will be uselessly retried, they are delivered into files from which they can be retrieved when the client host connects.

You do not have to specify a host list when using **manualroute** in this way. A route_list entry can be as simple as a single domain name in a configuration such as this:

```
route_append:
  driver = manualroute
  transport = batchsmtp_appendfile
  route_list = gated.domain.example
```

This router causes the **batchsmtp_appendfile** transport to be run for addresses in the domain *gated.domain.example*. Normally, instead of just a single domain, some kind of pattern would be used to match a set of domains, and a user must be specified for running the transport. A complete configuration might contain a transport such as this:

```
dialup_transport:
  driver = appendfile
  batch_max = 100
  use_bsmtp
  file = /var/dialups/$domain
  user = exim
```

and a router such as this:

```
route_dialup:
  driver = manualroute
  transport = dialup_transport
  route_list = *.dialup.example.com
```

The setting of batch_max in the transport allows up to 100 recipients in a single copy of the message, and the setting of use_bsmtp requests that the message's envelope be preserved in *batch SMTP* (BSMTP) format (☞ 9.2, 9.3.2).

When a local transport is used like this, a single host name may optionally be present in each routing rule. It is passed to the transport in the variable *$host*, and could, for example, be used in constructing the filename. The following router matches two sets of domains; for each set, a different value appears in *$host* when the transport is run:

```
route_dialup:
  driver = manualroute
  transport = dialup_transport
  route_list = *.dialup1.example.com host1; \
               *.dialup2.example.com host2
```

## 7.4.6 Using manualroute to route mail to UUCP

You can use **manualroute** for routing mail directly to UUCP software. Here is an example of one way this can be done. A **pipe** transport (☞ 9.5) is used to run the UUCP software directly:

```
uucp:
  driver = pipe
  user = nobody
  command = /usr/local/bin/uux -r - $host!rmail $local_part
  return_fail_output = true
```

This transport substitutes the values of *$host* and *$local_part* in the command:

```
/usr/local/bin/uux -r - $host!rmail $local_part
```

and then runs it as the user *nobody*. The message is piped to the command on its standard input. If the command fails, any output it produces is returned to the sender of the message. The corresponding router is:

```
uucphost:
  transport = uucp
  driver = manualroute
  route_data = ${lookup{$domain}lsearch{/usr/local/exim/uucphosts}}
```

The file */usr/local/exim/uucphosts* contains entries such as this:

```
darksite.ethereal.example:  darksite
```

When the router processes the address *someone@darksite.ethereal.example*, it passes the address to the **uucp** transport, setting *$host* to the string darksite.

## 7.4.7 Using manualroute on a mail hub

A *mail hub* is a host that receives mail for a number of domains (usually, but not necessarily, via MX records in the DNS), and delivers it using its own private routing mechanism. Often the final destinations are behind a firewall, with the mail hub being the one machine that can connect to machines both inside and outside the firewall. The **manualroute** router on the hub can be set to handle incoming mail like this:

```
through_firewall:
  driver = manualroute
  transport = remote_smtp
  route_data = ${lookup{$domain}lsearch{/internal/host/routes}}
```

If there are only a small number of domains, the routing could be specified inline, using the `route_list` option, but for a larger number, a lookup is easier to manage. If a routing file itself becomes large (more than, say, 20 to 30 entries), it is a good idea to turn it into one of the indexed formats (DBM or *cdb*) to improve performance. For this example, the file containing the internal routing might contain lines such as this:

```
abc.ref.example: m1.ref.example:m2.ref.example
```

The DNS would be set up with an MX record for *abc.ref.example* pointing to the mail hub, which would forward mail for this domain to one of the two specified hosts. They would be tried in order, because `hosts_randomize` is not set.

If the domain names are, in fact, the names of the machines to which the mail is to be sent by the mail hub, the configuration can be simplified. For example:

```
hub_route:
  driver = manualroute
  transport = remote_smtp
  route_list = *.rhodes.example  $domain
```

This configuration routes domains that end in *.rhodes.example* to hosts of the same name. A similar approach can be taken if the host name can be obtained from the domain name by any of the transformations that are available in Exim's string expansion mechanism.

## 7.4.8 Varying the transport

In addition to specifying how names are to be looked up, the options part of a rule may also contain a transport name. This is then used for domains that match the rule, overriding any setting of the generic `transport` option. For example, this router uses different local transports for each of its rules:

```
route_append:
  driver = manualroute
  route_list = \
    *.gated.domain1  $domain  batch_appendfile; \
    *.gated.domain2  ${lookup{$domain}dbm{/etc/domain2/hosts}\
                     {$value}fail}  batch_pipe
```

The first rule sends any address that it matches to the **batch_appendfile** transport, passing the domain in the *$host* variable, which does not achieve much (since it is also in *$domain*). The second rule does a file lookup to find a value to pass in *$host* to the **batch_pipe** transport, specifying that the router should decline to handle the address if the lookup fails.

## 7.4.9 Optimizing repeat routing

The **manualroute** router is similar to **dnslookup** in that addresses with the same domains are normally routed to the same list of hosts. Exim cannot assume that this is always true, because the router's options and preconditions may refer to the local part of an address. Therefore, each address is normally routed independently. However, **manualroute** has an option called `same_domain_copy_routing` that copies the routing for one address to all others in the same message that have the same domain, in the same way as the option of the same name does for **dnslookup**. This may give some performance improvement for messages with large numbers of recipients.

## 7.4.10 Summary of manualroute options

The options that are specific to **manualroute** are summarized in this section:

`host_find_failed` (string, default = freeze)

This option controls what happens when a host that **manualroute** tries to look up (because an address has been specifically routed to it) does not exist. The option can be set to one of the following:

```
decline
defer
fail
freeze
pass
```

This option applies only to a definite "does not exist" state; if a host lookup suffers a temporary error, delivery is deferred unless the generic `pass_on_timeout` option is set.

`hosts_randomize` (Boolean, default = false)

If `hosts_randomize` is false, the order in which hosts are listed is preserved as an order of preference for delivering the message; if it is true, the list is shuffled into a random order each time it is used.

`route_data` (string, default = unset)

If this option is set, it is expanded and must yield a hostlist and optional options. If the expansion is forced to fail, or the result is an empty string, the router declines.

`route_list` (string list, default = unset)

This string is a list of inline routing rules. Note that, unlike most string lists, the items are separated by semicolons by default. This is so that they may contain colon-separated host lists.

`same_domain_copy_routing` (Boolean, default = false)
When this option is set, only one routing operation is carried out for those addresses in a message that have the same domain. You must not set it if the configuration for the router refers to the local part of an address.

# 7.5 The queryprogram router

The **queryprogram** router routes an address by running an external command and acting on its output. The command's job is to make decisions about the routing of the address. It is not a command to perform message delivery; that function is available via the **pipe** transport.

Running an external command is an expensive way to route, because every address handled in this way requires a new process in which to run the command. If the command is actually a script in an interpreted language such as Perl or Python, the overhead is even greater.

The **queryprogram** router is intended mainly for use in lightly loaded systems, or for performing experiments. However, if it is possible to restrict this router to a few lightly used addresses by means of suitable preconditions, it could be in regular use, even on busy systems.

## 7.5.1 The queryprogram command

The command that is to be run is specified in the `command` option. This string is expanded; after expansion it must start with the absolute pathname of the command. An expansion failure causes delivery to be deferred and the message to be frozen. The command is run in a subprocess directly from Exim, without using an intervening shell. If you want a shell, you have to specify it explicitly; because this interposes yet another process, it increases the expense and is not recommended.

## 7.5.2 Running the queryprogram command

The command is run in a separate process under a uid and a gid that are specified by `command_user` and `command_group`, respectively. If the latter is not set, the gid associated with the user is used, as in this example:

```
pgm_router:
   driver = queryprogram
   transport = remote_smtp
   command = /usr/exim/pgmrouter $local_part $domain
   command_user = mail
```

The directory that is made current while running the command is specified by `current_directory`. It defaults to the root directory.

## 7.5.3 The result of the queryprogram command

The **queryprogram** router has a `timeout` option, which defaults to `1h` (1 hour). If the command does not complete in this time, its process group is killed and delivery is deferred. A zero time specifies no time limit, but this is not recommended. Delivery is also deferred if the command terminates in error (that is, if its return code is not zero).

No input is provided for the command, so any data it requires must be passed as arguments. The standard output of the command is read when the command terminates successfully. It should consist of a single line of output, starting with one of the following words:

`ACCEPT`

Routing succeeded; the rest of the line specifies what to do.

`DECLINE`

Routing did not succeed; offer the address to the next router unless `no_more` is set.

`DEFER`

Routing could not be completed at this time; try again later.

`FAIL`

Routing failed; do not pass the address to any more routers.

`FREEZE`

The same as `DEFER`, except that the message is frozen.

`PASS`

Pass the address to the next router, or the router specified by `pass_router`, overriding `no_more`.

`REDIRECT`

Redirect the address. The rest of the line is a list of new addresses, separated by commas. These must be regular addresses; files, pipes, and other special items are not permitted. The new addresses are routed independently, starting with the first router or the router specified by `redirect_router` if it is set.

When the first word is not `ACCEPT` or `REDIRECT`, the remainder of the line is an error message explaining what went wrong. For example:

```
DECLINE   cannot route to unseen.discworld.example
```

When the first word is `ACCEPT`, the rest of the line consists of a number of keyed data values, as follows (the line is split here in order to fit it on the page):

```
ACCEPT TRANSPORT=<transport-name> HOSTS=<host-list>
       LOOKUP=byname|bydns DATA=<text>
```

The fields may appear in any order, and all are optional. Quotes are required if the data for any field contains spaces. If `TRANSPORT` is not given, the transport specified by the generic `transport` option is used. The host list and lookup type are needed only if the transport is an **smtp** transport that does not itself have a host list. The lookup types operate in exactly the same way as in the **manualroute** router, described earlier in this chapter. For example:

```
ACCEPT TRANSPORT=remote_smtp HOSTS=gate.star.example LOOKUP=bydns
```

causes the message to be sent using the **remote_smtp** transport to the host *gate.star.example*, whose IP address is looked up using DNS address records. If the host turns out to be the local host, what happens is controlled by the generic `self` option.

The value of the `DATA` field, if present, is placed in the *$address_data* variable. For example:

```
ACCEPT HOSTS=x1.y.example:x2.y.example DATA="rule one"
```

routes the address to the default transport, using a host list that contains two hosts, whose IP addresses are looked up by calling the system host lookup function. When the transport runs, the string `rule one` is in *$address_data*.

## 7.5.4 Summary of queryprogram options

The options that are specific to **queryprogram** are summarized in this section:

`command` (string, default = unset)
This option must be set, and must, after expansion, start with a slash character. It specifies the command that is to be run.

`command_group` (string, default = unset)
This option specifies a gid to be set when running the command. If it begins with a digit, it is interpreted as the numerical value of the gid. Otherwise it is looked up in the password data.

`command_user` (string, default = unset)
This option specifies a uid to be set when running the command, and must always be set. If it begins with a digit, it is interpreted as the numerical value of the uid. Otherwise, the corresponding uid is looked up in the password data, and, if `command_group` is not set, a value for the gid is taken from the same entry.

`current_directory` (string, default = unset)
This option specifies an absolute path, which is made the current directory before running the command. If it is not set, the root directory is used.

timeout (time, default = 1h)
   If the command does not complete within the timeout period, its process group is
   killed and delivery is deferred. A value of zero time specifies no timeout.

# 7.6 The redirect router

The **redirect** router handles several kinds of address redirection and is the most
complex of Exim's routers. It normally uses the local part or the complete address to
find a list of new addresses or processing instructions. Its most common uses are for
resolving local part aliases from a central alias file (usually called */etc/aliases*), and
for handling users' personal *.forward* files, but it has many other potential uses. An
incoming address can be redirected in the following ways:

- It can be replaced by one or more new addresses that are themselves routed
  independently.

- It can be routed to be delivered to a given file or directory.

- It can be routed to be delivered to a specified pipe command.

- It can cause an automatic reply to be generated.

- It can be forced to fail, with a custom error message.

- It can be temporarily deferred.

- It can be discarded.

The generic transport option must not be set for **redirect** routers. However, there
are some private options that define transports for deliveries to files and pipes, and
for generating automatic replies.

## 7.6.1 Obtaining redirection data

The **redirect** router operates by interpreting a text string that is obtained either by
expanding the contents of the data option, or by reading the entire contents of a file
whose name is given in the file option. These two options are mutually exclusive.
Earlier (☞ 3.9), we discussed this router for handling system aliases:

```
system_aliases:
   driver = redirect
   data = ${lookup{$local_part}lsearch{/etc/aliases}}
```

and later in the same section the following router is used for handling users' *.forward*
files:

```
userforward:
   driver = redirect
   check_local_user
   file = $home/.forward
```

When data is used, if the expansion is forced to fail, or if it yields an empty string, the router declines. When file is used, the router declines if the file does not exist or if it is empty or consists only of comments.

Exim is not limited to a single alias file; you can have as many **redirect** routers as you like, each searching a different set of data. However, there is nothing special about such a sequence of routers; as soon as any one of them accepts an address, processing that address ceases.

Unless caseful_local_part is set, the local part is forced to lower case while running a router. Thus, the keys in alias files should normally be in lower case. For linearly searched files, this is not in fact necessary, because the searching is done in a case-independent manner, but it is relevant for other forms of lookup.

## 7.6.2 Including the domain in alias lookups

The earlier examples all use just the local part when looking up aliases, but there is nothing to stop you looking up the full address if you want to, using a router such as the following:

```
system_aliases:
  driver = redirect
  data = ${lookup{$local_part@$domain}lsearch{/etc/aliases.full}}
```

This makes it possible to hold aliases for several domains in a single file such as this:

```
postmaster@domain1:    jill@domain1
postmaster@domain2:    jack@domain2
```

If you want to mix the two types in the same file, you have to define an expansion that does a second lookup if the first one fails:

```
system_aliases:
  driver = redirect
  data = ${lookup{$local_part@$domain}lsearch{/etc/aliases.full}\
         ${$value}\
         {${lookup{$local_part}lsearch{/etc/aliases.full}}}}
```

## 7.6.3 Forward files and address verification

It is usual to set the verify option false for **redirect** routers that handle users' *.forward* files. There are two reasons for this:

- When Exim is receiving an incoming SMTP message from a remote host, it runs as *exim*, not as *root*. Therefore, it is unable to change uid to read the file as the user. As a result, it may not be able to read the file at all, which means that the router cannot operate.

- Even when the router can operate, the existence of a personal *.forward* file is unimportant when verifying an address. What should be checked is whether or not the local part is a valid user name, so cutting out the redirection processing saves some resources.

## 7.6.4 Child addresses in error messages

If Exim generates a delay or bounce message for an address that is generated by redirection, it normally quotes the child address in the message, as it does for a toplevel address. If you want to keep redirection information private, you can set `hide_child_in_errmsg` to be true. When this is done, delay and bounce messages refer to "an address generated from..." Of course, this applies only to messages generated locally. If a message is forwarded to another host, its bounce may well quote the generated address.

## 7.6.5 Interpreting redirection data

The data that **redirect** processes can be a simple list of items, separated by commas or newlines. However, it is also possible to request that Exim process the data as an *Exim filter*, which means that it is interpreted in a more complex way. In particular, conditions can be imposed on which deliveries are done. If the `allow_filter` option is set on the router, and the first line of the data starts with:

```
# Exim filter
```

it is interpreted as a filter rather than a simple list of addresses. The use of filters is described in chapter 10. We discuss the types of item that may appear in a non-filter redirection list later in this chapter.

## 7.6.6 Duplicate addresses

Exim removes duplicate addresses from the list of addresses to which it is delivering, so as to deliver just one copy to each unique address. This also applies to any items in redirection lists. For example, if a message is addressed to both *postmaster* and *hostmaster*, and these both happen to be aliased to the same person, a single copy of the message is delivered. This optimization does not apply to deliveries that are routed to pipes, provided the immediate parent addresses are different. Thus, if two different recipients of the same message happen to have set their *.forward* files to pipe to the same command,[1] two distinct deliveries are made. Within an alias file, a scheme such as:

```
localpart1: |/some/command
localpart2: |/some/command
```

does result in two different pipe deliveries, because the immediate parents of the pipes are distinct. However, an indirect aliasing scheme of the type:

---

[1]  */usr/bin/vacation* is a common example.

```
pipe:          |/some/command
localpart1: pipe
localpart2: pipe
```

does a single delivery only, because the intermediate local parts (the immediate parents of the pipe commands) are identical.

## 7.6.7 Items in redirection lists

The items in a non-filter redirection list are separated by newlines or commas.[1] Empty items are ignored. If an item is entirely enclosed in double quotes, these are removed. Otherwise, double quotes are retained because some forms of mail address require their use (but never to enclose the entire address). In the following description, "item" refers to what remains after any surrounding double quotes have been removed.

## 7.6.8 Including the incoming address in a redirection list

It is safe for an address to be redirected to itself, because Exim has a general mechanism for avoiding routing loops. A router is automatically skipped if any ancestor of the current address is identical to it and was processed by that router. Thus, a user with login name *spqr* who wants to preserve a copy of mail and also forward it somewhere else, can set up a *forward* file such as:

```
spqr, spqr@st.elsewhere.example
```

without provoking a loop, because when *spqr* is processed for the second time, the **redirect** router is skipped. A backslash before a local part with no domain is permitted. For example:

```
\spqr, spqr@st.elsewhere.example
```

---

 A backslash at the start of an item that is a qualified address (that is, with a domain) is not special; there are valid RFC 2822 addresses that start with a backslash.

---

A backslash is allowed for compatibility with other MTAs, but is not necessary in order to prevent a loop. However, the presence or absence of a backslash can make a difference when the router is handling more than one domain. If `qualify_preserve_domain` is set, a local part without a domain is qualified with the domain of the incoming address whether or not it is preceded by a backslash. If `qualify_preserve_domain` is not set, a local part without a leading backslash

---

[1] Newlines cannot be present in redirection lists obtained from linearly searched files, because they are removed by the continuation line processing.

is qualified with Exim's `qualify_recipient` value, whereas one with a leading backslash is qualified with the incoming domain.

## 7.6.9 A bad interaction between aliasing and forwarding

Care must be taken if there are alias names for local users who might have *.forward* files. For example, if the system alias file contains:

```
Sam.Reman: spqr
```

then:

```
Sam.Reman, spqr@reme.elsewhere.example
```

in *spqr*'s *.forward* file fails on an incoming message addressed to *Sam.Reman*. The incoming local part is turned into *spqr* by aliasing, and then the *.forward* file turns it back into *Sam.Reman*. When this "grandchild" address is processed, the system aliases router is skipped in order to break the loop, because it has previously handled *Sam.Reman*. This causes *Sam.Reman* to be passed on to subsequent routers, which probably cannot handle it. The *.forward* file should really contain:

```
spqr, spqr@reme.elsewhere.example
```

but because this is such a common user error, the `check_ancestor` option exists to provide a way around it (☞ 7.6.13).

## 7.6.10 Non-address items in redirection lists

The following types of non-address item may appear in a redirection list:

### Pathnames

A redirection item is interpreted as a pathname if it begins with / and does not parse as a valid RFC 2822 address that includes a domain. For example:

```
/home/world/minbari
```

is treated as a filename, but:

```
/s=molari/o=babylon/@x400gateway.example
```

is treated as an address. If a generated path is */dev/null*, delivery to it is bypassed at a high level, and the log entry shows `**bypassed**` instead of a transport name. This avoids the need to specify a user and group, which are necessary for a genuine delivery to a file. When the file name is not */dev/null*, either the router or the transport must specify a user and group under which to run the delivery.

## Pipe commands

A redirection item is treated as a pipe command if it begins with | and does not parse as a valid RFC 2822 address that includes a domain. Either single or double quotes can be used for enclosing the individual arguments of the pipe command; no interpretation of escapes is done for single quotes. If the command contains a comma character, it is necessary to put the whole item in double quotes because items are terminated by commas. For example:

```
"|/some/command ready,steady,go"
```

Do not, however, quote just the command. An item such as:

```
|"/some/command ready,steady,go"
```

is interpreted as a pipe with a rather strange command name, and no arguments.

## Including a sublist from a file

If a redirection item takes the form:

```
:include:<pathname>
```

a list of further items is taken from the given file and included at that point. If this is the first item in a redirection list taken from a linearly searched file, a colon must be used to terminate the alias name, as otherwise the first colon is taken as the alias terminator, and the item is not recognized. This example is incorrect:

```
eximlist    :include:/etc/eximlist
```

It must be written like this:

```
eximlist:   :include:/etc/eximlist
```

The use of :include: can be disabled by setting forbid_include on the router.

## Discarding an address

Sometimes you want to throw away mail to a particular address. Making the data option expand to an empty string does not work, because that causes the router to decline. Instead this special item:

```
:blackhole:
```

does what its name implies. No delivery is done, and no error message is generated. This has the same effect as routing to */dev/null*, but can be independently disabled by setting forbid_blackhole.

## Forcing delivery to be deferred or to fail

An attempt to deliver a particular address can be deferred or forced to fail by redirecting the address to:

```
:defer:
or
:fail:
```

However, you need to set `allow_defer` or `allow_fail`, respectively, to enable the use of these items. If an address is redirected to `:defer:`, it remains on the queue so that a subsequent delivery attempt can happen at a later time, but if it is redirected to `:fail:` it is immediately bounced. If an address is deferred for too long, it will ultimately fail, because normal retry rules apply.

When a list contains one of these two items, any prior items in the list are ignored. Text that follows `:defer:` or `:fail:` is placed in the error message that is associated with the failure. A comma does not terminate the error text, but a newline does.[1] For example, an alias file might contain these lines:

```
x.employee:   :fail:  Gone away, no forwarding address
j.caesar:     :defer: Mailbox is being moved today
```

If you want to include variable information in the message, you can arrange for it to be expanded by a setting of the `data` option like this:

```
data = ${expand:${lookup{$local_part}lsearch{/etc/aliases}}}
```

This would allow you to use alias entries such as:

```
j.caesar:     :defer: $local_part's mailbox is being moved today
```

In the case of an address that is being verified for the SMTP RCPT or VRFY commands, the text is included in the SMTP error response, which uses a 451 code for a deferral and 550 for a failure. If `:fail:` is encountered while a message is being delivered, the text is included in the bounce message that Exim generates; the text for `:defer:` appears in the log line for the deferral, but is not otherwise used.

## Bypassing lookup defaults

Sometimes it is useful to use a search type with a default for aliases, as in this example router we used earlier for virtual domains:

```
virtuals:
  driver = aliasfile
  domains = cdb;/etc/virtuals
  data = ${lookup{$local_part}lsearch*{/etc/$domain.aliases}}
  no_more
```

---

[1] Newlines are not normally present in alias expansions. In `lsearch` lookups, they are removed as part of the continuation process, but they may exist in other kinds of lookup and in included files.

However, there may be a need for exceptions to the default. These can be handled by redirecting them to:

```
:unknown:
```

For example:

```
*:              postmaster@virt3.example
postmaster: pat@dom5.example
jill:           jkr@dom4.example
jack:           :unknown:
```

This differs from `:fail:` in that it causes **redirect** to decline, so the address is offered to the next router, whereas `:fail:` forces routing to fail immediately.

## 7.6.11 Enabling and disabling certain features

The **redirect** router has a number of options for controlling which types of special redirection item are allowed to appear in redirection data (☞ 7.6.19). Some items are permitted by default, but can be disabled by options whose names start with `for-bid_` (for example, `forbid_include`). Other special items are forbidden by default, but can be enabled by options whose names start with `allow_` (for example, `allow_fail`).

Some of the options refer to items that may appear only in filter files. Filters have been mentioned briefly, but the full details are deferred until chapter 10, so these options probably will not make much sense at a first reading. Just remember that there are ways of locking out certain filtering features, and come back to this section when you need it.

## 7.6.12 Checks on file attributes

When the `file` option is used to specify the redirection data, Exim can be configured to carry out checks on the mode and ownership of the file. If these are incorrect, delivery is deferred.

The `modemask` option specifies mode bits that must *not* be set. For example:

```
modemask = 007
```

specifies that none of the "other" access bits must be set. The default value is 022, which specifies that neither the group nor the "other" write bit is permitted.

If `check_local_user` is set, Exim checks that the file is owned by the local user and, if the value of `modemask` permits the group write bit, that the group owner is the user's primary group. Additional owners and groups can be specified by the `owners` and `owngroups` options. If `check_local_user` is not set, these are the only permitted owners. For example:

```
owners = mail : root
owngroups = mail : root
```

Owner and group checking can be disabled by setting `check_owner` and `check_group` false, respectively.

## 7.6.13 Ancestor checking

Exim's default antilooping rule skips a router only when an ancestor that was processed by the router is the same as the current address. A wider condition for skipping a **redirect** router is provided by the `repeat_use` option. By default, it is true, but if it is set false, the router is skipped for a child address with *any* ancestor that was routed by the same router. This test happens before any of the generic preconditions are tested.

Earlier (☞ 6.2.1), we showed a use of the generic `redirect_router` option to avoid running a **redirect** router unnecessarily for a second time, by passing the new address directly to the next router. Setting `repeat_use` false has a similar effect, but in this case, the new address first has the opportunity to be processed by earlier routers.

In another earlier discussion (☞ 7.6.9), it was pointed out that a system alias file containing:

```
Sam.Reman: spqr
```

combined with a *.forward* file for *spqr* containing:

```
Sam.Reman, spqr@reme.elsewhere.example
```

did not work, because the alias *Sam.Reman* could be turned into the username *spqr* only once. This is such a common mistake that an option to get round it exists.

When `check_ancestor` is set, if a generated address is the same as any ancestor of the current address, it is not used; the current address is used instead. For this problem example, if `check_ancestor` is set on the router that handles *.forward* files, it prevents the router from turning *spqr* back into *Sam.Reman*. The default configuration sets `check_ancestor` on its **userforward** router so that it is more likely to "do what the user means".

## 7.6.14 Transports for pipes and files

When a **redirect** router generates deliveries directly to pipes or files, it is necessary to define the transports that are to be used by setting `pipe_transport` and `file_transport`, respectively. For example, the default Exim configuration handles system aliases by means of this router:

```
system_aliases:
  driver = redirect
  allow_fail
  allow_defer
  data = ${lookup{$local_part}lsearch{/etc/aliases}}
# user = exim
  file_transport = address_file
  pipe_transport = address_pipe
```

The presence of the final two options means that aliases such as:

```
fileit:    /some/file
pipeit:    |/some/command
```

are handled by the **address_file** and **address_pipe** transports, respectively. Either the router or the transports also need to set a user under which the delivery is to run. The default configuration shows a suggestion in the form of the commented-out setting of the user option.

## 7.6.15 Rewriting generated addresses

Generated addresses are normally rewritten according to the configured rewriting rules (see chapter 15), but if you do not want this to happen, you can set `rewrite` false in the router's configuration.

## 7.6.16 One-time redirection

When Exim has to retain a message for later delivery because it could not complete all the deliveries at the first attempt, it does not normally save the results of any redirection that was done. The next time it tries to deliver, each original recipient address is reprocessed afresh. This has the advantage that errors in alias lists and forward files can be corrected, but it has one disadvantage in the case of mailing lists that change frequently.

If one message is taking a very long time to be delivered to one subscriber, and new addresses are added to the list in the meantime, the new subscribers receive a copy of the old message, even though it dates from before their subscription. This can be avoided by setting the `one_time` option on the router that expands the mailing list. This changes Exim's behaviour so that, after a temporary delivery failure, it adds the undelivered "child" addresses to the top-level list of recipients, and marks the original address as delivered. Thus, subsequent changes to the mailing list no longer affect this message.

The original top-level address is remembered with each of the generated addresses, and is output in log messages. However, intermediate parent addresses are not recorded. This makes a difference to the log only if `all_parents` is set as a log selector. It is expected that `one_time` will typically be used for mailing lists, where there is normally just one level of expansion.

Setting `one_time` is possible only when there are no pipe or file deliveries in the redirection data, because it is not possible to turn these into top-level addresses. For this reason, `forbid_pipe` and `forbid_file` are forced to be true when `one_time` is set.

## 7.6.17 Syntax errors in redirection data

If Exim discovers a syntax error in a redirection list, it defers delivery of the original address. This is the safest action to take. However, in some circumstances this may not be appropriate. For example, if a mailing list is being maintained by some automatic subscription process, you do not want one subscriber's typo to hold up deliveries to the rest of the list.

If `skip_syntax_errors` is set, a malformed item is skipped, and an entry is written to the main log. If `syntax_errors_to` is also set, a mail message is sent to the address it contains, giving details of the failing address(es). Often it will be appropriate to set `syntax_errors_to` to the same address as `errors_to` (the address for delivery failures). If `syntax_errors_text` is set, its contents are expanded and placed at the head of the error message.

As long as there is at least one valid address, the router succeeds. However, if all the addresses in a redirection list are skipped because of syntax errors, the router declines. For a mailing list, this probably means that the message bounces, but having no valid addresses on a mailing list is rare. For a user's *.forward* file, the message would normally be delivered into the user's mailbox, which is a safe action to take.

If `skip_syntax_errors` is set when an Exim filter is interpreted, any syntax error in the filter causes filtering to be abandoned without any action being taken (except for sending a message if `syntax_errors_to` is set). That is, the router declines.

## 7.6.18 Telling users about broken .forward files

Users often introduce syntax errors into their *.forward* files. They also often test them from their own accounts, usually several times when they observe the messages are not getting through. Using `skip_syntax_errors`, it is possible to deliver error messages into such users' mailboxes, thus reducing the postmaster load. First, you must arrange a way of delivering messages that bypasses users' *.forward* files. A router that does this is described earlier (☞ 6.1.1):

```
real_users:
  driver = accept
  check_local_user
  local_part_prefix = real-
  transport = local_delivery
```

The setting of `local_part_prefix` means that this router is skipped unless the local part is prefixed with *real-*. If it is defined before the router that handles *.forward* files, it picks off such local parts and sets up a local delivery, thereby bypassing any forwarding that might exist.

With this in place, `syntax_errors_to` can be used on the **userforward** router to send a message to the user's inbox when there is a syntax error in the *.forward* file. Because we want to include newlines in the text string, it is given inside double quotes. When the value of an Exim option is quoted like this, a backslash inside the quotes is interpreted as an escape character. This provides a means of coding non-printing characters. In particular, `\n` becomes a newline character:

```
userforward:
  driver = redirect
  check_local_user
  file = $home/.forward
  skip_syntax_errors
  syntax_errors_to = real-$local_part@$domain
  syntax_errors_text = "\
    This is an automatically generated message. An error has\n\
    been found in your .forward file. Details of the error are\n\
    reported below. While this error persists, you will receive\n\
    a copy of this message for every message that is addressed\n\
    to you. If your .forward file is a filter file, or if it is\n\
    a non-filter file that contains no valid forwarding\n\
    addresses, a copy of each incoming message will be put in\n\
    your mailbox. If a non-filter file contains at least one\n\
    valid forwarding address, forwarding to the valid addresses\n\
    will happen, and those will be the only deliveries that\n\
    occur."
```

If a syntax error is encountered, the failing address is skipped, and the warning message is sent to the user's mailbox, using the *real-* prefix to bypass forwarding. A final cosmetic touch to this scheme is to rewrite the address in the warning message's headers so as to remove the *real-* prefix, using a rewriting rule such as this:

```
^real-([^@]+)@   $1@$domain  h
```

Exim's address rewriting facilities are described in chapter 15; the simple rule shown here rewrites addresses in header lines (leaving envelopes untouched) by removing `real-` from the start of the local part.

## 7.6.19 Summary of redirect options

The options that are specific to **redirect** are summarized in this section:

`allow_defer` (Boolean, default = false)
   Setting this option enables the use of `:defer:` in non-filter redirection data.

`allow_fail` (Boolean, default = false)
Setting this option enables the use of `:fail:` in non-filter redirection data, and the `fail` command in a filter file.

`allow_filter` (Boolean, default = false)
If this option is set, and the redirection data starts with the line:

```
# Exim filter
```

it is interpreted as a set of filtering commands instead of a list of redirection items. Details of the syntax and semantics of filter files are described in chapter 10.

`allow_freeze` (Boolean, default = false)
Setting this option enables the use of the `freeze` command in a filter. This is not something you normally want to let ordinary users do.

`check_ancestor` (Boolean, default = false)
This option is concerned with handling generated addresses that are the same as some address in the list of ancestors of the current address. When it is set, if a generated address is the same as any ancestor, it is replaced by a copy of the current address.

`check_group` (Boolean, default = see description)
When the `file` option is used, the group owner of the file is checked only when this option is set. If `check_local_user` is set, the user's default group is permitted; otherwise the group must be one of those listed in the `owngroups` option. The default setting for this option is true if `check_local_user` is set and the `modemask` option permits the group write bit, or if the `owngroups` option is set. Otherwise, it is false.

`check_owner` (Boolean, default = see description)
When the `file` option is used, the owner of the file is checked only when this option is set. If `check_local_user` is set, the local user is a valid owner; otherwise the owner must be one of those listed in the `owners` option. The default setting for this option is true if `check_local_user` or `owners` is set. Otherwise, it is false.

`data` (string, default = unset)
This option must be set if `file` is not set. Its value is expanded and used as a list of forwarding items or filtering instructions. If the expansion is forced to fail, or if the result of the expansion is empty, the router declines.

`directory_transport` (string, default = unset)
A **redirect** router sets up a delivery to a directory when a pathname ending with a slash is specified as a new "address". The transport used is specified by this option, which, after expansion, must be the name of a configured transport.

`file` (string, default = unset)

This option specifies the name of a file that contains the redirection data. It is mutually exclusive with the `data` option (that is, only one of them may be set). The string is expanded before use; if the expansion is forced to fail, the router declines. Other expansion failure cause delivery to be deferred. The result of a successful expansion must be an absolute path. The entire file is read and used as the redirection data. If the file does not exist, or is empty, or contains only comments, the router declines.[1]

`file_transport` (string, default = unset)

A **redirect** router sets up a delivery to a file when a pathname not ending in a slash is specified as a new "address". The transport used is specified by this option, which, after expansion, must be the name of a configured transport.

`forbid_blackhole` (Boolean, default = false)

If this option is true, the use of `:blackhole:` in a redirection list is disabled.

`forbid_file` (Boolean, default = false)

If this option is true, the router may not generate an item that specifies delivery to a local file or directory. If it attempts to do so, a delivery failure occurs.

`forbid_filter_existstest` (Boolean, default = false)

If this option is true, string expansions in filter files are not allowed to make use of the `exists` condition.

`forbid_filter_logwrite` (Boolean, default = false)

If this option is true, use of the logging facility in filter files is not permitted. This is in any case available only if the filter is being run under some unprivileged uid, which is normally the case for ordinary users' *forward* files.

`forbid_filter_lookup` (Boolean, default = false)

If this option is true, string expansions in filter files are not allowed to make use of `lookup` items.

`forbid_filter_perl` (Boolean, default = false)

This option is available only if Exim is built with embedded Perl support. If it is true, string expansions in filter files are not allowed to make use of the embedded Perl support.

`forbid_filter_readfile` (Boolean, default = false)

If this option is true, string expansions in filter files are not allowed to make use of the `readfile` item.

---

[1]  If an attempt to open the file fails with a "does not exist" error, Exim runs a check on the containing directory. If the directory does not appear to exist, delivery is deferred. This can happen when users' *forward* files are NFS-mounted directories and there is a mount problem.

`forbid_filter_reply` (Boolean, default = false)

If this option is true, this router may not generate an automatic reply message. If it attempts to do so, a delivery failure occurs. Automatic replies can be generated only from filter files, not from traditional forward files.

`forbid_filter_run` (Boolean, default = false)

If this option is true, string expansions in filter files are not allowed to make use of the `run` item.

`forbid_include` (Boolean, default = false)

If this option is true, the use of the special `:include:` item is not permitted.

`forbid_pipe` (Boolean, default = false)

If this option is true, the router may not generate an item that specifies delivery to a pipe. If it attempts to do so, a delivery failure occurs.

`hide_child_in_errmsg` (Boolean, default = false)

If this option is true, it prevents Exim from quoting a child address in a delay or bounce message.

`ignore_eacces` (Boolean, default = false)

If this option is set and an attempt to open the file named in the `file` option yields the `EACCES` error (permission denied), **redirect** behaves as if the file did not exist, and declines.

`ignore_enotdir` (Boolean, default = false)

If this option is set and an attempt to open the file named in the `file` option yields the `ENOTDIR` error (something on the path is not a directory), **redirect** behaves as if the file did not exist, and declines.

`include_directory` (string, default = unset)

If this option is set, the path names of any `:include:` items in a redirection list must start with this directory.

`modemask` (octal-integer, default = 022)

This specifies mode bits that must not be set for the file named in the `file` option. If they are set, delivery is deferred.

`one_time` (Boolean, default = false)

If `one_time` is set, and any addresses generated by the router fail to deliver at the first attempt, the failing addresses are added to the message as "top level" addresses, and the parent address that generated them is marked "delivered". Thus, redirection does not happen again at the next delivery attempt.

`owners` (string list, default = unset)

This specifies a list of permitted owners for the file named in the `file` option. This list is in addition to the local user when `check_local_user` is set.

owngroups  (string list, default = unset)
This specifies a list of permitted groups for the file named in the file option.
this list is in addition to the local user's primary group when
check_local_user is set.

pipe_transport  (string, default = unset)
A **redirect** sets up a delivery to a pipe when a string starting with a vertical bar
character is specified as a new "address". The transport used is specified by this
option, which, after expansion, must be the name of a configured transport.

qualify_preserve_domain  (Boolean, default = false)
If this option is set and an unqualified address (one without a domain) is generated, it is qualified with the domain of the incoming address instead of the value
of qualify_recipient.

repeat_use  (Boolean, default = true)
If this option is set false, the router is skipped for a child address that has any
ancestor that was routed by the same router.

reply_transport  (string, default = unset)
A **redirect** router sets up a delivery to an **autoreply** transport when a mail or
vacation command is used in a filter file. The transport used is specified by this
option, which, after expansion, must be the name of a configured transport.

rewrite  (Boolean, default = true)
If this option is set false, addresses generated by the router are not subject to
address rewriting. Otherwise, they are treated like new addresses, and the rewriting rules (see chapter 15) are applied to them.

skip_syntax_errors  (Boolean, default = false)
If skip_syntax_errors is set, a malformed address that causes a parsing
error is skipped, and an entry is written to the main log.

syntax_errors_text  (string, default = unset)
See syntax_errors_to.

syntax_errors_to  (string, default = unset)
This option applies only when skip_syntax_errors is set. If any addresses
are skipped because of syntax errors, a mail message is sent to the address
specified by syntax_errors_to, giving details of the failing addresses. If
syntax_errors_text is set, its contents are expanded and placed at the head
of the error message.

# 8

# Generic options that apply to all transports

Transports are the modules within Exim that carry out the actual message deliveries. Several examples are shown in earlier chapters; the next chapter discusses each transport in detail. In this chapter, we cover the generic options that apply to all transports, though some of them are used almost exclusively on local transports.

The only required option is `driver`, which defines which transport is being configured. For the **smtp** transport, this is often the only option you need to provide. In Exim's default configuration file, it is configured as follows:

```
remote_smtp:
   driver = smtp
```

In this case, the host to which the message is to be transported is expected to be supplied by a router (for example, as a result of a DNS lookup in **dnslookup**), and all the other transport options are defaulted.

## 8.1 Environment for running transports

Transports run in subprocesses of the main Exim delivery process. Before running a transport's code, Exim sets a specific uid and gid for the subprocess.[1] Exim also sets a current file directory; for some transports, a home directory setting is also relevant. For example, before running **appendfile** to write to a local user's mailbox, Exim normally switches to the uid and gid of that user, and sets the current directory to the user's home directory. This ensures that local deliveries are done "as the user", so that access to files and programs is controlled by the normal operating system protection mechanism.

The values used for the uid, the gid, and the directories may come from several different places. In many cases, the router that handles the address associates settings with that address. However, values may also be given in the transport's own configuration, and these override anything that comes with the address.

---

[1]  This assumes a conventional Exim installation, where Exim is privileged by virtue of being a setuid binary. In unconventional configurations this is not always true (☞ 19.1.3).

## 8.1.1 Uids and gids

Although you can change the uid and gid for remote transports, you should not do so unless you really understand what you are doing. By default these transports run under the Exim uid and gid. This gives them access to Exim's hints databases; these are needed for checking retry information for remote hosts. What follows in this section, therefore, is relevant mainly for local transports.

If the generic group option is set, it overrides any group that may be set in the address, even if user is not set. This makes it possible, for example, to run local mail delivery under the uid of the recipient, but in a special group, by using a transport such as this:

```
group_delivery:
  driver = appendfile
  file = /var/spool/mail/$local_part
  group = mail
```

You might want to do this if all the mailbox files are created in advance, and set up so that group *mail* can write to them (☞ 9.4.1). This example assumes that the router has set a value for the user (which will be the case if it is a router with check_local_user set), but it overrides any group setting that the router may have made.

Similarly, if the generic user option is set for a transport, its value overrides what is already set for the address. If user is non-numeric and group is not set, the gid associated with the user is used. If user is numeric, group must be set.

Every Unix process runs under a specific uid and gid, but in addition, a number of other groups can be associated with it. These are held in the *supplementary group access list*, and give the process privileges that are associated with those groups. For example, users who are members of the groups *staff*, *network*, and *admin* have all these groups set up in their login processes. Setting up the supplementary groups list uses resources, and is typically not needed for email delivery, so Exim does not do it by default.

For delivery via a pipe, however, you may sometimes want Exim to set up the supplementary groups list. The generic initgroups option lets you request this, but only when user is also specified on the transport. When the user is associated with the address by a router, the value of the initgroups option is taken from the router configuration.

## 8.1.2 Current and home directories

The generic current_directory and home_directory options can be used to specify the current and home directories for a transport, overriding any values that are set by the router. The home directory is placed in *$home* while expanding the transport's private options. If neither the router nor the transport sets a current directory, Exim uses the value of the home directory, if set. Otherwise, it sets the current directory to the root directory before running a local transport.

### 8.1.3 Expansion variables derived from the address

Normally, a local delivery handles a single address, and sets variables such as *$domain* and *$local_part* during the delivery. This is also the case when the max_rcpt option is set to one on an **smtp** transport. However, local transports can be configured to handle more than one address at once (for example, while writing in batch SMTP format for onward transmission by some other means), and the **smtp** transport normally operates with multiple addresses when they are routed to the same hosts.

When any transport is handling more than one address at once, the variables associated with the local part are never set, and *$domain* is set only if all the addresses have the same domain.

## 8.2 Debugging transports

The debug_print option operates just like the router option of the same name. Its sole purpose is to help debug Exim configurations. When Exim is run with debugging turned on (☞ 20.10), the string value of debug_print is expanded and added to the debugging output when the transport is run. This facility can be used to check that the values of certain variables are what you think they should be. For example, with this configuration:

```
remote_smtp:
  driver = smtp
  debug_print = self_hostname = $self_hostname
```

the value of the variable *$self_hostname* would be added to the debugging output at the time the transport was run.

## 8.3 Transporting only part of a message

Normally, the job of a transport is to copy an entire message. For special purposes, however, it is possible to transport only the header lines or only the body. Setting headers_only or body_only, respectively, achieves this, but only one of them may be set at once. For example, if copies of messages are being taken for some kind of header analysis, headers_only reduces the amount of data that is written.

# 8.4 Controlling message size

A transport can be configured to reject messages above a certain size by setting `message_size_limit` to a value greater than zero. The default is to apply no limit. Deliveries of messages that are above the limit fail and the address is bounced. If there is any chance that the bounce message (which contains a copy of the original message) could be routed to the same transport, you should ensure that the configuration option `return_size_limit` is less than the transport's `message_size_limit`, as otherwise the bounce message will also fail.

Note that there is a main configuration option for limiting the size of all messages processed by Exim, whose name is also `message_size_limit`. To have any effect, a local setting on a transport must naturally be less than the global limit.

# 8.5 Adding and removing header lines

During the delivery process, a transport can be configured to add or remove header lines. Three specific headers are commonly required to be added when a message is delivered into a local mailbox, and separate options are provided to request them. They are added at the very start of the message, before the *Received:* header lines.

### Delivery-date

The `delivery_date_add` option requests the addition of a header line of the form:

```
Delivery-date: Tue, 29 Feb 2000 16:14:32 +0000
```

This records the date and time that the message was delivered.

### Envelope-to

The `envelope_to_add` option requests the addition of a header line of the form:

```
Envelope-to: alex@troy.example
```

This records the original envelope recipient address that caused the delivery to occur. This may be an address that does not appear in the *To:* or *Cc:* header lines. In cases where a single batched delivery is being done for several recipient addresses, there may be more than one address listed. However, this is an unusual case, requiring the setting of the `batch_max` option (☞ 9.2); a normal local delivery is for just one recipient (even though the message may have several recipients).

## Return-path

The `return_path_add` option requests the addition of a header line of the form:

```
Return-path: <phil@thesa.example>
```

This records the sender address from the message's envelope. For a bounce message, the added header is:

```
Return-path: <>
```

RFC 2821 states:

> *When the delivery SMTP server makes the "final delivery" of a message, it inserts a return-path line at the beginning of the mail data.*

A *Return-path:* header line should not, therefore, be present in incoming messages. The other two added headers are not standardized (though they are used by some other MTAs) and also should not be present in incoming messages. Exim therefore removes all three of these headers from messages it receives, to allow messages that have already been delivered to be easily resent.[1]

## Other header lines

Other header lines can be added to the message by means of the `headers_add` option. If this is set, its contents are added at the end of the header section at the time the message is transported. Header lines added by a transport follow any that are added to an address by routers. Multiple lines can be added by coding \n. For example:

```
headers_add = X-added: this is a header added at $tod_log\n\
              X-added: this is another
```

Exim does not check the syntax of these added header lines; you should ensure that they conform to RFC 2822. A newline is supplied at the end if one is not present.

Original header lines (those that were received with the message) can be removed by setting `headers_remove` to a list of their names. For example:

```
headers_remove = return-receipt-to : acknowledge-to
```

The header names are given without their terminating colons (the colon in the example is a list separator character). These header lines are removed before the addition of any new ones specified by `headers_add`, so an individual header line can be removed and replaced by something different. However, it is not possible to refer to the old contents when defining the new line.

---

[1]  This behaviour can be prevented by setting the configuration options `return_path_remove`, `delivery_date_remove`, and `envelope_to_remove` false, respectively, but you should not normally do this.

Both `headers_add` and `headers_remove` are expanded before use. If the result is an empty string or if the expansion is forced to fail, no action is taken. Other kinds of failure (for example, an expansion syntax error) cause delivery to be deferred.

Header line additions and removals can also be specified on router configurations (☞ 6.3.2), in which case they are associated with the addresses that those drivers handle. If one router is associated with just one transport, it does not matter whether you specify header line changes on the transport or on the router. However, in configurations where several routers are using the same transport, where you specify header line changes obviously makes a difference.

At transport time, the removal list from the address is merged with the removal list from the transport before the relevant header lines are removed. Then the additions from the address and from the transport are made. It is not possible to use the transport's option to remove header lines added by a router.

## 8.6 Rewriting addresses in header lines

Some installations make a distinction between private email addresses that are used within a single host or within a local network, and public addresses that are used on the Internet. When a message passes from their private network to the outside world, they want internal addresses to be translated into external ones.

We have not yet talked about Exim's address rewriting facilities. Their main focus is on rewriting addresses at the time of a message's arrival, which means that every copy of a message that is delivered is affected. This is no good for solving the problem of internal and external addresses, because a single message may have both internal and external recipients. Some copies may need to be rewritten, whereas others may not.

To overcome this difficulty, a generic transport option called `headers_rewrite` exists. It allows addresses in header lines to be rewritten at transport time (that is, as the message is being copied to its destination). This means that the rewriting affects only those copies of the message that pass through the transport where the option is set. Copies that are delivered by other transports are unaffected.

There is a full discussion of this in chapter 15, so we will not say any more about it here.

## 8.7 Changing the return path

"Return path" is another name for the sender address carried in the message's envelope. If the `return_path` option is set for a transport, its contents are expanded, and the result replaces the existing return path. The expansion can refer to the existing value using the *$return_path* variable. If the expansion is forced to fail, no replacement occurs; if it fails for another reason, delivery is deferred.

The main use of this option is for implementing *Variable Envelope Return Paths* (VERP) for messages from mailing lists.[1] The problem with mailing list deliveries that bounce is that it is often difficult to discover which original recipient address provoked the bounce.

Suppose somebody subscribes to a mailing list using the address *J.Smith99@ alma.mater.example*, which is forwarded to *jan@plc.co.example*. All goes well until she changes jobs, her email account at *plc.co.example* is cancelled, and she forgets to update the forwarding because there is not much traffic on the list. When next a message is posted, the manager of the list receives a bounce message about a failure to deliver to *jan@plc.co.example*, an address that does not appear on the list. Finding out which original address caused the bounce may be possible by analysis of the *Received:* header lines that were added to the message; these sometimes contain the recipient address in copies of the message that have only one recipient, for example:

```
Received: from [192.168.247.11] (helo=mail.list.example ident=exim)
        by draco.alma.mater.example with esmtp (Exim 4.10)
        id 124h5o-0005wn-00
        for J.Smith99@alma.mater.example;
        Wed, 20 Jun 2001 10:46:44 +0100
```

However, if the message has more than one recipient, their addresses must not be placed in a *Received:* header because this would constitute a confidentiality exposure.[2] In any event, diagnosing the problem address is time-consuming, and not something that can easily be automated.

The VERP solution to this problem is to encode the subscriber's address in the envelope sender of the message, so that it is immediately available from any bounce messages. For example, suppose messages to the mailing list were previously sent out with the envelope sender set to:

```
somelist-request@list.example
```

After configuring VERP, the copy of the message that is sent to *J.Smith99@ alma.mater.example* has (for example) this envelope sender:

```
somelist-request=J.Smith99%alma.mater.example@list.example
```

If a bounce message is sent back to that address, the address of the subscriber that provoked it can easily be extracted in an automated way.

The downside of VERP is that a separate copy of every message must be sent to each list subscriber, so that it can have a customized sender address. For large lists

---

[1]  See *http://cr.yp.to/proto/verp.txt*.

[2]  Usually, subscribers to a mailing list are not shown the addresses of other subscribers.

that may have hundreds of subscribers in the same domain, this can use substantially more bandwidth and take longer in real time. There are two ways to alleviate this problem:

- Use VERP only for an occasional test message, say once a week. This need not be a special message; a normal post to the list could trigger it. Ignore bounces from non-VERP messages.

- Maintain a list of domains that have many subscribers, and send single copies to those domains. In other words, forgo the benefit of VERP for those domains.

VERP can be supported in Exim by using the `return_path` transport option to rewrite the envelope sender at transport time. For example, the following could be used:

```
return_path = \
  ${if match {$return_path}{^(.+?)-request@list.example\$}\
  {$1-request=$local_part%$domain@list.example}fail}
```

This has the effect of rewriting the return path (envelope sender) if the local part of the original return path ends in `-request` and the domain is *list.example*. The rewriting inserts the local part and domain of the recipient into the return path, in the format used in the previous example.

For this to work, you must arrange for outgoing messages that have `-request` in their return paths to be passed to the transport with just a single recipient, because *$local_part* and *$domain* are not set for messages that have multiple recipients. Local transports operate on one recipient at a time by default, but for an **smtp** transport you need to set:

```
max_rcpt = 1
```

in the transport's options. If your host does not handle much other traffic, you can just set this on the normal **remote_smtp** transport, but if you want to have the benefit of multiple recipients in other cases, you need to set up two **smtp** transports, like this:

```
normal_smtp:
  driver = smtp

verp_smtp:
  driver = smtp
  max_rcpt = 1
  return_path = {${local_part:$return_path}=\
                 $local_part%$domain@list.example}fail}
```

and then route mailing list messages to the second of them, using a router such as this:

```
verp_router:
  driver = dnslookup
  transport = verp_smtp
  condition = ${if match {$return_path}
              {^(.+?)-request@list.example\$}{yes}{no}}
```

The setting of `return_path` on the transport can be simpler, because the strict check is done by the router, so that it sends only addresses that have the `-request` suffix to the transport.

Of course, if you do start sending out messages with this kind of return path, you must also configure Exim to accept the bounce messages that come back to those addresses. Typically, this is done by setting a `local_part_prefix` or `local_part_suffix` option for a suitable router (☞ 6.1.1).

The overhead incurred in using VERP depends on the size of the message, the number of recipient addresses that resolve to the same remote host, and the speed of the connection over which the message is being sent. If many addresses resolve to the same host and the connection is slow, sending a separate copy of the message for each address may take substantially longer than sending a single copy with many recipients (for which VERP cannot be used).

# 8.8 Transport filters

If you want to make more extensive changes than can be achieved with the options just described, or if you want to modify the body of messages as they are transported, you can make use of a *transport filter*. This is a "filter" in the Unix sense of the word; it is unrelated to Exim's message filtering facilities that happen at routing time.

The `transport_filter` option specifies a command that is run at transport time. Instead of copying the message directly to its destination, Exim passes it to the command on its standard input. The standard output of the command is written to the destination. This is an expensive thing to do, and is made more so because Exim's delivery process cannot both read from and write to the filtering process, as doing so could lead to a deadlock. Exim therefore has to create a third process to do the writing, as shown in figure 8-1.

The entire message, including the header lines, is passed to the filter before any transport-specific processing (such as turning \n into \r\n and escaping lines starting with a dot for SMTP) is done. The filter can perform any transformations it likes, but, of course, it should take care not to break RFC 2822 syntax. A problem might arise if the filter increases the size of a message that is being sent down an SMTP channel. If the receiving SMTP server has indicated support for the SIZE parameter, Exim will have sent the size of the message at the start of the SMTP session. If what is actually sent is substantially more, the server might reject the

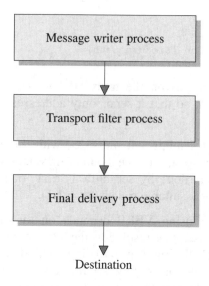

*Figure 8-1: Transport filtering*

message. You can work round this by setting the `size_addition` option on the **smtp** transport, either to allow for additions to the message or to disable the use of `SIZE` altogether.

The value of `transport_filter` is the command string for the program that is run in the process started by Exim. This program is run directly, not under a shell. The string is parsed by Exim in the same way as a command string for the **pipe** transport: Exim breaks it up into arguments and expands each argument separately. This means that the expansion cannot accidentally change the number of arguments. The special argument *$pipe_addresses* is replaced by a number of arguments, one for each address that applies to this delivery.[1]

The variables *$host* (containing the name of the remote host) and *$host_address* (containing the IP address of the remote host) are available for remote transports. For example:

```
transport_filter = /some/directory/transport-filter.pl \
    $host $host_address $sender_address $pipe_addresses
```

The filter process is run under the same uid and gid as the normal delivery. For remote deliveries, this is the Exim uid and gid.

---

[1]  *$pipe_addresses* is not an ideal name for this feature here, but as it was already implemented for the **pipe** transport, it seemed sensible not to change it.

## 8.8.1 Some uses for transport filters

Some administrators want to reduce the amount of information about their local networks that is contained in the headers of outgoing messages. If a message passes through several local MTAs before reaching the Internet gateway, it contains a number of *Received:* header lines that the administrator may want to modify. Using a transport filter is an easy way to do this.

Another possible application of transport filters is to encrypt the bodies of messages as they pass through certain transports. A transport such as:

```
encrypt_smtp:
  driver = smtp
  transport_filter = /usr/mail/encrypt/body $sender_address
```

could be selected by the routers for certain destination addresses, and the value of *$sender_address* could be used to control how the encryption was done.

A transport filter can also be used as a way of passing messages through a program that checks them for spam before delivery. The checking program adds header lines to suspect messages; these can subsequently be recognized by a recipient's filter file or user agent.[1] This is an alternative approach to what is described earlier (☞ 5.10.1), but much of the configuration is similar.

To operate like this, Exim has to deliver incoming messages to itself, via the filter, but in such a way that the filtered messages are recognized and delivered normally when they arrive for the second time. Furthermore, the messages' envelopes must be preserved during this process. You need to run the delivery as a *trusted user* in order to do this (☞ 19.3). Such users are allowed to forge sender addresses and set other message data, such as the protocol by which the message was received.

Suppose you have created a user called *spamkill* for the use of the checking program. To make it trusted, add it to the trusted_users option in the main part of Exim's configuration. For example:

```
trusted_users = spamkill : majordom : ...
```

The first router in the configuration could be

```
spamtest:
  driver = accept
  condition = ${if eq {$received_protocol}{spam-scanned}{no}{yes}}
  transport = spamcheck
```

This routes all addresses to the **spamcheck** transport, except when the value of *$received_prococol* is spam-scanned. Because only a trusted user can set the received protocol, you can be sure that the check cannot be bypassed. You can, of

---

[1]  See *http://spamassassin.org/* for details of one such program.

course, add further conditions such as a test that the message did not originate locally.

The **spamcheck** transport delivers messages back to Exim through a pipe, using the spam checker as a filter. The transport sets the received protocol to prevent the messages from being scanned again. The important options in the transport configuration are as follows:[1]

```
spamcheck:
  driver = pipe
  batch_max = 1000
  use_bsmtp
  command = /usr/sbin/exim -oMr spam-scanned -bS
  transport_filter = /usr/bin/spamc -s 500000
  user = spamkill
```

The setting of `batch_max` in the transport allows up to 1000 recipients in a single copy of the message, and the setting of `use_bsmtp` requests that the message's envelope be preserved in BSMTP format (☞ 9.2, 9.3.2).

The `-oMr` option in the *exim* command specifies that the received protocol is `spam-scanned`, and the `-bS` option tells Exim to expect batch SMTP on its standard input.

# 8.9 Shadow transports

A shadow transport is one that is run in addition to the main transport for an address. Shadow transports can be used for a number of different purposes, including keeping more detailed log information than Exim normally provides, and implementing automatic acknowledgement policies based on message headers. A local transport may set `shadow_transport` to the name of another local transport. Shadow remote transports are not supported.

When a shadow transport is defined, and a delivery to the main transport succeeds, the message is also passed to the shadow transport. However, this happens only if `shadow_condition` is unset, or its expansion does not result in a forced expansion failure, the empty string, or one of the strings 0, `no`, or `false`. This allows you to restrict shadowing to messages that match certain conditions.

If a shadow transport fails to deliver the message, the failure is logged, but it does not affect the subsequent processing of the message. Since the main delivery succeeded, the address is finished with. There is no retrying mechanism for shadow transports.

---

[1] If you copy this example, you should also consider the settings of other **pipe** options such as `home_directory`, `current_directory`, `log_output`, and `return_fail_output`.

Only a single level of shadowing is provided; the `shadow_transport` option is ignored on any transport when it is running as a shadow. Options concerned with output from pipes are also ignored. The log line for the successful delivery has an item added on the end, as follows:

```
ST=<<shadow transport name>>
```

If the shadow transport does not succeed, the error message is put in parentheses afterwards.

# 8.10 Control of retrying

When there is a temporary error for a remote delivery, Exim calculates a retry time based on the identity of the remote host. For temporary errors on local deliveries, on the other hand, the entire address (including the local part and the domain) is normally used. Chapter 12 has a detailed discussion of temporary errors and retrying.

A typical example of a temporary error for a local delivery is a failure caused by a full mailbox. Exim retries this delivery periodically according to its retry rules, but deliveries to other mailboxes should not be affected. For example, if the mailbox for *tweedledum@example.com* is full, Exim delays delivery attempts to that address, but this does not affect deliveries to *tweedledee@example.com* because the retry information is related to the entire address.

Sometimes, however, you may want to treat a temporary local delivery failure as a failure associated with the domain, and not with a particular local part. For example, suppose you are storing all the mail for some domain in a local file, awaiting connection from a dial-up host. When this temporary storage space fills up, you want to delay all delivery attempts for the domain, not just those for the first address that failed. You can do this by setting the option `retry_use_local_part` to be false.

# 8.11 Summary of generic transport options

The options that are common to all the transports are summarized in this section:

`body_only` (Boolean, default = false)
  If this option is set, the message's headers are not transported. The option is mutually exclusive with `headers_only`. If it is used with the **appendfile** or **pipe** transports, the settings of `message_prefix` and `message_suffix` should be checked, because this option does not automatically suppress them.

`current_directory` (string, default = unset)
  This specifies the current directory that is to be set while running the transport, overriding any value that may have been set by the router.

`debug_print` (string, default = unset)

If this option is set and debugging is enabled, the string is expanded and included in the debugging output when the transport is run.

`delivery_date_add` (Boolean, default = false)

If this option is true, a *Delivery-date:* header line is added to the message. This gives the actual time the delivery was made.

`driver` (string, default = unset)

This specifies which of the available transport drivers is to be used. There is no default, and this option must be set for every transport.

`envelope_to_add` (Boolean, default = false)

If this option is true, an *Envelope-to:* header line is added to the message. This gives the original address in the incoming envelope that caused this delivery to happen. More than one address may be present if `batch_max` is set greater than one, or if more than one original address was aliased or forwarded to the same final address.

`group` (string, default = see description)

This option specified a gid for running the transport process, overriding any value that the router supplies, and also overriding any value associated with `user`. If no group is otherwise specified, the Exim group is used.

`headers_add` (string, default = unset)

This option specifies a string of text that is expanded and added to the header portion of a message as it is transported. If the result of the expansion is an empty string, or if the expansion is forced to fail, no action is taken. Other expansion failures are treated as errors and cause the delivery to be deferred.

`headers_only` (Boolean, default = false)

If this option is set, the message's body is not transported. It is mutually exclusive with `body_only`.

`headers_remove` (string, default = unset)

This option is expanded; the result must consist of a colon-separated list of header names (without their terminating colons). Original header lines matching those names are omitted from any message that is transmitted by the transport. However, headers with these names may still be added.

`headers_rewrite` (string, default = unset)

This option allows addresses in header lines to be rewritten at transport time (that is, as the message is being copied to its destination). The value of `headers_rewrite` is a colon-separated list of rewriting rules, as described in chapter 15.

`home_directory` (string, default = unset)
   This specifies a home directory setting for the transport, overriding any value that may have been set by the router.

`initgroups` (Boolean, default = false)
   If this option is true and the uid for the delivery is provided by the transport, the *initgroups()* function is called when running the transport to ensure that any additional groups associated with the uid are set up.

`message_size_limit` (integer, default = 0)
   This option controls the size of messages passing through the transport. If its value is greater than zero and the size of a message exceeds the limit, the delivery fails.

`retry_use_local_part` (Boolean, default = see description)
   The default for this option is true for local transports and false for remote ones. When a delivery suffers a temporary failure, the retry information is keyed on the domain plus the local part if this option is true. When it is false, only the domain is used.[1]

`return_path` (string, default = unset)
   If this option is set, the string is expanded at transport time and replaces the existing return path (envelope sender) value. The expansion can refer to the existing value via *$return_path*. If the expansion is forced to fail, no replacement occurs; if it fails for another reason, Exim writes to its panic log and exits immediately.

`return_path_add` (Boolean, default = false)
   If this option is true, a *Return-path:* header line is added to the message. This is normally used only on transports that are doing final delivery into a mailbox. If the mailbox is a single file in Berkeley format, the return path is normally available in the separator line, but commonly this is not displayed by MUAs, and so the user does not have easy access to it. Other mailbox formats may not record the return path at all.

`shadow_condition` (string, default = unset)
   See `shadow_transport`.

`shadow_transport` (string, default = unset)
   A local transport may set the `shadow_transport` option to the name of another local transport. Whenever a delivery to the main transport succeeds, and either `shadow_condition` is unset, or its expansion does not result in a forced expansion failure, or the empty string, or one of the strings 0, or no, or `false`, the message is also passed to the shadow transport.

---

[1]   In the current implementation, this option is useful only for local transports. Its value is not inspected by remote transports.

transport_filter (string, default = unset)

This option sets up a filtering process (in the Unix shell sense) for messages at transport time. When the message is about to be written out, the command specified by transport_filter is started up in a separate process, and the entire message, including the headers, is passed to it on its standard input. The filter's standard output is read and written to the message's destination.

user (string, default = see description)

This option specifies the user under whose uid the delivery process is to run, overriding any uid that may have been set by the router. If the user is given as a name, the uid is looked up from the password data, and the associated group is taken as the value of the gid to be used if the group option is not set.

# 9

# The transports

In this chapter, we describe the functions and options of each of the available transports. There is only one transport for delivering messages to remote hosts, called **smtp**. The other transports do local deliveries, and are as follows:

**appendfile**

A transport that writes a message to a local file.

**autoreply**

A transport that generates an automatic reply to a message.

**lmtp**

A transport that passes a message to an external process via a pipe, using the LMTP protocol.

**pipe**

A transport that passes a message directly to an external process via a pipe.

**autoreply** is really a pseudotransport, because it does not actually deliver the message anywhere; instead it generates a new outgoing message (an automatic reply). It is included among the transports because its method of operation and configuration are the same, and it can include a copy of the original message in the reply.

## 9.1 The smtp transport

As the **smtp** transport is the only remote transport, it is used for all deliveries to remote hosts. However, more than one instance can be configured with different option settings if necessary. The most common configuration is very simple, usually this:

```
remote_smtp:
  driver = smtp
```

In this example, all the options that control the parameters of the SMTP connection take their default values. The list of remote hosts is set up by the router that handles the address, and it is passed to the transport along with the address(es) that are to be delivered.

However, the use of an **smtp** transport is not restricted to routers that set up host lists. To allow for this, the transport itself has options for specifying hosts. In addition, the characteristics of the SMTP connection can be modified in various ways. As a result, there are a lot of options for this transport.

## 9.1.1 Control of multiple addresses

The SMTP protocol allows any number of recipient addresses to be passed in a message's envelope, by means of multiple RCPT commands.[1] Exim normally does this when a message has more than one address that is routed to the same host, subject to the following options:

- max_rcpt specifies the maximum number of RCPT commands in one message transfer. The default value is 100; if max_rcpt is set to zero, there is no limit. When a message has more than max_rcpt recipients going to the same host, an appropriate number of separate copies of the message are sent. If max_rcpt is set to 1, a separate copy of the message is sent for each recipient. This is necessary if you want to implement VERP (☞ 8.7).

- When max_rcpt is greater than 1, the domains in the addresses need not be the same, provided that they all resolve to the same list of hosts. For example, a set of virtual domains that are all under one management usually all share the same MX hosts. However, if you want to make use of *$domain* in a transport option, you have to arrange that only one domain is ever involved, because otherwise *$domain* is not set. You can do this by setting The multi_domain option to be false. If you do this, a separate copy of the message is sent for each different domain.

The default action of using multiple addresses in a single transfer is the one recommended by RFC 2821. For personal messages (which rarely have more than a couple of recipients) that are traversing well-connected parts of today's Internet, it probably does not make much difference. However, for mailing lists with thousands of subscribers there can be a substantial cost if each is sent a separate copy, especially if many of the addresses are in the same domain.

## 9.1.2 Control of outgoing connections

Some large domains have very many MX records, each of which may refer to several IP addresses. When there are connection problems, trying every single one of these addresses is not sensible. If several IP addresses at the top of the list fail, it is reasonable to assume there is some problem that is likely to affect all of them, or at all least those with the same MX value.

The value of the hosts_max_try option is the maximum number of IP addresses that are initially tried. The default value for this option is five. Any addresses that are skipped because their retry times have not arrived are not counted. After this number

---

[1]  In practice, more than about a hundred recipients should be avoided, as this can lead to problems with some MTAs.

of IP addresses have been tried, Exim looks down the list for hosts with different MX values, and if it finds any, it tries one address for each value.

Because Exim operates in a distributed manner, if several messages for the same host arrive at around the same time, more than one simultaneous connection to the remote host can occur. This is not usually a problem except when there is a slow link between the hosts. In that situation, it may be helpful to restrict Exim to one connection at a time to certain hosts. This can be done by setting the `serialize_hosts` option to match the relevant remote hosts, for example:

```
serialize_hosts = 192.168.4.5 : my.slow.neighbour.example
```

Exim implements serialization by means of a hints database in which a record is written whenever a process connects to one of the restricted hosts, and is deleted when the connection is ended. Obviously, there is scope for records to be left lying around if there is a system or program crash, which would prevent Exim from contacting one of these hosts ever again. To guard against this, Exim ignores any records that are more than six hours old.

If the **smtp** transport finds that the host it is about to connect to has an existing connection, it skips that host and moves on to the next one as if a connection to the host had failed, except that it does not compute any retry information.

If you set up any serialization, you should also arrange to delete the relevant hints database whenever your system reboots. The names of the files start with *misc*, and they are kept in the *db* subdirectory in Exim's spool directory. There may be one or two files, depending on the type of DBM library in use.[1]

When a message has been successfully delivered over a TCP/IP connection, Exim looks in a different hints database to see if there are any other messages awaiting a connection to the same host. If there are, a new delivery process is started for one of them, and the current TCP/IP connection is passed to it. The new process may in turn create yet another process. Each time this happens, a sequence counter is incremented, and if it ever reaches the value of the `connection_max_messages` option (whose default value is 500), no further messages are sent on the same TCP/IP connection.

## 9.1.3 Control of each TCP/IP connection

When an outgoing SMTP connection is made from a host with a number of different TCP/IP interfaces (real or virtual),[2] the system's IP functions choose which interface to use for the sending IP address, unless told otherwise by a setting of the `interface` option. You may want to use this option if, for example, you are using certain IP addresses for web hosting only, and do not want them used for mail. The

---

[1]   The same files are used for ETRN serialization.

[2]   Such hosts are often called *multihomed* hosts.

`interface` option is set to a string that must be an IP address. For example, on a host that has IP addresses 192.168.123.123 and 192.168.9.9, you could set:

```
interface = 192.168.123.123
```

in which case all outgoing connections made by the transport would use that particular interface.

The `interface` option is an expanded string. This makes it possible to use different interfaces for different remote hosts, by making use of the *$host* or *$host_address* variables in the expansion.

In a system with IPv6 support, the type of interface specified must be of the same kind as the address to which the connection is being made. To allow for hosts that support both IPv4 and IPv6, the `interface` option is actually interpreted (after expansion) as a string of IP addresses. The first address in the list that is of the correct type (IPv4 or IPv6) is used. For example, if the setting is as follows:

```
interface = <; 3ffe:ffff:836f:0a00:000a:0800:200a:c031 ;\
            192.168.241.244
```

the first address is used for connections to IPv6 addresses, and the second is used for connections to IPv4 addresses.

The `port` option specifies the remote TCP/IP port to which Exim connects in order to send the message. For example:

```
port = 2525
```

If the value begins with a digit, it is taken as a port number; otherwise, it is looked up using the *getservbyname()* function, which looks at */etc/services* and possibly other system information sources such as NIS. The default setting for `port` is normally `smtp`, but if `protocol` is set to `lmtp`, the default changes to `lmtp`. This option is mainly used for testing, but is occasionally useful in other circumstances.

By default, Exim sets the socket option `SO_KEEPALIVE` on outgoing socket connections. This causes the kernel to probe idle connections periodically by sending packets with "old" sequence numbers. The other end of the connection should send an acknowledgement if the connection still exists, or a reset if it has been aborted.[1] You can set the `keepalive` option false to disable this, should it ever be necessary. (As far as I know, nobody has ever needed to.)

There are various timeouts associated with SMTP exchanges; normally these work well and you should not need to change them. However, they can be changed by

---

[1] The reason for doing this is that it has the beneficial effect of freeing up certain types of connection that can get stuck when the remote host is disconnected without tidying up the TCP/IP connection properly. Without `SO_KEEPALIVE`, there is no way of distinguishing between a connection that is idle and a connection that disconnected abnormally.

means of the following options (for the last three, the defaults in parentheses are the values recommended in RFC 2821):

`connect_timeout`

This option specifies how long to wait for the system's *connect()* function to establish a connection to a remote host. A setting of zero allows the system default timeout (typically several minutes) to act. However, because there have been problems with system default timeouts not working in some operating systems, Exim has a default of 5 minutes. Needless to say, this option has no effect unless its value is less than the system timeout.

`command_timeout` (5 minutes)

This option specifies how long to wait for a response to an SMTP command, and also how long to wait for the initial SMTP response after a TCP/IP connection has been established.

`data_timeout` (5 minutes)

This option specifies how long to allow for the transmission of one block of message data.[1] The overall transmission timeout for a message, therefore, depends on the size of the message.

`final_timeout` (10 minutes)

Specifies how long to wait for a response after the entire message has been sent.

## 9.1.4 Use of the SMTP SIZE option

If a remote SMTP server indicates that it supports the `SIZE` option of the `MAIL` command, Exim passes over the message size at the start of an SMTP transaction. If the message is too large for the receiving host, it can reject the `MAIL` command, which saves the client from transmitting a large message, only to have it rejected at the end.

The value of the `size_addition` option (default 1024) is added to the size of the message to obtain the argument for `SIZE`. This is to allow for headers and other text that may be added during delivery by configuration options or in a transport filter. It may be necessary to increase this value if a lot of text is added to messages. Alternatively, if the value of `size_addition` is negative, it disables the use of the `SIZE` option altogether.

---

[1]   Exim transmits messages in 8 KB blocks by default.

## 9.1.5 Use of the SMTP AUTH command

When Exim has been built to include support for at least one of the SMTP authentication mechanisms, the `hosts_require_auth` and `hosts_try_auth` options are available in the **smtp** transport. Each provides a list of servers to which Exim will attempt to authenticate as a client when it connects, provided the server announces authentication support.

The difference between the two options is in what happens if authentication fails. If the server is listed in `hosts_require_auth`, Exim defers delivery, and tries again later. This error is detectable in the retry rules, which means that the retry timeout can be set by the local administrator. If the server is listed in `hosts_try_auth`, on the other hand, Exim tries to deliver the message unauthenticated.

Details of SMTP authentication and how to configure Exim to use it are given in chapter 13.

## 9.1.6 Use of TLS encryption

The **smtp** transport has a number of options for controlling encryption in outgoing connections, but we leave their description until after the general discussion of SMTP encryption (☞ 13.1.4).

## 9.1.7 Use of the LMTP protocol

LMTP (RFC 2033) is a protocol for passing messages between an MTA and a "black box" method of storing mail such as the Cyrus IMAP message store. Later in this chapter (☞ 9.6) we discuss the background to LMTP, and describe how it can be used to pass messages to local processes. However, LMTP is similar to SMTP, and in some cases there is a requirement to pass messages to a message store over a TCP/IP connection, using LMTP instead of SMTP. You can configure Exim to do this by setting up an **smtp** transport with the following option:

```
protocol = lmtp
```

If you do this, the default value for `port` changes to `lmtp`, but everything else in the transport operates exactly as before. Of course, you must set up a special transport when you do this; LMTP is not used for the normal transmission of messages between MTAs.

## 9.1.8 Specifying hosts

There are two options for **smtp** that can specify lists of hosts: `hosts` and `fallback_hosts`.

## Specifying a primary host list

The most common situation in which `hosts` is set is when a router that cannot set up a host list is used to cause certain addresses to be delivered remotely. An example of this usage was given earlier (☞ 5.6), where we considered a corporate mail gateway that delivers some local parts in its local domain into local mailboxes, and sends others on to personal workstations. In the version of the example where an **accept** router is used, the `hosts` setting on the transport specifies the workstation.

## Overriding a router's host list

When an **smtp** transport is invoked from a router that sets up a host list, hosts that are set up by the router normally override hosts set in the transport. Sometimes, however, you may want a router to check for a valid destination, but have the message sent to a different host. If `hosts_override` is set, it is the router's hosts that are ignored.[1]

As an example of where this is useful, consider a host permanently connected to the Internet on a slow connection. This host sends all outgoing mail to a smart host so that queuing happens on the far side of the slow line. It is useful to be able to check that a remote domain exists before wasting bandwidth sending a message to the smart host. This can be done by using a router such as:

```
dnslookup:
  driver = dnslookup
  transport = smarthost
```

with this transport:

```
smarthost:
  driver = smtp
  hosts = the.smart.host
  hosts_override
```

The router uses the DNS to route addresses in the normal way, so any domains that do not exist fail to be routed and cause their addresses to fail. However, the host list that is set up by the router is ignored by the transport because `hosts_override` is set, thus causing all addresses with routeable domains to be delivered to the smart host.

## Specifying a fallback host list

The `fallback_hosts` option provides a "use a smart host only if delivery fails" facility. Earlier (☞ 6.3), we discussed an identically named option for routers. The option on the **smtp** transport has the same effect, but is overridden if fallback hosts are supplied by the router. The `hosts_override` option does not apply to `fallback_hosts`. Once normal deliveries are complete, the fallback queue is

---

[1]  If `hosts_override` is set without `hosts`, it has no effect.

delivered by rerunning the same transports with the new host lists. If several failing addresses have the same fallback hosts (and `max_rcpt` permits it), a single copy of the message is sent with multiple recipients.

## Randomizing host lists

When a `hosts` or `fallback_hosts` setting in an **smtp** transport specifies more than one host, they are tried in the order they are listed, unless `hosts_randomize` is set. In this case, the order of the list is randomized each time the transport is run. There is no facility for using the hosts in a "round-robin" fashion.

The `hosts_randomize` option also applies to host lists (both primary and fallback) that are set up by a router and passed to **smtp** with an address, except in the case of a host list derived from MX records, where the MX preferences specify the order.

The **manualroute** router also has an option called `hosts_randomize`. This causes it to reorder the host list it generates at routing time, which means that addresses whose host lists are specified as the same might end up with differently ordered lists. This prevents them being sent to an **smtp** transport in a batch. There are situations where this behaviour might be desirable.

## Looking up IP addresses

Three options in the **smtp** transport control the way IP addresses for host names (either from `hosts` or `fallback_hosts`) are looked up. The `gethostbyname` option specifies that IP addresses are looked up by calling the system's host lookup function instead of by calling the DNS resolver directly.[1]

The other two options operate in exactly the same way as the identically named options in the **dnslookup** router (☞ 7.2). These options are as follows:

`dns_qualify_single`

> Turns on the RES_DEFNAMES option of the DNS resolver, which causes it not to qualify domains that consist of just a single component.

`dns_search_parents`

> Turns on the RES_DNSRCH option of the DNS resolver, causing it to look in parent domains for unknown names.

---

[1]   The original function for doing this is called *gethostbyname()*, which is where the option name comes from. However, in modern IPv6 systems, *gethostbyname()* has been superseded by *getipnodebyname()*.

### Handling the local host

There is one final option concerned with hosts that are specified in the **smtp** transport. When any host specified in `hosts` or `fallback_hosts` turns out to be the local host, delivery is deferred by default. However, if `allow_localhost` is set, Exim goes on to do the delivery anyway. This should be used only in special cases when the configuration ensures that no looping will result (for example, a differently configured Exim is listening on the port to which the message is sent).

## 9.1.9 Control of retrying

Much of Exim's retrying logic is host-based rather than address- or message-based. This requires it to remember information about failing hosts, and the obvious place to implement the logic for this is in the **smtp** transport, where such failures are detected. There are, as a result, two options concerned with retrying: `retry_include_ip_address` and `delay_after_cutoff`.

Retries are normally based on both the host name and IP address, so that each IP address of a multihomed host is treated independently. However, in some environments, client hosts are assigned a different IP address each time they connect to the Internet. In this situation, the use of the IP address as part of the retry key on a server host leads to undesirable behaviour. Setting `retry_include_ip_address` false causes Exim to use only the host name. This should normally be done on a separate instance of the **smtp** transport, set up specially to handle these non-standard client hosts.

In order to understand `delay_after_cutoff`, you need to know how Exim handles temporary errors and retrying. This is explained later (☞ 12.10), so that is where a description of this option can be found.

## 9.1.10 Summary of smtp options

The options that are specific to the **smtp** transport are summarized in this section. Details of those that are concerned with TLS encryption can be found later (☞ 13.1.4). Of course, any generic transport option (☞ 8.11) may also be set for **smtp**.

`allow_localhost` (Boolean, default = false)
  When any host specified in `hosts` or `fallback_hosts` turns out to be the local host, Exim delays delivery by default. However, if `allow_localhost` is set, it carries on with the delivery.

`command_timeout` (time, default = 5m)
  This sets a timeout for receiving a response to an SMTP command that has been sent out. It is also used when waiting for the initial banner line from the remote host. Its value must not be zero.

`connect_timeout` (time, default = 5m)

This sets a timeout for the *connect()* function, which sets up a TCP/IP connection to a remote host. A setting of zero allows the system timeout (typically, several minutes) to operate. To have any effect, the value of this option must be less than the system timeout.

`connection_max_messages` (integer, default = 500)

This controls the maximum number of separate message deliveries that can take place over a single TCP/IP connection. If the value is zero, there is no limit.

`data_timeout` (time, default = 5m)

This sets a timeout for the transmission of each block in the data portion of the message. As a result, the overall timeout for a message depends on the size of the message. The value of this option must not be zero.

`delay_after_cutoff` (Boolean, default = true)

This option controls what happens when all remote IP addresses for a given domain have been inaccessible for so long that they have passed their retry cutoff times (☞ 12.10).

`dns_qualify_single` (Boolean, default = true)

If the `hosts` or `fallback_hosts` option is being used and `gethostbyname` is false, the option to cause the DNS resolver to qualify single-component names with the local domain is set if this option is true.

`dns_search_parents` (Boolean, default = false)

If the `hosts` or `fallback_hosts` option is being used and `gethostbyname` is false, the DNS resolver option to enable the searching of parent domains is set if this option is true.

`fallback_hosts` (string list, default = unset)

The value must be a colon-separated list of host names or IP addresses. String expansion is not applied. Fallback hosts can also be specified on routers; these associate such hosts with the addresses they process. Fallback hosts specified on the transport are used only if the address does not have its own associated fallback host list.

`final_timeout` (time, default = 10m)

This is the timeout that applies while waiting for the response after an entire message has been transported. Its value must not be zero.

`gethostbyname` (Boolean, default = false)

If this option is true when the `hosts` or `fallback_hosts` options are being used, IP addresses are looked up by calling the system host lookup function instead of using the DNS directly.

`hosts` (string list, default = unset)

This option specifies a list of hosts that are used if the address being processed does not have any hosts associated with it, or if the `hosts_override` option is set.

`hosts_avoid_tls` (host list, default = unset)

This option lists hosts for which TLS encryption is not to be used.

`hosts_max_try` (integer, default = 5)

This option specifies the maximum number of IP addresses to which the transport will try to connect.

`hosts_nopass_tls` (host list, default = unset)

This option lists hosts for which an encrypted session cannot be passed to a new process for sending a further message.

`hosts_override` (Boolean, default = false)

If this option is set and the `hosts` option is also set, any hosts that are attached to the address are ignored, and instead the hosts specified by the `hosts` option are used.

`hosts_randomize` (Boolean, default = false)

If `hosts_randomize` is false, the order in which hosts are listed in `hosts` or `fallback_hosts` is preserved as an order of preference for delivering the message; if the option is true, the list is shuffled into a random order each time it is used. Host lists that are associated with addresses (by routers) are also randomized, unless they were derived from MX records.

`hosts_require_auth` (host list, default = unset)

This option provides a list of servers for which authentication must succeed before Exim will transfer a message. An authentication failure causes the delivery to be deferred.

`hosts_require_tls` (host list, default = unset)

This option lists hosts for which TLS encryption is required.

`hosts_try_auth` (host list, default = unset)

This option provides a list of servers for which authentication is attempted before transferring a message. If authentication fails, Exim tries to deliver unauthenticated.

`interface` (string list, default = unset)

This option specifies which local interface to bind to when making an outgoing SMTP connection. If `interface` is not set, the system's IP functions choose which interface to use if the host has more than one. The first interface in the list that is of the correct type (IPv4 or IPv6) is used.

keepalive  (Boolean, default = true)
>    This option controls the setting of SO_KEEPALIVE on outgoing socket connections.

max_rcpt  (integer, default = 100)
>    This option limits the number of RCPT commands that are sent in a single SMTP message transaction. Each set of addresses is treated independently, and may cause parallel connections to the same host if remote_max_parallel permits this.

multi_domain  (Boolean, default = true)
>    When this option is set, the **smtp** transport can handle multiple addresses containing a mixture of different domains as long as they all resolve to the same list of hosts. Turning the option off restricts the transport to handling only one domain at a time.

port  (string, default = see description)
>    This option specifies the TCP/IP port that is used to send the message. If it begins with a digit, it is taken as a port number; otherwise, it is looked up using *getservbyname()*. The default is smtp unless the protocol option is set to lmtp, in which case the default for port changes to lmtp.

protocol  (string, default = smtp)
>    If this option is set to lmtp instead of smtp, the default value for the port option changes to lmtp, and the transport uses the LMTP protocol instead of SMTP.

retry_include_ip_address  (Boolean, default = true)
>    Setting this option false causes Exim to use only the host name instead of both the name and the IP address when constructing retry records (☞ 12.1).

serialize_hosts  (host list, default = unset)
>    This option lists the hosts to which only one TCP/IP connection at a time should be made.

size_addition  (integer, default = 1024)
>    The value of size_addition is added to the size of the message to create the value that Exim sends in the SIZE option of the SMTP MAIL command. This allows for headers and other text that may be added during delivery as a result of certain configuration options, and for text added by a transport filter. If the value of size_addition is negative, the use of the SIZE option is disabled.

tls_certificate  (string, default = unset)
>    This option names the file where the client's certificate is stored.

`tls_privatekey` (string, default = unset)
This option names the file where the client's private key is stored. If it is unset when `tls_certificate` is set, the private key is assumed to be in the same file as the certificate.

`tls_require_ciphers` (string, default = unset)
This option contains a list of permitted TLS ciphers.

`tls_tempfail_tryclear` (Boolean, default = true)
When the server host is not in `hosts_require_tls`, and there is a problem in setting up a TLS session, this option determines whether Exim should try to deliver the message in clear or not.

`tls_verify_certificates` (string, default = unset)
This option names the file where permitted server certificates are stored.

# 9.2 Address batching in the appendfile, lmtp, and pipe transports

When a message has several recipients that require local delivery, the transports normally handle one address at a time. That is, a separate instance of a transport is run for each address that is routed to it, and a separate copy of the message is written in each case. (This is in contrast to the **smtp** transport which by default handles multiple addresses that are routed to the same remote hosts as a single delivery.)

There are situations, however, in which it is useful to be able to run a local transport with multiple recipient addresses. For example:

- In an **appendfile** transport, when storing messages in files for later delivery to other hosts, a single copy of a message with multiple recipients saves space (☞ 12.12.1).

- In an **lmtp** transport, when delivering over "local SMTP" to a local process, a single copy saves time, and moreover is the normal way that the LMTP protocol is expected to work. A configuration example for **lmtp** is shown later (☞ 9.6).

- In a **pipe** transport, when passing a message to a scanning program or to some other delivery mechanism such as UUCP, multiple recipients may be desirable.

The **appendfile**, **lmtp**, and **pipe** transports have the same options for controlling multiple ("batched") deliveries. To save repeating the description for each transport, we cover these options in this section.

The `batch_max` option specifies the maximum number of addresses that can be delivered together in a single run of the transport. Its default value is one. When

more than one recipient address in a message is routed to a local transport that has a
batch_max value greater than one, the addresses are delivered in a batch (that is, in
a single run of the transport), but subject to these conditions:

- If any of the transport's options contain a reference to *$local_part*, no batching is possible.

- If any of the transport's options contain a reference to *$domain*, only addresses with the same domain are batched.

- If batch_id (whose value is a string) is set, it is expanded for each address, and only those addresses with the same expanded value are batched. This allows you to specify custom batching conditions.

- Batched addresses must have the same return path (where to send bounce messages), the same header additions and removals, the same user and group for running the transport, and if a host list is present, the first host must be the same.

The *$local_part* variable is never set when more than one address is being trans-
ported, and *$domain* is set only if all the addresses have the same domain. If the
generic envelope_to_add option is set for the transport, the *Envelope-to:* header
line that is added to the message contains all the addresses.

Local delivery batching is most commonly used in conjunction with batched SMTP.
Some examples are shown in chapter 5, and there is another example in section
9.3.2. As an example of the use of local delivery batching without BSMTP, suppose
you wanted to collect all messages for certain domains in files. First, set up a router
that picks off the domains and routes them to a special transport:

```
filed_domains_router:
  driver = accept
  domains = first.filed.example : second.filed.example : ...
  transport = filed_domains_transport
```

Now set up the transport, which in this example uses the domain to generate the
filename:

```
filed_domains_transport:
  driver = appendfile
  batch_max = 100
  file = /var/savedmail/$domain
  envelope_to_add
  return_path_add
  user = mail
```

There has to be a setting of user either on the router or the transport, to specify the
uid under which the delivery process runs. Setting envelope_to_add and
return_path_add ensures that the relevant parts of the message's envelope are
preserved in header lines.

This example assumes that all messages to one domain are stored in a single file. This does not have to be the case; **appendfile** can also operate by writing each message as a separate file (☞ 9.4.4).

# 9.3 Options common to the appendfile and pipe transports

The **appendfile** transport, which writes messages to files, and the **pipe** transport, which writes messages to pipes that are connected to other processes, have a number of options in common. To save repetition, they are collected together in this section.

## 9.3.1 Controlling the format of the message

As the message is written to a file or down a pipe, certain modifications can be made by the transport. Generic options for adding or removing header lines are covered in chapter 8; here we describe some options that apply only to local deliveries.

### Separating messages in a single file

When a mailbox consists of a single file that contains concatenated messages, there has to be some way of determining where one message ends and another begins. Several schemes have been used for this, the most common of which is the *Berkeley mailbox format*, in which a message begins with a line starting with the word From, followed by a space and other data, and ends with an empty line.

This format seems to have been adopted in the distant past because messages received by UUCP use such a line to contain the envelope sender address.[1] There is, however, no standard for it as a message separator, and several variants have been seen in practice. It is a most unfortunate choice of separator line, because lines within the bodies of messages that start with the word From are not uncommon. This means that such lines have to be escaped in some way (as described shortly), lest they be taken as the start of a new message.

Exim supports message separation by providing two options called message_prefix and message_suffix. Their contents are expanded and written at the start and end of every message, respectively. The default values depend on the settings of other transport options. If the **appendfile** transport is configured to append messages to a single mailbox file, and use_bsmtp is not set, the defaults are as follows:

```
message_prefix = "From ${if def:return_path{$return_path}\
        {MAILER-DAEMON}} $tod_bsdinbox\n"
message_suffix = "\n"
```

---

[1]  See RFC 976, *UUCP Mail Interchange Format Standard*.

These define Berkeley format message separation. The `message_prefix` setting places the envelope sender (return path) in the separator line, unless the message is a bounce message (where there is no return path). For bounce messages, `MAILER-DAEMON` is used, because some programs that read mailboxes do not work if nothing is inserted. The line ends with the date and time in a particular format required by this form of separator, which is made available in the variable *$tod_bsdinbox*. The `message_suffix` setting ensures that there is a blank line after every message.[1]

When **appendfile** is configured to deliver each message into a separate file, or if `use_bsmtp` is set, the default settings for `message_prefix` and `message_suffix` are empty, because in those cases no separators are needed. In all cases, however, the defaults can be overridden by explicit configuration settings.

Message separation is not an issue in the case of the **pipe** transport. However, some implementations of the commonly used */usr/ucb/vacation* command expect to see a `From` line at the start of messages that are piped to them. For this reason, the default values of the `message_prefix` and `message_suffix` options are the same as for **appendfile**. They define Berkeley format message separation except when `use_bsmtp` is set.

In many other applications of the **pipe** transport, however, the `From` line is not expected and should be disabled. An example of this was given earlier (☞ 5.4).

The Berkeley format is not the only one that uses textual separators between messages. In MMDF format, the beginnings and ends of messages are marked by lines containing exactly four non-printing characters whose numeric code value is 1. The **appendfile** transport can be configured to support this by setting the following options:

```
message_prefix = "\1\1\1\1\n"
message_suffix = "\1\1\1\1\n"
```

If you want to use such a format, you must be sure all your MUAs can interpret it.

## Escaping lines in the message

The mechanism provided for handling lines in the message that happen to look like message separators is a pair of options called `check_string` and `escape_string`. When batch SMTP delivery is configured, the contents of `check_string` and `escape_string` are forced to values that implement the SMTP escaping protocol for lines beginning with a dot. In this case, any settings made in the configuration file are ignored.

---

[1]  The message itself always ends with a newline, because the SMTP protocol is defined in terms of lines. For messages submitted locally, Exim adds a final newline if there isn't one.

Otherwise, the default for both these options is unset, except for an **appendfile** transport that is configured to append messages to a single mailbox file. In this case, the defaults are as follows:

```
check_string = "From "
escape_string = ">From "
```

As the transport writes a message, the start of each line is tested for matching check_string. If it does match, the initial matching characters are replaced by the contents of escape_string. The value of check_string is a literal string, not a regular expression. The default therefore inserts a single angle-bracket character before any line starting with From followed by a space. For example, if a message contains the line:

```
From the furthest reaches of the Galaxy, ...
```

**appendfile** actually writes:

```
>From the furthest reaches of the Galaxy, ...
```

If you are using MMDF mailbox separators, you need to change the default settings to:[1]

```
check_string  = "\1\1\1\1\n"
escape_string = "\1\1\1\1 \n"
```

### Control of line terminators

The final common option for **appendfile** and **pipe** that affects the contents of a message is use_crlf. When it is set, lines are terminated by CRLF instead of just a linefeed. Some external local delivery programs require this. It may also be useful in the case of batched SMTP, because the byte sequence written is then an exact image of what would be sent down a real SMTP connection.

---

 If you set use_crlf with message_prefix or message_ suffix, you must ensure that any occurrence of \n in those strings is changed to \r\n because they are written verbatim, without any special interpretation.

---

## 9.3.2 Use of batched SMTP (BSMTP)

Batched SMTP delivery is mentioned in several earlier sections, and a number of examples are shown (☞ 7.4.5). BSMTP is a convenient way to preserve envelopes in messages that are being temporarily stored in files, or to pass envelopes to processes

---

[1] If a message contains binary data, changing it in this way may damage the data, but that is probably better than a broken mailbox file.

such as virus scanners that can handle many recipients at once. This is particularly convenient if the message is subsequently going to be passed back to Exim, or to any program that transmits it over an SMTP connection.

In both the **appendfile** and **pipe** transports, the use_bsmtp option requests delivery in batched SMTP format. Messages are then written as if they were being transmitted over an SMTP connection. Each message starts with a MAIL command for the envelope sender, followed by a RCPT command for each recipient, and then DATA and the message itself, terminated by a dot. For example, a file written this way could contain:

```
MAIL FROM:<tom@abcd.example>
RCPT TO:<jerry@pqrs.example>
RCPT TO:<bugs@albuquerque.example>
DATA
<<message content>>
.
```

 Setting use_bsmtp does not of itself affect address batching. You need to set batch_max greater than one if you want to allow for more than one recipient in the SMTP envelope.

The default values of the message_prefix and message_suffix options are unset when use_bsmtp is set. However, some programs that read BSMTP files expect a HELO command to precede each message; the message_prefix option can be used to provide this. For example:

```
filed_domains:
  driver = appendfile
  file = /var/savedmail/$host
  batch_max = 100
  use_bsmtp
  message_prefix = HELO $primary_hostname
  user = mail
```

The settings of check_string and escape_string are forced to the following values when use_bsmtp is set:

```
check_string = .
escape_string = ..
```

These values implement the standard escaping mechanism for SMTP. Any values that are set in the configuration are ignored.

### 9.3.3 Summary of options common to appendfile and pipe

The options that are common to the **appendfile** and **pipe** transports are summarized in this section:

check_string (string, default = see description)

As the transport writes the message, the start of each line is tested for matching check_string, and if it does, the initial matching characters are replaced by the contents of escape_string. The value of check_string is a literal string, not a regular expression. For the **appendfile** transport, the default is From followed by a space when the transport is configured to append messages to a single mailbox file and use_bsmtp is not set. For the **pipe** transport, the default is always unset.

escape_string (string, default = see description)

See check_string. The default is >From when check_string's default is From, and unset otherwise.

message_prefix (string, default = see description)

The string specified here is expanded and output at the start of every message. When use_bsmtp is set, the default is unset. Otherwise, except when **appendfile** is configured to deliver each message into a separate file, the default setting is:

```
message_prefix = "From ${if def:return_path{$return_path}\
   {MAILER-DAEMON}} ${tod_bsdinbox}\n"
```

message_suffix (string, default = see description)

The string specified here is expanded and output at the end of every message. The default is \n when the default for message_prefix is not empty, and is unset otherwise.

use_bsmtp (Boolean, default = fails)

This option requests delivery of messages in batch SMTP format. It affects the default values of check_string, escape_string, message_prefix, and message_suffix.

use_crlf (Boolean, default = false)

This option causes lines to be terminated with the two-character CRLF sequence (carriage return, linefeed) instead of just a linefeed character.

## 9.4 The appendfile transport

Writing messages to files is the most complex operation of Exim's local transports; consequently, **appendfile** has a large number of options. This transport can operate in two entirely different ways:

- In "file" mode, the message is appended to the end of a file, which may pre-exist and contain other messages. Two major message formats are supported, with minor variations controllable by the `message_prefix` and `message_suffix` options.

- In "directory" mode, each message is written to an entirely new file within a specific directory. Three different file formats are supported.

When writing to a single file containing multiple messages, the file has to be locked so that neither MUAs nor other Exim processes can tamper with it while the delivery is taking place. This means that only one message at a time can be delivered to the mailbox, and while a message is being delivered, messages that are already in the mailbox cannot be removed. If, on the other hand, each message is written to a new file, no locking is required, multiple simultaneous deliveries can take place, and old messages can be deleted at any time.

## 9.4.1 Setting up a multimessage file for appending

When **appendfile** is called as a result of a filename item in a user's *.forward* file or as the result of a *save* command in a filter file, the router passes the name of the file to the transport, along with the address that is being delivered. In other cases, when no filename is already associated with the address, the `file` option specifies the name of the file to which the message is to be appended. An example that has been used several times for delivery to conventional mailboxes is:

```
file = /var/mail/$local_part
```

where the name of the file depends on the local part that is being delivered. This is a very simple example, but if necessary, the full power of string expansions can be used to compute the filename.

### Mailbox location

On hosts where the users have login access, some installations choose to locate users' mailboxes in their home directories. This has three benefits:

- There are no file permission complications, because users have full access to their own home directories.

- If there are a large number of users, you avoid the problems caused by a large number of files in one shared mailbox directory.

- The size of users' mailboxes can be constrained by the system file quota mechanism.

If you want to configure Exim this way, you can use a setting of the `file` option like this:

```
file = /home/$local_part/inbox
```

The disadvantages of this approach are as follows:

*   You may have to modify (or at least recompile) user agents so that they know where to find users' mailboxes.

*   If the home directories are automounted, there will be additional mounts and dismounts, because the home directory has to be mounted each time a new message arrives. On the other hand, if you allow users to have *.forward* files in their home directories, these mounts will occur anyway.

The alternative, and probably more common approach, is to locate all the mailboxes in a single directory, separate from the home directories. The directory is usually called */var/mail* or */var/spool/mail*, and most user agents expect to find mailboxes in one of these directories by default. This scheme works well enough for a moderate number of mailboxes, but when the number becomes large you normally have to find some way of splitting up the directory to avoid performance loss (☞ 4.12).

With all the mailboxes in a single directory, there has to be a way for an Exim delivery process, running as the recipient user, to create a new mailbox if it does not exist, and to be able to write to an existing mailbox.[1] Allowing all users full access to the directory is not the answer, because that would let one user delete another user's mailbox. Unix contains a file permission facility that is intended for just this situation. For historical reasons, it is known as the *sticky bit*. When a directory has this permission set, along with the normal write permission, any user may create a new file in the directory, but files can be deleted only by their owners. The letter t is used to indicate this permission, so a mailbox directory that is set up this way looks like this:

```
drwxrwxrwt   3 root      mail          512 Jul  9 13:48 /var/mail/
```

Exim's local delivery processes, which run using the uid and gid of the receiving user, can now create new mailboxes if necessary. Each mailbox will be owned by the local user, and by default will be accessible only to that user, who can modify it and also delete it.

There are some disadvantages to using "sticky" directories:

*   Users may try to use the directory as extra space to store files that are not mailboxes.

*   When a user's mailbox does not exist, a different user may maliciously create it, hoping to be able to access the first user's mail. This does not work, because Exim checks the ownership of existing files, but it does prevent the first user from receiving mail.

---

[1] Exim may also need to create and remove lock files (☞ 9.4.3).

Installations that find these possibilities unacceptable often adopt a different approach. Instead of using a "sticky" directory, they make use of the group access. The directory's permissions are set as shown here:

```
drwxrwx--x   3 root      mail            512 Jul  9 13:48 /var/mail/
```

The **appendfile** transport is configured to run under the group *mail* instead of the user's group, like this:

```
local_delivery:
  driver = appendfile
  file = /var/mail/$local_part
  group = mail
  mode = 660
```

It still runs with the user's uid, however. With this configuration, Exim can create new mailboxes because of the group write permission. Each mailbox is owned by the relevant user, but its group is set to *mail*. Exim can update an existing mailbox because the mode setting allows group *mail* to write to the file. The user's MUA can access the file as the owner. Nevertheless, there is still a disadvantage: the user cannot delete the file. Some MUAs do try to delete the file when all the messages it contains have been deleted or moved, which may give rise to error messages.

## Symbolic links for mailbox files

By default, **appendfile** will not deliver a message if the pathname for the file is that of a symbolic link. Setting allow_symlink relaxes that constraint, but there are security issues involved in the use of symbolic links. Be sure you know what you are doing if you allow them. The ownership of the link is checked, and the real file is subjected to the checks described below. The check on the top-level link ownership prevents one user from creating a link for another's mailbox in a "sticky" directory, though allowing symbolic links in this case is definitely not a good idea. If there is a chain of symbolic links, the intermediate ones are not checked.

## Delivering to named pipes (FIFOs)

As with symbolic links, **appendfile** will not deliver to a FIFO (named pipe) by default, but can be configured to do so by setting allow_fifo. If no process is reading the named pipe at delivery time, the delivery is deferred.

## Creating a non-existent file

The default action is to try to create the file and any superior directories if they do not exist. Several options give control over this process:

- If file_must_exist is set, an error occurs if the file does not exist. The delivery is deferred and the message is frozen.

- Otherwise, the value of `create_file` is inspected for constraints on where the file may be created. The option can be set to one of the following values:

  - `anywhere` means there is no constraint.

  - `inhome` means that the file may be created only if it is in the home directory.

  - `belowhome` means that the file may be created in the home directory or any directory below the home directory.

  In the second and third cases, a home directory must have been set up for the address by the router that handled it; this is the normal case when user forwarding or filtering is involved. The `create_file` option is not useful when an explicit filename is given for normal mailbox deliveries; it is intended for the case when filenames have been generated by user forwarding or filtering. In addition to this constraint, the file permissions must also permit the file to be created, of course. Remember that a local delivery always runs under some unprivileged uid and gid.

- The `create_directory` option controls whether superior directories may be created. It is true by default, but creation of directories occurs only when creation of the file is also permitted.

**The owner of an existing file**

If a file already exists, checks are made on its ownership and permissions. The owner must be the uid under which the delivery process is running, unless `check_owner` is set false. The uid is either set by the `user` option on the transport, or passed over with the address by the router. For the common cases of delivery into user mailboxes and deliveries to files specified in *.forward* files, the user is normally the local user that corresponds to the local part of the address. If `check_group` is set, the group ownership of the file is also checked. This is not the default, because the default file mode is 0600 (owner read/write only), for which the group is not relevant.

**The mode of the file**

If the delivery is the result of a *save* command in a filter file that specifies a particular mode for the file, a new file is created with that mode, and an existing file is changed to have that mode. Otherwise, if the file is created, its mode is set to the value specified by the `mode` option, which defaults to 0600. If the file already exists and has wider permissions (more bits set) than those specified by `mode`, they are reduced to the value of `mode`. If it has narrower permissions, an error occurs and delivery is deferred unless `mode_fail_narrower` is set false, in which case the delivery is attempted with the existing mode.

## 9.4.2 Format of appended messages

The default way of appending a message to a file is to write the contents of the
message_prefix option, followed by the message, followed by the contents of
message_suffix (☞ 9.3.1). The default values support traditional Berkeley Unix
mailboxes. Other formats that rely on textual separators can be used by changing
message_prefix and message_suffix, as was shown earlier in the MMDF
example (☞ 9.3.1).

### MBX format mailboxes

Another mailbox format that is supported by **appendfile** is MBX, which is requested
by setting mbx_format.[1] This single-file mailbox format is supported by Pine 4 and
its associated IMAP and POP daemons, and is implemented by the c-client library
that they all use.

Additional information about the lengths of messages is stored at the beginning of an
MBX mailbox. This makes it faster to access individual messages. Simultaneous
shared access to MBX mailboxes by different users is also possible. However, a
special form of file locking is required, and mbx_format should not be used if any
program that does not use this form of locking is going to access the mailbox. MBX
locking cannot be used if the mailbox file is NFS-mounted, because this type of
locking works only when the mailbox is accessed from a single host. There is more
discussion of MBX locking later in this chapter.

In order to maintain a mailbox in MBX format, Exim has to write the message to a
temporary file before appending it, so that it can obtain its exact length, including
any header lines that are added during the delivery process. This makes this form of
delivery slightly more expensive.

The message_prefix, message_suffix, and check_string options are
not automatically changed by the use of mbx_format; they should normally be set
empty because MBX format does not rely on the use of message separators. Thus, a
typical **appendfile** transport for MBX delivery might look like this:

```
local_delivery:
  driver = appendfile
  file = /var/mail/$local_part
  delivery_date_add
  envelope_to_add
  return_path_add
  mbx_format
  message_prefix =
  message_suffix =
  check_string =
```

---

[1]  The code for this is not built into Exim by default; it has to be requested in the build-time
configuration.

**Checking an existing file's format**

When Exim is adding a message to an existing mailbox file, the file is assumed to be in the correct format because normally only a single format is used on any one host. Sometimes, however, particularly during a transition from one format to another, files in different formats may coexist. In these situations, **appendfile** can be made to check the format of a file before writing to it, and if necessary, it can pass control to a different transport. For example, suppose that both Berkeley and MBX mailboxes exist on the system. The following could be added to the **local_delivery** transport we have just defined:

```
file_format = "*mbx*\r\n : local_delivery :\
              From     : local_bsd_delivery"
```

The items in a `file_format` list are taken in pairs. The first of each pair is a text string that is compared against the characters at the start of the file. If they match, the second string in the pair is the name of the transport that is to be used. In this example, if the file begins with `*mbx*\r\n`, the **local_delivery** transport is required. As this is the current transport, delivery proceeds. If, however, the file begins with `From`, control is passed to a transport called **local_bsd_delivery**, which might be defined thus:

```
local_bsd_delivery:
   driver = appendfile
   file = /var/mail/$local_part
   delivery_date_add
   envelope_to_add
   return_path_add
```

If the file does not exist or is empty, the format for the first mentioned transport is used, so in this example new files are created in MBX format. If the start of a file does not match any string, or if the transport named for a given string is not defined, delivery is deferred.

## 9.4.3 Locking a file for appending

In most Exim configurations, the parameters for controlling file locking can be left at their default values. Unless you want to understand the nitty-gritty of locking or have a special locking requirement, you can skip this section.

Mailbox files containing multiple messages are modified by both MTAs and MUAs. MTAs add messages, but MUAs can both add and remove messages, though removal is their most common action. When an MTA is updating a file by appending a message, it must ensure that it has exclusive control of the file, so that no other process can attempt to update it at the same time. Because of Exim's distributed nature, it is possible for several deliveries to the same file to be running simultaneously. This means that Exim has to coordinate its own processes, as well as interlocking against any MUAs that may be operating on the file.

Locking in Unix is a purely voluntary action on the part of a process. Its success relies on cooperative behaviour among all the processes that access a shared file. Two different conventions have arisen for locking mailbox files, and because it cannot assume that the MUAs on a system all use the same one, Exim normally obtains both kinds of lock before updating a file.

## Locking using a lock file

The first method of locking is to use a *lock file*. Unix contains a primitive operation that creates a file if it does not exist, or returns an error if it does exist. A process that needs exclusive access to a file called */a/b/c*, for example, attempts to create a file called */a/b/c.lock* by this method.[1] If creation succeeds, the process has ownership of the lock; if creation fails because the file already exists, some other process has the lock, and the first process must wait for a while and then try again. Once a process has finished updating the original file, it deletes the lock file. For this scheme to work, the following conditions must be met:

- All processes must use the same name for the lock file.

- The users running the processes must be able to create a new file (the lock file) in the directory that contains the original file.

There are two main problems with lock files:

- If a process crashes while it holds a lock, the lock file is not deleted. For this reason, most implementations use some kind of timeout to force the deletion of lock files that are too old.

- A process that is waiting for a lock has to wait for a fixed time before retrying; it cannot put itself onto some kind of queue and be automatically woken up when the lock becomes available.

Despite these problems, lock files are important because they are the only reliable way of locking that works over NFS when more than one host is accessing the same NFS file system.

## Using a locking function

The other method of locking operates only on an open file. For historical reasons, there are several different Unix calls for doing this; Exim uses the *fcntl()* function. This method of locking does not suffer from the problems of lock files because:

- No second filename is needed.

- The ability to create a new file is not needed.

---

[1] In practice, to cater for use over NFS, it is not quite as simple as just attempting to create the file, but the principle is the same.

The *fcntl()* function interworks with the *lockf()* function, but not with the older *flock()*. On some recent systems, *flock()* is just a veneer on top of *lockf()*.

- If a process crashes, the files it has open are automatically closed and their locks released.

- A call to lock a file can be queued, so that the lock is obtained as soon as it becomes available.

## Why use lock files?

Why isn't everybody using *fcntl()* locks exclusively, since they seem to be much better than lock files? One reason is history: lock files came first, and some older programs may still not be using anything else. A much more important reason is the widespread use of NFS. When more than one host is accessing the same NFS file system, *fcntl()* locks do not work. The reason is that the size of a file is saved in the NFS client host when the file is opened, so if two processes running on different hosts open a file simultaneously, they both receive the same size. If one then obtains a lock and updates the file while the other waits, the second one will have an incorrect size when it eventually acquires the lock. To update an NFS file safely from different hosts, it is necessary to obtain a lock before opening the file, and lock files provide the only way of doing this.

## Locking options for non-MBX mailboxes

The **appendfile** transport supports both kinds of lock for traditional mailbox formats, as well as a third variety for MBX mailboxes, which we will cover shortly. The default settings are to use both lock files and *fcntl()* locking, to cater for all possible situations, but options are provided for selecting one or the other kind of lock, and for changing some of the locking parameters. The mode of any created lock file is set by `lockfile_mode`.

If `use_lockfile` is set false, lock files are not used, and if `use_fcntl_lock` is set false, locking by *fcntl()* is disabled. Only one kind of locking can be turned off at once, but in most cases you should not do either of these things. You should only contemplate turning one of them off if you are absolutely sure that the remaining locking is sufficient for all programs that access the mailbox.

Various timeouts are used when attempting to lock a mailbox, and their values can be changed if necessary. If an existing lock file is older than `lockfile_timeout`, Exim assumes it has been left behind by accident, and attempts to remove it.

By default, non-blocking calls to *fcntl()* are used. If a call fails, Exim sleeps for `lock_interval`, and then tries again, up to `lock_retries` times. Non-blocking calls are used so that the file is not kept open during the wait for the lock; the reason for this is to make it as safe as possible for NFS deliveries in the case when processes might be accessing an NFS mailbox without using a lock file.[1]

On a busy system, sleeping and retrying does not give such good performance as using a blocking call to *fcntl()* with a timeout. This is particularly relevant when only *fcntl()* locks are in use (for lock files, the only possibility is to sleep and retry). One symptom of a problem with mailbox locking is the frequent appearance of the error message "failed to lock mailbox" in Exim's log. If this message is followed by "(fcntl)", indicating that the problem is with *fcntl()* locking, you should try changing the way *fcntl()* is used, by setting `lock_fcntl_timeout`. When this option is set to a non-zero time, blocking calls with the given timeout are used. There may still be some retrying: the maximum number of retries is computed as:

```
(lock_retries * lock_interval) / lock_fcntl_timeout
```

rounded up to the next whole number. In other words, the total time during which **appendfile** is trying to obtain a lock is roughly the same with blocking or non-blocking calls, unless `lock_fcntl_timeout` is set very high.

## Locking options for MBX mailboxes

When **appendfile** is configured for MBX mailboxes (by setting `mbx_format`), the default locking rules are different. If none of the locking options are mentioned in the configuration, `use_mbx_lock` is assumed, and the other locking options default to false. It is possible to use the other kinds of locking with `mbx_format`, but `use_fcntl_lock` and `use_mbx_lock` are mutually exclusive. MBX locking follows the locking rules of the c-client library.

Exim takes out a shared *fcntl()* lock on the mailbox file, and an exclusive lock on the file whose name is */tmp/.<device-number>.<inode-number>*, where the device and inode numbers are those of the mailbox file. The shared lock on the mailbox stops any other MBX client from acquiring an exclusive lock on it and expunging it (removing messages). The exclusive lock on the */tmp* file prevents any other MBX client from updating the mailbox in any way. When writing is finished, if an exclusive lock on the mailbox itself can be obtained, indicating there are no current sharers, the */tmp* file is unlinked (deleted). Otherwise it is left, because one of the other sharers might be waiting to lock it. The *fcntl()* calls for obtaining these locks are non-blocking by default, but can be made to block by setting the `lock_fcntl_timeout` option.

---

[1]  This should not be done, but accidents do happen, and an inexperienced administrator might end up with such a configuration.

MBX locking interoperates correctly with the c-client library, providing for shared access to the mailbox. It should not be used if any program that does not use this form of locking is going to access the mailbox, nor should it be used if the mailbox file is NFS-mounted, because it works only when the mailbox is accessed from a single host.

If you set `use_fcntl_lock` with an MBX-format mailbox, you cannot use an MUA that uses the standard version of the c-client library, because as long as it has a mailbox open (this means for the whole of a Pine or IMAP session, for example), Exim is unable to append messages to it.

## 9.4.4 Delivering each message into a separate file

So far, we have been considering cases where a mailbox consists of a single file and new messages are delivered by appending. This is by far the most common type of configuration, but there is an alternative, which is to deliver each message into a separate new file. The mailbox then consists of an entire directory, with each message in its own file. There are advantages and disadvantages to this approach. The advantages are as follows:

- No locking by the MTA is required when delivering. A consequence of this is that more than one message can be delivered into the mailbox simultaneously, which is beneficial on very busy systems.

- Deleting messages is easy and quick, since it does not require any rewriting, and it is not necessary to hold up new deliveries while it happens.

- Incomplete deliveries (which can arise as a result of a system failure, for example) can be handled better.

- The problems concerning message separators that arise in single-file mailboxes are all bypassed.

The disadvantages are as follows:

- If a mailbox contains a large number of messages, the number of files in the directory may impact performance.[1]

- Most common MUAs support only the single-file type of mailbox.

As a consequence of the last point, systems that use this kind of delivery for local mailboxes are usually those where access to the mailboxes is carefully controlled, for example, by providing only POP or IMAP access.[2] However, delivery into separate files is also commonly used in an entirely separate situation: when messages are being stored temporarily for a dial-up host (☞ 12.12).

---

[1]   Different operating systems, and indeed different filesystems, have different thresholds beyond which performance degrades.

[2]   The POP and IMAP daemons that are used must, of course, be able to handle multifile mailboxes.

The **appendfile** transport can be configured to deliver each message into a separate file by replacing the `file` option with the `directory` option. The setting of `create_directory` determines whether the directory may be created if it does not exist, and if it is created, `directory_mode` specifies its mode. The data that is written is identical to the single-file mailbox case; in particular, `message_prefix` and `message_suffix` data is written if configured, and `check_string` is respected. Normally, these features are not required when each message is in its own file, so the default values for these options are unset when `directory` is set.

Three different separate-file formats are available, but only the most commonly used one is discussed here, because the others are not widely used.

## 9.4.5 Maildir format

One separate-file delivery mode for local mailboxes that is gaining general acceptance (not just with Exim) is called *maildir*. This is more complicated than just delivering into individual files, and it operates as follows:

* Within the designated directory, three subdirectories called *tmp*, *new*, and *cur* are created.

* A message is delivered by writing it to a new file in *tmp*, and then renaming it into the *new* directory. The filename usually includes the host name, the time, and the process ID, but the only requirement is that it be unique.

* Once a mail-reading program has seen a new message in *new*, it normally moves it to *cur*. This reduces the number of files it has to inspect when it starts up.

Files in the *tmp* directory that are older than, say, 36 hours should be deleted; they represent delivery attempts that failed to complete.

Exim delivers in maildir format if the `maildir_format` option is set. This is a typical configuration:

```
maildir_delivery:
  driver = appendfile
  directory = /home/$local_part/maildir
  maildir_format
  delivery_date_add
  envelope_to_add
  return_path_add
```

The presence of `directory` rather than `file` specifies one file per message, and `maildir_format` specifies that the maildir rules should be followed. Messages delivered by this transport end up in files with names such as:

```
/home/caesar/maildir/new/955429480.9324.host.example
```

An additional string can be added to the name by setting `maildir_tag`. The contents of this option are expanded and added to the filename when the file is moved into the *new* directory. The tag may contain any printing characters except a forward slash; if it starts with an alphanumeric character, a leading colon is inserted. By this time, the file has been written to the *tmp* directory (using just the basic name) and so its exact size is known. This value is made available in the *$message_size* variable. An example of how this can be used is described in the next section.

The filename used in maildir delivery should always be unique; however, in the unlikely case that such a file already exists, or if it fails to create the file, Exim waits for two seconds, and tries again with a new filename. The number of retries is controlled by the `maildir_retries` option (default 10). If this is exceeded, delivery is deferred.

## 9.4.6 Mailbox quotas

If a system disk quota is exceeded while **appendfile** is writing to a file, the delivery is aborted and tried again later. A quota error is detectable by the retry rules (see chapter 12), so the configuration file can specify special handling of these errors if necessary. After a quota error, **appendfile** does its best to clean up a partial delivery. Any temporary files are deleted, and if **appendfile** is appending to a mailbox file, it resets the length and the time of last access to what they were before.

In some configurations, it may not be possible to make use of system quotas. To allow the sizes of mailboxes to be controlled in these cases, **appendfile** has its own quota mechanism.[1] The `quota` option imposes a limit on the size of the file to which Exim is appending, or to the total space used in the directory tree if the `directory` option is set. In the latter case, computation of the space used is expensive, because all the files in the directory (and any subdirectories) have to be individually inspected and their sizes added up.[2] Also, there is no interlock against two simultaneous deliveries. It is preferable to use the operating system's quota mechanism if you can.

The cost of adding up the sizes of individual files can be lessened on systems where maildir delivery is in use and the users have no direct access to the files. Setting the option:

```
maildir_tag = ,S=$message_size
```

causes the size of each message to be added to its name, leading to message files with names such as:

```
/home/caesar/maildir/new/955429480.9324.host.example,S=3265
```

---

[1]   Of course, if system quotas are also in force, you cannot specify a quota that exceeds a system quota.

[2]   This is done using the system's *stat()* function.

When Exim needs to find the size of a file, it first checks `quota_size_regex`. This should be set to a regular expression that matches the filename. If it captures one string (by means of a parenthesized subexpression), that string is interpreted as a representation of the file's size. For example:

```
quota_size_regex = S=(\d+)$
```

could be used with the `maildir_tag` just shown. This approach is not safe if the users have any kind of access that permits them to rename the files, but in environments where this is not the case, it saves having to run *stat()* for each file, which is of considerable benefit. The value of `quota_size_regex` is not expanded.

The value of the `quota` option itself is expanded, and the result must be a numerical value (decimal point allowed), optionally followed by one of the letters K or M. Thus, this sets a fixed quota of 10 MB for all users:

```
quota = 10M
```

The expansion happens while Exim is running as root, before it changes uid and gid in order to run the delivery, so files or databases that are inaccessible to the end user can be used to hold quota values that are looked up in the expansion. For example:

```
quota = ${lookup pgsql {select quota from users \
        where id='${quote_pgsql:$local_part}'}{$value}{500K}}
```

When delivery fails because an Exim quota is exceeded, the handling of the error is exactly as for system quota failures, and so it can be subject to special retry rules. The value specified is not accurate to the last byte, because the check is done before actually delivering the message. During delivery, separator lines and additional header lines may be added, thereby increasing the message's size by a small amount.

When messages are being delivered into individual files, the total number of files in the directory can also be controlled by setting the value of `quota_filecount` greater than zero. This can be used only if `quota` is also set.

## 9.4.7 Inclusive and exclusive quotas

As described so far, Exim's quota system operates in a similar way to system disk quotas: it prevents the mailbox from ever exceeding a certain size. This means that when a mailbox is nearly full, it may be possible to deliver small messages into it, but not large ones. Some administrators do not like this way of working; they would rather have a hard cutoff of all mail delivery when a quota is reached. The `quota_is_inclusive` option provides a way of changing Exim's behaviour. By default it is set to true, which retains the default behaviour. If you change the default by setting:

```
quota_is_inclusive = false
```

the check for exceeding the quota does not include the current message. Thus, deliveries continue until the quota has been exceeded; thereafter, no further messages are delivered.

## 9.4.8 Quota warnings

Users are often unaware of how large their mailboxes are becoming, particularly when attachments are involved. In the case of a single file, allowing a mailbox to exceed a few megabytes often causes the user's MUA to run slowly when initializing or when removing messages. This effect is often incorrectly reported as a slow-running system. The **appendfile** transport can be configured to send a warning message when the size of a mailbox crosses a given threshold. It does this only once, because repeating such a warning for mailboxes that are above the threshold would only exacerbate the problem.

The quota_warn_threshold option is expanded in the same way as quota. If the resulting value is greater than zero, and a successful delivery of the current message causes the size of the file or total space in the directory tree to cross the given threshold, a warning message is sent. It is not necessary to set quota in order to use this option,[1] but if quota is set, the threshold may be specified as a percentage by following the value with a percent sign. For example:

```
quota = 10M
quota_warn_threshold = 75%
```

The warning message itself is specified by the quota_warn_message option, which must start with a *To:* header line containing the recipient(s). A *Subject:* line should also normally be supplied. The default is:

```
quota_warn_message = \
   To: $local_part@$domain\n\
   Subject: Your mailbox\n\
   \n\
   This message is automatically created by mail delivery\
   software.\n\n\
   The size of your mailbox has exceeded a warning threshold that\n\
   is set by the system administrator.\n
```

## 9.4.9 Notifying comsat

*comsat* is a server process that listens for reports of incoming mail and notifies logged-on users who have requested to be told when mail arrives. It does this by writing "You have mail" messages to their terminals. If notify_comsat is set, **appendfile** informs *comsat* when a successful delivery has been made.

---

[1] It can therefore be used with system quotas.

## 9.4.10 Summary of appendfile options

The options that are specific to the **appendfile** transport are summarized in this section. Other options that can be set for **appendfile** are described earlier (☞ 9.2, 9.3). Of course, any generic transport option (☞ 8.11) may also be set for **appendfile**.

allow_fifo (Boolean, default = false)
 If you want to deliver messages to FIFOs (named pipes), you must set this option to true, because **appendfile** will not deliver to a FIFO by default. If no process is reading the named pipe at delivery time, the delivery is deferred.

allow_symlink (Boolean, default = false)
 If you want to deliver messages to files using symbolic links, you must set this option true, because **appendfile** will not deliver to such files by default.

check_group (Boolean, default = false)
 The group owner of the file is checked to see that it is the same as the group under which the delivery process is running when this option is set. The default setting is unset because the default file mode is 0600, which means that the group is irrelevant.

check_owner (Boolean, default = true)
 If this option is turned off, the ownership of an existing mailbox file is not checked.

create_directory (Boolean, default = true)
 When this option is true, Exim creates any missing parent directories for the file that it is about to write. A created directory's mode is given by the directory_mode option.

create_file (string, default = anywhere)
 This option constrains the location of files that are created by the transport. It must be set to one of the value anywhere, inhome, or belowhome.

directory (string, default = unset)
 This option is mutually exclusive with the file option. When it is set, the string is expanded, and the message is delivered into a new file or files in or below the given directory, instead of being appended to a single mailbox file.

directory_mode (octal integer, default = 0700)
 If **appendfile** creates any directories as a result of the create_directory option, the mode is specified by this option.

file (string, default = unset)
 This option is mutually exclusive with the directory option. It need not be set when **appendfile** is being used to deliver to files whose names are obtained from forwarding, filtering, or aliasing address expansions, since in those cases the

filename is associated with the address. Otherwise, either the `file` option or the `directory` option must be set.

`file_format` (string, default = unset)

This option requests the transport to check the format of an existing file before adding to it. The check consists of matching a specific string at the start of the file.

`file_must_exist` (Boolean, default = false)

If this option is true, the file specified by the `file` option must exist, and an error occurs if it does not. Otherwise, it is created if it does not exist.

`lock_fcntl_timeout` (time, default = 0s)

If this option is set to a non-zero time, blocking calls to *fcntl()* with that timeout are used to lock mailbox files. Otherwise, non-blocking calls with sleeps and retries are used.

`lock_interval` (time, default = 3s)

This specifies the time to wait between attempts to lock the file.

`lock_retries` (integer, default = 10)

This specifies the maximum number of attempts to lock the file. A value of zero is treated as 1.

`lockfile_mode` (octal integer, default = 0600)

This specifies the mode of the created lock file, when a lock file is being used.

`lockfile_timeout` (time, default = 30m)

When a lock file is being used, if a lock file already exists and is older than this value, it is assumed to have been left behind by accident, and Exim attempts to remove it.

`maildir_format` (Boolean, default = false)

If this option is set with the `directory` option, delivery is into a new file in the maildir format that is used by some other mail software.

`maildir_retries` (integer, default = 10)

This option specifies the number of times to retry when writing a file in maildir format.

`maildir_tag` (string, default = unset)

This option applies only to deliveries in maildir format. It is expanded and added onto the names of newly delivered message files.

`mbx_format` (Boolean, default = false)

If `mbx_format` is set with the `file` option, the message is appended to the mailbox file in MBX format instead of traditional Berkeley Unix format. If none of the locking options are mentioned in the configuration, `use_mbx_lock` is assumed and the other locking options default to false.

`mode` (octal integer, default = 0600)
If a mailbox file is created, it is given this mode. If it already exists and has wider permissions, they are reduced to this mode. If it has narrower permissions, an error occurs unless `mode_fail_narrower` is false. However, if the delivery is the result of a `save` command in a filter file specifying a particular mode, the mode of the output file is always forced to take that value, and this option is ignored.

`mode_fail_narrower` (Boolean, default = true)
This option applies when an existing mailbox file has a narrower mode than that specified by the `mode` option. If `mode_fail_narrower` is true, the delivery is deferred ("mailbox has the wrong mode"); otherwise Exim continues with the delivery attempt, using the existing mode of the file.

`notify_comsat` (Boolean, default = false)
If this option is true, the *comsat* daemon is notified after every successful delivery to a user mailbox. This is the daemon that notifies logged-on users about incoming mail.

`quota` (string, default = unset)
This option imposes a limit on the size of the file to which Exim is appending, or to the total space used in the directory tree if the `directory` option is set. After expansion, the string must be numeric, optionally followed by K or M.

`quota_filecount` (integer, default = 0)
This option applies when the `directory` option is set. It limits the total number of files in the directory (like the inode limit in system quotas). It can only be used if `quota` is also set. A value of zero specifies no limit.

`quota_is_inclusive` (Boolean, default = true)
This option controls whether the current message is included when checking whether a mailbox has exceeded its quota. If the value is false, the check does not include the current message. In this case, deliveries continue until the quota has been exceeded; thereafter, no further messages are delivered.

`quota_size_regex` (string, default = unset)
This option is used when Exim is computing the amount of space used in a directory by adding up the sizes of all the message files therein. It is not expanded, but is interpreted as a regular expression that is applied to every file name. If it matches and captures one string, that string is interpreted as a textual representation of the file's size.

`quota_warn_message` (string, default = see description)

This string is expanded and inserted at the start of warning messages that are generated as a result of the `quota_warn_threshold` setting. It should start with a *To:* header line that defines the recipient of the message.

`quota_warn_threshold` (string, default = 0)

This option is expanded in the same way as `quota`. If the resulting value is greater than zero, and delivery of the message causes the size of the file or total space in the directory tree to cross the given threshold, a warning message is sent. The content and recipients of the message are defined by `quota_warn_message`. If `quota` is also set, the threshold may be specified as a percentage of it by following the value with a percent sign.

`use_fcntl_lock` (Boolean, default = true)

This option controls the use of the *fcntl()* function to lock a file for exclusive use when a message is being appended.

`use_lockfile` (Boolean, default = true)

If this option is turned off, Exim does not attempt to create a lock file when appending to a file.

`use_mbx_lock` (Boolean, default = see description)

Setting this option specifies that special MBX locking rules are to be used. It is set by default if `mbx_format` is set and none of the locking options are mentioned in the configuration. The locking rules are the same as are used by the c-client library that underlies Pine4 and the IMAP4 and POP daemons that come with it. The rules allow for shared access to the mailbox. However, this kind of locking does not work when the mailbox is NFS-mounted.

# 9.5 The pipe transport

The **pipe** transport delivers a message by creating a pipe and a new process that runs a given program. The message is written to the pipe by the transport, and read from the other end of the pipe by the external program. There are many common uses for this mechanism. For example:

- An individual user can set up a pipe delivery from a *.forward* file in order to process incoming messages automatically, perhaps to sort them into different folders or to generate automatic replies.[1]

- Messages addressed to mailing lists can be piped to a list handling program such as Majordomo or Listman.

---

[1]  Some of this functionality is also available in Exim filter files.

- Messages addressed to domains reached by other transport mechanisms (such as UUCP) can be piped to programs that implement such transports.

- Local deliveries can be done by passing messages to an external local delivery agent (such as *procmail*), instead of using **appendfile**.

## 9.5.1 Defining the command to run

When a pipe is set up by aliasing or forwarding, or from a filter file, the command to run is defined by that mechanism. For example, an alias file could contain the line:

```
majordomo: |/usr/local/mail/majordomo
```

which causes messages addressed to the local part *majordomo* to be passed to a process running the command */usr/local/mail/majordomo*. As another example, a user's filter file could contain the command:

```
pipe /usr/bin/vacation
```

which passes the message to */usr/bin/vacation*. A suitable transport for use in these cases is the one in the default configuration:

```
address_pipe:
  transport = pipe
  ignore_status
  return_output
```

where no command is specified, because the command comes with the address that is being delivered (the other options are explained later in this chapter).

If the command name is not an absolute path, Exim looks for it in the directories listed by the colon-separated `path` option, whose default setting is:

```
path = /usr/bin
```

Thus, the filter example could actually be given as:

```
pipe vacation
```

If a router passes a message to a **pipe** transport directly, without involving aliasing or forwarding, the command is specified by the `command` option on the transport itself. For example, if you want your host to do all local deliveries using *procmail*, you can set up a transport like this:

```
procmail_pipe:
  driver = pipe
  command = /opt/local/bin/procmail -d $local_part
  return_path_add
  delivery_date_add
  envelope_to_add
  check_string = "From "
  escape_string = ">From "
  group = mail
```

The router for accepting addresses for this transport might look like this:

```
procmail:
  driver = accept
  check_local_user
  transport = procmail_pipe
```

In this example, the pipe is run as the local user, but with the group set to *mail*. An alternative is to run the pipe as a specific user such as *mail* or *exim*. However, in this case you must arrange for *procmail* to trust that user to supply a correct sender address. If you do not specify either a `group` or a `user` option, the pipe command is run as the local user. The home directory is the user's home directory by default.

## 9.5.2 The uid and gid for the command

The process that **pipe** sets up for its command runs under the same uid and gid as the **pipe** transport itself. As is the case for any local delivery, this user and group can be specified by the `user` and `group` options, either on the transport or on the router that calls it, or they can be taken from a local user's password data by a router that has `check_local_user` set.

## 9.5.3 Running the command

Exim does not by default run the command for a **pipe** transport under a shell. This has two benefits:

- The additional cost of a shell process is avoided.

- Characters inserted into the command from the incoming message cannot be misinterpreted as shell metacharacters.

In the documentation for programs that expect to be run from an MTA via a pipe (for example, *procmail*), you often find a recommendation to place:

```
IFS=" "
```

at the start of the command. This assumes that the command will be run under a shell, and it is ensuring that the `IFS` shell variable (which defines the argument separator) is set to a space. When using the **pipe** transport in its default mode (that is, without using a shell), not only is this setting not required, but it will cause the command to fail, because no shell is used.

### Parsing the command line

String expansion is applied to the command line except when it comes from a traditional *.forward* file (commands from a filter file are expanded). However, before the expansion is done, the command line is broken down into a command name and a list of arguments. Unquoted arguments are delimited by whitespace. If an argument contains whitespace, it must be enclosed in either single or double quotes. In double-quoted arguments, a backslash is interpreted as an escape character in the usual way. This does not happen for single-quoted arguments.

The string expansion is applied to the command name, and to each argument in turn rather than to the whole line. Because the command name and arguments are identified before expansion, any expansion item that contains whitespace must be quoted, so as to be contained within a single argument. A setting such as:

```
command = /some/path ${if eq{$local_part}{ab123}{xxx}{yyy}}
```

will not work, because it is split into the three items:

```
/some/path
${if
eq{$local_part}{ab123}{xxx}{yyy}}
```

and the second and third are not valid expansion items. You have to write:

```
command = /some/path "${if eq{$local_part}{ab123}{xxx}{yyy}}"
```

to ensure that the expansion is all in one argument. The expansion is done in this way, argument by argument, so that the number of arguments cannot be changed as a result of expansion, and quotes or backslashes in inserted variables do not interact with external quoting.

Special handling takes place when an argument consists precisely of the text $pipe_addresses. This is not a general expansion variable; the only place this string is recognized is when it appears as an argument for a pipe or transport filter command. It causes each address that is being handled to be inserted in the argument list *as a separate argument*. This makes it easy for the command to process the individual addresses, and avoids any problems with spaces or shell metacharacters. It is of use when a **pipe** transport is handling groups of addresses in a batch (☞ 9.2).

### Using a shell

If a shell is needed in order to run the command, it can of course be explicitly specified as part of the command. There are also circumstances where existing commands (for example, in existing *.forward* files) expect to be run under a shell and cannot easily be modified. To allow for these cases, there is an option called use_shell, which changes the way the **pipe** transport works. Instead of breaking up the command line as just described, it expands it as a single string and passes the result to */bin/sh*. This mechanism is inherently less secure, and in addition uses an extra process.

## 9.5.4 The command environment

The message that is being delivered is supplied to the command on its standard input stream, and the standard output and standard error streams are both connected to a single pipe that is read by Exim. The handling of output is described later in this section. The environment variables that are set up when the command is invoked are shown in table 9-1.

*Table 9-1: Environment variables for pipe commands*

| Environment variable | Contents |
|---|---|
| DOMAIN | The domain of the address |
| HOME | The "home" directory |
| HOST | The host name if supplied by the router |
| LOCAL_PART | See the description later in this section |
| LOCAL_PART_PREFIX | See the description later in this section |
| LOCAL_PART_SUFFIX | See the description later in this section |
| LOGNAME | See the description later in this section |
| MESSAGE_ID | The message's ID |
| PATH | As specified by the path option |
| QUALIFY_DOMAIN | The configured qualification domain |
| RECIPIENT | The complete recipient address |
| SENDER | The sender of the message (empty if a bounce) |
| SHELL | /bin/sh |
| TZ | The value of the timezone option, if set |
| USER | See the description later in this section |

The environment option can be used to add additional variables to this environment; its value is a colon-separated list of <name>=<value> settings, for example:

```
environment = SENDER_HOST=$sender_host_address
```

When more than one address is being processed by a single run of the **pipe** transport (as a consequence of batch_max being set greater than one), the variables that depend on the local part are not set, and DOMAIN is set only if all the addresses have the same domain.

In the case of a single recipient address, LOCAL_PART is set to the local part of the address with any prefix or suffix removed. The affixes are placed in LOCAL_PART_PREFIX and LOCAL_PART_SUFFIX, respectively. LOGNAME and USER are set to the same value as LOCAL_PART for compatibility with other MTAs. The RECIPIENT variable contains the complete address, including the local part affixes and the domain.

HOST is set only when a **pipe** transport is called from a router that supplies a host name (for example, when handling batched SMTP).

If the transport's `home_directory` option is set, its value is used for the HOME environment variable. Otherwise, any value that was set by the router (☞ 6.3.4) is used.

The file creation mask (umask) setting in the pipe process is taken from the value of the `umask` option, which defaults to the value 022. This value means that any files that the process creates do not have the group- or world-writable permission bits set.

## 9.5.5 Timing the command

A default timeout of one hour is imposed on the process that runs the command. If the command fails to complete within this time, it is killed. This normally causes the delivery to fail. The value of the timeout can be changed by the `timeout` option. A zero time interval specifies no timeout, but this is not recommended. In order to ensure that any further processes created by the command are also killed, Exim makes the initial process a process group leader, and kills the whole process group on a timeout. However, this action is undermined if any of the processes starts a new process group.

## 9.5.6 Restricting which commands can be run

When users are permitted to set up pipe commands from forward or filter files, you may want to restrict which commands they may specify. The `allow_commands` and `restrict_to_path` options provide two different ways of doing this. If neither are set, there is no restriction on which commands may be executed; otherwise, only commands that are permitted by one or other of these options are allowed.

The `allow_commands` value is expanded, and then interpreted as a colon-separated list of permitted command names. They need not be absolute paths; the `path` option is used to resolve relative paths. If `restrict_to_path` is set, any command name not listed in `allow_commands` must contain no slashes (that is, it must be a simple command name); it is searched for only in the directories listed in the `path` option. For example, consider this setting:

```
allow_commands = /usr/ucb/vacation
```

If `restrict_to_path` is not set, the only permitted command is */usr/ucb /vacation*. If, however, the configuration is:

```
allow_commands = /usr/ucb/vacation
path = /usr/local/bin
restrict_to_path
```

then in addition to */usr/ucb/vacation*, any command from */usr/local/bin* may be specified.

Enforcing the restrictions specified by `allow_commands` and `restrict_to_` `path` can be done only when the command is run directly from the **pipe** transport, without an intervening shell. Consequently, these options may not be set if `use_shell` is set.

## 9.5.7 Handling command errors

If `ignore_status` is true, the status (exit code) returned by the process that runs the command is ignored, and Exim always behaves as if zero (success) had been returned. If `ignore_status` is false (the default value), the status returned by the process can indicate a temporary or a permanent failure.

Temporary failures are the values listed in the `temp_errors` option. This contains a colon-separated list of numbers or an asterisk, meaning "all errors". The default list contains the values of the errors `EX_TEMPFAIL` and `EX_CANTCREAT`, which are commonly defined in *usr/include/sysexits.h*. After one of these errors, Exim defers delivery and tries again later.

Any other status value is treated as a permanent error, and the address is bounced. Failure to execute the command in a **pipe** transport is by default treated as a permanent failure. The most common causes of this are non-existent commands and commands that cannot be accessed because of their permission settings. However, if `freeze_exec_fail` is set, failure to execute is treated specially, and causes the message to be frozen, whatever the setting of `ignore_status`.

## 9.5.8 Handling output from the command

Anything that the command writes to its standard error or standard output streams is "caught" by Exim. The maximum amount of output that the command may produce is limited by `max_output` (default 20 KB), as a guard against runaway programs. If the limit is exceeded, the process running the command is killed. This normally causes a delivery failure. Because of buffering effects, the amount of output may exceed the limit by a small amount before Exim notices.

You can control what happens to the output by setting a number of options. Three options set conditions under which the first line of any output is written to Exim's main log:

```
log_defer_output    log if delivery deferred
log_fail_output     log if delivery failed
log_output          log always
```

The output is converted to a single string of printing characters before being written to the log, using escape character sequences as necessary, in order not to disturb the layout of the log.

You can also arrange for the output to be returned to the sender of the message as part of a delivery failure report. If you set `return_output` true, the production of any output whatsoever is treated as constituting a delivery failure, independently of the return code from the command. The `return_fail_output` option operates in the same way, but applies only when the command process returns a non-temporary error code (that is, the return code is non-zero and is not one of those listed in `temp_errors`).

The `return_output` and `return_fail_output` options apply only when the message has a non-empty sender (that is, when it is not itself a bounce message). If neither of them is set, the output is discarded (after optional logging). However, even in this configuration, if the amount of output exceeds `max_output`, the command is killed on the grounds that is it probably misbehaving.

## 9.5.9 Summary of pipe options

The options that are specific to the **pipe** transport are summarized in this section. Other options that can be set for **pipe** are described earlier (☞ 9.2, 9.3). Of course, any generic transport option (☞ 8.11) may also be set for **pipe**.

`allow_commands`  (string, default = unset)
   The string is expanded, and then is interpreted as a colon-separated list of permitted commands. If `restrict_to_path` is not set, the only commands permitted are those in the `allow_commands` list. They need not be absolute paths; the `path` option is used for relative paths.

`command`  (string, default = unset)
   This option need not be set when **pipe** is being used to deliver to pipes obtained from address expansions (usually under the instance name **address_pipe**). In other cases, the option must be set, to provide a command to run. It need not yield an absolute path (see the `path` option).

`environment`  (string, default = unset)
   This option is used to add additional variables to the environment in which the command runs. Its value is a string that is expanded, and then interpreted as a colon-separated list of environment settings of the form *<name>=<value>*.

`freeze_exec_fail`  (Boolean, default = false)
   Failure to execute the command in a **pipe** transport is by default treated like any other failure while running the command. However, if `freeze_exec_fail` is set, failure to execute is treated specially, and causes the message to be frozen, whatever the setting of `ignore_status`.

`ignore_status`  (Boolean, default = false)
   If this option is true, the status returned by the process that is set up to run the command is ignored, and Exim behaves as if zero had been returned.

`log_defer_output` (Boolean, default = false)

If this option is set and the status returned by the command is one of those listed in `temp_errors`, and any output was produced, the first line of it is written to the main log.

`log_fail_output` (Boolean, default = false)

If this option is set, and the command terminates with a return code that is neither zero nor one of those listed in `temp_errors`, the first line of any output is written to the main log.

`log_output` (Boolean, default = false)

If this option is set and the command returns any output, the first line of output is written to the main log, whatever the return code.

`max_output` (integer, default = 20K)

This specifies the maximum amount of output that the command may produce on its standard output and standard error file combined. If the limit is exceeded, the process running the command is killed.

`path` (string list, default = `/usr/bin`)

This option specifies the string that is set up in the `PATH` environment variable of the subprocess. If the `command` option does not yield an absolute pathname, the command is sought in the `PATH` directories.

`restrict_to_path` (Boolean, default = false)

When this option is set, any command name not listed in `allow_commands` must contain no slashes. The command is sought only in the directories listed in the `path` option.

`return_fail_output` (Boolean, default = false)

If this option is true, and the command terminates with a return code other than zero or one of those listed in `temp_errors`, any output is returned in the delivery error message. However, if the message has no sender (that is, it is a bounce message), output from the command is discarded.

`return_output` (Boolean, default = false)

If this option is true, and the command produces any output, the delivery is deemed to have failed whatever the return code from the command, and the output is returned in the bounce message. Otherwise, the output is just discarded. However, if the message has no sender (that is, it is itself a bounce message), output from the command is always discarded, whatever the setting of this option.

`temp_errors` (string, default = see description)

This option contains a colon-separated list of numbers. If `ignore_status` is false and the command exits with a return code that matches one of the numbers, the failure is treated as temporary and the delivery is deferred. The default setting contains the codes defined by `EX_TEMPFAIL` and `EX_CANTCREAT` in *sysexits.h*.

If Exim is compiled on a system that does not define these macros, it assumes values of 75 and 73, respectively.

`timeout` (time, default = 1h)
   If the command fails to complete within this time, it is killed. This normally causes the delivery to fail. A zero time interval specifies no timeout.

`umask` (octal integer, default = 022)
   This specifies the umask setting for the process that runs the command.

`use_shell` (Boolean, default = false)
   If this option is set, it causes the command to be passed to */bin/sh* instead of being run directly from the transport. This is less secure, but is needed in some situations where the command is expected to be run under a shell and cannot easily be modified. You cannot make use of the `allow_commands` and `restrict_ to_path` options, or the *$pipe_addresses* facility if you set the `use_shell` option to be true. The command is expanded as a single string, and handed to */bin/sh* as data for its `-c` option.

# 9.6 The lmtp transport

When an installation supports a very large number of accounts, keeping individual mailboxes as separate files or directories is no longer feasible because of the problems of scale. One solution to this problem is to use an independent *message store*, which is a software product for managing mailboxes. It provides interfaces for adding, reading, and deleting messages, but how they are stored internally is not defined, and the mailboxes cannot be accessed as regular files. One such product is the Cyrus IMAP server.[1]

When an MTA delivers a message to a message store of this type, it has to pass over the envelope just as it does when delivering to a remote host, and the existing SMTP protocol seems like a good candidate for a means of doing this. However, for messages with multiple recipients, there are some technical problems in using SMTP in this way, which led to the definition of a new protocol called LMTP.[2] This is very similar to SMTP, and Exim's **smtp** transport has an option for using LMTP instead of SMTP over a TCP/IP connection (☞ 9.1.7).

LMTP is also intended for communication between two processes running on the same host, and this is where the **lmtp** transport comes in.[3] It is in effect a cross between the **pipe** and **smtp** transports, with the additional ability to access a Unix

---

[1]   See *http://asg.web.cmu.edu/cyrus*.

[2]   If you are interested in the detailed arguments, read RFC 2033, which defines LMTP.

[3]   Because LMTP is not required in the majority of installations, the code for the **lmtp** transport is not included in Exim unless specially requested at build time.

domain socket. When it is used like **pipe**, it runs a command in a new process and sends the message to it, but instead of just writing the message down the pipe, it interacts with the command, using the LMTP protocol. Here is an example of a typical **lmtp** transport that uses a command in this way:

```
local_lmtp:
  driver = lmtp
  command = /some/local/lmtp/delivery/program
  batch_max = 20
  user = exim
```

This delivers up to 20 addresses at time, in a mixture of domains if necessary, running as the user *exim*.

The **lmtp** transport has only three options of its own: command, timeout, and socket. The first two operate in exactly the same way as the **pipe** options of the same names, so the discussion is not repeated here.

The socket option is mutually exclusive with command. It specifies the path of a Unix domain socket that is to be used for the LMTP conversation, instead of running a command.

Since the whole point of LMTP is to be able to pass a single copy of a message with more than one recipient, batch_max should normally be set to a value other than the default. As for other local transports, if user or group is not set, values must be set up by the router that passes addresses to this transport.

# 9.7 The autoreply transport

The **autoreply** transport is not a true transport in that it does not cause the message to be delivered in the usual sense. Instead, it generates another, new mail message. However, the original message can be included in the generated message.

This transport is commonly run as the result of mail filtering, where sending a "vacation" message is a common example. What the user wants to do is to send an automatic response to incoming mail, saying that he or she is away and therefore will not be able to read the mail for a while. In the next chapter, we go into mail filtering in depth, but here is an extract from a filter file that does this job:

```
if personal and not error_message then
  mail
  to $reply_address
  subject "Re: $h_subject"
  text "I'm away this week, but I'll get back to you asap."
endif
```

When activated from a user's filter file like this, **autoreply** runs under the uid and gid of the local user, with appropriate current and home directories.

In an attempt to reduce the possibility of message cascades, messages created by the **autoreply** transport always take the form of delivery error (bounce) messages. That is, the envelope sender field is empty. This should stop hosts that receive them from generating new automatic responses in turn.

There is a subtle difference between routing a message to a **pipe** transport that generates some text to be returned to the sender, and routing it to an **autoreply** transport. This difference is noticeable only if more than one address from the same message is so handled. In the case of a **pipe**, the separate outputs from the different addresses are gathered up and returned to the sender in a single message, whereas if **autoreply** is used, a separate message is generated for each address that is passed to it.

If any of the generic options for manipulating headers (for example, `headers_add`) are set on an **autoreply** transport, they apply only to the copy of the original message that is included in the generated message when `return_message` is set. They do not apply to the generated message itself, and are therefore not really useful.

Having no recipients for the message that an **autoreply** transport generates is not treated as an error. The message is just discarded. This means that autoreplies that are addressed to *$sender_address* when this is empty (because the incoming message is a bounce message) do not cause problems.

## 9.7.1 The parameters of the message

There are two possible sources of the data for constructing the new message: the incoming address and the options of the transport. When a user's filter file contains a *mail* or *vacation* command, all the data from the command (recipients, header lines, body) is attached to the address that is passed to the **autoreply** transport. In this case, the transport's options are ignored.

On the other hand, when the transport is activated directly by a router (that is, not from a filter file), the data for the message is taken from the transport's options. In other words, the options in the transport's configuration are used only when it receives an address that does not contain any reply information of its own. Thus, the message is specified entirely by the filter file or entirely by the transport; it is never built from a mixture of data.

When the data has not come from a filter command, the transport options that specify the message are as follows:

`bcc, cc, to`

These options specify recipients and the corresponding header lines.

`from`

> This option specifies the *From:* header line; if this does not correspond to the user running the transport, a *Sender:* header is added by Exim by default, but this behaviour can be changed by setting the `local_from_check` and `local_from_prefix` options (☞ 20.2.1).

`reply_to`

> This option specifies the *Reply-To:* header line. Note that the option name contains an underscore, not a hyphen.

`subject`

> This option specifies the *Subject:* header line.

`text`

> This option specifies a short text to appear at the start of the body.

`file`

> This option specifies a file whose contents form the body of the message. If `file_optional` is set, no error is generated if the file does not exist or cannot be read. If `file_expand` is set, the contents of the file are passed through the string expander, line by line, as they are added to the message. This makes it possible to vary the contents of the message according to the circumstances.

`headers`

> This option specifies additional header lines that are to be added to the message. Several headers can be added by enclosing the text in quotes and using \n to separate them.

`return_message`

> This option specifies that the original message is to be added to the end of the newly created message. The amount that is returned is subject to the general `return_size_limit` option.

For example, here is a transport that could be used to send back a message explaining that a particular mailing list no longer exists:

```
auto_message:
  driver = autoreply
  to = $sender_address
  subject = The mailing list $local_part is no more
  text = Your message to $local_part@$domain is being returned\n\
    because the $local_part mailing list is no longer in use.
  return_message
  user = exim
```

You could send messages to this transport by a router such as this:

```
old_lists:
  driver = accept
  domains = mailing.list.domain
  local_parts = /etc/dead/lists
  transport = auto_message
```

This runs only for the one domain, for local parts that are listed in the file.

## 9.7.2 Once-only messages

The traditional "vacation" use of **autoreply** is to send a message only once, or no more than once in a certain time interval, to each different sender. This can be configured by setting the once option to the name of a file, which is then used to record the recipients of messages that are created, together with the times at which the messages are sent. By default, only one message is ever sent to a given recipient. However, if once_repeat is set to a time greater than zero, another message may be sent if that much time has elapsed since the previous message. For example:

```
once_repeat = 10d
```

The settings of once and once_repeat are used only if the data for the message is being taken from the transport's own options. For calls of **autoreply** that originate in message filters, the settings from the filter are used.

## 9.7.3 Keeping a log of messages sent

The log option names a file in which a record of every message that is handled by the transport is logged. The value of the option is expanded, and the file is created if necessary, with a mode specified by mode.

The setting of log is used only if the data for the message is being taken from the transport's own options. For calls of **autoreply** that originate in message filters, the settings from the filter are used.

## 9.7.4 Summary of autoreply options

The options that are specific to the **autoreply** transport are summarized in this section. Of course, any generic transport option (☞ 8.11) may also be set for **autoreply**.

bcc  (string, default = unset)
    This option specifies the addresses that are to receive "blind carbon copies" of the message when the message is specified by the transport. The string is expanded.

cc  (string, default = unset)
    This option specifies recipients of the message and the contents of the *Cc:* header when the message is specified by the transport. The string is expanded.

file  (string, default = unset)
   The contents of the file are sent as the body of the message when the message is
   specified by the transport. The string is expanded. If both file and text are set,
   the text string comes first.

file_expand  (Boolean, default = false)
   If this is set, the contents of the file named by the file option are subjected to
   string expansion as they are added to the message.

file_optional  (Boolean, default = false)
   If this option is true, no error is generated if the file named by the file option
   does not exist or cannot be read.

from  (string, default = unset)
   This option specifies the contents of the *From:* header when the message is
   specified by the transport. The string is expanded.

headers  (string, default = unset)
   This option specifies additional RFC 2822 headers that are to be added to the
   message when the message is specified by the transport. The string is expanded.

log  (string, default = unset)
   This option names a file in which a record of every message sent is logged when
   the message is specified by the transport. The string is expanded.

mode  (octal integer, default = 0600)
   If either the log file or the "once" file has to be created, this mode is used.

once  (string, default = unset)
   This option names a DBM database in which a record of each recipient is kept
   when the message is specified by the transport. The string is expanded.

once_repeat  (time, default = 0s)
   This option specifies the time interval after which another message may be sent to
   the same recipient, when the message is specified by the transport.

reply_to  (string, default = unset)
   This option specifies the contents of the *Reply-To:* header when the message is
   specified by the transport. The string is expanded.

return_message  (Boolean, default = false)
   If this is set, a copy of the original message is returned with the new message,
   subject to the maximum size set in the return_size_limit general configuration option.

subject  (string, default = unset)
   This option specifies the contents of the *Subject:* header line when the message is
   specified by the transport. The string is expanded.

`text`  (string, default = unset)

This specifies a single string to be used as the body of the message when the message is specified by the transport. The string is expanded. If both `text` and `file` are set, the text comes first.

`to`  (string, default = unset)

This option specifies recipients of the message and the contents of the *To:* header when the message is specified by the transport. The string is expanded.

# 10

# Message filtering

As a message passes through Exim, it can be inspected by a number of different *message filters*. We have already discussed transport filters, which occur as a message is transported (☞ 8.8). In this chapter, we are concerned with a different kind of filtering, which happens while a message is being processed to determine where it should be delivered. Filtering at this stage provides another way of controlling a message's delivery. We have already mentioned user and system filters without much explanation; now is the time to rectify that omission. These filters work as follows:

- Provided the configuration permits it, users may place filtering instructions in their *.forward* files instead of just a list of forwarding destinations.[1] User filters are obeyed when Exim is routing addresses; they extend the concept of forwarding by allowing conditions to be tested. A user filter is run as a consequence of routing one address. The constituent parts of the address are available in *$local_part* and *$domain* (and, if relevant, *$local_part_prefix* and/or *$local_part_suffix*).

- A system filter can be set up by the administrator. This uses the same filtering commands as a user filter (with a few additions), but is obeyed just once per delivery attempt, before any routing is done. Because there may be many recipients for a message, address-related variables such as *$local_part* and *$domain* are not set when a system filter is run, but a list of all the recipients is available in the variable *$recipients*.

Before describing the syntax of filtering commands in detail, we work through a few straightforward examples to give you a flavour of how filtering operates.

## 10.1 Examples of filter commands

These examples are written from the perspective of a user's filter file. First, a simple forwarding:

```
# Exim filter
deliver baggins@rivendell.middle-earth.example
```

The first line indicates that the file is a filter file rather than a traditional *.forward* file. The only command in this file is an instruction to deliver the message to a specific

---

[1] The filename *.forward* is the one most commonly used, but it is not hardwired into Exim. The configuration could specify a different name.

address. This particular file does nothing that a traditional *.forward* could not do, and is exactly equivalent to a file containing:

```
baggins@rivendell.middle-earth.example
```

The next example shows vacation handling using traditional means (that is, by running */usr/ucb/vacation*), assuming that *.vacation.msg* and other files have been set up in the home directory:

```
# Exim filter
unseen pipe "/usr/ucb/vacation $local_part"
```

The *pipe* command is an instruction to run the given program and pass the message to it via a pipe. The arguments given to filter commands are always expanded so that references to variables such as *$local_part* can be included.

The word `unseen` that precedes the command tells Exim not to treat this command as *significant*. This means that after filtering, Exim goes on to deliver the message in the normal way. That is, one copy of the message is sent to the pipe, and another is added to the user's mailbox. Without `unseen`, the pipe delivery would be the only delivery that is done.

This example also does not do anything that a traditional *.forward* could not do. For the user *spqr*, it is equivalent to:

```
\spqr, |/usr/ucb/vacation spqr
```

Vacation handling can, however, be done entirely inside an Exim filter, without running another program. If there is a file called *.vacation.msg* in the home directory, this filter file suffices:

```
# Exim filter
if personal then vacation endif
```

This example shows something that a traditional *.forward* file cannot do. The *if* command allows a filter to test certain conditions before taking action. In this example, it is testing the `personal` condition. We explain what this means in detail later on, but for now you just need to know that it is distinguishing between messages that are personally addressed to the user, and those that are not (for example, messages from a mailing list). If the incoming message is personal, the filter command *vacation* is run. This command generates an automatic response message to the sender of the incoming message, in the same way that */usr/ucb/vacation* does.

As well as sending the vacation message, we want Exim to continue processing the message, and carry on with the normal delivery. In this case, it happens automatically, because the *vacation* command is not a significant action. There is no need to use `unseen`, because it is the default.

There are several conditions that you can test with the *if* command. The next example examines the contents of the *Subject:* header line, and for certain subjects, arranges to deliver the message to a specific file instead of the normal mailbox:

```
# Exim filter
if $header_subject: contains "empire" or
   $header_subject: contains "foundation"
then
    save $home/mail/f+e
endif
```

Saving to a file like this is a significant action, so no other deliveries are done for messages that match the test. If the *save* command were preceded by unseen, it would take a copy of the relevant messages, without affecting normal delivery.

The following example illustrates the use of a regular expression for a slightly unusual purpose. It extracts the day of the week from the variable *$tod_full*, which contains the date and time in this format:

```
Wed, 16 Oct 2002 09:51:40 +0100
```

The filter command looks for messages that are not marked "urgent", and saves them in files whose names contain the day of the week:

```
# Exim filter
if $header_subject: does not contain "urgent" and
   $tod_full matches "^(...),"
then
    save $home/mail/$1
endif
```

The matches condition tests a string using a regular expression. In this example, the regular expression always matches, and its parentheses extract the day name (the first three characters of *$tod_full*) into the *$1* variable. This can then be used in the command that follows.

Suppose you want to throw away all messages from a certain domain that is bombarding you with junk, but nevertheless want to accept messages from the postmaster. You could use this filter file:

```
# Exim filter
if $sender_address contains "@spam.site.example" and
   $sender_address does not contain "postmaster@"
then
    seen finish
endif
```

The *finish* command ends filtering. Putting the word seen in front of it makes it into a significant action, which means that normal message delivery will not take place. As no deliveries are set up by the filter when the condition matches, the message is discarded.

This final example is a reminder of how a user can handle multiple personal
mailboxes, as described in section 5.5:

```
# Exim filter
if $local_part_suffix is "-foo"
then
    save $home/mail/foo
elif $local_part_suffix is "-bar"
then
    save $home/mail/bar
endif
```

The remainder of this chapter covers the format of filter files and the individual
filtering commands in detail.

# 10.2 Filtering compared with an external delivery agent

It is important to realize that no deliveries actually happen while a system or user
filter file is being processed. The result of filtering is a list of destinations to which a
message should be delivered; the deliveries themselves take place later, along with all
other deliveries for the message. This means that it is not possible to test for
successful deliveries while filtering. It also means that duplicate addresses generated
by filtering are dropped, as with any other duplicate addresses.

If a user needs to be able to test the result of a delivery in some automatic way, an
external delivery agent such as *procmail* must be used instead of an Exim filter
(☞ 5.4). At first sight, *procmail* and Exim filters appear to provide much the same
functionality, albeit with very different syntax. However, there are some important
differences:

- Forwarding from an Exim filter is "true forwarding" in the sense that the
  envelope sender is not changed; the message is just redirected to a new recipient. An unprivileged external delivery agent cannot do this because any message it resubmits has the local user's address as its envelope sender.

- Because an external delivery agent has to submit a new message in order to
  achieve additional deliveries, duplicate addresses are not detected. For example,
  if a message arrives addressed to both *bob* and *alice*, and *bob* forwards it to
  *alice* from *procmail*, two copies are delivered, whereas if the forwarding happens in an Exim filter, only one copy is delivered.

- As mentioned earlier, the results of a delivery (for example, the return code
  from the command to which a message is piped) can be inspected by an
  external delivery agent, but not in an Exim filter.

The use of Exim filters and external delivery agents is not mutually exclusive. You should use whichever of them best provides the features you need.

# 10.3 Setting up a user filter

User filters are handled by the **redirect** router as an alternative form of forwarding information. If the `allow_filter` option is set for the router, and the first line of the redirection data begins with the text:

```
# Exim filter
```

in any capitalization and with any spacing, the file is interpreted as a filter file instead of a conventional forwarding list. The remainder of the filter must conform to the filtering syntax, which is described later in this chapter.

> In most cases, user filters are kept in files that are specified by the `file` option of the **redirect** router, and for this reason the phrase "filter file" is commonly used. However, from the point of view of the **redirect** router, all that matters is that the redirection data has the correct syntax. This means that a filter can equally well be set up using the `data` option instead of the `file` option (for example, by extracting the filter text from a database).

As in the case of a conventional redirection list, if the filter sets up any deliveries to pipes or files, the router must have settings of `pipe_transport` or `file_transport` to specify how such deliveries are to be done. A third transport, specified by `reply_transport`, is required for filters that generate automatic replies to messages (something a conventional redirection list cannot do).

Some administrators may not wish to support automatic replies or deliveries to files and pipes in user filters. Also, in some environments it may be desirable to disable certain types of string expansion. For example, on a host where the users do not have login accounts but can provide their own filters via FTP, the administrator may want to lock out the reading of arbitrary files and the running of commands. The following options of the **redirect** router are provided for disabling certain features of user filters:

`forbid_file`

This option disables the use of the *save* command in filters. It also disables the use of pathnames in non-filter redirection data.

`forbid_filter_existstest`

This option disables the `exists` condition in expansion strings in filters.

`forbid_filter_lookup`

This option disables the use of `lookup` in expansion strings in filters.

`forbid_filter_perl`

This option disables the use of embedded Perl in expansion strings in filters.[1]

`forbid_pipe`

This option disables the use of the *pipe* command in filters. It also disables the use of a pipe in non-filter redirection data.

`forbid_filter_readfile`

This option disables the use of `readfile` in expansion strings in filters.

`forbid_filter_run`

This option disables the use of `run` in expansion strings in filters.

`forbid_filter_reply`

This option disables the use of the *mail* and *vacation* commands in filters.

## 10.4 Setting up a system filter

A system filter is different to a user filter in that it runs only once per delivery process, however many recipients a message might have. Because it runs right at the start of delivery, before the recipient addresses are routed, the options for setting it up appear in the main section of the runtime configuration file.

A system filter is enabled by setting the option `system_filter` to the path of the file that contains the filter instructions. For example:

```
system_filter = /etc/mail/exim.filter
```

There are several other options for controlling the system filter. They are as follows:

`system_filter_directory_transport` (string, default = unset)

This option sets the name of the transport that is used when the *save* command in a system filter specifies a path ending in /, implying delivery of each message into a separate file in some directory.

---

[1]  Embedded Perl support is in any case only available if Exim is built specifically to include it.

`system_filter_file_transport` (string, default = unset)
: This option sets the name of the transport that is used when the *save* command in a system filter specifies a path not ending in /.

`system_filter_group` (string, default = unset)
: This option sets the gid under which the system filter is run. The same gid is used for any pipe, file, or autoreply deliveries that are set up by the filter, unless the transport overrides them.

`system_filter_pipe_transport` (string, default = unset)
: This option sets the name of the transport that is used when a *pipe* command is used in a system filter.

`system_filter_reply_transport` (string, default = unset)
: This option sets the name of the transport that is used when a *mail* command is used in a system filter.

`system_filter_user` (string, default = unset)
: This option sets the uid under which the system filter is run. The same uid is used for any pipe, file, or autoreply deliveries that are set up by the filter, unless the transport overrides them. If `system_filter_user` is not set, the system filter runs as root.

# 10.5 Testing filter files

Filter files, especially the more complicated ones, should always be tested, as it is easy to make mistakes. Exim provides a facility for preliminary testing of a filter file before installing it. This tests the syntax of the file and its basic operation, and can also be used with ordinary (non-filter) *.forward* files.

Because a filter can test the contents of messages, a test message is required. Suppose you have a new user filter file called *new-filter* and a test message in a file called *test-message*. The following command can be used to test the filter:

```
exim -bf new-filter <test-message
```

The `-bf` option tells Exim that the following item on the command line is the name of a filter file that is to be tested. The test message itself is supplied on the standard input. If there are no message-dependent tests in the filter, an empty test message can be used; otherwise the message must start with header lines or the `From` message separator line that is found in traditional multimessage folder files. A warning is given if no header lines are read.

The result of running this command, provided no syntax errors are detected in the filter file, is a list of the actions that Exim would try to take if presented with the message for real. For example, the output:

```
Deliver message to: gulliver@lilliput.example
Save message to: /home/lemuel/mail/archive
```

means that one copy of the message would be sent to *gulliver@lilliput.example*, and another would be added to the file */home/lemuel/mail/archive*.

The actions themselves are not attempted while testing a filter file in this way; there is no check, for example, that any forwarding addresses are valid. If you want to know why a particular action is being taken, add the -v option to the command. This causes Exim to output the results of any conditional tests and to indent its output according to the depth of nesting of *if* commands in the filter file. Further additional output from a filter test can be generated by the *testprint* command, which is described later.

When Exim is outputting a list of the actions it would take, if any text strings are included in the output, non-printing characters therein are converted to escape sequences. In particular, if any text string contains a newline character, this is shown as \n in the testing output.

When testing a filter, Exim makes up an envelope for the message. The recipient is by default the user running the command, and so is the sender, but the command can be run with the -f option to supply a different sender. For example:

```
exim -bf new-filter -f islington@neverwhere.example <test-message
```

Alternatively, if the -f option is not used, but the first line of the supplied message is a From separator from a message folder file (not the same thing as a *From:* header line), the sender is taken from there. If -f is present, the contents of any From line are ignored.

The return path is the same as the envelope sender, unless the message contains a *Return-path:* header, in which case it is taken from there. You need not worry about any of this unless you want to test out features of a filter file that rely on the sender address or the return path.

It is possible to change the envelope recipient by specifying further options. The -bfd option changes the domain of the recipient address, while the -bfl option changes the local part. An adviser could make use of these options to test someone else's filter file.

The -bfp and -bfs options specify the prefix or suffix for the local part. These might be relevant when testing the handling of multiple user addresses (☞ 5.5).

If the filter tests information about the source of the message (for example, the name or the IP address of the host from which it was received), you may want to set up specific values for it to test. This can be done by making use of several command-line options whose names begin with -oM. For example, -oMa sets the remote host address. See chapter 20 for details of these options.

## 10.5.1 Testing a system filter file

A system filter can be tested in the same way as a user filter, but you should use the command-line option `-bF` instead of `-bf`. This allows Exim to recognize those commands and other features of a system filter that are not available in user filters.

## 10.5.2 Testing an installed filter file

Testing a filter file before installation cannot find every potential problem; for example, it does not actually run commands to which messages are piped. Some "live" tests should therefore also be done once a filter is installed.

If at all possible, users should test their filter files by sending messages from other accounts. If a user sends a test message from the filtered account and delivery fails, the bounce message is sent back to the same account, which may cause another delivery failure. This does not cause an infinite sequence of messages, because a new bounce message is never created for a failed bounce message. However, it does mean that the original failure is not returned to the sender, and also that the postmaster has to investigate the stuck bounce message.

A sensible precaution against this occurrence is to include the line:

```
if error_message then finish endif
```

as the first filter command, at least while testing. This causes filtering to be abandoned for a bounce message, and since no destinations are generated by the filter, the message goes on to be delivered to the original address. Unless there is a good reason for not doing so, it is recommended that this line be present at the start of all user filter files.

# 10.6 Format of filter files

Apart from leading whitespace, the first text in a filter file must be:

```
# Exim filter
```

This is what distinguishes it from a conventional *.forward* file (assuming the configuration has enabled filtering). If the file does not have this initial line, it is treated as a conventional *.forward* file, both when delivering mail and when using the `-bf` testing mechanism. The whitespace in the line is optional, and any capitalization may be used. Further text on the same line is treated as a comment. For example, you could have:

```
#   Exim filter   <<== do not edit or remove this line!
```

The remainder of the file is a sequence of filtering commands. These consist of keywords and data values separated by whitespace or line breaks, except in the case of conditions for the *if* command, where parentheses also act as separators. For example, in the command:

```
deliver gulliver@lilliput.example
```

the keyword is `deliver` and the data value is `gulliver@lilliput.example`. The commands are in free format, and can be spread over more than one line; there are no special terminators. If the character # follows a separator, everything from # up to the next newline is ignored. This provides a way of including comments in a filter file.

There are two ways in which a data value can be input:

- If the text contains no whitespace, it can be typed verbatim. However, if it is part of a condition, it must also be free of parentheses, because these are used for grouping in conditions. The examples shown so far have all been of this type.

- Otherwise, a data value must be enclosed in double quotation marks, as in this example:

```
if $h_subject: contains "Free Gift" then
   save /dev/null
endif
```

When quotes are used, backslash is treated as an "escape character" within the string, thereby allowing special characters such as newline to be included. A data item enclosed in double quotes can be continued onto the next line by ending the first line with a backslash. Any leading whitespace at the start of the continuation line is ignored.

In addition to the escape character processing that occurs when strings are enclosed in quotes, most data values are also subject to string expansion. In an expanded string, both the dollar and backslash characters are interpreted specially. This means that if you really want a dollar in a data item in a filter file, you have to escape it. The command:

```
if $h_subject: contains \$\$\$\$ then seen finish endif
```

tests for the string $$$$. If quotes are used, an additional level of escaping is necessary:

```
if $h_subject: contains "\\$\\$\\$\\$" then
   seen finish
endif
```

If a backslash is required in a quoted data string, as can happen if the string is to be interpreted as a regular expression, \\\\ has to be entered.[1]

---

[1] The \N feature of string expansions, which disables the expansion of part of the string, is sometimes more convenient.

# 10.7 Significant actions

When, in the course of delivery, a message is processed by a filter file, what happens next (that is, after the filter file has been processed), depends on whether the filter has taken any *significant action* or not. For a user filter, if there is at least one significant action, the filter is considered to have handled the entire delivery arrangements for the current address, and no further routing of the address takes place. In the case of a system filter, if any significant actions are taken, the original recipient addresses are ignored.

If, on the other hand, no significant actions happen, Exim continues processing as if there were no filter file. For a user filter, the address is offered to subsequent routers, and normally this eventually sets up delivery of a copy of the message into a local mailbox. For a system filter, the original recipient addresses are routed, and delivery proceeds as normal.

The delivery commands *deliver*, *save*, and *pipe* are by default significant actions. For example, if the command:

```
deliver hatter@wonderland.example
```

is obeyed in a user's filter file, the address is not offered to subsequent routers. However, if the command is preceded by the word unseen, for example:

```
unseen deliver hatter@wonderland.example
```

the delivery is not considered to be significant. In effect, a filter containing only an "unseen" delivery takes a copy of a message, without affecting the normal delivery. This can be used in a system filter for making archive copies of messages.

The other filter commands (those that do not specify a delivery of the message) are not significant actions by default, but they can be made significant by putting the word seen before them. For example, obeying a *finish* command terminates the running of a filter; it is not itself a significant action, so whether the filter as a whole has taken any significant action depends on the previously obeyed commands (if any). However, if the command:

```
seen finish
```

is obeyed, the filter ends with a significant action, and no further delivery processing takes place. A filter containing only this command is a black hole; it is most commonly used after testing some characteristic of the message.

# 10.8 Filter commands

The filter commands described in subsequent sections are as follows:

| | |
|---|---|
| *add* | Increment a user variable |
| *deliver* | Deliver to an email address |
| *fail* | Fail delivery (system filter only) |
| *finish* | End processing |
| *freeze* | Freeze delivery (system filter only) |
| *headers* | Add/remove header lines (system filter only) |
| *if* | Test condition |
| *logfile* | Define log file |
| *logwrite* | Write to log file |
| *mail* | Send a reply message |
| *pipe* | Pipe to a command |
| *save* | Save to a file |
| *testprint* | Print while testing |
| *vacation* | Tailored form of *mail* |

# 10.9 The add command

The *add* command provides a primitive means of counting within a filter file.

```
add <number> to <user variable>
```

For example:

```
add 2 to n3
```

The names of the user variables consist of the letter n followed by a single digit.
There are therefore 10 user variables of this type, and their values can be obtained by
the normal expansion syntax (for example *$n4*) in other commands. At the start of
filtering, these variables all contain zero. At the end of a system filter, their values
are copied into *$sn0* to *$sn9* so that they can be referenced in users' filter files. Thus,
a system filter can set up "scores" for a message, to which a user filter can refer.
Both arguments of the *add* command are expanded before use, making it possible to
add variables to each other. Subtraction can be obtained by adding negative numbers.
The following example is not realistic, but shows the kind of thing that can be done:

```
if $h_subject: does not match "(?-i)[a-z]" then
  add 1 to n1
endif
if $h_subject: contains "make money" then
  add 1 to n2
endif
add $n2 to n1
if $n1 is above 3 then seen finish endif
```

The first command tests the subject of the message for the presence of a lower-case letter. If there are none (that is, if the subject is entirely in upper case), the variable *$n1* is incremented. The second command increments *$n2* if the subject contains a specific string. Then the contents of *$n2* are added to *$n1*, and the sum is tested.

Notice that the variable names are given without a leading dollar sign for variables that are being incremented. If you wrote:

```
add 1 to $n1
```

the string expansion that is applied to each argument would turn it into a command such as:

```
add 1 to 0
```

which is an invalid command that provokes a syntax error.

# 10.10 Delivery commands

The following filter commands set up message deliveries (that is, they arrange for copies of the message to be transported somewhere). Such deliveries are significant actions unless the command is preceded by unseen.

## 10.10.1 The deliver command

```
deliver <mail address>
```

For example:

```
deliver "Dr Livingstone <David@darkest.africa.example>"
```

This command provides a forwarding operation. The message is sent to the given address. For a user filter, this is exactly the same as putting the address in a traditional *.forward* file. To deliver a copy of the message to a user's normal mailbox, the user's login name can be given, just as in a traditional *.forward* file. This does not cause a loop because Exim notices that the address has already been processed by the router that runs the filter, and it skips the router the next time round.

An optional addition to a *deliver* command is:

```
errors_to <mail address>
```

In a system filter, the given address is not restricted, but in the case of a user filter, it must be the address that is in the process of being routed. That is, the only valid usage is:

```
errors_to $local_part@$domain
```

(or the equivalent using a literal string) in a user filter. This facility allows users to change the envelope sender of a message to be their own address when forwarding it, so that any subsequent delivery failure reports are sent to the forwarding user, instead of to the original sender. This is useful only when the forwarding is conditional, of course, so that bounce messages are not themselves forwarded.

Only a single address may be given to a *deliver* command, but multiple occurrences of the command may be used to cause the message to be delivered to more than one address. However, duplicate addresses are discarded.

## 10.10.2 The save command

```
save <file name>
```

For example:

```
save $home/mail/bookfolder
```

This command causes a copy of the message to be appended to the given file (that is, the file is used as a mail folder). More than one *save* command may appear; each one causes a copy of the message to be written to its argument file, provided they are different (duplicate *save* commands are ignored).

The ability to use the *save* command in a user filter is controlled by the system administrator; it may be forbidden by setting `forbid_file` on the router.

An optional mode value may be given after the filename, for example:

```
save /some/folder 0640
```

This makes it possible for users to override the systemwide mode setting for file deliveries (normally `0600`). If an existing file does not have the correct mode, it is changed. The value for the mode is interpreted as an octal number, even if it does not begin with a zero.

For a system filter, the filename in a *save* command must be an absolute path. For a user filter, if the filename does not start with a slash character, the directory specified by the *$home* variable is prepended. The user must of course have permission to write to the file, and (in a conventional configuration) the writing of the file takes place in a process that is running with the user's uid and the user's primary gid. Any secondary groups to which the user may belong are not normally taken into account, though the system administrator can configure Exim to set them up (☞ 6.3.4).

An alternative form of delivery may be enabled, in which each message is delivered into a new file in a given directory. For a system filter, this requires a setting of `system_filter_directory_transport`, whereas for a user filter it requires a setting of `directory_transport` on the **redirect** router. If this is the case, the functionality can be requested by giving the directory name terminated by a slash after the *save* command, for example:

```
save separated/messages/
```

There are several different possible formats for such deliveries (☞ 9.4). If this functionality is not enabled, the use of a pathname ending in a slash causes an error.

## 10.10.3 The pipe command

```
pipe <command>
```

For example:

```
pipe "$home/bin/countmail $sender_address"
```

This command causes a separate process to be run, and a copy of the message is passed to it on its standard input. More than one *pipe* command may appear; each one causes a copy of the message to be written to its argument pipe, provided they are different (duplicate *pipe* commands are ignored).

The command supplied to *pipe* is split up by Exim into a command name and a number of arguments, delimited by whitespace, except for arguments enclosed in double quotes (in which case backslash is interpreted as an escape), or in single quotes (in which case no escaping is recognized). Note that as the whole command is normally supplied in double quotes, a second level of quoting is required for internal double quotes. For example:

```
pipe "$home/myscript \"size is $message_size\""
```

String expansion is performed on the separate components after the line has been split up, and the command is then run directly by Exim; it is not run under a shell. This means that substitutions in the expansions cannot change the number of arguments, nor can substituted quotes, backslashes, or other shell metacharacters cause confusion. Documentation for some programs that are normally run via this kind of pipe often suggest that the command should start with:

```
IFS=" "
```

This is a shell command, and should *not* be present in Exim filter files, because Exim does not normally run the command under a shell.

The preceding paragraph assumes a default configuration for the **pipe** transport that is being used for pipe deliveries from filters. If use_shell is set on the transport, things are different. A number of other options on the transport can affect the way the command is run, including applying restrictions as to which commands may be run, and how any output from the command is handled (☞ 9.5).

### 10.10.4 Ignoring delivery errors

As explained earlier in this chapter, filtering just sets up addresses for delivery; no deliveries actually happen while a filter file is active. If any of the generated addresses subsequently suffers a delivery failure, an error message is generated in the normal way. However, if the filter command which sets up a delivery is preceded by the word `noerror`, locally detected errors for that delivery, and any deliveries consequent on it (that is, from alias, forwarding, or filter files it invokes) are ignored. For example, suppose a user wants to scan all incoming messages using some program, as well as having them delivered into the normal mailbox. A command such as:

```
unseen noerror pipe $home/bin/mailscan
```

can be used; `unseen` ensures that normal delivery is not affected, and `noerror` ensures that a failure of the pipe does not cause a bounce message to be generated.

## 10.11 Mail commands

There are two commands that cause the creation of a new mail message, neither of which are significant actions unless the command is preceded by the word `seen`. Sending messages automatically is a powerful facility, but it should be used with care, because of the danger of creating infinite sequences of messages. The system administrator can forbid the use of these commands in users' filter files, by setting `forbid_filter_reply` on the **redirect** router.

To help prevent runaway message sequences, these commands have no effect when the incoming message is a bounce message, and messages sent by this means are treated as if they were reporting delivery errors (that is, their envelope senders are empty). Thus, they should never themselves cause a bounce message to be returned. The basic mail-sending command is:

```
mail to <address-list>
     cc <address-list>
     bcc <address-list>
     from <address>
     reply_to <address>
     subject <text>
     text <text>
     [expand] file <filename>
     return message
     log <log file name>
     once <note file name>
     once_repeat <time interval>
```

For example:

```
mail text "Got your message about $h_subject:"
```

All the keywords that can follow *mail* are optional; you need only specify those whose defaults you want to change. As a convenience for use in one common case, there is also a command called *vacation*. It behaves in the same way as *mail*, except that the defaults for the `file`, `log`, `once`, and `once_repeat` keywords are:

```
expand file .vacation.msg
log   .vacation.log
once .vacation
once_repeat 7d
```

respectively. These are the same filenames and repeat period used by the traditional Unix *vacation* command. The defaults can be overridden by explicit settings, for example:

```
vacation once_repeat 14d
```

The *vacation* command is normally used conditionally, subject to the `personal` condition, so as not to send automatic replies to non-personal messages from mailing lists or elsewhere.

For both commands, the key/value argument pairs can appear in any order. At least one of `text` or `file` must appear (except with *vacation*, where `file` can be defaulted); if both are present, the text string appears first in the message. If `expand` precedes `file`, each line of the file is subject to string expansion as it is included in the message.

If no `to` keyword appears, the message is sent to the address in the *$reply_address* variable, which is the contents of the *Reply-To:* header line if it exists, or otherwise the contents of the *From:* header line. An *In-Reply-To:* header is automatically included in the created message, giving a reference to the message identification of the incoming message.

Several lines of text can be supplied to `text` by including the escape sequence \n in the string where newlines are required, for example:

```
mail text
  "This is an automatic response to your message.\n\
I am very busy, but will look at it eventually."
```

If the command is output during filter file testing, newlines in the text are shown as \n.

Note that the keyword for creating a *Reply-To:* header line is `reply_to`, because Exim keywords may contain underscores, but not hyphens. If the `from` keyword is present and the given address does not match the user under which the filter is running, Exim adds a *Sender:* header line to the message by default. This behaviour can be changed by setting the `local_from_check` and `local_from_prefix` options (☞ 20.2.1). If `from` is not specified, a *From:* header is constructed from the login name and the value of `qualify_domain`.

If `return_message` is specified, the incoming message that caused the filter file to be run is added to the end of the newly created message, subject to the maximum size limitation for returned messages, which is controlled by the `return_size_ limit` option in Exim's main configuration.

If a log file is specified, an entry is added to it for each message sent. The entry contains several lines as in this example:

```
2000-05-01 14:04:06
To: John Doe <jd@somewhere.example>
Subject: Re: wish list for exim
```

If a `once` file is specified, it is used to hold a database for remembering who has received a message, and no more than one message is ever sent to any particular address, unless `once_repeat` is set. This specifies a time interval after which another copy of the message may be sent. For example:

```
once_repeat = 5d4h
```

causes a new message to be sent if five days and four hours have elapsed since the last one was sent. There must be no whitespace in a time interval.

The filename specified for `once` is used as the basename for direct-access (DBM) file operations. Exim creates and maintains the DBM file or files automatically. There are a number of different DBM libraries in existence. Some operating systems provide one as a default, but even in this case a different one may have been used when building Exim. With some DBM libraries, specifying `once` results in two files being created, with the suffixes *.dir* and *.pag* being added to the given name. With some others a single file with the suffix *.db* is used, or the name is used unchanged.

If `once` is used in a "vacation" scenario, the DBM file must be deleted by the user when the vacation is over and the filter file has been changed so as not to send any more messages.

More than one *mail* or *vacation* command may be obeyed in a single filter run; they are all honoured, even when they are to the same recipient.

# 10.12 Logging commands

A log can be kept of actions taken by a filter file. For user filters, the system administrator may choose to disable this feature by setting `forbid_filter_ logwrite` on the **redirect** router. Logging takes place while the filter file is being interpreted. It does not queue up for later as the delivery commands do. The reason for this is so that a log file need be opened only once for several write operations.

There are two commands, neither of which constitutes a significant action. The first defines a file to which logging output is subsequently written:

```
logfile <file name>
```

For example:

```
logfile $home/filter.log
```

The filename may optionally be followed by a mode for the file, which is used if the file has to be created. For example:

```
logfile $home/filter.log 0644
```

The number is interpreted as octal, even if it does not begin with a zero. The default for the mode is `0600`. It is suggested that the *logfile* command should normally appear as the first command in a filter file. Once *logfile* has been obeyed, the *logwrite* command can be used to write to the log file:

```
logwrite <"some text string">
```

For example:

```
logwrite "$tod_log $message_id processed"
```

It is possible to have more than one *logfile* command, to specify writing to different log files in different circumstances. Writing takes place at the end of the file, and a newline character is added to the end of each string if there is not one already. Newlines can be put in the middle of the string by using the \n escape sequence. Lines from simultaneous deliveries may be interleaved in the file, as there is no interlocking, so you should plan your logging with this in mind. However, data should not be lost.

# 10.13 The testprint command

It is sometimes helpful to be able to print out the values of variables when testing filter files. The command:

```
testprint <"text">
```

For example:

```
testprint "home=$home reply_address=$reply_address"
```

does nothing when mail is being delivered. However, when the filtering code is being tested by means of the -bf or -bF options, the value of the string is written to the standard output.

# 10.14 The finish command

The command *finish*, which has no arguments, causes Exim to stop interpreting the filter file. What happens next depends on whether any significant actions have been taken. The *finish* command itself is not a significant action unless preceded by the word seen. Reaching the end of a filter file has the same effect as obeying a *finish* command.

# 10.15 Obeying filter commands conditionally

Most of the power of filtering comes from the ability to test conditions and obey different commands depending on the outcome. The *if* command is used to specify conditional execution, and its general form is:

```
if     <condition>
then   <commands>
elif   <condition>
then   <commands>
else   <commands>
endif
```

There may be any number of *elif-then* sections (including none) and the *else* section is also optional. Any number of commands, including nested *if* commands, may appear in any of the <commands> sections.

Conditions can be combined by using the words and and or, and parentheses can be used to specify how several conditions are to combine. Without parentheses, and is more strongly binding than or. Here is an example that uses parentheses:

```
if $h_subject: contains [EXIM] and
   (
   $return_path is exim-users-admin@exim.org or
   $h_to:$h_cc: contains exim-users@exim.org
   )
then
   save $home/Mail/exim-list
endif
```

If any string in a condition contains parentheses, it must be quoted to avoid misinterpretation.

A condition can be preceded by not to negate it, and there are also some negative forms of condition that are more English-like. For example:

```
if not personal and $h_subject: does not contain [EXIM]
   then save $home/Mail/other-lists
endif
```

The following descriptions show just the individual conditions, not the complete *if* commands.

## 10.15.1 String testing conditions

There are a number of conditions that operate on text strings, using the words
begins, ends, is, contains, and matches. If the condition names are written
in lower case, the testing of letters is done without regard to case; if they are written
in upper case (for example, CONTAINS), the case of letters is significant.

### Start of string test

```
<text1> begins <text2>
<text1> does not begin <text2>
```

For example:

```
if $header_from: begins "Friend@"
```

A begins test checks for the presence of the second string at the start of the first,
with both strings having been expanded.

### End of string test

```
<text1> ends <text2>
<text1> does not end <text2>
```

For example:

```
if $header_from: ends "@public.example.com"
```

An ends test checks for the presence of the second string at the end of the first, with
both strings having been expanded.

### Exact string test

```
<text1> is <text2>
<text1> is not <text2>
```

For example:

```
if $local_part_suffix is "-foo"
```

An is test does an exact match between the strings, having first expanded both of
them.

### Partial string test

```
<text1> contains <text2>
<text1> does not contain <text2>
```

For example:

```
if $header_subject: contains "evolution"
```

A contains test does a partial string match, having expanded both strings.

## Regular expression string test

```
<text1> matches <text2>
<text2> does not match <text2>
```

For example:

```
if $sender_address matches "(Bill|John)@"
```

For a matches test, after expansion of both strings, the second one is interpreted as a regular expression, and matched against the first. Care must be taken if you need a backslash in a regular expression, because backslashes are interpreted as escape characters both by the string expansion code and by Exim's normal string reading code when a string is given in quotes. For example, if you want to test the sender address for a domain ending in *.com*, the regular expression is:

```
\.com$
```

The backslash and dollar sign in that expression have to be escaped when used in a filter command, because otherwise they would be interpreted by the expansion code. You can escape each of them individually, as follows:

```
if $sender_address matches \\.com\$
```

Alternatively, you can make use of the \N facility to disable expansion in part of the string. This is usually more convenient for regular expressions, because the expression itself is unmodified. For example:

```
if $sender_address matches \N\.com$\N
```

Any part of a string that lies between two occurrences of \N is copied without change by the string expander. However, if the string is given in quotes (mandatory only if it contains whitespace or parentheses) you have to double all the backslashes, and write:[1]

```
if $sender_address matches "\\N\\.com$\\N"
```

If the regular expression contains parenthesized subexpressions to capture parts of the matching string, numeric variable substitutions such as *$1* can be used in the actions that follow a successful match. If the match fails, the values of the numeric variables remain unchanged. Previous values are not restored after *endif*; in other words, only one set of values is ever available. If the condition contains several subconditions connected by and or or, it is the strings extracted from the last successful match that are available in subsequent actions. String expansion of a condition occurs just before it is tested, which means that numeric variables from one subcondition are available for use in subsequent subconditions.

---

[1]  Without the use of \N you would have to write \\\\ for a backslash and \\$ for a dollar sign.

## 10.15.2 Numeric testing conditions

The following conditions are available for performing numerical tests:

```
<number1> is above <number2>
<number1> is not above <number2>
<number1> is below <number2>
<number1> is not below <number2>
```

For example:

```
if $message@_size is not above 10k
```

The `<number>` arguments must expand to strings of digits, optionally followed by one of the letters K or M (in upper case or lower case), which cause multiplication by 1024 and 1024×1024, respectively.

## 10.15.3 Testing for personal mail

A common requirement in user filters is to distinguish between incoming personal mail and mail from a mailing list. In particular, this test is normally required before sending "vacation messages", so as to avoid sending them to mailing lists. The condition:

```
personal
```

is a shorthand for:

```
$header_to: contains $local_part@$domain and
$header_from: does not contain $local_part@$domain and
$header_from: does not contain server@ and
$header_from: does not contain daemon@ and
$header_from: does not contain root@ and
$header_subject: does not contain "circular" and
$header_precedence: does not contain "bulk" and
$header_precedence: does not contain "list" and
$header_precedence: does not contain "junk"
```

This condition tests for the appearance of the current user in the *To:* header, checks that the sender is not the current user or one of a number of common daemons, and checks the contents of the *Subject:* and *Precedence:* headers. It is useful only in user filter files, because a unique recipient (from which to set *$local_part* and *$domain*) does not exist during the running of a system filter.

If prefixes or suffixes are in use for local parts (something that depends on the configuration of Exim), the first two tests are also done with:

```
$local_part_prefix$local_part$local_part_suffix
```

instead of just *$local_part*. If the system is configured to rewrite local parts of mail addresses (for example, to rewrite *dag46* as *Dirk.Gently*), the rewritten form of the address is also used in these tests.

This example shows the use of `personal` in a filter file that is sending out vacation messages:

```
if personal then
  mail
   to $reply_address
   subject "Re: $h_subject:"
   file $home/vacation/message
   once $home/vacation/once
   once_repeat 10d
endif
```

It is quite common for people who have mail accounts on a number of different systems to forward all their mail to one host, and in this case a check for personal mail should test all their mail addresses. To allow for this, the `personal` condition keyword can be followed by:

```
alias <address>
```

any number of times, for example:

```
if personal
  alias smith@else.where.example
  alias jones@other.place.example
then ...
```

This causes messages containing the alias addresses to be treated as personal. The aliases are used when checking both the *To:* and the *From:* headers.

## 10.15.4 Testing for significant actions

Whether or not any previously obeyed filter commands have resulted in a significant action can be tested by the condition `delivered`, for example:

```
if not delivered then save mail/anomalous endif
```

## 10.15.5 Testing for error messages

The condition `error_message` is true if the incoming message is a mail bounce message, that is, if its envelope sender address is empty. Putting the command:

```
if error_message then finish endif
```

at the head of a filter file is a useful insurance against things going wrong in such a way that you cannot receive bounce messages, and it is highly recommended. Note that `error_message` is a condition, not an expansion variable, and therefore is not preceded by $.

## 10.15.6 Testing delivery status

There are two conditions that are intended mainly for use in system filter files but which are available in users' filter files as well. The condition `first_delivery` is true if this is the first attempt to deliver the message, and false otherwise.

The condition `manually_thawed` is true only if the message was frozen for some reason, and was subsequently released by the system administrator. It is unlikely to be of use in users' filter files. An explicit forced delivery counts as a manual thaw, but thawing as a result of the `auto_thaw` option does not.

## 10.15.7 Testing a list of addresses

There is a facility for looping through a list of addresses and applying a condition to each of them. It is executed as a condition that is part of an `if` command, and takes the form:

```
foranyaddress <string> (<condition>)
```

where *<string>* is interpreted as a list of RFC 2822 addresses, as in a typical header line or the value of *$recipients* in a system filter, and *<condition>* is any valid filter condition or combination of conditions. The parentheses surrounding the condition are mandatory, to delimit it from possible further subconditions of the enclosing *if* command. Within the condition, the expansion variable *$thisaddress* is set to the non-comment portion of each of the addresses in the string in turn. For example, if the string was as follows (split over two lines here):

```
B.Simpson <bart@springfield.example>,
   lisa@springfield.example (his sister)
```

then *$thisaddress* would take on the values `bart@springfield.example` and `lisa@springfield.example` in turn.

If there are no valid addresses in the list, the whole condition is false. If the internal condition is true for any one address, the overall condition is true and the loop ends. If the internal condition is false for all addresses in the list, the overall condition is false. In other words, the overall condition succeeds if, and only if, at least one address in the list satisfies the internal condition.

This example tests for the presence of an eight-digit local part in any address in a *To:* header:

```
if foranyaddress $h_to: ( $thisaddress matches ^\\d{8}@ ) then ...
```

When the overall condition is true, the value of *$thisaddress* in the commands that follow `then` is the last value it took inside the loop. At the end of the *if* command, the value of *$thisaddress* is reset to what it was before. It is best to avoid the use of multiple occurrences of `foranyaddress`, nested or otherwise, in a single *if* command, if the value of *$thisaddress* is to be used afterwards, because it is not always clear what the value will be. Nested *if* commands should be used instead.

Header lines can be joined together if a check is to be applied to more than one of them. For example:

```
if foranyaddress $h_to:,$h_cc: ....
```

scans through the addresses in both the *To:* and the *Cc:* headers.

# 10.16 Additional features for system filters

During the running of a system filter, the variable *$recipients* contains a list of all the envelope recipients of the message, separated by commas and whitespace. There are also some additional filtering commands. These are normally permitted only in system filters, and attempts to use them in a user filter, or when testing using -bf, are faulted. However, the allow_fail and allow_freeze options of the **redirect** router can be set true to permit the use of the *fail* and *freeze* commands in non-system filters. This facility is intended for use on systems where centrally managed per-user filter files are run; it is not normally sensible to enable these commands when users can modify their own filter files.

## 10.16.1 The fail command

```
fail text <"text">
```

For example:

```
fail text "Administrative rejection"
```

This command prevents any deliveries of the message from taking place, except for those that may have previously been set up in the filter. It is similar to seen finish, but in this case a bounce message is generated. The text string (which can be omitted if not required) is included in the bounce message. No further commands in the filter file are obeyed, so if, for example, you want to use *logwrite* to keep a log of forced failures, you must place that command before *fail*.

The text given with a *fail* command is also used as part of the failure message that is written to the log. If the message is quite long, this can fill up a lot of log space when such failures are common. To reduce the size of the log message, Exim interprets the text in a special way if it starts with the two characters << and contains >> later. The text between these two strings is written to the log, and the rest of the text is used in the bounce message. For example:

```
fail "<<filter 1>>Your message is not being delivered because \
    it contains attachments that we do not like."
```

Take great care with the *fail* command when basing the decision to fail on the contents of the message, because the normal delivery error bounce message includes the contents of the original message, and will therefore trigger the *fail* command again (causing a mail loop) unless steps are taken to prevent this. Testing the error_message condition is one way to prevent this. You could use, for example:

```
if $message_body contains "this is spam" and not error_message
then
   fail text "spam is not wanted here"
endif
```

## 10.16.2 The freeze command

```
freeze text <"text">
```

For example:

```
freeze text "Administrative rejection"
```

This command prevents any deliveries other than those previously set up in the filter from taking place, but the message is not bounced. Instead, after any deliveries that were set up by the filter have been attempted, the message remains in the queue and is frozen. No further commands in the filter file are obeyed, so if, for example, you want to use *logwrite* to keep a log of freezing actions, you must place that command before *freeze*.

The *freeze* command is ignored if the message has been manually unfrozen and not subsequently manually frozen. This means that automatic freezing in a system filter can be used as a way of checking out suspicious messages. If a frozen message is found on inspection to be valid after all, manually unfreezing it (using the -Mt option, or via the Exim monitor) allows it to be delivered. A forced delivery attempt (using -M or -qff, for example) also counts as manual unfreezing, but reaching the auto_thaw time does not.

## 10.16.3 The headers add command

```
headers add <"text">
```

For example:

```
headers add "X-Filtered: checked on $primary_hostname"
```

The string is expanded and added to the end of the message's header lines. It is the responsibility of the filter maintainer to make sure the new header conforms to RFC 2822 syntax. Leading whitespace is ignored, and if the string is otherwise empty, or if the expansion is forced to fail, the command has no effect. A newline is added at the end of the string if it lacks one. More than one header line may be added in one command by including \n within the string.

Header lines that are added by a system filter are visible during the subsequent delivery process, and can be referred to in expansion strings. This is different from header lines that are added by routers, which apply only to individual addresses and are not generally visible.

## 10.16.4 The headers remove command

```
headers remove <"text">
```

For example:

```
headers remove "Return-Receipt-To"
```

The string is expanded, and is then treated as a colon-separated list of header names. Any header lines with those names are removed from the message. This command applies only to the original header lines that are stored with the message; others such as *Envelope-to:* and *Return-path:* that are added at delivery time cannot be removed by this means.

The header lines that are removed by a system filter become invisible during the subsequent delivery process, and cannot be referred to in expansion strings. This is different from headers that are specified for removal by routers, which remain visible and are removed only when the message is transported.

# 11

# Shared data and Exim processes

In the overview of Exim's operation in chapter 3, the use of multiple processes is mentioned. In this chapter, we describe the different types of process that are used for handling messages. This is background information about the way Exim works, which may be useful when you want to understand exactly what it is doing. The four process types are as follows:

*The daemon process*

The daemon process listens for incoming SMTP connections, and starts a reception process for each one. The daemon may also periodically start queue runner processes. There is normally only one daemon process.

*Reception processes*

A non-SMTP reception process accepts one incoming message and stores it on Exim's spool disk. An SMTP reception process can accept several messages from the same source.

*Queue runner processes*

A queue runner process scans the list of waiting messages, and starts a delivery process for each one in turn.

*Delivery processes*

A delivery process performs one delivery attempt on a single message.

Most Exim processes are short-lived. They perform one task, such as receiving or delivering a message, and then exit. The only exception is the daemon process, which, as its name implies, runs continuously.

Each Exim process that is receiving or delivering a message operates, for the most part, independently of other Exim processes that are working on different messages. Nevertheless, Exim processes do interact with each other by referring to shared files. Before going into the details of each process type, we first describe the shared files, because their contents affect the way the processes operate. The files fall into three categories, as shown in figure 11-1.

- Log files record actions that Exim has taken.

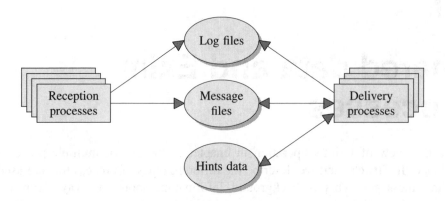

*Figure 11-1: Shared data*

- Message files contain the messages that are in the process of being received or delivered.

- Hints files contain information about delivery problems that were encountered earlier.

The message files and hints files are held in subdirectories inside Exim's spool directory, whose name is configurable, though it is most commonly called */var/spool/exim*. You can find the name of the spool directory by running the command:

```
exim -bP spool_directory
```

In some configurations, the log files are here as well, in another subdirectory, but Exim can be configured to put them elsewhere. In configurations where the log information is being written only to *syslog*, there are no log files.

# 11.1 Message files

Each message is held in two separate files, whose names consist of the message's unique identifier followed by -D and -H, respectively. For example, the message 12b2ie-0000GI-00 is held in the two files:

```
12b2ie-0000GI-00-D
12b2ie-0000GI-00-H
```

The first line of each file is the file's own name. This self-identification is an insurance against a disk crash that destroys the directory, but not the files themselves. The -D file contains the body of the message and may be very large. It is never updated after the message has been received.

The -H file contains the message's envelope and header lines, together with other information about the message, such as the host it arrived from and those addresses to which it has already been delivered. The exact format is described in the reference manual. This file is normally fairly small, and is updated during the lifetime of a message that cannot be delivered to all its recipients at the first attempt, in order to record which addresses have been dealt with. The existence of a -H file is sufficient to indicate the presence of a message on the queue. No separate list of messages is maintained.

The *input* directory within Exim's spool directory is used to hold the message files, which under normal circumstances are continually being created and deleted as mail passes through the system. If a large amount of mail is being handled, there will be contention between different Exim processes for access to the *input* directory. Furthermore, if the total number of messages on the queue at any time is large, updating the directory may take a long time, and thus may lead to poor performance. The size of directory that provokes a degradation in performance varies between different operating systems. Solaris, for example, can handle bigger directories than GNU/Linux (using its default file system) before it starts to degrade. To improve matters when the queue is large, the option:

```
split_spool_directory = true
```

can be set. When this is done, an extra directory level is used. Within the *input* directory, 62 subdirectories are created, with names consisting of a single letter or digit, and the message files are distributed among them. The sixth character in the message ID is used to determine the subdirectory in which a message is stored. For example, the message 12b2ie-0000GI-00 is stored in *input/e*. The sixth character is chosen because it is the least significant base-62 digit of the time of the message's arrival and changes every second. Splitting the *input* directory like this reduces the number of files in any one directory, and also reduces the amount of contention between processes that are trying to create or delete files in the directory. One disadvantage is that more work is required to scan the queue, either for listing it or for performing a queue run, but these operations are relatively infrequent.

During delivery, Exim creates two other files for each message. A third file in the *input* directory (or a subdirectory thereof) with suffix -J (for "journal") is used to record each recipient address as soon as it is delivered. If the message has to be retained for a subsequent delivery attempt at the end of a delivery run, the contents of the -J file are merged into the -H file, and the -J file is deleted. There are two reasons for the use of journal files:

- If there is a crash of any sort between the time a delivery completes and the time that this fact is recorded on disk, an unwanted second copy of the message will be delivered later.[1] Appending a single line to the -J file is a quick operation compared with updating the -H file, which involves writing a number of pieces of data to a new file and then renaming it. The use of a journal therefore minimizes the possibility of duplicate deliveries.

- Another reason for using a journal is that when several remote deliveries of the same message are taking place in parallel, in multiple processes, they can all add to the same -J file easily, without the need for explicit locking, because the operating system ensures that only one update happens at once.

The final per-message file is the *message log*, which contains log entries that record the progress of the message's delivery. For example, for every successful or unsuccessful delivery, a line is written to this file. The same information is also recorded on Exim's main log, but keeping copies in message log files makes it easy for an administrator to check the progress, or lack of it, of individual messages. Message logs are kept in a subdirectory called *msglog* in Exim's spool directory, and their names are the relevant message IDs. A message's log file is deleted when processing of the message is complete.[2] If the `split_spool_directory` option is set, the *msglog* directory is subdivided in the same way as the *input* directory.

You can disable the use of per-message logs by setting the `message_logs` option false. This reduces the number of files that Exim uses to process a message, which could be beneficial on a heavily loaded system.

# 11.2 Locking message files

When an Exim process is working on a message, it locks the -D file to prevent any other Exim process from trying to deliver the same message.[3] If another delivery process is started for the message, for example, by a queue runner, it notices the lock, and exits without doing anything, logging the message:

```
Spool file is locked (another process is handling this message)
```

This is a normal occurrence and does not indicate an error, though if it continues to occur for the same message over a long period of time, it might mean that there is some problem with the delivery process. You can turn off these log entries by unsetting the `skip_delivery` log selector (☞ 21.2.2).

---

[1] Even if Exim and all the other software in the system were bug-free, hardware failures and power losses can cause this effect.

[2] There is an option called `preserve_message_logs` that causes them to be moved to a spool directory called *msglog.OLD* instead, for statistical or debugging uses. It is then the administrator's responsibility to ensure that they are deleted.

[3] The -H file cannot be used for locking a message, because it can be updated during a delivery process, and the updating is carried out by writing a temporary file and renaming. This changes the underlying identity (inode) of the file, which is what locking is based on.

# 11.3 Hints files

Exim collects data about previously encountered delivery problems, in order to adapt its behaviour to changing circumstances. It remembers, for example, the hosts to which it has been unable to connect, so as not to keep trying them too often. The term "hints" is used to describe this data, because it is not critical for Exim's operation. If, for example, information about a failing host is lost, Exim will try to deliver to it at the next opportunity, instead of waiting for a previously calculated retry time. However, all this means is that the system is doing more work than it would otherwise have done. The pattern of delivery attempts is affected, but no messages are damaged or lost.

Because of the non-critical nature of the hints data, Exim maintains it by simple system I/O calls; there is no need for the sort of heavyweight transaction-based apparatus that would be necessary if the data had to be managed in the safest possible manner. This means that the overhead of maintaining the hints is minimal.

The hints data is kept in a number of files in a subdirectory of the spool directory called *db*. These files are not read or written sequentially like conventional files, because that would be very slow. Instead, the data they contain is held in indexed DBM files. Exim uses three different kinds of hints database, as follows:

- The *retry* database holds information about temporary delivery failures. These hints can be related to a particular host, mail address, or message (sometimes to a combination of host and message). The database records the type of error, the time of the first failure, the time of the last delivery attempt, and the earliest time it is reasonable to try again. A discussion of how this data is created and used is given in chapter 12.

- There is a database that contains lists of messages that are awaiting delivery to specific hosts, after having failed at their first attempt. In normal circumstances, this is updated only when a message fails to be delivered, though it is possible to force new messages to be added before their first delivery attempt.[1] The data is keyed by host name and IP address, and consists of a list of message IDs. The name of the database is *wait-*, followed by the name of the transport that attempted the delivery. A discussion of how this data is created and used is also given in chapter 12.

- The *misc* database is used for miscellaneous ephemeral data that Exim needs to record. So far, it has two uses:

    - The SMTP ETRN command allows a connected client host to request the server to attempt to deliver mail for a specific domain using a special kind of queue runner process. ETRN is mainly of use when the client is a dial-up host (☞ 13.3.3). The database is used to ensure that a client host

---

[1] See the `queue_smtp_domains` and `-odqs` options.

cannot cause more than one queue runner process to run at once by issuing multiple ETRNs.

– The `serialize_hosts` option of the **smtp** transport defines a set of hosts to which no more than one connection at once should be made. Typically, these are hosts that are connected over slow lines. The database is used to ensure that only one delivery process at a time connects to one of these hosts.

 If you are running a server that accepts ETRN or are making use of `serialize_hosts`, you should arrange to delete all the files whose names start with *misc* in the *db* subdirectory of Exim's spool directory whenever your host reboots. Otherwise, records that were never deleted will delay serialized deliveries or the use of ETRN until Exim decides that they are too old to be valid any longer (it waits six hours).

The exact names of the files in the *db* directory depend on the DBM library that is in use. Two filenames are used by some libraries, with the extensions *.dir* and *.pag*, whereas others use *.db* or no extension at all. Thus, the *retry* database, for example, might be held in *retry.dir* and *retry.pag*, or *retry.db*, or just *retry*. You will also see files whose names end in *.lock* in the *db* directory. These are used to ensure that only one process writes to a database at once when Exim is updating the hints files.[1]

Every delivery process consults the *retry* hints, and after any SMTP deliveries, the *wait-* hints are checked. If the system is running normally, the majority of these accesses are read-only, using shared locks that do not hold processes up. Only when there is a temporary failure or a successful delivery after a previous failure is it necessary for a process to gain exclusive access in order to update the hints. The hope is that this is a relatively rare occurrence.

Hints files accumulate out-of-date information that needs to be cleared out from time to time. For example, if a number of hosts are set up to accept mail for a certain domain, but all are unreachable at some time, retry data for each host is created. However, when the waiting message is subsequently delivered to one of them, the information for the others remains. There is a utility called *exim_tidydb* that clears away "dead wood" (data that has not been updated for a long time) in hints files; it should be run at regular intervals (for instance, daily or weekly). There are also some other utilities for inspecting and modifying the contents of hints files (☞ 21.10).

---

[1] Conventional locking of the files themselves cannot be used because Exim accesses them indirectly via a DBM library, and not all the DBM libraries provide integrated locking facilities. For simplicity, therefore, an external lock is used.

# 11.4 Log files

Unless Exim has been configured to use only *syslog*, it writes logging data to three files in its log directory, whose location is configurable at build time or at runtime. The most common locations are the *log* subdirectory within Exim's spool directory (which is the default), or a location such as */var/log/exim* on systems that keep all their logs in one place. The contents of Exim's logs are described later (☞ 21.1).

Exim processes all write to the same log files, but no Exim process ever reads any log data. Interlocking between processes is achieved by opening log files for appending, and ensuring that each log line is written in a single write operation. The operating system then ensures that only one update happens at once, and there is no need for the processes to do any locking of their own.

Log files are normally cycled on a regular (usually daily) basis by renaming. An Exim utility called *exicyclog* (☞ 21.4) is provided for this purpose, but if your operating system has its own log cycling facilities, they can be used instead. After a log file is renamed, a new file is created as soon as any Exim process has something to be logged. Existing Exim processes that have already opened the old file may keep it open, but will not write to it again; as soon as these processes have completed, the file becomes dormant. A common practice is to compress the previous-but-one log file 24 hours after it was renamed; the *exicyclog* script does this automatically.

# 11.5 User and group IDs for Exim processes

Exim is normally installed as a "setuid *root*" program, with permissions set like this:

```
-rwsr-xr-x  1 root  mail   561952 Nov 30 09:53 exim
```

The s permission means that whenever Exim starts up, it acquires *root* privilege, without which (for example) it cannot write into every user's mailbox. However, it is desirable on general security principles that any Exim process should stop running as *root* as soon as it no longer needs the privilege. In order to do this, it needs to have some other uid to use instead. Therefore, as part of the process of building Exim (described in chapter 22), a uid and gid must be defined; these are referred to in this book as "the Exim uid" and "the Exim gid".[1]

# 11.6 Process relationships

Although there is no central process that has overall control of what Exim is doing, Exim processes do interact with each other in various ways. The connections are illustrated in figure 11-2. The upper part of the figure is concerned with message reception, and the lower part with delivery. The solid lines indicate data flows, while

---

[1]  There is a general discussion of security later (☞ 19.1).

dashed ones are used to show where one process creates another without passing any message data. For example, the daemon process creates a new process for each incoming SMTP connection, and local reception processes can be created by any other process such as a user's MUA or a script that sends a message.

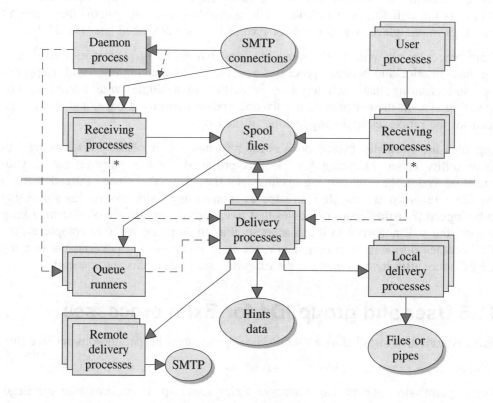

*Figure 11-2: Process relationships*

Delivery processes are started as a result of the arrival of a new message (the two lines marked *), or by a queue runner process. Exim also has command-line options that can be used by privileged users or by some automatic mechanism external to Exim itself to start delivery processes or queue runners. Immediate delivery can be suppressed by setting options in the configuration file, either unconditionally or under specific circumstances (☞ 11.8).

A delivery process performs one delivery attempt for one message. Each local and remote delivery of the message is done in a separate subprocess of the main delivery process. In the case of remote deliveries, several may be run at once, depending on the value of remote_max_parallel.

# 11.7 The daemon process

The daemon performs two tasks: listening for incoming SMTP connections and periodically starting queue runner processes. It is possible to run two separate daemons for these tasks, but there seems little advantage in doing so. This description assumes the common style of usage, where the daemon is started by a command such as:

```
exim -bd -q15m
```

The -bd option sets up a daemon that is listening for incoming SMTP, while -q15m specifies that it should start a new queue runner process every 15 minutes. These options are compatible with Sendmail, so the command:

```
/usr/sbin/sendmail -bd -q15m
```

that appears in the boot scripts in most operating systems will correctly start an Exim daemon, provided that */usr/sbin/sendmail* has been converted into a symbolic link to the Exim binary.

When a daemon starts up, unless debugging is enabled, it disconnects itself from any controlling terminal. After this, it writes its process ID into a file so that it can easily be found. The location of this file is configured either at build time, or by setting pid_file_path, but if no location is specified, the pid file is written in Exim's spool directory using the name *exim-daemon.pid*. This makes it easy to find when you want to kill the daemon, or send it a HUP signal after changing Exim's configuration file.

If you are running a host that uses different IP addresses (on virtual interfaces) to support a number of virtual web servers, you may not want to have incoming SMTP connections on all the virtual interfaces. If you set local_interfaces to a list of IP addresses, the daemon listens only on those interfaces. Otherwise, all interfaces are used.

By default, the same port number is used for all interfaces. It defaults to the standard SMTP port (25). The default can be changed by the daemon_smtp_port option or by the use of -oX on the command line that starts the daemon. Other ports can be useful for special applications, or for testing.

If you want to have a daemon that listens on more than one port, you can do so by setting local_interfaces appropriately or by using the extended form of the -oX command line option, which takes the same settings as local_interfaces. For each interface listed, a port number can be given; this overrides the default. Two different formats can be used, as shown in this example:

```
local_interfaces = <; 192.168.3.4.1234; \
                   [192.168.112.124]:5678
```

The first (adding a dot and the port number to the IP address) avoids the need to change the list separator.[1] The second is the same format in which the combination of an IP address and a port is shown in log files and *Received:* header lines.

You can configure multiple ports on a single interface by repeating the IP address, like this:

```
local_interfaces = 192.168.2.5.25 : 192.168.2.5.26
```

The variables *$interface_address* and *$interface_port* contain the interface address and port for each message that is received over TCP/IP.

The following checks are performed when the daemon receives an incoming SMTP connection:

- If the maximum permitted number of simultaneous incoming SMTP connections, as set by the `smtp_accept_max` option, is exceeded, the connection is rejected with the error response:

  ```
  421 Too many concurrent SMTP connections;
      please try again later.
  ```

  You should set `smtp_accept_max` to a value that is appropriate to the power of your host and the speed of your network connection. The default value of 20 is on the small side.

- If `smtp_accept_max_per_host` is set, the list of current connections is scanned to find out how many are from the incoming IP address. If the new connection would cause the limit to be exceeded, the connection is rejected with the error:

  ```
  421 Too many concurrent SMTP connections from one IP address;
      please try again later.
  ```

  There is no default limit on the number of connections from a single host.

- If `smtp_accept_queue` is greater than zero, and the number of incoming SMTP connections exceeds its value, no delivery processes are started for messages that are received. Instead, they remain on the queue until picked up by a queue runner process. This value is useful only if it is less than `smtp_accept_max`. It can help to keep the system load down at times of high SMTP input.

- If `smtp_accept_reserve` is greater than zero, Exim reserves that number of incoming SMTP connections (out of the maximum set in `smtp_accept_max`) for the hosts listed in `smtp_reserve_hosts`. This does not limit the number of connections from those hosts; rather, it ensures that other hosts

---

[1] It is also convenient when using -oX, because it avoids the use of shell metacharacters.

cannot use all the available connections. For example, consider the following settings:

```
smtp_accept_max = 100
smtp_accept_reserve = 15
```

Once there are 85 incoming connections, new ones are accepted only from the favoured hosts. This can be useful on clusters of hosts that are interchanging mail. For example, if the hosts on a LAN are interacting with a server that also acts as an Internet gateway, reserving some of the server's connections for the local hosts prevents external hosts from blocking internal mail by using all the server's SMTP slots.

*   The value of `smtp_load_reserve` is a system load average.[1] When the system's actual one-minute load average is above this value, connections are accepted only from hosts that are defined by `smtp_reserve_hosts` (if any). Other hosts are rejected with the error:

    ```
    421 Too much load; please try again later.
    ```

If none of the checks fail, a new process is created to continue handling the incoming connection; the daemon is now ready to accept another SMTP connection. Although it does very little processing before forking, other incoming connections may arrive during that time. The operating system maintains a queue of waiting connections, the length of which is specified by `smtp_connect_backlog`. Once this number of connections are waiting, subsequent connection attempts are supposed to be refused at the TCP/IP level. However, on some operating systems, attempts to connect have been seen to time out in such circumstances. The default value of 20 is a conservative one. For large systems, it is probably a good idea to increase this, possibly substantially (50 is a reasonable number).

Apart from incoming TCP/IP connections, there are two other events that wake up a daemon process. The first is its timer, in the case when it is configured to start queue runner processes periodically. Whenever the timer expires, a new queue runner process is created, unless `queue_run_max` is greater than zero and the number of queue runner processes that are still running is greater than or equal to its value.

The other useful event is the arrival of a SIGHUP signal. You should send a SIGHUP signal to the daemon whenever Exim's configuration file has been updated. The daemon reacts by closing down any sockets that it is listening on and re-executing itself, thereby rereading the configuration file. It is a good idea to inspect the end of the main log to check that the daemon has restarted successfully. A consequence of the way SIGHUP is handled is that the memory of the number of incoming SMTP connections and running queue runner processes is lost after a SIGHUP.

---

[1]   See the Unix *uptime* command for details of system load averages.

The daemon has to take notice of the completion of SMTP reception processes and queue runner processes in order to maintain its counts of active processes, so that it can refrain from starting new ones when the limits are reached. However, termination of these processes does not wake up the daemon. Instead, the daemon checks for completed processes whenever it wakes up for any other reason, which on busy systems happens frequently. On systems where not much is happening, "zombie" (defunct) processes that are children of the daemon can sometimes be seen. This is perfectly normal; they are tidied away the next time the daemon wakes up.

## 11.7.1 Summary of options for the daemon

Here is a summary of the configuration options that are relevant to the daemon process and the reception processes it creates:

daemon_smtp_port (string, default = unset)
> This option specifies the default SMTP port on which the daemon listens. It can be overridden by giving a port number with an IP address in the local_ interfaces option, or by using -oX on the command line. If this option is unset, the standard SMTP port 25 is used.

local_interfaces (string, default = unset)
> The string must be a colon-separated list of IP addresses. Each address may optionally include a port, using either of these formats:

```
<ip address>.<port number>
[<ip address>]:<port number>
```

> If local_interfaces is unset, the daemon issues a generic *listen()* that accepts incoming SMTP connections on any interface, using the default port. Otherwise, it listens only on the interfaces (and ports) identified here. An error occurs if it is unable to bind a listening socket to any listed interface. The contents of local_interfaces are also used as a list of the local host's addresses when routing mail and checking for mail loops (☞ 6.5).

queue_run_max (integer, default = 5)
> This option controls the maximum number of queue runner processes that an Exim daemon will run simultaneously. This does not mean that it starts them all at once, but rather that if the maximum number are still running when the time comes to start another one, it refrains from starting it. This can happen with very large queues and/or very sluggish deliveries. Remember that Exim is not a centralized system. This limit applies only to a single daemon process. If a queue runner is started by another means (for example, by hand by the administrator), it does not count towards this limit. Also, if the daemon is restarted or sent a SIGHUP signal, it loses its memory of previously started queue runners.

`smtp_accept_max` (integer, default = 20)

This specifies the maximum number of simultaneous incoming SMTP connections that Exim will accept. It applies only to the listening daemon; there is no control (in Exim) when incoming SMTP is being handled by *inetd*. If the value is set to zero, no limit is applied, but this is not recommended.

`smtp_accept_max_per_host` (string, default = unset)

This option restricts the number of simultaneous IP connections from a single host (strictly, from a single IP address) to the Exim daemon. The string is expanded, to enable different limits to be applied to different hosts by reference to *$sender_host_address*. Once the limit is reached, additional connection attempts from the same host are rejected with error code 421. No limit is imposed by default. If this option is used, `smtp_accept_max` must be non-zero.

`smtp_accept_queue` (integer, default = 0)

If the number of simultaneous incoming SMTP connections handled via the listening daemon exceeds this value, messages received are simply placed on the queue; no delivery processes are started automatically. A value of zero implies no limit, and clearly any non-zero value is useful only if it is less than the `smtp_accept_max` value (unless that is zero). See also `queue_only`, `queue_only_load`, `queue_smtp_domains`, and the various `-od` command-line options.

`smtp_accept_reserve` (integer, default = 0)

When `smtp_accept_max` is set greater than zero, this option specifies a number of SMTP connections that are reserved for connections from the hosts that are specified in `smtp_reserve_hosts`.

`smtp_connect_backlog` (integer, default = 20)

This specifies a maximum number of waiting SMTP connections. Exim passes this value to the TCP/IP system when it sets up its listener. Once this number of connections are waiting for the daemon's attention, subsequent connection attempts are refused at the TCP/IP level.

`smtp_load_reserve` (fixed point, default = unset)

Whenever the system load average is higher than this value, incoming SMTP connections are accepted only from those hosts that match an entry in `smtp_reserve_hosts`.

`smtp_reserve_hosts` (host list, default = unset)

This option defines hosts for which SMTP connections are reserved; see `smtp_accept_reserve` and `smtp_load_reserve`.

# 11.8 Reception processes

Reception processes for handling incoming SMTP messages from remote hosts are started by the daemon or by *inetd*.[1] A single SMTP reception process can receive any number of messages. However, if the number received exceeds the value of `smtp_accept_queue_per_connection` (default 10), no automatic delivery processes are started for the remainder. They are just put on the queue for the next queue runner to deal with.

A TCP/IP connection from a local process is treated in the same way as a connection from a remote host, even if it uses the loopback address 127.0.0.1 (or ::1 on an IPv6 system).

The other way a local process can send a message is by starting an Exim reception process itself (that is, by running */usr/sbin/sendmail* or */usr/lib/sendmail* in a new process). The message is passed to the Exim process on its standard input. There are several different ways in which this can be done (☞ 14.3).

Receiving a message consists of copying its contents to a pair of -D and -H files in Exim's spool area. Once these files have been successfully written, reception is complete, and Exim returns a success response to the sender.

The existence of an -H file signifies the presence of a message on the queue. There is no separately maintained list of messages; the files *are* the queue. As soon as the -H file comes into existence (by renaming from a temporary name), it is legitimate for another Exim process to start work delivering the message. A process that receives a message creates a delivery process before it finishes, except in the following circumstances:

- If `queue_only` is set, or the reception process was started with the -odq option, incoming messages are placed on the queue without an automatic delivery process being started. Deliveries then occur only via queue runner processes, or manual intervention. On very busy systems, this may lead to better throughput because the total number of delivery processes can be controlled.

- If `queue_only_load` is set to some positive value, and the system load is greater than this value, incoming messages are queued without immediate delivery. For example:

  ```
  queue_only_load = 8
  ```

  specifies that no immediate deliveries are to take place when the system load is greater than 8.

---

[1] Most Exim installations use a daemon, and that is generally assumed in this book. Nevertheless, if an administrator wants to route all incoming TCP/IP connections through *inetd* for whatever reason, Exim can handle this way of working. However, it is likely to be less efficient on a busy system.

- If `queue_only_file` names an existing file, no immediate delivery takes place. This facility is intended for use on dial-up hosts, where a configuration such as this:

    ```
    queue_only_file = /etc/not-dialed-up
    ```

    can be used in conjunction with commands in the dial-up starting and stopping scripts to remove and create the file. A colon-separated list of files may be given, in which case the existence of any one of them is enough to provoke queuing.

There are two other options that may delay some deliveries of a message until the next queue run, while not necessarily delaying all of them. These options are `queue_domains` and `queue_smtp_domains` (or `-odqs`) (☞ 12.12).

## 11.9 Queue runner processes

The job of a queue runner process is to start delivery processes for all the messages that are on Exim's spool, waiting for each process to complete before starting the next. In other words, a single queue runner process works its way through the queue, attempting to deliver just one message at time. It does not (by default) distinguish between messages that have suffered a failed delivery attempt and those that were put on the queue without an immediate delivery process being started. However, it does skip over frozen messages.

Notice that the queue runner does not itself do any of the work of delivering. That is left to the delivery processes that it creates. All the queue runner does is to arrange for delivery processes to be run for all the waiting messages, in a controlled manner.

Queue runner processes should be started at regular intervals, and the most common way of doing this is to use an option such as `-q15m` (every 15 minutes) on the command that starts the Exim daemon. However, external mechanisms such as *cron* can be used to start queue runners by means of the command:

```
exim -q
```

Multiple queue runner processes may be active simultaneously. The daemon does not start a new one if the maximum number (specified by `queue_run_max`) are still active. Queue runners that are not started by the daemon are not included in this count.

In very busy environments, it may be desirable to control the total number of Exim delivery processes that run simultaneously. If you set `queue_only`, immediate delivery on reception is suppressed, so the only delivery processes are those that are started by queue runners. If you configure the daemon to start queue runners frequently (say every minute by starting it with `-q1m`), but limit the maximum number that may be simultaneously active, for example, by setting:

```
queue_run_max = 10
```

there will never be more than 10 delivery processes running at once, though additional subprocesses will be created to carry out the actual deliveries.[1]

## 11.9.1 Special kinds of queue run

Additional queue running options are available for special purposes; these are not normally used in regular periodic queue runs, but are either specified for one-off queue runs by the system administrator, or generated in response to some specific event such as the connection of a dial-up host.

In a normal queue run, the delivery processes inspect the retry data for addresses and hosts, and refrain from attempting deliveries for those addresses whose retry times have not yet arrived. This can be overridden by starting a queue runner with `-qf`, which forces a delivery attempt for all addresses. An even more powerful option is `-qff`, which, in addition to overriding retry times, causes frozen messages not to be skipped.

If `i` (for "initial delivery") is added to any of the `-q` options, messages that have previously been tried are skipped. This can be useful if you are putting messages on the queue without an immediate delivery (for example, by using `queue_only` or `-odq`), and want a queue runner to process just the new messages. If `l` (a lower case letter L) is added to the end of any of the `-q` options, only local deliveries take place. These variants of the `-q` option are summarized in table 11-1.

*Table 11-1: Queue runner options (-q)*

| Option | Meaning |
|---|---|
| `-q` | Single queue run, respect retry times |
| `-qf` | Single queue run, override retry times |
| `-qff` | Single queue run, override retry times, include frozen messages |
| `-qi, -qfi, -qffi` | First delivery attempts only |
| `-ql, -qfl, -qffl` | Local deliveries only |
| `-qil, -qfil, -qffil` | Both of the above |

It is possible to run only part of the queue, or to select only messages whose senders or recipients match certain patterns (☞ 20.5).

---

[1] If `remote_max_parallel` is greater than one, there may also be multiple subprocesses for remote deliveries (☞ 4.9).

Normal queue runners process the waiting messages in an arbitrary order that is likely to be different each time. This is beneficial when there is one particular message that is provoking delivery failures for some address. For example, very large messages sometimes cause timeouts or other problems when transmitted to remote hosts, whereas smaller messages to the same hosts might get through. After a temporary error such as a timeout, Exim is not prepared to try the same host again for some time, so any other messages for the same address are likely to be passed over in the same queue run. By processing the messages "randomly", there is a chance that in some future queue run the trouble-free messages will be handled first, and so be delivered instead of being delayed behind the problem message.

You can specify that Exim should not do this randomizing, and instead should process the messages in order of their IDs, which is in effect the order of their arrival, by setting `queue_run_in_order`. However, there is rarely a good reason for doing this, and it can degrade performance on systems with a large queue where `split_spool_directory` is set. The reason is that all the subdirectories of the *input* directory have to be scanned before any deliveries can start, in order to obtain the complete list of messages and sort them by ID. When the order is not constrained, the subdirectories can be tackled one at a time.

## 11.10 Delivery processes

Delivery processes are the most complex of Exim's processes. Each delivery process handles one delivery attempt for one message only, though there may be many recipients for the message and therefore many delivery actions, all of which take place in subprocesses. Delivery processes may be started as a result of a message's arrival, by a queue runner process, or by an administrator using the -M option. For example:

```
exim -M 11wO3z-00042J-00
```

starts a delivery process for the given message, overriding any retry times.

When a delivery process starts up, it normally checks first to see if the message it is working on is frozen. If it is, it writes to the log:

```
Message is frozen
```

and exits without doing anything. However, a delivery process can be told to process frozen messages regardless (this happens if it is running as a result of -M or -qff, for example), and there is also an `auto_thaw` option, which automatically "thaws" (unfreezes) messages after they have been frozen for a certain length of time.

Before proceeding to the normal delivery actions, a delivery process runs the system filter if one is configured. Exim's filtering features are described in chapter 10. The system filter may add or remove header lines, modify the list of recipients, or cause a message to be frozen or all its recipient addresses to be failed.

After system filtering, before any deliveries occur, a delivery process determines what must be done for every recipient by running the routers for each address in turn. This allows for optimization when more than one address is routed to the same host, and it also means that duplicate addresses generated by aliasing or forwarding can be discarded.

If a message is to be delivered to more than one remote host, Exim can be configured to run several SMTP deliveries at once by setting `remote_max_parallel` to a value greater than one, as in this example:

```
remote_max_parallel = 5
```

When this is done, and there are multiple remote deliveries to be made, a delivery process forks several subprocesses at a time, up to the maximum specified. The value of `remote_max_parallel` controls the maximum number of parallel deliveries created by a single Exim delivery process only. Because Exim has no central queue manager, there is no way of controlling the total number of simultaneous deliveries running on the local host if immediate delivery of incoming messages is configured.

Once all the delivery attempts are complete, if any of them failed outright, a bounce message is created and sent to the envelope sender address. It contains information about all the addresses that failed in this delivery run, and is created by calling Exim in a subprocess and writing to its standard input. If there is no sender address (that is, if the message that is failing to be delivered is itself a bounce message), no new bounce message can be sent. The failing message is left on the queue and frozen so that no further delivery attempts are made and the administrator's attention is drawn to it.

The final actions of the delivery process depend on whether all the message's recipients have been completely handled (either delivered or bounced). If there are no remaining addresses, all the spool files for the message are deleted, and "Completed" is written to the main log. Otherwise there are some addresses that have suffered temporary errors, or which were skipped for some reason. A warning message about the delivery delay is sent to the message's sender if appropriate (☞ 19.8.3), and the spool files are updated to record those addresses that have been delivered or bounced in the current delivery attempt.

## 11.10.1 Variations on delivery

A delivery process normally operates on all the recipient addresses in a message. On a host that is not permanently connected to the Internet, this is inappropriate; you want to deliver to the local addresses, but save the remote ones until the host is online. The `queue_domains` and `queue_smtp_domains` options allow you to specify this behaviour (☞ 12.12).

Sometimes it may be beneficial to specify the order in which remote deliveries take place. This is done by setting `remote_sort_domains` to a list of domains; remote deliveries to addresses in those domains are then carried out in that order. Other remote deliveries take place afterwards, in an unpredictable order. For example, you could specify that deliveries to hosts on your local network happen first by a setting such as:

```
remote_sort_domains = *.mydomain.example
```

Finally, there is an option called `hold_domains` that specifies a list of domains that Exim is not to deliver, except when a delivery is forced by an administrator. An address in these domains is deferred every time a delivery process encounters it. This feature is intended as a temporary operational measure for delaying the delivery of mail while some problem is being sorted out or some new configuration is being tested.

# 11.11 Summary of message handling process types

Whenever the Exim binary is run, the type of process is controlled by the command line options with which it is called. The options for the four kinds of message handling process are summarized in table 11-2.

*Table 11-2: Message handling process types*

| Option | Meaning |
|---|---|
| `-bd` | Daemon process, listening for SMTP, forks SMTP reception processes |
| `-bs` from *inetd* | SMTP reception process |
| `-bs` (not *inetd*) | Local SMTP reception process |
| `-bS` | Local batch SMTP reception process |
| `-M` | Forced delivery process for specific message |
| `-q` | Single queue runner process, starts delivery processes |
| `-q` *<time>* | Daemon process, starts queue runners periodically |
| `-t` or none | Local reception process |

A local reception process can be created by any other process, but creating the other kinds of process requires the caller to have Exim administration privileges (☞ 19.3).

# 11.12 Other types of process

In addition to message handling, some other kinds of process are used for administering Exim or for debugging the configuration. Special configuration options are used for setting these up (for details, see chapter 20). For example, the -bp option causes Exim to list the messages on its queue.

# 12

# Delivery errors and retrying

This chapter is all about temporary delivery errors, and how Exim deals with them. In an ideal world, every message would either be delivered at the first attempt, or be bounced, and temporary errors would not arise. In the real world, this does not happen; hosts are down from time to time, or are not responding, and network connections fail. An MTA has to be prepared to hold on to messages for some time, while trying every now and again to deliver them. Some rules are needed for deciding how often the retrying is to occur and when to give up because the retrying has been going on for too long.

A related topic is how to handle messages destined for hosts that are connected to the Internet only intermittently (for example, by dial-up lines). In this case, incoming messages have to be kept on some server host because they cannot be delivered immediately. Exim was not designed for this, and is not ideal for it, but because it is being used in such circumstances, the final section of this chapter discusses how it can best be configured.

## 12.1 Retrying after errors

Delivering a message costs resources, so it is a good idea not to retry unreasonably often. Trying to deliver a failing message every minute for several days, for example, is not sensible. Even trying as often as every 15 minutes is wasteful over a long period. Furthermore, if one message has just suffered a temporary connection failure, immediately trying to deliver another message to the same host is also a waste of resources.

A number of MTAs use *message-based* retrying; they apply a retry schedule to each message independently. This can cause hosts to be tried several times in quick succession. Exim is not like this; for failures that are not related to a specific message, it uses *host-based* retrying. If delivery to a host fails temporarily, all messages that are routed to that host are delayed until its next retry time arrives.

In practice, Exim normally bases retry operations on the failing IP address, rather than the host name. If a host has more than one IP address, each is treated separately as far as retrying is concerned. In the discussion that follows, we use the word "host" when talking about remote delivery errors, to make it easier to read. It should be understood, however, that this refers to a single IP address, so that a host with several network interfaces is, in effect, treated as several independent hosts.

Information about temporary delivery failures is kept in a hints database called *retry* in the *db* subdirectory of Exim's spool directory. You can read the contents of this if you want to, using the *exinext* utility (☞ 21.6.2). The information includes details of the error, the time of the first failure, the time of the most recent failure, and the time before which it is not reasonable to try again.

Exim uses a set of configurable *retry rules* in a separate section of the configuration file to decide when next to try a failing delivery. These rules allow you to specify fixed or increasing retry intervals, or a combination of the two. Details of the rules are given later in this chapter, after the different kinds of error are described.

## 12.2 Remote delivery errors

Most, but not all, delays and retries are concerned with deliveries to remote hosts. Three different kinds of error are recognized during a remote delivery: host errors, message errors, and recipient errors.

### 12.2.1 Host errors

A host error is not associated with a particular message, nor with a particular recipient of a message. The host errors are as follows:

- Refusal of connection to a remote host.

- Timeout of a connection attempt.

- An error code in response to setting up a connection.

- An error code in response to EHLO or HELO.

- Loss of connection at any time except after the final dot that ends a message.

- I/O errors at any time.

- Timeout during the SMTP session, other than in response to MAIL, RCPT, or the dot at the end of the data.

When a permanent SMTP error code ($5<xx>$) is given at the start of a connection or in response to an EHLO or HELO command, all the addresses that are routed to the host are failed, and returned to the sender in a bounce message.

The other kinds of host error are treated as temporary, and they cause all addresses routed to the host to be deferred. Retry data is created for the host, and it is not tried again, for any message, until its retry time arrives. If the current set of addresses are not all delivered to some backup host by the current delivery process, the message is added to a list of those waiting for the failing host.[1] This is a hint that Exim uses if it

---

[1]   Strictly, the list is of messages routed through the current transport that are waiting for the specific host, but in the great majority of configurations, there is usually only one **smtp** transport.

makes a subsequent successful delivery to the host. It checks to see if there are any other messages waiting for the same host, and if so, sends them using the same SMTP connection.

## 12.2.2 Message errors

A message error is associated with a particular message when sent to a particular host, but not with a particular recipient of the message. The message errors are as follows:

- An error code in response to MAIL, DATA, or the dot that terminates the data.

- Timeout after sending MAIL.

- Timeout or loss of connection after the dot that terminates the data. A timeout after the DATA command itself is treated as a host error, as is loss of connection at any other time.

For a temporary message error, all addresses that are routed to the host are deferred. Retry data is not created for the host, but instead, a retry record for the combination of the host name and the message ID is created. The message is not added to the list of those waiting for this host. This ensures that the failing message will not be sent to this host again until the retry time arrives. However, other messages that are routed to the host are not affected, so if it is some property of the message that is causing the error, this does not stop the delivery of other mail.

If the remote host specifies support for the SIZE parameter in its response to EHLO, Exim adds SIZE=<*nnn*> to the MAIL command. Thus, an overlarge message causes a permanent message error because it arrives as a response to MAIL. However, when SIZE is not in use, some hosts respond to unacceptably large messages by just dropping the connection. This leads to a temporary message error if it is detected after the whole message has been sent. Better behaved hosts give a permanent error return after the end of the message; this allows the message to be bounced without retries.

## 12.2.3 Recipient errors

A recipient error is associated with a particular recipient of a message. The recipient errors are as follows:

- An error code in response to RCPT.

- Timeout after RCPT.

For temporary recipient errors, the failing address is deferred, and routing retry data is created for it. This delays processing of the address in subsequent queue runs, until its routing retry time arrives. The delay applies to all messages, but because it operates only in queue runs, one attempt is made to deliver a new message to the failing address before the delay starts to operate. This ensures that, if the failure is really related to the message rather than the recipient ("message too big for this recipient" is a possible example), other messages have a chance of being delivered. If a delivery to the address does succeed, the retry information is cleared, after which all stuck messages are tried again in the next queue run.

The message is not added to the list of those waiting for this host. Use of the host for other recipient addresses is unaffected, and except in the case of a timeout, other recipients are processed independently, and may be successfully delivered in the current SMTP session. After a timeout, it is, of course, impossible to proceed with the session, so all addresses are deferred. However, those other than the one that failed do not suffer any subsequent retry delays. Therefore, if one recipient is causing trouble, the others have a chance of getting through when a subsequent delivery attempt occurs before the failing recipient's retry time.

## 12.2.4 Problems of error classification

Some hosts have been observed to give temporary error responses to every MAIL command at certain times ("insufficient space" has been seen). These are treated as message errors. It would be nice if such circumstances could be recognized instead as host errors, and retry data for the host itself created, but this is not possible within the current Exim design. What actually happens is that retry data for every (host, message) combination is created.

The reason that timeouts after MAIL and RCPT are treated specially is that these can sometimes arise as a result of the remote host's verification procedures taking a very long time. Exim makes this assumption, and treats them as if a temporary error response had been received. A timeout after the final dot is treated specially because it is known that some broken implementations fail to recognize the end of the message if the last character of the last line is a binary zero. Thus, is it helpful to treat this case as a message error.

Timeouts at other times are treated as host errors, assuming a problem with the host, or the connection to it. If a timeout after MAIL, RCPT, or the final dot is really a connection problem, the assumption is that at the next try, the timeout is likely to occur at some other point in the dialogue, causing it to be treated as a host error.

There is experimental evidence that some MTAs drop the connection after the terminating dot if they do not like the contents of the message for some reason. This is in contravention of the RFC, which indicates that a 5<xx> response should be given. That is why Exim treats this case as a message error rather than a host error, in order not to delay other messages to the same host.

## 12.2.5 Delivery to multiple hosts

In all cases of temporary delivery error, if there are other hosts (or IP addresses) available for the current set of addresses (for example, from multiple MX records), they are tried in the current run for any undelivered addresses, subject of course to their own retry data. This means that newly created recipient error retry data does not affect the current delivery process; instead, it takes effect the next time a delivery process for the message is run.

# 12.3 Local delivery errors

Remote deliveries are not the only cases where a temporary error may be encountered; such errors can also arise during local deliveries. The two most common cases are as follows:

- A delivery to a mailbox file fails because the user is over quota.

- A delivery to a command via a pipe fails, with the command yielding a return code that is defined as "temporary" (☞ 9.5).

The mechanism for computing retry times is the same as for remote delivery errors, but retry delays apply only to deliveries in queue runs. When a delivery is not part of a queue run (typically, an immediate delivery on receipt of a message), the routers are always run, and local deliveries are always attempted, even if retry times are set for them. This makes for better behaviour if one particular message is causing problems (for example, causing quota overflow, or provoking an error in a filter file). If such a delivery suffers a temporary failure, the retry data is updated as normal, and subsequent delivery attempts from queue runs occur only when the retry time for the local address is reached.

# 12.4 Routing errors

Temporary errors are also possible during routing. They are most commonly caused by:

- A problem with a DNS lookup (either a timeout or a "try again" DNS error). A name server may be down for some reason, or it may be unreachable owing to a network problem. Mistakes in zone files also sometimes cause name servers to issue temporary errors.

- A problem with a lookup in a local database. The database server may be down, or, if it is on some other host, it may be unreachable.

- Mistakes in Exim's configuration (for example, a syntax error in an expansion string).

Retry processing applies to routing an address as well as to transporting a message, but only for delivery processes started in queue runs (as explained in the previous section). The retry rules do not distinguish between routing and transporting, so it is not possible, for example, to specify different behaviour for failures to route the domain *snark.example* and failures to deliver to the host *snark.example*. However, although they share the same retry rule, the actual retry times for routing and transporting a given domain are maintained independently.

## 12.5 Retry rules

The rules for controlling how often Exim retries a temporarily failing address are contained in a separate part of the configuration file, introduced by the line "begin retry". Each retry rule occupies one line and consists of three parts: a pattern, an error name, and a list of retry parameters. Figure 12-1 shows the single rule that is provided in the default configuration file. Many installations operate with just this default rule.

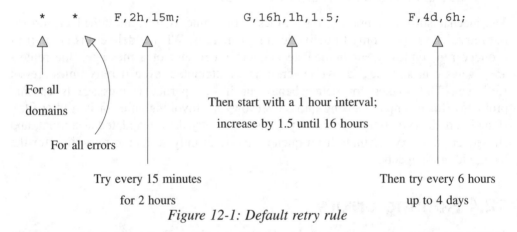

*Figure 12-1: Default retry rule*

When Exim needs to calculate when next to try to deliver a particular address, it searches the retry rules in order, and uses the first one it encounters that matches certain criteria, depending on the particular error that was encountered. If no suitable rule is found, a temporary error is converted into a permanent error, and the address is bounced after the first delivery attempt. Therefore, the final rule should normally contain asterisks in the first two fields, as shown in figure 12-1, so that it applies to all cases that are not covered by earlier rules.

## 12.5.1 Retry rule patterns

The pattern that starts a retry rule can be any item that may appear in an address list. The possibilities include regular expressions and several forms of lookup (☞ 18.7). However, a domain name (possibly wildcarded) is the most common type of retry pattern. The pattern is processed as a one-item address list, which means that it is expanded before being tested against an address.

### Retry rules for remote deliveries

When looking for a retry rule after a routing attempt for a remote domain has failed (for example, after a DNS timeout), each line in the retry configuration is tested only against the domain in the address. However, when looking for a retry rule after a remote delivery attempt has failed (for example, a connection timeout), each line in the retry configuration is first tested against the remote host name, and then against the domain name in the address. For example, if the MX records for *a.b.c.d* are:

```
a.b.c.d.  MX  5  x.y.z.
          MX  6  p.q.r.
          MX  7  m.n.o.
```

and the retry rules are:

```
p.q.r    *      F,24h,30m;
a.b.c.d  *      F,4d,45m;
```

then failures to deliver the address *xyz@a.b.c.d* to the host *p.q.r* use the first rule to determine retry times, but for all the other hosts for the domain *a.b.c.d*, the second rule is used. The second rule is also used if routing to *a.b.c.d* suffers a temporary failure.

A domain may route to a number of hosts, and each host may have more than one IP address. Retry algorithms are selected on the basis of the domain name, but are applied to each IP address independently. If, for example, a host has two IP addresses and one is broken, Exim will generate retry times for that IP address, and will not try to use it until its next retry time comes. Thus, the good IP address is likely to be tried first most of the time.

### Retry rules for local deliveries

In the case of domains that are handled locally, temporary failures are usually associated with both the local part and the domain. For example, a delivery failure caused by an overfull mailbox is specific to one user. Therefore, when dealing with this type of error, we need to set up retry times for one particular address instead of for the whole domain. Exim handles this requirement by means of an option called `retry_use_local_part`, which exists as a generic option for both routers and transports. The default value is true for local transports and for routers that have check_local_user set, and false in all other cases. The default is therefore true for "normal" deliveries to local mailboxes or pipe commands.

When Exim is dealing with a temporary delivery failure for an address that was handled by a driver with retry_use_local_part set true, the complete address (*user@domain*) is matched against any retry rules that start with regular expressions or patterns containing local parts. However, if there is no local part in a pattern that is not a regular expression, the local part of the address is not used in the matching. Thus, an entry such as:

```
lookingglass.example        *  F,24h,30m;
```

matches any address whose domain is *lookingglass.example*, whether or not retry_use_local_part is set, whereas:

```
alice@lookingglass.example  *  F,24h,30m;
```

applies only when the local part is *alice* and the driver that detects the temporary failure has retry_use_local_part set.

---

 If local delivery is being used to collect messages for onward trans-mission by some other means (for example, as batched SMTP), a tem-porary failure may not be dependent on the local part after all. For example, a file in which all messages for a particular domain are being collected may have reached a quota limit. If this is the case, and you want to avoid independent retrying for each different local part, you should arrange for such deliveries to be carried out by a special trans-port with retry_use_local_part set false. Exim will then retry on the basis of the domain only.

---

## 12.5.2 Retry rule error names

The second field in a retry rule is the name of a particular error, or an asterisk, which matches any error. The errors that can be specified are listed in table 12-1.

This field makes it possible to apply different retry algorithms to different kinds of error; some examples are shown in the following section. The authentication failure error applies when a server is listed in hosts_require_auth in an **smtp** trans-port, but the client could not authenticate. The quota errors apply both to system-enforced quotas and to Exim's own quota mechanism in the **appendfile** transport.

*Table 12-1: Error field in retry rules*

| Error | Meaning |
|---|---|
| `auth_failed` | Authentication failed |
| `quota` | Quota exceeded in local delivery |
| `quota_<time>` | Quota exceeded in local delivery, and the mailbox has not been read for `<time>` |
| `refused_MX` | Connection refused; host obtained from an MX record |
| `refused_A` | Connection refused; host not obtained from an MX record |
| `refused` | Any connection refusal |
| `timeout_connect` | Connection timed out |
| `timeout_DNS` | DNS lookup timed out |
| `timeout` | Any timeout |

## 12.5.3 Retry rule parameter sets

The remainder of a retry rule is a sequence of retry parameter sets, separated by semicolons and optional whitespace. For example:

```
F,3h,10m; G,16h,40m,1.5; F,4d,6h
```

Each set consists of:

```
<letter>,<cutoff time>,<arguments>;
```

For example, in:

```
F,8h,15m;
```

the letter is F, the cutoff time is 8 hours, and there is just one argument. The letter identifies the algorithm for computing a new retry time; the cutoff time is the time beyond which this algorithm no longer applies, and the arguments vary the algorithm's action. There are two available algorithms:

- The letter F specifies retrying at fixed intervals. There is a single argument, which specifies the interval. In the previous example, `15m` sets up retries every 15 minutes.

- The letter G specifies retrying at increasing intervals.[1] The first argument specifies a starting value for the interval, and the second a multiplier. For example:

```
G,16h,40m,1.5;
```

---

[1]  G was chosen because it is next to F, and because the intervals form a geometric progression.

specifies an initial interval of 40 minutes that is increased each time by a factor of 1.5. The actual intervals used are therefore 40 minutes, 60 minutes, 90 minutes, and so on.

A retry rule may contain any number of parameter sets of either type, in any order. If none are provided, no retrying is done for addresses and errors that match the rule, thereby immediately turning temporary errors into permanent errors.

## 12.6 Computing retry times

When Exim computes a retry time from a retry rule, the parameter sets are scanned from left to right until one whose cutoff time has not yet passed is reached. The cutoff time is measured from the time that the first failure for the host or domain (combined with the local part if relevant) was detected, not from the time the message was received.

This set of parameters is then used to compute a new retry time that is later than the current time. In the case of fixed interval retries, this just means adding the interval to the current time. For geometrically increasing intervals, retry intervals are computed from the rule's parameters until one that is greater than the previous interval is found. Consider the rule in the default configuration:

```
*   *   F,2h,15m; G,16h,1h,1.5; F,4d,6h;
```

For the first 2 hours after a failure is detected, the next retry time is computed as 15 minutes after the most recent failure. After that, there is an interval of 1 hour before the next retry, and this is increased by a factor of 1.5 each time, until 16 hours have passed since the first failure. Thereafter, retries happen every 6 hours, until 4 days have passed.

At this point, Exim has run out of retry algorithms for the address. In this state, if any delivery suffers a temporary failure, it is converted into a permanent timeout failure, and the address is bounced. What happens if a new message for the same address arrives is described in section 12.10.

Because a geometric retry rule might "run away" and generate enormously long retry intervals, there is a configuration option called `retry_interval_max` that limits the maximum interval between retries. Its default value is `24h`, ensuring that all temporarily failing addresses are tried at least once a day.

## 12.7 Using retry times

The retry times that are computed from the retry rules are hints rather than promises. Exim does not make any attempt to run deliveries exactly at the computed times. Instead, a queue runner process starts delivery processes for delayed messages periodically, and these processes attempt new deliveries only for those addresses that have passed their next retry time. If a new message arrives for an address that had a temporary failure earlier, local deliveries are tried immediately (because retry times apply to local deliveries only in queue runs), but remote deliveries are tried only if the retry time for that address has been reached. A continual stream of messages for a broken host does not therefore cause a continual sequence of delivery attempts.

If no new messages for a failing address arrive, the minimum time between retries is the interval between queue runner processes. There is not much point in setting retry times of 5 minutes if your queue runners happen only once an hour, unless there are a significant number of incoming messages (which might be the case on a system that is sending everything to a smart host, for example).

## 12.8 Retry rule examples

Here are some example retry rules suitable for use when *wonderland.example* is a domain that is delivered locally:

```
alice@wonderland.example quota     F,7d,3h
wonderland.example        quota_5d
wonderland.example        *         F,1h,15m; G,2d,1h,2;
lookingglass.example      *         F,24h,30m;
*                         refused_A F,12h,20m;
*                         *         F,2h,15m; G,16h,1h,1.5; F,5d,6h;
```

The first rule sets up special handling for mail to *alice@wonderland.example* when there is an over-quota error. Retries continue every 3 hours for 7 days. The second rule handles over-quota errors for other local parts at *wonderland.example* in the case when the mailbox has not been read for 5 days. The absence of a local part in the pattern has the same effect as supplying *@. As no retry algorithms are supplied, messages that fail for quota reasons are bounced immediately if the mailbox has not been read for at least 5 days. If the mailbox has been read within the last 5 days, this rule does not apply, and the next rule is used instead.

The third rule handles all other errors for *wonderland.example*; retries happen every 15 minutes for an hour, then with geometrically increasing intervals until 2 days have passed since a delivery first failed.

The fourth rule controls all retries for the domain *lookingglass.example*, and the remaining two rules handle all other domains, with special action for connection refusal from hosts that were not obtained from an MX record. The "connection refused" error means that a host is up and running, but is not listening on the SMTP port. This state exists for a short while when a host is restarting, but if it continues for some time, it is increasingly likely that the host is a workstation whose name has crept into an email address in error, because it is never going to accept SMTP connections. It therefore makes sense to bounce such addresses more quickly than normal.

The final rule in a retry configuration should always have asterisks in the first two fields so as to provide a general catchall for any addresses and errors that do not have their own special handling, unless, of course, you want such addresses never to be retried. This example tries every 15 minutes for 2 hours, then at intervals starting at 1 hour and increasing by a factor of 1.5 up to 16 hours, then every 6 hours up to 5 days.

## 12.9 Timeout of retry data

One problem with Exim's use of a host-based rather than a message-based retrying scheme arises when a host is tried only infrequently. A common example is an MX secondary host for some domain. Suppose there is a period of network failure, such that both the primary and the secondary host for a domain are unreachable. Retry data for both of them is computed. When the network comes back, mail is delivered to the primary server, leaving the retry information for the secondary still set. It could be weeks or months before the secondary is tried again. If it then fails, Exim could be in danger of concluding that it had been down all that time.

To circumvent this problem, Exim timestamps the data that it writes to its retry hints database. When it consults the data during a delivery, it ignores any that is older than the value set in `retry_data_expire` (default 7 days). If, for example, a host has not been tried for 7 days, Exim will try it immediately when a message for it arrives, and if that fails, it will calculate a retry time as if it were failing for the first time.

If a host really is permanently dead, this behaviour causes a burst of retries every now and again, but only if messages routed to it are rare. If there is a message at least once every 7 days, the retry data never expires.

## 12.10 Long-term failures

Special processing happens when an address has been failing for so long that the cutoff time for the last algorithm has been reached. This is independent of how long any specific message has been failing; it is the length of continuous failure for the address that counts. For routing or local deliveries, a subsequent failure causes Exim to time out the address, and it is bounced. For remote deliveries, it is a bit more complicated, because a remote domain may route to more than one host, each of which may have more than one IP address. The address is timed out only when the cutoff times for all the IP addresses have been passed. For example, if the domain *lookingglass.example* is routed by MX records to both *tweedledum.example* and *tweedledee.example*, and the retry rules are:

```
tweedledum.example   *   F,1d,30m;
tweedledee.example   *   F,5d,2h;
```

then the address *alice@lookingglass.example* does not time out until *tweedledum.example* has been down for more than one day and *tweedledee.example* has been down for more than five days.

Suppose there are a number of messages on the queue that are waiting to deliver to the same address, and that eventually the address times out when one message attempts a delivery. What should happen to the others? Should further deliveries be tried, or should the addresses be bounced without trying to deliver? What should happen when new messages arrive for the timed out address?

One possibility is to try a delivery for each message, although this could result in many failed delivery attempts. Local deliveries do not use many resources, so Exim always tries a local delivery, even when the address timed out earlier. If the delivery fails, the address is bounced.

Remote deliveries are handled differently, in order to avoid making too many potentially expensive delivery attempts. For every IP address that has passed its cutoff time, Exim continues to compute retry times, based on the final retry algorithm. Until the post-cutoff retry time for one of the IP addresses is reached, the failing address is bounced without actually trying to deliver to a remote host. This means that a new message can arrive and be bounced without any delivery attempt taking place at all. In effect, Exim is saying: "This host has been dead for five days and I tried it recently, so it is not worth trying again yet." If a new message arrives after the retry time for at least one of the IP addresses, one new delivery attempt is made to those IP addresses that are past their retry times, and if that still fails, the address is bounced, and new retry times are computed.

The final interval in a retry rule is often quite long (in the default rule, it is 6 hours). If you feel that this is too long to wait between retries of a failed host, you can add an additional parameter set specifically to shorten this time. Consider, for example, the default rule with one additional parameter set:

```
*   *   F,2h,15m; G,16h,1h,1.5; F,4d,6h; F,4d1h,1h;
```

This rule carries on trying for 4 days and 1 hour, instead of 4 days. That in itself does not make much difference, of course, but when this rule times out, the final retry interval is 1 hour instead of 6. This means that, from then on, Exim tries to deliver to a host if at least an hour has elapsed since the last failure. If less than an hour has passed, it will bounce an address without trying a delivery.

A similar kind of behaviour can be specified in a different way, by setting:

```
delay_after_cutoff = false
```

in an **smtp** transport. When `delay_after_cutoff` is false, if all the IP addresses to which a domain routes are past their final cutoff time, Exim tries to deliver to those IP addresses that have not been tried since the message arrived. If there are none, or if they all fail, the address is bounced. In other words, it does not delay when a new message arrives, but tries the expired IP addresses immediately, unless they have been tried since the message arrived (presumably in delivering some other message). If there is a continuous stream of messages for the failing domains, unsetting `delay_after_cutoff` means that there will be many more attempts to deliver to failing IP addresses than in the default case when `delay_after_cutoff` is true. However, if a clump of messages arrive more or less simultaneously, some of them may be bounced without a delivery attempt.

# 12.11 Ultimate address timeout

The retry rules we have been describing work well in most normal circumstances, but there is one case where messages can be left on the queue for extended periods, potentially leading to an ever-increasing queue. This is the case where a host is intermittently available, or when a message has some attribute that prevents its delivery when others to the same address get through.

For example, if the destination's connection to the Internet is of poor quality and suffers frequent failures, short messages might be deliverable, while longer ones almost always fail. Whenever a message is successfully delivered, the "retry clock" for the host is restarted, and so it never times out. As a result, the failing messages could remain on the queue for ever. To prevent this, Exim uses another rule, called the *ultimate address timeout*, which has two parts:

- If a message has been on the queue for longer than the cutoff time of every applicable retry rule for an address (if more than one host is involved, there may be more than one retry rule), a delivery is attempted for that address to all possible hosts, even if the normal retry time has not been reached.

- After any temporary delivery failure, if the message has been on the queue for longer than the cutoff time of every applicable retry rule for the address, the address is timed out, even if there is an unexpired retry rule. New retry times are not computed in this case.

Recall an earlier example where the domain *lookingglass.example* was routed by MX records to two hosts, whose retry times were set by these rules:

```
tweedledum.example  *  F,1d,30m;
tweedledee.example  *  F,5d,2h;
```

Using this configuration, if Exim finds that a message addressed to the *lookingglass.example* domain has been on its queue for more than five days, it forces a delivery attempt for that address, regardless of the current retry times. If the delivery fails, Exim bounces the address, whatever the retry state of the two hosts.

# 12.12 Intermittently connected hosts

Exim was designed for running in an environment where all hosts are permanently connected to the Internet. However, hosts that use dial-up to connect to the Internet only intermittently have become quite common, because this way of working is cheaper. There are also hosts with ISDN connections whose administrators want to control when ISDN is used. For example, they do not want a connection to be made every time a local user submits a message for a remote destination.

If Exim is run in such an environment, the retrying mechanisms are not really adequate. Despite this, people are running Exim, both on intermittently connected hosts and on the servers that support them. The following sections contains some guidance on how to do this, but do bear in mind that it is stretching the purpose for which Exim was designed.

## 12.12.1 Incoming mail for an intermittently connected host

Incoming mail for intermittently connected hosts accumulates on a server that is permanently connected, and the client host collects the mail when it connects. There are two ways in which this can be done:

- Mail for each connecting host is delivered into files on the server. Sometimes a single mailbox is used for each host, independent of the local parts in the addresses. In other configurations, each message is delivered into a separate file. The MTA on the server is not involved in storing the mail, because as far as it is concerned, the messages have been delivered. Therefore, no special attention to the retry rules is needed.

- Mail remains in the MTA's queue and is delivered using SMTP when the client connects. This requires special configuration for Exim, to avoid too much pointless retrying.

If you are using Exim on the server, the first method is strongly recommended, especially if there are likely to be more than a trivial number of messages waiting for a client to connect. Exim's simple queuing strategy is based on the premise that most messages can be delivered quickly, and that therefore queue sizes will normally be small. Scanning large queues can slow things down. Furthermore, if you use the second approach, you are mixing up two kinds of message in the queue: those that are having delivery problems, and those that are waiting for a client host to connect. This makes administration harder.

If you do use Exim's queue as a place to hold messages for dial-up clients (and despite the earlier remarks, this is not unreasonable if, say, there is just one client that receives a handful of messages a day), there are some configuration options that can improve its performance. You should set a long retry period for the intermittent hosts. For example:

```
cheshire.wonderland.example    *    F,5d,24h
```

This stops a lot of failed delivery attempts from occurring, but Exim remembers which messages it has queued up for that host. Once the client comes online, delivery of one message can be forced (either by using the -M or -R options, or by using the ETRN SMTP command). This causes all the queued up messages to be delivered, often down a single SMTP connection. While the host remains connected, any new messages are delivered immediately.

If the connecting hosts do not have fixed IP addresses (that is, if a host is issued with a different IP address each time it connects), Exim's retry mechanisms on the holding host become confused, because the IP address is normally used as part of the key string for holding retry information. This can be avoided by setting retry_include_ip_address false on the **smtp** transport. When this is done, the retrying is based only on the host name. This has disadvantages for permanently connected hosts that have more than one IP address, so it is best to arrange a separate transport for these intermittently connected hosts. For example, a configuration could have two **smtp** transports, like this:

```
normal_smtp:
  driver = smtp

special_smtp:
  driver = smtp
  no_retry_include_ip_address
```

and could either use two routers for handling the different kinds of host, or a single router with a transport setting that selects the appropriate transport, like this:

```
dnslookup:
  driver = dnslookup
  transport = ${if match{$domain}\
               {\N\.variable\.example$\N}\
               {special_smtp}{normal_smtp}}
```

This does conventional DNS routing, but selects the **special_smtp** transport for domains whose names end with *.variable.example*, and the **normal_smtp** transport for all others.

## 12.12.2 Exim on an intermittently connected host

On an intermittently connected client host, Exim must be configured so that local deliveries take place immediately, but remote deliveries are not attempted until a queue run is explicitly started. None of the retrying mechanism is relevant. The simplest configuration is to set queue_domains, which provides a list of domains for which immediate delivery is not to be done. For example, on a single host that is not part of a local network, the setting should be:

```
queue_domains = ! +local_domains
```

so that all remote domains are queued. If there are several hosts on a local network that exchange mail among themselves, queue_domains can be set to exclude their domains from queuing:

```
queue_domains = ! *.local.hosts : ! +local_domains
```

When a connection to the Internet is made, if a queue run is started by obeying:

```
exim -qf
```

each message is likely to be sent in a separate SMTP session, because no routing was previously done. (It is best to use -qf instead of just -q, in case there were any earlier failed delivery attempts, because -qf overrides retry times.) Messages from intermittently connected hosts are often all sent to a single smart host, and it is more efficient if they can all be sent in a single SMTP connection. This can be arranged by running the queue with:

```
exim -qqf
```

instead. In this case, the queue is scanned twice. In the first pass, routing is done, but no deliveries take place. It is as if every remote delivery suffered a temporary failure, and Exim updates its hints file that contains a list of which messages are waiting for which hosts. The second pass is a normal queue run; since all the messages were routed earlier, those destined for the same host are likely to be sent as multiple deliveries in a single SMTP connection.

Another way of arranging for remote routing to be done in advance is to use queue_smtp_domains instead of queue_domains. You can do this only if it is possible to route the remote addresses when the client is not connected to the Internet. For example, if you want to send everything to a single smart host, whose IP address you know, you can use a router such as:

```
remotes:
  driver = manualroute
  route_list = * 192.168.4.5
```

where the IP address of the smart host is given explicitly. Unless you put the smart host in your /etc/hosts file, giving its name instead of its IP address would cause a DNS lookup that would not work when the client was offline. The difference from queue_domains is that Exim does the routing when the message arrives, so the queue run can be done with -qf instead of -qff, which is faster (though marginally so if there are only a few messages).

## The daemon on an intermittently connected host

If you run an Exim daemon on an intermittently connected host, it should not be configured to start up any queue runner processes. That is, it should be started with just the -bd option. You may want to do this if you have user agents that use SMTP to transfer messages to the MTA via the loopback interface, or if you have incoming mail from other hosts on a local network.

## Incoming mail on an intermittently connected host

If incoming mail from the Internet is received using SMTP, the server is likely to send many messages over a single connection. The default behaviour of Exim is to suspend automatic delivery of messages after a certain number have been received in one connection. This prevents too many local delivery processes from being started by a single remote host. This is not as relevant on a host that receives mail from just one source, so the value of smtp_accept_queue_per_connection should be increased or even set to zero (that is, disabled), so that all incoming messages down a single connection are delivered immediately.

# 13

# Encryption, authentication, and other SMTP processing

We mention SMTP encryption and authentication in earlier chapters, and also mention several aspects of the other processing that happens when Exim sends or receives messages using SMTP. In this chapter, we describe how SMTP encryption and authentication work, and how you can configure Exim so that it makes use of them. In the next chapter, when we discuss access control lists, we show how you can test whether an incoming SMTP connection is encrypted or authenticated and use this information to decide whether or not to accept an incoming message.

After the discussion of encryption and authentication, the rest of this chapter contains some further detail about general SMTP processing, for those that want to know more about the nitty-gritty.

## 13.1 Encrypted SMTP connections

RFC 3207 defines how SMTP connections can be set up so that the data that passes between two hosts is encrypted in transit. Once a connection is established, the client issues a STARTTLS command. If the server accepts this, the two hosts negotiate an encryption mechanism to be used for all subsequent data transfers.[1] The SMTP session then reverts to an initial state, and the client starts again by sending a new EHLO command over the encrypted connection.

 This mechanism provides security only when data is in transit between two hosts. It does not provide end-to-end encryption from the original sender to the final mailbox.

Encryption on SMTP connections uses a protocol known as TLS (Transport Layer Security), which is defined in RFC 2246. This is a standardized protocol that is a derivative of Netscape's Secure Sockets Layer (SSL). TLS is implemented in Exim

---

[1] Some legacy clients do not support STARTTLS, but instead connect to a different port and expect to negotiate an encryption mechanism immediately. Such clients can be supported by means of the -tls-on-connect command line option, which is described in the reference manual.

by making use of the OpenSSL or GnuTLS library.[1] There is no cryptographic code in the Exim distribution itself.

In order to use encryption you must install OpenSSL or GnuTLS, and then build a version of Exim that includes TLS support. You also need to understand the basic concepts of encryption at a managerial level, and in particular, the way that public keys, private keys, and certificates are used, including the concepts of certificate signing and certificate authorities. If you do not understand about certificates and keys, please try to find a source of this background information, which is not specific to Exim or even to mail processing. Some helpful introductory material can be found in the FAQ for the SSL addition to the Apache web server.[2] Other parts of this documentation are also helpful, and contain links to further files. Eric Rescorla's book *SSL and TLS* (Addison-Wesley, 2001) contains useful introductory material as well as in-depth discussions of encryption protocols.

You can create a private key and a self-signed certificate using the *req* command provided with OpenSSL, like this:

```
openssl req -x509 -newkey rsa:1024 -keyout file1 -out file2 \
            -days 9999 -nodes
```

*file1* and *file2* can be the same file; the key and the certificate are delimited and so can be identified independently. The -days option specifies a period for which the certificate is valid; here we are specifying a long time. The -nodes option is important: if you do not set it, the key is encrypted with a pass phrase that you are prompted for, and any use that is made of the key causes more prompting for the pass phrase. This is not helpful if you are going to use this certificate and key in an MTA, where prompting is not possible.

A self-signed certificate made in this way is sufficient for testing, and may be adequate for all your requirements if you are mainly interested in encrypting transfers and not in secure identification. For example, you may want to use encryption only for the purpose of protecting the passwords used in SMTP authentication.

---

Some clients require that the certificate presented by the server be a user (or "leaf") certificate, and not a self-signed certificate. In this situation, you have to use the self-signed certificate to sign a user certificate, and install the self-signed certificate on the client as a trusted root certification authority.

---

[1]  See *http://www.openssl.org/* or *http://www.gnu.org/software/gnutls/gnutls.html*, respectively.

[2]  See *http://www.modssl.org/docs/2.7/ssl_faq.html#ToC24*.

## 13.1.1 Configuring Exim to use TLS as a server

When Exim has been built with TLS support, it advertises the availability of the STARTTLS command to client hosts that match `tls_advertise_hosts`, but not to any others. The default value of this option is unset, which means that STARTTLS is not advertised at all. This default is chosen because it is sensible for hosts that want to use TLS only as a client, and also because TLS cannot work as a server without additional information.

To support TLS on a server, you must set `tls_advertise_hosts` to match some hosts, and you must also specify files that contain one or more certificates and a private key. For example:

```
tls_advertise_hosts = *
tls_certificate = /etc/secure/exim/certs
tls_privatekey = /etc/secure/exim/privkey
```

The first file contains the server's X509 certificate and any intermediate certificates that are needed for its verification. The second file contains the server's private key. These files must be readable by the Exim user. The certificates and key can be all be stored in the same file; if `tls_privatekey` is not set, it is assumed that this is the case.

With just these options set, Exim will work as an encrypting server with clients such as Netscape. It does not require the client to have a certificate (but see the next section for how to insist on this). There is one other option that may be needed in other situations. If `tls_dhparam` is set to a filename, the SSL library is initialized for the use of Diffie–Hellman ciphers with the parameters contained in the file. This increases the set of ciphers that the server supports.[1]

The strings supplied for the options that specify files are expanded every time a client host connects. It is therefore possible to use different certificates and keys for different hosts, if you so wish, by making use of the client's IP address (*$sender_host_address*) to control the expansion. If a string expansion is forced to fail, Exim behaves as if the option is not set.

## 13.1.2 Requesting client certificates

If you want an Exim server to request a client's certificate when negotiating a TLS session, you must set either `tls_verify_hosts` or `tls_try_verify_hosts` to match the relevant clients. By default these host lists are unset; you can, of course, set either of them to * to make it apply to all TLS connections. Client certificates are verified by comparing them with a list of expected certificates that is specified by `tls_verify_certificates`, which contains the name of a file or a directory.

---

[1]  See the command *openssl dhparam* for a way of generating this data.

A single file can contain multiple certificates, concatenated end to end. If a directory is used, each certificate must be in a separate file with a name (or a symbolic link) of the form `<<hash>>.0`, where `<<hash>>` is a hash value constructed from the certificate. You can compute the relevant hash by running the command:

```
openssl x509 -hash -noout -in /cert/file
```

where */cert/file* contains just one certificate.

The difference between `tls_verify_hosts` and `tls_try_verify_hosts` is in what happens when the client does not supply a certificate, or if the certificate does not match any of those in the collection named by `tls_verify_certificates`.

- If the client matches `tls_verify_hosts`, the attempt to set up a TLS session is aborted, and the incoming connection is dropped.

- If the client matches `tls_try_verify_hosts`, the (encrypted) SMTP session continues.

In the second case, ACLs that run for subsequent SMTP commands can detect the fact that no certificate was verified, and vary their actions accordingly. For example, you can insist on a verified client certificate before accepting an address for relaying, but not require it for local delivery.

## 13.1.3 Variables that are set for a TLS connection

The variable *$tls_cipher* is set to the name of the cipher that was negotiated for an incoming TLS connection. It is included in the *Received:* header line of an incoming message (by default; you can, of course, change this). It is also included in the log line that records a message's arrival, keyed by X=. If you do not want this, you can unset the `tls_cipher` log selector (☞ 21.2.2).

When an SMTP connection is not encrypted, the value of *$tls_cipher* is the empty string. This provides a way of testing for encryption in string expansions.

When Exim receives a certificate from a client (whether or not it is verified), the value of the Distinguished Name is made available in the variable *$tls_peerdn*. Because it is often a long text string, it is not included in the log line or the *Received:* header line by default. You can arrange for it to be logged (keyed by DN=), by setting the `tls_peerdn` log selector, and you can use `received_header_text` to change the contents of the *Received:* header line.

## 13.1.4 Configuring Exim to use TLS as a client

The log selectors for TLS data apply to outgoing SMTP deliveries as well as to incoming messages, with `log_peerdn` causing logging of the server certificate's

Distinguished Name. The remaining client configuration for TLS is all within the **smtp** transport.

It is not necessary to set any options to have TLS work in the **smtp** transport. If TLS is advertised by a server, the **smtp** transport will automatically attempt to start a TLS session. However, this can be prevented by setting hosts_avoid_tls (an option of the transport) to a list of server hosts for which TLS should not be used.

If you want to insist that encryption be used for delivering to certain servers, you can set hosts_require_tls to match them. Exim will not deliver messages in clear to any hosts that match this option. If there is an error of any sort in setting up TLS for a host that matches hosts_require_tls, delivery to that host is not attempted. If there are alternative hosts, they are tried; otherwise delivery is deferred.

When the server host does not match hosts_require_tls, Exim may try to deliver the message unencrypted. It always does this if the response to STARTTLS is a 5<xx> code. For a temporary error code, or for a failure to negotiate a TLS session after a success response code, what happens is controlled by the tls_tempfail_tryclear option of the **smtp** transport. If it is false, delivery to this host is deferred, and other hosts (if available) are tried. If it is true, Exim attempts to deliver in clear.

You can provide the client with a certificate and private key by setting tls_certificate and (optionally) tls_privatekey as options on the **smtp** transport. The certificate is passed to the server only if it requests it. (If the server is Exim, it will request a certificate if tls_verify_hosts or tls_try_verify_ hosts matches the client.)

You can cause the server's certificate to be verified by setting tls_verify_ certificates to the name of a file that contains expected certificates. You can restrict TLS connections to use specific ciphers by setting tls_require_ ciphers to a colon-separated list. If either of these checks fails, delivery to the current host is abandoned.

All the client options are expanded before use, with *$host* and *$host_address* containing the name and IP address of the server to which the client is connected. Forced failure of an expansion causes Exim to behave as if the relevant option were unset.

# 13.2 SMTP authentication

The original SMTP protocol, designed for a small, cooperative Internet consisting mostly of fairly large, multi-user hosts, had no concept of authentication. All hosts were equal, and any host could send mail to any other for local or onward delivery as best it could. Today's Internet is very different. The concept of *servers* and *clients* has arisen, and hosts that relay mail are servers that are configured to allow it to happen only when the mail arrives from an approved client.

Exim uses ACLs to control which incoming messages it accepts, both for relaying and for local delivery. The full details are covered in the next chapter, but we give an example here to show the need for SMTP authentication.

One way of controlling relaying is by checking the sending host. For example, you might want to permit relaying only from clients on your local network. You can do this using a statement such as:

```
accept hosts = 192.168.5.224/27
```

in the ACL that is run for every SMTP RCPT command. This accepts any recipient address if the sending host matches the given network. (If it does not, subsequent ACL statements are applied to decide whether or not to accept the address.)

However, checking by sending host address does not work in cases such as the following:

*   An employee with a laptop is away from base, and wants to be able to connect from arbitrary locations and send outgoing mail via the server back at home. Even without a laptop, someone might want to do this from a cybercafe, or other "foreign" client.

*   An employee has a dial-up ISP account at home that uses a different IP address each time a new connection is made, so an IP address check cannot be used.

*   The local network is not a strong enough restriction; only those persons who are authorized may send mail via the server from a workstation.

SMTP authentication (RFC 2554) was invented as one way of solving these problems.[1] It works like this:

*   When a server that supports authentication is sent an EHLO command, it advertises a number of authentication *mechanisms*. For example, the response to EHLO might be:

    ```
    250-server.test.example Hello client.test.example [10.0.0.1]
    250-SIZE
    250-PIPELINING
    250-AUTH LOGIN CRAM-MD5
    250 HELP
    ```

    The second-to-last line advertises the LOGIN and CRAM-MD5 authentication mechanisms.

*   When a client wants to authenticate, it sends the SMTP command AUTH, followed by the name of an authentication mechanism, for example:

---

[1]  Another possibility is to use encryption with verified certificates.

```
AUTH LOGIN
```

The command may optionally contain additional authentication data.

- The server replies with a response code beginning with the digit 3 (indicating "more data needed") and an associated *challenge* string. The challenge string may be a simple prompt such as "Please enter a password".

- The client answers the challenge by sending a response string.

- The server may send another challenge, and the challenge–response sequence can be repeated any number of times, including zero. If, for example, all the authentication data is sent in the AUTH command, no more may be needed, so there are no challenges. All the data is encoded in base-64 so that it can include all 256 byte values. Note that this is not encryption. Anybody who intercepts the transmission is able to decode it into its original form.

- Eventually, the server responds with a return code indicating success or failure of the authentication attempt, or a temporary error code if authentication could not be completed.

Once a client has authenticated, the server may permit it to do things that unauthenticated clients are not allowed to do. What these are is entirely up to the management of the server. Exim uses ACLs to implement this kind of control.

## 13.2.1 Authentication mechanisms

Several different authentication mechanisms have been published. Exim supports three of them: PLAIN, LOGIN, and CRAM-MD5.[1] These mechanisms are used by various popular user agents that submit mail to a server using SMTP. However, since not everybody is interested in SMTP authentication, the code for these mechanisms is not included in the Exim binary unless the build-time configuration explicitly requests it.

Before describing how Exim is configured to support SMTP authentication, we need to explain how the three common authentication mechanisms work.

## 13.2.2 PLAIN authentication

PLAIN authentication is described in RFC 2595. It requires that three concatenated data strings be sent, separated by binary zero characters. These are either sent with the AUTH command itself, or as a response to an empty challenge string. The second and third data strings are a user/password pair that can be checked by the server. The

---

[1] Exim also supports the *Secure Password Authentication* method (SPA, also known as NTLM or NTCR), but it is not covered in this book. The details are in the reference manual. This mechanism is used by some Microsoft servers.

first string is not relevant to SMTP authentication, and is normally empty.[1] Here is an example of an authentication exchange, where the concatenated data string is sent as part of the AUTH command and the lines sent by the client and the server are identified by C and S, respectively:

```
C: AUTH PLAIN AHBoMTAAc2VjcmV0
S: 235 Authentication successful
```

The base-64 string AHBOMTAAc2VjcmV0 is an encoding of:

```
<nul>ph10<nul>secret
```

where <nul> represents a binary zero byte. The first data string is empty, the username is ph10, and the password is secret.

PLAIN authentication is efficient in that it requires only a single command and response. The password must be held in clear on the client host, but can be kept encrypted on the server, exactly as it is for login passwords. However, unless an encrypted SMTP connection is used, the data travels over the network unencrypted, and is vulnerable to eavesdropping. For this reason, PLAIN authentication is often made available only when the SMTP connection is encrypted using TLS, as described earlier in this chapter.

## 13.2.3 LOGIN authentication

LOGIN authentication is not described in any RFC, but it is used by the user agent Pine. Like PLAIN authentication, it is based on a user/password combination, but each of these is prompted for separately, so an authentication exchange might look like this:

```
C: AUTH LOGIN
S: 334 VXNlcm5hbWU6
C: cGgxMA==
S: 334 UGFzc3dvcmQ6
C: c2VjcmV0
S: 235 Authentication successful
```

Unencoded, this is:

```
C: AUTH LOGIN
S: 334 Username:
C: ph10
S: 334 Password:
C: secret
S: 235 Authentication successful
```

LOGIN authentication is less efficient than PLAIN, because three interactions are required. Like PLAIN authentication, the username and password are transmitted in

---

[1]  The mechanism is designed for use in protocols other than SMTP, where a specific user identity is used for subsequent operations (for example, to run a login session); the first string can specify a different user from the one whose password was checked.

clear. Some people have argued that it is "safer" because the username and password do not travel in the same packet, though this does not seem to be a very strong argument.

## 13.2.4 CRAM-MD5 authentication

CRAM-MD5 authentication (RFC 2195) avoids transmitting unencrypted passwords over the network. The server sends a single challenge string, and the client sends back a username, followed by a space and the MD5 digest[1] of the challenge string concatenated with a password. The server computes the MD5 digest of the same string and compares this with what it has received. For example:

```
C: AUTH CRAM-MD5
S: 334 PDE4OTYuNjk3MTcwOTUyQHBvc3RvZmZpY2UucmVzdG9uLm1jaS5uZXQ+
C: dGltIGRkOTJiNGJiMzRhZmFhBmMjkwNWVkZDMxOTZhNTU3
S: 235 Authentication successful
```

Unencoded, this is:

```
C: AUTH CRAM-MD5
S: 334 <1896.697170952@postoffice.reston.example>
C: tim dd92b4bb34afaa70f2905edd3196a557
S: 235 Authentication successful
```

The string `dd92b4bb34afaa70f2905edd3196a557` is the MD5 digest of:

```
<1896.697170952@postoffice.reston.example>secret
```

However, if the digest is intercepted, the original string cannot be extracted from it, so the password remains secure. In addition, the digest cannot be reused, because the challenge string is different each time.

CRAM-MD5 requires only two interactions, and avoids transmitting the password in clear, but the disadvantage is that the password must be held in clear on the server as well as on the client.

## 13.2.5 Advertising authentication

If Exim is configured as an authenticating server, it normally advertises the mechanisms it supports in response to an EHLO command. However, there are circumstances where this is not always wanted.

Consider a configuration where some hosts are permitted to relay without authentication (because they are on a local network, for example), whereas others are required to authenticate. What happens when a client host that does not need to authenticate connects? Some client software, on seeing the support for authentication,

---

[1] An MD5 digest is a 16-byte cryptographic hash computed from an arbitrary text string in such a way as to minimize the chances of two strings having the same digest. See RFC 1321.

insists on attempting to authenticate, and there is no way to configure it otherwise. This may cause it to prompt the user for authentication data unnecessarily.

To avoid this problem, you can set the `auth_advertise_hosts` option to define the hosts to which the advertisement should be sent. For example, to exclude the hosts on a local LAN you could use a setting such as this:

```
auth_advertise_hosts = ! 192.168.33.0/24
```

As happens for all host lists, the contents of `auth_advertise_hosts` are expanded before each use, and the list is checked afresh for each EHLO command. This allows you to use different values for encrypted and unencrypted sessions. Consider this setting:

```
auth_advertise_hosts = ${if eq{$tls_cipher}{}{}{*}}
```

The expansion tests the contents of *$tls_cipher* by comparing it with the empty string (the second pair of braces after `eq`). If *$tls_cipher* is empty, implying an unencrypted session, the value of the expansion is empty, so it matches no hosts. However, in a TLS session, *$tls_cipher* is not empty, so the value of the expansion is *, which matches all hosts. Thus, the effect of this setting is that authentication is not advertised when a client sends the first EHLO command, but if a TLS session is negotiated, authentication *is* advertised in response to the second EHLO that the client sends.

## 13.2.6 Choice of authentication mechanism

If you are setting up an Exim client to use a remote server, and you do not know which authentication mechanisms it supports, you can use Telnet to find out:

```
$ telnet some.server.example 25
220 some.server.example ESMTP Exim 4.05 Mon, 13 May 2002 10:24:18 +0100
EHLO client.domain.example
250-some.server.example Hello client.domain.example [192.168.8.20]
250-SIZE 20971520
250-PIPELINING
250-AUTH PLAIN CRAM-MD5
250 HELP
quit
```

If you are setting up an Exim server, you often do not have much choice about which authentication mechanism to use; in practice, you are stuck with whatever your clients' software supports. It is, however, worth thinking about the issues.

The main difference between the mechanisms is whether passwords are transmitted in clear or not. How serious an exposure this is depends on the passwords you are using and the networks over which they travel. If the networks are private and secure, or if all the data being transferred is encrypted, this is a less serious concern than if you are using unencrypted connections over the public Internet.

In any case, it is a good idea to use a different set of passwords from the normal login passwords, so that the consequences of disclosure of an SMTP password are limited to potential abuse of mail submission. This is particularly relevant if you require your users to use an encrypted connection for normal logins, but not for SMTP authentication.

Using an alternative password set with CRAM-MD5 authentication means that you do not have to keep normal passwords in clear on the server (just the SMTP passwords); this is probably the safest of the currently supported mechanisms when encryption is not in use. Using encrypted connections, PLAIN or LOGIN are better, because they do not require passwords to be stored in clear on the server.

## 13.2.7 Exim authenticators

The section of the runtime configuration file that starts with "begin authenticators" is where you specify the parameters for SMTP authentication. This contains definitions for a number of *authenticators*, each of which specifies an authentication mechanism.

The authenticators are defined using the same syntax as the definitions of routers and transports. When Exim is receiving SMTP mail, it is acting as a server; when it is sending out messages over SMTP, it is acting as a client. Configuration options are provided for use in both these circumstances, and a single version of Exim can act both as a client and as a server at different times. Each authenticator can have both server and client functions.

To make it clear which options apply to which function, the prefixes `server_` and `client_` are used on option names that are specific to either the server or the client function, respectively. Server and client functions are disabled if none of their options are specified. If an authenticator is to be used for both server and client functions, a single definition, using both sets of options, is required. For example:

```
cram:
   driver = cram_md5
   public_name = CRAM-MD5
   server_secret = ${if eq{$1}{ph10}{secret}fail}
   client_name = ph10
   client_secret = secret2
```

The `server_` option is used when Exim is acting as a server, and the `client_` options are used when it is acting as a client. An explanation of this example follows later, with the description of the CRAM-MD5 authenticator.

## 13.2.8 Authentication on an Exim server

When a message is received from an authenticated host, the value of *$received_protocol* is set to `asmtp` instead of `esmtp` or `smtp`, and *$sender_host_* *authenticated* contains the name of the authenticator that successfully authenticated the client. It is empty if there was no successful authentication.

When a client host has authenticated itself, Exim pays attention to the AUTH parameter on incoming SMTP MAIL commands, for example:

```
MAIL FROM:<theboss@acme.com.example> AUTH joker@edu.example
```

The address given in the AUTH parameter is supposed to identify the authenticated original submitter of the message, but this feature does not seem to be in widespread use. The special value <> means "no authenticated sender available". If the client host is not authenticated, Exim accepts the syntax of the AUTH parameter, but ignores the data.

If accepted, the value is available during delivery in the *$authenticated_sender* variable, and is passed on to other hosts to which Exim authenticates as a client. Do not confuse this value with *$authenticated_id*, which is a string obtained from the authentication process (see later in this chapter), and which is not usually a complete email address.

## 13.2.9 Testing server authentication

Exim's -bh option can be useful for testing server authentication configurations (☞ 20.9.3). The data for the AUTH command has to be sent encoded in base 64. If you have the *mimencode* command installed on your host, a quick way to produce such data is (for example):

```
echo -e -n '\0name\0password' | mimencode
```

The command *echo -e -n* works in most shells (that is, it interprets backslashes in the text, and outputs the result without a terminating newline). However, in some shells (for example, the Solaris Bourne shell), no options are recognized. In these cases, backslashes are often interpreted automatically, but you have to add \c to avoid the terminating newline:

```
echo '\0name\0password\c' | mimencode
```

In the absence of the *mimencode* command, the following Perl script can be used:

```
use MIME::Base64;
printf ("%s", encode_base64(eval "\"$ARGV[0]\""));
```

This interprets its argument as a Perl string and then encodes it. The interpretation as a Perl string allows binary zeros, which are required for some kinds of authentication, to be included in the data. For example, a command line to run this script using the name *encode* might be:

```
encode '\0user\0password'
```

Single quotes are required in all these examples to prevent the shell from interpreting the backslashes. If either the user or the password string starts with an octal digit, you must use three zeros instead of one after the backslash.

## 13.2.10 Authentication by an Exim client

The **smtp** transport has two options called `hosts_require_auth` and `hosts_try_auth`. When the **smtp** transport connects to a server that announces support for authentication and also matches one of these options, Exim (as a client) tries to authenticate as follows:

- For each authenticator that is configured as a client, it searches the authentication mechanisms announced by the server for one whose name matches the public name of the authenticator.

- When it finds one that matches, it runs the authenticator's client code. The variables *$host* and *$host_address* are available for any string expansions that the client might do. They are set to the server's name and IP address. If any expansion is forced to fail, the authentication attempt is abandoned. Otherwise an expansion failure causes delivery to be deferred.

- If the result is a temporary error or a timeout, Exim abandons trying to send the message to the host for the moment. It will try again later. If there are any backup hosts available, they are tried in the usual way.

- If the response to authentication is a permanent error (5*xx* code), Exim carries on searching the list of authenticators. If all authentication attempts give permanent errors, or if there are no attempts because no mechanisms match, Exim tries to deliver the message unauthenticated if the host matches `hosts_try_auth`, but not if it matches `hosts_require_auth`.

The authentication error that occurs when a delivery is deferred can be detected in a retry rule (☞ 12.5.2). This means you can control how much retrying takes place, or (by specifying no retries) turn the temporary error into a permanent one.

When Exim has authenticated itself to a remote server, it adds the `AUTH` parameter to the `MAIL` commands it sends if it has an authenticated sender for the message. If a local process calls Exim to send a message, the sender address that is built from the login name and `qualify_domain` is treated as authenticated.

## 13.2.11 Options common to all authenticators

Configured authenticators have names, just like routers and transports. The following options are common to all authenticators:

driver (string, default = unset)
> This option must always be set. It specifies which of the available authenticators (**plaintext** or **cram_md5**) is to be used.

public_name (string, default = unset)
> This option specifies the name of the authentication mechanism that the driver implements, and by which it is known to the outside world. These names should contain only upper-case letters, digits, underscores, and hyphens (RFC 2222), but Exim in fact matches them caselessly. If public_name is not set, it defaults to the driver instance's name.

> The public names of authenticators that are configured as servers are advertised by Exim when it receives an EHLO command, in the order in which they are defined. When an AUTH command is received, the list of authenticators is scanned in definition order for one whose public name matches the mechanism given in the AUTH command.

server_set_id (string, default = unset)
> When an Exim server successfully authenticates a client, this string is expanded using data from the authentication, and preserved for any incoming messages in the variable *$authenticated_id*. It is also included in the log lines for incoming messages. For example, a user/password authenticator configuration might preserve the username that was used to authenticate, and refer to it subsequently during delivery of the message.

## 13.2.12 Using the plaintext authenticator in a server

When running as a server, the **plaintext** authenticator collects one or more data strings from the client, and places them in *$1*, *$2*, and so on. The number of data strings required is controlled by the setting of server_prompts, which contains a colon-separated list of prompt strings. However, the prompts are not necessarily sent as challenges because any strings that are sent with the AUTH command are used first.

Data supplied on the AUTH command line is treated as a list of NUL-separated strings. If there are more strings in server_prompts than the number of strings supplied with the AUTH command, the remaining prompts are used to obtain more data. Each response from the client may be a list of NUL-separated strings. This general approach allows **plaintext** to be configured to support either PLAIN or LOGIN authentication.

Once a sufficient number of data strings have been received, the contents of `server_condition` are expanded. Failure of the expansion (forced or otherwise) causes a temporary error code to be returned. If the result of a successful expansion is an empty string, `0`, `no`, or `false`, authentication fails. If the result of the expansion is `1`, `yes`, or `true`, authentication succeeds and the contents of `server_set_id` option are expanded and saved in *$authenticated_id*. For any other result, a temporary error code is returned, with the expanded string as the error text.

For the PLAIN authentication mechanism, three data strings are required. These are sent either with the `AUTH` command or in a separate response following an empty challenge.[1] The second and third data strings are treated as a user/password pair. Using a single fixed user and password as an example, a PLAIN authenticator can be configured as follows:

```
fixed_plain:
   driver = plaintext
   public_name = PLAIN
   server_prompts = :
   server_condition = ${if and {{eq{$2}{ph10}}{eq{$3}{secret}}}{yes}{no}}
   server_set_id = $2
```

The setting of `server_prompts` specifies just one (empty) prompt string because empty strings at the ends of lists are always ignored in Exim. This authenticator would be advertised in the response to `EHLO` as:

```
250-AUTH PLAIN
```

A client host could authenticate itself by sending the command:

```
AUTH PLAIN AHBoMTAAc2VjcmV0
```

The argument string is encoded in base 64, as required by the RFC. This example, when decoded, is `<nul>ph10<nul>secret`, where `<nul>` represents a zero byte. This is split up into three strings, the first of which is empty. As there is only one prompt string, no further prompts are sent. If the client does not send data with the command, the server prompts for it with an empty challenge, as in this example (where the client commands and server responses are indicated by C and S):

```
C: AUTH PLAIN
S: 334
C: AHBoMTAAc2VjcmV0
```

---

[1] There is a common misconception that the data has to be sent with the `AUTH` command. This arises because the RFC that defines PLAIN authentication (RFC 2595) is written using SASL (Simple Authentication and Security Layer) terminology, and talks about "a single message". This is misinterpreted in the SMTP context as "a single SMTP command".

Once the data has been received, the contents of `server_condition` are expanded. This example checks that the second and third data strings are `ph10` and `secret`, respectively.

For the LOGIN authentication mechanism, no data is sent with the `AUTH` command. Instead, a username and password are supplied separately, in response to prompts. The plaintext authenticator can be configured to support this as follows:

```
fixed_login:
  driver = plaintext
  public_name = LOGIN
  server_prompts = Username:: : Password::
  server_condition = \
    ${if and {{eq{$1}{ph10}}{eq{$2}{secret}}}{yes}{no}}
  server_set_id = $1
```

This authenticator would in fact accept data as part of the `AUTH` command, but if the client does not supply it (as is the case for LOGIN clients), the prompt strings are used to obtain the two data items.

---

 Some clients are sensitive to the exact contents of the prompt strings, and variations such as "User Name:" are not always accepted. The example shown is known to work with several different clients.

---

## 13.2.13 Checking passwords in plaintext authenticators

The **plaintext** examples just shown are unrealistic because they admit just one user/password combination. In practice, you usually want to be able to authenticate a number of users, each with their own password. Several features of expansion strings are provided to help with this. They can be combined with the lookup facilities to provide many different ways of authenticating users.

For example, if encrypted passwords are available in */etc/passwd*, you can use the following setting in a **plaintext** authenticator:

```
server_condition = ${if crypteq{$3}\
  {${extract{1}{:}{${lookup{$2}lsearch{/etc/passwd}{$value}}}}}\
  }{yes}{no}}
```

The expansion string uses a lookup to obtain the user data from the file, extracts the first data field (the encrypted password), and compares it with the authentication password using the `crypteq` expansion condition. This condition encrypts the subject password and compares the result with what was obtained from the file.

However, many operating systems no longer keep encrypted passwords directly in */etc/passwd* as implied by this example. Instead, the passwords are held in "shadow" files that are not readable by ordinary users. Processes that handle incoming SMTP connections run under the Exim user, so any files that are referenced by the expansion of `server_condition` must be accessible to that user. If a shadow password file cannot be read by the Exim user, this technique cannot be used.

One way round this is to use a different set of passwords for authentication, and keep them in a file that Exim can read. This is in any case more secure than sharing login passwords because exposure of one does not compromise the other. Exim also has support for *Pluggable Authentication Modules* (PAM), authentication using LDAP, the Cyrus *pwcheck* authentication daemon, and RADIUS (☞ 17.7.5).

## 13.2.14 Using the plaintext authenticator in a client

The **plaintext** authenticator has just one client option, called `client_send`. Its value is a colon-separated list of authentication data strings. Each string is independently expanded before being sent to the server. The first string is sent with the AUTH command; subsequent strings are sent in response to prompts from the server.

Because the PLAIN authentication mechanism requires bytes containing binary zeros in the data, further processing is applied to each string before it is sent. If there are any single circumflex characters in the string, they are converted to zero bytes. Should an actual circumflex be required as data, it must be doubled in the string.

This is an example of a client configuration that implements PLAIN authentication mechanism with a fixed name and password:

```
fixed_plain:
  driver = plaintext
  public_name = PLAIN
  client_send = ^ph10^secret
```

The lack of colons in `client_send` means that the entire text is sent with the AUTH command, with the circumflex characters converted to zero bytes. A similar example that uses the LOGIN mechanism is:

```
fixed_login:
  driver = plaintext
  public_name = LOGIN
  client_send = : ph10 : secret
```

The initial colon ensures that no data is sent with the AUTH command itself. The remaining strings are sent in response to prompts.

## 13.2.15 Using the cram_md5 authenticator in a server

The **cram_md5** authenticator has one server option, called `server_secret`. When the server receives the client's response to the CRAM-MD5 challenge, the "username" is placed in the expansion variable *$1*, and `server_secret` is expanded to obtain the password for that user. The server then computes the CRAM-MD5 digest that the client should have sent, and checks that it received the correct string. If the expansion of server_secret is forced to fail, authentication fails. If the expansion fails for some other reason, a temporary error code is returned to the client.

For example, the following authenticator checks that the username given by the client is ph10, and if so, uses secret as the password. For any other username, authentication fails:

```
fixed_cram:
  driver = cram_md5
  public_name = CRAM-MD5
  server_secret = ${if eq{$1}{ph10}{secret}fail}
  server_set_id = $1
```

If authentication succeeds, the setting of server_set_id preserves the username in *$authenticated_id*. A more sophisticated version might look up the secret string in a file or database, using the username as the key.

### 13.2.16 Using the cram_md5 authenticator in a client

When used as a client, the **cram_md5** authenticator has two options, client_name and client_secret, which must both be set. They are expanded and used as the username and secret strings, respectively, when computing the response to the server's challenge.

Forced failure of either expansion string is treated as an indication that this authenticator is not prepared to handle this case. Exim moves on to the next configured client authenticator. Any other expansion failure causes Exim to give up trying to send the message to the current server.

A simple example configuration of a **cram_md5** client authenticator, using fixed strings, is as follows:

```
fixed_cram:
  driver = cram_md5
  public_name = CRAM-MD5
  client_name = ph10
  client_secret = secret
```

Most authenticating clients connect only to a single server to deliver their mail, in which case this kind of simple configuration is sufficient. If several servers are involved, the conditional features of expansion strings can be used to select the correct data for each server by referring to *$host* or *$host_address* in the options.

# 13.3 SMTP over TCP/IP

SMTP over TCP/IP is the only way of transferring messages between hosts that Exim supports. Outgoing SMTP over TCP/IP is described earlier (☞ 9.1). The next few sections cover some of the detailed processing that occurs for incoming SMTP over TCP/IP. After that, we discuss some other uses of SMTP where a remote host is not involved.

## 13.3.1 Incoming SMTP messages over TCP/IP

Incoming SMTP messages over TCP/IP can be accepted in one of two ways: by running a listening daemon or by using *inetd*. In the latter case, the entry in */etc/inetd.conf* should be like this:

```
smtp  stream  tcp  nowait  exim  /usr/exim/bin/exim  in.exim  -bs
```

Exim distinguishes between this case and the case of a local user agent using the -bs option by checking whether the standard input is a socket.

By default, Exim does fairly minimal logging of incoming SMTP connections. For example, it does not write a log entry when a remote host connects or disconnects (either via the daemon or *inetd*), unless the disconnection is unexpected. A number of log selectors are available for increasing the amount of logging information (☞ 21.2.2).

The amount of disk space that is available is checked whenever SIZE is received on a MAIL command, independently of whether message_size_limit or check_spool_space is configured, unless smtp_check_spool_space is set false. A temporary error is given if there is not enough space. The check is for the amount specified in check_spool_space plus the value given with SIZE, that is, it checks that the addition of the incoming message will not reduce the space below the threshold.

When a message is successfully received, Exim includes the local message ID in its response to the final dot that terminates the data, for example:

```
250 OK id=13M6GM-0005kt-00
```

If the remote host logs this text, it can help with tracing what has happened to a message if a query is raised.

Exim can be configured to rewrite addresses as they are received in SMTP commands, before any syntax checking is done (☞ 15.6.3). It can also be configured to verify addresses in incoming SMTP commands (☞ 14.9).

## 13.3.2 The VRFY and EXPN commands

RFC 2821 defines two SMTP commands that were originally intended to be helpful aids in debugging delivery problems: VRFY verifies an email address, and EXPN lists the expansion of an alias or mailing list. In former times, when the Internet was a friendlier place where messages were often delivered directly to their destination hosts, mail administrators made use of these commands regularly. Nowadays, with so much more mail being delivered indirectly via mail hubs and gateways, their potential usefulness has declined, and in addition, many administrators regard them as security exposures.

Exim supports neither of these commands by default. It responds to a VRFY command in this way:

```
252 VRFY not available
```

A success code (252) rather than an error code is used because some broken clients issue a VRFY command before attempting to send a message.

If you want to make VRFY or EXPN available on your server, you must set up appropriate access control lists that accept these commands under appropriate conditions. For example, you might allow them from hosts on your local network, but not otherwise, or only for connections to the loopback interface.

When VRFY is accepted, exactly the same code as when Exim is called with the -bv option is run. Conversely, EXPN is treated as an address test (similar to the -bt option) rather than a verification (the -bv option). A single-level expansion of the address is done. If an unqualified local part is given as the argument to EXPN, it is qualified with qualify_domain.

## 13.3.3 The ETRN command

RFC 821 (the original SMTP RFC) describes a command called TURN, which reverses the roles of the client and server. The idea was that a client could connect, send its outgoing mail, and then use TURN to become the server to receive incoming messages. However, without authentication this has serious security problems and is deprecated in RFC 2821.

RFC 1985 describes an SMTP extension called ETRN that is intended to overcome the security problems of the original TURN command, while still permitting a client to connect and request that pending mail be delivered. This has found some favour in communities where clients connect to servers by dial-up methods.

The ETRN command is concerned with "releasing" messages that are awaiting delivery to certain hosts. They are not sent down the same connection that issued the ETRN command, but are routed in the normal way over fresh TCP/IP connections, thus avoiding the security problems of TURN. Exim contains support for ETRN, but it does not fit naturally into the way Exim is designed. Because Exim does not organize its message queue by host, it is not straightforward to find "all messages waiting for this host". If you run a server that is a holding system for dial-up systems, and there is more than a trivial amount of mail to be kept, you should consider delivering the pending mail into local files, using a different directory for each host, say, as discussed earlier (☞ 12.12). ETRN can still be used to start up a delivery program that reads messages from these files.

The ETRN command can be used in several formats in which its argument is defined to be a host or a domain name. The only form that is supported entirely within Exim is the one where the text starts with the # prefix, in which case the interpretation of the remainder of the text is not defined and is specific to the SMTP server. A valid ETRN command causes a run of Exim with the -R option, with the remainder of the ETRN text as its argument. For example:

```
ETRN #brigadoon
```

runs the command:

```
exim -R brigadoon
```

which causes a delivery attempt on all messages with undelivered addresses containing the text brigadoon. All addresses in the messages are considered for delivery, not just the ones that trigger the selection. Note that the supplied string is not necessarily a host or domain name.

Exim uses an ACL to control the use of ETRN. By default, this command is rejected and the attempt is logged on the main and reject logs. If you want to use ETRN, you need to set up an ACL that recognizes the hosts that are permitted to use it. When ETRN is accepted, it is logged on the main log.

When smtp_etrn_serialize is set (the default), it prevents the simultaneous execution of more than one queue run for the same argument string as a result of an ETRN command. This stops a misbehaving client from starting more than one queue runner at once. Exim implements the serialization by writing a hints record whenever a process is started by ETRN, and deleting it when the process completes.

Obviously, there is scope for hints records to be left lying around if there is a system or program crash. To guard against this, Exim ignores any records that are more than six hours old, but you should normally arrange to delete any files in the *spool/db* directory whose names begin with misc after a system reboot.

For more control over what ETRN does, the smtp_etrn_command option can be used. This specifies a command that is run whenever ETRN is accepted, whatever the form of its argument. For example:

```
smtp_etrn_command = /etc/etrn_command $domain $sender_host_address
```

The string is split up into arguments that are independently expanded. The variable *$domain* is set to the argument of the ETRN command, but no syntax checking is done on the contents of this argument.

# 13.4 Local SMTP

Some user agents use SMTP to pass messages to their local MTA using the standard input and output, as opposed to passing the envelope on the command line and writing the message to the standard input. This is supported by the -bs command-line option. This form of SMTP is handled in the same way as incoming messages over TCP/IP, except that all host-specific processing is bypassed, and any envelope sender given in a MAIL command is ignored unless the caller is trusted.

Conversely, some software applications for managing message stores accept incoming messages from an MTA using a variation of SMTP known as LMTP (RFC 2033). Exim supports this either via the **lmtp** transport for communicating with a local process over a pipe (☞ 9.6), or by the protocol option of the **smtp** transport for using LMTP over TCP/IP (☞ 9.1).

# 13.5 Batched SMTP

Batched SMTP is a format for storing messages or passing them to other processes in which the envelopes are prepended to the message in the form of SMTP commands (☞ 9.3.2). It is mostly used as an intermediate format between Exim and other forms of transport such as UUCP or a private delivery agent for dial-up clients.

Messages that are in batch SMTP format can be passed to Exim by means of the -bS command-line option. This causes Exim to accept one or more messages by reading SMTP on the standard input, but to generate no SMTP responses. If the caller is trusted, the senders in the MAIL commands are believed; otherwise, the sender is always the caller of Exim. Unqualified senders and receivers are not rejected (there seems little point) but instead are automatically qualified. HELO and EHLO act as RSET; VRFY, EXPN, ETRN, HELP, and DEBUG act as NOOP; QUIT quits.

If any error is detected while reading a message, including a missing dot at the end, Exim gives up immediately. It writes details of the error to the standard output in a stylized way that the calling program should be able to make some use of automatically, for example:

```
554 Unexpected end of file
Transaction started in line 10
Error detected in line 14
```

It writes a more verbose version for human consumption to the standard error file, for example:

```
An error was detected while processing a file of BSMTP input.
The error message was:

  501 '>' missing at end of address

The SMTP transaction started in line 10.
The error was detected in line 12.
The SMTP command at fault was:

    rcpt to:<malformed@in.com.plete

1 previous message was successfully processed.
The rest of the batch was abandoned.
```

The return code from Exim is zero only if there were no errors. It is 1 if some messages were accepted before an error was detected, and 2 if no messages were accepted.

# 14

# Message reception and policy controls

Once upon a time, when the Internet was young and innocent, MTAs accepted any message that was sent to them and did their best to deliver it, including sending it on to another host. This process is known as *relaying*. This cooperative approach has been so much abused in recent times that it is now viewed as a bad thing for an MTA to be unselective in the messages it is prepared to accept.

A host that accepts arbitrary messages for relaying is called an *open relay*; such hosts used to be common, but as levels of abuse have risen, they have almost all been eliminated. In today's Internet, hosts that relay mail must ensure that they do so only in the specific cases they are expecting to handle, for example, only relaying to certain domains or from certain hosts.

The general increase in unsolicited mail has also caused MTAs to tighten up their controls on all incoming messages, even when relaying is not involved. Much junk mail arrives with bogus sender addresses or syntactically invalid header lines; such mail can be kept out by checking before accepting messages. No such checks can be perfect, because a clever forger can usually find a way round them, but they do reduce the size of the problem.

This chapter is concerned with the way in which Exim accepts incoming messages, including the checks that may be applied during the reception process. These are specified by means of *Access Control Lists* (ACLs). When installed "out of the box", Exim is configured not to allow any relaying, and to impose some standard checks on incoming messages from other hosts. The system administrator can customize these checks by modifying the default ACLs.

This chapter also covers changes that may be made to messages at the time of their reception, other than address rewriting, which is covered in the next chapter.

## 14.1 Message sources

Messages received over TCP/IP are treated differently from those that are received from local processes directly, and we point out some of these differences shortly. A local process can, of course, make a TCP/IP connection to the local host, either using the loopback interface or using the host's external IP address. Messages received over such connections are treated in the same way as those that are received from remote hosts. In particular, note that the loopback address is not treated as special. If you want, for example, to allow relaying for messages received on the loopback interface, you have to configure this explicitly.[1]

SMTP is the only way of transferring a message over a TCP/IP connection, but when a message is passed from a local process without using TCP/IP, several formats are supported, including the use of SMTP over a pipe connection. If SMTP is used in this way, the message is still treated as originating from a local user process; only input over TCP/IP is considered "remote". However, all SMTP input (whether local or remote) is subject to the checks defined by the ACLs. Non-SMTP input is not checked.

Unlike some other MTAs, Exim never changes the bodies of messages in any way. In particular, it does not attempt to convert one form of encoding into another. It is "8-bit clean", which means that the only characters it treats specially are those that it is required to interpret, such as CR (carriage return) and LF (linefeed). All other character values are treated as data.

## 14.2 Message size control

It is a good idea to set a limit to the size of message that Exim will handle. The `message_size_limit` option controls this limit. For example:

```
message_size_limit = 12M
```

sets a limit of 12 MB (the default limit is 50 MB). Messages that are larger than the limit are not accepted.[2]

When Exim creates a bounce message, it appends the original message to the end of the error message text. To avoid sending excessively large bounce messages, there is a limit to the amount of original message that is copied. This is set by `return_size_limit`, which defaults to 100 KB. The body of the original message is truncated when the limit is reached,[3] and a comment pointing this out is added at the top. The value of `return_size_limit` should always be somewhat smaller than `message_size_limit`.

---

[1]   It is allowed by the default configuration.

[2]   There is a transport option, also called `message_size_limit`, which limits the size of message a particular transport will handle. To have any effect, this must, of course, be less than the global limit.

[3]   The limit is not exact to the last byte, owing to the use of buffering for transferring the message in chunks.

# 14.3 Messages from local processes

An Exim reception process may be started by any locally running process. Most commonly, this happens when a user instructs a user agent to send a message, but other processes are also able to send messages if they wish. For example, if a command that is automatically run by *cron* produces output, it is mailed to the user. For historical reasons, processes that send messages in this way call the local MTA using one of the paths */usr/sbin/sendmail* or */usr/lib/sendmail*. Whichever of these paths is conventional in your operating system should be set up as a symbolic link to Exim, which is compatible with the Sendmail interface for accepting messages in this way.

Exim can be run directly from a shell, passing options and arguments on the command line, and the message on the standard input. This is generally useful only for testing, because you have to supply the entire message, including all the header lines. For sending "real" messages from a shell, it is better to use a user agent such as the Unix *mail* command.

## 14.3.1 Addresses in header lines

In a locally submitted message, if an unqualified address is found in any of the header lines that contain addresses, it is qualified using the domain defined by `qualify_domain` (for senders) or `qualify_recipient` (for recipients) at the time the message is received. For example, on a host called *ahost.plc.example*, you might have configured:

```
qualify_domain = plc.example
qualify_recipient = ahost.plc.example
```

If an incoming message contained:

```
From: theboss
To: thedogsbody
```

Exim would convert these lines into:

```
From: theboss@plc.example
To: thedogsbody@ahost.plc.example
```

## 14.3.2 Specifying recipient addresses

There are a number of different ways of passing recipient envelope addresses to Exim from a local process. In all cases, unqualified addresses are permitted; they are qualified using the domain defined by the `qualify_recipient` option. This defaults to the value of `qualify_domain`, which in turn defaults to the name of the local host.

- If none of -bs, -bS, or -t are present as options, the recipients are passed as the command's arguments. Each argument may be a comma-separated list of

RFC 2822 addresses. In other words, if Exim is called directly from a shell, either commas or spaces can be used to separate the addresses. For example, one could type:

```
exim  user1@example.com,user2@another.example.com  user3
```

followed by the message, complete with RFC 2822 header lines. The message is terminated by an end-of-file indication, or, unless the -oi option is given, by a line consisting of a single dot character.

- If the -t option is present on the command line, no arguments are normally given. Exim constructs the list of envelope recipients by extracting all the addresses from any *To:*, *Cc:*, and *Bcc:* header lines within the message. Then it removes any *Bcc:* header lines. This is the only case where *Bcc:* lines are removed from messages; if they are present in messages received in any other way, they are preserved.

  If the command does have arguments, they are interpreted as addresses *not* to send to; in other words, any argument addresses that also appear in the header lines are ignored. This action, removing any argument addresses from the recipients list, accords with published Sendmail documentation, but it appears that some versions of Sendmail *add* addresses given on the command line, instead of removing them. Exim can be made to behave in this fashion by setting:

  ```
  extract_addresses_remove_arguments = false
  ```

- If the -bs option is present on the command line, Exim expects to receive SMTP commands on its standard input, and it writes responses to the standard output.[1]

- If the -bS option is present on the command line, Exim expects to receive SMTP commands on its standard input, but it does not write any responses. This is so-called *batch SMTP*, where the SMTP commands are just being used as a convenient way of encoding the envelope addresses.

For both kinds of SMTP, more than one message can be passed in one connection, whereas the other cases are limited to one message at a time. Further details about SMTP handling are given in chapter 13. The sources of recipient addresses for locally submitted messages and the command-line options that affect them are summarized in table 14-1.

---

[1]  This option is also used when running Exim under *inetd*; Exim can tell the difference, because, in the *inetd* case, the standard input is a socket with an associated remote IP address. When started from *inetd*, Exim treats the message as coming from a remote host.

*Table 14-1: Recipient address sources for locally submitted messages*

| Option | Meaning |
|--------|---------|
| *none* | Command arguments are recipients |
| -t | Recipients from headers (Bcc: removed) |
| -bs | Recipients from local SMTP RCPT commands |
| -bS | Recipients from batch SMTP RCPT commands |

## 14.3.3 Local sender addresses

The source of the envelope sender address for messages submitted locally (that is, not over TCP/IP) depends on whether or not the calling user is trusted (☞ 19.3). A trusted user is permitted to supply a sender address, via the MAIL command if the message is being received using SMTP, or otherwise in one of the following ways:

- By including a line in one of the following forms at the start of the message, preceding the RFC 2822 header lines:

```
From <address> Fri Dec 31 23:59 GMT 1999
From <address> Fri, 31 Dec 99 23:59:59
```

The origin of the use of this line is the transfer of mail using UUCP (see RFC 976). It was then adopted as a message separator line in "Berkeley format" mailbox files, so is frequently found in saved messages. Because several different formats are encountered, Exim recognizes this line by matching it against a regular expression that is defined by the uucp_from_pattern option. The default pattern matches the two formats shown, leaving the value of the address in the *$1* variable.

If uucp_from_pattern matches, Exim expands the contents of uucp_from_sender (whose default value is $1) to obtain a sender address for the message. The expanded string is parsed as an RFC 2822 address. For example, if the message starts with:

```
From a.oakley@berlin.example Fri Jan  5 12:35 GMT 1996
```

and uucp_from_pattern is set to its default value, expanding the contents of uucp_from_sender yields *a.oakley@berlin.example*. If there is no domain in the result, the local part is qualified with qualify_domain unless it is the empty string.

- By supplying a sender address using the -f command-line option. For example:

```
exim -f '<f.butler@berlin.example>'
```

If -f is present, it overrides any From line that may be in the message.

If the caller of Exim is not trusted, a sender address supplied in any of these ways is recognized, but ignored. Instead, Exim creates an envelope sender for the message using the login ID of the process that called it, and the domain specified by `qualify_domain`.

# 14.4 Unqualified addresses from remote hosts

The RFCs specify that all the addresses in a message that is received from another host, both in the envelope and in the header lines, must be fully qualified (that is, they must contain both a local part and a domain). There is only one exception: the unqualified address *postmaster* is required to be accepted. Other unqualified addresses, such as those in the following SMTP commands:

```
MAIL FROM:<caesar>
RCPT TO:<brutus>
```

cause error responses because of the lack of a domain. However, when SMTP is being used as a submission protocol from local workstations, there is sometimes a need to relax this restriction. You can allow certain hosts to send messages containing unqualified addresses by setting either or both of `sender_unqualified_hosts` or `recipient_unqualified_hosts` to lists of such hosts. For example, a gateway on the local network 192.168.45.0 might permit its local clients to send unqualified addresses by setting:

```
sender_unqualified_hosts = 192.168.45.0/24
recipient_unqualified_hosts = 192.168.45.0/24
```

Unqualified addresses are not retained in the messages Exim receives. Each such address is qualified as soon as it is accepted, using the domain specified in `qualify_domain` for sender addresses, and that in `qualify_recipient` for recipients. The value of `qualify_domain` defaults to the name of the local host, and the value of `qualify_recipient` defaults to the value of `qualify_domain`.

On a host called *delta.plc.example*, if neither of these options is set, the unqualified address *apollo* becomes *apollo@delta.plc.example*, but if:

```
qualify_domain = plc.example
```

is set, it becomes *apollo@plc.example* in all cases. However, with the following:

```
qualify_domain = plc.example
qualify_recipient = delta.plc.example
```

the shorter domain is used only for sender addresses. By the time a message comes to be delivered, its envelope contains only fully qualified addresses.

If there are any unqualified addresses in header lines, they too are qualified, provided the message came from a host that is permitted to send unqualified addresses. If not, unqualified addresses in header lines are left untouched; they are neither qualified nor subjected to rewriting.

# 14.5 Checking a remote host

In this section, we cover a number of different checks that can be applied to a remote host when it connects to Exim in order to send a message. These are independent checks that are not part of ACL processing.

## 14.5.1 Explicit host blocking

The `host_reject_connection` option causes Exim to reject SMTP connections from specific hosts as soon as they are received. For example:

```
host_reject_connection = 192.168.34.5 : *.enemy.example
```

This option is for use in exceptional circumstances. Normally, SMTP connections are accepted, and checks are carried out later (using ACLs) during message transfer. This allows for more flexibility. For example, you can accept messages to *postmaster* from certain hosts, but block everything else.

When a connection is rejected by `host_reject_connection`, the message remains on the remote host, which may try to deliver it to alternative MX hosts or may try to redeliver it again later.[1] This is another reason for rejecting at a later stage. Unless the remote host is seriously broken, a permanent rejection of every recipient causes the message to be bounced and not retried.

## 14.5.2 Verifying a host's name

On receiving a TCP/IP connection, the only identification for a remote host that Exim has is an IP address. The host should give its name as the data in an EHLO or HELO command, but there is no guarantee that this is the name by which it is registered. Workstations that are using SMTP to submit mail commonly send the wrong name.

The name supplied by EHLO or HELO is placed in the variable *$sender_helo_name*. The only way Exim can find a properly registered name for the host is to look for a name that is associated with the IP address. This might be found in a local hosts table in */etc/hosts*, but more commonly a DNS lookup is required. This raises two problems: first, that DNS lookups can be expensive and take time, and second, that substantial numbers of Internet hosts are only registered "one way" in the DNS. That is, you can look up their names to find an IP address, but not *vice versa*.

---

[1]  However, if the remote host is running Exim, it will bounce the message on receiving an initial 550 response.

For this reason, Exim does not try to find the registered name of a connecting host unless its configuration requires it. If you can arrange your configuration to avoid these lookups, you will gain some extra efficiency. The default configuration file is designed for use on small client hosts, and it contains the setting:

```
host_lookup = *
```

This forces Exim to look up a host name for every incoming connection. If you are running a busy server, it is probably a good idea to remove this setting, or modify it to be less general. For example, you could use a setting like the following:

```
host_lookup = 192.168.3.0/24
```

to constrain the lookup to hosts on your local network. Although host_lookup can contain any item that is allowed in a host list, it normally contains only IP addresses. There is not much point in including host names, because this implies finding a host name in order to check whether to find a host name!

When a host name is found by looking up the IP address, it is placed in the variable *$sender_host_name*. If no lookup is done, or if the lookup fails, this variable is empty. Failure to find a host name does not itself cause a connection to be rejected immediately, but it might cause a later rejection if a host name is needed for one of the checks described in the following sections.

When a host does not match host_lookup, Exim does not look for its name at the start of a connection. However, if one of the conditions in an ACL requires knowledge of the host name, a lookup is done at that point. The most common example is the presence of a host list that contains wildcard entries (☞ 18.6.4).

In Exim's log files, host names that have not been verified, but which are just the data from EHLO or HELO commands, are shown in parentheses. Some broken client hosts have been observed to specify the server's name, or one of its local domains, instead of their own name in EHLO or HELO commands. Suppose the host *server.plc.example* is handling the domain *plc.example*. A client host called *broken.example*, which is broken in this way, may send this command:

```
ehlo server.plc.example
```

when what it is supposed to send is:

```
ehlo broken.example
```

Using the supplied name in log lines (even in parentheses) is likely to cause confusion, so there is a facility for causing Exim to look up the correct name in this situation. If the argument specified by EHLO or HELO matches the domain list helo_lookup_domains, a lookup is forced. The default value for this option is as follows:

```
helo_lookup_domains = @ : @[]
```

The @ item matches the server's host name, and the @ [] item matches any of its IP addresses in brackets (☞ 18.5).

## 14.5.3 Verifying EHLO or HELO

The RFCs specifically state that mail should not be refused on the basis of the data contents of the EHLO or HELO commands. However, there are installations that do want to be strict in this area, and Exim has the helo_verify_hosts and helo_try_verify_hosts options in order to support them. The values of these options are lists of hosts for which stricter checking is required.

The difference between the two options is in what happens when the check fails. For hosts that match helo_verify_hosts, failure provokes a permanent error (550 error code); an entry is written in the main and reject logs. For hosts that match helo_try_verify_hosts, processing continues after a failed check (with no logging). This state can be detected in a subsequent ACL (☞ 14.8.15), allowing it to be used to accept or reject recipient addresses in conjunction with other conditions.

When a sending host matches helo_verify_hosts or helo_try_verify_hosts, the argument supplied by EHLO or HELO is verified. If it is in the form of a literal IP address in square brackets, it must match the actual IP address of the sending host. If it is a domain name, the sending host's name is looked up from its IP address and compared against it. If the lookup or the comparison fails, the IP addresses associated with the EHLO or HELO name are looked up and compared against the sending host's IP address. If none of them match, the check fails.

Even when helo_verify_hosts and helo_try_verify_hosts are not used, Exim rejects EHLO and HELO commands that contain syntax errors. One common mistake is the appearance of underscore characters in domain names.[1] Because this error is so very widespread, there is an option to specify additional characters that are permitted. This setting allows underscores:

```
helo_allow_chars = _
```

Occasionally, there is a need to allow some hosts to send real junk in EHLO or HELO commands (including no data at all); such hosts can be accommodated by setting helo_accept_junk_hosts. For example:

```
helo_accept_junk_hosts = 192.168.5.224/27
```

removes the syntax check entirely for hosts on that network.

---

[1] There is a common misconception that not allowing underscores is a DNS restriction. It is not; a domain name in the DNS may contain a wide variety of characters (see RFC 2181). However, there is a restriction in RFC 2821, the specification of SMTP, which permits only letters, digits, dots, and hyphens in domain names that are used in SMTP transactions.

# 14.6 Limiting the rate of message arrival

Some sites find it helpful to be able to limit the rate at which certain hosts can send them messages, and the rate at which an individual message can specify recipients. For example, by slowing down the rate at which their customers can send messages with large numbers of recipients, ISPs may be able to reduce the amount of spam they transmit.

When a host matches `smtp_ratelimit_hosts`, the values of `smtp_ratelimit_mail` and `smtp_ratelimit_rcpt` are used to control the rate of acceptance of MAIL and RCPT commands, respectively. These options apply independently to individual SMTP connections; there is no sharing of data between different connections from the same host.

Each of these options, if set, must contain four comma-separated values:

*A threshold*

This number specifies how many MAIL commands in a single connection or how many RCPT commands in a single message can be accepted before the rate limiting kicks in.

*An initial time delay*

This is the amount of time by which to delay the first command after the threshold has been reached. Unlike other times in Exim, numbers with decimal fractional parts are allowed here.

*A multiplier*

This number, which may contain a fractional part, is the factor by which the delay is increased for each subsequent command.

*A maximum value for the delay*

This should normally be less than five minutes, because after that time, the client is liable to timeout the SMTP command.

For example, these settings have been used successfully at the site which first suggested this feature, for controlling mail from their customers:

```
smtp_ratelimit_mail = 2,0.5s,1.05,4m
smtp_ratelimit_rcpt = 4,0.25s,1.015,4m
```

The first setting specifies delays that are applied to MAIL commands after two have been received over a single connection. The initial delay is 0.5 seconds, increasing by a factor of 1.05 each time to a maximum of four minutes. The second setting applies delays to RCPT commands when more than four occur in a single message.

# 14.7 Relay control

The default Exim configuration permits no relaying of messages from other hosts. It assumes the simplest kind of environment, where all mail that is accepted from other hosts is addressed to a single local domain that is the same as the host's name. The host is "at the end of the line" for mail delivery. This does not mean that all incoming mail from outside has to be locally delivered; there may be aliases or users' *.forward* files that cause messages to be delivered to other hosts. Such *redirection* is not classed as relaying.

Relaying occurs when a message that is received from another host is passed on to a third host without any reference to a local domain in the recipient address. If a message is sent from *alpha.example* to *beta.example*, with recipient address *homer@beta.example*, no relaying is involved, even if the user *homer* on *beta* has a *.forward* file that sends the message on to another host, because the original recipient address is in a local domain.

However, if the recipient is *odysseus@gamma.example*, then we have a case of relaying by *beta*:

```
alpha -> beta -> gamma
```

A single message may have many recipients; some may require relaying whereas others may not. Checking for relay permission must therefore happen for each recipient address independently. The checks are specified in ACLs, which are described shortly.

## 14.7.1 Incoming and outgoing relaying

From Exim's point of view, there are two kinds of message relaying, as illustrated in figure 14-1.

A host that is acting as a gateway or as an MX backup relays messages from arbitrary hosts to a specific set of domains. This is called *incoming relaying*. On the other hand, a host that is acting as a smart host for a number of clients relays messages from those clients to the Internet at large. This is called *outgoing relaying*. What is not wanted is the transmission of mail from arbitrary remote hosts through your system to arbitrary domains.

The same host may fulfil both the incoming and outgoing relay functions, as shown in the figure, but in principle these two kinds of relaying are entirely independent. Large installations often use different hosts for handling incoming and outgoing relaying.

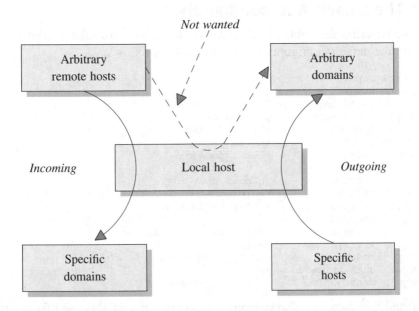

*Figure 14-1: Message relaying*

# 14.8 Access control lists

Access control lists provide flexibility in the way Exim checks incoming messages. The majority of them apply to non-batch SMTP input, whether from remote hosts or from the local host. There is also one ACL that can be used to check batch SMTP and non-SMTP messages.

ACLs are defined in a separate section of the runtime configuration file, headed by begin acl. Each ACL definition starts with a name, terminated by a colon. Here is a complete ACL section containing just one very small ACL:

```
begin acl

small_acl:
  accept    hosts = one.host.example
```

You can have as many ACLs as you like in the ACL section, and the order in which they appear does not matter. The lists are self-terminating.

Most ACLs are used to control Exim's behaviour when it receives certain SMTP commands. The most common use is for controlling which recipients are accepted in incoming messages (that is, which RCPT commands are accepted).

## 14.8.1 The default ACL configuration

Before we describe the contents of ACLs in detail, we will take a brief look at the ACL from the default configuration file, which is as follows:

```
acl_check_rcpt:
  accept  hosts          = :
  deny    local_parts    = ^.*[@%!/|] : ^\\.
  accept  local_parts    = postmaster
          domains        = +local_domains
  require verify          = sender
  accept  domains         = +local_domains
          endpass
          message         = unknown user
          verify          = recipient
  accept  domains         = +relay_to_domains
          endpass
          message         = unrouteable address
          verify          = recipient
  accept  hosts           = +relay_from_hosts
  accept  authenticated   = *
  deny    message         = relay not permitted
```

In the actual file, there are also copious comments. This ACL is used for every RCPT command in an incoming SMTP message. For each recipient, the ACL statements are considered in order, until the recipient address is either accepted or rejected. The RCPT command is then accepted or rejected, according to the result of the ACL processing.

```
acl_check_rcpt:
```

This line, consisting of a name terminated by a colon, marks the start of the ACL, and names it.

```
accept  hosts = :
```

This ACL statement accepts the recipient if the sending host matches the given host list. But what does that strange list mean? It does not actually contain any host names or IP addresses. The presence of the colon puts an empty item in the list; Exim matches this only if the incoming message did not come from a remote host (because the host name and IP address are empty in this case). The colon is important. Without it, the list itself is empty, and can never match anything.

What this statement is doing is accepting unconditionally all recipients in messages that are submitted by SMTP from local processes using the standard input and output (that is, not using TCP/IP). A number of MUAs operate in this manner.

```
deny    local_parts  = ^.*[@%!/|] : ^\\.
```

The first item in this statement uses a regular expression to reject recipient addresses with local parts that contain any of the characters @, %, !, /, or |. Although these characters are entirely legal in local parts (in the case of @ only if correctly quoted), they do not normally occur in Internet mail addresses.

The first three have in the past been associated with explicit message routing, and addresses containing these characters are regularly tried by spammers in an attempt to bypass relaying restrictions. Such addresses are also used by open relay testing programs. Unless you really need them, it is safest to reject these characters at this early stage. Slash is included in the list to avoid problems in local parts that are used to construct file names. Vertical bar is included because of its use as a pipe symbol in shell commands.

The second item in the deny statement uses another regular expression to reject recipient addresses with local parts that start with a dot. This is a precaution against attempts to abuse configurations where the local part is used as a file name (for example, when it is the name of a mailing list).

This configuration is heavy-handed in rejecting these characters for all messages it accepts from remote hosts. This is a deliberate policy of being as safe as possible. By moving the test elsewhere in the ACL, you can relax the restriction so that, for example, it applies only to addresses in your local domains.

```
accept  local_parts   = postmaster
        domains       = +local_domains
```

This statement, which has two conditions, accepts an incoming address if the local part is *postmaster* and the domain is one of those listed in the local_domains domain list. The presence of this statement means that mail to the local postmaster is never blocked by any of the subsequent tests. This can be helpful while sorting out problems in cases where the subsequent tests are incorrectly denying access.

```
require verify        = sender
```

This statement requires the sender address to be verified before any subsequent ACL statement can be used. If verification fails, the incoming recipient address is refused. Verification consists of trying to route the address, to see if a message could be delivered to it. In the case of remote addresses, basic verification checks only the domain, but *callouts* can be used for more verification if required. The details of address verification are discussed later (☞ 14.9).

```
accept  domains       = +local_domains
        endpass
        message       = unknown user
        verify        = recipient
```

This statement accepts the incoming recipient address if its domain is one of the local domains, but only if the address can be verified. Verification of local addresses normally checks both the local part and the domain.

The endpass line needs some explanation: if the condition above endpass fails, that is, if the address is not in a local domain, control is passed to the next ACL statement. However, if the condition below endpass fails, that is, if a recipient in a local domain cannot be verified, access is denied and the recipient is rejected. The message line provides a customized error message for the failure. Thus, if a recipient address gets past this statement in the ACL, we know that it must be for a non-local domain. The remaining ACL statements, therefore, are concerned with checking for valid relaying.

```
accept  domains      = +relay_to_domains
        endpass
        message      = unrouteable address
        verify       = recipient
```

This statement accepts the incoming recipient address if its domain is one of the domains for which this host is a relay, but again, only if the address can be verified. In the default configuration, relay_to_domains is defined by this line:

```
domainlist relay_to_domains =
```

That is, it is an empty list that matches no domains.

```
accept  hosts        = +relay_from_hosts
```

Control reaches this statement only if the recipient's domain is neither a local domain, nor a relay domain. The statement accepts the address if the message is coming from one of the hosts that are defined as being allowed to relay through this host. The default configuration defines relay_from_hosts like this:

```
hostlist relay_from_hosts = 127.0.0.1
```

This allows processes on the local host to submit outgoing messages via the loopback interface. Exim does not treat a loopback address in any special way, so it is necessary to enable this kind of relaying explicitly, because some user agents, notably MH and NMH, send mail by connecting to the loopback address on the local host.

Recipient verification is omitted in this ACL statement, because in many cases of message submission, the clients are dumb MUAs that do not cope well with SMTP error responses. If you are actually relaying out from MTAs, you should probably add recipient verification to this ACL statement.

```
accept  authenticated = *
```

Control reaches here when an arbitrary host tries to relay to an arbitrary domain. The statement accepts the address only if the client host has authenticated itself (☞ 13.2). The default configuration does not define any authenticators, which means that no client can in fact authenticate. You need to add authenticator definitions to the configuration if you want to make use of this ACL statement.

```
deny    message      = relay not permitted
```

The final statement denies access, giving a specific error message. Reaching the end of the ACL also causes access to be denied, but with the generic message "administrative prohibition".

## 14.8.2 Specifying when ACLs are used

Defining an ACL in the ACL section of the runtime configuration does not of itself cause the ACL to be used. You also have to tell Exim when to use it. Global options are used to specify which ACL to use in different circumstances. They are shown in table 14-2.

*Table 14-2: ACL selection options*

| Option | Specifies |
|---|---|
| acl_smtp_auth | ACL to run for AUTH commands |
| acl_smtp_connect | ACL to run at the start of an SMTP connection |
| acl_smtp_data | ACL to run after DATA is complete |
| acl_smtp_etrn | ACL to run for ETRN commands |
| acl_smtp_expn | ACL to run for EXPN commands |
| acl_smtp_mail | ACL to run for MAIL commands |
| acl_not_smtp | ACL to run for non-SMTP messages |
| acl_smtp_rcpt | ACL to run for RCPT commands |
| acl_smtp_starttls | ACL to run for STARTTLS commands |
| acl_smtp_vrfy | ACL to run for VRFY commands |

For example, with this setting:

```
acl_smtp_rcpt = acl_check_rcpt
```

the default ACL described earlier is used whenever Exim receives a RCPT command in an SMTP dialogue. The majority of policy tests on incoming messages can be carried out when RCPT commands arrive. A rejection of RCPT should cause the sending MTA to give up on that recipient address.

Rejecting a MAIL command should cause an entire message to be rejected, but some MTAs do not implement this correctly, and instead continue to try to send the message. It is better, therefore, to reject RCPT commands instead.

However, you cannot test the contents of a message (for example, to verify addresses in the header lines) at RCPT time, because the message itself has not yet been transferred. Such tests have to appear in the ACL that is run before the final response to the DATA command is sent. This is the ACL specified by acl_smtp_data. At this time, it is no longer possible to reject individual recipients; an error response rejects the entire message. Unfortunately, it is known that some MTAs do not treat a permanent error correctly when received at this stage. Instead, they keep the message on their queue and try again later, just as some do for a rejected `MAIL` command. However, that is their problem, though it does waste some of your resources.

The ACL specified by `acl_not_smtp` is run for incoming messages that are not received via interactive SMTP, that is, for non-SMTP messages and batch SMTP messages. The ACL is run after the message has been read, just before it is finally accepted. A rejection either causes Exim to end with a non-zero return code, or it causes a bounce message to be sent to the sender, depending on the `-oex` option with which Exim was called (☞ 20.4).

The ACL specified by `acl_smtp_connect` is run at the start of an SMTP connection. A rejection at this time normally causes the client host to try again later.

The remaining ACL selection options control the use of the SMTP commands `AUTH`, `ETRN`, `EXPN`, `STARTTLS`, and `VRFY`.

## 14.8.3 Use of the ACL selection options

The values of the global ACL selection options are expanded before use, so you can use different ACLs in different circumstances. The most common usage is for the expanded string to name an ACL that is defined in the configuration, as in the examples shown earlier. However, this is not the only possibility. Having expanded the string, Exim searches for an ACL as follows:

- If the string begins with a slash, Exim assumes that it is a file name; it attempts to open the file and read its contents as an ACL. If the file does not exist or cannot be read, an error occurs (typically causing a temporary failure of whatever caused the ACL to be run). If an ACL is successfully read from a file, it is retained in memory, so that it can be reused within the current process without having to reread the file. Consider this example:

```
acl_smtp_data = /etc/acls/\
  ${lookup{$sender_host_address}lsearch\
  {/etc/acllist}{$value}{default}}
```

This looks up an ACL file to use on the basis of the host's IP address, falling back to a default file if the lookup does not succeed.

- If the string does not start with a slash, and does not contain any spaces, Exim searches the ACL section of the configuration for an ACL whose name matches the string.

- If no named ACL is found, or if the string contains spaces, Exim parses the string as an inline ACL. This simplifies the configuration in cases where the ACL is very short, such as this example:

```
acl_smtp_vrfy = accept
```

This setting allows free use of the VRFY command.

## 14.8.4 ACL return codes

The result of running an ACL is either "accept" or "deny", or, if some test cannot be completed (for example, if a database is down), "defer". These results cause 2*xx*, 5*xx*, and 4*xx* return codes, respectively, to be used in the SMTP dialogue. A fourth return, "error", occurs when there is a configuration error such as invalid syntax in the ACL. This also causes a 4*xx* return code.

## 14.8.5 Unset ACL options

For most of the available ACLs, if the associated global acl_... option is unset, no check is applied, and the relevant action is allowed to proceed. However, this is not the case for the ETRN, EXPN, RCPT, and VRFY commands. If no ACL is set up for them, they are rejected. This means that acl_smtp_rcpt must be defined before Exim can receive any messages over an SMTP connection.

## 14.8.6 Available data for message ACLs

When an ACL for MAIL, RCPT, or DATA is being run, the variables that contain information about the host and the message's sender (for example, $sender_host_address$ and $sender_address$) are set, and can be used in ACL statements. In the case of RCPT (but not MAIL or DATA), $domain$ and $local_part$ are set from the recipient address.

The $message_size$ variable is set to the value of the SIZE parameter on the MAIL command at MAIL and RCPT time, or to -1 if that parameter was not given. Its value is updated to the true message size by the time the ACL after DATA is run.

The $rcpt_count$ variable increases by one each time a RCPT command is received. While an ACL for RCPT is being processed, the value of $rcpt_count$ includes the current command. The $recipients_count$ variable, on the other hand, increases by one each time a RCPT command is accepted, so while an ACL for RCPT is being processed, it contains the number of previously accepted recipients. During the processing of the first RCPT command, therefore, $rcpt_count$ has a value of one, whereas $recipients_count$ has a value of zero. At DATA time, $recipients_count$ contains the total number of accepted recipients.

## 14.8.7 Available data for non-message ACLs

When an ACL for AUTH, ETRN, EXPN, STARTTLS, or VRFY is being run, the remainder of the SMTP command line is placed in $smtp_command_argument$. An example of how this can be used to decide whether or not to accept the command is shown in section 14.8.20.

## 14.8.8 Format of an ACL

An individual ACL consists of a number of statements. Each statement starts with a verb, optionally followed by a number of conditions and other modifiers. If all the conditions are met, the verb is obeyed. If there are no conditions, the verb is always obeyed. What happens if any of the conditions are not met depends on the verb (and in the case of `accept`, on the special `endpass` modifier). Not all the conditions make sense at every testing point. For example, you cannot test a sender address in the ACL that is run for a `VRFY` command.

As you can see from the examples already discussed, the conditions and modifiers are written one to a line, with the first one on the same line as the verb, and subsequent ones on following lines. If you have a very long condition, you can continue it onto several physical lines by the usual \ continuation mechanism. It is conventional to align the conditions vertically.

## 14.8.9 ACL verbs

The ACL verbs are as follows:

accept

> If all the conditions are met, the ACL returns "accept". If any of the conditions are not met, what happens depends on whether `endpass` appears among the conditions. If the failing condition precedes `endpass`, control is passed to the next ACL statement; if it follows `endpass`, the ACL returns "deny". An example of this was discussed in section 14.8.1.

defer

> If all the conditions are met, the ACL returns "defer". If any of the conditions are not met, control is passed to the next ACL statement. A result of "defer" causes a temporary rejection of the SMTP command by means of a 4xx error code.

deny

> If all the conditions are met, the ACL returns "deny". If any of the conditions are not met, control is passed to the next ACL statement. For example:

```
deny dnslists = blackholes.mail-abuse.org
```

> rejects commands from hosts that are on a DNS black list.

drop

> If all the conditions are met, the action is the same as for `deny`, except that after a permanent error code is sent, the SMTP connection is dropped.

require

> If all the conditions are met, control is passed to the next ACL statement. If any of the conditions are not met, the ACL returns "deny". For example, when checking a RCPT command:
>
>     require verify = sender
>
> passes control to subsequent statements only if the message's sender can be verified. Otherwise, it rejects the command.

warn

> If all the conditions are met, the contents of the message and log_message modifiers (described shortly) are used to add a warning header line to the incoming message, or write to the main log, respectively. No action is taken if there is a temporary problem with one of the conditions, but the incident is logged. In all cases, control passes to the next ACL statement. For example, the following statement:
>
>     warn message = X-blacklisted-at: $dnslist_domain
>          dnslists = blackholes.mail-abuse.org : \
>                     dialup.mail-abuse.org
>
> adds an *X-blacklisted-at:* header line to messages received from hosts that are on one of the given DNS black lists. The ACL for RCPT commands may be run many times for a single message, but any given header line is added only once.
>
> Header lines that are added by an ACL for a RCPT command are visible when a subsequent ACL is run at the end of the DATA command. This provides a way of passing data between the two ACLs.

At the end of each ACL there is an implicit unconditional deny.

## 14.8.10 Condition and modifier processing

Not all conditions are relevant in all circumstances. For example, testing senders and recipients does not make sense in an ACL that is being run as the result of the arrival of an ETRN command, and checks on message headers can be carried out only in an ACL specified by acl_smtp_data or acl_not_smtp.

An exclamation mark preceding a condition negates its result. For example:

    deny   domains = *.dom.example
           !verify = recipient

causes the ACL to return "deny" if the recipient domain ends in *dom.example* and the recipient address cannot be verified.

The arguments of conditions and modifiers are expanded. A forced failure of an expansion causes a condition to be ignored, that is, it behaves as if the condition is true. Consider these two statements:

```
accept  senders = ${lookup{$host_name}lsearch\
                   {/some/file}{$value}fail}
accept  senders = ${lookup{$host_name}lsearch\
                   {/some/file}{$value}{}}
```

Each attempts to look up a list of acceptable senders. If the lookup succeeds, the returned list is searched, but if the lookup fails, the behaviour is different in the two cases. The `fail` in the first statement causes the condition to be ignored, leaving no further conditions. The `accept` verb therefore succeeds. The second statement, however, generates an empty list when the lookup fails. No sender can match an empty list, so the condition fails and therefore the `accept` also fails.

## 14.8.11 ACL modifiers

The ACL modifiers are `control`, `delay`, `endpass`, `log_message`, and `message`. They operate as follows:

### The control modifier

This modifier has an argument that is either `freeze` or `queue_only`. It may appear only in the ACLs for commands relating to an incoming message. For example:

```
accept  hosts   = +queue_hosts
        control = queue_only
```

The `control` modifier causes the message to be frozen or just queued (without immediate delivery), respectively, assuming that the message is accepted. Once one of these controls is set, it remains set for the message, and cannot be unset by other ACLs.

You can use `control` with the `warn` verb to apply the control, while leaving the decision to accept or deny to a subsequent verb. For example:

```
warn    hosts   = +freeze_hosts
        control = freeze
accept  ...
```

If `warn` has neither `message` nor `log_message` modifiers (as in this example), it does not add anything to the message and does not write a log entry.

### The delay modifier

This modifier, which has an argument that specifies a time interval, causes Exim to wait for the time interval before proceeding. The time is given in the usual Exim notation. This modifier may appear in any ACL. Like `control`, you can use `delay` with a `warn` verb to cause a delay without taking a decision about accepting or denying.

The delay happens as soon as the modifier is processed; this is unlike `message` and `log_message` (see below), which do not get used until all the conditions have been evaluated. For example:

```
deny  condition = ${if > {$rcpt_count}{20}{yes}{no}}
      delay = 30s
```

In this example, if there are more than 20 `RCPT` commands, the current command is rejected after a 30-second pause. Some administrators like to include delays of this type to slow down junk mailers.

## The endpass modifier

This modifier, which has no argument, is recognized only in `accept` statements. It marks the boundary between the conditions whose failure causes control to pass to the next statement, and the conditions whose failure causes the ACL to return "deny".

## The log_message modifier

For a `warn` statement, this modifier specifies a message that is written to the main log if the conditions are true. "Warning:" is added to the start of the message. For example, to permit all `AUTH` commands, while also logging their contents, you could use the following ACL:

```
acl_check_auth:
   warn    log_message = received from $sender_fullhost: \
                         AUTH $smtp_command_data
   accept
```

For statements other than `warn`, the `log_message` modifier sets up text to be used as part of the log message when access is denied. For `accept` and `require` statements, the message is used only if it precedes the condition that causes rejection. For example:

```
require log_message = wrong cipher
        encrypted   = DES-CBC3-SHA
```

This statement denies access, including the text "wrong cipher" in the log line, unless the SMTP session is encrypted using the DES-CBC3-SHA cipher suite.

`log_message` adds to any underlying error message that may exist because of the condition. For example, while verifying a recipient address, a redirection using the `:fail:` facility might have already set up a message.

Although `log_message` specifies the text before the conditions to which it applies, the expansion does not happen until after a condition has failed. This means that any variables that are set by the condition are available for inclusion in the message. For example, a number of variables whose names begin with *$dnslist* are set after a DNS black list lookup succeeds.

## The message modifier

For a `warn` statement, this modifier specifies a header line that is to be added to an incoming message if the conditions are true. An example is shown earlier with the description of the `warn` verb. The `message` modifier is ignored if used with a `warn` statement in an ACL that is not associated with an incoming message.

For statements other than `warn`, the `message` modifier sets up a message that is used as an error message if the current statement causes the ACL to deny access. The message is returned as part of the SMTP response. For `accept` and `require` statements, the most recent `message` modifier that precedes the failing condition is used. Consider this version of an earlier example, which has the `message` and `verify` lines swapped round:

```
accept   domains        = +local_domains
         endpass
         verify         = recipient
         message        = unknown user
```

This does not work as expected; the supplied message is never used because the rejection happens before the `message` modifier is reached.

The `accept` and `require` statements may usefully contain more than one `message` modifier, each applying to the failure of a different condition. A `deny` statement, on the other hand, tests all its conditions before access is denied. Consequently, the last `message` modifier is always the one that is used, even if it appears after all the conditions.

The text of the `message` modifier is literal; any quotes are taken as literals, but because the text is expanded, backslash escapes are always processed. A message containing newlines gives rise to a multi-line SMTP response. Like `log_message`, the contents of `message` are not expanded until after a condition has failed.

If `message` is specified on an ACL statement that denies access because of an address verification failure, the supplied message overrides the error message from the verification process. In particular, it overrides a message that is set by the use of `:fail:` in a **redirect** router. However, the original message is available in *$acl_verify_message*, so you can use it as part of, or instead of, your message if you want to.

### Interaction of message and log_message

If `log_message` is not present when access is denied, but `message` is present, the `message` text is used for logging. However, if it contains newlines, only the first line of the text is logged. In the absence of both `log_message` and `message`, a default built-in message is used. Neither `log_message` nor `message` are used if they are empty strings, or if their expansions fail.

## 14.8.12 ACL conditions

Several of the more common ACL conditions are shown in earlier examples. A complete list is shown in table 14-3. The use of these conditions is described in the following sections.

*Table 14-3: ACL conditions*

| Condition | Use |
|-----------|-----|
| acl | Allows one ACL to call another |
| authenticated | Tests for SMTP authentication |
| condition | A general customizable condition |
| dnslists | Checks DNS black lists |
| domains | Tests the domain of a recipient address |
| encrypted | Tests for an encrypted SMTP session |
| hosts | Tests for specific sending hosts |
| local_parts | Tests the local part of a recipient address |
| recipients | Tests a recipient address |
| sender_domains | Tests the domain of a sender address |
| senders | Tests the sender address |
| verify | Verifies sender and recipient addresses |
| | Verifies syntax and sender addresses in header lines |
| | Tests for certificate and `HELO` verification |

## 14.8.13 Checking the identity of the client host

The `hosts` condition checks that the calling host matches a given host list. This test is most commonly used to allow relaying from hosts on a local network, using an ACL fragment such as this line from the default configuration (described earlier):

```
accept hosts = +relay_from_hosts
```

If you include name lookups or wildcarded host names in a host list that also contains IP addresses, you should normally put the IP addresses first. For example, you could have the following:

```
accept hosts = 10.9.8.7 : dbm;/etc/friendly/hosts
```

The reason for this lies in the left-to-right way that Exim processes lists. It can test IP addresses without any DNS lookups, but when it reaches an item that requires a host name, it fails if it cannot find a host name to compare with the pattern. If you put this list in the opposite order, as follows:

```
accept hosts = dbm;/etc/friendly/hosts : 10.9.8.7
```

the `accept` statement fails for a host whose name cannot be found, even if its IP address is 10.9.8.7, because a host name is required for the lookup that comes first.

If you really want to do the name check first, and still recognize the IP address even if the name lookup fails, you can rewrite the ACL like this:

```
accept hosts = dbm;/etc/friendly/hosts
accept hosts = 10.9.8.7
```

The default action on failing to find the host name is to assume that the host is not in the list, so the first `accept` statement fails. The second statement then checks the IP address.

## 14.8.14 Using DNS black lists

As a service to the Internet community, a number of organizations are maintaining lists of hosts from which it might be desirable not to accept connections. Some of these lists may be freely used; others provide the service only on payment of a subscription.

The lists are maintained in the DNS, to make them easily accessible, with the hosts being indexed by IP address. The original list that started this trend is called the Realtime Blackhole List. This is a hand-maintained "black list" of hosts that, in the judgement of the list maintainers, have been misbehaving. Another list that is now managed by the same site is the *Dial-up User List* (DUL).[1] This list contains IP addresses that are used by ISPs for their dial-up customers. Many administrators configure their MTAs to refuse direct SMTP connections from such hosts, arguing that dial-up users should send out mail via their ISP's servers, where it can be better controlled. Several of the other lists use automatic means for detecting open relays; some of their policies have proved controversial.

### Checking a DNS list in an ACL

The `dnslists` ACL condition checks for entries in DNS black lists. In its simplest form, the condition tests whether the calling host is on a DNS black list by looking up the inverted IP address in one or more DNS domains. For example, if the calling host's IP address is 192.168.62.43, and the ACL statement is as follows:

---

[1]   See *http://mail-abuse.org/rbl/* and *http://mail-abuse.org/dul/*.

```
deny dnslists = blackholes.mail-abuse.org : \
                dialups.mail-abuse.org
```

the following domains are looked up:

```
43.62.168.192.blackholes.mail-abuse.org
43.62.168.192.dialups.mail-abuse.org
```

If a DNS lookup times out or otherwise fails to give a decisive answer, Exim behaves as if the host is not on the relevant list. This is usually the required action when `dnslists` is used with `deny` (which is the most common usage), because it prevents a DNS failure from blocking mail. However, you can change this behaviour by putting one of the following special items in the list:

| | |
|---|---|
| +include_unknown | behave as if the item is on the list |
| +exclude_unknown | behave as if the item is not on the list (default) |
| +defer_unknown | give a temporary error |

Each of these applies to any subsequent items on the list. For example:

```
deny dnslists = +defer_unknown : foo.bar.example
```

Testing the list of domains stops as soon as a record is found in the DNS. If you want to warn for one list and block for another, you can use two different statements, as in this example:

```
deny  dnslists = blackholes.mail-abuse.org
warn  dnslists = dialups.mail-abuse.org
```

Some DNS lists are keyed on domain names rather than inverted IP addresses.[1] You can change the name that is looked up by adding additional data to a `dnslists` item, introduced by a slash. For example:

```
deny  message  = Sender's domain is listed at $dnslist_domain
      dnslists = dsn.rfc-ignorant.org/$sender_address_domain
```

This particular example is useful only in ACLs that are obeyed after RCPT or DATA commands, when a sender address is available. If the message's sender is *user@tld.example*, the domain that is looked up in this example is *tld.example. dsn.rfc-ignorant.org*. You can mix entries with and without additional data in the same `dnslists` condition.

You can, of course, combine `dnslists` with any other ACL condition. For example, you might want to exclude connections from hosts on your local network from this check. This ACL fragment:

```
deny  hosts    = !192.168.56.224/28
      dnslists = rbl-plus.mail-abuse.example
```

---

[1]  See, for example, the *domain based zones* link at *http://www.rfc-ignorant.org/*.

specifies that the DNS list check happens only for connections from hosts that are not in the 192.168.56.224/28 network.

## Data obtained from a DNS black list

When an entry is found in a DNS black list, *$dnslist_domain* contains the name of the domain that matched, *$dnslist_value* contains the data from the DNS record, and *$dnslist_text* contains the contents of any associated TXT record. You can use these variables in message or log_message modifiers. Although these appear before the condition in the ACL, they are not expanded until after it has failed. For example:

```
deny    hosts   = !+local_networks
        message = $sender_host_address is listed at $dnslist_domain
        dnslists = rbl-plus.mail-abuse.example
```

DNS black list lookups are cached by Exim during the running of a reception process, so a lookup based on the IP address or sender address happens at most once for any incoming connection, even if it appears in the ACL that runs for every recipient.

## Restricting dnslists to specific data values

DNS black lists are constructed using address records in the DNS. The original RBL just used the address 127.0.0.1 on the right-hand side of the records, but the RBL+ list and some other lists use a number of values with different meanings. The values used in the RBL+ list are shown in table 14-4.

*Table 14-4: RBL+ address usage*

| Address   | Meaning             |
|-----------|---------------------|
| 127.1.0.1 | RBL                 |
| 127.1.0.2 | DUL                 |
| 127.1.0.3 | DUL and RBL         |
| 127.1.0.4 | RSS                 |
| 127.1.0.5 | RSS and RBL         |
| 127.1.0.6 | RSS and DUL         |
| 127.1.0.7 | RSS and DUL and RBL |

If you add an equals sign and an IP address after a dnslists domain name, you can restrict its action to DNS records with a matching right-hand side. For example, this statement:

```
deny dnslists = rblplus.mail-abuse.org=127.1.0.2
```

rejects only those hosts that yield 127.1.0.2. More than one address may be given, using a comma as a separator. These are alternatives; if any one of them matches, the RBL entry operates. If there are no addresses, any address record is considered to be a match.

If you want to specify a constraining address and also change the name that is looked up, the address list must be specified first. For example:

```
deny dnslists = dsn.rfc-ignorant.org=127.0.0.3/$sender_address_domain
```

## 14.8.15 Checking the state of the SMTP connection

There are several ACL conditions for checking the state of the SMTP connection.

### Checking for an encrypted connection

The `encrypted` condition tests for an encrypted SMTP connection, and, optionally, which cipher suite is in use. To test for encryption without testing for any specific ciphers, use this setting:

```
encrypted = *
```

If the SMTP connection is encrypted, the asterisk matches any cipher suite, so the condition is true. If the SMTP connection is not encrypted, the condition is false. A list of cipher suite names can be given instead of an asterisk. For example:

```
encrypted = IDEA-CBC-MD5:DES-CBC3-SHA
```

The condition is then true only if one of the listed suites is being used.

### Checking for a verified certificate

The `tls_try_verify_hosts` option is described in section 13.1.2. For matching hosts, it causes Exim to request a client certificate when setting up an encrypted session, but not to fail if no certificate is supplied, or if the certificate is not the one that is expected. The following ACL condition:

```
verify = certificate
```

is true only if the session is encrypted and a certificate was received from the client and verified.

You could use this condition (for example) to insist on a verified certificate for addresses that are being relayed, while still accepting addresses for local delivery on encrypted connections without a verified client certificate.

## Checking for SMTP authentication

The `authenticated` ACL condition is used to test whether the incoming SMTP connection is authenticated. This example succeeds if any authenticator has been used:

```
accept authenticated = *
```

You can restrict the test to specific authenticators by listing their names as the argument for the condition. For example, you might allow relaying from a local host that uses an unencrypted authentication mechanism, but require CRAM-MD5 authentication otherwise. This ACL fragment shows how such a test might be written:

```
accept hosts         = +local_lan_hosts
       authenticated = *
accept authenticated = cram_md5
```

 The names given to the `authenticated` condition are the names of Exim authenticators, not the authentication mechanism names.

## Verifying the EHLO command

The `helo_try_verify_hosts` option is described in section 14.5.3. For matching hosts, it causes Exim to verify the data supplied in the `EHLO` or `HELO` command, but to carry on even if verification fails. The following ACL condition:

```
verify = helo
```

is true only if an `EHLO` or `HELO` command has been received and its contents have been verified.

# 14.8.16 Checking sender addresses

There are ACL conditions that test for specific sender addresses, and there is also the possibility of verifying sender addresses. The "sender address" in all these cases is taken from the message envelope, not from any header line.

## Testing for specific sender addresses

The `senders` condition tests whether the sender of an incoming message matches a given address list. For example, to block messages from *spammer@coldmail.example* and from any local part at *spamhaus.example* you could use this ACL statement:

```
deny senders = spammer@coldmail.example : \
               *@spamhaus.example
```

To test for a bounce message, which has an empty sender, the following condition can be used:

```
senders = :
```

The colon is required in order to set up an empty list item. A completely empty list never matches any sender.

There is also a condition called `sender_domains` that tests the domain of the sender address. This allows you to use the domain list format for testing senders. Suppose you are using the default configuration, and have defined a list of domains for incoming relaying and a list of hosts for outgoing relaying like this:

```
domainlist relay_to_domains = dom1.example : dom2.example
hostlist   relay_from_hosts = 127.0.0.1 : 192.168.23.0/24
```

You might want to check that outgoing relayed messages have senders that are in the incoming relay domains. You could do this by changing this ACL statement:

```
accept  hosts = +relay_from_hosts
```

into this ACL statement:

```
accept  hosts           = +relay_from_hosts
        endpass
        message         = Invalid sender domain
        sender_domains  = +relay_to_domains
```

---

 You should never use a test on a sender address as the only condition for accepting a message, because envelope sender addresses can be trivially forged.

---

## Verifying sender addresses

The sender address in a message's envelope is the address to which bounce messages are sent. If a host accepts a message with a bad sender address, but subsequently cannot deliver the message, the result is an undeliverable bounce message that the postmaster has to sort out. On very busy hosts, such problems are often simply ignored by setting `ignore_bounce_errors_after` to a zero time interval, but it is also reasonable to do some checking on a sender address before accepting a message.

The most common causes of bad sender addresses are as follows (not in order):

•   Misconfigured mail software, frequently an MUA running on a single-user workstation, especially when this is shared between several users so that each one has to set up their own address every time they use it.

- The use of domains that are not registered in the DNS.

- Misconfigured name servers; hostmasters are only human, and typos in zone files can arise.

- Broken gateways from other mail systems that fail to create a valid SMTP envelope sender.

- Forgery, which is very common in spam mail.

You can configure Exim to verify sender addresses by including the following condition in an ACL:

```
verify = sender
```

If the message's sender is empty (that is, the incoming message is a bounce message), the condition is always true. Otherwise, the sender address is verified. The idea of verification is to try to detect those sender addresses to which a bounce message could not be delivered, so what Exim does is to run the address through the routers, as if it were being asked to deliver a message to it.

Verification can also be used for recipient addresses, so we leave discussion of its details until later in this chapter (☞ 14.9). Exim caches the result of sender verification, to avoid doing it more than once per message.

## 14.8.17 Checking recipient addresses

The earlier discussion of the default ACL describes the use of the domains and local_parts conditions for checking incoming recipient addresses in SMTP RCPT commands. A typical example, from the default configuration, is as follows:

```
accept   local_parts   = postmaster
         domains       = +local_domains
```

When either of these conditions succeeds with a lookup, the result of the lookup is placed in *$local_parts_data* or *$domain_data*, respectively.

There is also a recipients condition that checks the entire recipient address against an address list of recipients. Suppose you have a file of recipients who have asked you to block messages from a specific sender. You could use an ACL statement like this:

```
deny   sender      = badguy@evil.example
       recipients = lsearch;/etc/blockbadguy
```

You can also ask Exim to verify each recipient before accepting it, by including the following condition in a suitable ACL statement:

```
verify = recipient
```

The default ACL contains examples of this. There is a discussion of the details of verification later in this chapter.

## 14.8.18 Automatic detection of MX backup domains

If a host is acting as an MX backup for a large number of domains that change frequently, maintaining a list of them for Exim to consult, in addition to the related MX records in the DNS, is a duplication of effort. You can avoid this by using the special item @mx_any in a domain list, as in this example:

```
accept domains = @mx_any
```

This ACL statement accepts any recipient whose domain has an MX pointing to the local host. The items @mx_primary and @mx_secondary are similar, except that the first matches only when a primary MX target is the local host, and the second matches only when no primary MX target is the local host, but a secondary target is. "Primary" means an MX record with the lowest preference value; there may of course be more than one such MX record.

---

 Using @mx_any (or @mx_secondary) to allow relaying opens your server to the possibility of abuse. Anyone with access to a DNS zone can list your server in a secondary MX record as a backup for their domain, without your permission. This is not a huge exposure because first, it requires the cooperation of a hostmaster to set up, and second, their mail is passing through your server, so they run the risk of your noticing and (for example) throwing it all away. Nevertheless, the insecurity is there. A safer way of avoiding the maintenance of two different sets of data is to generate both the DNS zone data and Exim's relaying data from a single source.

---

## 14.8.19 Checking message header lines

A common spamming ploy is to send syntactically invalid header lines such as the following examples:[1]

```
To: @
To: <>
```

In addition, some MUAs have been observed to send invalid header lines of these types:[2]

---

[1]   The first is invalid because there is no local part or domain. An empty address, as in the second example, is not allowed in header lines (it is permitted only in the SMTP MAIL command).

[2]   In the first, a special character (the at sign) appears unquoted in the "phrase" part of the RFC 2822 address. In the second, a special character (the colon) appears unquoted in the local part.

```
To: user@domain.example <user@domain.example>
To: <mailto:user@domain>
```

Exim can test for such syntax errors in an ACL that is run after a message has been received, that is, in an ACL specified by `acl_smtp_data`. For example, the following statement rejects messages with syntactically invalid header lines:

```
require verify = header_syntax
```

This checks the syntax of all header lines that can contain lists of addresses (*Sender:*, *From:*, *Reply-To:*, *To:*, *Cc:*, and *Bcc:*). This is a syntax check only; no verification of the addresses takes place.

Another condition that is relevant only in an ACL that is run after a message has been received is as follows:

```
verify = header_sender
```

This checks that there is a verifiable sender address in at least one of the *Sender:*, *Reply-To:*, or *From:* header lines. Details of address verification are given later in this chapter. You can combine this condition with the `senders` condition to restrict it to bounce messages only (where there is no verifiable sender in the envelope). For example:

```
deny    senders = :
        message = A valid sender header is required for bounces
        !verify = header_sender
```

## 14.8.20 Custom ACL checks

The `condition` condition allows you to create customized tests in ACLs, using any of the available string expansion items and variables. The value of the condition is expanded, and if the result is an empty string, the number zero, `no`, or `false`, the condition is false. If the result is a non-zero number, `yes`, or `true` the condition is true. Any other value is assumed to indicate some kind of configuration error, and so the ACL yields "defer".

For example, suppose you want to allow any authentication mechanism to be used on an encrypted connection, but only CRAM-MD5 when the connection is not encrypted. The best way to do this is to refuse the AUTH command when the conditions are not met. You could do this by creating an ACL to check the AUTH command as follows:

```
acl_check_auth:
  accept encrypted = *
  accept condition = ${if eq {${uc:$smtp_command_argument}}\
                     {CRAM-MD5}{yes}{no}}
  deny    message = Require CRAM-MD5 or TLS encrypted connection
```

The first statement in this example accepts the AUTH command if the connection is encrypted. The second statement uses a custom test to see if the argument of the AUTH command is CRAM-MD5. The result of the expansion is yes only if the argument matches.

## 14.8.21 Calling nested ACLs

One ACL can call another ACL in the manner of a "subroutine" by means of the acl condition. This can simplify the running of different ACLs for different recipients or different domains or different sending hosts. It can also be used to split up long ACLs into more manageable pieces. For example, the default ACL could be rewritten so as to separate out the ACLs for local and remote addresses as follows:

```
acl_check_rcpt:
  accept  hosts = :
  deny    local_parts  = ^.*[@%!/|] : ^\\.
  accept  domains      = +local_domains
          endpass
          acl          = acl_local
  accept  acl          = acl_relay
```

The "subroutines" are as follows:

```
acl_local:
  accept  local_parts  = postmaster
  require verify        = sender
  accept  verify        = recipient
  deny    message       = unknown user

acl_relay:
  require verify        = sender
  accept  domains       = +relay_to_domains
          endpass
          message       = unrouteable address
          verify        = recipient
  accept  hosts         = +relay_from_hosts
  accept  authenticated = *
  deny    message       = relay not permitted
```

A message set up in a nested ACL is overridden by a message specified at a higher level.

The possible values for the argument of an acl condition are the same as for the ACL selection options (☞ 14.8.3). To test the condition, the named or inline ACL is run. If it returns "accept", the condition is true; if it returns "deny", the condition is false; if it returns "defer", the calling ACL returns "defer". ACLs may be nested up to 20 deep; the limit exists purely to catch runaway loops.

# 14.9 Address verification

Verification is the process of validating a sender or recipient address by checking as far as possible whether Exim could deliver a message to it. A successful verification cannot guarantee that an address is deliverable, but a failure to verify does guarantee that it is not deliverable.

Several of the `verify` conditions described in the previous section cause addresses to be verified. These conditions can be followed by a number of options that modify the verification process. The options are separated from the keyword and from each other by slashes. For example:

```
verify = sender/callout
verify = recipient/defer_ok/callout=10s
```

The first stage of verification is carried out by passing the address to the configured routers, in the same way as when delivering a message. However, there are router options that can be used to change the behaviour of routers when they are verifying, as opposed to routing an address for delivery (☞ 6.1.2, 6.2.3).

If there is a defer error while doing this verification routing, the ACL normally returns "defer". However, if you include `defer_ok` in the options, the condition is forced to be true instead.

## 14.9.1 Verification callouts

For local addresses, routing normally checks the validity of the local part of the address. However, for remote addresses, routing verifies the domain, but is unable to do any checking of the local part. There are situations where some means of verifying the local part of remote addresses is desirable. One way this can be done is to make an SMTP *callback* to the sending host (for a sender address) or a *callforward* to a subsequent host (for a recipient address), to see if the host accepts the address in an SMTP command. We use the term *callout* to cover both cases.

If the `callout` option is present on an ACL condition that verifies an address, a second stage of verification occurs if the address is successfully routed to one or more remote hosts. Exim makes SMTP connections to the remote hosts, to test whether the address is acceptable. For a sender address, it behaves as if transmitting a bounce message and sends:

```
HELO <primary host name>
MAIL FROM:<>
RCPT TO:<<the address to be tested>>
QUIT
```

When verifying a recipient address, the MAIL command in the callout contains the sender address of the message. If the response to the RCPT command is a 2*xx* code, the verification succeeds. If it is 5*xx*, the verification fails. For any other condition,

Exim tries the next host, if any. If there is a problem with all the remote hosts, the ACL yields "defer", unless the callout option `defer_ok` is given, in which case the condition is forced to succeed.

Callout options are specified following an equals sign after `callout`, and separated by commas if there is more than one of them. For example:

```
deny   !verify = sender/callout=defer_ok
```

 A successful callout does not guarantee that the remote will accept and deliver messages to the address. Some hosts make no checks on recipient addresses at SMTP time.

There is a default timeout of 30 seconds for each host connection in a callout attempt. This can be changed by specifying a different time on the `callout` option. For example:

```
require verify = sender/callout=5s
```

For SMTP callout connections, the port to connect to and the outgoing interface are taken from the transport to which the address was routed, if it is a remote transport. Otherwise port 25 is used, and the interface is not specified.

The callout facility allows you to reject some senders with valid domains but invalid local parts, something that is commonly encountered in spam messages. However, callouts should be used with care, because they use more resources to verify an address.

You can reduce the cost of callouts by restricting their use to certain domains or certain sending hosts. For example, one instance where the cost of callout might be acceptable is a corporate gateway that checks addresses in domains that are local to the corporation, but not local in the Exim sense, using ACL statements such as these:

```
deny   sender_domains = +corporate_domains
       !verify         = sender/callout
deny   domains         = +corporate_domains
       !verify         = recipient/callout
```

The assumption is that any of the corporate domains resolves to a host on the local LAN, so that making an SMTP connection to it is relatively cheap.

## Additional callout features

Some additional features that were added to Exim after release 4.10 are briefly described in this section.

Current releases of Exim cache the results of callouts by default, so as to reduce the overall cost. The expiry times for the different cache records can be set by several options whose names begin with callout_. You can suppress caching by setting no_cache as a callout option, as in this example;

```
deny    domains  = +corporate_domains
        !verify  = recipient/callout=no_cache,10s
```

If random is specified as a callout option, a check using a recipient with a "random" local part is done first. This is not really random – it is defined by the expansion of the option callout_random_local_part, which defaults to the following string:

```
$primary_host_name-$tod_epoch-testing
```

The idea here is to try to determine whether the remote host accepts all local parts without checking. If it does, there is no point in doing callouts for specific local parts. If the "random" check succeeds, no further testing is done. The result is cached, and used to force subsequent callout checks to succeed without a connection being made, until the cache record expires.

If postmaster is specified as a callout option, a successful callout check is followed by a similar check for the local part *postmaster* at the same domain. If this address is rejected, the callout fails. This enforces the RFC requirement that *postmaster* should be a valid local part in all email domains.

## 14.9.2 Redirection while verifying

A dilemma arises when a local address is redirected by aliasing or forwarding during verification: should the generated addresses themselves be verified, or should the successful expansion of the original address be enough to verify it? Exim takes the following pragmatic approach:

- When an incoming address is redirected to just one child address, verification continues with the child address, and if that fails to verify, the original verification also fails.

- When an incoming address is redirected to more than one child address, verification does not continue. A success result is returned.

This seems the most reasonable behaviour for the common use of aliasing as a way of redirecting different local parts to the same mailbox. It means, for example, that a pair of alias entries of this form:

```
A.Wol:   aw123
aw123:   :fail: Gone away, no forwarding address
```

work as expected, with both local parts causing verification failure. When a redirection generates more than one address, the behaviour is more like a mailing list, where the existence of the alias itself is sufficient for verification to succeed.

### 14.9.3 Testing address verification

You can test how Exim would respond to a request to verify a particular sender or recipient address by using the -bvs or -bv options, respectively. For example:

```
exim -bvs homer@greece.example
exim -bv  virgil@rome.example
```

There is a difference between -bvs and -bv only if your configuration distinguishes between senders and recipients when verifying (for example, by the use of verify_sender on one or more routers).

If the configuration of your routers includes any tests of values associated with a sending host, for example, checking the contents of *$sender_host_address*, you can supply values for the test using one of the command-line options whose names start with -oM (☞ 20.2.3).

# 14.10 The local_scan() function

The ACLs that are run for RCPT and DATA provide facilities for simple, straightforward checks on incoming messages. However, their design is not suitable for more sophisticated checking, such as scanning the contents of messages.

The methods for message scanning that are described in section 5.10 require the message to be accepted so that it can be delivered to the scanning program. You can, however, arrange to scan incoming messages just before they are accepted, by providing your own *local_scan()* function. This function is written in C and linked with the Exim binary. However, a description of the programming interface is beyond the scope of this book; you can find these details in the Exim reference manual.

# 14.11 Incoming message processing

Exim performs various transformations on the original sender and recipient addresses of all messages that it handles, as well as on the messages' header lines. Some of these changes are optional and configurable, while others always take place. All of this processing happens at the time a message is received, before it is first written to the spool. Address rewriting is covered in chapter 15; the other changes are described here.

## 14.11.1 Resent- header lines

RFC 2822 makes provision for header lines starting with the string Resent- to be added to a message when it is resent by the original recipient to somebody else. These headers are *Resent-Date:*, *Resent-From:*, *Resent-Sender:*, *Resent-To:*, *Resent-Cc:*, *Resent-Bcc:* and *Resent-Message-ID:*. The RFC says this about these header lines:

> *Resent fields are strictly informational. They MUST NOT be used in the normal processing of replies or other such automatic actions on messages.*

This leaves things rather vague as far as other processing actions such as address rewriting are concerned. Exim treats *Resent-:* header lines as follows:

- A *Resent-From:* line that just contains the login id of the submitting user is automatically rewritten in the same way as *From:* (described shortly).

- If there's a rewriting rule for a particular header line, it is also applied to *Resent-:* header lines of the same type. For example, a rule that rewrites *From:* also rewrites *Resent-From:*.

- For local messages, if *Sender:* is removed on input, *Resent-Sender:* is also removed.

- If there are any *Resent-:* header lines but no *Resent-Date:*, *Resent-From:*, or *Resent-Message-ID:*, they are added as necessary. It is the contents of *Resent-Message-ID:* (rather than *Message-ID:*) that are included in log lines in this case.

- The logic for adding *Sender:* is duplicated for *Resent-Sender:* when any *Resent-:* header lines are present.

## 14.11.2 The UUCP "From" line

Messages that have come from UUCP (and some other applications) often begin with a line containing the envelope sender and a timestamp, following the word From and a space.[1] Earlier in this chapter (☞ 14.3.3), we discussed how this line could be used by a trusted user to supply an envelope sender address for a locally generated message.

For incoming SMTP messages, a UUCP From line is not normally recognized. It is syntactically invalid as a header line, so it is treated as the first line of the message's body. However, because there are broken programs that send out SMTP messages with leading From lines, there are options to make Exim recognize them in SMTP input. Their contents, however, are always ignored and removed from the message.

---

[1] A similar line is also used as a separator in "Berkeley format" mailbox files. Do not confuse this with the *From:* header line.

For incoming SMTP over TCP/IP, `ignore_fromline_hosts` can be set to a list of hosts for which a From line is ignored; for SMTP over the standard input and output (the `-bs` option), `ignore_fromline_local` must be set true. These options should be used only as a last resort when broken sending software must be used and cannot be fixed.

In all cases, only one From line is recognized. If there is more than one, the second is treated as a data line that starts the body of the message.

## 14.11.3 The From: header line

If an incoming message does not contain a *From:* header line, Exim adds one containing the sender's address. This is obtained from the message's envelope in the case of remote messages; for locally generated messages, the calling user's login name and full name are used to construct an address, using the format of this example:

```
From: Zaphod Beeblebrox <zaphod@end.univ.example>
```

The user's full name is obtained from the `-F` command-line option, if set. Otherwise it is obtained by looking up the calling user and extracting the "gecos" field from the password entry. If the "gecos" field contains an ampersand character, this is replaced by the login name with the first letter converted to upper case, as is conventional in a number of operating systems.

In some environments, the "gecos" field is used to hold more than just the user's name; it might also contain a departmental affiliation or an office or telephone number. The `gecos_pattern` and `gecos_name` options make it possible to extract just the username in such cases. When they are set, `gecos_pattern` is treated as a regular expression that is to be applied to the field, and if it matches, `gecos_name` is expanded and used as the user's name.[1] Numeric variables such as *$1*, *$2*, and so on, can be used in the expansion to pick up subfields that were matched by the pattern. In HP-UX, where comma separators are conventionally found, the following can be used:

```
gecos_pattern = ^([^,]*)
gecos_name = $1
```

This extracts everything before the first comma as the user's full name.

In all cases, the username is made to conform to RFC 2822 by quoting all or parts of it if necessary. If characters with values greater than 127 appear in a username, Exim encodes it as described in RFC 2047, which defines a way of including non-ASCII characters in header lines. However, if `print_topbitchars` is set, these characters are treated as normal printing characters.

---

[1] Before matching, any ampersand in the "gecos" field is replaced by the login name, as previously described.

For compatibility with Sendmail, if an incoming non-SMTP message has a *From:* header containing just the unqualified login name of the calling user, this is replaced by an address containing the user's login name and full name, as just described.

## 14.11.4 The Sender: header line

The *Sender:* header line is supposed to contain the address of the originator of a message when this is different to the contents of the *From:* header line. On multi-user systems, it is helpful to record the true identity of the person who sent a message. If one out of several thousand users sends a message containing:

```
From: god@heaven.com
```

and this causes offence, the local postmaster may be grateful for the *Sender:* header when seeking the culprit. However, *Sender:* is of little relevance for messages that originate on single-user systems.

The default behaviour of Exim is appropriate for multi-user systems, which is probably what the author of RFC 822 had in mind in the 1980s. *Sender:* header lines are left untouched in messages that arrive over TCP/IP. For other messages, however, unless they are sent by a trusted user using the `-f` or `-bs` command-line option, or `local_sender_retain` is set true, any existing *Sender:* header lines are removed.

For non-trusted callers, a check is made to see if the address given in the *From:* header line is the correct (local) sender of the message. If not, a *Sender:* line giving the true sender address is added to the message. This can be disabled by setting the following:

```
local_from_check = false
```

However, the envelope sender is still forced to be the login ID at the qualify domain for locally submitted messages.

The sender address that is expected in *From:* is the login ID, qualified with the contents of `qualify_domain`. Some installations may permit the use of prefixes or suffixes to local parts. For example, the addresses:

```
user@example.com
home-user@example.com
work-user@example.com
```

may all refer to the same user, who can make use of the prefix in a filter file to carry out some automatic mail management. If you do not want the appearance of a prefix in a *From:* line to trigger the addition of a *Sender:* line, you can set `local_from_prefix`. For example:

```
local_from_prefix = *-
```

permits any prefix that ends in a hyphen, so that a message containing:

```
From: anything-user@example.com
```

does not cause a *Sender:* header to be added if *user@example.com* matches the actual sender address that is constructed from the login name and qualify domain. The option `local_from_suffix` provides the same facility for suffixes.

## 14.11.5 The Bcc:, Cc:, and To: header lines

If Exim is called with the `-t` option, to take recipient addresses from the header lines of a locally submitted message, it removes any *Bcc:* header line that may exist (after extracting its addresses), unless the message has no *To:* or *Cc:* header lines, in which case a *Bcc:* header line with no addresses is left in the message.

If Exim is called to receive a message with the recipient addresses given on the command line, and there is no *Bcc:*, *To:*, or *Cc:* header line in the message, an empty *Bcc:* header line is added.

Insisting on the presence of at least an empty *Bcc:* line makes messages conform to RFC 822, though this requirement has in fact been removed in RFC 2822.

## 14.11.6 The Return-path:, Envelope-to:, and Delivery-date: header lines

A *Return-path:* header line is defined in the RFCs as something the MTA should insert when it does the final delivery of a message, in order to record the envelope sender address.

An *Envelope-to:* header line is not part of the standard RFC 2822 header set, but Exim can be configured to add one to the final delivery of a message, in order to record the envelope recipient address.

A *Delivery-date:* header line is not part of the standard RFC 2822 header set, but Exim can be configured to add one to the final delivery of a message, to record the time it was delivered.

None of these three header lines should be present in messages in transit, and Exim normally removes any that it finds. This action can be disabled by specifying any or all of the following:

```
return_path_remove = false
envelope_to_remove = false
delivery_date_remove = false
```

## 14.11.7 The Date: header line

If a message has no *Date:* header line, Exim adds one, giving the current date and time.

## 14.11.8 The Message-ID: header line

If an incoming message does not contain a *Message-ID:* header line, Exim constructs one and adds it to the message. The ID is constructed from Exim's internal message ID, preceded by the letter E to ensure that it starts with a letter, and followed by @ and the primary host name. Additional information can be included in this header by setting the `message_id_header_text` option.

## 14.11.9 The Received: header line

A *Received:* header is added at the start of every message that Exim processes. The contents of this header are defined by the `received_header_text` option; Exim automatically adds a semicolon and a timestamp to the configured string. The default setting of this option is:

```
received_header_text = Received: \
    ${if def:sender_rcvhost {from $sender_rcvhost\n\t}\
    {${if def:sender_ident {from $sender_ident }}\
    ${if def:sender_helo_name {(helo=$sender_helo_name)\n\t}}}}\
    by $primary_hostname \
    ${if def:received_protocol {with $received_protocol}} \
    ${if def:tls_cipher {($tls_cipher)\n\t}}\
    (Exim $version_number)\n\t\
    id $message_id\
    ${if def:received_for {\n\tfor $received_for}}
```

The reference to *$tls_cipher* is omitted when Exim is not compiled to support TLS encryption. The use of conditional expansions ensures that this setting works for both locally generated messages and messages received from remote hosts. It creates header lines such as the following:

```
Received: from scrooge.example ([192.168.12.25] ident=root)
          by marley.example with smtp (Exim 4.10)
          id E0tS3Ga-0005C5-00
          for cratchit@dickens.example; Mon, 25 Dec 2000 14:43:44 +0000
Received: from ebenezer by scrooge.example with local (Exim 4.04)
          id E0tS3GW-0005C2-00; Mon, 25 Dec 2000 14:43:41 +0000
```

Note the automatic addition of the date and time in the required format.

# 15

# Rewriting addresses

There are a number of circumstances in which addresses in messages are altered as they are handled by Exim. This can apply both to the messages' envelopes and to their headers. The header lines that may be affected are *Bcc:*, *Cc:*, *From:*, *Reply-To:*, *Sender:*, and *To:*. Some of these changes happen automatically, whereas others are explicitly configured by the administrator.

## 15.1 Automatic rewriting

One case of automatic rewriting is the addition of a domain to an unqualified address. This qualification is applied to addresses in header lines as well as to those in envelopes. For example, if a message is sent on a host where `qualify_domain` is set to *crete.example* by this command:

```
$ exim daedalus
To: daedalus
...
```

the unqualified local part *daedalus* is transformed into the fully qualified address *daedalus@crete.example*, both in the envelope and in the *To:* header line. Messages that arrive from other hosts should not contain unqualified addresses; you need to set `sender_unqualified_hosts` and/or `recipient_unqualified_hosts` if you want to allow such messages to be accepted (☞ 14.4).

The other case in which automatic rewriting happens is when an incomplete domain is given. The routing process may cause this to be expanded into the full domain name within the current encompassing domain. For example, a header such as:

```
To: minos@knossos
```

might be rewritten as:

```
To: minos@knossos.crete.example
```

if encountered on a host within the *crete.example* domain. Strictly, an MTA should not carry out any deliveries of a message until all its addresses have been routed, in case any of the header lines have to be changed as a result of routing. Otherwise it runs the risk of sending different copies of the message to different recipients.

However, doing this in practice could hold up many deliveries for unreasonable amounts of time in messages when one address could not immediately be routed (because of DNS timeouts, for example). Exim therefore does not delay other deliveries when the routing of one or more addresses is deferred. Addresses that cannot immediately be routed are usually for distant domains; as such addresses are not normally rewritten by this process, the chance of getting things "wrong" is fairly small.

# 15.2 Configured rewriting

Some people believe that configured rewriting is a Mortal Sin, because "MTAs should not tamper with messages". Others believe that life is not possible without it. Exim provides the facility; you do not have to use it. In general, rewriting addresses from your own domains has some legitimacy. Rewriting other addresses should be done only with great care and in special circumstances. My own view is that rewriting should be used sparingly, and mainly for "regularizing" addresses in your own domains. Although rewriting recipient addresses can be used as a routing tool, it is not intended for this purpose, and this use of rewriting is not recommended.

There are two commonly encountered circumstances where address rewriting is used, as illustrated by these examples:

- The company whose domain is *hitch.example* has a number of hosts that exchange mail with each other behind a firewall, using the host names as mail domains, but there is only a single gateway to the outer world. The gateway removes the local host names from addresses in outgoing messages, so that, for example, *fp42@vogon.hitch.example* becomes *fp42@hitch.example*. A rewriting rule that implements this is:

```
*@*.hitch.example   $1@hitch.example
```

- A host rewrites the local parts of its own users to remove login names and replace them by real-world names, so that, for example, *fp42@hitch.example* becomes *Ford.Prefect@hitch.example*. This can be done by a rewriting rule of this form:

```
*@hitch.example   ${lookup{$1}dbm{/etc/realnames.db}\
                  {$value}fail}@hitch.example frsF
```

We explain shortly how these rewriting rules operate. The two kinds of rewriting are not mutually exclusive, and very often both are done by having both rules in the configuration.

The order in which addresses in a message are rewritten is undefined, except that the envelope sender address is always rewritten before any header lines. If a rewrite of an address in a header line refers to *$sender_address*, it is the rewritten value that is used. However, you cannot assume that, for example, the *From:* header line is always rewritten before the *To:* header line, or *vice versa*.

Configured address rewriting can take place at several different stages of a message's processing. Rewriting happens when a message is received, but it can also happen when a new address is generated during routing (for example, by aliasing), and when a message is transported.

Two different kinds of address rewriting can be set up by an Exim administrator. They are called *general* and *in-transport* rewriting. They operate in a similar way, but at different times. General rewriting applies to all copies of a message, whereas in-transport rewriting applies only to those copies of a message that pass through a particular transport.

## 15.2.1 General rewriting

General rewriting is defined by a set of rules that are given in a section of the runtime configuration file introduced by `begin rewrite`. Each rule specifies the types of address on which it operates, and Exim applies the rules to each address when it first encounters it.

* A message's sender address, its original recipient addresses, and the addresses in its header lines are rewritten as soon as the message is received, before the start of any delivery processing. This happens only once. If the message is received from a host that is permitted to send unqualified addresses, they are qualified before rewriting. Other hosts are required to send fully qualified addresses in the envelope for the message to be accepted, but there may still be unqualified addresses in the header lines. Such addresses are left entirely alone; they are neither qualified nor rewritten.

* During delivery, recipient addresses that are generated by redirection (aliasing or forwarding) are rewritten at the time they are generated, unless `rewrite` is set false on the relevant router.

Addresses in header lines that are generated during delivery (that is, those that are added by routers, transports, or a system filter), are not subject to general rewriting.

## 15.2.2 In-transport rewriting

If the corporate gateway that was used as an earlier example is a host that does nothing but relay mail to the outside world, general rewriting rules can be used because rewriting is required for all deliveries.

However, not every site has the luxury of a separate host just to relay outgoing mail. If the same host is handling both onsite and offsite deliveries, there is a problem if the requirement is to rewrite addresses only in those copies of messages that are going offsite. The problem arises because Exim keeps only one copy of a message, however many recipients it has. If a message has both local and remote recipients, the requirement for rewriting only for remote delivery cannot be met by general rewriting. Instead, you must use in-transport rewriting.

This allows addresses in header lines to be rewritten at transport time (that is, as the message is being copied to a destination). Unlike general rewriting, envelope addresses cannot be rewritten by this means. You can, however, rewrite the envelope sender by using the `return_path` option on a transport, but you cannot rewrite recipient addresses at transport time.

In-transport rewriting is configured by setting the `headers_rewrite` option on a transport to a colon-separated list of rewriting rules. Each rule is in exactly the same form as one of the general rewriting rules that are applied when a message is received (see the following section). For example:

```
headers_rewrite = a@b c@d f : \
                  x@y w@z
```

changes *a@b* into *c@d* in *From:* header lines, and *x@y* into *w@z* in all address-bearing header lines. However, only the message's original header lines and any that were added by a system filter are rewritten. Note that this is different to general rewriting, which does not apply to header lines added by a system filter. If a router or transport adds header lines, they are not affected by this rewriting.

## 15.3 Rewriting rules

For both general and in-transport rewriting, the entire set of rules is applied to one address at a time. In other words, Exim does not go through the rules once, applying each one to every relevant address (which is one way it might have worked). Instead, it completely rewrites each address before moving on to the next one.

For each address, the rules are scanned in order of definition, with each one potentially changing the address, so that a replacement address from an earlier rule can itself be rewritten as a result of the application of a later rule. However, there are some cases where scanning stops after a particular rule has been applied.

Here is a very simple rewriting rule that just turns one explicit address into another:

```
ph10@workshop.exim.example    P.Hazel@exim.example
```

As a general rewriting rule, this would occupy a line by itself and apply to all instances of the address. As an in-transport rule, it would be the value of `headers_rewrite`:

```
headers_rewrite = ph10@workshop.exim.example  P.Hazel@exim.example
```

In this case, it would apply only to addresses in header lines. Further examples are shown here as general rewriting rules, but they could equally be used as in-transport rules.

In many cases, some kind of wildcard matching is employed in rewriting rules, and lookups can be used to vary the replacement address. The following configuration uses two rules to implement the most common forms of rewriting for the domain *exim.example*:

```
*@*.exim.example  $1@exim.example
*@exim.example    ${lookup{$1}dbm{/etc/realnames.db}\
                  {$value}fail}@exim.example frsF
```

The first rule removes the first component of domain names that end in *.exim.example*, and the second rule converts the local part by means of a file lookup. Thus, addresses in the *exim.example* domain are rewritten in two stages. The `frsF` that appears at the end of the second rule is a string of flag characters, which are explained in the following section.

### 15.3.1 Format of rewriting rules

In general, each rewriting rule is of the form:

```
<pattern>  <replacement>  <flags>
```

The pattern is terminated by whitespace, and it matches those addresses that are to be rewritten by this rule. The flags are single characters, some of which indicate the address location (header line, envelope field) to which the rule applies; other flags control how the rewriting takes place. Both the pattern and the address location flags must match for a rule to be "triggered". The allowed formats for patterns and flags are described later.

The replacement string is also terminated by whitespace. If either the pattern or the replacement string contain whitespace, they must be enclosed in double quotes. Within quotes, normal quoting conventions apply. A common configuration error is to forget to quote patterns or replacement strings that contain whitespace.

## 15.4 Rewriting patterns

The pattern in a rewriting rule is processed as a one-item address list, and can be any item that may appear in an address list (☞ 18.7).

 Address lists are always expanded before matching, and rewriting patterns are no exception. Thus, you must take care if your pattern contains dollar or backslash characters. In the case of a regular expression, it is usually simplest to use the `\N` facility for suppressing expansion.

After a rewriting pattern has been matched, the numerical variables (*$1*, *$2*, and so on) may be set, depending on the type of match that occurred. These can be used in the replacement string to insert portions of the subject address. The following examples cover some of the most common cases:

- If the pattern:

  ```
  *queen@*.example
  ```

  is matched against the address *hearts-queen@wonderland.example*, the three variables are set as follows:

  ```
  $0 = hearts-queen@wonderland.example
  $1 = hearts-
  $2 = wonderland
  ```

  Note that if the local part does not start with an asterisk, but the domain does, it is *$1* that contains the wild part of the domain.

- If the domain is specified as a lookup, and the lookup is a partial one, the wild part of the domain is placed in the next numerical variable, and the fixed part of the domain is placed in the succeeding variable. If the address *foo@bar.baz.example* is processed by a rewriting rule using the pattern:

  ```
  *@partial-dbm;/some/dbm/file
  ```

  and the key in the file that matches the domain is `*.baz.example`, the three variables are set as follows:

  ```
  $1 = foo
  $2 = bar
  $3 = baz.example
  ```

  The address *foo@baz.example* matches the same wildcard file entry; in this case *$2* is set to the empty string but *$3* is still set to `baz.example`. If a non-wild key is matched in a partial lookup, *$2* is again set to the empty string and *$3* is set to the whole domain. For non-partial lookups, no numerical variables are set.

- A regular expression is matched against the entire address, with the domain part lower-cased. After matching, the numerical variables refer to the bracketed capturing subexpressions, with *$0* referring to the entire address. For example, if the following pattern:

  ```
  \N^(red|white)\.king@(wonderland|lookingglass)\.example$
  ```

  is matched against the address *red.king@lookingglass.example*, the variables are set as follows:

  ```
  $0 = red.king@lookingglass.example
  $1 = red
  $2 = lookingglass
  ```

Note the use of \N to ensure that the backslash and dollar characters in the regular expression are left alone when the pattern is expanded.

# 15.5 Applying rewriting rules

If the replacement string for a rule is a single asterisk, an address that matches is not rewritten by that rule, and no subsequent rewriting rules are scanned for the address. For example:

```
hatta@lookingglass.example  *
```

specifies that *hatta@lookingglass.example* is never to be rewritten.

Otherwise, the replacement string is expanded; during the expansion, the variables *$local_part* and *$domain* refer to the address that is being rewritten. Any letters in these variables retain their original case; they are not lower-cased.

The expansion must either yield a fully qualified address or be terminated by a forced failure in a lookup or conditional expansion item. A forced failure causes the rewriting rule not to modify the address; it is equivalent to generating the following:

```
$local_part@$domain
```

as a replacement (but a bit more efficient). Any other kind of expansion failure (for example, a syntax error) causes the entire rewriting operation to be abandoned, and an entry to be written to the panic log.

## 15.5.1 Conditional rewriting

The behaviour of forced expansion failures means that the conditional features of string expansion can be used to implement conditional rewriting. For example, the following applies a rewriting rule only to messages that originate outside the local host:

```
*@*.hitch.example  "${if !eq {$sender_host_address}{}\
                   {$1@hitch.example}fail}"
```

The value of *$sender_host_address* is the empty string for locally originated messages; this rule restricts rewriting to cases when it is not empty (that is, to cases where the message came from a remote host). The forced failure causes the rewriting rule to be abandoned for locally originated messages, but subsequent rules are still applied to the address. Note that quotes have to be used for the rule in this example because it contains whitespace characters.

## 15.5.2 Lookup-driven rewriting

Rewriting that is entirely lookup-driven can be implemented by a rule of the form:

```
*@*    ${lookup...
```

with a lookup key derived from *$local_part* and *$domain*. The pattern matches every address, so the behaviour is entirely controlled by the expansion of the replacement string.

# 15.6 Rewriting flags

There are several different kinds of flag that may appear on rewriting rules:

- Flags that specify header lines and envelope fields to which the rule applies (shown in table 15-1): E, F, T, b, c, f, h, r, s, t

- Flags that control the rewriting process: Q, q, R, w

- A flag that specifies rewriting at SMTP time: S

*Table 15-1: Flags to select addresses*

| Flag | Meaning |
|------|---------|
| E | Rewrite all envelope fields |
| F | Rewrite the envelope From field |
| T | Rewrite the envelope To field |
| b | Rewrite the *Bcc:* header line |
| c | Rewrite the *Cc:* header line |
| f | Rewrite the *From:* header line |
| h | Rewrite all header lines |
| r | Rewrite the *Reply-To:* header line |
| s | Rewrite the *Sender:* header line |
| t | Rewrite the *To:* header line |

For in-transport rewriting rules, which apply only to header lines, the flags E, F, S, and T are not permitted.

## 15.6.1 Flags specifying what to rewrite

If none of the flag letters in table 15-1, nor the S flag (see later in this chapter) are present, the rewriting rule applies to all header lines and (for general rewriting but not for in-transport rewriting) to both the sender and recipient fields of the envelope. Otherwise, the rewriting rule is used only when rewriting addresses from the appropriate sources. Thus, in this example, which was given earlier:

```
*@*.exim.example   $1@exim.example
*@exim.example     ${lookup{$1}dbm{/etc/realnames.db}\
                   {$value}fail}@exim.example frsF
```

the first rule applies to all addresses, but the second one is used only for the *From:*, *Reply-to:*, and *Sender:* header lines, and the envelope sender (From) field.

## 15.6.2 Flags controlling the rewriting process

There are four flags that control the way the rewriting process works. These take effect only when a rule is invoked. For this to happen, the address must be of the correct type (match the selection flags) and also match the pattern:

- If the Q flag is set on a rule, the rewritten address is permitted to be an unqualified local part. It is qualified with qualify_recipient. In the absence of Q, the rewritten address must always include a domain. There is not much point in writing a rule such as:

  ```
  aaaa@domain.example   bbbb    Q
  ```

  because you might just as well write the qualifying domain in the replacement address. However, the flag can be useful if the replacement involves a file lookup that just produces local parts.

- If the q flag is set on a rule, no further rewriting rules are considered for the current address, even if no rewriting actually takes place because of a forced failure in the expansion. The q flag does not apply if the address is of the wrong type (does not match the selection flags) or does not match the pattern.

- The R flag causes a successful rewriting rule to be reapplied to the new address, up to 10 times. It can be combined with the q flag, to stop rewriting once it fails to match (after at least one successful rewrite). The R flag is generally of use in gateway environments where different styles of addressing are used. An example is given in connection with the S flag later.

- When an address in a header line is rewritten, the rewriting normally applies only to the working part of the address, with any comments and RFC 2822 "phrase" left unchanged. For example, the rule:

  ```
  fp42@*.hitch.example  prefect@hitch.example
  ```

  would change the following:

  ```
  From: Ford <fp42@restaurant.hitch.example>
  ```

  into:

  ```
  From: Ford <prefect@hitch.example>
  ```

Sometimes there is a need to replace the whole RFC 2822 address item, and this can be done by adding the flag letter w to a rule. If this is set on a rule that causes an address in a header line to be rewritten, the whole address is replaced, not just the working part. For example, the rule:

```
fp42@*.hitch.example  "\"F.J. Prefect\" <prefect@hitch.example>"  w
```

changes the following:

```
From: Ford <fp42@restaurant.hitch.example>
```

into:

```
From: "F.J. Prefect" <prefect@hitch.example>
```

The replacement must be a complete RFC 2822 address, including the angle brackets if necessary. When the w flag is set on a rule that causes an envelope address to be rewritten, all but the working part of the replacement address is discarded because envelope addresses do not contain "phrase" or comment items.

## 15.6.3 The SMTP-time rewriting flag

The rewrite flag S specifies a rule that applies to incoming envelope addresses at SMTP time, as soon as each MAIL or RCPT command is received and before any other processing; even before syntax checking. This form of rewrite rule allows for the handling of addresses that are not compliant with RFC 2821 (for example, UUCP "bang paths" in SMTP input, or malformed addresses from broken SMTP clients).

Because the input for a rewriting rule with the S flag is not required to be a syntactically valid address, the pattern must be a regular expression, and the variables *$local_part* and *$domain* are not available during the expansion of the replacement string. The pattern is matched against the entire text supplied by a MAIL or RCPT command, including any enclosing angle brackets, and the result of rewriting replaces the original address in the MAIL or RCPT command. For example, suppose one of your local SMTP clients is broken and sends malformed SMTP commands such as this:

```
RCPT TO: internet:ceo@plc.example
```

There are two things wrong with this address: the lack of surrounding angle brackets and the presence of the unwanted string internet: at the beginning. Obviously, the best thing would be to fix the client, but sometimes this is not possible, at least not quickly. Using the S rewriting flag you can arrange for Exim to patch up such bad addresses:

```
\N^\s*internet:(.*)$  <$1>  S
```

The regular expression pattern matches addresses that start with `internet:` (with optional leading whitespace), and arranges to capture the remainder by means of the parentheses. The replacement string wraps the captured substring in the angle brackets that are required in SMTP commands, so the result is treated as if the command were:

```
RCPT TO:<ceo@plc.example>
```

Another case where this kind of rewriting is useful is when interfacing to systems that use UUCP bang-path addressing, in which addresses are of the form:

```
host1!host2!host3...!user
```

Exim supports only Internet domain-based addressing, and so does not recognize bang paths. However, in some cases, rewriting can be used to convert bang-path addresses. If this is done at SMTP time using the S flag, the rewritten addresses are subject to the normal verification and relay checking, which is what you want.[1] The following rules convert bang paths into more conventional Internet addresses at SMTP time:

```
\N^(?=.*?!)(?!.*?@)(.*)$           $1@bang.path         S
\N^([^!]+)!([^%]+)([^@]*)@bang\.path$  $2%$1$3@bang.path   SR
\N^(.*)%([^@]*)@bang\.path$        $1@$2                S
```

The first rule recognizes strings that contain at least one exclamation mark but no @ characters, and adds the pseudodomain *bang.path*, thereby allowing the other two rules to operate on them. Conventional Internet addresses that happen to contain exclamation marks are not affected by this rewriting.

The second rule changes the local part of these special addresses by reversing the order of the parts and replacing the exclamation marks with percent signs. For example, *a!b@bang.path* becomes *b%a@bang.path*, and *a!b!c!d@bang.path* becomes *d%c%b%a@bang.path*. This rule needs the R (repeat) flag, because each time it runs, it handles only one exclamation mark. The final rule removes the pseudodomain, and changes the final percent sign into an @.

Using these rules, a two-part bang path such as *a!b* is turned into *b@a*, and a longer path such as *a!b!c!d* becomes *d%c%b@a*. This notation is sometimes called the "percent hack", and has been used in Internet addressing for explicit routing of mail, though it is not a standard. Nowadays it is falling out of use.

---

[1] Since a bang-path address is a syntactically valid local part, you could configure Exim to accept unqualified addresses, and then later rewrite local parts containing exclamation marks. This is not, however, a good idea, because it bypasses relay checking.

# 15.7 A further rewriting example

The ability to rewrite addresses may be used in many different ways. The most common use of rewriting is for removing local host names, and converting login names to "real names" in messages that are leaving a local network for the wider Internet. Earlier, we showed a simple way of implementing such rewriting:

```
*@*.exim.example  $1@exim.example
*@exim.example    ${lookup{$1}dbm{/etc/realnames.db}\
                  {$value}fail}@exim.example frsF
```

This example can be extended to provide additional functionality, such as rejecting messages whose local sender addresses cannot be recognized. We show the complete configuration first, and then explain how it works. There are five rules:

```
\N^(?>.*)(?<!\.exim\.example)   *
root@*.exim.example "admin@exim.example (root@$1)"  hFwq
*@*.exim.example \
  ${lookup{$local_part@$2}lsearch{/etc/realnames}{$value}\
  {"$1@$2-is-not-known"}}@exim.example  Fq
*@*.exim.example \
  ${lookup{$local_part@$2}lsearch{/etc/realnames}{$value@exim.example}\
  {$sender_address}}  fsrq
*@*.exim.example \
  ${lookup{$local_part@$2}lsearch{/etc/realnames}{$value}{unknown}}\
  @exim.example
```

Because we are rewriting only those addresses that end in *.exim.example*, we can save some resources by having an initial rule that recognizes other domains and abandons any attempt to rewrite them:

```
\N^(?>.*)(?<!\.exim\.example)   *
```

The pattern is a regular expression that matches all addresses that do not end in *.exim.example*, and the single asterisk as a replacement string means "do not rewrite this address and do not scan any more rules". This means that only addresses that end with *.exim.example* are passed to the remaining rules.

Some explanation of the regular expression is needed. There are several ways you can write a pattern to implement "ends with", but this is the most efficient. \N at the start of the pattern stops the string expander from making any changes to it. The regular expression itself starts with this sequence:

```
^(?>.*)
```

which matches the entire string. ^ matches the start of the string, and .* matches any number of arbitrary characters, but because it is enclosed in (?>) parentheses, no backtracking is permitted, so having reached the end of the string, the current point stays there. However, the pattern itself is not finished. We still have:

```
(?<!\.exim\.example)
```

This is a negative backward assertion; it checks that the characters immediately preceding the current position (that is, those at the end of the string) are `.exim.example`. If it fails, the pattern match fails (because no backtracking is permitted to try this test at any other position). If this test succeeds, the pattern match succeeds because the end of the pattern has been reached.

The more "obvious" regular expression for checking that a string ends with `.exim.example` is:

```
\.exim\.example$
```

This is less efficient because it scans through the string character by character, looking for a dot; whenever it finds one, it checks to see if it is followed by `exim.example` and the end of the string. This is more work than a single check at the end of the string.

The second rewriting rule in this example handles mail from *root*. Such mail may be generated by *cron* or other system jobs on local hosts. Although it is usually addressed to local users, there is always the possibility that such users have forwarded their mail offsite. If there is more than one local host, rewriting *root* in the same way as a user login name loses information about which local host's *root* actually sent the message. This rewriting rule is one way of preserving this information:

```
root@*.exim.example "admin@exim.example (root@$1)"  hFwq
```

The pattern matches *root* at any of the local hosts, and the hF flags restrict this rule to header lines and the envelope sender. The new address is a standard one, but retains the original host name in a comment. The w flag ensures that the comment is retained in any header lines that are rewritten, so that, for example:

```
From: Charlie Root <root@host1.exim.example>
```

is rewritten as:

```
From: admin@exim.example (root@host1)
```

This does, of course, allow the local host name to remain in the message. Sites that are paranoid about hiding their local host names would not want to do this.[1] The q flag on this rule causes rewriting to cease after the rule has been obeyed, so the subsequent rules do not apply to *root* addresses.

The third rule rewrites the envelope sender of the message by looking up the address, minus the terminating *.exim.example*, in a file containing lines such as this:

```
jc@host1:    J.Caesar
jc@host2:    Jiminy.Cricket
```

---

[1]  They would probably also want to remove the *Received:* header lines that show local host names.

which might be called */etc/realnames*. In other words, it allows for non-unique local parts among the local hosts. Provided this file is not too big, using a linear search is acceptable.[1] The pattern does not need to test the domain, because we know that the rule is applied only to domains ending in *.exim.example*, so the rule is as follows:

```
*@* ${lookup{$local_part@$2}lsearch{/etc/realnames}{$value}\
   {"$1@$2-is-not-known"}}@exim.example  Fq
```

The F flag ensures that this rule is applied only to envelope senders. If the address cannot be found in the file, it is rewritten to a magic sequence. An unknown sender address such as *xxxx@host1.exim.example* is turned into the following:

```
"xxxx@host1-is-not-known"@exim.example
```

by this rule. The idea here is that, provided incoming sender addresses are being verified, this rewritten address will fail to verify, and so the message will not be accepted by the gateway for onward transmission if its sender address is not in the list of local addresses.

The fourth rule rewrites sender addresses within the message's *From:*, *Sender:*, and *Reply-To:* header lines. It is almost the same as the previous rule, except that failure to look up the original address is not treated as such a serious error here; an unknown address is replaced by the sender address from the envelope:

```
*@* ${lookup{$local_part@$2}lsearch{/etc/realnames}\
   {$value@exim.example}{$sender_address}}     fsrq
```

Exim always rewrites the envelope sender address before it rewrites header lines,[2] so we know that the sender address has been validated.

The final rule has no flags, and so in theory applies to all addresses, but because of the use of the q flag in previous rules, it is only ever applied to envelope recipients and the addresses in the recipient header lines *To:* and *Cc:* (and *Bcc:* if present). It replaces local parts in our domain from the list of real names, substituting unknown for any that it cannot find:

```
*@* ${lookup{$local_part@$2}lsearch{/etc/realnames}{$value}{unknown}}\
   @exim.example
```

# 15.8 Testing rewriting rules

Exim's general rewriting configuration can be tested by the -brw command-line option. This takes an address (which can be a full RFC 2822 address) as its argument. The output is a list of how the address would be transformed by the general rewriting rules for each of the different places it might appear (that is, for

---

[1]  Once it is above a hundred lines or so, it should be converted into some kind of indexed lookup, for example, a *cdb* or DBM file (see chapter 16).

[2]  This is the only ordering of rewrites that is specified.

each different header line and for the envelope sender and recipient fields). For example:

```
exim -brw ph10@workshop.exim.example
```

might produce the output:

```
    sender: Philip.Hazel@exim.example
      from: Philip.Hazel@exim.example
        to: ph10@workshop.exim.example
        cc: ph10@workshop.exim.example
       bcc: ph10@workshop.exim.example
  reply-to: Philip.Hazel@exim.example
  env-from: Philip.Hazel@exim.example
    env-to: ph10@workshop.exim.example
```

which shows that general rewriting has been set up for that address when used in any of the source fields, but not when it appears as a recipient address. If the S flag is set for any rewriting rules, another line is added to the output, showing the rewriting that would occur at SMTP time.

# 16

# File and database lookups

We have introduced and given brief explanations of the way Exim can be configured to look up data in files and databases in earlier chapters. Lookups give you flexibility in the way you store the data that controls Exim's behaviour. They also allow Exim to make use of common, companywide databases that can be shared with other programs. Lookups can be used in several different kinds of configuration item, but they operate in the same way in each case. This chapter covers the underlying lookup mechanisms in detail; there are many examples of lookup usage throughout the book.

You can specify lookups in two different types of configuration item:

- Any string that is to be expanded may contain explicit lookup requests, which make it possible to replace portions of the string by data read from a file or database (☞ 17.8).

- A number of configuration options and ACL conditions contain lists of domains, hosts, or mail addresses that are to be checked against some item of data related to a message. These lists can contain lookup items as a way of avoiding excessively long linear lists in the configuration file (☞ 18.3). The item being checked is used as a key for the lookup, and if the lookup succeeds, the item is taken as being in the list. For long lists, an indexed lookup gives much improved performance over a linear scan. When Exim is using a lookup to check whether something is in a list, any data that is returned by the lookup is discarded; whether the lookup succeeds or fails is all that counts.[1]

There are a number of different types of lookup, and each is implemented by a separate module of code that is included in Exim only if it is requested when the binary is built. This makes it easy to add new kinds of lookup, while at the same time not requiring every Exim binary to include all possible lookups. The default build-time configuration includes only the lsearch and dbm lookups, so if you want to use any other kind, you must ensure that Exim has been built to include them. In most cases, you will also need to install some other software (such as a specific database package).

There are two different ways in which the main part of Exim can call a lookup module, but each individual module uses just one of them. This is known as the *style* of the lookup.

---

[1] This is a simplification; there are in fact two special cases, the domains and local_parts options in routers (and the similarly named ACL conditions), where the data is preserved for later use.

- Modules that support the *single-key* style are given the name of a file in which to look, and a key to search for. The lookup type determines how the file is searched. If the key is found in the file, a single data string is returned. This style handles plain files, indexed files, NIS maps, and directory searches.

- Modules that support the *query* style accept a generalized query, and they may return more than one item of data. This style is used to access databases such as those held by NIS+, LDAP, MySQL, PostgreSQL, or Oracle, and also for some other special forms of lookup.

To perform a lookup, Exim hands over the necessary data to the relevant lookup module, and receives in return a string of data that was looked up, or an indication that the lookup did not succeed. Each lookup, even when coded entirely within Exim itself, is treated as a "black box" whose internals are not visible to the rest of the program. This is illustrated in figure 16-1.

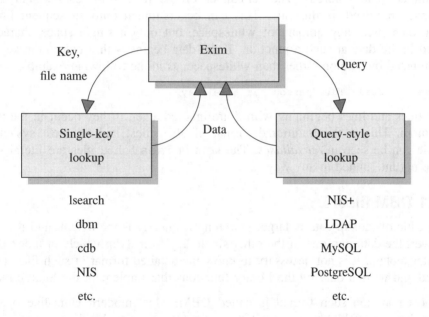

*Figure 16-1: File and database lookups*

There are no restrictions on where the different kinds of lookup can be used. Any kind of lookup can be used wherever a lookup is permitted.

# 16.1 Single-key lookup types

A single-key lookup provides a way of searching a set of data consisting of (*key*, *value*) pairs, where the keys are fixed strings. Such data is often shown as a sequence of lines with a key at the start of each line, separated from its data by a colon, even if in operation the data is actually stored in some other way, such as in a NIS map. For example:

```
root:           postmaster@simple.example,
postmaster:     simon@simple.example
```

A file that contains data in this format can, in fact, be searched directly by means of the `lsearch` lookup type, which generalizes the format slightly. The file is searched linearly from the start for a line beginning with the key, which is terminated by a colon or whitespace or the end of the line. Whitespace between the key and the colon is permitted (and ignored). The remainder of the line, with leading and trailing whitespace removed, is the data. This can be continued onto subsequent lines by starting them with any amount of whitespace, but only a single space character is retained in the data at such a junction. If the data begins with a colon, the key must be terminated by a colon rather than whitespace, as in the following example:

```
exuser:  :fail: This person has gone away.
```

Empty lines and lines beginning with # are ignored, even if they occur in the middle of an item. This is the traditional format of alias files, and on most systems, an example can be seen in */etc/aliases*. The keys in `lsearched` files are literal strings and are not interpreted in any way.

## 16.1.1 DBM files

When a file of lookup data is large, searching it linearly is inefficient, and it is better to convert the data into one of the other single-key formats in which an index is used for faster lookup. It is not necessary to know the detailed format of such files, as they are read and written only by the library functions that implement the lookup method.

The most common such format is called DBM. Most modern Unix-like operating systems have a DBM library installed as standard, though this is not true of some older systems. The two most common DBM libraries are *ndbm* (standard on Solaris and IRIX) and Berkeley DB Version 2, 3 or 4 (standard on several free operating systems).[1] Exim supports both of these, as well as the older Berkeley DB Version 1, *gdbm*, and *tdb*. The choice of which DBM library to use is made when Exim is built.

Because DBM is so commonly used, Exim comes with a utility called *exim_dbmbuild*, which creates a DBM file (or files – some DBM libraries use more than one file) from a file in traditional alias format. For example:

---

[1]  You can find information about Berkeley DB at *http://www.sleepycat.com*.

```
exim_dbmbuild /etc/aliases /etc/aliases.db
```

builds a DBM version of the system aliases file and calls it */etc/aliases.db*. This can then be used by changing the search type and filename in the router that handles aliases, so that instead of a linear search, a keyed DBM lookup is now used:

```
system_aliases:
  driver = redirect
  data = ${lookup{$local_part}dbm{/etc/aliases.db}}
  ...
```

One complication in the implementation of DBM lookups is whether the key strings include a terminating binary zero byte or not. Both Exim itself and the *exim_dbmbuild* utility include a terminating zero. However, if you use some other means of creating DBM files (for example, the DBM functions in Perl), you may end up with files that do not have this extra character in the keys. Such files can be read by Exim using the dbmnz lookup type instead of dbm.

Using a DBM file is more efficient than a linear search if the file has more than a few dozen entries in it. However, because DBM libraries provide both reading and updating facilities, it is not as efficient as a read-only indexed file format, which requires less overhead. This is where the next lookup type comes in.

## 16.1.2 cdb files

The cdb lookup type searches a Constant DataBase file.[1] The *cdb* format is designed for indexed files that are read frequently and never updated, except by total re-creation. As such, it is particularly suitable for large files containing aliases or other indexed data referenced by an MTA.

The *cdb* distribution is not needed in order to build Exim with *cdb* support, because the code for reading *cdb* files is included directly in Exim itself. However, no means of building or testing *cdb* files is provided with Exim because these are available within the *cdb* distribution. The usual way to build a *cdb* file from a "flat" file is to run a command of the following form:

```
cdbmake-12 /etc/aliases.cdb /etc/aliases.tmp < /etc/aliases
```

This uses a utility that is part of the *cdb* distribution. However, it works only on input files that have spaces separating the keys and data (a colon is not treated specially), and no continuation lines, so conventional alias files may need editing first. The *cdbmake-12* command first converts the flat file into a format containing the lengths of the key and data at the start of each line. It then pipes this data to the *cdbmake* command, which uses it to create a *cdb* file in the temporary file whose name is the second argument. If this is successful, the temporary file is renamed to the first argument.

---

[1]  Information about *cdb* is found at *http://www.pobox.com/~djb/cdb.html*.

### 16.1.3 NIS maps

The `nis` lookup type specifies a call to NIS, using the filename as the name of a NIS map in which to look up the key.[1] Exim does not recognize aliases for NIS map names; the full name must always be used, as in this router:

```
system_aliases:
  driver = redirect
  data = ${lookup{$local_part}nis{mail.aliases}}
  ...
```

### 16.1.4 Directory lookups

The `dsearch` lookup type searches a directory for a file whose name matches the key. It can be useful in configurations for virtual domains. For example, we discussed the following virtual domain router earlier (☞ 5.2):

```
virtuals:
  driver = redirect
  domains = cdb;/etc/virtuals
  data = ${lookup{$local_part]lsearch{/etc/$domain.aliases}}
  no_more
```

This requires the maintenance of a separate file (*/etc/virtuals*) containing a list of virtual domains. If, instead, we place the alias files in a separate directory, naming each one after its domain, we can use a `dsearch` lookup to search that directory, and thereby avoid having to maintain a separate list of domains. The following router shows this approach:

```
virtuals:
  driver = redirect
  domains = dsearch;/etc/valiases
  data = ${lookup{$local_part]lsearch{/etc/valiases/$domain}}
  no_more
```

The `dsearch` lookup in the `domains` option causes Exim to search the directory */etc/valiases* for a file whose name is the same as the domain of the address it is handling. If the file is found, there is a match, and the router is run. Thus, the existence of a virtual domain is now dependent only on the existence of its alias file.

## 16.2 Query-style lookup types

Query-style lookups give access to collections of data where the search function processes a generalized query, as opposed to the simple filename and key string that the single-key lookups use. In addition, some query-style lookups can return more than one value at once. You can pick out individual values from such data using the `extract` feature of string expansions (☞ 17.10).

---

[1]  The terminating zero is normally excluded from the key, but there is a variant called `nis0`, which does include the terminating binary zero in the key.

The query-style lookup interface allows Exim to read data from a number of general database servers and other information sources, brief descriptions of which are included in the following sections. Before using any of the databases with Exim, you should first become familiar with the concepts and mode of operation from the database's own documentation.

## 16.2.1 Quoting lookup data

When data from an incoming message is included in a query-style lookup, special characters in the data can cause syntax errors in the query. For example, a NIS+ query that contains:

```
[name=$local_part]
```

will be broken if the local part happens to contain a closing square bracket. For NIS+, data can be enclosed in double quotes as in this example:

```
[name="$local_part"]
```

but this then leaves the problem of a double quote in the data. The rule for NIS+ is that double quotes must be doubled. Other lookup types have different rules and, to cope with the differing requirements, an expansion operator that quotes according to the lookup's rules is provided for each query-style lookup. For example, the safe way to write the NIS+ query is:

```
[name="${quote_nisplus:$local_part}"]
```

A quote operator can be used for all lookup types, but has no effect for single-key lookups, because no quoting is ever needed in their key strings.

## 16.2.2 NIS+

Although NIS+ does not seem to have become as popular as NIS, it is nevertheless used by some sites. Using NIS+ jargon, a query consists of an *indexed name* followed by an optional colon and field name. If a field name is included, the result of a successful query is the contents of the named field; if a field name is not included, the result consists of a concatenation of *field-name=field-value* pairs, separated by spaces. Empty values and values containing spaces are quoted. For example, the following query:

```
[name=mg1456],passwd.org_dir
```

might return the string:

```
name=mg1456 passwd="" uid=999 gid=999 gcos="Martin Guerre"
home=/home/mg1456 shell=/bin/bash shadow=""
```

(split over two lines here to fit on the page), whereas:

```
[name=mg1456],passwd.org_dir:gcos
```

would just return the gcos field as:

```
Martin Guerre
```

with no quotes. A NIS+ lookup fails if NIS+ returns more than one table entry for the given indexed name. The following example shows a router that uses NIS+ to handle aliases:

```
system_aliases:
  driver = redirect
  data = ${lookup nisplus \
    {[name="${quote_nisplus:$local_part}"],aliases.org_dir:address}}
```

This query assumes there is a NIS+ table called *aliases.org_dir* containing at least two fields, *name* and *address*.

## 16.2.3 LDAP

An increasingly popular protocol for accessing databases that hold information about users is LDAP. Exim supports LDAP queries in the form of a URL, as defined in RFC 2255. For example, in the configuration of an aliasing router, one might have these settings:

```
system_aliases:
  driver = redirect
  data = ${lookup ldap {ldap:///\
             cn=${quote_ldap:$local_part},o=University%20of%20Cambridge,\
             c=UK?mailbox?base?}}
```

This searches for a record whose cn field is the local part, and extracts its mailbox field. This example does not specify which LDAP server to query, but a specific LDAP server can be specified by starting the query with:

```
ldap://hostname:port/...
```

If the port (and preceding colon) are omitted, the standard LDAP port (389) is used.

When no server is specified in a query, a list of default servers is taken from the ldap_default_servers configuration option. This supplies a colon-separated list of servers that are tried in turn until one successfully handles a query or there is a serious error. Successful handling either returns the requested data or indicates that it does not exist. Serious errors are syntactical, or finding multiple values when only a single value is expected. Errors that cause the next server to be tried are connection failures, bind failures, and timeouts. In other words, the servers in the list are expected to contain identical data, with the later ones acting as backups for the earlier ones.

For each server name in the list, a port number can be given. The standard way of specifying a host and port is to use a colon separator (RFC 1738). Because `ldap_default_servers` is a colon-separated list, such colons have to be doubled. For example:

```
ldap_default_servers = \
   ldap1.example.com::145 : ldap2.example.com
```

If `ldap_default_servers` is unset, a URL with no server name is passed to the LDAP library with no server name, and the library's default (normally the local host) is used.

The LDAP URL syntax provides no way of passing authentication and other control information to the server. To make this possible, the URL in an LDAP query may be preceded by any number of *name=value* settings, separated by spaces. If a value contains spaces, it must be enclosed in double quotes. The following names are recognized:

*user*

Sets the Distinguished Name for authenticating the LDAP bind.

*pass*

Sets the password for authenticating the LDAP bind.

*size*

Sets the limit for the number of entries returned.

*time*

Sets the maximum waiting time for a query.

The values may be given in any order. Here is the `data` option of the previous example with added authentication data:

```
data = ${lookup ldap {\
        user="cn=admin,o=University of Cambridge,c=UK" \
        pass = secret \
        ldap:///\
        cn=${quote_ldap:$local_part},o=University%20of%20Cambridge,\
        c=UK?mailbox?base?}}
```

A problem with placing a password directly in a query such as this is that the values of Exim's configuration settings can be obtained by using the `-bP` command-line option, so any user of the system who can run Exim can see this information. You can prevent this by putting the word `hide` in front of the option setting:

```
hide data = ${lookup ldap {\
    ...
```

When `hide` is present, only admin users can extract the value using `-bP`. Another way of keeping the password secret is to place it in a separate file, accessible only to the Exim user, and use a `readfile` expansion item to obtain its value.

The LDAP authentication mechanism can be used to check passwords as part of SMTP authentication, using the `ldapauth` expansion condition (☞ 17.7.5).

## 16.2.4 Data returned by an LDAP lookup

Although in many cases, such as the earlier example, an LDAP query is expected to find a single entry and extract the value of just one of its attributes, an LDAP lookup may in fact find multiple entries in the database, each with any number of attributes. However, if a lookup finds an entry with no attributes, it behaves as if the entry did not exist.

You can control what happens if more than one entry is found, by varying the lookup type. There are three LDAP lookup types; they behave differently in the way they handle the results of a query:

`ldap`

> This type requires the result to contain just one entry; if there are more, it gives an error. However, more than one attribute value may be taken from the entry.

`ldapdn`

> This type also requires the result to contain just one entry, but it is the Distinguished Name that is returned rather than any attribute values.

`ldapm`

> This type permits the result to contain more than one entry; the attributes from all of them are returned, with a newline inserted between the data from each entry.

In the common case where you specify a single attribute in your LDAP query, the result is not quoted, and if there are multiple values, they are separated by commas. If you specify multiple attributes, they are returned as space-separated, quoted strings, each preceded by the attribute name and an equals sign. For example:

```
ldap:///o=base?attr1,attr2?sub?(uid=fred)
```

might yield:

```
attr1="value one" attr2="value2"
```

If you do not specify any attributes in the search, this same format is used for all attributes in the entry. For example:

```
ldap:///o=base??sub?(uid=fred)
```

might yield:

```
objectClass="top" attr1="value one" attr2="value2"
```

The `extract` operator in string expansions can be used to pick out individual fields from such data.

## 16.2.5 MySQL, PostgreSQL, and Oracle

MySQL, PostgreSQL, and Oracle are database packages whose queries are expressed in the SQL language. The first two are open source software. Handling aliases using MySQL could be configured like this:

```
system_aliases:
  driver = redirect
  data = ${lookup mysql \
          {select mailbox from userdata \
           where id='${quote_mysql:$local_part}'}}
```

This example assumes the existence of a table called `userdata`, with fields called `mailbox` and `id`. You can, of course, use any table and field names you like. For PostgreSQL or Oracle, the configuration is identical, except that `mysql` is replaced by `pgsql` or `oracle`, respectively, wherever it appears.

If the result of the query contains more than one field, the data for each field in the row is returned, preceded by its name, so the result of the following query:

```
select home,name from userdata where id='ph10'
```

might be:

```
home=/home/ph10 name="Philip Hazel"
```

Empty values and values containing spaces are double-quoted, with embedded quotes escaped by backslash.

If the result of the query contains just one field, the value is passed back verbatim, without a field name, for example:

```
Philip Hazel
```

If the result of the query yields more than one row, it is all concatenated, with a newline between the data for each row.

Before it can use MySQL, PostgreSQL, or Oracle lookups, Exim has to be told where the relevant servers are. There is no default server as for LDAP. Exim also needs to know which username and password to use when connecting to a server, and which database to search. This is done by setting `mysql_servers`, `pgsql_servers`, or `oracle_servers` (respectively) to a colon-separated list of data for each server. Each item contains a host name, database name, username, and password, separated by slashes. This example lists two servers:

```
hide pgsql_servers = localhost/userdb/root/secret:\
                     otherhost/userdb/root/othersecret
```

Note the use of the `hide` prefix to protect the value of the variable. When `hide` is present, only admin users can extract the value using `-bP`. For each query, the servers are tried in order until a connection and a query succeeds. A host may be specified as `<name>:<port>`, but because this is a colon-separated list, the colon has to be doubled.

For MySQL, the database name may be empty, as in the following example:

```
hide mysql_servers = localhost//root/secret
```

In this case, the identity of the database must be specified in every query. For example:

```
select mailbox from userdb.userdata where ...
```

is a query that selects from the table called `userdata` in the database called `userdb`. This facility is not available in PostgreSQL or Oracle.

## 16.2.6 DNS lookups

Direct access to the DNS is available within Exim's configuration through a query-style lookup called `dnsdb`. A query consists of a DNS record type name and a DNS domain name, separated by an equals sign. The result of a lookup is the right-hand side of any DNS records that are found, separated by newlines if there is more than one of them, in the order they were returned by the DNS resolver. For example, this string expands into the MX hosts for the domain *a.b.example*:

```
${lookup dnsdb{mx=a.b.example}{$value}}
```

The DNS types that are supported are A (IPv4 address), AAAA (IPv6 address, available when Exim is compiled with IPv6 support), CNAME (canonical name), MX (mail exchanger), NS (name server), PTR (pointer), and TXT (text). When the type is MX, the data for each record consists of the preference value and the host name, separated by a space. When the type is PTR, the address should be given as normally written; it is converted to the necessary *in-addr.arpa* (IPv4) or *ip6.arpa* (IPv6) format internally. For example:

```
${lookup dnsdb{ptr=192.168.4.5}{$value}}
```

If the type is omitted, it defaults to TXT for backwards compatibility with earlier versions of Exim.

## 16.2.7 Whoson lookups

*Whoson*[1] is a proposed Internet protocol that allows server programs to check whether a particular dynamically allocated IP address is currently allocated to a known (trusted) user and, optionally, to obtain the identity of the said user. In Exim,

---
[1]   See *http://whoson.sourceforge.net*.

this can be used to implement "POP before SMTP" checking, using ACL statements such as the following:

```
require condition = \
  ${lookup whoson {$sender_host_address}{yes}{no}}
```

The query consists of a single IP address. If the lookup succeeds, the value returned is the name of the authenticated user. If the IP address is not currently allocated to a known user, the lookup fails.

# 16.3 Temporary errors in lookups

Lookup functions can return temporary error codes if the lookup cannot be completed. For example, a database server might be unavailable. When this occurs in a transport or router, delivery of the message is deferred, as for any other temporary error. In other circumstances, Exim generates a temporary error if possible. It is not advisable to use a lookup that might defer for critical configuration data such as a list of local domains in an ACL.

# 16.4 Default values in single-key lookups

In this context, a "default value" is a value specified by the administrator to be used instead of the result of a lookup if the lookup fails to find any data. This section applies only to single-key lookups; for query-style lookups there is usually some feature in the query language that can provide similar facilities.

If an asterisk is added to a single-key lookup type name (for example, lsearch*), and the initial lookup fails, the key that consists of the literal string * is looked up in the file to provide a default value.

If *@ is added to a single-key lookup type name (for example dbm*@), and the initial lookup fails, and the key contains an @ character, a second lookup is done with everything before the last @ in the key replaced by *. If the second lookup fails (or does not take place because there is no @ in the key), * is looked up as an ultimate default.

If the original key is *jim@domain1.example*, for instance, a single-key search type such as cdb*@ looks up the following keys:

```
jim@domain1.example
*@domain1.example
*
```

The first one that succeeds provides the result of the lookup. Examples of uses for these defaulting features are discussed in section 5.2.1.

# 16.5 Partial matching in single-key lookups

Normally, a single-key lookup searches the file for an exact match with the given key. However, in a number of situations where domains are being looked up, it is useful to be able to do partial matching, where only the final components of the search key match a key in the file. Suppose, for instance, you want to match all domains that end in *dates.example*. First, you must create the special key:

```
*.dates.example
```

in the file. No normal search for a domain can ever match that item, because domains cannot contain asterisks. However, if you add the string `partial-` to the start of a single-key lookup type, Exim behaves in a different way. For example, in an ACL you might have the following:

```
accept domains = partial-lsearch;/etc/relay/domains
```

When `partial-` is specified, Exim first looks up the original key; if that fails, an asterisk component is added at the start of the key, and it is looked up again. If that fails, Exim starts removing dot-separated components from the start of the key, one-by-one, and adding an asterisk component on the front of what remains.

---

 Keys in the file that do not begin with an asterisk are matched only by unmodified original keys even when partial matching is in use. You must include keys starting with asterisks to enable partial matching to take place.

---

A default minimum number of two non-asterisk components are required. If the original key is *2250.future.dates.example*, Exim does the following lookups, in this order:

```
2250.future.dates.example
*.2250.future.dates.example
*.future.dates.example
*.dates.example
```

As soon as one key in the sequence matches a key in the file, the lookup finishes. The minimum number of components can be adjusted by including a number before the hyphen in the search type. For example, `partial3-lsearch` specifies a minimum of three non-asterisk components in the modified keys. If `partial0-` is used, the original key is shortened right down to the null string, and the final lookup is for an asterisk on its own.

If the search type ends in `*` or `*@` (☞ 16.4), the search for an ultimate default that this implies happens after all partial lookups have failed. If `partial0-` is specified, adding * to the search type has no effect, because the * key is already included in the sequence of partial lookups.

The use of * in partial matching differs from its use as a wildcard in domain lists and the like, where it just means "any sequence of characters". Partial matching works only in terms of dot-separated components, and the asterisk in a partial matching subject key must always be followed by a dot. For example, you could not use the following:

```
*key.example
```

as a key in a file to match partial lookups of *donkey.example* and *monkey.example*.

# 16.6 Lookup caching

An Exim process caches the most recent lookup result on a per-file basis for single-key lookup types, and keeps the relevant files open. In some types of configuration, this can lead to many files being kept open for messages with many recipients. To avoid hitting the operating system limit on the number of simultaneously open files, Exim closes the least recently used file when it needs to open more files than its own internal limit, which can be changed via the lookup_open_max option. For query-style lookups, a single data cache per lookup type is kept for each Exim process.

# 17

# String expansion

The combination of expansions and lookups makes it possible to configure Exim in many different ways. If you want to explore these different possibilities, you need to understand what string expansions can do for you. A number of examples are covered in earlier chapters; this chapter contains a full explanation of the mechanism, and descriptions of all the different expansion items. A reference summary of string expansion, including a list of all the expansion variables, is given in appendix A.

When Exim is expanding a string, special processing is triggered by the appearance of a dollar sign. The expander copies the string from left to right until it hits a dollar, at which point it reads to the end of the expansion item, does whatever processing is required, and adds the resulting substring to its output before continuing to read the rest of the original string. Most, but not all, expansion items involve the use of curly brackets (braces) as delimiters. For example, when expanding the following string:

```
Before-${substr_4_2:$local_part}-After
```

the expander copies the initial substring `Before-`, then processes the expansion item `${substr_4_2:$local_part}` to produce the next part of the result, and finally adds the substring `-After` at the end.

In the following sections, we cover the various different kinds of item that can occur in expansion strings. Whitespace may be used to improve readability between subitems that are keywords, or between substrings enclosed in braces inside an outer set of braces, but any other whitespace is taken as part of the string.

## 17.1 Escaping literal substrings

To make it possible to include literal dollar and brace characters in the output of an expansion, backslash is treated as an escape character by the expander. A number of special sequences, such as `\n` for newline, are recognized.[1] If any other character follows a backslash, it is treated as a literal with no special meaning. Thus, a literal dollar sign is entered as `\$` and a literal backslash as `\\`.

Escaping individual characters can be tedious and error-prone if the string contains many literal dollars or backslashes. In this case, it is usally easier to use the special escape sequence `\N`. This causes subsequent characters to be copied literally until the next occurrence of `\N`. For example, the expansion of `\NA$B\C\N` is `A$B\C`. This feature is particularly useful for regular expressions, which is where most literal

---

[1] These are exactly the same set as those that are recognized by the string-reading code.

dollar and backslash characters are found in expanded strings. For example, the regular expression:

```
^\d{8}@example\.com$
```

matches an email address where the local part consists of precisely eight digits, and the domain is *example.com*. Suppose that you wanted to place the mailboxes for such users in a special directory. Whereas an ordinary user's mailbox is:

```
/var/mail/$local_part
```

you want to arrange for this group of users' mailboxes to be:

```
/var/mail/special/$local_part
```

You could use a value like this for the `file` option in an **appendfile** transport:

```
file = /var/mail/\
  ${if match {$local_part}{^\d{8}@example\.com$}\
  {special/}}$local_part
```

The details of how the `if` expansion item works are described later, in the section on conditionals, but the idea is to match the local part against the regular expression, and if it matches, to insert `special/` into the filename.

However, this option setting does not work, because when the string is expanded, the dollar and backslashes that are part of the regular expression are interpreted by the expander before it attempts the regular expression match, and an error occurs, because `$}` is not a valid expansion item. The most convenient solution is as follows:

```
file = /var/mail/\
  ${if match {$local_part}{\N^\d{8}@example\.com$\N}\
  {special/}}$local_part
```

This "protects" the regular expression from expansion by enclosing it between two instances of `\N`. The alternative is to use individual escapes as follows:

```
file = /var/mail/\
  ${if match {$local_part}{^\\d{8}@example\\.com\$}\
  {special/}}$local_part
```

where an extra backslash has been inserted before every dollar and backslash in the regular expression.[1]

---

[1] If you enclose the value in double quotes, you have to insert yet more backslashes because they are also special inside double quotes. This is a good reason for avoiding quotes unless you really need their backslash interpretation.

## 17.2 Variable substitution

We use the variable *$local_part* many times in configuration examples, and also
mention several other variables. In fact, a large number of variables exist, containing
data that might be of use in configuration files, and also in system and user filters. A
complete list is given in appendix A.

In most cases, we have been able to reference *$local_part* by including:

```
$local_part
```

in the configuration settings we have used. This format is fine, provided that what
follows the variable name is not a letter, digit, or underscore. If it is, the alternative
syntax:

```
${local_part}
```

must be used, so that the end of the variable's name can be distinguished. An
expansion syntax error occurs if the name is unknown to Exim. You can test whether
a variable contains any data by means of the def condition, which is described later
in this chapter.

## 17.3 Header insertion

The contents of a specific message header line can be inserted into a string by an
item of the form:

```
$header_from:
```

The abbreviation $h can be used instead of $header, and header names are not
case-sensitive. This example inserts the contents of the *From:* header line. It is
similar to the insertion of the value of a variable, but there are some important
differences:

*   The name must be terminated by a colon, and curly brackets must *not* be used
    because they are permitted in header names.[1] The colon is not included in the
    expanded text. If the name is followed by whitespace, the colon may be
    omitted; in this case the whitespace *is* included in the expanded text. However,
    it is best to get into the habit of including the colon, so that you do not leave it
    out when it is really needed.

*   If the message does not contain a header with the given name, the expansion
    item adds nothing to the string; it does not fail. Thus, use of the correct spelling
    of header names is vital. If you use $header_reply_to:, for example, it
    does not insert the contents of the *Reply-To:* header. You can test for the

---

[1] Any printing characters except colon and whitespace are permitted by RFC 2822.

presence of a particular header by means of the `def` condition, which is described later in this chapter.

The contents of header lines are most frequently referenced from filter files (see chapter 10) in commands such as:

```
if "$h_subject:" contains "Make money fast" then ...
```

but there are also situations where it can be useful to refer to them in driver configurations.

If there is more than one header line with the same name (common with *Received:* headers), they are concatenated and inserted together, up to a maximum length of 64 KB. A newline is inserted at each junction. In addition, for those that are known to contain lists of addresses (for example, *To:* and *Cc:*), a comma is inserted as well.[1]

# 17.4 Operations on substrings

A number of expansion items perform some operation on a portion of the expansion string, having first expanded it in its own right. They are all of the form:

```
${<operator-name>:<substring>}
```

In some cases, the operator name is followed by one or more argument values, separated by underscores. The substring starts immediately after the colon, and may have significant leading and/or trailing whitespace. In a real configuration, it always contains at least one expansion item; there is little point in writing a literal string to be operated on, because you could do the operation yourself and write the result instead.

## 17.4.1 Extracting the initial part of a substring

Consider this common setting of the `file` option in an **appendfile** transport:

```
file = /var/mail/$local_part
```

On a system with very many mailboxes, it is desirable not to keep them all in the same directory, but rather to split them among several directories. A simple scheme for doing this would be:

```
file = /var/mail/${length_1:$local_part}/$local_part
```

which interposes another directory level. The name of the intermediate directory is computed from the local part by means of the `length` expansion operator, which extracts an initial substring from its argument, having first expanded it. Suppose the local part is *caesar*. On encountering the following:

---

[1] RFC 2822 specifies that there should only be one instance of such header lines, but this rule is often ignored.

```
${length_1:$local_part}
```

during the expansion process, Exim first expands the operator's argument, converting the item to:

```
${length_1:caesar}
```

The `length_1` operator then extracts the first character of `caesar`, before carrying on with the rest of the string, so that the final mailbox name becomes:

```
/var/mail/c/caesar
```

Assuming all local parts start with a letter, this distributes the user mailboxes among 26 subdirectories. If this were not enough, more characters from the local part could be used:

```
file = /var/mail/${length_2:$local_part}/$local_part
```

This in theory produces 676 (26×26) subdirectories. The problem with this approach is that letters in usernames are not usually spread evenly over the alphabet, and so some subdirectories are more heavily used than others. In section 17.4.3 we will discuss a better way of handling this.

## 17.4.2 Extracting an arbitrary part of a substring

In addition to `length`, Exim has a `substr` operator that can be used to extract arbitrary substrings. For example:

```
${substr_3_2:$local_part}
```

extracts two characters starting at offset 3 in the local part. The first character in the string has offset zero. Suppose you want to include the name of the month in a filename for some reason. The variable *$tod_full* contains the current date and time in the form:

```
Fri, 07 Apr 2000 14:25:48 +0100
```

from which the month can be extracted by:

```
${substr_8_3:$tod_full}
```

If the starting offset of `substr` is greater than the string length, the result is an empty string; if the length plus starting offset is greater than the string length, the result is the right-hand part of the string, starting from the offset.

The `substr` operator can take negative offset values to count from the right-hand end of its operand. The last character is offset -1, the second-to-last is offset -2, and so on. For example:

```
${substr_-5_2:1234567}
```

yields 34. If the absolute value of a negative offset is greater than the length of the string, the substring starts at the beginning of the string, and the length is reduced by the amount of overshoot. For example:

```
${substr_-5_2:12}
```

yields an empty string, but:

```
${substr_-3_2:12}
```

yields 1. If the second number is omitted from substr, the remainder of the string is taken if the offset is positive. If it is negative, all characters in the string preceding the offset point are taken. For example:

```
${substr_4:penguin}    yields  uin
${substr_-4:penguin}   yields  pen
```

That is, an offset of -*n* with no length yields all but the last *n* characters of the substring.

### 17.4.3 Hashing operators

For historical reasons, Exim has two hashing functions, one of which produces a string consisting of letters and digits, whereas the other produces one or two strings that are numbers. The following setting for the one-letter mailbox subdirectory discussed earlier gives a more even spread:

```
file = /var/mail/${hash_1:$local_part}/$local_part
```

The hash_1 operator applies a hashing algorithm that produces a hash string of length 1, chosen from the set of upper and lower case letters and digits. The subdirectory name is now a single character, out of 62 possibilities. Longer hash strings can be requested by giving different numbers after hash, and the character set from which they are chosen can be controlled by a second parameter.

However, the newer, numeric hashing function (nhash) gives a more even spread of results and can handle larger numbers of possibilities. Using the numeric hash, the setting:

```
file = /var/mail/${nhash_62:$local_part}/$local_part
```

achieves a similar effect, though now the names of the subdirectories are numerical strings in the range 0–61. For use on very large systems, nhash can be requested to produce two numbers computed from a single hash of the string. For example:

```
file = /var/mail/${nhash_8_64:$local_part}
```

When this is done, the two numbers are separated by a slash, so *caesar*'s mailbox might now be:

```
/var/mail/7/49/caesar
```

### 17.4.4 Forcing the case of letters

Two other operators that are sometimes useful are `uc` and `lc`. These force their arguments to upper or lower case, respectively. As an example, suppose a user wants to use a filter to file incoming messages in different mail folders for different senders, in a case-independent manner. A filter command such as this could be used:

```
save $home/mail/${lc:$sender_address}
```

The `lc` operator ensures that the entire sender address is in lower case when it is used in the filename.

# 17.5 Character translation

The `tr` expansion item translates single characters in strings into different characters, according to its arguments. The first argument is the string to be translated, and this is followed by two translation strings, normally of the same length. For example, the following translates a comma-separated list into a colon-separated list:

```
${tr {a,b,c}{,}{:}}   yields  a:b:c
```

The second and third strings can contain more than one character. They correspond one-to-one, and each character in the second string that is found in the first string is replaced by the corresponding character in the third string. If there are duplicates in the second string, the last occurrence is used. If the third string is shorter than the second, its last character is replicated. However, if it is empty, no translation takes place.

# 17.6 Text substitution

A general string substitution facility is available. It is called `sg` because it operates like *sed* and Perl's `s` operator with the `/g` (global) option. It takes three arguments: the subject string, a regular expression, and a replacement string. For example:

```
${sg {abcdefabcdef}{abc}{**}}   yields  **def**def
```

The pattern is matched against the subject string, and the matched portion is replaced by the replacement string. A new match is then begun on the remainder of the subject, and this continues until the end of the subject is reached. If there are no matches, the yield is the unaltered subject string. Within the replacement string, the numeric variables *$1*, *$2*, and so on can be used to refer to captured substrings in the regular expression match. Because all three arguments are expanded before use, any $ characters that are required in the regular expression or in the replacement string have to be escaped or protected by `\N`. For example:

```
${sg {abcdef}{^(...)(...)\$}{\N$2$1\N}}   yields  defabc
```

# 17.7 Conditional expansion

A great deal of the power of the expansion mechanism comes from its ability to vary the results of expansion items depending on certain conditions. The basic conditional expansion item takes the following form:

```
${if <condition> {<string1>}{<string2>}}
```

The condition is tested, and if it is true, *<string1>* is expanded and used as the replacement for the whole item; if not, *<string2>* is used instead. You can omit *<string2>* and its surrounding braces completely if it is an empty string. A number of different conditions are available.

## 17.7.1 Testing for a specific string

To test the exact value of a string, the eq condition is used. Here is an easy way to implement an exceptional mailbox location for just one user:

```
file = ${if eq{$local_part}{john}\
       {/home/john/inbox}\
       {/var/mail/$local_part}}
```

The condition that is tested is eq{$local_part}{john}; following the condition name eq, two substrings are given in curly brackets. Each is separately expanded and then they are compared for equality. If they are equal, the first of the following substrings is used; otherwise the second is used. In this example, if the local part is *john*, the mailbox is */home/john/inbox*, whereas for all other local parts it is the result of expanding /var/mail/$local_part.

It is often useful to lay out conditions and other complicated expansion strings over several lines like this, because it makes them easier to read. Because the substrings are independently expanded, they may contain their own conditional expansions, which can make for very unreadable text. For example, if you want an exceptional mailbox location for two users, it can be done by setting:

```
file = ${if eq{$local_part}{john}\
       {/home/john/inbox}\
       {\
         ${if eq{$local_part}{jack}\
         {/home/jack/inbox}\
         {/var/mail/$local_part}}\
       }}
```

Laid out like this it is fairly easy to understand, compared with:

```
file = ${if eq{$local_part}{john\
       }{/home/john/inbox}{${if eq\
       {$local_part}{jack}{/home/jack/inbox}{\
       /var/mail/$local_part}}}}
```

Clearly, this approach to this particular requirement is usable only for a few cases, because it does not scale very well. For large numbers of exceptions, another technique should be used. For local parts that match a pattern, you could use a regular expression. Otherwise a file lookup could be used.

## 17.7.2 Negated conditions

A separate condition for testing inequality is not provided because there is a general negation mechanism for conditions. Any condition preceded by an exclamation mark is negated, like this:

```
${if ! eq{$local_part}{john}{...
```

Of course, in the case of eq, another way of achieving the same effect is to transpose the order of the two strings that follow the condition.

## 17.7.3 Regular expression matching

If you want to test a string for something other than simple equality, you can use a regular expression. The match condition, like eq, takes the next two brace-enclosed substrings as its arguments. The second is interpreted as a regular expression and is matched against the first. For example:

```
${if match {$local_part}{\N^x\d\d\N}{...
```

tests whether a local part begins with x followed by at least two digits. The regular expression is enclosed by \N to protect the internal backslashes from being interpreted by the expander. Appendix B contains a reference description of the regular expressions supported by Exim.

If the regular expression contains capturing parentheses, the captured substrings are available in the variables *$1*, *$2*, and so on during the expansion of the "success" string. For example:

```
${if match {$local_part}{\N^x(\d\d)\N}{$1}}
```

not only tests *$local_part* as before, but yields the value of the two digits as its result via the expansion of *$1*. If there is no match, its yield is the empty string. When tests of this kind are nested, the values of the numeric variables (*$1*, *$2*, and so on) are remembered at the start of processing an if item, and restored afterwards.

## 17.7.4 Encrypted string comparison

When an Exim server is authenticating an SMTP connection (☞ 13.2), it may need to compare a cleartext password with one that has been encrypted (for example, a user password from */etc/passwd* or equivalent). This is done by encrypting the cleartext and comparing the result with the encrypted value Exim already has. It might seem that all that is needed is an operator to encrypt a string, but because of the way Unix passwords are encrypted, that is not sufficient. An encrypted password is stored with a two-character "salt" string, and the same value is needed in order to encrypt the string to be tested in the same way. The stored string contains both the salt and the result of the encryption.[1] To save having to quote it twice (once to encrypt and once to compare), there is a single condition called crypteq that does both jobs at once. Its first argument is the cleartext, and its second is the encrypted text, like this:

```
${if crypteq {mysecret}{ksUCNd4Cs6lSI}{...
```

In this example, the cleartext mysecret is first encrypted by the *crypt()* function, using the salt ks, and the result is then compared with UCNd4Cs6lSI. In most real cases, of course, the encrypted value is not included directly in the string like this. The second argument for crypteq is more likely to be a subexpansion that looks up a value in a file or database.

Forms of encryption other than that used by the *crypt()* function are used in some installations. LDAP has introduced a notation whereby an encrypted string is preceded by a string in braces that states how it was encrypted. Fortunately, an opening brace character is not valid as a "salt" character. If the encrypted string does not begin with a brace, encryption by *crypt()* is assumed by the crypteq condition. Otherwise, the contents of the braces must either be crypt (which has the same effect), sha1, or md5, as in the following example:

```
{md5}CY9rzUYh03PK3k6DJie09g==
```

This indicates that the encrypted string is an MD5 hash of the cleartext; sha1 would indicate a SHA-1 hash. If you include such a string directly into an expanded string, you will have to quote the braces using backslashes, because they will otherwise be taken as part of the expansion syntax. For example:

```
${if crypteq{test}{\{md5\}CY9rzUYh03PK3k6DJie09g==}{1}{0}}
```

The crypteq condition is automatically included in the Exim binary when it is built with SMTP authentication support, but otherwise it has to be specially requested at build time.

## 17.7.5 Other authentication tests

Several other expansion conditions support different types of user authentication. None of these conditions are included in the Exim binary by default because the relevant libraries are not available on all systems. If you want to use any of these conditions, you must ensure that your binary is built with the appropriate support.

---

[1] For details of password encryption, see the specification of the *crypt()* function for your operating system.

## PAM authentication

The pam condition provides an interface to the *PAM* library that is available on some operating systems. PAM stands for *Pluggable Authentication Modules*, and it provides a framework for supporting different methods of authentication. The caller of PAM supplies a *service name* and an initial string that identifies a user. The authentication function then requests zero or more data strings from the caller, and it uses these as input to its authentication logic. In the most common case, a single data string is requested, which is in effect a password.

The pam expansion condition has a single argument that consists of a colon-separated list of strings. PAM is called with the service name exim and the first of the strings as the username. The remaining strings are passed to PAM in response to its data requests. The condition is true if PAM authenticates successfully. For example:

```
${if pam{mylogin:mypassword}{yes}{no}}
```

yields yes if the user *mylogin* successfully authenticates with the single data string mypassword, and no otherwise. The data for pam is rarely a fixed string like this; usually it is made up of variables containing values from the SMTP AUTH command (☞ 13.2).

If passwords that are to be used with PAM contain colon characters, the example just given will not work, because a colon in the password is interpreted as a delimiter in the list of strings to pass to PAM. This problem can be avoided by doubling any colons that may be present. If the password is in *$2* for example, this could be used:

```
${if pam{mylogin:${sg{$2}{:}{::}}}{yes}{no}}
```

In some operating environments, PAM authentication can be used only by a root process. When Exim is receiving incoming mail from remote hosts, it runs as the Exim user, which sometimes causes problems with PAM in these environments. There is as yet no easy resolution of this problem, though one possible solution is to use the Cyrus *pwcheck* daemon.

## pwcheck authentication

When passwords are kept in "shadow" files for security purposes, non-root users such as *exim* cannot access them. Using the Cyrus *pwcheck* daemon is one way of making it possible for passwords to be checked by a process that is not running as root. This is supported by an expansion condition called pwcheck. It takes one argument, which must be the user name and password, separated by a colon. For example, in a LOGIN authenticator configuration, you might have this:

```
server_condition = ${if pwcheck{$1:$2}{1}{0}}
```

You do not need to install the full Cyrus software suite in order to use the *pwcheck* daemon. You can compile and install just the daemon alone from the Cyrus SASL library. Ensure that *exim* is the only user that has access to the */var/pwcheck* directory.

### Radius authentication

Radius authentication (RFC 2865) is supported in a similar way to PAM and *pwcheck*. The radius condition has a single argument. This must expand to a user name and password, colon separated. They are passed to the Radius client library, which calls the Radius server. The condition is true if the authentication is successful. For example, in a LOGIN authenticator you might have the following:

```
server_condition = ${if radius{$1:$2}{yes}{no}}
```

### LDAP authentication

The ldapauth condition supports user authentication using LDAP. Details of how to use LDAP in lookups, and the syntax of LDAP queries is described in section 16.2.3. When used with the ldapauth condition, the query must contain a user name and password. The main part of the query is not used, and can be empty. The condition is true if the user name and password are accepted by the LDAP server, and false otherwise. The following example shows a typical setting from a LOGIN authenticator:

```
server_condition = ${if ldapauth \
  {user="uid=${quote_ldap:$1},ou=people,o=example.org" \
  pass="$2" \
  ldap://ldap.example.org/}{yes}{no}}
```

## 17.7.6 Numeric comparisons

Exim provides a number of conditions that test numeric values. These use familiar symbols such as > and =. They are written in a prefix notation, with the condition first, followed by two substrings that must (after their own subexpansion) take the form of optionally signed decimal integers. These may optionally be followed by one of the letters K or M (in either upper or lower case), signifying multiplication by 1024 or 1024×1024, respectively. For example:

```
${if > {$message_size}{10M}{...
```

tests whether the size of the message (which is contained in the *$message_size* variable) is greater than 10 MB. The available numeric conditions are:

```
=    equal
==   equal
>    greater
>=   greater or equal
<    less
<=   less or equal
```

The general negation facility provides for inequality testing.

## 17.7.7 Empty variables and non-existent header lines

The def condition tests whether a variable contains any value, or whether a particular header line exists in a message. In the first case, def is followed by a colon and the variable name, and it is true only if the variable is not empty. For example:

```
${if def:sender_host_address {remote}{local}}
```

yields the string remote if *$sender_host_address* is not empty (indicating that the message did not originate on the local host), and local otherwise. Note that the variable name is given in the condition without a leading $ character. If the variable does not exist, an error occurs.

In its second guise, def is followed by a colon, the string header_ or h_, and the name of a message header line terminated by another colon, as in the following example:

```
${if def:header_reply-to:{$h_reply-to:}{$h_from:}}
```

The condition tests for the existence of the header line in the message being processed, so in this case the yield of the expansion is the contents of *Reply-To:* if it exists; otherwise it is the contents of *From:*. The expander does not check whether there are actually any data characters in the header line or not.

## 17.7.8 File existence

There are times when you may want to adopt different strategies depending on whether or not a specific file or directory exists. The exists condition has a single string as an argument. It calls the *stat( )* function to see if the string exists as a pathname in the filesystem, and is true if the function succeeds. Suppose you are moving user mailboxes from one directory to another. If a mailbox exists in the old directory, you want Exim to use it; otherwise you want to use or create a mailbox in the new directory. A setting of the file option like this could be used:

```
file = /var/\
  ${if exists{/var/oldmail/$local_part}{old}{new}}\
  mail/$local_part
```

For the local part *sue*, this expands to */var/oldmail/sue* if that file exists; otherwise to */var/newmail/sue*.

## 17.7.9 The state of a message's delivery

There are two conditions that have no data associated with them: first_ delivery is true during the first delivery attempt on a message, but is false during any subsequent delivery attempts; queue_running is true during delivery attempts that have been started by a queue runner process, but is false otherwise. These allow you to adopt different routing strategies at different times, if you want to. If you want a router to be used only at the first delivery attempt, you can set an option like this:

```
condition = ${if first_delivery {yes}{no}}
```

During the first delivery, the condition is true and the string expands to yes. In subsequent delivery attempts, the result is no, and so the router is skipped.

## 17.7.10 Combining expansion conditions

Several conditions can be combined into a single condition using the logical operators and and or. Each of these is followed by any number of conditions, each enclosed in braces. The entire list is also enclosed in braces, to show where it ends. This can make for some very unreadable text unless one is careful. The and condition is true only if all of its subconditions are true, whereas the or condition is true if any one subcondition is true. Here is a fanciful example that tests whether today is a leap day, spread over several lines for readability:

```
${if and
    {
    {eq {${substr_5_2:$tod_log}}{02}}
    {eq {${substr_8_2:$tod_log}}{29}}
    }
    {Today's the day}{Not today}}
```

The *$tod_log* variable contains the current date and time in this format:

```
2000-02-29 14:42:00
```

The first condition tests the two digits for the month, and the second one tests the day number. The subconditions are tested from left to right, and only as many as necessary to establish the overall condition are fully evaluated. Subconditions may themselves use and and or if necessary.

## 17.7.11 Forcing expansion failure

We defined the conditional expansion item as a condition followed by two substrings: a "true" string and a "false" string. If the second string is empty (that is, if it would be coded as {}), it can be omitted. Sometimes, however, you do not want to use an empty string if the condition fails; you want to take more drastic action. Instead of a second string, you can supply the word fail, not in braces. This causes the entire expansion to fail, but in a way that the calling code can detect. We say "the expansion is forced to fail".

The result of this kind of failure depends on what the expanded string is being used for. In some cases it is no different from a failure caused by a syntax error, but in a number of other cases it causes whatever is being done to be skipped. For example, you can cause headers to be added to a message by setting the `headers_add` option on a router or transport, containing a string to be added to the header section of a message. If you use a setting such as this:

```
headers_add = ${if eq {$sender_host_address}{}\
   {X-Postmaster: <postmaster@example.com>}\
   fail}
```

Exim adds an *X-Postmaster:* header to any messages received locally (host address empty). When *$sender_host_address* is not empty, `fail` causes the string expansion to fail, which in this particular circumstance causes the addition of headers to be cancelled. Whenever `fail` in an expansion has a special effect like this, it is documented along with the option to which it applies.

## 17.8 Lookups in expansion strings

The ability to call Exim's lookup functions while expanding a string is a powerful feature. A portion of the string can be replaced by data obtained from a file or database, or the existence of a particular key in a file or database can be used to influence the result of the expansion.

The `lookup` expansion item is a form of conditional expansion, containing two substrings following the specification of the lookup. If the lookup succeeds, the first substring is expanded and used; during its expansion, the variable *$value* contains the data that was looked up. If the lookup fails, the second substring is expanded and used. Just as in the case of an `if` condition, the second substring may be absent, or the word `fail` may be used, as described in the previous section.

If you also omit the first substring, Exim behaves as if it were `{$value}`. For example, the normal router for handling aliases is as follows:

```
system_aliases:
   driver = redirect
   data = ${lookup{$local_part}lsearch{/etc/aliases}}
```

This is exactly the same as the following, which has the substrings explicitly included:

```
system_aliases:
   driver = redirect
   data = ${lookup{$local_part}lsearch{/etc/aliases}{$value}{}}
```

There are two different formats for `lookup` items in expanded strings, depending on whether a single-key or query-style lookup is being used. We will introduce them by extending an example that was used earlier.

## 17.8.1 Single-key lookups in expansion strings

Recall that the following setting:

```
file = ${if eq{$local_part}{john}\
       {/home/john/inbox}\
       {/var/mail/$local_part}}
```

provides an easy way of specifying an exceptional location for the mailbox of just
one user. With any more than a handful of exceptions, this technique does not work
well. Instead, it would be better to create an indexed file containing the locations of
all the special mailboxes. Laid out as a flat file, it might contain lines such as this:

```
john:       /home/john/inbox
jill:       /home/jill/inbox
alex:       /home/alex/mail/inbox
```

This file could be used directly in an **appendfile** transport:

```
file = ${lookup {$local_part} lsearch {/the/file} \
       {$value}{/var/mail/$local_part}}
```

For a single-key lookup type, the introductory $ { lookup is followed by a substring
in braces that defines the key to be looked up, after it has been separately expanded.
In this case, it is the local part of the address that is being routed. Then there is a
word that specifies the type of lookup, in this case lsearch, followed by a
substring containing data for the search which, for a single-key search type, is the
name of the file to be searched.

In our example, if the local part is *jill*, the lookup succeeds, and *$value* contains
/home/jill/inbox during the expansion of the first replacement string. As this
consists of $value only, the result of the entire lookup is /home/jill/inbox. If
a local part that is not in the file is looked up, no data is found, and so the second
replacement string, /var/mail/$local_part, is expanded and used.

## 17.8.2 Partial lookups in expansion strings

Partial lookups (☞ 16.5) can be used for single-key lookup types, and when a partial
lookup succeeds, the variables *$1* and *$2* contain the wild and non-wild parts of the
key during the expansion of the replacement substring. They return to their earlier
values at the end of the lookup item. Consider a file of domain names containing:

```
one.example
*.two.example
```

and a lookup item of the form:

```
${lookup {$domain} partial-lsearch {/the/file}{wild="$1" notwild="$2"}}
```

When *$domain* contains one.example, the result is:

```
wild="" notwild="one.example"
```

because no partial matching was done. However, if *$domain* contains `twenty.`
`two.example`, the result is:

```
wild="twenty" notwild="two.example"
```

### 17.8.3 Single-key lookup failures

If Exim cannot attempt the lookup because of some problem (for example, if it
cannot open the file), the entire string expansion fails, in a similar way to a syntax
error. You can guard against the particular case of a non-existent file by using the
`exists` test described earlier. For example:

```
file = ${if exists{/the/file}\
       {\
       ${lookup {$local_part} lsearch {/the/file} \
       {$value}\
       {/var/mail/$local_part}}\
       }\
       {/var/mail/$local_part}}
```

### 17.8.4 Query-style lookups in expansion strings

A large linear file should be turned into an indexed structure of some kind (DBM or
*cdb*) to improve performance, or the data could be stored in one of the databases
Exim supports. Here is a configuration setting that looks up a mailbox using MySQL:

```
file = ${lookup mysql \
       {select mbox from users where \
       id='${quote_mysql:$local_part}'} \
       {$value} \
       {/var/mail/$local_part}}
```

This example assumes there is a table called `users` with fields called `id` and `mbox`.
When a query-style lookup is used in an expansion string, you do not specify a
separate key. Instead, the lookup type name follows `${lookup` immediately and is
followed by a substring that forms the database query. The success and failure
substrings then follow as before.

### 17.8.5 Reducing the number of database queries

On a busy system, a lookup such as the previous example, which requires a database
call for every delivery, might result in poor performance. An improvement could be
obtained by dumping the data from the database every night, and building (for
example) a *cdb* file that would give much better performance. However, additions to
the database would not then take immediate effect. The best of both worlds could be
achieved by checking the *cdb* file first, and doing a database lookup only if that
failed. For example:

```
file = \
  ${lookup {$local_part} cdb {/the/cdb/file} \
    {$value}\
      {\
      ${lookup mysql \
      {select mbox from users where \
      id='${quote_mysql:$local_part}'} \
      {$value} \
      {/var/mail/$local_part}}\
      }\
  }
```

There are some further remarks on the topic of reducing the number of database queries in section 17.10.2.

## 17.8.6 Defaults for lookups in expansion strings

When using single-key lookups in expansion strings, the lookup type name may be followed by * or *@ to request default lookups (☞ 16.4). Alternatively, the "false" substring can contain an explicit second lookup to be done if the first one fails, and this works for both single-key and query-style lookups.

# 17.9 Inserting whole files

You can insert the entire contents of a file into an expansion string by an item of the following form:

```
${readfile{<file name>}{<end-of-line string>}}
```

The file name and end-of-line string are first expanded separately. The file is then read, and its contents replace the entire item. All newline characters in the file are replaced by the end-of-line string if it is present. If it is an empty string, newlines are removed.

# 17.10 Extracting fields from substrings

There are several expansion items that extract data fields from substrings, having first expanded them.

## 17.10.1 Splitting up addresses

local_part and domain are operators that extract the local part and the domain from an address, respectively. For example, if the sender of a message is *brutus@rome.example.com*, then:

```
local part is ${local_part:$sender_address}
domain is ${domain:$sender_address}
```

expands to:

```
local part is brutus
domain is rome.example.com
```

## 17.10.2 Extracting named fields from a line of data

Suppose you want to pick out individual field values from a data file containing lines such as this:

```
trajan: uid=142 gid=241 home=/homes/trajan
```

An `lsearch` lookup on the key `trajan` returns the rest of the line of data; the `extract` expansion item can be used to split it up. For example, to obtain the value of the `uid` field:

```
${extract{uid}{${lookup{trajan}lsearch{/the/file}{$value}fail}}}
```

There are two substrings that follow `extract`; the first is a name, and the second is a string of `<name>=<value>` items from which it extracts the value that matches the given name. In this example, the string is obtained by a lookup, which is the most common case. The lookup of the key `trajan` yields:

```
uid=142 gid=241 home=/homes/trajan
```

so the `extract` item becomes:

```
${extract{uid}{uid=142 gid=241 home=/homes/trajan}}
```

before the extraction operation is applied. If any of the values in the data contain whitespace, they must be enclosed in double quotes, and within double quotes, normal escape processing takes place.[1]

If the name is not found in the data string, the item is replaced by the empty string. However, the `extract` item can also be used in a similar way to a lookup or conditional item. If two further argument strings are given, the first is used when the extraction succeeds, with *$value* containing the extracted substring, and the second is used when the extraction fails. For example:

```
${extract{uid}{uid=142 gid=241 home=/homes/trajan}{userid=$value}}
```

yields `userid=142`. Once again, "fail" can be specified instead of a second substring, to force expansion failure.

If you are using query-style lookups, you can often select individual fields within the query language. However, if a number of fields are required, it is better to read them from the database together and use `extract` to separate them, because the results of database lookups are cached. Consider the following two settings, which might

---

[1]   \n is turned into newline, for example, and backslash must appear as \\.

appear on a local transport's configuration, to specify the uid and gid under which it is to run:

```
user  = ${lookup mysql \
  {select uid from accounts where \
   id='${quote_mysql:$local_part}'}}
group = ${lookup mysql \
  {select gid from accounts where \
   id='${quote_mysql:$local_part}'}}
```

Two separate database queries are required, one for each option. If instead these settings are used:

```
user  = ${extract{uid}{\
        ${lookup mysql \
        {select uid,gid from accounts where \
          id='${quote_mysql:$local_part}'}}\
        }}
group = ${extract{gid}{\
        ${lookup mysql \
        {select uid,gid from accounts where \
          id='${quote_mysql:$local_part}'}}\
        }}
```

only a single database call actually occurs, because the two queries are identical, so the cached result is used for the second one. Exim caches only the most recent query, but this is sufficient to give substantial benefit.

Another way of retaining the result of a lookup during the routing and delivery of an address is to make use of the address_data option (☞ 6.3.1).

## 17.10.3 Extracting unnamed fields from a line of data

There is a second form of the extract expansion item that can be used on data strings that are separated by particular characters. A good example is the password file, */etc/passwd*, where the fields are separated by colons. To extract a user's real name from this file, an expansion such as this can be used:

```
${extract{4}{:}{${lookup{hadrian}lsearch{/etc/passwd}{$value}fail}}}
```

If the line in */etc/passwd* is:

```
hadrian:x:42:99:Hadrian IV::/bin/bash
```

the lookup yields:

```
x:42:99:Hadrian IV::/bin/bash
```

and the result of the extraction is the fourth colon-separated field in this data, namely, Hadrian IV.

This form of extract is distinguished from the other by having a first argument consisting entirely of digits. The second argument is a list of field separator characters, any one of which can be used in the data. In other words, the separators are always a single character, not a string. Two successive separators mean that the field between them is empty (the fifth field in the previous example). If the field number in the expansion is zero, the entire string is returned; if it is greater than the number of fields, an empty string is returned. A negative number can be used to count fields from the right; -1 extracts the last field, -2 the second-to-last field, and so on.

As in the case of the other form of `extract`, you can optionally supply two additional substrings that are used in a similar way to the substrings in a lookup or conditional item. The first is used if the field is found, with *$value* containing the extracted data, and the second substring is used otherwise. Once again, "fail" can be specified instead of a second substring, to force expansion failure.

## 17.11 IP address masking

An IP network is defined using an IP address and a mask. For example, 192.168.34.192/26 defines the network consisting of all IP addresses whose most significant 26 bits are the same as those of 192.168.34.192. To check whether a given host is in this network, it is necessary to mask the least significant bits of its IP address (that is, convert them into zeros) before comparing it with the network address. There are some built-in host tests that automatically take care of masking, but in order to let you write custom tests, a masking expansion operator exists. When processing a message that came from the host 192.168.34.199, the string:

```
${mask:$sender_host_address/26}
```

expands to the string `192.168.34.192/26`. This could be compared against a fixed value, or looked up in a file. This poses a small problem in the case of IPv6 addresses, which are normally written using colons to separate the components, because a colon is the key terminator in data files that are in `lsearch` format (that is, in the same form as alias files). A normal IPv6 address cannot therefore be a key in such a file. In order to make it possible to use IPv6 addresses as `lsearch` keys, the `mask` operator outputs them using dots as separators instead of colons. For example, the string:

```
${mask:3ffe:ffff:836f:0a00:000a:0800:200a:c031/99}
```

expands to:

```
5f03.1200.836f.0a00.000a.0800.2000.0000/99
```

Letters in IPv6 addresses are always output in lower case by the `mask` operator.

# 17.12 Quoting

When data from a message is included in an expansion string by a variable or header insertion, problems can occur if the inserted data contains unanticipated characters. Local parts can contain all manner of special characters if they are correctly quoted using RFC 2822's rules. The following addresses are all valid:

```
O'Reilly@ora.com.example
double\"quote@weird.example
"two words"@weird.example
"abc@pqr"@some.domain.example
abc\@pqr@some.domain.example
```

When Exim receives an address, it strips out the RFC 2822 quoting so as to obtain a "canonical" representation of the local part. The last two examples have the same canonical local parts. Suppose that *$local_part* was being used in a MySQL lookup query containing the following fragment:

```
... where id='$local_part' ...
```

The first example would break this query because the local part contains an apostrophe. Such problems can be avoided by using the appropriate quoting mechanism in the string expansion. Several are provided, for use in different circumstances.

## 17.12.1 Quoting addresses

The quote operator puts its argument into double quotes if it contains anything other than letters, digits, underscores, dots, or hyphens. Any occurrences of double quote or backslash are escaped with a backslash. This kind of quoting is useful if a new mail address is being created from an old one for some reason. For example, suppose you wanted to send unknown local parts in your local domain to some other domain, retaining the same local part, but changing the domain. You could do this using a **redirect** router such as this as your final router:

```
send_elsewhere:
  driver = redirect
  data = $local_part@dead-letter.example.com
```

As this is the last router, local parts that the other routers could not handle would be passed to it. The example would work fine until somebody sent a message with a local part containing an @ character, for example:

```
"malicious@example"@your.domain
```

Exim would report a syntax error in the new address, because the value of *$local_part* would be malicious@example after removing the RFC 2822 quoting. To guard against this, the option is better defined as follows:

```
data = ${quote:$local_part}@dead-letter.example.com
```

This causes the local part to be quoted if necessary.

## 17.12.2 Quoting data for regular expressions

The `rxquote` operator inserts backslashes before any non-alphanumeric characters in its argument. As its name suggests, it is used when inserting data that is to be interpreted literally into regular expressions. If you want to check whether the current delivery address is mentioned in the *To:* header of a message, you can write an expansion conditional such as the following:

```
${if match{$h_to:}{^.*$local_part@$domain} {...
```

Note that in this case, \N is not used to protect the regular expression from expansion, because we are using expansion to construct the expression. However, any regular expression metacharacters in the local part or the domain would break the regular expression, and as a dot is such a character, the domain is almost certain to cause trouble. The correct way to write this example is as follows:

```
${if match{$h_to:}{^.*${rxquote:$local_part@$domain}} {...
```

## 17.12.3 Quoting data in lookup queries

There are special quoting operators for each of the query-style lookup types:

*NIS+*

The effect of the `quote_nisplus` expansion operator is to double any quote characters within the text.

*LDAP*

Two levels of quoting are required in LDAP queries, the first for LDAP itself, and the second because the LDAP query is represented as a URL. The `quote_ldap` expansion operator implements the following rules:

- For LDAP quoting, the characters #,+"\<>;*() have to be preceded by a backslash.[1]

- For URL quoting, all characters except alphanumerics and !$'()*+-._ are replaced by %*xx*, where *xx* is the hexadecimal character code. Note that backslash has to be quoted in a URL, so characters that are escaped for LDAP end up preceded by %5C in the final encoding.

*MySQL*

The `quote_mysql` expansion operator converts newline, tab, carriage return, and backspace to \n, \t, \r, and \b, respectively, and the characters ' "\ are

---

[1]  In fact, only some of these need be quoted in Distinguished Names, and others in LDAP filters, but it does no harm to have a single quoting rule for all of them.

escaped with backslashes. Percent and underscore are special only in contexts where they can be wildcards, and MySQL does not permit them to be quoted elsewhere, so they are not affected by the `quote_mysql` operator.

*Oracle*

The `quote_oracle` expansion operator has exactly the same effect as `quote_mysql`.

*PostgreSQL*

The `quote_pgsql` expansion operator converts newline, tab, carriage return, and backspace to \n, \t, \r, and \b, respectively, and the characters ' " \ are escaped with backslashes, as for `quote_mysql`. However, percent and underscore are treated differently. PostgreSQL allows them to be quoted in contexts where they are not special. For example, an SQL fragment such as:

```
where id="ab\%cd"
```

has the same effect as:

```
where id="ab%cd"
```

which is not the case for MySQL. Percent and underscore are therefore escaped by `quote_pgsql`.

## 17.12.4 Quoting printing data

The final quoting operator is called `escape`, and it is for use when inserted data is required to contain printing characters only. It converts any non-printing characters into escape sequences starting with a backslash.[1] For example, a newline character is turned into \n, and a backspace into \010. Local parts that are quoted in email addresses may contain such characters, though usually it is only persons bent on mischief that create them. Message header lines are another place where non-printing characters may occur. As an example of where `escape` might be used, consider the creation of an automatic reply to an incoming message. The details of how to do this can be found earlier (☞ 9.7), but you do not need to know them to follow this example, which just shows how the *Subject:* line of the reply might be specified:

```
subject = Re: message from $sender_address to $local_part
```

That should not cause any delivery trouble, whatever the contents of the local part and sender address, but it could be very confusing if there were backspaces, for example, in one of the variables. A safer way to write this is:

```
subject = Re: message from ${escape:$sender_address} \
   to ${escape:$local_part}
```

---

[1] Whether characters with the most significant bit set (so-called "8-bit" characters) count as printing or non-printing is controlled by the `print_topbitchars` option.

# 17.13 Re-expansion

The expand operator first expands its argument substring like all the other operators, but then passes the result through the expander for a second time. The most common use is when the first expansion does a lookup, because it allows the data that is looked up to contain expansion variables. Suppose the file option for local delivery is written like this:

```
file = ${lookup{$local_part}lsearch{/etc/mailboxes}\
       {${expand:$value}}{/var/mail/$local_part}}
```

To find the name of the mailbox file, the local part is looked up in /etc/mailboxes. If no data is found, the string /var/mail/$local_part is expanded and used. Otherwise the value that was looked up is used, but it is first re-expanded. The file /etc/mailboxes could contain lines such as this:

```
jim:    /home/jim/inbox
```

for which the additional expansion would have no effect, but it could also contain lines like this:

```
jon:    ${if eq{$h_precedence:}{bulk}{/dev/null}{/var/mail/jon}}
```

which discards messages with a *Precedence:* header line whose value is bulk, by causing them to be written to */dev/null*.[1]

# 17.14 Calling external code

The facilities available for string expansion allow for quite sophisticated transformations on strings. Nevertheless, there is always somebody who wants to do more. The ultimate sledgehammer is to run an external program or a Perl function as part of a string expansion.

## 17.14.1 Running an external program

The run expansion item allows the result of running an external command to be incorporated into a string. The syntax is as follows:

```
${run {<command> <args>}{<string1>}{<string2>}}
```

The command and its arguments are first expanded separately, and then the command is run in a separate process, but under the same uid and gid as the calling process. As in other command executions from Exim, a shell is not used by default. If you want a shell, you must explicitly code it.

---

[1]  This is not a recommended way of achieving this effect; it is just an example to demonstrate the expand operator.

If the command succeeds (gives a zero return code) the first string is expanded and replaces the entire item; during this expansion, the standard output from the command is in the variable *$value*. If the command fails, the second string, if present, is expanded. If it is absent, the result is empty. Alternatively, the second string can be the word `fail` (not in braces) to force expansion failure if the command does not succeed. If both strings are omitted, the result is the standard output on success, and nothing on failure.

The return code from the command is put in the variable *$runrc*, and this remains set afterwards, so in a filter file you can write commands such as the following:

```
if "${run{x y z}{}}$runrc" is 0 then ...
  elif $runrc is 1 then ...
  ...
endif
```

When expanding the first string, Exim runs the command *x* with two argument strings, *y* and *z*. The empty pair of braces causes any output from the command to be discarded; the value of the whole expanded string is therefore just the return code, taken from *$runrc*.

## 17.14.2 Running embedded Perl

If you want to make use of Perl from within expansion strings, Exim has to be built with support for embedded Perl (see chapter 22). Access to Perl subroutines is via a configuration option called `perl_startup`, which defines a set of Perl subroutines, and the expansion string operator `${perl...}`, which causes them to be run. If there is no `perl_startup` option in the Exim configuration file, no Perl interpreter is started, and there is almost no overhead for Exim (since none of the Perl library is paged in unless it is used).

If there is a `perl_startup` option, the associated value is taken to be Perl code, which is executed in a newly created Perl interpreter. It is not expanded in the Exim sense, so you do not need backslashes before any characters to escape special meanings. The option should usually be something such as the following:

```
perl_startup = do '/etc/exim.pl'
```

where */etc/exim.pl* contains Perl code that defines the subroutines you want to use. Exim can be configured either to start up a Perl interpreter as soon as it starts to execute, or to wait until the first time the interpreter is needed. Starting the interpreter at the beginning ensures that it is done while Exim still has its setuid privilege, which might be needed to gain access to initialization files, but imposes an unnecessary overhead if Perl is not used in a particular run. By default, the interpreter is started only when it is needed, but this can be changed, as follows:

- Setting `perl_at_start` true in the configuration requests a startup when Exim starts.

- The command-line option -ps also requests a startup when Exim starts, over-riding a false setting of perl_at_start.

- There is also a command-line option -pd (for delay), which suppresses the initial startup, even if perl_at_start is set.

When the configuration file includes a perl_startup option, string expansion items can call the Perl subroutines defined by the perl_startup code like this:

```
${perl{func}{argument1}{argument2} ... }
```

An item such as this calls the subroutine *func* with the given arguments (having first expanded the arguments). A minimum of zero and a maximum of eight arguments may be passed. Passing more than this results in an expansion failure. The return value of the subroutine is inserted into the expanded string, unless the return value is undef. In this case, the expansion fails in the same way as an explicit fail on an if or lookup item. If the subroutine aborts by obeying Perl's *die* function, the expansion fails with the error message that was passed to *die*.

The Perl interpreter is not run in a separate process, so when it is called from an expansion string, its uid and gid are those of the Exim process. In particular, initializing the interpreter when Exim starts to run causes it to run as *root* during its initialization only; it does not cause subsequently called subroutines to run as *root*.

Within any Perl code called from Exim, the function *Exim::expand_string* is avail-able to call back into Exim's string expander. This helps to reduce the number of arguments you need to pass to a Perl subroutine. For example, the Perl code:

```
my $lp = Exim::expand_string('$local_part');
```

makes the current value of *$local_part* available in the Perl variable *$lp*. Note the use of single quotes to protect against *$local_part* being interpolated as a Perl variable.

If the string expansion is forced to fail, the result of *Exim::expand_string* is undef. If there is a syntax error in the expansion string, the Perl call from Exim's expansion string fails with an appropriate error message, in the same way as if *die* were used.

# 17.15 Locking out certain expansion items in filter files

Some system administrators may wish to lock out the use of the more powerful string expansion features in users' filter files. For example, the use of run and perl may be considered undesirable, and on a system where users do not have login accounts, it may be desirable to stop users from attempting to access arbitrary files. The **redirect** router has a number of options whose names begin with forbid_ that are used to disable individual expansion items (☞ 7.6.19).

# 17.16 Testing string expansions

If you are setting up some complicated expansion string, perhaps involving lookups, conditionals, or regular expressions, it is helpful to be able to test it in isolation before you try it in an Exim configuration file. If Exim is called with the -be option, as in this example:

```
exim -be
```

it does not perform any mail handling functions at all. Instead, if there are any command-line arguments, it expands each one and writes it as a separate line to the standard output. Otherwise, it reads lines from its standard input, expands them, and writes them to the standard output. It prompts for each line with an angle bracket. For example:

```
$ exim -be '$tod_log'
2000-02-10 15:51:00
$ exim -be
> ${lookup{root}lsearch{/etc/passwd}}
x:0:1:Super-User:/:/bin/sh
>
```

This facility allows you to test the general expansion functionality, but, because no message is being processed, you cannot make use of variables such as *$local_part* that relate to messages.

# 18

# Domain, host, and address lists

Lists of domains, hosts, addresses, and local parts are used in a number of Exim's options, and are shown in examples throughout this book. In this chapter, we will explore all the types of item that you can use in these lists, which are always expanded before being searched.

Each list can be thought of as defining a set of domains, hosts, addresses, or local parts, respectively. When Exim is testing to see whether a domain (or host, address, or local part) matches an item in a list, it asks the question "Is this domain (or host, address, or local part) in the set defined by this list?" It scans the list from left to right, checking against each item in turn. As soon as an item matches, the scan stops.

All lists use colons as separator characters by default, and whitespace at either end of an item is ignored. If you need to include a literal colon in an item, it must be doubled. Unfortunately, this is necessary for all colons that appear in IPv6 addresses. For example:

```
local_interfaces = 127.0.0.1: ::::1
```

contains two items: the IPv4 address `127.0.0.1` and the IPv6 address `::1`. The space after the first colon is vital; without it, the list would be incorrectly interpreted as the two items `127.0.0.1::` and `1`.

An alternative to doubling colons is to change the separator character for the list. If a list starts with a < character that is immediately followed by a non-alphanumeric printing character (excluding whitespace), that character is used as the separator. The `local_interfaces` example could be rewritten to use + as the separator as follows:

```
local_interfaces = <+ 127.0.0.1 + ::1
```

## 18.1 Negative items in lists

Sometimes it is useful to have exceptions to wildcard patterns. For example, suppose all domains ending in *.cities.example* are local domains. We might have the following setting on a router, to cause it to process addresses in those domains:

```
domains = *.cities.example
```

Now suppose that we want to exclude *athens.city.example*, while retaining all the others. The existing list item is a *positive* item. If it matches, the answer to the question "Is the domain in this list?" is "yes". It is also possible to have *negative* items, which, if they match, cause the answer to be "no", and this provides exactly the feature we need. An exclamation mark preceding any item negates it.[1] Consider this example:

```
domains = !athens.cities.example:\
          *.cities.example
```

If the domain is *athens.cities.example*, the first item matches. Because it is negated, this causes the answer to be "no". Otherwise the domain is matched against *\*.cities.example*.

 If you are using a macro (☞ 4.3.5) in your configuration file to define a number of items for a list, you cannot negate all of them by putting an exclamation mark in front of the macro name, because macros work by simple text substitution. For example, if you have defined:

```
LOCAL = domain1 : domain2
```

then:

```
domains = !LOCAL
```

is *not* the same as:

```
domains = !domain1 : !domain2
```

For this kind of requirement, a named list (described later) should be used.

If the last item in a list is a negative item, it changes what happens when the end of the list is reached without anything matching. In the examples we have used so far, reaching the end of the list provokes a "no" answer. However, for a list such as this:

```
queue_domains = !*.mydomain.example
```

reaching the end of the list causes a "yes" answer because that seems the natural interpretation of such a list. In effect, a list that ends with a negative item is treated as if it had an additional "matches everything" item at the end, so this example behaves exactly the same as:

```
queue_domains = !*.mydomain.example : *
```

---

[1] There may be optional whitespace between the exclamation mark and the item.

Another way of thinking about positive and negative items in lists is to read the connector as "or" after a positive item and as "and" after a negative item.

# 18.2 List items in files

In any of these lists, an item beginning with a slash is interpreted as the name of a file that contains out-of-line items, one per line. Empty lines in the file are ignored. The other lines are interpolated into the list exactly as if they appeared inline, except that they are not expanded, and the file is read afresh each time the list is scanned. A file may not, however, contain the names of other files.

For domain and host lists, if a # character appears anywhere in a line of the file, it and all following characters on the line are ignored. For address and local part lists, # must be at the start of a line or be preceded by whitespace to be recognized as introducing a comment, because # can legitimately appear in a local part. If a plain filename is preceded by an exclamation mark, the sense of any match within the file is inverted. For example, with the setting:

```
hold_domains = !/etc/nohold-domains
```

and a file containing the lines:

```
!a.b.c
*.b.c
```

*a.b.c* is in the set of domains defined by `hold_domains`, whereas any domain matching *\*.b.c* is not.

# 18.3 Lookup items in lists

Lists may also contain lookup items; these operate differently for the four kinds of list, so they are described separately later. However, it is important to realize that a lookup, even if it uses the `lsearch` lookup method, is not the same as an interpolated file, as just described. The example file shown could not be used for an `lsearch` lookup because the data in a lookup file is fixed: it cannot contain any negation or wildcarding.[1] Consequently, there is an important difference between (for example):

```
hold_domains = /etc/hold-domains
```

and:

```
hold_domains = lsearch;/etc/hold-domains
```

---

[1]  The partial and default features of single-key lookups are implemented by multiple probes of the file.

even though the file is read sequentially in both cases. In the first case, each line is interpolated just as if it appeared inline, and the file may contain any item type other than a further filename. For example, it could contain items beginning with asterisks, or regular expressions. However, if a lookup is used (the second case), the keys in the file are not interpreted specially; they are always literal strings.

# 18.4 Named lists

Named lists were introduced earlier (☞ 4.4), using the following example:

```
domainlist local_domains = localhost:my.dom.example
```

Any list of domains, hosts, email addresses, or local parts can be given a name that is used with a plus sign to refer to the list elsewhere in the configuration, as in the first router in the default configuration, which is as follows:

```
dnslookup:
  driver = dnslookup
  domains = ! +local_domains
  transport = remote_smtp
  no_more
```

The four kinds of named list are created by configuration lines starting with the words domainlist, hostlist, addresslist, or localpartlist, respect-ively. Then there follows the name that you are defining, followed by an equals sign and the list itself. For example:

```
hostlist    relay_hosts = 192.168.23.0/24 : my.friend.example
addresslist bad_senders = cdb;/etc/badsenders
```

A named list may refer to other named lists, as in the following example:

```
domainlist  dom1 = first.example : second.example
domainlist  dom2 = +dom1 : third.example
domainlist  dom3 = fourth.example : +dom2 : fifth.example
```

Named lists may have a performance advantage. When Exim is routing an address or checking an incoming message, it caches the result of tests on named lists. So, if you have a setting such as the following:

```
domains = +local_domains
```

on several of your routers, the actual test is done only for the first one. However, the caching works only if there are no expansions within the list itself or any sublists that it references. In other words, caching happens only for lists that are known to be the same each time they are referenced.

By default, there may be up to 16 named lists of each type. This limit can be extended by changing a compile-time variable. The use of named lists is recom-

If the last item in a referenced list is a negative one, the effect may not be what you intended, because the negation does not propagate out to the higher level. For example, consider:

```
domainlist  dom1 = !a.b
domainlist  dom2 = +dom1 : *.b
```

The second list specifies "either in the `dom1` list or matches `*.b`". The first list specifies "does not match `a.b`", so the domain *x.y* matches it. That means that *x.y* matches the second list as well. The effect is not the same as this list:

```
domainlist  dom2 = !a.b : *.b
```

where *x.y* does not match. It is best to avoid negation altogether in referenced lists if you can.

---

mended for concepts such as local domains, relay domains, and relay hosts. The default configuration is set up like this.

# 18.5 Domain lists

Domain lists are used for specifying sets of mail domains for various purposes, such as which domains are local, or which are acceptable for relaying. Here is an (unrealistic) example of a domain list that uses several different kinds of item:

```
domainlist local_domains = \
   @:\
   lib.unseen.edu.example:\
   *.foundation.fict.example:\
   \N^[1-2]\d{3}\.fict\.example$\N:\
   partial-dbm;/opt/penguin/example:\
   nis;domains.byname:\
   nisplus;[name=$domain,status=local],domains.org_dir
```

There are some fairly obvious processing trade-offs among the various matching modes. Using an asterisk is faster than using a regular expression, and listing a few names explicitly probably is too. The use of a file or database lookup is expensive, but it may be the only option if hundreds of names are required. Because the items are tested in order, it makes sense to put the most commonly matched items earlier in the string.

Some domain lists are scanned frequently by Exim. It is therefore important that any lookups they use be quick and unlikely to defer. You should not, for instance, put the list of local domains on a heavily loaded database server that is running on a host on a remote network. For the best performance, lookups should normally use a local file or a server running on the local host, or at least a host on the local LAN.

## 18.5.1 Domain list items

There are a number of different types of item that may appear in a domain list.

### Matching the local host name

If an item consists of a single @ character, it matches the local host name, as set in the `primary_hostname` option. This makes it possible to use the same configuration file on several different hosts that differ only in their names. The following example:

```
domainlist local_domains = @ : plc.com.example
```

ensures that the local host name is a local domain.

### Matching local IP interfaces

If an item consists of the string @[] it matches any local IP interface address, enclosed in square brackets, as in an email address that contains a domain literal. The use of domain literals is dying out in today's Internet, and is not recommended.

### Matching domains MX'd to the local host

If an item consists of the string @mx_any it matches any domain that has an MX record pointing to the local host, or to any host that is listed in `hosts_treat_as_ local`. The items @mx_primary and @mx_secondary are similar, except that the first matches only when a primary MX target is the local host, and the second only when no primary MX target is the local host, but a secondary MX target is. "Primary" means an MX record with the lowest preference value; there may of course be more than one of them.

### Matching the ends of domain names

If an item starts with an asterisk, the remaining characters of the item are compared with the terminating characters of the domain. The use of an asterisk in domain lists differs from its use in partial matching lookups. In a domain list, the character following the asterisk need not be a dot, whereas partial matching works only in terms of dot-separated components. For example, a domain list such as:

```
domainlist local_domains = *key.example
```

matches *donkey.example* as well as *cipher.key.example*.

An asterisk may appear only at the start of an item, where it encodes the commonly required "ends with" test. More complex wildcard matching requires the use of a regular expression.

## Matching by regular expression

If an item starts with a circumflex character, it is treated as a regular expression, and matched against the domain using a regular expression matching function. Because lists are always expanded before being scanned, you must either protect the regular expression from expansion with \N, or escape any backslash, dollar, and curly bracket (brace) characters to prevent them from being interpreted by the string expander (unless you really do want to build a regular expression by expansion).

Expansion happens before each item is interpreted, so \N can be placed before the leading circumflex, as in the following example:

```
domainlist local_domains = \N^mta\d{3}\.plc\.example$\N
```

This specifies that any domain whose name is *mta* followed by three digits and *.plc.example* is a local domain. The circumflex that introduces a regular expression is treated as part of the expression. This means that it "anchors" the expression to the start of the domain name. However, you can start with ^.* to accommodate arbitrary leading characters if you need to. A description of the regular expressions that Exim supports can be found in appendix B.

## Matching by single-key lookup

If an item starts with the name of a single-key lookup type followed by a semicolon (for example, dbm; or lsearch;), the remainder of the item must be a filename in a suitable format for the lookup type. For example, for dbm; it must be an absolute path:

```
hold_domains = dbm;/etc/holddomains.db
```

The appropriate type of lookup is done on the file using the domain name as the key. If the lookup succeeds, the domain matches the item.

## Matching by partial single-key lookup

Any of the single-key lookup type names may be preceded by partial<n>-, where the <n> is optional, for example:

```
partial-dbm;/partial/domains
```

This causes partial matching logic to be invoked (☞ 16.5).

### Matching by query-style lookup

If the item starts with the name of a query-style lookup type followed by a semicolon (for example, `nisplus;` or `ldap;`), the remainder of the item must be an appropriate query for the lookup type. For example:

```
domainlist local_domains = \
   mysql; select domain from localdomains where \
   domain='$domain';
```

If the lookup succeeds, the domain that is being tested matches the item. Note that this is not looking up a list of domains to test; it is testing a single domain by running a query (which normally would refer to the domain).[1]

### Matching a literal domain name

If none of the earlier cases apply, a case-insensitive textual comparison is made between the item and the domain.

## 18.5.2 Data from lookups in domain lists

Lookups in domain lists are a way of obtaining a "yes" or "no" answer about a domain's membership of a particular set of domains. The data that is looked up as part of the test is normally discarded. However, there is one case when it is retained. If either the `domains` or `local_parts` option on a router, or one of the identically named conditions in an ACL, is matched by means of a lookup, Exim sets the *$domain_data* and *$local_part_data* variables, respectively, to the data that was looked up. In a router, these values last for the duration of the router, and, if it routes the address to a transport, are also set while the transport is running. In an ACL, the values last for the remainder of the ACL statement.

# 18.6 Host lists

Host lists are used to control what remote hosts are allowed to do (for example, use the local host as a relay, or issue an *ETRN* command). Hosts can be identified in two different ways, by IP address or by name. In a host list, some types of item are matched to an IP address, and some are matched to a name. You need to be particularly careful with this when single-key lookups are involved, to ensure that the correct value is being used as the key.

---

[1]  If you do want to use a lookup to construct a domain list, you can use the normal `${lookup...}` expansion syntax.

## 18.6.1 Special host list patterns

If a host list item is the empty string, it matches only when no remote host is involved. This is the case when a message is received from a local process on the standard input (with or without the use of SMTP), that is, when a TCP/IP connection is not used. An example of this can be seen in an ACL in the default configuration, which contains this statement:

```
accept  hosts = :
```

The other special item in a host list is a single asterisk, which matches any host or no host, as in this example:

```
auth_advertise_hosts = *
```

Neither the IP address nor the name is actually inspected for this item.

## 18.6.2 Host checks by ip address

When Exim receives an SMTP connection from another host, the only reliable identification it initially has for the host is its IP address. This is used for checking the types of item described in this section.

### Matching an IP address

If the item is an IP address, it is compared with the IP address of the subject host. In an ACL, for example, the following statement:

```
accept hosts = 10.8.43.23
```

could be used to allow relaying from the host with that particular IP address.

### Matching the IP address of a local interface

If the pattern is @[], it matches the IP address of any IP interface on the local host. For example, if the host has one external interface address 10.45.23.56, these two ACL statements have the same effect:

```
accept hosts = 127.0.0.1 : 10.45.23.56
accept hosts = @[]
```

### Matching a masked IP address

If the item is an IP address followed by a slash and a mask length, for example:

```
host_lookup = 10.11.42.0/24
```

it is matched against the IP address of the subject host under the given mask. The mask is specified in CIDR notation, with its value being interpreted as the number of address bits that must match, starting from the most significant end. Thus, an entire network of hosts can be included (or excluded) by a single item.

The mask is *not* a count of addresses, nor is it the high number of a range of addresses. It is the number of bits in the network portion of the address. The example shown specifies a 24-bit netmask, so it matches all 256 addresses in the 10.11.42.0 network. An item such as

```
192.168.23.236/30
```

matches just two addresses, 192.168.23.236 and 192.168.23.237. A mask value of 32 for an IPv4 address is the same as no mask at all; just a single address matches.

IPv4 addresses in host lists are given in the normal "dotted-quad" notation. IPv6 addresses are given in colon-separated format, but the colons have to be doubled so as not to be taken as item separators. This example shows both kinds of address:

```
recipient_unqualified_hosts = 192.168.0.0/12: \
                      3ffe::ffff::836f::::/48
```

Colons in IPv6 addresses must be doubled only when such addresses appear inline in a host list. Doubling is not required (and must not be done) when IPv6 addresses appear in a file. For example:

```
recipient_unqualified_hosts = /opt/exim/unqualnets
```

could make use of a file containing:

```
192.168.0.0/12
3ffe:ffff:836f::/48
```

to have exactly the same effect as the earlier example, though it is of course less efficient for a small number of addresses. Alternatively, you can change the separator character in the list to avoid having to double colons in IPv6 addresses. For example:

```
recipient_unqualified_hosts = <+ 192.168.0.0/12+ \
                      3ffe:ffff:836f::/48
```

## Matching by masked IP address single-key lookup

A single-key lookup using the IP address as the basis for the key can be specified by an item of the following form:

```
net<number>-<search-type>;<search-data>
```

For example:

```
net24-dbm;/etc/networks.db
```

First, the IP address of the subject host is masked using *<number>* as the mask length. Then a textual string is constructed from the masked value, followed by the mask, and this is used as the key for the lookup. For example, if the host's IP address is 192.168.34.6, the key that is looked up for this example is `192.168.34.0/24`.

IPv6 addresses are converted to a text value using lower-case letters and dots as separators instead of the more common colon because a colon is the key terminator in `lsearch` files. This prevents any string containing a colon from being used as a key. Full, unabbreviated IPv6 addresses are always used.

## Matching by unmasked IP address single-key lookup

If a single-key lookup is specified without a mask, as in the following example:

```
net-cdb;/etc/spechosts
```

the text form of the IP address of the subject host is used unmasked as the lookup key string. This is not the same as specifying `net32` for an IPv4 address or `net128` for an IPv6 address, because the mask value is not included in the key. However, IPv6 addresses are still converted to an unabbreviated form using lower-case letters, with dots as separators.

## Matching by IP address query-style lookup

The same form can be used for query-style lookups, as in the following example:

```
accept hosts = net-mysql;select host from relays \
               where ip='$sender_host_address'
```

You can use the expansion string `mask` operator if you want to use masked IP addresses in this kind of lookup.

---

 Although *$sender_host_address* appears explicitly as part of the query, you still need to precede the search type with `net-`, because if you do not, Exim assumes the host name is needed, and tries to look it up before running the query. This may waste some resources, but more importantly, if the host name cannot be found, the host list match fails.

---

# 18.6.3 Host checking using forward lookup

If an item in a host list is a plain domain name, for example:

```
accept hosts = my.friend.example
```

Exim calls the system host lookup function to find its IP addresses. This typically causes a forward DNS lookup of the name. In some cases other sources of information such as */etc/hosts* may be used, depending on the way your operating system is set up. The result is compared with the IP address of the host being checked. The primary name of the local host can be included in a host list by an item consisting of just the character @; this makes it possible to use the same configuration on several hosts that differ only in their names.

## 18.6.4 Host checking using reverse lookup

The remaining types of item that can appear in host lists are wildcard patterns for matching against the host name. If this is not already known, Exim calls the system function to obtain it from the IP address. This typically causes a reverse DNS lookup to occur, though other sources of information such as */etc/hosts* may be used, depending on the configuration of your operating system.

If the lookup fails (that is, if Exim cannot find a host name for the IP address), it behaves as if the host does not match the list. One side effect of this is that subsequent items in the list are not examined, even if they do not require the host name to be known.[1] For this reason, you should always put items involving IP addresses first if you can. Suppose you have the following setting in an ACL:

```
accept hosts = *.myfriend.example : 192.168.5.4
```

When a connection from any host arrives, Exim has to find a host name before it can test the first item in the list. If a name cannot be found, the condition fails, even if the host's IP address is 192.168.5.4. Putting the items in the opposite order makes the accept succeed for connections from that host, whether or not its name can be found. It is also more efficient, because the reverse lookup is not even attempted.

If you really do want to do the name check first, and still recognize the IP address when a reverse lookup fails, you can rewrite the ACL like this:

```
accept hosts = *.myfriend.example
accept hosts = 192.168.5.4
```

If the first accept fails, Exim goes on to try the second one.

In some circumstances, it may be desirable to treat the host as matching the list if a reverse lookup fails. To allow this, the special item +include_unknown may appear in a host list at top level; it is not recognized in an interpolated file. If any subsequent items require a host name and the reverse lookup fails, the host is assumed to match the list (that is, the behaviour is the opposite to the default). For example:

```
deny hosts = +include_unknown : *.enemy.example
```

denies access from any host whose name matches *.enemy.example, but only if it can find a host name from the incoming IP address. This is a dangerous thing to do if you really are dealing with a malicious enemy, because the block can easily be

---

[1] The order of items in a list matters because of the existence of negative items, so an unresolvable item cannot just be skipped.

circumvented by unregistering the calling hosts. However, if you must accept mail from unregistered hosts, but also need to block other registered hosts by name, this facility can be useful.

As a result of aliasing, hosts may have more than one name. When processing any of the following items, all the host's names are checked.

## Matching the ends of host names

If an item in a host list starts with an asterisk, the remainder of the item must match the end of the host name. For example, `*.b.c` matches all hosts whose names end in *.b.c*. The asterisk may appear only at the start of the item; this special simple form is provided because this is a very common requirement. Other kinds of wildcarding require the use of a regular expression.

## Matching by regular expression

If an item starts with a circumflex, it is taken to be a regular expression that is matched against the host name. For example:

```
accept hosts = \N^[ab]\.c\.d$\N
```

matches either of the two hosts *a.c.d* or *b.c.d*. As in the case of a domain list, the circumflex is interpreted as part of the regular expression.

## Matching by host name lookup

If an item is of the form `<search-type>;<filename-or-query>`, as in the following example:

```
accept hosts = dbm;/host/accept/list
```

the host name is looked up using the search type and file name or query (as appropriate). If the lookup succeeds, the item matches. The retrieved data is not used.

When using this kind of item with a single-key lookup, you must have host *names* as keys in the file, not IP addresses. If you want to do lookups based on IP addresses, you must precede the search type with `net-` (☞ 18.6.2). There is, however, no reason why you could not use two items in the same list, one doing an address lookup and one doing a name lookup, with both using the same file.

For a query-style lookup, what to lookup is given explicitly in the query, but Exim always ensures that the host name is available before running the query for this type of pattern. If you are not using the host name in your query, you should be using the `net-` form of search described earlier, so that Exim does not look up the host name unnecessarily.

# 18.7 Address lists

Address lists are used in a number of options to vary Exim's behaviour for certain sender or recipient addresses. For example, in an ACL you might have the following statement, in order to deny access by certain senders:

```
deny senders = cleo@egypt.example : tony@egypt.example
```

The rewriting and retry sections of the configuration file both contain rules that require an address list item as their first component. Only a single item may appear in these cases, but it can be of any type that is described in this section.

There is one special case to be considered: the sender address of a bounce message is always empty. You can test for this by providing an empty item in an address list. For example, you can constrain a router to handle only bounce messages by using the following option:

```
senders = :
```

The presence of the colon creates an empty item. If you do not provide any data at all, the list is empty and matches nothing. In other cases, each item in an address list is matched against a mail address in the form *<local_part>@<domain>*.

## Matching by regular expression

If an item starts with a circumflex, a regular expression match is done against the complete address, using the entire item as the regular expression. For example:

```
deny senders = \N^(cleo|tony)@egypt\.example$\N
```

As in the case of domain and host lists, the circumflex is interpreted as part of the regular expression.

## Matching a list of local parts per domain

If the item starts with @@ followed by a single-key lookup item (for example, @@lsearch;/some/file), the address being checked is split into a local part and a domain. The domain is looked up in the file. If it is not found, there is no match. If it is found, the data that is looked up is treated as a colon-separated list of local part items, each of which is matched against the subject local part in turn. As in all colon-separated lists in Exim, a colon can be included in an item by doubling.

The lookup may be partial, or may cause a search for a default keyed by *. The local part items that are looked up can be regular expressions, or begin with *, or even be further lookups. They may also be independently negated. For example, with:

```
deny senders = @@dbm;/etc/reject-by-domain
```

the data from which the DBM file is built could contain lines such as this:

```
baddomain.example:  !postmaster : *
```

If a sender's domain is *baddomain.example*, that line of local part items is retrieved and scanned. In this case, if the local part is *postmaster* it matches the negated item, so the whole address fails to match the list. Any other local part matches the asterisk. If a local part that actually begins with an exclamation mark is required, it has to be specified using a regular expression.

If the last item in a list of local parts starts with a right angle bracket, the remainder of the item is taken as a new key to look up in order to obtain a continuation list of local parts. This is called *chaining*. The new key can be any sequence of characters. Thus, one might have entries such as the following:

```
h1.example.com: spammer1 : spammer2 : >*
h2.example.com: spammer3 : >*
*:          ^\d{8}$
```

These specify a match for eight-digit local parts for all domains, in addition to the specific local parts listed for each individual domain. Of course, using this feature costs another lookup each time a chain is followed, but the effort needed to maintain the data is reduced. It is possible to construct loops using this facility, and in order to catch them, the number of times Exim follows a chain is limited to 50.

The @@<*lookup*> style of item can also be used with a query-style lookup, but in this case, the chaining facility is not available. The lookup can only return a single list of local parts.

## Matching by address lookup

Complete addresses can be looked up by using an item that consists of a lookup type, a semicolon, and the data for the lookup. For example:

```
deny senders = cdb;/etc/blocked.senders : \
   mysql;select address from blocked where \
   address='${quote_mysql:$sender_address}'
```

For a single-key lookup type, Exim uses the complete address as the key. Partial matching cannot be used, and is ignored if specified, with an entry being written to the panic log.

## Matching local part and domain separately

If an item contains an @ character, but is not a regular expression or a lookup as just described, the local part of the subject address is compared with the local part of the item, which may start with an asterisk. If the local parts match, the domain is checked in exactly the same way as for an item in a domain list. For example, the domain can be wildcarded, refer to a named list, or be a lookup, as in the following example:

```
deny senders = *@*.spamsite.example:\
               *@+hostile_domains:\
               bozo@partial-lsearch;/list/of/dodgy/sites
```

If a local part that begins with an exclamation mark is required, it has to be specified using a regular expression, because otherwise the exclamation mark is treated as a sign of negation.

### Matching the domain only

If an item is not one of the syntax forms so far described, that is, if an item that is not a regular expression or a lookup does not contain an @ character, it is matched against the domain part of the subject address. The local part is not checked. The only two formats that are recognized this way are a literal domain, or a domain pattern that starts with *.

## 18.7.1 Case of letters in address lists

Domains in email addresses are always processed without regard to the case of any letters in their names, but the case of local parts may be significant on some systems (☞ 5.9). However, RFC 2505 (*Anti-Spam Recommendations for SMTP MTAs*) suggests matching addresses to blocking lists should be done in a case-insensitive manner. Since most address lists in Exim are used for this kind of control, Exim attempts to do this by default.

The domain portion of an address is always converted to lower case before matching it to an address list. The local part is converted to lower case by default, and any string comparisons that take place are done case-insensitively. This means that the data in the address list itself, in interpolated files, and in any file that is looked up using the @@ mechanism, can be in either case. However, the keys in files that are looked up by a search type other than lsearch (which works case-insensitively) must be in lower case, because these types of lookup are case sensitive.

To allow for case-sensitive address list matching, if the string +caseful is included as an item in an address list, the original case of the local part is restored for any comparisons that follow, and string comparisons become case-sensitive. This does not affect the domain, which remains in lower case.

## 18.7.2 Local part lists

Local part lists are matched in the same way as domain lists, except that the special items that refer to the local host (@, @[], @mx_any, @mx_primary, and @mx_secondary) are not recognized. That is, as well as literal matches, items starting with an asterisk, regular expressions, and lookups are supported.

Case-sensitivity in local part lists is handled in the same way as for address lists, and the +caseful item can be used if required.

# 19

# Miscellany

This chapter contains a number of items that do not fit naturally into the other chapters, but which are too small to warrant individual chapters of their own.

## 19.1 Security issues

We use the word "security" to cover aspects of the operation of Exim that are concerned with keeping messages and other data secure, and with letting Exim perform privileged actions that are not permitted to ordinary user programs. There are three main issues:

- An MTA requires privilege in order to carry out the full range of expected functions, but it must take care to prevent its privilege being abused. If possible, it should relinquish privilege whenever it does not need it.

- An MTA must keep the files containing the messages it handles from being accessed by ordinary user programs. Under some countries' data protection legislation, messages and even mail logs are considered to be personal data, so they must be processed with appropriate care.

- An MTA must provide extra facilities for its administrators (for example, the ability to delete a message on the queue) that are safe from abuse by ordinary users.

Security is an important issue because breaches of security can lead to serious consequences. The full details of the security aspects of Exim are quite involved and allow for some variation in the way it is configured. However, there are some standard recommendations you should normally follow, unless you are sure you understand the consequences of doing otherwise. They are as follows:

- Exim requires a special user (uid) and group (gid) for it own use. Many sites set up a user and a group called *exim*; others use *mail*. If you build Exim from source (see chapter 22), define the user in your *Local/Makefile* as shown in this example:

      EXIM_USER=exim

  If you do not specify the group separately (by setting EXIM_GROUP), the user's default group is used. If you are using a precompiled version of Exim that does not contain the settings you want to use, you can redefine them in the runtime configuration file as in this example:

```
    exim_user = mail
```

However, this does not completely hide the built-in values, because they are still used to check the ownership of Exim's configuration file. Changing the user at runtime is also less safe, because if that setting is lost, Exim may run under the wrong uid and gid.

- Add your system administrators to the Exim group. This allows them to read Exim's log files and carry out Exim administration functions without needing to know the *root* password; for more detail, see the discussion of privileged users (☞ 19.3).

- If you want your administrators to be able to run the *eximon* monitoring tool, they need to have read access to the message files on Exim's spool. The Exim group is set for these files, but the default mode is 0600, which gives access only to the Exim user (and *root*, of course). You need to change the mode to 0640; this can be done only if you build Exim from source (☞ 22.3.5).

- Install Exim as *root*, using `make  install`. This ensures that the binary is owned by *root* and has the setuid bit set.

The following sections discuss security issues in more depth.

## 19.1.1 Use of root privilege

Before we go into the details of how Exim uses the *root* privilege, we give a brief review of the Unix features that are used.

### How Unix uses uids to control privilege

From the start, Unix had the concept of a *real* uid and an *effective* uid for every process. These are both set to the same value when a user logs in. The effective uid is the one used for privilege checking (for example, file access), and it can be changed when a new program is run by setting the *setuid* flag in the owner permissions of the executable file. This causes the effective uid to be set to that of the file's owner; the real uid is unchanged. Modern versions of Unix also have a *saved* uid, which is set to the same value as the effective uid when the latter is changed at program startup.

The ways in which programs can manipulate these uids while they are running are not exactly the same in all Unix-like systems, but a process whose effective uid is *root* is able to set all the uids to any value, and any process can change its effective uid to its real or saved uid as and when it chooses. This means that there are two different ways in which a process with *root* privilege (one whose effective uid is *root*) can give up the privilege:

- If all three uids are changed to something other than *root*, the abdication is permanent within the current program; privilege cannot be regained except by executing a new program that is owned by *root* and has the setuid flag set.

- If the real or saved uid is set to *root* and the effective uid is set to something else, the abdication is only temporary. Because any process may change its effective uid to its real or saved uid, privilege can be regained at any time.

Relinquishing the privilege temporarily is a less secure action because an error could cause it to be reinstated at the wrong time.[1] Earlier versions of Exim used both kinds of privilege abdication for various purposes, but Exim 4 uses only the permanent kind.

## Why does Exim need root privilege?

Exim does two thing that require it to be privileged:

- When started as a daemon, Exim sets up a socket connected to the SMTP port (port 25). This can be done only by a privileged process because the port number is less than 1024.

- An Exim delivery process sets up subprocesses that run as specified users. These unprivileged processes are used for reading users' forward files, and for doing actual deliveries. By default, local delivery processes run as the receiving user, whereas remote delivery processes run as the Exim user. The main delivery process runs as *root* so that it can set up these subprocesses with appropriate uids.

Because of these requirements, the Exim binary is normally setuid to *root*. In some special circumstances (for example, when the daemon is not in use and there are no conventional local deliveries), it may be possible to run it setuid to some user other than *root* (usually the Exim user). This possibility is discussed later, but in the vast majority of Exim installations, the output of the *ls -l* command should look like this:

```
-rwsr-xr-x  1 root     smd        560300 Jun 14 08:53 exim
```

That is, the binary is owned by *root*, and the s flag is set for the owner. This means that whenever the program is started, the effective uid is changed to *root*. The group (smd in this case) is not normally relevant. Although it always starts as *root*, Exim gives up *root* privilege when it no longer needs it, by changing uid to the Exim user. In particular, it does this when receiving messages from any source.

---

[1]  For those who know about Unix system functions: permanent abdication is implemented by calling *setuid()*, whereas temporary abdication is implemented by calling *seteuid()* (or, on a few systems, *setresuid()*).

## 19.1.2 Running local deliveries as root

It is generally considered to be a bad idea to run local deliveries as *root*, on the grounds of avoiding excessive privilege where it is not needed. Most installations set up *root* as an alias for the system administrator, which bypasses this problem, but just in case this is not done, Exim's default configuration contains a "trigger guard" in the form of the following setting:

```
never_users = root
```

Whenever Exim is about to run a delivery process, it checks to see if the required uid is one of those listed in `never_users`. If it is, an error is logged and the delivery is deferred.

## 19.1.3 Running an unprivileged exim

In some restricted environments, it is possible to run Exim without any privilege at all, or by retaining privilege only when starting a daemon process. This gives added security, but restricts the actions Exim is able to take. A host that does no local deliveries is a good candidate for this kind of configuration. There are two possibilities if you want to run Exim in this way:

*   Keep the binary setuid to *root*, as in other configurations, but set the `deliver_drop_privilege` option to be true. In all cases, except when starting the daemon, this setting causes Exim to give up privilege as soon as it starts, and thereafter it runs under the Exim uid and gid. In the case of the daemon, Exim behaves as normal; *root* privilege is retained until Exim has bound its listening socket to the SMTP port. The daemon can respond correctly to a SIGHUP signal requesting that it restart (to reload its configuration), because the reinvocation regains *root* privilege.

*   Make the Exim binary setuid and setgid to the Exim user and group:

    ```
    -rwsr-sr-x  1 exim   exim    560300 Jun 14 08:53 exim
    ```

    This means that it always runs under the Exim uid and gid and cannot start up as a daemon unless it is called by a process that is running as *root*. A daemon cannot restart itself as a result of SIGHUP because it is no longer a *root* process at that point. You should still set `deliver_drop_privilege` to be true in this case, because this setting stops Exim from trying to reinvoke itself to do a delivery after a message has been received. Such a reinvocation is a waste of time because it would have no effect. Instead, Exim just carries on in the same incarnation of the program.

If the second approach is chosen, unless Exim is invoked from a *root* process, it ends up running with the real uid and gid set to those of the invoking process, and the effective uid and gid set to Exim's values. Ideally, any association with the values of the invoking process should be dropped (that is, the real and saved uid and gid should be reset to the effective values). Some operating systems have a function that permits this action for a non-*root* effective uid, but a number of them do not. Because of this lack of standardization, Exim does not address this problem. For this reason, the first approach is perhaps the better one to take if you are concerned about this issue.

Setting `deliver_drop_privilege` true is more efficient than the normal mode of operation, because Exim no longer needs to reinvoke itself when starting a delivery process after receiving a message. However, to achieve this extra efficiency, you have to submit to some restrictions, which are all concerned with handling local addresses and local deliveries. There are no special restrictions on message reception or remote delivery, because these run as the Exim user in all configurations.

The restrictions are as follows:

- All local deliveries have to be run under the Exim uid and gid. You should use the `user` and `group` options to override routers or transports that normally deliver as the recipient. Any implicit or explicit specification of a different user causes an error.

- Use of *.forward* files is severely restricted, such that it is usually not worth including a **userforward** router in the configuration. Users who wished to use *.forward* would have to make their home directories and the files themselves accessible to the Exim user. Even if this is done, pipe and file items in *.forward* files, and their equivalents in Exim filters, cannot be permitted in practice. Although such deliveries could be allowed to run as the Exim user, that would be insecure and probably not very useful.

- Unless user mailboxes are all owned by the Exim user, which is possible in some POP3-only or IMAP-only environments:

    - They must be owned by the Exim group and be writable by that group. This implies that you must set `mode` in the **appendfile** configuration, as well as the mode of the mailbox files themselves.

    - You must set `check_owner` false in the **appendfile** configuration, because most or all of the files will not be owned by the Exim user.

    - You must set `file_must_exist` true in the **appendfile** configuration, because Exim cannot set the owner correctly on a new mailbox when unprivileged. This also implies that new mailboxes must be created manually.

# 19.2 Use of RFC 1413 identification

RFC 1413 (*Identification Protocol*) is much misunderstood. It defines a protocol (usually called *ident*) by which a server, on receiving a connection from a client, can make an IP call back to the client and retrieve identification information relating to the original connection. In the context of SMTP, the following sequence occurs:

(1)   Host C (client) connects to the SMTP port on host S (server) from an arbitrary port.

(2)   Host S connects to host C's ident port, passing the number of host C's calling port.

(3)   Host C sends host S identification data relating to the SMTP connection.

(4)   Host S records the data with the incoming message.

A common misunderstanding is to think that the information is supposed to be of use to the server. It is not; it is something the server can record and pass back to the client's administrator if there is a query.

Consider a large shared machine with thousands of registered users who have login accounts. If a user of that system makes a TCP/IP connection to another host and abuses it in some way, the manager of the shared system, when investigating the resulting complaint, has a much easier task if the called host recorded RFC 1413 identification information obtained from the calling host.

Many hosts simply send out login names in response to RFC 1413 connections, in which case the culprit is immediately identifiable. Some hosts include more information, such as time and source of login, and for privacy reasons, some hosts encrypt the information. RFC 1413 is an aid to finding the human responsible for a particular TCP/IP connection from a multi-user system. It is not relevant in the context of single-user clients.

Exim makes RFC 1413 callbacks by default; any identification information that is received is included in the log line for each incoming message received. You can restrict Exim's RFC 1413 callbacks to certain hosts by setting `rfc1413_hosts`. This option defaults to:

```
rfc1413_hosts = *
```

that is, the callbacks are made for all hosts. A timeout is applied to these connections, controlled by `rfc1413_query_timeout`. This defaults to `30s` (30 seconds). If it is set to a zero length of time, no RFC 1413 connections are made. This is the recommended way of disabling these callbacks.

# 19.3 Privileged users

A privileged user is one who is permitted to ask Exim to do things that normal users may not. There are two different kinds of action involved, so there are two different classes of privileged user, called *trusted* users and *admin* users. In the descriptions of the command-line options in chapter 20, a restriction to trusted or admin users is noted for those options to which it applies.

## 19.3.1 Trusted users

Trusted users are allowed to override certain information when submitting messages via the command line (that is, other than over TCP/IP). The Exim user and *root* are automatically trusted, and additional trusted users can be defined by the `trusted_users` option, for example:

```
trusted_users = uucp : majordom
```

In addition, if the current group or any of the supplementary groups of the process that calls Exim is the Exim group, or any group listed in the `trusted_groups` option, the caller is trusted.

### Setting the sender of a locally submitted message

When an ordinary (non-trusted) user submits a message locally, a sender address is constructed from the login name of the real user of the calling process and the default qualifying domain. This address is set as the sender in the message's envelope. It is also placed in an added *Sender:* header line (☞ 14.11.4) if the *From:* header does not contain it, though this can be disabled by setting the `local_from_check` option to be false.

A trusted user may override the sender address by using the `-f` option. For example:

```
exim -f 'alice@carroll.example' ...
```

forces the sender address to be *alice@carroll.example*. If you are running mailing list software that is external to Exim, you should arrange for it to run as a trusted user so it can specify sender addresses when passing messages to Exim for delivery to subscribers.

The origin of the concept of trusted users lies in multi-user systems, where the administration wants to ensure that an authenticated sender address is present in every message that is sent out.[1] In this kind of environment, trusted users are those who are allowed to "forge" sender addresses when submitting messages using the command line interface.

---

[1]  For messages sent directly over TCP/IP from user processes, the *ident* protocol can help provide similar accountability (☞ 19.2).

On small workstations where everything that is done can be accounted to a few people, the distinction between trusted and non-trusted users is less useful, especially in the case of sender addresses. If you are running such a system, you may want to remove the restriction on the use of -f. You can do this by setting the untrusted_set_sender option. The value of untrusted_set_sender is an address list containing patterns matching the addresses that untrusted users are allowed to set. If you want to allow untrusted users to set envelope sender addresses without restriction, you can set it as follows:

```
untrusted_set_sender = *
```

On the other hand, the following example restricts users to setting senders that start with their login id followed by a hyphen:

```
untrusted_set_sender = ^$sender_ident-
```

The *$sender_ident* variable contains the login id for locally submitted messages.

### Setting other information in a locally submitted message

In addition to a sender address, a trusted user may supply additional information, such as an IP address, as if the message had been received from a remote host (☞ 20.2).

These facilities are provided to make it possible for administrators to inject messages with "remote" characteristics using the command line. This can be useful when passing on messages that have arrived via some other transport system, such as UUCP, or when reinjecting messages that have initially been delivered to a virus scanner (☞ 5.10.1).

## 19.3.2 Admin users

Admin users are permitted to use options that affect the running of Exim, for example, to start daemon and queue runner processes, or to remove messages from the queue. The Exim user and *root* are automatically admin users and additional admin users can be set up by adding them to the Exim group.

If you want to, you can "open up" two actions normally permitted only to admin users so that any user can request them:

- If prod_requires_admin is set false, any user may start an Exim queue run by means of the -q option, and may also request the delivery of an individual message by means of the -M option.

- If queue_list_requires_admin is set false, any user may list the messages on the queue by means of the -bp option.

If you want to make all members of an existing group into admin users, you can do so by specifying the group in the admin_groups option. The current group does not have to be one of these groups in order for an admin user to be recognized. For example, setting:

```
admin_groups = sysadmin
```

makes every user in the *sysadmin* group an Exim admin user. However, there is an advantage in doing it the other way (that is, in adding all your administrators to the *exim* group explicitly). If you do this, and if you arrange for Exim's spool and log files to have mode 0640, it gives the administrators read access to these files, which is necessary if they want to run the *eximon* monitor program or examine log files directly.

# 19.4 RFC conformance

The original RFCs that define basic Internet mail services are now very old. RFCs 821 and 822 were published in 1982; some clarifications were published in RFC 1123 in 1989. Subsequent RFCs were mostly concerned with adding functionality such as MIME and extending the SMTP protocol.

The Internet has changed dramatically since 1982 and MTAs have had to change with it, in some cases adopting new conventions that are not in the RFCs, and in others choosing to ignore the RFCs' recommendations or relax their restrictions. Some, but not all, of these changes are incorporated into the revised versions of RFCs 821 and 822. These were published as RFCs 2821 and 2822 in April, 2001.

It is important to remember that the RFCs are not legally binding contracts; their intent is to facilitate widespread interworking over the network. If software conforms to the relevant RFCs, the chances that it can interwork successfully are high. However, you may find that not following an RFC in some particular instance extends interworking between your host and those with which it communicates. If such a change is widely adopted, it may eventually be sanctioned as a standard, though there are some cases where widely used practice is frowned on by the purists. Any particular piece of software must steer a middle course between strict adherence to the RFCs on the one hand, and total disregard on the other.

There are a number of ways in which Exim does not conform strictly to the RFCs. Some of them are very minor, others you can control by setting options, but a few are fundamental to the way the program works and cannot be disabled. These distinctions reflect the prejudices of the author.

## 19.4.1 8-bit characters

Although TCP/IP has always been an 8-bit transport medium, the mail RFCs still insist that mail is a 7-bit service. Characters with the most significant bit set (that is, with a value greater than 127) are forbidden.

The transfer of 8-bit material can be negotiated in some circumstances, but otherwise an MTA is supposed to encode 8-bit characters in some way before transmitting them. Note that this does not apply to binary attachments (which are already encoded into 7-bit characters by the MUA that creates the message), but rather to "raw" 8-bit characters received by the MTA. The most common reason why these are encountered is the use of accented and other special letters in European languages and names.

Requiring an MTA not to pass on 8-bit characters without special action raises technical problems and issues of design principle. If an MTA has received a message containing 8-bit characters and the remote MTA to which it wants to send the message has not indicated support for 8-bit transfers (which is an SMTP extension), the sending MTA must choose between three possibilities:

- Bounce the message.

- Translate the message into a 7-bit format, making an arbitrary choice of encoding mechanism.

- Just send the 8-bit characters anyway.

Strict adherence to the RFCs permits only the first two of these. However, the first is not very helpful, and the second may well turn the message into a form that is not displayed correctly to the final recipient.[1] Breaking the rules, however (sending the 8-bit characters as they are), has a high probability of achieving the result that is intended, namely, the transfer of these characters from sender to recipient.

To make any decisions about 8-bit characters, an MTA has to check a message's body for their presence. Some people (including this author) feel strongly that the job of an MTA is to move messages about, not to spend resources inspecting or modifying their content. For this reason, Exim is "8-bit clean". It makes no modification to message bodies and it pays no attention to 8-bit characters contained therein; they are transported unmodified.

There is, however, an option that is concerned with 8-bit characters. When Exim acts as a server, it happily accepts 8-bit characters in messages in accordance with the philosophy just described, but not all clients are prepared to send such characters in the way Exim does. The RFCs specify an SMTP extension called 8BITMIME for the transmission of 8-bit data. If `accept_8bitmime` is set true in Exim's runtime configuration file, Exim advertises the 8BITMIME extension in its response to the EHLO command. This causes certain clients to send 8-bit data unmodified instead of encoding it; they use the BODY= parameter on MAIL commands to indicate this. Exim recognizes this parameter, but it does not affect its actions in any way. Thus, setting `accept_8bitmime` is just a way of persuading clients not to encode 8-bit

---

[1] Converting messages into "quoted-printable" format is notorious for this.

data. Exim processes such data in the same way, whether or not the `BODY` parameter is used.

## 19.4.2 Address syntax

Syntactically invalid addresses, both in envelopes and header lines, are a depressingly common occurrence. Exim performs syntax checks on all RFC 2821 addresses received in SMTP commands, but it does not check header lines unless

```
verify = header_syntax
```

is specified in an ACL, or it is extracting envelope addresses from header lines as a result of the -t option.

### Built-in address syntax extensions

A number of extensions to the syntax specified in the RFCs are always permitted:

(1)  Exim accepts a header line such as:

```
To: A.N.Other <ano@somewhere.example>
```

which is strictly invalid because dot is a special character in RFC 2822; the line should really be:

```
To: "A.N.Other" <ano@somewhere.example>
```

but many mail programs allow the unquoted form.

(2)  Strictly, an unquoted local part may not start or end with a dot or contain adjacent dots, for example:

```
.ABC@somewhere.example
P.H.@somewhere.example
A..Z@somewhere.example
```

Again, these forms are accepted because of widespread use. However, the ACL in the default configuration file rejects local parts starting with a dot, because these can cause trouble when local parts are being used as file names (for example, in a mailing list configuration).

(3)  "Quoted pairs" in unquoted local parts, for example:

```
abc\@xyz@somwhere.example
```

are permitted by RFC 2821 but not by RFC 2822; for simplicity, Exim always accepts them.

(4)  When reading SMTP `MAIL` and `RCPT` commands, Exim does not insist that addresses be enclosed in angle brackets.

## Configurable address syntax extensions

Two other address extensions can be enabled by setting options:

(1)   Misconfigured mailers occasionally send out addresses within additional pairs of angle brackets, as in the following example:

```
MAIL FROM:<<xyz@bad.example>>
```

This normally causes a syntax error, but if `strip_excess_angle_brackets` is set true, the excess brackets are removed by Exim.

(2)   The DNS use of a trailing dot to indicate a fully qualified domain sometimes causes confusion and leads to the use of mail addresses that end with a dot, as in the following example:

```
dotty@dot.example.
```

Again, this normally causes a syntax error, but if `strip_trailing_dot` is set true, the trailing dot is quietly removed.

## Domain literal addresses

The RFCs permit the use of *domain literal* addresses, which are of the following form:

```
shirley@[10.8.3.4]
```

That is, instead of a domain name, an IP address enclosed in brackets is used. This causes the message to be sent to the host with that IP address. Even in 1982, when RFC 822 was written, the use of domain literals was deprecated. The RFC says:

> *The use of domain-literals is strongly discouraged. It is permitted only as a means of bypassing temporary system limitations, such as name tables which are not complete.*

In the modern Internet, addressing messages to specific hosts by their IP addresses is seen by many as highly undesirable. For this reason, Exim does not recognize domain literal syntax by default. If you want to permit the use of this feature, you must set `allow_domain_literals` true in the runtime configuration. This just allows the syntax to be recognized; you must also adjust your configuration so that domain literal addresses are appropriately routed.

- If you want to deliver domain literal addresses for your own host, you must include the domain literals in an appropriate domain list, as in this example:

  ```
  domainlist local_domains = myhost.example : [192.168.10.8]
  ```

  Alternatively, you can set:

  ```
  domainlist local_domains = myhost.example : @[]
  ```

which causes all the IP addresses for your host to be recognized in domain literal format.

• If you want to deliver domain literal addresses to remote hosts, you must ensure that an **ipliteral** router is defined, in order to route them.

### Source routed addresses

Finally, while on the subject of address syntax, Exim recognizes so-called "source routed" addresses of the form:

```
@relay1,@relay2,@relay3:user@domain
```

However, the use of such addresses has been discouraged since RFC 1123, and an MTA is entitled to ignore all the routing information and treat such an address as:

```
user@domain
```

This is what Exim does.

## 19.4.3 Canonicizing addresses

When a mail domain is the name of a CNAME record in the DNS, the original RFCs suggest that an MTA should automatically change it to the "canonical name" as a message is processed, and there are MTAs that do make this change. However, the new RFCs do not contain this suggestion, and Exim does not perform this rewriting.

## 19.4.4 Coping with broken MX records

The right-hand side of an MX record is defined to be a host name. Some DNS administrators fail to appreciate this and set up MX records with IP addresses on the right-hand side, like this:

```
clueless.example.   MX  1   192.168.43.26
```

Unfortunately, there are broken MTAs in use that do not object to these records, leading people to think that they will always work. Exim is not one of them; it treats the right-hand side as a domain name, tries to look up its address records, and naturally fails.[1]

If you are in a situation in which you just have to deliver mail to such domains (perhaps you want to send a message to a postmaster pointing out the error), you can get Exim to misbehave by setting `allow_mx_to_ip` true in the runtime configuration. This setting is not recommended for general use.

---

[1]  It does, however, notice what is going on and adds a suitable comment to the failure message.

## 19.4.5 Line terminators in SMTP

The specification of SMTP states that lines are terminated by the two-character sequence consisting of carriage return (CR) followed by linefeed (LF), and this is what Exim uses when it sends out SMTP. For incoming SMTP, however, there are clients that are known to break the rules by just using linefeed alone to terminate lines. For this reason, Exim accepts such input.

## 19.4.6 Syntax of HELO and EHLO

One of the more common errors in client SMTP implementations is sending syntactically invalid EHLO or HELO commands. The most common error is the use of underscores in the host name that is the command's argument. Exim rejects syntactically invalid EHLO and HELO commands by default, but there are some options that can be used to change this behaviour (☞ 14.5.3).

# 19.5 Timestamps

Exim uses a timestamp for every line it writes to any of its log files and for every *Received:* header it creates. By default, these timestamps are in the local wallclock time zone. However, you can change this by setting the timezone option. For example, if you set:

```
timezone = EST
```

timestamps are in Eastern Standard Time. If you want all timestamps to be in Universal Coordinated Time (UTC, also known colloquially as GMT), this setting:

```
timezone = UTC
```

Unfortunately, there is apparently no standard way a program on a Unix-like system can specify the use of local wallclock time without knowing what the local time zone is. It can be done in some operating systems, but not in others. For this reason, the default setting for timezone is taken from the setting of the TZ environment variable at the time Exim is built, in the hope that this does the correct thing in most cases.

If TZ is unset when Exim is built or if timezone is set to the empty string, Exim removes any existing TZ variable from the environment when it is called. On GNU/Linux, Solaris, and BSD-derived operating systems, this causes wallclock time to be used.

## 19.6 Checking spool space

Checking available spool space was mentioned earlier in connection with the SIZE option of the MAIL command (☞ 13.3.1). This is just one particular case in which this happens. There are four options that request checks on disk resources before accepting a new message.

If either check_spool_space or check_spool_inodes contains a value greater than zero, for example:

```
check_spool_space = 50M
check_spool_inodes = 100
```

the free space in the disk partition that contains the spool directory is checked to ensure that there is at least as much free space and as many free inodes as specified. The check happens at the start of accepting a message from any source. The check is not an absolute guarantee because there is no interlocking between processes handling messages that arrive simultaneously.

If you have configured Exim to write its log files in a different partition to the spool files, you can set check_log_space and check_log_inodes in the same way, in order to check that partition.

If there is less space or fewer inodes than requested, Exim refuses to accept incoming mail. In the case of SMTP input, this is done by giving a 452 temporary error response to the MAIL command. If there is a SIZE parameter on the MAIL command, its value is added to the check_spool_space value and the check is performed even if check_spool_space is zero, unless smtp_check_spool_space is set false.

For non-SMTP input and for batched SMTP input, the test is done at startup; on failure, a message is written to the standard error stream and Exim exits with a non-zero code, as it obviously cannot send an error message of any kind.

## 19.7 Control of DNS lookups

In a conventional configuration, Exim makes extensive use of the DNS when handling mail. Most of the time this "just happens", and you do not need to be concerned with the details of DNS lookups. However, DNS problems are not entirely unknown; they can sometimes be alleviated by changing the way Exim does its DNS lookups.

Whereas the DNS itself can store domain names that contain almost any character, domains used in email are restricted to letters, digits, hyphens, and dots. Some DNS resolvers have been observed to give temporary errors if asked to look up a domain name (for an MX record, say) that contains other characters. To avoid this problem, Exim checks domain names before passing them to the resolver by matching them against a regular expression specified by `dns_check_names_pattern`. The default setting is:

```
dns_check_names_pattern = \
  (?i)^(?>(?(1)\.|())[^\W_](?>[a-z0-9-]*[^\W_])?)+$
```

which permits only letters, digits, and hyphens in domain name components, and requires them neither to start nor end with a hyphen. If a name contains invalid characters, Exim behaves as if the DNS lookup had returned "not found". This checking behaviour can be suppressed by setting `dns_check_names_pattern` to an empty string.

Badly set-up name servers have been seen to give temporary errors for domain lookups for long periods of time. This causes messages to remain on the queue and be retried until they time out. Sometimes you may know that a particular domain does not exist. If you list such domains in `dns_again_means_nonexist`, a temporary DNS lookup error is treated as a non-existent domain, causing messages to bounce immediately. This option should be used with care because there are many legitimate cases of temporary DNS errors.

Finally, the options `dns_retrans` and `dns_retry` can be used to set the retransmission and retry parameters for DNS lookups. Values of zero (the defaults) leave the system default settings unchanged. The value of `dns_retrans` is the time in seconds between retries and `dns_retry` is the number of retries. Exactly how these settings affect the total time a DNS lookup may take is not clear.

# 19.8 Bounce message handling

This section covers several options that alter the way Exim handles or generates bounce messages (that is, delivery failure reports). This also includes warning messages, which are sent after a message has been on the queue for a specific time. Warning messages have the same format as bounce messages.

## 19.8.1 Replying to bounce messages

When Exim generates a bounce message, it inserts a *From:* header line specifying the sender as *Mailer-Daemon* at the default qualifying domain. For example:

```
From: Mail Delivery System <Mailer-Daemon@myhost.example>
```

Experience shows that many people reply, either accidentally, or out of ignorance, to such messages.[1] You should normally arrange for *mailer-daemon* to be an alias for *postmaster* if you want to see these messages. Another thing you can do is to set

---

[1]   In addition, some software, in contravention of the RFCs, generates automatic replies to bounce messages by extracting an address from the header lines.

`errors_reply_to`, which provides the text for a *Reply-To:* header line in bounce messages. For example:

```
errors_reply_to = postmaster@myhost.example
```

## 19.8.2 Taking copies of bounce messages

Sometimes there is a requirement to monitor the bounce messages that Exim is creating. The `errors_copy` option can be used to cause copies of locally generated bounce messages that are sent to particular addresses to be copied to other addresses. The value is a colon-separated list of items; each item consists of a pattern and a list of addresses, separated by whitespace. If the pattern matches the recipient of the bounce, the message is copied to the addresses on the list. The items are scanned in order, and once a match is found, no further items are examined. For example:

```
errors_copy = spqr@mydomain   postmaster@mydomain :\
              rqps@mydomain   postmaster@mydomain,\
                              hostmaster@mydomain
```

takes copies of any bounces sent to *spqr@mydomain* or *rqps@mydomain*. The bounces are copied to *postmaster@mydomain* in both cases; those for *rqps@mydomain* are also copied to *hostmaster@mydomain*. To send copies of all bounce messages to the postmaster you could use:

```
errors_copy = *@*  postmaster
```

In each item, the pattern can be any single item that may appear in an address list. The list of addresses is expanded, and must end up as a comma-separated list. The expansion variables *$local_part* and *$domain* are set from the original recipient of the error message, and if there is any wildcard matching in the pattern, the expansion variables *$0*, *$1*, etc. are set in the normal way.

## 19.8.3 Delay warning messages

When a message is delayed (that is, if it remains on Exim's queue for a long time), Exim sends a warning message to the sender at intervals specified by the `delay_warning` option, provided certain conditions (described later) are met. The default value for `delay_warning` is 24 hours; if it is set to a zero time interval, no warnings are sent. The data is a colon-separated list of times after which to send warning messages. Up to ten times may be given. If a message has been on the queue for longer than the last time, the last interval between the times is used to compute subsequent warning times. For example, with:

```
delay_warning = 1h
```

warnings are sent every hour, whereas with:

```
delay_warning = 4h:8h:24h
```

the first message is sent after 4 hours, the second after 8 hours, and subsequent ones every 16 hours thereafter. To stop warnings after a given time, set a huge subsequent time, for example:

```
delay_warning = 4h:24h:99w
```

Nowadays, when most messages are delivered very rapidly, users appreciate warnings of delay, but on the whole they do not usually like them to be repeated too often. On the other hand, sending such warnings to the managers of mailing lists is usually counterproductive. To ensure that warnings are sent only in appropriate circumstances, Exim has the `delay_warning_condition` option.

This string is expanded at the time a warning message might be sent. If all the deferred addresses have the same domain, it is set in *$domain* during the expansion; otherwise *$domain* is empty. If the result of the expansion is a forced failure, an empty string, or a string matching any of 0, no, or `false` (the comparison being done caselessly), the warning message is not sent. The default setting for the option is:

```
delay_warning_condition = \
  ${if match{$h_precedence:}{(?i)bulk|list|junk}{no}{yes}}
```

which suppresses the sending of warnings for messages that have `bulk`, `list`, or `junk` in a *Precedence:* header line. This covers most mailing lists.

## 19.8.4 Customizing bounce messages

Default text for the message that Exim sends when an address is bounced is built into the code of Exim, but you can change it, either by adding a single string or by replacing each of the paragraphs by text supplied in a file.

If `bounce_message_text` is set, its contents, which are not expanded, are included in the default message immediately after "This message was created automatically by mail delivery software." For example:

```
bounce_message_text = If you don't understand it, please ask your \
                      postmaster for help.
```

Alternatively, you can set `bounce_message_file` to the name of a template file for constructing error messages. The file consists of a series of text items, separated by lines consisting of exactly four asterisks. If the file cannot be opened, default text is used and a message is written to the main and panic logs. If any text item in the file is empty, default text is used for that item.

Each item of text that is read from the file is expanded, and there are two expansion variables that can be of use here: *$bounce_recipient* is set to the recipient of an error message while it is being created, and *$return_size_limit* contains the value of the `return_size_limit` option, rounded to a whole number. The items must appear in the file in the following order:

- The first item is included in the header lines of the bounce message and should include at least a *Subject:* header. Exim does not check the syntax of these lines.

- The second item forms the start of the error message. After it, Exim lists the failing addresses with their error messages.

- The third item is used to introduce any text from **pipe** transports that is to be returned to the sender. It is omitted if there is no such text.

- The fourth item is used to introduce the copy of the message that is returned as part of the error report.

- The fifth item is added after the fourth one if the returned message is truncated because it is bigger than `return_size_limit`.

- The sixth item is added after the copy of the original message.

The default state (`bounce_message_file` unset) is equivalent to the following file, in which the sixth item is empty. The *Subject:* line and the line that begins "A message" have been split to fit them on the page:

```
Subject: Mail delivery failed
  ${if eq{$sender_address}{$bounce_recipient}
  {: returning message to sender}}
****
This message was created automatically by mail delivery software (Exim).

A message
${if eq{$sender_address}{$bounce_recipient}{that you sent }{sent by

  <$sender_address>

}}could not be delivered to all of its recipients.
This is a permanent error. The following address(es) failed:
****
The following text was generated during the delivery attempt(s):
****
------ This is a copy of the message, including all the headers. ------
****
------ The body of the message is $message_size characters long; only
------ the first $return_size_limit or so are included here.
****
```

## 19.8.5 Customizing warning messages

The text of delay warning messages (those sent as a result of the `delay_warning` option) can be customized in a similar manner to bounce messages. You can set `warn_message_file` to the name of a template file, which in this case contains only three text sections:

- The first item is included in the header lines and should include at least a *Subject:* header line. Exim does not check the syntax of these lines.

- The second item forms the start of the warning message. After it, Exim lists the delayed addresses.

- The third item ends the message.

During the expansion of this file, *$warn_message_delay* is set to the delay time in one of the forms `<n>` `minutes` or `<n>` `hours`, and *$warn_message_recipients* contains a list of recipients for the warning message. There may be more than one if multiple recipient addresses have different `errors_to` settings on the routers that handled them. The default state is equivalent to the file:

```
Subject: Warning: message $message_id delayed $warn_message_delay
****
This message was created automatically by mail delivery software (Exim).

A message
${if eq{$sender_address}{$warn_message_recipients}{that you sent }
{sent by

  <$sender_address>

}}has not been delivered to all of its recipients after
more than $warn_message_delay on the queue on $primary_hostname.

The message identifier is:     $message_id
The subject of the message is: $h_subject
The date of the message is:    $h_date

The following address(es) have not yet been delivered:
****
No action is required on your part. Delivery attempts will continue for
some time, and this warning may be repeated at intervals if the message
remains undelivered. Eventually the mail delivery software will give up,
and when that happens, the message will be returned to you.
```

# 19.9 Miscellaneous controls

This section contains brief descriptions of some minor options that do not merit a section to themselves, but which may be of general interest. The Exim reference manual describes additional, minority-interest options.

`max_username_length` (integer, default = 0)

Some operating systems are broken in that they truncate the argument to *getpwnam()* (the function that reads information about a login name) to eight characters, instead of returning "no such user" for longer names. If this option is set to a value greater than zero, any attempt to call *getpwnam()* with an argument that is longer than its value behaves as if *getpwnam()* failed.

received_headers_max (integer, default = 30)

When a message is to be delivered, the number of *Received:* headers is counted. If it is greater than this parameter, a mail loop is assumed to have occurred, the delivery is abandoned, and an error message is generated.

smtp_banner (string, default = built-in)

This string, which is expanded every time it is used, is output as the initial positive response to an SMTP connection. The default setting is:

```
smtp_banner = $primary_hostname ESMTP Exim $version_number $tod_full
```

Failure to expand the string causes Exim to write to its panic log and exit immediately. If you want to create a multiline response to the initial SMTP connection, use \n in the string at appropriate points, but not at the end. Note that the 220 code is not included in this string. Exim adds it automatically (several times in the case of a multiline response).

smtp_receive_timeout (time, default = 5m)

This sets a timeout value for SMTP reception. If a line of input (either an SMTP command or a data line) is not received within this time, the SMTP connection is dropped and the message is abandoned. For non-SMTP input, reception timeout is controlled by receive_timeout.

# 20

# Command-line interface to Exim

Whenever Exim is called, it is passed options and arguments specifying what the caller wants it to do. Because you can call Exim from a shell in this way, this is called the *command-line interface*. In practice, most calls of Exim come directly from other programs such as MUAs, and do not involve an actual "command line". However, the options and arguments are the same.

Many command-line options are compatible with Sendmail, so Exim can be a drop-in replacement, but there are additional options specific to Exim. Some options can be used only when Exim is called by a privileged user, and these are noted in what follows.

The command-line options are many, but they can be divided into a number of functional groups as follows:

*Input mode control*

Options to start processes for receiving incoming messages

*Additional message data*

Options to supply information to be incorporated into an incoming message that is submitted locally

*Immediate delivery control*

Options to control whether a locally submitted message is delivered immediately on arrival, possibly depending on the type of recipient addresses

*Error routing*

Options to control how errors in a locally submitted message are reported

*Queue runner processes*

Options for starting queue runners and selecting which messages they process

*Configuration overrides*

Options for overriding the normal configuration file

*Watching Exim*

>   Options for inspecting messages on the queue

*Message control*

>   Options for forcing deliveries and doing other things to messages

*Testing*

>   Options for testing address handling, filter files, string expansion, and retry rules

*Debugging*

>   Options for debugging Exim and its configuration

*Internal*

>   Options that are only useful when one instance of Exim calls another

*Miscellaneous*

>   A few oddities

*Compatibility with Sendmail*

>   Options that are recognized because they are used by Sendmail, but which do
>   nothing useful in Exim

In this chapter, we discuss the options by functional group. You can find a complete
list of options in alphabetical order in the reference manual.

# 20.1 Input mode control

Four mutually exclusive options control the way messages are received.

## 20.1.1 Starting a daemon process

If -bd is specified, a daemon process is started in order to receive messages from
remote hosts over TCP/IP connections. It normally listens on the SMTP port (25),
but the -oX option can be used to specify a different port. For example:

```
exim -bd -oX 1225
```

starts up a daemon that listens on port 1225. This can be useful for some non-
standard applications, and also for testing Exim as a daemon without disturbing the
running mail service. A detailed discussion of the daemon was given earlier
(☞ 11.7). Only admin users are permitted to start daemon processes.

## 20.1.2 Interactive SMTP reception

If -bs is specified, a reception process that reads SMTP commands on its standard input and writes the responses to its standard output is started. This option can be used by any local process; however, if any messages are submitted during the SMTP session, the senders supplied in the MAIL commands are ignored unless the caller is trusted. The -bs option is also used to start up reception processes from *inetd* to receive mail from remote hosts as an alternative to using a daemon. The necessary entry in */etc/inetd.conf* should be along these lines:

```
smtp stream tcp nowait /usr/exim/bin/exim in.exim -bs
```

Exim can tell the difference between the two uses of -bs by inspecting its standard input. If there is an associated IP address, the input must be a socket and the process must have been started by *inetd*. In this case, sender addresses from MAIL commands are honoured.

The -os option can be used to set a timeout for receiving an SMTP message; this overrides the smtp_receive_timeout configuration option.

## 20.1.3 Batch SMTP reception

If -bS is specified, a reception process that reads SMTP commands on its standard input, but does not write any responses, is started. This is so-called "batch SMTP", which is really just another way of injecting messages in a non-interactive format. This is commonly used for messages received by other transport mechanisms, such as UUCP, or for messages that have been temporarily stored in files. Once again, the senders supplied in the MAIL commands are ignored unless the caller is trusted. More details about the handling of all forms of SMTP are given in chapter 13.

## 20.1.4 Non-SMTP reception

If -bm is specified, a reception process that reads the body of the message from the standard input and the list of recipients from the command's arguments is started. This option is assumed if no other conflicting options are present, so it is possible to inject a message by a simple command like:

```
exim theodora@byzantium.example
<message>
.
```

where *<message>* contains all the necessary RFC 2822 header lines, though Exim does add certain headers if they are missing. By default, the message is terminated either by end-of-file (which can be signalled from a terminal by typing CTRL-D) or by a line containing only a single dot, as shown here. The second form of termination is turned off if -i or -oi is present, and this should be used whenever messages of unknown content are submitted by this means. Otherwise, a line in the message that consists of a single dot causes the message to be truncated.

The -t option provides an alternative way of supplying the message's envelope recipients. If it is present, it implies -bm, but the recipients are taken from the *To:*, *Cc:*, and *Bcc:* header lines instead of from the command arguments. Any *Bcc:* header lines are then removed from the message. For example:

```
exim -t
From: caesar@rome.example
To: theodora@byzantium.example
Bcc: cleopatra@cairo.example
...
```

submits a message to be delivered to *theodora@byzantium.example* and to *cleopatra@cairo.example*; neither copy will contain the *Bcc:* line. This is the only circumstance in which Exim removes *Bcc:* lines. If they are present in messages received through other interfaces, they are left intact.

If addresses are supplied as command arguments when -t is used, there are two possibilities: they can be added to or subtracted from the list of addresses obtained from the header lines. By default, Exim follows the behaviour that is documented for many versions of Sendmail; it subtracts them from the list. Furthermore, if one of the other addresses subsequently generates one of the argument addresses as a result of aliasing or forwarding, it is also discarded. For example:

```
exim -t brutus@rome.example
From: caesar@rome.example
To: anthony@rome.example
Cc: senate-list@rome.example
...
```

submits a message that is not delivered to *brutus@rome.example*, even if that address appears in the expansion of *senate-list*. Of course, this works only if aliases are expanded on the same host; if the message is dispatched to another host with the address *senate-list@rome.example* intact, the exception is lost. The feature therefore seems to be of little use.

In practice, a number of versions of Sendmail do not follow the documentation. Instead, they add argument addresses to the recipients list. Exim can be made to behave in this way by setting:

```
extract_addresses_remove_arguments = false
```

in its configuration file. When this is done, argument addresses that do not also appear in *To:* or *Cc:* headers behave like additional *Bcc:* recipients.

Exim expects that messages submitted using -bm or -t contain lines terminated by a single linefeed character, according to the normal Unix convention, and most user agents that use the interface conform to this usage. However, there are some programs that supply lines terminated by two characters, carriage return and linefeed (CRLF), as if in an SMTP session. To cope with these maverick cases, Exim supports the -dropcr option. When this is set, any carriage return character that immediately precedes a linefeed in the input is dropped.

The -or option can be used to set a timeout for receiving a non-SMTP message; this overrides the receive_timeout configuration option. If no timeout is set, Exim waits forever for data on the standard input.

### 20.1.5 Summary of reception options

The options used to control the way in which reception processes operate are summarized in table 20-1.

*Table 20-1: Input mode options*

| Option | Meaning |
|--------|---------|
| -bd | Start listening daemon |
| -bs | SMTP on stdin and stdout, from local process or via *inetd* |
| -bS | Batch SMTP from local process |
| -bm | Message on standard input, recipients as arguments |
| -t | Message on standard input, recipients from header lines |
| -dropcr | Drop carriage return characters |
| -or | Set non-SMTP timeout |
| -os | Set SMTP timeout |

# 20.2 Additional message data

Several options provide additional data to be incorporated into a message received from a local process (that is, not over TCP/IP).

### 20.2.1 Sender address

The -f option supplies a sender address to override the address computed from the caller's login name, but only if the caller is a trusted user. For example, on a host whose default mail domain is *elysium.example*, if a *root* process obeys:

```
exim -f zeus@olympus.example apollo@olympus.example
```

the envelope sender of the message is set to *zeus@olympus.example* instead of *root@elysium.example* because *root* is always a trusted user. The -f option is ignored by default for non-trusted users, but the untrusted_set_sender option can be used to relax this restriction (☞ 19.3.1).

Even when this option is not set, untrusted callers are always permitted to use one special form of -f. A call of the form:

```
exim -f '<>' apollo@olympus.example
```

specifies an empty envelope sender for the message.[1] Empty envelope senders are used as a way of identifying messages that must never give rise to bounce messages. This usage is prescribed in the RFCs for bounce messages themselves, and it has also been adopted for other kinds of message, such as delivery delay warnings. If a non-trusted user calls Exim in this way, the -f option is honoured in that the envelope sender is emptied, but unless local_from_check is set false, there is still a comparison of the real sender with the contents of the *From:* header, and a *Sender:* header line is added if necessary. This does not happen if the caller is trusted.

If a -f option is present on the command line, it overrides any sender information obtained from an initial From line at the start of the message.

## 20.2.2 Sender name

When Exim constructs a *Sender:* header, or a *From:* header (which it does if one is missing) for a local sender, it reads the system's password information to obtain the caller's real name from the so-called "gecos" field, leading to lines of the form:

```
Sender: The Boss <zeus@olympus.example>
```

The username part of this (The Boss) can be overridden by means of the -F command-line option, for example:

```
exim -F 'The Big Cheese' apollo@olympus.example
```

Because users are normally permitted to change the values of their gecos fields in the password information, this option is not restricted to trusted users.

## 20.2.3 Remote host information

There are a number of options starting with -oM that trusted users can use when submitting a message locally to set values that are normally obtained from an incoming SMTP connection. The message then has the characteristics of one that was received from a remote host. These options are as follows:

- -oMa sets the field that contains the IP address of the remote host.

- -oMaa sets the field that contains the authenticator name, making the message appear to have arrived over an authenticated connection.

- -oMai sets the authenticated id value.

---

[1]  The angle brackets < > are quoted to make this a valid shell command line.

- `-oMas` sets the authenticated sender value.

- `-oMi` sets the field that holds the IP address of the interface on the local host that was used to receive the message.

- `-oMr` sets the protocol used to receive the message. This value is useful for logging and for identifying messages from specific local sources such as mailing list managers or virus checkers; there is no restriction on what it may contain. An example of the use of `-oMr` was shown earlier (☞ 5.10.1).

- `-oMs` sets the field that holds the verified name of the remote host.

- `-oMt` sets the field that holds the identification string obtained by an RFC 1413 (ident) callback to the sending host.

If any of these options are used by a non-trusted caller, or for SMTP input over TCP/IP, they are ignored, except that a non-trusted caller is permitted to use them in conjunction with the `-bh`, `-bf`, and `-bF` options, for testing host checks and filter files.

Apart from testing, the `-oM` options are useful when submitting mail received from remote hosts by some non-SMTP protocol. Suppose a batch of mail has been received by UUCP from the host *fleeting.example*, whose IP address is 192.168.23.45, and stored in batch SMTP format in a file called */etc/uucp/received*. This could be passed to Exim by a trusted user running the command:

```
exim -bS -oMa 192.168.23.45 -oMs fleeting.example \
   -oMr uucp < /etc/uucp/received
```

The log entries and the *Received:* header line that is added to every message would show the values supplied by the `-oM` options.

# 20.3 Immediate delivery control

These options control what happens to a message immediately after it has been received; specifically, whether a delivery process is started for it or not. They are rarely needed except for testing.

The `-odb` option applies to all modes in which Exim accepts incoming messages, including the listening daemon. It requests "background" delivery of such messages, which means that the accepting process automatically starts a delivery process for each message received, but Exim does not wait for such processes to complete (they carry on running "in the background"). This is the default action if none of the `-od` options are present.

The -odf and -odi options, which are synonymous,[1] request "foreground" (synchronous) delivery when Exim has accepted a locally generated message.[2] For each message received on the standard input, Exim creates a new delivery process, but waits for it to complete before proceeding. The effect is that the original reception process does not finish until the delivery attempt does.

The -odq option applies to all modes in which Exim accepts incoming messages, including the listening daemon. It specifies that the accepting process should not automatically start a delivery attempt for each message received. Messages are placed on the queue and remain there until a subsequent queue runner process encounters them. The queue_only configuration option has the same effect.

In contrast, if -odqs is set, recipient addresses are processed and local deliveries are done in the normal way. However, if any SMTP deliveries are required, they are not done at this time. Such messages remain on the queue until a subsequent queue runner process encounters them. Because routing was done, Exim knows which messages are waiting for which hosts, so if there are a number of messages destined for the same host, they are sent in a single SMTP connection. The queue_smtp_domains option has the same effect for specific domains. See also the -qq option (☞ 20.5.4).

# 20.4 Error routing

If Exim detects an error while receiving a non-SMTP message (for example, a malformed recipient address), it can report the problem either by writing a message on the standard error file or by sending a mail message to the sender. Which of these two actions it takes is controlled by the following options:

- If -oem is set, the error is reported by sending a message. The return code from Exim is 2 if the error was that the original message had no recipients, or 1 otherwise. This is the default action if none of these options are given.

- If -oee is set, the error is again reported by sending a message, but this time the return code from Exim is zero if the error message was successfully sent. If sending an error message fails, the return code is as for -oem.

- If -oep is set, the error is reported by writing a message to the standard error stream and giving a return code of 1.

Errors are handled in a special way for batch SMTP input (☞ 13.5).

---

[1]  -odf is compatible with Smail 3; -odi is compatible with Sendmail.

[2]  If given for a daemon process, these are the same as -odb.

If there is a problem with the sender address, which can only happen when it is supplied via the -f option, an error message is written to the standard error stream, independently of the setting of these options.

# 20.5 Queue runner processes

Queue runner processes are normally started periodically by the daemon, or by a *cron* job if you are not using a daemon. They can also be started manually by an admin user, if necessary. For example, the command:

```
exim -q
```

creates a single queue runner process that scans the queue once. This is the command that a daemon issues whenever it is time to start a queue runner.

## 20.5.1 Initial deliveries only

A queue runner can be restricted to those messages that have not previously been tried by adding the letter i (for "initial delivery") after -q. This is useful only in special configurations where messages are placed on the queue without an automatic delivery attempt (for example, by setting the queue_only option true).

## 20.5.2 Overriding retry times and freezing

A normal queue runner processes only unfrozen messages and addresses whose retry times have been reached. Additional letters can be added to -q to change this. If a single f follows -q, delivery attempts are forced for all addresses (whether or not they have reached their retry times), but frozen messages are still skipped. However, if ff follows -q, frozen messages are automatically thawed and included in the processing. Thus:

```
exim -qff
```

ensures that a delivery attempt is made for every address in every message.

## 20.5.3 Local deliveries only

A queue runner can be restricted to local deliveries only by adding the letter l (ell), following f or ff, if present. Thus:

```
exim -qfl
```

processes all unfrozen messages, and does local deliveries, but skips remote deliveries.

456                                    Chapter 20: Command-line interface to Exim

## 20.5.4 Two-pass processing for remote addresses

In a conventional queue run, each message is processed only once. If a number of messages have remote addresses that route to the same host and none of them have previously been processed, each is sent in a separate SMTP connection. This circumstance is quite common in some configurations, such as a host that is connected to the Internet only intermittently (☞ 12.12.2).

For better performance, it is desirable that Exim should know that it has several messages for the same host, so that they can be sent in a single SMTP connection. If any of the -q options is specified with an additional q (for example, -qqff), the resulting queue run is done in two stages. In the first stage, remote addresses are routed, but no transportation is done. The database that remembers which messages are waiting for specific hosts is updated, as if delivery to those hosts had been deferred. When this is complete, a second, normal queue scan happens, and normal routing and delivery takes place. Messages that are routed to the same host are delivered down a single SMTP connection because of the hints that were set up during the first queue scan.

## 20.5.5 Periodic queue runs

On most installations, queue runner processes should be started at regular intervals. You can request that an Exim daemon do this job by following -q with a time value. For example:

```
exim -q20m
```

creates a daemon that starts a queue runner process every 20 minutes (and does nothing else). This form of the -q option is usually combined with -bd in order to start a single daemon that listens for incoming SMTP as well as periodically starting queue runners. For example:

```
exim -bd -q30m
```

In practice, the command that starts this kind of daemon is usually the standard one that appears in the operating system's boot scripts, which refer to */usr/sbin/sendmail* or */usr/lib/sendmail*. Usually, such scripts are able to start up Exim instead, without needing modification, provided that the Sendmail path has been symbolically linked to the Exim binary.

You can, if you wish, use a time value with any of the variants of -q discussed so far, for example:

```
exim -qff4h
```

forces a delivery attempt of every address on the queue every four hours.

## 20.5.6 Processing specific messages

By default, a queue runner process scans the entire queue of messages in an unpredicatable order. Sometimes you may want to do a queue run that looks at only the most recently arrived messages on the queue. For example, you might learn that a host that has been offline for a few hours is now working again, but you also know that the older messages are for a host that is still down.

If you follow -q (or -qf, and so on) with a message ID, as in the following example, all messages whose IDs are lexically less are skipped:

```
exim -qf 0t5C6f-0000c8-00
```

Because message IDs start with the time of arrival, this skips any messages that arrived before 0t5C6f-0000c8-00. If a second message ID is given, messages whose IDs are greater than it are skipped. However, the queue is still processed in an arbitrary order.

## 20.5.7 Processing specific addresses

A queue runner process can be instructed to process only those messages whose senders or recipients match a particular pattern. The -S and -R options specify patterns for the sender and recipients, respectively. If both -S and -R are specified, both must be satisfied. In the case of -R, a message is selected as long as at least one of its undelivered recipients matches. For example:

```
exim -R zalamea.example
```

starts a delivery process for any message with an undelivered address that contains *zalamea.example*. It is a straightforward textual check; the string may be found in the local part or in the domain (or in both, if it contains an @).

If you want to use a more complicated pattern, you can specify that the string you supply is a regular expression, by following -R or -S by the letter r For example:

```
exim -Rr '(major|minor)\.zalamea\.example$'
```

selects messages that contain an undelivered address that ends with major. zalamea.example or minor.zalamea.example.

Once a message is selected for delivery, a normal delivery process is started and all the recipients are processed, not just those that matched -R. For the first selected message, Exim overrides any retry information and forces a delivery attempt for each undelivered address. If -S or -R is followed by f or ff, the forcing applies to all selected messages; in the case of ff, frozen messages are also included.

The -R option makes it straightforward to initiate delivery of all messages to a given domain after a host has been down for some time.

## 20.5.8 Summary of queue runner options

The options for queue runner processes are summarized in table 20-2.

*Table 20-2: Queue runner options*

| Option | Meaning |
|--------|---------|
| -q | Normal queue runner |
| -qf | Queue run with forced deliveries |
| -qff | Forced deliveries and frozen messages |
| -ql | Local deliveries only |
| -qfl | Forced local deliveries |
| -qffl | As -qfl, but include frozen messages |
| -R | Select on recipient, literal string |
| -Rf | Ditto, with forcing |
| -Rff | Ditto, with forcing and frozen messages |
| -Rr | Select on recipient, regular expression |
| -Rrf | Ditto, with forcing |
| -Rrff | Ditto, with forcing and frozen messages |
| -S | Select on sender, literal string |
| -Sf | Ditto, with forcing |
| -Sff | Ditto, with forcing and frozen messages |
| -Sr | Select on sender, regular expression |
| -Srf | Ditto, with forcing |
| -Srff | Ditto, with forcing and frozen messages |

Any of the -q... options can be given as -qq... to cause a two-stage queue run, and any of them may also be followed by a time, in order to set up a daemon that periodically repeats the queue run with the same option.

# 20.6 Configuration overrides

The name of Exim's runtime configuration file is defined in the build-time configuration and embedded in the binary. This is necessary because Exim is normally a setuid program with *root* privilege that can be called by any process. Allowing the use of arbitrary runtime configurations would be a huge security exposure. However, it is sometimes useful to be able to use an alternative configuration file or to vary the contents of the standard file, either for testing or for some special purpose.

The name of the runtime configuration file can be changed by means of the -C option:

```
exim -C /etc/exim/alt.config ...
```

If the caller is not *root* or the Exim user and the filename is different to the built-in name, Exim immediately gives up its *root* privilege permanently and runs as the calling user.

The runtime configuration file can contain macro definitions (☞ 4.3.5). Their values can be overridden by means of the -D option, for example:

```
exim -DLOG_SELECTOR=+filter ...
```

but again, unless the caller is *root* or the Exim user, Exim gives up its root privilege when this option is used. The -D option can be repeated up to ten times in a command line.

# 20.7 Watching Exim's queue

Admin users can use the next set of options to inspect the contents of Exim's queue. If you have access to an X Window server, an alternative way of looking at this information is to run the Exim monitor (*eximon*). However, anything that *eximon* can do can also be done from the command line.

The -bpc option outputs a single number, which is the count of messages on the queue. The -bp option outputs a complete list. Each message is displayed as in this example:

```
25m  2.9K  0t5C6f-0000c8-00 <caesar@rome.example>
             brutus@rome.example
             ...
```

The first line shows the length of time the message has been on the queue (in this case, 25 minutes), the size (2.9 KB), the local ID, and the envelope sender. For bounce messages that have no sender, <> appears here. The remaining lines contain the envelope recipients, one per line. Those to whom the message has already been delivered are marked with the letter D; in the case of an address that is expanded by aliasing or forwarding, this happens only when deliveries to all its children are complete.

If -bpu is used instead of -bp, only undelivered addresses are shown. If -bpa is used, delivered addresses that were generated from the original addresses are added. If -bpr is used, the output is not sorted into chronological order of message arrival. This can speed things up if there are many messages on the queue, and is particularly useful if the output is going to be postprocessed in a way that does not require sorting. You can also use -bpra and -bpru, which act like -bpa and -bpu, but again without sorting.

# 20.8 Message control

There is a set of options, all beginning with -M, that permit admin users to inspect the contents of messages that are on the queue and perform certain actions on them.

## 20.8.1 Operations on a list of messages

The options described in this section can all take a list of message IDs as arguments; the action is performed on each message that is not in the process of being delivered. For example:

```
exim -M 123H3N-0003mY-00 0t5C6f-0000c8-00
```

-M creates a delivery process for each message in turn, thawing it first if necessary. During delivery, retry times are overridden and options such as queue_domains and hold_domains are ignored. In other words, Exim carries out a delivery attempt for every undelivered recipient. This is often called "forcing message delivery".

-Mf and -Mt freeze and thaw messages, respectively. When -Mt has been applied to a message, the condition manually_thawed is true in an Exim filter.

-Mg and -Mrm both cause messages to be abandoned. The difference between them is that -Mg (g stands for "give up") fails each address with the error "delivery cancelled by administrator", and generates a bounce message to the sender, whereas -Mrm just removes messages from the spool without sending bounces.

If a delivery process is already working on a message, none of these options has any effect and an error message is output. Actions other than -M are logged in the main log, along with the identity of the admin user who requested them.

## 20.8.2 Inspecting a queued message

The contents of a message's spool files can be inspected by an admin user; the options -Mvb, -Mvh, and -Mvl, followed by a message ID, output the body (-D file), header (-H file) or message log file, respectively. For example:

```
exim -Mvl 123H3N-0003mY-00
```

shows the message log for message 123H3N-0003mY-00.

## 20.8.3 Modifying a queued message

The options described in this section allow an admin user to modify a message on the queue, provided that it is not in the process of being delivered. They all require a message ID as their first argument; some of them need additional data as well.

The recipients of a message can be changed by -Mar, -Mmd, and -Mmad. The first of these adds an additional recipient. For example:

```
exim -Mar 123H3N-0003mY-00 extra@xyz.example
```

adds the recipient *extra@xyz.example* to message 123H3N-0003mY-00. There is no way to remove recipients, but Exim can be told to pretend that it has delivered to them. The command:

```
exim -Mmad 123H3N-0003mY-00
```

marks all recipient addresses as delivered, whereas:

```
exim -Mmd 123H3N-0003mY-00 godot@waiting.example
```

marks just the address *godot@waiting.example* as delivered. If you need to divert a message to one or more new recipients, perhaps because the original addresses are known to be invalid, the safe way to do it is as follows:

- Freeze the message using -Mf to ensure that no Exim process tries to deliver it while you are working on it.

- Use -Mmad to mark all the existing recipients as delivered, or use -Mmd to do that to certain recipients only.

- Use -Mar as many times as necessary to add new recipients.

- Thaw the message using -Mt, or force a delivery with -M.

You can also change the envelope sender of a message using the -Mes option. For example:

```
exim -Mes 123H3N-0003mY-00 newsender@new.domain.example
```

To remove the sender altogether (that is, to make the message look like a bounce message), the new sender may be specified as <>.

### 20.8.4 Summary of message control options

The options for message control are summarized in table 20-3.

# 20.9 Testing options

There are a number of options to help you test out Exim and its configuration, or to find out why it did what it did. Sometimes the options in the next section (☞ 20.10) can be helpful too.

### 20.9.1 Testing the configuration settings

If you want to be sure that the Exim binary is usable and that it can successfully read its configuration file, run:

```
exim -bV
```

*Table 20-3: Message control options*

| Option | Meaning |
|--------|---------|
| -M     | Force delivery |
| -Mar   | Add recipient |
| -Mes   | Edit sender |
| -Mf    | Freeze |
| -Mg    | Give up (bounce) |
| -Mmad  | Mark all delivered |
| -Mmd   | Mark delivered |
| -Mrm   | Remove message (no bounce) |
| -Mt    | Thaw |
| -Mvb   | View message body |
| -Mvh   | View message header |
| -Mvl   | View message log |

Exim writes its version number, compilation number, and compilation date to the standard output, reads its configuration file, and exits successfully if no problems are encountered. Errors in the configuration file cause messages to be written to the standard error stream.

You can also check what it has read from the configuration file. If -bP is given with no arguments, it causes the values of all Exim's main configuration options to be written to the standard output. However, if any of the option settings are preceded by the word hide, their values are shown only to admin users. You should use hide when you place sensitive information, such as passwords for access to databases, in the configuration file.

The values of one or more specific options can be requested by giving their names as arguments, for example:

```
exim -bP qualify_domain hold_domains
```

The name of the configuration file can be requested as follows:

```
exim -bP configure_file
```

Configuration settings for individual drivers can be obtained by specifying one of the words router, transport, or authenticator, followed by the name of an appropriate driver instance. For example:

```
exim -bP transport local_delivery
```

The generic driver options are output first, followed by the driver's private options. A complete list of all drivers of a particular type, with their option settings, can be obtained by using `routers`, `transports`, or `authenticators`. For example:

```
exim -bP authenticators
```

Finally, a list of the names of drivers of a particular type can be obtained by using one of the words `router_list`, `transport_list`, or `authenticator_list`. For example:

```
exim -bP router_list
```

might output:

```
dnslookup
system_aliases
cancelled_users
real_localuser
userforward
localuser
```

## 20.9.2 Testing routing

In most common cases, it is not necessary to send a message to find out how Exim would route a particular address; the `-bt` option does this for you. For example:

```
$ exim -bt ph10@exim.example
ph10@exim.example
  deliver to ph10@exim.example
  router = dnslookup, transport = remote_smtp
  host ppsw.exim.example   [10.111.8.38]    MX=7
  host ppsw.exim.example   [10.111.8.40]    MX=7
```

This tells you that the **dnslookup** router was the one that handled the address, routing it to the **remote_smtp** transport with the given host list. For more information about how this outcome was reached, you can set debugging options (☞ 20.10).

The `-bv` and `-bvs` options allow you to check what Exim would do when verifying a recipient or a sender address, respectively, as opposed to processing the address for delivery. If you have not used options that cause routers to behave differently when verifying (for example, `verify_only`), the result is the same as for `-bt`. There is a difference between `-bv` and `-bvs` only if you have set `verify_sender` or `verify_recipient` on a router, in order to make a distinction between these two cases.

There is one shortcoming of all these address tests. If you set up a configuration so that the routing process makes use of data from within a message that is being delivered, this cannot be simulated in the absence of a message. For example, suppose you want to send all output from your mailing lists to a central server that has plenty of disk for holding a large queue (because deliveries to a large list can take some time), but you want to deliver other messages directly to their destinations. You can identify mailing list messages by the fact that they contain the header line:

```
Precedence: list
```

Configuring Exim to do this is straightforward, using a router of this kind:

```
list_to_server:
  driver = manualroute
  condition = ${if eq {$h_precedence:}{list}{yes}{no}}
  transport = remote_smtp
  route_list = * server.name.example
```

However, when you use -bt to test addresses, this router is never run because the condition never matches. See the description of -N (☞ 20.10.1) for an alternative approach to testing that could be more useful here.

## 20.9.3 Testing incoming connections

If you set up verification and rejection policies for use when mail is received from other hosts, following through exactly how the checks are going to be applied can sometimes be quite tricky. The -bh option is there to help you. You specify an IP address, and Exim runs a fake SMTP session, as if it had received a connection from that address. While it is doing so, it outputs comments about the checks that it is applying, so you can see what is happening. You can go through the entire SMTP dialogue if you want to; if you want to check on relay controls, you have to proceed at least as far as the RCPT commands.[1]

Nothing is written to the log files and no data is written to Exim's spool directory. This is all totally fake, and is purely for the purpose of testing. Here is a transcript of part of a testing session, interspersed with comments:

```
$ exim -bh 192.203.178.4
```

This command starts up a fake SMTP session, as if a connection from 192.203.178.4 has been received.

```
**** SMTP testing session as if from host 192.203.178.4
**** but without any ident (RFC 1413) callback.
**** This is not for real!
```

Exim is reminding you that this is all make-believe. RFC 1413 callbacks cannot be done, because there is no real TCP/IP connection.

```
>>> host in host_lookup? yes (end of list)
```

---

[1] If all you are interested in is whether a particular recipient address is accepted or rejected, you can use the *exim_checkaccess* utility command, which is a "packaged" version of the -bh test (☞ 21.8).

Exim checks to see if the calling host matches anything in the `host_lookup` option. The answer is "yes", but what it has matched is the end of the list. How can this be? The final item in `host_lookup` must have been a negative item (starting with an exclamation mark). When this is the case, reaching the end of the list yields "yes" rather than "no".

```
>>> looking up host name for 192.203.178.4
>>> IP address lookup yielded dul.crynwr.com
```

Because the IP address matched `host_lookup`, Exim did a reverse DNS lookup to find the host name, and what it found was *dul.crynwr.com*. This is a test host that is guaranteed to be on the MAPS DUL (dial-up user list), so that people can test their configurations.

```
>>> host in host_reject_connection? no (option unset)
```

Another configuration option is checked; it is unset, so the host does not match. Several other similar options are checked at this point.

```
220 libra.test.example ESMTP Exim 4.10 ...
```

Exim has now finished its preliminary testing, and this is the initial response it would send to the remote host. You now have to play the part of the client by typing SMTP commands, the first of which should be HELO or EHLO:

```
helo dul.crynwr.com
250 libra.test.example Hello dul.crynwr.com [192.203.178.4]
```

After a successful HELO (or EHLO) you can try passing a message to Exim, using the MAIL, RCPT, and DATA commands. However, any messages that are "accepted" are discarded. During the message transaction, Exim outputs comments about the checks it performs on the addresses and gives the appropriate responses. You can end the testing session with the QUIT command, or by breaking out using CTRL-C.

## 20.9.4 Testing retry rules

You can check which retry rule will be used for a particular address by means of the `-brt` option, which must be followed by at least one argument. Exim outputs the applicable retry rule. For example:

```
$ exim -brt bach.comp.example
Retry rule: *.comp.example  F,2h,15m; F,4d,30m;
```

The argument can be a complete email address or just a domain name. Another domain name can be given as an optional second argument; if no retry rule is found for the first argument, the second is tried. This ties in with Exim's behaviour when looking for retry rules for remote hosts. If no rule is found that matches the host, one that matches the mail domain is sought.

A third optional argument, the name of a specific delivery error, may also be given. So the following:

```
exim -brt host.comp.example comp.example timeout_connect
```

asks the question "Which retry rule will be used if a connection to the host *host.comp.example* times out while attempting to deliver a message with a recipient in the *comp.example* domain?"

## 20.9.5 Testing rewriting rules

The -brw option for testing address rewriting rules is described in section 15.8.

## 20.9.6 Testing filter files

The -bf and -bF options for testing user and system filters are described in section 10.5.

## 20.9.7 Testing string expansion

The -be option for testing string expansions is described in section 17.16.

# 20.10 Options for debugging

It is helpful, both to its author and to its users, if a complicated program like Exim can output information about what it is doing, to make it easier to track down problems. Any user can ask Exim to write minimal tracing information to the standard error stream by setting the -v option. If any SMTP message deliveries are involved, the SMTP dialogue is shown.

Admin users can request more detailed information by setting -d. When this option is given on its own, a large amount of standard debugging data is output. This can be reduced, or increased to include some more rarely needed information, by following -d with a string made up of names preceded by plus or minus characters. These add or remove sets of debugging data, respectively. For example, -d+filter adds filter debugging, whereas -d-all+filter selects only filter debugging. The available debugging categories are shown in table 20-4.

Unfortunately, the DNS resolver writes its debugging output to the standard output rather than the standard error stream.

The default (-d with no argument) omits expand, filter, interface, load, local_scan, memory, pid, timestamp, and resolver. However, if a daemon is started with debugging turned on, pid is forced, to ensure that the different subprocesses can be distinguished.

*Table 20-4: Debugging selectors*

| Selector | Show debug information for |
|---|---|
| acl | ACL interpretation |
| auth | Authenticators |
| deliver | General delivery logic |
| dns | DNS lookups (see also resolver) |
| dnsbl | DNS black list code |
| exec | Arguments for *execv()* calls |
| expand | Details of string expansion |
| filter | Filter handling |
| hints_lookup | Hints data lookups |
| host_lookup | All types of name-to-IP address handling |
| ident | RFC 1413 (ident) lookups |
| interface | Lists of local interfaces |
| lists | Matching things in lists |
| load | System load checks |
| local_scan | Debugging in the *local_scan()* function |
| lookup | General lookup code and all lookups |
| memory | Memory handling |
| process_info | Setting info for the process log |
| queue_run | Queue runs |
| pid | Add pid (process id) to debug lines |
| receive | General message reception logic |
| resolver | The DNS resolver's debugging output |
| retry | Retry handling |
| rewrite | Address rewriting |
| route | Address routing |
| timestamp | Timestamp debug lines |
| tls | TLS logic |
| transport | Transports |
| uid | Changes of uid/gid and looking up uid/gid |
| verify | Address verification logic |
| all | All of the above, and also -v output |

The debugging output is designed primarily to help Exim's author track down problems, but much of it should be understandable by most administrators. In particular, if you turn on debugging in conjunction with -bt or when delivering a message, you can track the flow of control through the various routers as an address is processed. If the debug_print option is set in any router or transport, it produces output whenever any debugging is selected, or if -v is used.

### 20.10.1 Suppressing delivery

In the discussion of -bt and -bv (☞ 20.9.2), it was pointed out that they cannot be used to test any address processing that involves the contents of a message. One way this can be tested is to use the -N option. This is a debugging option that inhibits delivery of a message at the transport level. It implies -v, but higher levels of debugging output can be requested if needed. Exim goes through many of the motions of delivery but does not actually transport the message. Instead, it behaves as if it had successfully done so. However, it does not make any updates to the retry database, and the log entries for deliveries are flagged with *> instead of =>.

Once -N has been used on a message, it can never be delivered normally. If the original delivery is deferred, subsequent delivery attempts are automatically done with -N.

Because -N throws away mail, only *root* and the Exim user are allowed to use it in conjunction with -bd, -q, -R, or -M (that is, to "deliver" arbitrary messages in this way). Any other user can use -N only when supplying an incoming message.

## 20.11 Terminating the options

There is a special option whose name consists of two hyphens. Its only purpose is to terminate the options, and therefore to cause subsequent command-line items to be treated as arguments rather than options, even if they begin with a hyphen. It is possible (though unlikely) for the local part of an email address to begin with a hyphen; to send a message to such an address, you would need to call Exim like this:

```
exim -- -oddname@wherever.example
```

## 20.12 Embedded Perl options

The -pd and -ps options, which control the way an embedded Perl interpreter is initialized, are described in section 17.14.2.

## 20.13 Compatibility with Sendmail

Many of Exim's command-line options are directly compatible with Sendmail, so that Exim can be installed as a "drop-in" replacement. However, because Exim's design is different, some Sendmail options are not relevant, or operate in a different way in

Exim. Sendmail also has a number of obsolete options and synonyms that still seem to be used by some older MUAs.

- The following options are recognized by Exim, but do nothing: -B, -G, -h, -n, -m, -om, -oo, -U, and -x.

- Any option that begins with -e is treated as a synonym for the corresponding option that begins -oe.

- -i and -oitrue are synonyms for -oi.

- -oeq is synonymous with -oep and -oew is synonymous with -oem.

- -ov is synonymous with -v.

- -qR and -qS are synonyms for -R and -S, respectively.

- -r is a synonym for -f.

Sendmail interprets a call with the -bi option as a request to rebuild its alias file, and there is often a command called *newaliases* whose action is something like "rebuild the data base for the mail aliases file".

Exim does not have the concept of *the* alias file; you can configure as many aliasing routers as you like, though in practice just one is most common. "Rebuilding" may be relevant if you are using a DBM or *cdb* file for aliases, but not if you are using NIS or a database such as MySQL.

Scripts that are run when the system boots (or at other times) may call *newaliases* or */usr/sbin/sendmail* with the -bi option. Exim does nothing if called with -bi, unless you specify:

```
bi_command = /the/path/to/some/command
```

in which case it runs the given command, under the uid and gid of the caller of Exim. The value of bi_command is just a command name with no arguments. If an argument is required, it must be given by the -oA option on the command line.

## 20.14 Calling Exim by different names

There are some fairly common command names that are used by other MTAs for performing various mail actions. If you are running Exim, the actions can be requested by means of command-line options, and it would be possible to use shell scripts to set this up. However, there is an easier way. If you call the Exim binary under certain other names, by means of symbolic links, it assumes specific options. The supported names are:

*mailq*

> This name assumes the -bp option, which causes Exim to list the contents of the
> queue.

*rsmtp*

> This name assumes the -bS option, which causes Exim to read batch SMTP from
> the standard input (this is for Smail compatibility).

*rmail*

> This name assumes the -i and -oee options; the former turns off the recognition
> of a single dot as a message terminator, and the latter changes the handling of
> errors that are detected on input. The name *rmail* is used by some UUCP systems.

*runq*

> This name assumes -q and causes a single queue run (this is for Smail
> compatibility).

None of these alternative names are set up by the standard installation scripts. If you
want to use them, you must create the symbolic links yourself.

# 21

# Administering Exim

Once Exim is up and running, there are a few things that must be done regularly to ensure that it keeps on handling your mail the way you want it to. How much regular attention it needs very much depends on the nature of your installation and the volume of mail you are handling.

One thing you might want to do is to watch what Exim is actually in the process of doing or what it has just done. You can check up on Exim processes using the *exiwhat* utility and you can read the log files directly, or use the Exim monitor to display a rolling main log. A utility script called *exigrep* provides a packaged way of extracting log entries for messages that match a given pattern.

Log files can become very large; normally they are "cycled" on a regular (usually daily) basis so that logs for previous days can be compressed. Some operating systems have standard procedures for cycling log files; for those that do not, a utility script called *exicyclog* is provided.

In this chapter, we describe Exim's logging mechanism, the format of the entries that are written when messages are received or delivered, and the options you can use to control what is logged. The available utilities for extracting and displaying log information are also described. After that, the facilities for finding out what Exim processes are doing are covered, including use of the Exim monitor, which is an X11 application for Exim administration. Finally, there is a discussion of the maintenance needs of alias and other files, hints databases, and user mailboxes.

## 21.1 Log files

Exim writes three different logs, referred to as the *main*, *reject*, and *panic* logs.

- The main log records the arrival of each message and each delivery in a single logical line in each case. The format is as compact as possible in an attempt to keep down the size of log files. Two-character flag sequences make it easy to pick out these lines. A number of other events are also recorded in the main log, some of which are conditional on the setting of the log_selector option (☞ 21.2.2).

- The reject log records information about addresses and messages that are rejected for policy reasons. Most of its contents are copies of lines that are also written to the main log; having a separate copy makes it easier to check how your rejection policies are working. However, if a message's header has been read at the time a line is written to the reject log, the header is copied to the reject (but not the main) log.

• An entry is written to the panic log when Exim suffers a disastrous error (such as a syntax error in its configuration file). Often (but not always) it bombs out afterwards. When all is going well, the panic log should be empty. You should check its contents regularly, in order to pick up any problems.[1] If Exim cannot open a panic log file, it tries as a last resort to write to the system log (*syslog*).

In addition to these three log files, Exim normally writes a log file for each message it handles. The names of these per-message logs are the message IDs, and they are kept in the *msglog* subdirectory of the spool directory. The contents of the message log are a copy of the main log's delivery entries for the message in question, though repeated "retry time not reached" messages are omitted. These files are written to make it easy for the administrator to find the history of what has happened to a particular message. Unless `preserve_message_logs` is set, a message log is deleted when the message to which it refers is complete.

The use of message logs can be disabled by setting the `message_logs` option to be false. This reduces the amount of disk I/O, which should improve performance on busy, disk-limited systems.

## 21.2 Log destination control

Exim's logs may be written to local files, to *syslog*, or to both. However, it should be noted that many *syslog* implementations use UDP as a transport. They are therefore unreliable in the sense that messages are not guaranteed to arrive at the log host, nor is the ordering of messages necessarily maintained.[2]

The destination for Exim's logs can be configured when the binary is built, or by setting `log_file_path` in the runtime configuration. This latter string is expanded so it can contain, for example, references to the host name:

```
log_file_path = /var/log/$primary_hostname/exim_%slog
```

It is generally advisable, however, for the log destination to be included in the binary rather than setting it at runtime because then the setting is available right from the start of Exim's execution. Otherwise, if there is something it wants to log before it has read the configuration file (for example, an error in the configuration file), it will not use the path you want, and may not be able to log at all.

---

[1]  For example, you could set up a *cron* job to mail you if it finds a non-empty panic log.

[2]  It has also been reported that for large log files (tens of megabytes), you may need to tweak *syslog* to prevent it from syncing the file with each write; on Linux, this has been seen to make *syslog* take over 90% of CPU time.

The value of `log_file_path` is a colon-separated list, currently limited to two items at most.[1] If an item is `syslog`, then *syslog* is used; otherwise the item must either be an absolute path, containing `%s` at the point where `main`, `reject`, or `panic` is to be inserted, or be empty, implying the use of the default path (which is `log/%slog` in the spool directory). The default path is used if nothing is specified. Here are some examples of possible settings:

```
log_file_path=/usr/log/exim_%s
log_file_path=syslog
log_file_path=:syslog
log_file_path=syslog : /usr/log/exim_%s
```

Log data is written only to files for the first of these settings, and only to *syslog* for the second. The third setting uses the default path and *syslog*, and the fourth uses *syslog* and a file path. If there is more than one path in the list, the first is used and a panic error is logged.

## 21.2.1 Logging to syslog

The use of *syslog* does not change what Exim logs or the format of its messages. The same strings are written to *syslog* as to log files. However, if you set `syslog_timestamp` false, Exim does not add a timestamp to the log lines that it writes to *syslog*.

The *syslog* "facility" is set to `LOG_MAIL` and the program name to `exim`. On systems that permit it (all except ULTRIX), the `LOG_PID` flag is set so that the *syslog* call adds the pid as well as the time and host name to each line. The three log streams are mapped onto *syslog* priorities as follows:

- The main log is mapped to `LOG_INFO`.
- The reject log is mapped to `LOG_NOTICE`.
- The panic log is mapped to `LOG_ALERT`.

Many log lines are written to both the main and the reject logs, so there will be duplicates if these are routed by *syslog* to the same place.

Exim's log lines can sometimes be very long, and some of its reject log entries contain multiple lines when headers are included. To cope with both these cases, entries written to *syslog* are split into separate *syslog* calls at each internal newline, and also after a maximum of 1000 characters. To make it easy to reassemble them later, each component of a split entry starts with a string of the form `[<n>/<m>]` or `[<n>\<m>]`, where `<n>` is the component number and `<m>` is the total number of components in the entry. The separator is / when the line is split because it is too long; if it is split because of an internal newline, the separator is \.

---

[1]   The delimiter for most lists in Exim can be changed from a colon to another character, but this option
    is an exception. A colon *must* be used.

For example, if the length limit were 70 instead of 1000, the following would be the result of a typical rejection message to the main log (LOG_INFO), each line in addition being preceded by the time, host name, and pid as added by *syslog*:

```
[1/3] 1999-09-16 16:09:43 11RdAL-0006pc-00 rejected from [127.0.0.1] (ph10):
[2/3]  syntax error in 'From' header when scanning for sender: missing or ma
[3/3] lformed local part in "<>" (envelope sender is <ph10@cam.example>)
```

The same error might cause the following lines to be written to the reject log (LOG_NOTICE):

```
[1/14] 1999-09-16 16:09:43 11RdAL-0006pc-00 rejected from [127.0.0.1] (ph10):
[2/14]  syntax error in 'From' header when scanning for sender: missing or ma
[3\14] lformed local part in "<>" (envelope sender is <ph10@cam.example>)
[4\14] Recipients: ph10@some.domain.cam.example
[5\14] P Received: from [127.0.0.1] (ident=ph10)
[6\14]       by xxxxx.cam.example with smtp (Exim 3.22 #27)
[7\14]       id 11RdAL-0006pc-00
[8\14]       for ph10@cam.example; Mon, 16 Apr 2001 16:09:43 +0100
[9\14] F From: <>
[10\14]   Subject: this is a test header
[11\14]   X-something: this is another header
[12\14] I Message-ID: <E11RdAL-0006pc-00@xxxxx.cam.example>
[13\14] B Bcc:
[14/14]   Date: Mon, 16 Apr 2001 16:09:43 +0100
```

Log lines that are neither too long nor contain newlines are written to *syslog* without modification, for example:

```
 1999-09-16 16:09:47 SMTP connection from [127.0.0.1] closed by QUIT
```

The times added by *syslog* are normally the same as Exim's timestamps (though in a different format and without the year), so setting `syslog_timestamp` false reduces the amount of data written without much loss of information.

## 21.2.2 Reducing or increasing what is logged

By setting the `log_selector` global option, you can disable some of Exim's default logging, or you can request additional logging. The value of `log_ selector` is made up of names preceded by plus or minus characters, as in the following example:

```
 log_selector = +arguments -retry_defer
```

The arguments are processed from left to right, with the positive ones increasing and the negative ones decreasing the amount of logging. The available names are shown in table 21-1, with the default selection marked by asterisks.

More details on each of these items follows:

*Table 21-1: Optional logging items*

| Name | Information logged |
|------|-------------------|
| address_rewrite | Address rewriting |
| all_parents | All parents in => lines |
| arguments | Command line arguments |
| *connection_reject | Connection rejections |
| *delay_delivery | Immediate delivery delayed (message queued) |
| delivery_size | Add S=<*nnn*> to => lines |
| *dnslist_defer | Defers of DNS list (aka RBL) lookups |
| *etrn | ETRN commands |
| incoming_interface | Incoming interface on <= lines |
| incoming_port | Incoming port on <= lines |
| *lost_incoming_connection | As it says (includes timeouts) |
| *queue_run | Start and end queue runs |
| received_recipients | Recipients on <= lines |
| received_sender | Sender on <= lines |
| *retry_defer | "retry time not reached" messages |
| sender_on_delivery | Add sender to => lines |
| *size_reject | Rejection because message too big |
| *skip_delivery | "message is frozen", "spool file is locked" |
| smtp_confirmation | SMTP confirmation on <= lines |
| smtp_connection | SMTP connections |
| smtp_protocol_error | SMTP protocol errors |
| smtp_syntax_error | SMTP syntax errors |
| subject | Contents of *Subject:* on <= lines |
| *tls_cipher | TLS cipher suite on <= lines |
| tls_peerdn | TLS peer DN on <= lines |
| all | All of the above |

## address_rewrite

This causes all address rewriting to be logged as an aid to debugging rewriting rules. It applies both to global rewrites and in-transport rewrites.

## all_parents

Normally only the original and final addresses are logged on delivery lines; with this selector, intermediate parents are given in parentheses between them.

`arguments`

Setting this option causes Exim to write the options and arguments with which it was called to the main log. This is a debugging feature, added to make it easy to find out with what arguments certain MUAs call the MTA. The logging does not happen if Exim has given up *root* privilege because it was called with the `-C` or `-D` options. This facility cannot log unrecognized arguments because the arguments are checked before the configuration file is read. The only way to log such cases is to interpose a script between the caller and Exim.[1]

`connection_reject`

A log entry is written whenever an incoming SMTP connection is rejected, for whatever reason.

`delay_delivery`

A log entry is written whenever a delivery process is not started for an incoming message because the load is too high or too many messages were received on one connection. Logging does not occur if no delivery process is started because `queue_only` is set or `-odq` was used.

`delivery_size`

For each delivery, the size of message delivered is added to the `=>` line, tagged with `S=`.

`dnslist_defer`

A log entry is written if an attempt to look up a host in a DNS black list suffers a temporary error.

`etrn`

Every legal `ETRN` command that is received is logged, before the ACL is run to determine whether or not it is actually accepted. An invalid `ETRN` command, or one received within a message transaction, is not logged by this selector (see `smtp_syntax_error` and `smtp_protocol_error`).

`incoming_interface`

The interface on which a message was received is added to the `<=` line as an IP address in square brackets, tagged by `I=` and followed by a colon and the port number.

`incoming_port`

The remote port number from which a message was received is added to log entries and *Received:* header lines, following the IP address in square brackets,

---

[1]  An example of such a script, called *logargs.sh*, is provided in Exim's utility directory.

and separated from it by a colon. This is implemented by changing the value that is put in the *$sender_fullhost* and *$sender_rcvhost* variables. Recording the remote port number has become more important with the widening use of NAT (see RFC 2505).

`lost_incoming_connection`

A log line is written when an incoming SMTP connection is unexpectedly dropped.

`queue_run`

The start and end of every queue run are logged.

`received_recipients`

The recipients of a message are listed in the main log as soon as the message is received. The list appears at the end of the log line that is written when a message is received, preceded by the word "for". The addresses are listed after they have been qualified, but before any rewriting has taken place.

`received_sender`

The unrewritten original sender of a message is added to the end of the log line that records the message's arrival, after the word "from" (before the recipients if `received_recipients` is also set).

`retry_defer`

A log line is written if a delivery is deferred because a retry time has not yet been reached. However, this "retry time not reached" message is always omitted from individual message logs after the first delivery attempt.

`sender_on_delivery`

The message's sender address is added to every delivery and bounce line, tagged by F= (for "from").

`size_reject`

A log line is written whenever a message is rejected because it is too big.

`skip_delivery`

A log line is written whenever a message is skipped during a queue run because it is frozen or because another process is already delivering it.

`smtp_confirmation`

The response to the final dot in the SMTP dialogue for outgoing messages is added to delivery log lines in the form `C="<text>"`. A number of MTAs (including Exim) return an identifying string in this response.

`smtp_connection`

This turns on more verbose logging of incoming SMTP connections. It does not apply to batch SMTP, but it does apply to SMTP connections from local processes that use the `-bs` option, including incoming connections using *inetd*. A log line is written whenever a connection is established or closed. If a connection is dropped in the middle of a message, a log line is always written, but otherwise nothing is written at the start and end of SMTP connections unless this selector is set.

`smtp_protocol_error`

A log line is written for every SMTP protocol error encountered.

`smtp_syntax_error`

A log line is written for every SMTP syntax error encountered. An unrecognized command is treated as a syntax error. For an external connection, the host identity is given; for an internal connection using `-bs`, the sender identification (normally the calling user) is given.

`subject`

The subject of the message is added to the arrival log line, preceded by `T=` (T for "topic", because S is already used for "size").

`tls_cipher`

When a message is sent or received over an encrypted connection, the cipher suite used is added to the log line, preceded by `X=`.

`tls_peerdn`

When a message is sent or received over an encrypted connection, and a certificate is supplied by the remote host, the peer DN is added to the log line, preceded by `DN=`.

## 21.2.3 Unprintable characters in log lines

There is one final option that affects logging. When Exim includes data from a message within a log entry, it takes care to ensure that unprintable characters are escaped, so as not to mess up the format of the log. For example, if a message contains these lines in its header:

```
Subject: This subject covers
  more than one line
```

and the `subject` selector is set, the text that is written to the log is:

```
T="This subject covers\n  more than one line"
```

Characters whose values are greater than 127 (so-called "8-bit" or "top-bit" characters) are by default printed using octal escape sequences. However, if you set `print_topbitchars` true, these characters are considered to be printing characters and are sent to the log unmodified.

# 21.3 Format of main log entries

Each entry in the main log is a single line of text. Some of the lines are quite long, but it is done this way to make it easier to parse the lines in programs that analyse the data. Every line starts with a timestamp of the form:

```
2000-06-30 01:07:31
```

The time zone used for Exim's timestamps is discussed in section 19.5. Log lines that relate to the reception or delivery of messages have a two-character "flag" after the timestamp to make them readily identifiable. The flags are:

| | |
|---|---|
| <= | for an arrival |
| => | for a successful delivery |
| == | for deferment of delivery till later |
| ** | for a delivery failure |

In addition, -> and *> are used for some special kinds of delivery, as described later in this chapter.

## 21.3.1 Logging message reception

The arrival of a message that is not received over TCP/IP is logged by a line of the form shown in this example, which is split over several lines here in order to fit it on the page:

```
2000-06-30 00:11:51 137nTL-0005br-00 <= holly@dwarf.example
    U=holly P=local S=811
    id=Pine.SOL.3.96.1000630001852.21797A-100000@dwarf.example
```

The address that immediately follows <= is the envelope sender address (after any rewriting rules have been applied), and the U field records the login name of the process that called Exim to submit the message.

When a message arrives from another host, the U field records the RFC 1413 identity of the user that sent the message, if one was received, and an H field identifies the sending host:

```
2000-06-30 08:57:53 137CW1-0005MB-00 <= kryten@dwarf.example
    H=mailer.dwarf.example [192.168.123.123] U=exim
    P=smtp S=5678 id=20000630091558.B12616@dwarf.example
```

The number given in square brackets is the IP address of the client host. If there is just a single name in the H field, as shown here, Exim has verified that it corresponds to the IP address. If the name is in parentheses, it is the name that was quoted by the remote host in the EHLO or HELO command, and has not been verified.[1]

If verification yields a different name to that given for EHLO or HELO, the verified name appears first, followed by the EHLO or HELO name in parentheses. In this example, the client did not give its fully qualified name:

```
H=mm272.lucy.example (mm272) [192.168.215.229]
```

Misconfigured hosts (and mail forgers) sometimes put an IP address, with or without brackets, in the EHLO or HELO command, leading to entries in the log containing extracts such as this:

```
H=(10.21.32.43) [192.168.8.34]
H=([10.21.32.43]) [192.168.8.34]
```

Such entries can be confusing. Only the final address in square brackets can be relied on.

For all messages, the P field specifies the protocol used to receive the message. This is set to asmtp for messages received from hosts that have authenticated themselves using the SMTP AUTH command. In this case, the name of the authenticator that was used is logged with A as the field name. If an authenticated identification was set up by the authenticator's server_set_id option, this is logged too, separated by a colon from the authenticator name. For example:

```
A=fixed_plain:ph10
```

If you are using a version of Exim that supports encrypted transfers, the cipher that was used for an incoming message is logged with X as the field name. For example:

```
X=TLSv1:DES-CBC3-SHA:168
```

If you do not want this, remove tls_cipher from the log selector. Nothing is logged by default when Exim requests a certificate from a client, but if you add tls_peerdn to the log selector, the Distinguished Name is logged with DN as the field name.

The size of the received message is given in bytes by the S field. When the message is delivered, headers may be removed or added. This means that the size of delivered copies of the message may be different to the value logged on arrival (and indeed may be different to one another).

The ID field records the contents of any existing *Message-ID:* header line. If the message does not contain such a line, nothing is logged, but Exim adds one before delivering the message.

---

[1] Looking up a client host name from its IP address occurs only if Exim's configuration requires the name, in order to check it against a host list, or if the host matches the host_lookup option.

A delivery error (bounce) message is shown with the sender address < >, and if it is a locally generated message, this is normally followed by an R field, which is a reference to the local identification of the message that caused the error message to be sent. For example:

```
2000-06-30 00:49:27 137o3j-0005mU-00 <= <> R=137o3e-0005mO-00 U=root
   P=local S=1239
```

records the arrival of a bounce message that was provoked by the message with the ID 137o3e-0005mO-00.

You can request that additional data be added to the message reception log line by setting certain log selectors, as described earlier.

## 21.3.2 Logging deliveries

Here are examples of delivery log lines for a local and a remote delivery, respectively:

```
1995-10-31 08:59:13 0tACW1-0005MB-00 => marv <marv@hitch.example>
   R=localuser T=local_delivery
1995-10-31 09:00:10 0tACW1-0005MB-00 => monk@holistic.example
   R=dnslookup T=remote_smtp H=holistic.example [192.168.234.234]
```

The R and T fields identify the router and the transport that were used for the delivery. The H field identifies the remote host.

For a local delivery, the field that immediately follows => is either just a local part, the name of a file, or a pipe command. This is followed by the original address, in angle brackets, as in the first line in this example. If (as a result of aliasing or forwarding) intermediate addresses exist between the original and the final address, the last of these is given in parentheses after the final address. However, the log selector all_parents can be set to cause all intermediate addresses to be logged.

The generation of a reply message by a filter file gets logged as a "delivery" to the addressee, preceded by >. The R and T items record the router and transport. For example:

```
2000-06-30 09:42:35 137wNf-0000ng-00 => >hermione@hws.thaum.example
   <harry@hws.thaum.example> R=userforward T=address_reply
```

shows that user *harry* has a filter file that used a *reply* command to generate a message to *hermione@hws.thaum.example*. Nearby in the log, often immediately preceding such a line, you will find the entry recording the arrival of the generated message.

If a shadow transport is run after a successful local delivery, the log line for the successful delivery has an item added on the end, of the form:

```
ST=shadow transport name
```

If the shadow transport does not succeed, the error message is put in parentheses afterwards.

For remote deliveries, if the final delivery address is not the same as the original address (owing to changes made by routers), the original is shown in angle brackets.

When more than one address is included in a single delivery (for example, two SMTP RCPT commands are used in one transaction), the second and subsequent addresses are flagged with -> instead of => so that statistics gathering programs can draw a distinction between copies delivered and addresses delivered. If two or more messages are delivered down a single SMTP connection, an asterisk follows the IP address in the log lines for the second and subsequent messages.

When a delivery is discarded as a result of the command *seen finish* being obeyed in a user's filter file that generates no deliveries, a log entry of the form:

```
1998-12-10 00:50:49 0znuJc-0001UB-00 => discarded
    <low.club@trick4.bridge.example> R=userforward
```

is written, to record why no deliveries are logged for that address. If a system filter discards all deliveries for a message, the log line is:

```
1999-12-14 00:30:42 0znuKe-0001UB-00 => discarded (system_filter)
```

Finally, when the -N debugging option is used to prevent deliveries from actually occurring, log entries are flagged with *> instead of => or ->.

## 21.3.3 Deferred deliveries

When a delivery is deferred, a line of the following form is logged:

```
2002-12-19 16:20:23 16aiQz-0002Q5-00 == marvin@@endrest.example
    R=dnslookup T=smtp defer (146): Connection refused
```

In the case of remote deliveries, the error is the one that occurred for the last IP address that was tried. Details of individual SMTP failures are also written to the log, so this line would be preceded by a line such as this:

```
2002-12-19 16:20:23 16aiQz-0002Q5-00 Failed to connect to
    mail1.endrest.example [192.168.239.239]: Connection refused
```

When a delivery is deferred because a retry time has not been reached, a defer message is written to the log, but only if the log selector retry_defer is set.

- "Retry time not reached" means that the address previously suffered a temporary error during routing or local delivery and the time to retry it has not yet arrived.

- "Retry time not reached for any host" means that the address previously suffered temporary errors during remote delivery and the retry time has not yet arrived for any of the hosts to which it is routed.

## 21.3.4 Delivery failures

If a delivery fails because an address cannot be routed, a line of the following form is logged:

```
1995-12-19 16:20:23 0tRiQz-0002Q5-00 ** jim@trek99.example
  <jim@trek99.example>: unknown mail domain
```

If a delivery fails at transport time, the router and transport are shown, and the response from the remote host is included, as in this example:

```
2002-07-11 07:14:17 17SXDU-000189-00 ** ace400@pb.example R=dnslookup
  T=remote_smtp: SMTP error from remote mailer after
  RCPT TO:<ace400@pb.example>: host pbmail3.py.example [192.168.63.111]:
  553 5.3.0 <ace400@pb.example>... Addressee unknown
```

The log lines for all forms of delivery failure are flagged with **.

## 21.3.5 Message completion

A line of the form:

```
1995-10-31 09:00:11 0tACW1-0005MB-00 Completed
```

is written to the main log when a message is about to be removed from the spool at the end of its processing. This guarantees that no further log entries for that message will be written.

## 21.3.6 Other log entries

Various other types of log entry are written from time to time. Most should be self-explanatory. One that sometimes causes worry is "Spool file is locked". This is not normally an error; it means that an attempt to deliver a message cannot proceed because some other Exim process is already working on the message. This log entry can be quite common if queue runner processes are started at frequent intervals. It can be suppressed by unsetting the log selector skip_delivery.

However, if you see this log line repeating for the same message for an unreasonable amount of time, there may be a problem. You can use the *exiwhat* utility to find out what the Exim process that is working on the message is trying to do.

## 21.3.7 Summary of fields in log lines

A summary of the field identifiers that are used in log lines is shown in table 21-2.

*Table 21-2: Fields in log lines*

| Field flag | Information |
|---|---|
| A | Authenticator name (and optional id) |
| C | SMTP confirmation on delivery |
| DN | DN from peer certificate |
| F | Sender address (on delivery lines) |
| H | Host name and IP address |
| id | Message id for incoming message |
| P | Protocol for incoming message |
| R | On <= lines: reference for local bounce; on => lines: router name |
| S | Size of message |
| ST | Shadow transport name |
| T | On <= lines: message subject (topic); on => lines: transport name |
| U | Local user or RFC 1413 identity |
| X | TLS cipher suite |

# 21.4 Cycling log files

If you are using local files rather than *syslog* to record Exim's logs (the most common configuration), you should normally "cycle" the main log and the reject log periodically. The cycling process consists of renaming the current log file and deleting previous ones that are too old. Most sites do this by setting up a *cron* job that runs once a day, commonly at midnight, so that each file contains the log for one day.[1]

An Exim delivery process opens the main log when it first needs to write to it, and it keeps the file open in case subsequent entries are required (for example, if a number of different deliveries are being done for the same message). However, remote SMTP deliveries can take a long time, and this means that the file might be kept open and used long after it was renamed. To avoid this, Exim checks the main log file by name before reusing an open file. If the file does not exist, or if its inode has changed (that is, although it has the same name, it is actually a different file), Exim closes the old file and opens the new one instead. Thus, an old log file may remain open for quite some time, but no Exim processes should write to it once it has been renamed.

---

[1] You cannot, of course, ensure that the renaming happens on the dot of midnight, nor can you synchronize with any Exim processes that might be in the process of writing to the log, so, in practice, there will usually be a few log lines in the "wrong" file.

Some operating systems have standard scripts for log cycling, which of course can be used. For those that do not, a utility script called *exicyclog* is provided as part of the Exim distribution. It cycles both the main log and the reject log files. You can run it from a root *crontab* entry of the form:

```
1 0 * * *  su exim -c /usr/exim/bin/exicyclog
```

This example runs the script at 00:01 every day. The script does not need to be run as root because the log files are owned by the Exim user.

If no main (or reject) log file exists, the script does nothing (for that set of files). Otherwise, each time *exicyclog* is run, the files get "shuffled down" by one: *mainlog* becomes *mainlog.01*, the previous *mainlog.01* becomes *mainlog.02*, and so on, up to a limit that is set in the script when it is built (the default is 10). All the old files except for yesterday's log (*mainlog.01*) are automatically compressed to save disk space.[1]

# 21.5 Extracting information from log files

Two Perl scripts for extracting information from main log files are provided in the Exim distribution. They provide fairly basic facilities, but you can modify them or write your own if you need additional functionality.

## 21.5.1 The exigrep utility

The *exigrep* utility extracts from one or more log files all entries relevant to any message whose entries contain at least one that matches a given pattern. For example:

```
exigrep 'H=orange\.csi\.example' /var/spool/exim/log/mainlog
```

not only picks out the lines containing the string H=orange.csi.example, but also all the other lines for the messages that have a matching entry. Thus, the output would be the complete set of log lines for all messages involving that particular host. The entries are sorted so that all the entries for each message are printed together, and there is a blank line between each message's entries.

*exigrep* makes it easy to search for all mail for a given user or a given host or domain. The script's usage is as follows:

```
exigrep [-l] <pattern> [<log file>] [<log file>] ...
```

where the -l flag means "literal", that is, treat all characters in the pattern as standing for themselves. Otherwise the pattern must be a Perl regular expression. The log files can be compressed or uncompressed; those that are compressed are piped

---

[1] We have used the default filename, *mainlog*, in this description, but the script works fine with whatever log filenames you choose to use.

through the *zcat* utility as they are read.[1] If no filenames are given on the command line, the standard input is read.

## 21.5.2 The eximstats utility

A Perl script called *eximstats* is supplied with the Exim distribution. It extracts statistics from Exim log files. Originally, *eximstats* was intended merely as a demonstration of how this could be done, but it has found its way into regular use, and over time, it has been hacked about and substantially extended. *eximstats* gives a large amount of information by default, but there are options for suppressing various parts of it; these are summarized in table 21-3.

*Table 21-3: Eximstats options*

| Option | Effect |
|---|---|
| -bydomain | League tables by superior domain |
| -byemail | League tables by email address |
| -byhost | League tables by host (default) |
| -h0 | Suppress histograms |
| -h<n> | Control histogram interval |
| -help | Show help information |
| -html | Output in HTML |
| -ne | Suppress output for errors |
| -nr | Suppress output for relays |
| -nr[pattern>/ | Ditto, for those that match the pattern |
| -nt | Suppress output for deliveries by transport |
| -q0 | Suppress time-on-queue output |
| -q<n1,n2...> | Control time-on-queue intervals |
| -t<n> | Set length of league tables |
| -tnl | Omit local information from league tables |
| -t_remote_users | Include non-local local parts |

By default the output is in plain text, but the -html option causes it to be written in HTML. A brief description of the output and the main options is given here. More details can be found in the Exim manual.

Following any options, the arguments to the script are a list of files, which should be main log files. For example:

```
eximstats -nr -ne /var/spool/exim/log/mainlog.01
```

---

[1]   This assumes that the location of *zcat* was known at the time Exim was built.

*eximstats* extracts information about the number and volume of messages received from or delivered to various hosts. The information is sorted both by message count and by volume, and the top 50 hosts in each category are listed on the standard output. For messages delivered and received locally, similar statistics are produced per user.

The output also includes total counts and statistics about delivery errors and histograms showing the number of messages received and deliveries made in each hour of the day. A delivery with more than one address in its envelope (for example, an SMTP transaction with more than one RCPT command) is counted as a single delivery.

Though normally more deliveries than receipts are reported (because messages may have multiple recipients), it is possible for *eximstats* to report more messages received than delivered, even though the spool is empty at the start and end of the period in question. If an incoming message contains no valid recipients, no deliveries are recorded for it. An error report is handled as a separate message.

*eximstats* outputs a grand total summary giving the volume and number of messages received and deliveries made and the number of hosts involved in each case. It also outputs the number of messages that were delayed (that is, not completely delivered at the first attempt), and the number that had at least one address that failed. Here is an example of this initial output:

```
Exim statistics from 1999-01-21 00:11:08 to 1999-01-22 00:10:46

Grand total summary
-------------------
                                              At least one address
   TOTAL       Volume     Messages     Hosts    Delayed       Failed
   Received    153MB        16520      2341   53  0.3%    104  0.6%
   Delivered   182MB        23197      1513
```

The remainder of the output is in sections that can be independently disabled or modified by various options. First, there is a summary of deliveries by transport:

```
Deliveries by transport
-----------------------
                      Volume    Messages
   **bypassed**          960           1
   :blackhole:          27KB           4
   address_file       1665KB         425
   address_pipe       2134KB         417
   address_reply        4368           3
   local_delivery      135MB       16141
   remote_smtp          43MB        6206
```

`**bypassed**` is recorded when a message is routed to */dev/null*, which Exim recognizes as a special case. `:blackhole:` records the use of the special

:blackhost: feature of alias files. This part of the output can be suppressed by setting the -nt option.

The next part of the output consists of two textual histograms, showing the number of messages received and delivered per hour, respectively. They are automatically scaled, which is why the numbers of messages per dot in these examples are rather strange:

```
Messages received per hour (each dot is 27 messages)
-----------------------------------------------------
00-01    342 ...........
01-02    249 .........
02-03    206 .......
03-04    154 .....
04-05    134 ....
05-06    160 .....
06-07    141 .....
07-08    245 .........
08-09    562 ....................
09-10   1208 ............................................
10-11   1228 .............................................
11-12   1300 ................................................
12-13   1242 .............................................
13-14   1070 .......................................
14-15   1320 ................................................
15-16   1335 .................................................
16-17   1281 ..............................................
17-18   1026 .....................................
18-19    890 ................................
19-20    597 ......................
20-21    452 ................
21-22    448 ................
22-23    467 .................
23-24    463 .................

Deliveries per hour (each dot is 47 deliveries)
-----------------------------------------------
00-01    411 ........
01-02    266 .....
02-03    236 .....
03-04    189 ....
04-05    139 ..
05-06    208 ....
06-07    164 ...
07-08    263 .....
08-09    985 ....................
09-10   1801 ......................................
10-11   1780 .....................................
11-12   1916 ........................................
12-13   1624 ..................................
13-14   1607 ..................................
14-15   2087 ............................................
15-16   2373 ..................................................
16-17   1764 .....................................
```

```
17-18    1299 ...........................
18-19    1118 ......................
19-20     693 ..............
20-21     579 ...........
21-22     524 ..........
22-23     634 ............
23-24     537 ..........
```

By default, the time interval is one hour. If -h0 is given, the histograms are suppressed; if -h followed by a number is given, the value gives the number of divisions per hour, so -h2 sets an interval of 30 minutes. The default is equivalent to -h1.

Next, there is an analysis of the time spent on the queue, first by all messages:

```
Time spent on the queue: all messages
-------------------------------------

Under    1m    16271  98.5%   98.5%
         5m      168   1.0%   99.5%
        15m       30   0.2%   99.7%
        30m       19   0.1%   99.8%
         1h       10   0.1%   99.9%
         3h       10   0.1%   99.9%
         6h        4   0.0%  100.0%
        12h        3   0.0%  100.0%
         1d        1   0.0%  100.0%
Over     1d        1   0.0%  100.0%
```

and then by messages that had at least one remote delivery:

```
Time spent on the queue: messages with at least one remote delivery
-------------------------------------------------------------------

Under    1m     5073  95.6%   95.6%
         5m      167   3.1%   98.7%
        15m       27   0.5%   99.2%
        30m       12   0.2%   99.5%
         1h       10   0.2%   99.7%
         3h       10   0.2%   99.8%
         6h        4   0.1%   99.9%
        12h        3   0.1%  100.0%
Over     1d        1   0.0%  100.0%
```

These particular statistics were recorded on a good day. This output can be suppressed by the -q0 option. Alternatively, -q can be followed by a list of time intervals for this analysis. The values are separated by commas and are in seconds, but can involve arithmetic multipliers, so, for example, you can set 3*60 to specify 3 minutes. A setting such as:

```
-q60,5*60,10*60
```

causes *eximstats* to give counts of messages that stayed on the queue for less than one minute, less than 5 minutes, less than 10 minutes, and over 10 minutes.

Unless -nr is specified, there follows a list of all messages that were relayed via the
local host, starting off like this:

```
Relayed messages
----------------

    5 (rosemary) [192.168.182.138] jcbreb@cus.example
      => green.gra.example [192.168.8.57] r5j4m@herm.gra.example
    ...

Total: 1949 (plus 0 unshown)
```

The relay information lists messages that were actually relayed (that is, they came
from a remote host and were directly delivered to some other remote host). Each pair
of lines represents a single relay route; the leading number shows how many different messages were delivered over this route. The rest of the first line contains the
sending host name and IP address and the envelope sender address.

Sometimes you only want to know about certain relays. You can selectively omit
relay information by providing a regular expression after -nr, like this:

```
eximstats '-nr/busy\.host\.name/' /var/spool/exim/log/mainlog.01
```

The pattern is matched against a string of the following form (here split over two
lines):

```
H=<host> [<ip address>] A=<sender address> => H=<host>
  A=<recipient address>
```

for example:

```
H=in.host [10.2.3.4] A=from@some.where => H=out.host A=to@else.where
```

The sending host name appears in parentheses if it has not been verified as matching
the IP address. The mail addresses are taken from the envelope, not the headers.
Relays that are suppressed by this mechanism contribute to the "unshown" count in
the final total line.

The next part of the output consists of "league tables", starting with:

```
Top 50 sending hosts by message count
-------------------------------------

  323    3834KB    purple.csi.example
  314    5710KB    maroon.csi.example
  170    1853KB    local
   29      97KB    mta1.cl.example
   28    3653KB    pml20.acad.abc.example
   28     725KB    hutmail.com.example
  ...
```

which lists the hosts from which the most messages were received. It is followed by:

- Top 50 sending hosts by volume.

- Top 50 local senders by message count; this lists the local parts for messages originating on the local host.

- Top 50 local senders by volume.

- Top 50 destinations by message count; this is by host.

- Top 50 destinations by volume.

- Top 50 local destinations by message count; this is by local part.

- Top 50 local destinations by volume.

You can change the number 50 by means of the -t option; for example, -t10 lists only the top 10 in each category. If you set -t0, this part of the output is suppressed; if you set -tnl, the information about local senders and destinations is suppressed.

By default, the league tables are compiled for individual hosts. If you set the -bydomain option, the first component of each host name is removed, so the information is aggregated for the superior domains instead. If you want both kinds of information, you can give both -bydomain and -byhost. You can also request league tables on the basis of individual email addresses, by setting -byemail.

The final section of output from *eximstats* is a list of delivery errors:

```
List of errors
--------------

     1 " peter"@cus.example R=unknownuser T=unknownuser_pipe:
       return message generated

     1 1996@southwest.cim.example R=dnslookup T=smtp: SMTP error
       from remote mailer after RCPT TO: <1996@southwest.cim.example>:
       host tuert.southwest.cim.example [192.168.9.19]:
       550 <1996@southwest.cim.example>...
       User unknown

     ...

Errors encountered: 118
-----------------------
```

The number at the start of each item is a count of the number of identical errors. This output can be suppressed by specifying -ne.

# 21.6 Watching what Exim is doing

There are two aspects to watching what Exim is actually doing at any time. The message files in its spool directory contain the work that it has undertaken to do.

These represent its activity on a relatively long time scale, whereas the current set of Exim processes are what it is actually doing at this instant. Facilities are provided for looking at both of these kinds of activity.

## 21.6.1 The exiqsumm utility

One way of watching what Exim is doing is to inspect the list of messages it is in the process of handling. The -bp command-line option and its variants (☞ 20.7) provide this information. There is also a short utility script called *exiqsumm* that postprocesses the -bp output to provide a summary. The following command:

```
exim -bp | exiqsumm
```

produces output lines of this form:

```
    3    2322    74m    66m    wek.example
```

This means that three messages on the queue have undelivered addresses in the *wek.example* domain. Their total size is 2322 bytes; the oldest has been queued for 74 minutes and the newest for 66 minutes.

## 21.6.2 The exinext utility

If you want to know when Exim will next try a particular delivery that has suffered a temporary error, you can use a utility called *exinext*, which is mostly a Perl script, to extract information from Exim's retry database. Given a mail domain or a complete address, it looks up the hosts for the domain and outputs any retry information that it may have. At present, the retry information is obtained by running the basic *exim_dumpdb* utility (described in the reference manual) and post-processing the output. *exinext* is not particularly efficient, but then it is not expected to be run very often. Here is an example of its use:

```
$ exinext piglet@milne.fict.example
kanga.milne.fict.example:192.168.8.1 error 146: Connection refused
  first failed: 21-Feb-1996 14:57:34
  last tried:   21-Feb-1996 14:57:34
  next try at:  21-Feb-1996 15:02:34
roo.milne.fict.example:192.168.8.3 error 146: Connection refused
  first failed: 20-Jan-1996 13:12:08
  last tried:   21-Feb-1996 11:42:03
  next try at:  21-Feb-1996 19:42:03
  past final cutoff time
```

The phrase "past final cutoff time" means that an error has been occurring for longer than the maximum time mentioned in the relevant retry rule. You can give *exinext* a local part, without a domain, to obtain retry information for a local delivery that has been failing temporarily. A message ID can be given to obtain retry information pertaining to a specific message. This exists only when an attempt to deliver a message to a remote host suffers a message-specific error (☞ 12.2.2).

## 21.6.3 Querying Exim processes

You can, of course, use the Unix *ps* command to obtain a list of Exim processes. Typically, this is combined with *grep* to form a command such as:

```
ps -ef | grep exim
```

The output might contain lines such as this:

```
exim   295      1  0    Jul 01 ?         0:05 /usr/sbin/sendmail -bd -q15m
exim  4240    295  0  10:09:40 ?         0:00 /usr/sbin/sendmail -bd -q15m
exim  4342    295  0  10:10:59 ?         0:00 /usr/exim/bin/exim -q
exim  4345   4342  0  10:10:59 ?         0:00 /usr/exim/bin/exim -q
exim  4376    295  0  10:11:13 ?         0:00 /usr/sbin/sendmail -bd -q15m
```

These processes are all running as the Exim user, and none of them has an associated terminal (that is what the question marks mean). You can deduce that process 295 is a daemon process because its parent is process number 1, the *init* process that becomes the parent of all daemon processes. Also, it was started some days ago, so its starting time is given as a date rather than a time.

Processes 4240, 4342, and 4376 are all children of the daemon. The first and the third must be reception processes for incoming SMTP connections because the command that is shown is the same as the daemon's. This means that it has forked new processes, but has not executed a new command. Process 4342, however, although also forked from the daemon, is running a different command (namely, a queue runner process). It has created process 4345 to deliver a message.

This information from *ps* is rather limited. You cannot tell, for example, from which remote hosts messages are arriving, or which messages a queue runner is delivering. A technique that is adopted by some programs for making information about their activity available is to change the values of the argument variables with which they are called, so that the output from *ps* changes as the program proceeds. Unfortunately, this technique does not work on all operating systems, so Exim does not use it.

Instead, Exim processes respond to the SIGUSR1 signal by writing a line of text describing what they are doing to the file *exim-process.info* in Exim's spool directory. This facility is packaged up for use via a utility script called *exiwhat*. You must run this command as *root*, so that it has the privilege to send a signal to processes running under any uid.[1]

The first thing *exiwhat* does is empty the process information file. Then it finds all the Exim processes and sends each one a SIGUSR1 signal. The script waits for one second to allow the processes to react, then copies the file to the standard output. It might look like this:

---

[1]  This is different from restarting the daemon using SIGHUP, which can be done either as *root* or as *exim*.

```
 295 daemon: -q15m, listening on port 25
4240 handling incoming connection from [192.168.243.242]
4342 running queue: waiting for 0tAycK-0002ij-00 (4345)
4345 delivering 0tAycK-0002ij-00 to mail.ref.example [192.168.42.42]
  (editor@ref.example)
4375 handling incoming connection from [192.168.234.111]
```

The number at the start of each output line is the process number. The fourth line has been split here, in order to fit it on the page.

Some operating systems have a command for identifying all processes running a specific program, and sending them a signal. On Linux and FreeBSD this is *killall*; on Solaris it is *pkill*.

---

 Note that *killall* on Solaris is very different; it kills *all* processes. You do not want to run it by mistake.

---

Exim makes use of a multiple-kill command when it can. For other systems, a combination of *ps* and *egrep* are used to find all the Exim processes. Unfortunately, the *ps* command varies between different operating systems. Not only are different options used, but the format of the output is different. If *exiwhat* does not seem to work for you, check the first few lines of the shell script, which should contain something like this:

```
multikill_cmd=pkill
multikill_arg='exim( |$|-)'

ps_cmd=/bin/ps
ps_arg=-e
egrep_arg=' exim( |$|-)'

signal=-USR1
```

If `multikill_cmd` is not empty, it specifies a multiple-kill command, and `multikill_arg` is its argument. Otherwise, the next three settings are used. The first of them sets the path to the *ps* command and the second is the argument for *ps*. The third is the argument for *egrep* to make it extract the list of Exim processes from the *ps* output. In both cases, the final setting specifies the signal to be sent. The actual values may vary, depending on which operating system you are running.

If you find you need to change these values, and you have compiled and installed Exim from the source code, you should change the defaults at compile time so that the correct values will be used when you build the next release.

# 21.7 The Exim monitor

The Exim monitor is an X Window application that continuously displays information about what Exim is doing. An admin user can perform certain operations on messages from this GUI interface; however, all such facilities are also available from the command line, and, indeed, the monitor itself makes use of the command-line interface to carry out these operations.

## 21.7.1 Running the monitor

The monitor is started by running the script called *eximon*. This is a shell wrapper script that sets up a number of environment variables and then runs the binary called *eximon.bin*. The environment variables are a way of configuring the monitor, for example, specifying the size of its window. Their default values are specified when Exim is built. However, even if you are using a precompiled version of Exim, the parameters that are built into the *eximon* script at compile time can be overridden for a particular invocation by setting up environment variables of the same names, preceded by EXIMON_. For example, a shell command such as:

```
EXIMON_LOG_DEPTH=400 eximon
```

(in a Bourne-compatible shell) runs *eximon* with an overriding setting of the LOG_DEPTH parameter.

If EXIMON_LOG_FILE_PATH is set in the environment, it overrides the Exim log file configuration. This makes it possible to have *eximon* tailing log data that is written to *syslog*, provided that MAIL.INFO *syslog* messages are routed to a file on the local host. Otherwise, if only *syslog* is used to record logging data, the Exim monitor is unable to provide a log tail display.

X resources can be used to change the appearance of the window in the normal way. For example, a resource setting of the form:

```
Eximon*background: grey94
```

changes the colour of the background to light grey rather than white. The stripcharts are drawn with both the data lines and the reference lines in black. This means that the reference lines are not visible when on top of the data. However, their colour can be changed by setting a resource called "highlight" (an odd name, but that is what the Athena stripchart widget uses). For example, you can set up lighter reference lines in the stripcharts by obeying the following command:

```
xrdb -merge <<End
Eximon*highlight: grey50
End
```

In order to see the contents of messages on the spool and to operate on them, *eximon* must either be run as *root* or by a user who is a member of the Exim group.

The monitor's window is divided into three parts, as shown in figure 21-1, which is an actual screen shot taken on a live system. However, mail addresses, host names, and IP addresses have been hidden with x's for privacy reasons.

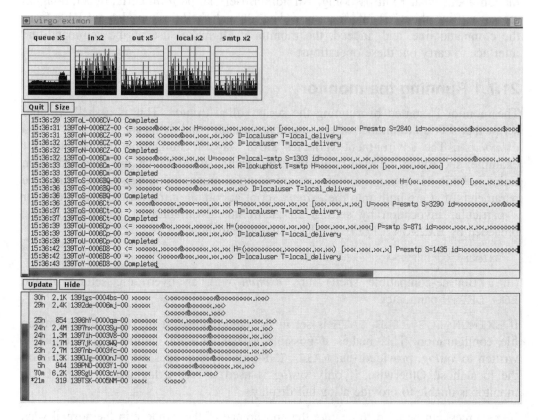

*Figure 21-1: Monitor screenshot*

The first part contains one or more stripcharts and two action buttons, the second contains a "tail" of the main log file, and the third is a display of the queue of messages awaiting delivery, with two more action buttons.

## 21.7.2 The stripcharts

The first stripchart is a count of messages on the queue. The remaining stripcharts are defined in the configuration script by regular expression matches on log file entries, making it possible to display, for example, counts of messages delivered to certain hosts or using certain transports. The supplied defaults display counts of received and delivered messages, and of local and SMTP deliveries. The default period between stripchart updates is one minute.

The stripchart displays rescale themselves automatically as the value they are displaying changes. There are always 10 horizontal lines in each chart; the title string indicates the value of each division when it is greater than one. For example, x2 means that each division represents a value of 2.

It is also possible to have a stripchart that shows the percentage fullness of a particular disk partition, which is useful when local mailboxes are confined to a single partition. This relies on the availability of the *statvfs( )* function or equivalent in the operating system. Most, but not all, versions of Unix that support Exim have this. For this particular stripchart, the top of the chart always represents 100%, and the scale is given as x10%. You can start up *eximon* with this additional stripchart by a command of this form:

```
EXIMON_SIZE_STRIPCHART=/var/mail eximon
```

assuming you are running a Bourne-compatible shell. This example monitors the size of the partition containing the */var/mail* directory. If you build Exim from source, you can specify in the build-time configuration that this is to be the default. The name of the chart is the last component of the path, but you can change this by setting EXIMON_SIZE_STRIPCHART_NAME if you want to.

### 21.7.3 Main action buttons

Below the stripcharts is an action button for quitting the monitor. Next to this is another button marked Size. They are placed here so that shrinking the window to its minimum size leaves just the queue count stripchart and these two buttons visible. The Size button is a toggle that causes the window to flip between its maximum and minimum sizes. When expanding to the maximum, if the window cannot be fully seen where it currently is, it is moved back to where it was the last time it was at full size. The old position is remembered; next time the window is reduced to the minimum, it is moved back.

The idea is that you can keep a reduced window just showing one or two stripcharts at a convenient place on your screen, easily expand it to show the full window when required, and just as easily put it back to what it was. This feature is copied from what the *twm* window manager does for its f.fullzoom action. The minimum size of the window can be changed by setting the environment variables EXIMON_MIN_HEIGHT and EXIMON_MIN_WIDTH when starting the monitor.

### 21.7.4 The log display

The second section of the window is an area in which a display of the last few lines of the main log is maintained. This is not available when the only destination for logging data is *syslog*, unless the *syslog* lines are routed to a local file whose name is passed to *eximon* via the EXIMON_LOG_FILE_PATH environment variable.

The log subwindow has a scrollbar at its left-hand side that can be used to move back to look at earlier text, and the up and down arrow keys also have a scrolling effect. If new text arrives in the window when it is scrolled back, the caret remains where it is, but if the window is not scrolled back, the caret automatically moves to the end of the new text.

The amount of log that is kept depends on the setting of EXIMON_LOG_BUFFER, which specifies the amount of memory to use. When this is full, the earlier 50% of data is discarded; this is much more efficient than throwing it away line by line. The subwindow also has a horizontal scrollbar for accessing the ends of long log lines. This is the only means of horizontal scrolling; the right and left arrow keys are not available. Text can be cut from this part of the window using the mouse in the normal way. The size of this subwindow is controlled by EXIMON_LOG_DEPTH.

Searches of the text in the log window can be carried out by means of the CTRL-R and CTRL-S keystrokes, which default to a reverse and forwards search, respectively. The search covers only the text that is displayed in the window. It cannot go further back up the log. The point from which the search starts is indicated by a caret marker. This is normally at the end of the text in the window, but it can be positioned explicitly by pointing and clicking with the left mouse button, and it is moved automatically by a successful search.

Pressing CTRL-R or CTRL-S pops up a window into which the search text can be typed. There are buttons for selecting forward or reverse searching, for carrying out the search, and for cancelling. If the Search button is pressed, the search happens and the window remains so that further searches can be done. If the Return (or Enter) key is pressed, a single search is done and the window is closed. If CTRL-C is pressed the search is cancelled.[1]

## 21.7.5 The queue display

The bottom section of the monitor window contains a list of all messages that are on the queue, including those currently being delivered, as well as those awaiting delivery in the future.

The depth of this subwindow is controlled by EXIMON_QUEUE_DEPTH, and the frequency with which it is updated is controlled by EXIMON_QUEUE_INTERVAL; the default is 5 minutes because queue scans are quite expensive. However, there is an Update action button just above the display that can be used to force an update of the queue display at any time.

---

[1]   The searching facility is implemented using the facilities of the Athena text widget. By default, this pops up a window containing both "search" and "replace" options. In order to suppress the unwanted "replace" portion for *eximon*, a modified version of the *TextPop* widget is distributed with Exim. However, the linkers in BSDI and HP-UX seem unable to handle an externally provided version of *TextPop* when the remaining parts of the text widget come from the standard libraries. On these systems, therefore, *eximon* has to be built with the standard widget, which results in these unwanted items in the search pop-up window.

When a host is down for some time, pending mail can build up for it, and this can make it hard to deal with other messages on the queue. To help with this situation, there is a button next to Update called Hide. If pressed, a dialogue box called "Hide addresses ending with" is opened. If you type anything in here and press Return (or Enter), the text is added to a chain of such texts, and if every undelivered address in a message matches at least one of the texts, the message is not displayed.

If there is an address that does not match any of the texts, all the addresses are displayed as normal. The matching happens on the ends of addresses so, for example, `foo.com.example` specifies all addresses in that domain, whereas `xxx@foo.com.example` specifies just one specific address. When any hiding has been set up, a button called Unhide is displayed. If pressed, it cancels all hiding. Also, to ensure that hidden messages are not forgotten, a hide request is automatically cancelled after one hour.

While the dialogue box is displayed, you cannot press any buttons or do anything else to the monitor window. For this reason, if you want to cut text from the queue display to use in the dialogue box, you must do the cutting before pressing the Hide button.

The queue display contains, for each unhidden queued message, the length of time it has been on the queue, the size of the message, the message ID, the message sender, and the first undelivered recipient, all on one line. If it is a delivery error message, the sender is shown as < >. If there is more than one recipient to which the message has not yet been delivered, subsequent recipients are listed on additional lines, up to a maximum configured number, following which an ellipsis is displayed. Recipients that have already received the message are not shown. If a message is frozen, an asterisk is displayed at the left-hand side.

The queue display has a vertical scrollbar and can also be scrolled by means of the arrow keys. Text can be cut from it using the mouse in the normal way. The text searching facilities, as described earlier for the log window, are also available, but the caret is always moved to the end of the text when the queue display is updated.

## 21.7.6 The queue menu

If the Shift key is held down and the left button is clicked when the mouse pointer is over the text for any message in the queue window, an action menu pops up and the first line of the queue display for the message is highlighted. This does not affect any selected text. If you want to use some other event for popping up the menu, you can set EXIMON_MENU_EVENT in the environment before starting the monitor. The value set in this parameter is a standard X event description. For example, to run *eximon* using Ctrl rather than Shift you could use:

```
EXIMON_MENU_EVENT='Ctrl<Btn1Down>' eximon
```

An example of an *eximon* menu is shown in figure 21-2.

```
17QQLC-0005Xc-00
Message log
Headers
Body
Deliver message
Freeze message
Thaw message
Give up on msg
Remove message
_____

Add recipient
Mark delivered
Mark all delivered
Edit sender
```

*Figure 21-2: Monitor menu*

The title of the menu is the message ID, and it contains entries that act as follows:

*Message log*

The contents of the message log for the message are displayed in a new text window.

*Headers*

Information from the spool file containing the envelope information and header lines is displayed in a new text window.

*Body*

The contents of the spool file containing the body of the message are displayed in a new text window. There is a default limit of 20 KB to the amount of data displayed. This can be changed by setting EXIMON_BODY_MAX.

*Deliver message*

A call to Exim is made using the -M option to request delivery of the message. This causes an automatic thaw if the message is frozen. The -v option is also set. The output from Exim is displayed in a new text window. The delivery is run in a separate process, so as to avoid holding up the monitor while the delivery proceeds.

*Freeze message*

A call to Exim is made using the -Mf option to request that the message be frozen.

*Thaw message*

A call to Exim is made using the -Mt option to request that the message be thawed.

*Give up on msg*

A call to Exim is made using the -Mg option to request that Exim gives up trying to deliver the message. A delivery failure report is generated for any remaining undelivered addresses.

*Remove message*

A call to Exim is made using the -Mrm option to request that the message be deleted from the system without generating any failure reports.

*Add recipient*

A dialogue box is displayed into which a recipient address can be typed. Pressing Return (or Enter) causes a call to Exim to be made using the -Mar option, which requests that an additional recipient be added to the message. However, if the entry box is empty, no action is taken.

*Mark delivered*

A dialogue box is displayed into which a recipient address can be typed. Pressing Return (or Enter) causes a call to Exim to be made using the -Mmd option, which marks the given recipient address as already delivered. However, if the entry box is empty, no action is taken.

*Mark all delivered*

A call to Exim is made using the -Mmad option to mark all recipient addresses as already delivered.

*Edit sender*

A dialogue box is displayed initialized with the current sender's address for you to edit. Pressing Return (or Enter) causes a call to Exim to be made using the -Mes option, which replaces the sender address. However, if the entry box is empty, no action is taken.

In cases when a call to Exim is made, if the call results in any output from Exim (in particular, if the command fails), a window containing the command and the output is displayed. When a delivery is forced, there is always output because of the use of the -v option. In any text window that is displayed as a result of a menu action, the normal cut-and-paste facility is available and searching can be carried out using CTRL-R and CTRL-S, as described earlier for the log tail window.

The results of the action are normally apparent from the log and queue displays. The latter is automatically updated for actions such as freezing and thawing, unless EXIMON_ACTION_QUEUE_UPDATE=no has been set. In this case, the Update button has to be used to force an update to the display after freezing or thawing.

# 21.8 Checking relay access

The -bh command line option allows you to run a fake SMTP session with debugging output, in order to check what Exim is doing when it is applying policy controls to incoming SMTP mail. However, not everybody is sufficiently familiar with the SMTP protocol to be able to make full use of -bh, and sometimes you just want to answer the question *Does this address have access?* without bothering with any further details.

The *exim_checkaccess* utility is a "packaged" version of -bh. It takes two arguments, an IP address and an email address, as in the following example:

```
exim_checkaccess 10.9.8.7 A.User@a.domain.example
```

The utility runs a call to Exim with the -bh option, to test whether the given email address would be accepted in a RCPT command in a TCP/IP connection from the host with the given IP address. The output of the utility is either the word "accepted", or the SMTP error response, as in this example:

```
Rejected:
  550 Relay not permitted
```

When running this test, the utility uses <> as the envelope sender address for the MAIL command, but you can change this by providing additional options. These are passed directly to the Exim command. For example, to specify that the test is to be run with the sender address *himself@there.example* you can use this command:

```
exim_checkaccess 10.9.8.7 A.User@a.domain.example \
                 -f himself@there.example
```

---

 The additional Exim command line items must be given *after* the two mandatory arguments.

---

# 21.9 Maintaining alias and other files

Although Exim uses just one runtime configuration file, this generally refers to other files containing various kinds of data (for example, alias lists). If you update any of these referenced files, Exim processes will pick up the new contents immediately; you do not need to take special action. However, if you update the runtime configuration itself, or any files that are included by the `.include` mechanism, you must send a `SIGHUP` signal to the daemon process. You need to be *root* or *exim* to do this, using a command such as:

```
kill -HUP `cat /var/spool/exim/exim-daemon.pid`
```

This command causes the daemon to restart and reread the configuration. It is a good idea to check the log after you have done this, so as to ensure that the daemon has restarted successfully. All Exim processes other than the daemon are short-lived, so as new ones start, they will see the new configuration.

## 21.9.1 Maintaining DBM files

If you are using DBM files for aliases or any other data, you need to rebuild them from source files if you want to change their contents. A utility program called *exim_dbmbuild* is provided for doing this. It reads an input file in the format of an alias file and writes a DBM database, using the lower-cased alias names as keys, and the remainder of the information as data. The lowercasing can be prevented by calling the program with the `-nolc` option.

A terminating zero is included as part of the key string. This is expected by the dbm lookup type. However, if the option `-nozero` is given, *exim_dbmbuild* creates files without terminating zeros in either the key strings or the data strings. The dbmnz lookup type can be used with such files.

The program requires two arguments: the name of the input file (which can be a single hyphen to indicate the standard input) and the name of the output database. It creates the database under a temporary name and then renames the file(s) if all goes well. If the native Berkeley DB interface is in use (common in free operating systems), the two filenames must be different because in this mode the Berkeley DB functions create a single output file using exactly the name given. For example:

```
exim_dbmbuild /etc/aliases /etc/aliases.db
```

reads the system alias file and creates a DBM version of it in */etc/aliases.db*.

In systems that use the *ndbm* routines (mostly proprietary versions of Unix), DBM databases consist of two files with suffixes *.dir* and *.pag*. In this environment, the suffixes are added to the second argument of *exim_dbmbuild*, so it can be the same as the first.

The program outputs a warning if it encounters a duplicate key. By default, only the first of a set of duplicates is used; this makes it compatible with `lsearch` lookups. An option called `-lastdup` causes it to use the last instead. There is also an option `-nowarn`, which stops it from listing duplicate keys to the standard error stream. If any duplicates are encountered, the return code is 1, unless `-noduperr` is used. For other errors (when it has not actually made a new file), the return code is 2.

# 21.10 Hints database maintenance

Exim uses DBM files to hold the data for its hints databases. Under normal circumstances you do not have to worry very much about these, except in one respect: they need "tidying" periodically. Out-of-date information accumulates in the files; if they are not tidied, their size keeps on increasing. This is usually quite gradual, so that weekly tidying is often sufficient, though some sites prefer to do it daily. A utility program called *exim_tidydb* is provided to do this job.

Deleting unwanted information from a DBM file does not normally reduce the size of the file. However, it does make the space for the deleted items available for subsequent reuse.

There is also a utility for dumping the contents of a hints database and one for making modifications. However, you are most unlikely to want to use either of them, so they are not described here. The reference manual has details if you need them.

The *exim_tidydb* utility program requires two arguments. The first specifies the name of Exim's spool directory, and the second is the name of the database that *exim_tidydb* is to operate on. These names are as follows:

`retry:`

   The database of retry information.

`wait-<transport-name>:`

   Databases of information about messages waiting for remote hosts, using particular transports. Usually there is only one remote transport, so there is just one such database with a name such as `wait-remote_smtp`.

`misc:`

   A database containing miscellaneous information that Exim needs to remember, such as a list of current connections to hosts that are restricted to one outgoing connection at a time by the `serialize_hosts` option of the **smtp** transport.

If *exim_tidydb* is run with no options, it removes all records from the database that are more than 30 days old. For example:

```
exim_tidydb  /var/spool/exim  retry
```

The cutoff date can be altered with the -t option, which must be followed by a time. For example, to remove all records older than a week from the retry database, use the following:

```
exim_tidydb -t 7d /var/spool/exim retry
```

Some of the hints databases contain data pertaining to specific messages. For these, a check is made to ensure that message IDs in database records are those of messages still on the queue. The hints concerning messages that no longer exist are automatically removed.

The *exim_tidydb* utility outputs comments on the standard output whenever it removes information from the database. However, this output is not normally needed, and can be discarded. You should normally run this utility periodically on all databases, but at a quiet time of day, since it requires a database to be locked (and therefore be inaccessible to Exim) while it does its work. It can be run as the Exim user. For example, if you have just one remote transport called **remote_smtp**, these commands would be appropriate:

```
exim_tidydb /var/spool/exim retry            >/dev/null
exim_tidydb /var/spool/exim wait-remote_smtp >/dev/null
exim_tidydb /var/spool/exim misc             >/dev/null
```

You can put these commands in a file (called */usr/exim/bin/tidy_alldb*, for example) and have it run daily by a root *crontab* entry such as:

```
10 3 * * * su exim -c /usr/exim/bin/tidy_alldb
```

You have to make sure that *exim_tidydb* can be found, either by using an absolute pathname or by setting PATH in the script. Alternatively, you can use a *crontab* entry for *exim* instead of *root*, and, of course, you can put the individual commands directly into the *crontab* if you want to.

# 21.11 Mailbox maintenance

Now and again there are occasions when you want to prevent any new messages from being delivered into a user's mailbox because you want to carry out some maintenance activity on it, or investigate a problem. You could modify Exim's configuration file to defer deliveries to that user, but then you would have to remodify it afterwards, and in any case, this would not prevent user agents from modifying the mailbox. A better approach is to lock the mailbox.[1]

The *exim_lock* utility locks a mailbox file using the same algorithm as Exim. This prevents modification of a mailbox by Exim or a user agent. The utility requires the name of the file as its first argument. If the locking is successful, the second

---

[1]  Locking only works, of course, if the mailbox is a single file. If you are using multifile mailboxes, another approach must be found.

argument is run as a command. If there is no second argument, the value of the SHELL environment variable is used; if this is unset or empty, */bin/sh* is run. When the command finishes, the mailbox is unlocked and the utility ends. For example:

```
exim_lock /var/spool/mail/spqr
```

runs an interactive shell while the file is locked, whereas:

```
exim_lock -q /var/spool/mail/spqr <<End
some commands
End
```

runs a specific non-interactive sequence of commands while the file is locked. The -q ("quiet") option suppresses verification output. A single command can be run while the file is locked by a command such as:

```
exim_lock -q /var/spool/mail/spqr "cp /var/spool/mail/spqr /some/where"
```

Note that if a command is supplied, it must be entirely contained within the second argument; hence the quotes.

Without -q, some verification output is written. More detailed verification of the locking process can be requested with -v. There are also some options that are similar to the options on the **appendfile** transport for controlling the way the mailbox is locked. Unless you have made changes to the locking options of **appendfile**, you should not need to specify any of these options. For details, see the reference manual.

# 22

# Building and installing Exim

So far, we have talked only about how to use Exim, assuming that it is already installed on your system. We have not yet covered the installation process. There are three possibilities:

- Some operating systems (for example, Debian GNU/Linux) are now distributed with Exim already installed. If yours is one of these, you do not need to do anything, unless you want to use some of the optional code that is not included in your binary or you want to upgrade to a later release. If you do, you will have to fetch the source and compile it yourself.

- Some operating systems (for example, FreeBSD) have a standardized "ports" mechanism, with a simple command that fetches the Exim source, compiles it with a particular set of options, and installs it for you. Again, if the options are suitable, you need do no more; if not, you must recompile, but in this scenario, the source is already available on your host. However, if you want to upgrade to a later release, you will have to fetch a new source.

- If neither of these apply to you, you will have to fetch a copy of the source yourself, and then compile and install it.

This chapter describes the process of building and installing Exim from the source distribution.

## 22.1 Prerequisites

You need to have a working ANSI/ISO C compiler installed before you can build Exim. If you do not have a compiler, either consult your vendor or consider installing *gcc*, the GNU C compiler. You can find information about *gcc* at *http://www.fsf.org /order/ftp.html*. If you want to build the Exim monitor, the X Window libraries and header files must also be available.

You will need *gunzip* (or *bunzip*) and *tar* to unpack the source. The building process assumes the availability of standard Unix tools such as *make* and *sed*. You do not need Perl in order to build or run Exim, but as some of the associated utilities are Perl scripts, it is a good idea to make sure that it is installed as well.

Finally, even if you do not use DBM lookups in your configuration, Exim requires a DBM library, because it uses DBM files for holding its hints databases. Licenced versions of Unix normally contain a library of DBM functions operating via the *ndbm* interface. Free operating systems vary in what they contain as standard. Some older versions of Linux have no default DBM library at all, and different distributors have chosen to include different libraries. However, the more recent releases of all the free operating systems seem to have standardized on the Berkeley DB library.

The original Berkeley DB package reached Version 1.85 before being superseded by Release 2 and then Releases 3 and 4. The older versions are no longer maintained. You can find information about Berkeley DB at *http://www.sleepycat.com*.

## 22.2 Fetching and unpacking the source

The "Availability" link on the Exim home page (*http://www.exim.org*) leads to a page containing a list of sites from which the source may be downloaded. The home page also contains information about the status of different versions. You can use your browser to download a distribution into an appropriate directory such as */usr/source /exim*. The distribution is a single compressed *tar* file, for example:

```
/usr/source/exim/exim-4.10.tar.gz
```

Move to that directory, and unpack Exim using *gunzip* and *tar*:[1]

```
$ cd /usr/source/exim
$ gunzip exim-4.10.tar.gz
$ tar -xf exim-4.10.tar
```

You should now have a directory called *exim-4.10*, which is the distribution file tree. You can delete the *tar* file to save space, and then move into the distribution directory:

```
$ rm exim-4.10.tar
$ cd exim-4.10
```

You should see the following files:

| | |
|---|---|
| CHANGES | information about changes |
| LICENCE | the GNU General Public License |
| Makefile | top-level makefile |
| NOTICE | conditions for the use of Exim |
| README | list of files, directories, and simple build instructions |

Other files whose names begin with *README* may also be present. The following subdirectories should be present:

| | |
|---|---|
| Local | empty; you put local building configuration here |
| OS | OS-specific files |
| doc | documentation files |

---

[1] The distribution is available in *bzip2* as well as *gzip* format; the former is substantially smaller, and therefore quicker to download. The final file extension is *.bz2*, instead of *.gz*, and you decompress it using *bunzip* instead of *gunzip*.

| | |
|---|---|
| `exim_monitor` | source files for the Exim monitor |
| `scripts` | scripts used in the building process |
| `src` | source files for Exim and some utilities |
| `util` | independent utilities |

The *doc* directory contains a copy of the reference manual as a plain text file called *spec.txt*. This is provided more for convenient searching than for sequential reading. You can download copies of the manual in various other formats from the ftp sites; to save space, these are not included in the source distribution. PostScript or PDF is best if you want to make a printed copy, whereas HTML and Texinfo are indexed formats for reading online.[1] The *doc* directory also contains information about changes and new additions to Exim. A complete list of runtime and build-time options can be found in the file *doc/OptionLists.txt*.

Most utilities are contained in the *src* directory and are built with the Exim binary; those distributed in the *util* directory are example scripts that do not depend on any compile-time configuration.

# 22.3 Configuration for building

The configuration that you set up for building Exim is placed in the directory called *Local*, which is empty initially. For Exim itself there must be a file called *Local/Makefile*, and for the Exim monitor a file called *Local/eximon.conf*. You should never need to modify any of the original distribution files. If something in your operating system requires a different setting, do not modify the default; instead insert an overriding setting in *Local/Makefile*. If you do things this way, you will be able to copy the contents of the *Local* directory and reuse them when the time comes to build the next release.

## 22.3.1 The contents of Local/Makefile

The contents of *Local/Makefile* are a series of settings such as:

```
BIN_DIRECTORY=/usr/exim/bin
```

The settings can be in any order, and you can insert comment lines starting with # if you wish. A template for *Local/Makefile* is supplied in *src/EDITME*. It contains sample settings and comments describing what they are for. One way of creating your *Local/Makefile* is to copy the template and then edit the copy:

```
$ cp src/EDITME Local/Makefile
$ vi Local/Makefile
```

However, you can, of course, create *Local/Makefile* from scratch. There are a number of different types of setting that it can contain:

---

[1]   Later in this chapter there is more on the Texinfo documentation (☞ 22.8).

*Mandatory*

These are settings without which Exim will not build.

*Drivers*

These settings specify which drivers are included in the binary.

*Modules*

These settings specify which optional modules (for example, lookup types) are included in the binary.

*Recommended*

There are some values that can be set either at build time or in the runtime configuration. It is recommended they be set here if possible.

*Optional*

These settings are simply a matter of choice.

*System*

These settings depend on the configuration of your operating system.

The contents of *Local/Makefile* are combined with files from the *OS* directory to arrive at the settings to be used for building Exim in the following way:

- *OS/Makefile-Default* contains a common list of default settings. For example, it contains:

  ```
  CC=gcc
  ```

  to specify *gcc* as the default C compiler.

- Settings in the OS-specific *Makefile* can override the common defaults for a particular operating system. For example, in *OS/Makefile-IRIX65*, there is:

  ```
  CC=cc
  ```

  This specifies *cc* as the default C compiler when building under Irix 6.5.

- Finally, settings in *Local/Makefile* can override anything previously set. Suppose you wanted to use *gcc* under Irix 6.5 after all. The correct way to do this is not to delete the setting in *OS/Makefile-IRIX65*, but instead to add:

  ```
  CC=gcc
  ```

  in *Local/Makefile*, so as to leave the distribution files unchanged.

Some option settings are for use in special cases, and are rarely needed. The following sections cover briefly those that are more commonly required. The *src/EDITME* and *OS/Makefile-Defaults* files contain more details, in the form of extended comments.

## 22.3.2 Mandatory Local/Makefile settings

There are only three settings that you must include in *Local/Makefile*. They specify the directory into which Exim will be installed, the location of its runtime configuration file, and the identity of the Exim user. For example:

```
BIN_DIRECTORY=/usr/exim/bin
CONFIGURE_FILE=/usr/exim/configure
EXIM_USER=exim
```

EXIM_USER defines the uid and gid for the Exim user (that is, the identity under which Exim runs when it does not need *root* privilege). If you define the user numerically, you also need to specify EXIM_GROUP. However, if you build Exim with just these settings, it will not be very useful, because the resulting binary contains no drivers and no code for any lookup types. It would be capable of receiving messages, but not delivering them.

## 22.3.3 Driver choices in Local/Makefile

In practice, most people take the default settings in *src/EDITME* when it comes to choosing which routers and transports to include. These are as follows:

```
ROUTER_ACCEPT=yes
ROUTER_DNSLOOKUP=yes
ROUTER_IPLITERAL=yes
ROUTER_MANUALROUTE=yes
ROUTER_QUERYPROGRAM=yes
ROUTER_REDIRECT=yes

TRANSPORT_APPENDFILE=yes
TRANSPORT_AUTOREPLY=yes
TRANSPORT_PIPE=yes
TRANSPORT_SMTP=yes
```

If you want to include support for SMTP authentication, you must add one or both of the following:

```
AUTH_CRAM_MD5=yes
AUTH_PLAINTEXT=yes
```

## 22.3.4 Module choices in Local/Makefile

The default settings for lookup types are:

```
LOOKUP_DBM=yes
LOOKUP_LSEARCH=yes
```

which cause the inclusion of code for lsearch and dbm lookup types. Other possibilities are as follows:

```
LOOKUP_CDB=yes
LOOKUP_DNSDB=yes
LOOKUP_DSEARCH=yes
LOOKUP_LDAP=yes
LOOKUP_MYSQL=yes
LOOKUP_NIS=yes
LOOKUP_NISPLUS=yes
LOOKUP_ORACLE=yes
LOOKUP_PGSQL=yes
LOOKUP_WHOSON=yes
```

Apart from LOOKUP_DNSDB, you should set these only if you have the relevant software installed on your system. It is usually also necessary to specify where the appropriate library and include files may be found. For example, if you want to include support for MySQL, you might use:

```
LOOKUP_MYSQL=yes
LOOKUP_INCLUDE=-I /usr/local/mysql/include
LOOKUP_LIBS=-L/usr/local/lib -lmysqlclient
```

## 22.3.5 Recommended Local/Makefile settings

A few important settings can be specified either at build time or at runtime. It is recommended that you set these at build time if their values are fixed, for two reasons:

- Runtime settings can be lost accidentally, which might lead to serious misbehaviour.

- A change to the log file path at runtime cannot take effect until the runtime configuration has been read. If there is a serious problem before this (for example, inability to read the runtime configuration), Exim cannot log it to the correct place, and maybe cannot log it at all.

If it is so dangerous, why can these settings be changed at runtime? There are two reasons:

- Some administrators need to distribute copies of the binary to a number of hosts with slightly different requirements. They are prepared to accept the risk.

- It makes certain kinds of testing easier.

Examples of the settings that are in this recommended category are as follows:

```
LOG_FILE_PATH=/var/log/exim_%slog
SPOOL_DIRECTORY=/var/spool/exim
SPOOL_MODE=0640
```

You do not need to set `LOG_FILE_PATH` at all if you are happy with the default, which is to use a subdirectory of the spool directory, equivalent in this example to:

```
LOG_FILE_PATH=/var/spool/exim/log/%slog
```

You do not need to set `SPOOL_MODE` if you are happy with the default value of 0600. Setting it to 0640 allows members of the Exim group to read spool files, which is necessary for running the Exim monitor.

## 22.3.6 A plausible minimal Local/Makefile

Here is an example of a minimal *Local/Makefile* that includes the recommended settings as well as the default drivers and lookups:

```
BIN_DIRECTORY=/usr/exim/bin
CONFIGURE_FILE=/usr/exim/configure
EXIM_USER=exim

LOOKUP_DBM=yes
LOOKUP_LSEARCH=yes

ROUTER_ACCEPT=yes
ROUTER_DNSLOOKUP=yes
ROUTER_IPLITERAL=yes
ROUTER_MANUALROUTE=yes
ROUTER_QUERYPROGRAM=yes
ROUTER_REDIRECT=yes

SPOOL_DIRECTORY=/var/spool/exim
SPOOL_MODE=0640

TRANSPORT_APPENDFILE=yes
TRANSPORT_AUTOREPLY=yes
TRANSPORT_PIPE=yes
TRANSPORT_SMTP=yes
```

Building Exim with this file produces a usable binary that can carry out straightforward mail delivery.

## 22.3.7 System-related Local/Makefile settings

The C compiler is called either *cc* or *gcc*, or sometimes something else again, and different compilers accept different option settings. The system-related settings allow you to specify the name of your compiler and its options, as in the following example:

```
CC=cc
CFLAGS=-Otax -4
```

On some operating systems, additional libraries must be specified. For example, Solaris keeps the socket-related functions in a separate library. The OS-dependent makefiles use `LIBS` for these settings. For example, the Solaris file contains:

```
LIBS=-lsocket -lnsl -lkstat
```

If you want to add yet more libraries of your own, you should use EXTRALIBS rather than LIBS, but you can of course use LIBS if you want to override what is in the distribution files.

The settings in LIBS and EXTRALIBS are used for every binary that is built, which includes some of the utilities. If you want to restrict the use of certain libraries to just the Exim binary or just the *eximon* binary, you can use EXTRALIBS_EXIM and EXTRALIBS_EXIMON, respectively.

Settings for the DBM library are also commonly required:

```
USE_DB=yes
DBMLIB=-ldb
```

The defaults for these settings are taken from the system-specific makefiles in the *OS* directory, so, in most cases, you should not need to set them in *Local/Makefile*.

If you want Exim to use wallclock time for its timestamps, you might want to set TIMEZONE_DEFAULT in *Local/Makefile*, for example:

```
TIMEZONE_DEFAULT=EST
```

This provides the default value for the timezone option (☞ 19.5). If it is not included, the value of the TZ environment variable at the time Exim is built is used.

## 22.3.8 Optional settings in Local/Makefile

The remaining settings in *Local/Makefile* are simply a matter of choice. For example:

```
EXICYCLOG_MAX=28
```

specifies that the *exicyclog* utility should keep a maximum of 28 old log files (the default is 10). The comments in *src/EDITME* explain what the settings do in each case.

## 22.3.9 Configuration for building the Exim monitor

The Exim monitor is built along with Exim, and if you want to do this, you must set up a suitable configuration for it. There are only two things that are mandatory:

- In the main configuration file, *Local/Makefile*, you must include:

```
EXIM_MONITOR=eximon.bin
```

  If this setting is not present, the monitor is omitted from the building process. You may also need to specify the whereabouts of the X11 library and include files if the defaults are not correct. For example:

```
X11=/opt/X11R6.3
XINCLUDE=-I$(X11)/include
XLFLAGS=-L$(X11)/lib
X11_LD_LIB=$(X11)/lib
```

- You must create *Local/eximon.conf*, which is a configuration file containing your choices.

A commented template for *Local/eximon.conf* is supplied in *exim_monitor/EDITME*. In this case, there are no mandatory settings, so the file can be completely empty, though it must exist. You can set up an empty file with the command:

```
touch Local/eximon.conf
```

The available settings allow you to change the size of the window and the appearance of some of the data. Descriptions of each setting appear as comments in *exim_monitor/EDITME*.

## 22.3.10 Building Exim for multiple systems

If you are building Exim for just a single operating system on a single host, you can skip this section entirely. If, on the other hand, you have a single source directory that is accessible to a number of hosts running different operating systems, or using different hardware architectures, you may want to set different values for the different cases.

So far, we have talked about a single *Local/Makefile* containing all the local settings. You can, in fact, supply separate files for each operating system, each hardware architecture, and each combination of operating system and architecture, if you so wish. These are optional files that are consulted in addition to *Local/Makefile* only if they exist. The full list of all possible files is as follows:

```
Local/Makefile
Local/Makefile-ostype
Local/Makefile-archtype
Local/Makefile-ostype-archtype
```

where *ostype* is the operating system type (for example, Linux), and *archtype* is the hardware architecture type (for example, i386). The files are used in that order. In other words, settings in *Local/Makefile* apply to all cases, but can be overridden by settings in *Local/Makefile-ostype*, which in turn can be overridden by the other two files. Thus, a single set of files can contain the correct settings for all the different cases, with a minimum of repetition.

A similar scheme is used for the Exim monitor, where the filenames are as follows:

```
Local/eximon.conf
Local/eximon.conf-ostype
Local/eximon.conf-archtype
Local/eximon.conf-ostype-archtype
```

The values that are used for *ostype* and *archtype* are obtained from scripts called *scripts/os-type* and *scripts/arch-type*, respectively. If either of the environment variables EXIM_OSTYPE or EXIM_ARCHTYPE is set, their values are used instead, thereby providing a means of forcing particular settings. Otherwise, the scripts try to find suitable values by running the *uname* command. If this fails, the shell variables OSTYPE and ARCHTYPE are inspected. A number of ad hoc transformations are then applied, to produce the standard names that Exim expects. You can run these scripts directly from the shell in order to find out what values will be used on your system.

The toplevel makefile copes with rebuilding Exim correctly if any of the configuration files are edited. However, if an optional configuration file is deleted, it is necessary to *touch* the associated non-optional file (that is, *Local/Makefile* or */Local /eximon.conf*) before rebuilding.

## 22.4 The building process

Once you have created the appropriate configuration files in the *Local* directory, you can run the building process by the single command:

```
$ make
```

The first thing this does is to create a "build directory" whose name is *build-ostype-archtype* (for example *build-SunOS5-5.8-sparc*). Links to the source files are installed in this directory, and all the files that are created while building are written here. This way of doing things means that you can build Exim for different operating systems and different architectures from the same set of shared source files if you want to.

If this is the first time *make* has been run, it calls a script that builds a makefile inside the build directory, using the configuration files from the *Local* directory.[1] The new makefile is passed to another instance of *make*, which does the real work. First, it builds a header file called *config.h*, using values from *Local/Makefile*, and then it builds a number of utility scripts. Next, it compiles and links the binaries for the Exim monitor (if configured), a number of utilities, and finally Exim itself. If all goes well, the last line of output on your screen should be:

```
>>> exim binary built
```

If you have problems building Exim, check for any comments there may be in the *README* file concerning your operating system, and also take a look at the FAQ, where some common problems are covered. It is available from any of the FTP sites, and it is also online at *http://www.exim.org*.

---

[1] The command *make makefile* can be used to force a rebuild of the makefile in the build directory, should this ever be necessary. If you make changes to *Local/Makefile*, it is automatically rebuilt when next you run *make*.

# 22.5 Installing Exim

The command:

```
$ make install
```

runs a script called *scripts/exim_install*, which copies the binaries and scripts into the directory whose name is specified by BIN_DIRECTORY in *Local/Makefile*.

Files are copied only if they are newer than any versions already in the directory. Old versions of the utility programs are renamed by adding the suffix *.O* to their names. The Exim binary itself, however, is handled differently. It is installed under a name that includes the version number and the compile number, for example *exim-4.10-1*. The script then arranges for a symbolic link called *exim* to point to the binary. If you are updating a previous version of Exim, the script takes care to ensure that the name *exim* is never absent from the directory (as seen by other processes). This means you can safely install a new version of Exim on a live system.

You need to be *root* when you run this command, because, for most configurations, the main Exim binary is required to be owned by *root* and have the setuid bit set. The install script therefore sets *root* as the owner of the main binary makes it setuid. If you want to see what the script will do before running it for real, run it from the build directory, using the -n option (for which *root* privilege is not needed):

```
$ (cd build-SunOS5-5.5.1-sparc; ../scripts/exim_install -n)
```

The -n option causes the script to output a list of the commands it would obey, without actually obeying any of them.

If the runtime configuration file, as defined by CONFIGURE_FILE in *Local/Makefile*, does not exist, the default configuration file *src/configure.default* is copied there by the installation script. If a runtime configuration file already exists, it is left alone.

The default configuration uses the local host's name as the only local domain, and is set up for delivering locally into the shared directory */var/mail*, running as the local user. Aliases in */etc/aliases* and *.forward* files in users' home directories are supported. Remote domains are routed using the DNS, with delivery over SMTP. There is an ACL that accepts incoming SMTP mail for the local domain only; relaying from other hosts is locked out.

You do not need to create the spool directory when installing Exim. When it starts up, Exim creates the spool directory if it does not exist. Subdirectories are automatically created in the spool directory as necessary.

If you are installing Exim on a system that is running some other MTA, installing the files by running *make install* does not of itself cause Exim to supersede the other MTA. Once you get this far, it is all ready to go, but it still needs to be "turned on" before it will start handling your mail. Before you take this final step, it is a good idea to do some testing.

# 22.6 Testing before turning Exim on

When all the files are in place, you can run various tests, including passing messages to Exim directly and having it deliver them. You can then inspect the log files or run the monitor if you wish. The one thing you cannot do while another MTA is running is to run a daemon on the standard SMTP port, but if you wish to test the daemon, an alternative port can be used.

First, check that the runtime configuration file is syntactically valid by running the command:

```
exim -bV
```

If there are any errors in the configuration file, Exim outputs error messages, which are also written to the panic log. Otherwise, it just outputs the version number and build date. Routing tests can be done by using the address testing option. For example:

```
exim -v -bt user@your.domain
```

checks that it recognizes a local mailbox, and:

```
exim -v -bt user@somewhere.else.example
```

a remote one. Then try using Exim to deliver mail, both locally and remotely. This can be done by passing messages directly to Exim, without going through a user agent. For example:

```
exim postmaster@your.domain
From: user@your.domain
To: postmaster@your.domain
Subject: Testing Exim

This is a test message.
:.:
```

If you encounter problems, look at Exim's log files to see if there is any relevant information there, and use the -bp option to see if the message is still on Exim's queue. Another source of information is running Exim with debugging turned on by the -d option (you need to be an admin user to do this). Amongst other things, this shows the sequence of routers that process an address. If a message is stuck on Exim's spool, you can force a delivery with debugging turned on by a command of the form:

```
exim -d -M 13A918-0000iT-00
```

One specific problem that has shown up on some sites is the failure of local deliveries into a single shared mailbox directory that does not have the "sticky bit" (☞ 9.4.1) set on it. By default, Exim tries to create a lock file before writing to a mailbox file, and if it cannot create the lock file, the delivery is deferred. To work round this problem, either set the "sticky bit" on the directory, or set a specific group for local deliveries and allow that group to create files in the directory (see the comments about the **local_delivery** transport in the default configuration file). For further discussion of locking issues, see section 9.4.3.

You can test a daemon by running it on a non-standard port by a command such as the following:

```
exim -bd -oX 1225
```

and then using *telnet* to connect to port 1225.[1] However, if you want to test out policy controls for incoming mail, the -bh option is better, because it allows you to simulate an incoming connection from any IP address you like.

A new version on a system that is already running Exim can most easily be tested by building a binary with a different CONFIGURE_FILE setting. From within the runtime configuration, all other file and directory names that Exim uses can be altered, in order to keep it entirely clear of the production version.

# 22.7 Turning Exim on

The conventional pathname that is used to call the MTA on Unix-like systems is either */usr/sbin/sendmail* or */usr/lib/sendmail*. In some cases, both paths exist, usually pointing to the same file. User agents use one of these names to send messages, and there is usually a reference from one of the system boot scripts that starts a listening daemon.

The process of "turning Exim on" consists of changing these paths so that they refer to Exim instead of to the previous MTA. This is commonly done by renaming the existing file and setting up a symbolic link. You need to be *root* to do this. It is also a good idea to remove the setuid bit from the previous MTA, and/or make it inaccessible. For example:

```
$ mv /usr/sbin/sendmail /usr/sbin/sendmail.old
$ chmod 0600 /usr/sbin/sendmail.old
$ ln -s /usr/exim/bin/exim /usr/sbin/sendmail
```

Once this is done, any program that calls */usr/sbin/sendmail* actually calls Exim.

Some operating systems have introduced alternative ways of switching MTAs. For example, if you are running FreeBSD, you need to edit the file */etc/mail/mailer.conf*

---

[1]   It is often useful to add -d to such a command to turn on debugging; this leaves the testing daemon connected to the terminal, so you can easily kill it with CTRL-C.

instead of setting up a symbolic link as just described. A typical example of the contents of this file for running Exim is as follows:

```
sendmail            /usr/exim/bin/exim
send-mail           /usr/exim/bin/exim
mailq               /usr/exim/bin/exim -bp
newaliases          /usr/bin/true
```

Once you have set up the symbolic link, or edited */etc/mail/mailer.conf*, your Exim installation is "live". Check it by sending a message from your favourite user agent.

There is one more thing to do once you have Exim running on your host, and that is to set up *cron* jobs. You need these to cycle the log files (unless you are using *syslog* only) and to tidy the hints databases from time to time (☞ 21.4, 21.10).

# 22.8 Installing documentation in info format

Some operating systems have standardized on the GNU *info* system for documentation, and if yours is one of these, you probably want to install Exim's documentation in this format. You can arrange for this to happen as part of the Exim installation process by making a few preliminary preparations.

The source of the *info* version of the documentation is not included in the Exim distribution, because not everybody wants it, so you have to fetch it separately. The site from which you obtained Exim should also have a file with a name such as this:

```
exim-texinfo-4.10.tar.gz
```

This unpacks into two files called:

```
exim-texinfo-4.10/doc/filter.texinfo
exim-texinfo-4.10/doc/spec.texinfo
```

The version number will always end in a zero, because the main documentation is not updated for intermediate releases where the version number ends with a non-zero digit. Copy or move these into the *doc* directory of the source tree that you are using (which may have a later version number):

```
$ mv exim-texinfo-4.10/doc/* exim-4.12/doc
```

Then add to your *Local/Makefile* a line of the form:

```
INFO_DIRECTORY=/usr/local/info
```

to define the location of the *info* files on your system. Once this is done, running the following:

```
$ make install
```

automatically builds the *info* files from the *texinfo* sources, and installs them in */usr/local/info*.

# 22.9 Upgrading to a new release

Once you have fetched and unpacked the source of a new release, you should read the file called *README.UPDATING*. This contains information about changes that might affect the way Exim runs or that require changes to the configuration. Most releases of Exim are entirely backwards-compatible with their predecessors, though there was an incompatible change to the runtime configuration at the introduction of Release 3.00, and a further major change for Release 4.00.

You can normally just copy the files in your *Local* directory to the source tree for the new release in order to build it with the same settings as before. You may, of course, need to add to them in order to take advantage of new features that require configuration at build time.

After you have built a new release, provided that it is compatible with the old runtime configuration, you can install it "on the fly" without having to stop anything. There have only been two new releases (3.00 and 4.00) where this was not possible. If it happens again, you can be sure that *README.UPDATING* will warn you about it, and tell you how to proceed. Otherwise, just run:

```
$ make install
```

Once this has been done, programs that call the MTA immediately start using the new version instead of the old. However, the daemon process will continue to run the old version until you tell it to reload itself by sending it a HUP signal.

# Appendix A

# Summary of string expansion

This appendix contains a list of all the available expansion items, conditions, and variables, in alphabetical order in each case, with brief descriptions. A more detailed discussion of the expansion items and conditions can be found in chapter 17.

## A.1 Expansion items

The following items are recognized in expanded strings. Whitespace may be used between subitems that are keywords or substrings enclosed in braces inside an outer set of braces, to improve readability.

`$<variable-name>` or `${<variable-name>}`

The contents of the named variable are substituted. An unknown variable name causes an error.

`${address:<string>}`

The string is expanded; it is then interpreted as an RFC 2822 address and the effective address is extracted from it.

`${base62:<string>}`

The expanded string must consist entirely of decimal digits. The number is converted to base 62 and output as a string of six characters, including leading zeros.

`${domain:<string>}`

The string is expanded; it is then interpreted as an RFC 2822 address and the domain is extracted from it.

`${escape:<string>}`

If the expanded string contains any non-printing characters, they are converted to escape sequences starting with a backslash.

`${expand:<string>}`

The string is expanded twice.

`${extract{<key>}{<string>}}`

The subfield identified by the key is extracted from the expanded string. If the subfield is not found, the result is an empty string.

`${extract{<key>}{<string1>}{<string2>}{<string3>}}`

The subfield identified by the key is extracted from *<string1>*. If the subfield is found, its value is placed in *$value* and *<string2>* is then expanded; otherwise *<string3>* is expanded.

`${extract{<number>}{<separators>}{<string>}}`

The subfield numbered *<number>* is extracted from the expanded string. If there are insufficient fields, nothing is inserted.

`${extract{<number>}{<separators>}{<string1>}{<string2>}{`
`<string3>}}`

The subfield numbered *<number>* is extracted from the expanded *<string1>* and placed in *$value*. Then *<string2>* is expanded. If there are insufficient fields, *<string3>* is expanded instead.

`${hash_<n>_<m>:<string>}`

A textual hash of length *<n>* is generated, using characters from the first *<m>* characters of the concatenation of lower case letters, upper case letters, and digits. See also `nhash`.

`$header_<header-name>:` or `$h_<header-name>:`

The contents of the named message header are substituted. If there is no such header, no error occurs, and nothing is substituted.

`${if <condition> {<string1>}{<string2>}}`

If *<condition>* is true, *<string1>* is expanded; otherwise *<string2>* is expanded.

`${lc:<string>}`

The letters in the expanded string are forced into lower case.

`${length_<number>:<string>}`

The initial *<number>* characters of the expanded string are substituted.

`${local_part:<string>}`

The expanded string is interpreted as an RFC 2822 address, and the local part is extracted from it.

`${lookup{<key>} <single-key-lookup-type> {<file>}{<string1>}{<string2>}}`

The key is looked up in the given file using the given lookup type. If it is found, `<string1>` is expanded with *$value* containing the data; otherwise `<string2>` is expanded.

`${lookup <query-style-lookup-type> {<query>}{<string1>}{<string2>}}`

The query is passed to the given query-style lookup. If it succeeds, `<string1>` is expanded with *$value* containing the data; otherwise `<string2>` is expanded.

`${mask:<IP address>/<bitcount>}`

An IP address where all but the most significant `<bitcount>` bits are forced to zero is substituted, followed by `/<bitcount>`.

`${md5:<string>}`

The MD5 hash of the expanded string is inserted as a 32-digit hexadecimal number.

`${nhash_<n>:<string>}`

The string is expanded and then processed by a hash function that returns a numeric value in the range 0 to `<n-1>`.

`${nhash_<n>_<m>:<string>}`

The string is expanded and then processed by a div/mod hash function that returns two numbers, separated by a slash, in the ranges 0 to `<n-1>` and 0 to `<m-1>`, respectively.

`${perl{<subroutine>}{<arg>}{<arg>}...}`

The Perl subroutine is called with the given arguments, up to a maximum of eight. The arguments are first expanded.

`${quote:<string>}`

The string is expanded and then substituted, in double quotes if it contains anything other than letters, digits, underscores, dots, and hyphens. Any occurrences of double quotes and backslashes are escaped with a backslash.

`${quote_<lookup-type>:<string>}`

Lookup-specific quoting rules are applied to the expanded string.

`${readfile{<filename>}{<eol string>}}`

The contents of the file are inserted, with all newlines replaced by *<eol string>*.

`${run{<command args>}{<string1>}{<string2>}}`

The command is run in a separate process. If it succeeds, its output is placed in *$value* and *<string2>* is expanded. Otherwise, *<string2>* is expanded.

`${rxquote:<string>}`

A backslash is inserted before any non-alphanumeric characters in the expanded string.

`${sg{<subject>}{<regex>}{<replacement>}}`

The regular expression is repeatedly matched against the expanded subject string, and for each match, the expanded replacement is substituted. *$1*, *$2*, and so on can be used in the replacement to insert captured substrings.

`${substr_<offset>_<length>:<string>}`

A substring of length *<length>* starting at offset *<offset>* is extracted from the expanded string. Negative offsets count backwards from the end of the string.

`${tr{<subject>}{<string1>}{<string2>}}`

The expanded *<subject>* is translated by replacing characters found in *<string1>* by the corresponding characters in *<string2>*.

`${uc:<string>}`

The letters in the expanded string are forced into upper case.

# A.2 Expansion conditions

The following conditions are available for testing by the `${if` item while expanding strings:

`!<condition>`

Preceding any condition with an exclamation mark negates the result of the condition.

`<symbolic operator> {<string1>}{<string2>}`

There are a number of symbolic operators for numeric comparisons. They are:

|     |                           |
| --- | ------------------------- |
| =   | equal to                  |
| ==  | equal to                  |
| >   | greater than              |
| >=  | greater than or equal to  |
| <   | less than                 |
| <=  | less than or equal to     |

The two strings must take the form of optionally signed decimal integers, option-ally followed by one of the letters K or M (in either upper or lower case), signifying multiplication by 1024 or 1024×1024, respectively.

`crypteq {<string1>}{<string2>}`

The `crypteq` condition has two arguments. The first is encrypted and compared against the second, which is already encrypted. This condition is included in the Exim binary if it is built to support any authentication mechanisms. Otherwise, it is necessary to define `SUPPORT_CRYPTEQ` in *Local/Makefile* to have `crypteq` included in the binary.

`def:<variable-name>`

This form of the `def` condition must be followed by the name of one of the expansion variables (☞ A.3). The condition is true if the named expansion vari-able does not contain the empty string. The variable name is given without a leading dollar character. If the variable does not exist, the expansion fails.

`def:header_<header-name>:` or `def:h_<header-name>:`

This form of the `def` condition is true if a message is being processed and the named header exists in the message. No dollar appears before `header_` or `h_` in the condition, and the header name must be terminated by a colon if whitespace does not follow.

`eq {<string1>}{<string2>}`

The two substrings are first expanded. The condition is true if the two resulting strings are identical, including the case of letters.

`exists {<filename>}`

The substring is first expanded and then interpreted as an absolute path. The condition is true if the named file (or directory) exists.

`first_delivery`

This condition, which has no data, is true during a message's first delivery attempt. It is false during any subsequent delivery attempts.

`ldapauth{<LDAP query>}}`

This condition is true if the user and password in the LDAP query are successfully authenticated by the LDAP server.

`match {<string1>}{<string2>}`

The two substrings are first expanded. The second is treated as a regular expression and applied to the first. Because of the pre-expansion, if the regular expression contains dollar, or backslash characters, they must be escaped with backslashes. Care must also be taken if the regular expression contains braces (curly brackets). A closing brace must be escaped so that it is not taken as a premature termination of `<string2>`. It does no harm to escape opening braces, but this is not strictly necessary. The condition is true if the match succeeds.

`pam {<string1>:<string2>:...}`

The *Pluggable Authentication Module* (PAM) is initialized with the service name "exim" and the username taken from the first item in the colon-separated data string (that is, `<string1>`). The remaining items in the data string are passed over in response to requests from the authentication function. In the simple case, there will only be one request (for a password), so the data will consist of two strings only.[1]

`pwcheck{<user:password>}}`

This condition performs user authentication by calling the Cyrus *pwcheck* daemon.

`queue_running`

This condition, which has no data, is true during delivery attempts that are initiated by queue runner processes, and false otherwise.

`radius{<authentication string>}}`

This condition performs user authentication by calling the Radius server.

## A.2.1 Combining conditions

Two or more conditions can be combined using `and` and `or`:

`and {{<cond1>}{<cond2>}...}`

The subconditions are evaluated from left to right. The condition is true if all of the subconditions are true. If there are several `match` subconditions, the values of the numeric variables afterwards are taken from the last one. When a false subcondition is found, the following ones are parsed but not evaluated.

---

[1]  Pluggable Authentication Modules (*http://ftp.kernel.org/pub/linux/libs/pam/*) are a facility that is available in the latest releases of Solaris and in some GNU/Linux distributions.

```
or {{<cond1>}{<cond2>}...}
```

The subconditions are evaluated from left to right. The condition is true if any one of the subconditions is true. When a true subcondition is found, the following ones are parsed but not evaluated. If there are several `match` subconditions, the values of the numeric variables afterwards are taken from the first one that succeeds.

Note that `and` and `or` are complete conditions on their own, and precede their lists of subconditions. Each subcondition must be enclosed in braces within the overall braces that contain the list. No repetition of `if` is used.

# A.3 Expansion variables

The variable substitutions available for use in expansion strings are as follows:

*$0, $1,* and so on

When a `matches` expansion condition succeeds, these variables contain the captured substrings identified by the regular expression during subsequent processing of the success string of the containing `if` expansion item. They may also be set externally by some other matching process that precedes the expansion of the string.

*$acl_verify_message*

During the expansion of the `message` modifier in an ACL statement after an address verification has failed, this variable contains the original failure message that will be overridden by the expanded string.

*$address_data*

This variable is set by means of the `address_data` option in routers. The value then remains with the address while it is processed by subsequent routers and eventually a transport.

*$address_file*

When a message is routed to a specific file as a result of aliasing or forwarding, this variable holds the name of the file when the transport is running. For example, using the default configuration, if user *r2d2* has a *.forward* file containing:

```
/home/r2d2/savemail
```

then when the **address_file** transport is running, *$address_file* contains */home/r2d2/savemail*. At other times, the variable is empty.

*$address_pipe*

When a message is routed to a pipe (as a result of aliasing or forwarding), this variable holds the pipe command when the transport is running.

*$authenticated_id*

When a server successfully authenticates a client, it may be configured to preserve some of the authentication information in the variable *$authenticated_id*. For example, a user/password authenticator configuration might preserve the username for use in the routers.

*$authenticated_sender*

When a client host has authenticated itself, Exim pays attention to the AUTH= parameter on the SMTP MAIL command. Otherwise, it accepts the syntax, but ignores the data. Unless the data is the string < >, it is set as the authenticated sender of the message, and the value is available during delivery in the *$authenticated_sender* variable.

*$body_linecount*

This variable holds the number of lines in the body of a message.

*$bounce_recipient*

This is set to the recipient address of a bounce message while Exim is creating it. It is useful if a customized error message text file is in use.

*$caller_gid*

This variable holds the group ID under which the process that called Exim was running. This is not the same as the group ID of the originator of a message (see *$originator_gid*). If Exim re-execs itself, this variable in the new incarnation normally contains the Exim gid.

*$caller_uid*

This variable holds the user ID under which the process that called Exim was running. This is not the same as the user ID of the originator of a message (see *$originator_uid*). If Exim re-execs itself, this variable in the new incarnation normally contains the Exim uid.

*$compile_date*

This variable holds the date on which the Exim binary was compiled.

*$compile_number*

The building process for Exim keeps a count of the number of times Exim has been compiled. This serves to distinguish different compilations of the same version of the program.

*$dnslist_domain*

When a client host is found to be on a DNS black list, the list's domain name is put into this variable so that it can be included in the rejection message.

*$dnslist_text*

When a client host is found to be on a DNS black list, the contents of any associated TXT record are placed in this variable.

*$dnslist_value*

When a client host is found to be on a DNS black list, the IP address from the resource record is placed in this variable.

*$domain*

When an address is being routed or delivered on its own, this variable contains the domain. In particular, it is set during user filtering, but not during system filtering, since a message may have many recipients and the system filter is called just once.

When a remote or local delivery is taking place, if all the addresses that are being handled simultaneously contain the same domain, it is placed in *$domain*. Otherwise, this variable is empty while a transport is running. Transports should be restricted to handling only one domain at once if its value is required at transport time. This is the default for local transports.

At the end of a delivery, if all deferred addresses have the same domain, it is set in *$domain* during the expansion of `delay_warning_condition`.

The *$domain* variable is also used in some other circumstances that are not connected with message delivery:

- When an ACL is running for a `RCPT` command, *$domain* contains the domain of the recipient address.

- When an address rewriting configuration item is being processed, *$domain* contains the domain portion of the address that is being rewritten; it can be used in the expansion of the replacement address.

- Whenever a domain list is being scanned, *$domain* contains the subject domain.

- When the `smtp_etrn_command` option is being expanded, *$domain* contains the complete argument of the `ETRN` command.

*$domain_data*

When a router has a setting of the `domains` option or an ACL uses the `domains` condition, and the domain is matched by a file lookup, the data obtained from the lookup is placed in *$domain_data*. For a router, the value remains available during the running of the router, and any subsequent transport. For an ACL, the value remains available while the rest of the statement is processed.

*$home*

When the `check_local_user` option is set for a router, the user's home directory is placed in *$home* when the check succeeds. In particular, this means it is set during the running of users' filter files. A router may also explicitly set a home directory for use by a transport; this can be overridden by a setting on the transport itself.

*$host*

When the **smtp** transport is expanding its options for encryption using TLS, *$host* contains the name of the host to which it is connected. Likewise, when used in the client part of an authenticator configuration, *$host* contains the name of the server to which the client is connected.

When used in a transport filter *$host* refers to the host involved in the current connection. When a local transport is run as a result of a router that sets up a host list, *$host* contains the name of the first host.

*$host_address*

This variable is set to the remote host's IP address whenever *$host* is set for a remote connection.

*$host_lookup_failed*

This variable contains "1" if the message came from a remote host and there was an attempt to look up the host's name from its IP address, but the attempt failed. Otherwise the value of the variable is "0".

*$interface_address*

For a message received over a TCP/IP connection, this variable contains the address of the IP interface that was used.

*$interface_port*

For a message received over a TCP/IP connection, this variable contains the port that was used.

*$local_part*

When an address is being routed or delivered on its own, this variable contains the local part. If a local part prefix or suffix has been recognized, it is not included in the value. When a number of addresses are being delivered in a batch by a local or a remote transport, *$local_part* is not set.

When a message is being delivered to a **pipe**, **appendfile**, or **autoreply** transport as a result of redirection, *$local_part* is set to the local part of the parent address.

When an ACL is running for a RCPT command, *$local_part* contains the local part of the recipient address.

When a configuration rewrite item is being processed, *$local_part* contains the local part of the address that is being rewritten.

*$local_part_data*

When a router has a setting of the local_parts option or an ACL uses the local_parts condition, and the local part is matched by a file lookup, the data obtained from the lookup is placed in *$local_part_data*. For a router, the value remains available during the running of the router, and any subsequent transport. For an ACL, the value remains available while the rest of the statement is processed.

*$local_part_prefix*

When an address is being routed or delivered, and a specific prefix for the local part is recognized, it is available in this variable, having been removed from *$local_part*.

*$local_part_suffix*

When an address is being routed or delivered, and a specific suffix for the local part is recognized, it is available in this variable, having been removed from *$local_part*.

*$local_scan_data*

This variable contains the text returned by the *local_scan()* function when a message is received. A description of *local_scan()* can be found in the reference manual; it is not covered in this book.

*$localhost_number*

This contains the expanded value of the `localhost_number` option. The expansion happens after the main options have been read.

*$message_age*

This variable is set at the start of a delivery attempt to contain the number of seconds since the message was received. It does not change during a single delivery attempt.

*$message_body*

This variable contains the initial portion of a message's body while it is being delivered, and is intended mainly for use in filter files. The maximum number of characters of the body that are used is set by the `message_body_visible` configuration option; the default is 500. Newlines are converted into spaces to make it easier to search for phrases that might be split over a line break, and binary zeros are also converted into spaces.

*$message_body_end*

This variable contains the final portion of a message's body while it is being delivered. The format and maximum size are as for *$message_body*.

*$message_body_size*

When a message is being received or delivered, this variable contains the size of the body in bytes. The count starts from the character after the blank line that separates the body from the header lines. Newlines are included in the count. See also *$message_size*.

*$message_headers*

This variable contains a concatenation of all the header lines when a message is being processed. They are separated by newline characters.

*$message_id*

When a message is being received or delivered, this variable contains the unique message ID that is used by Exim to identify the message.

*$message_size*

When a message is being received or delivered, this variable contains its size in bytes. The size includes those headers that were received with the message, but not those (such as *Envelope-to:*) that are added to individual deliveries. See also *$message_body_size*.

*$n0* to *$n9*

These variables are counters that can be incremented by means of the *add* command in filter files.

*$original_domain*

When a top-level address is being processed for delivery, this contains the same value as *$domain*. However, if a "child" address (for example, generated by an alias, forward, or filter file) is being processed, this variable contains the domain of the original address. This differs from *$parent_domain* when there is more than one level of aliasing or forwarding. When more than one address is being delivered in a batch by a local or remote transport, *$original_domain* is not set.

Address rewriting happens as a message is received. Once it has happened, the previous form of the address is no longer accessible. It is the rewritten top-level address whose domain appears in this variable.

*$original_local_part*

This is the counterpart of *$original_domain*, and contains the local part of the original top-level address.

*$originator_gid*

This is the value of *$caller_gid* that was set when the message was received. For messages received via the command line, this is the gid of the sending user. For messages received by SMTP over TCP/IP, this is the gid of the Exim user.

*$originator_uid*

The value of *$caller_uid* that was set when the message was received. For messages received via the command line, this is the uid of the sending user. For messages received by SMTP over TCP/IP, this is the uid of the Exim user.

*$parent_domain*

This variable is empty, except when a "child" address (generated by aliasing or forwarding, for example) is being processed, in which case it contains the domain of the immediately preceding parent address.

*$parent_local_part*

This variable is empty, except when a "child" address (generated by aliasing or forwarding, for example) is being processed, in which case it contains the local part of the immediately preceding parent address.

*$pid*

This variable contains the current process id.

*$pipe_addresses*

This is not an expansion variable, but is mentioned here because the string `$pipe_addresses` is handled specially in the command specification for the **pipe** transport and in transport filters. It cannot be used in general expansion strings, and provokes an "unknown variable" error if encountered.

*$primary_hostname*

This variable holds the value set in the configuration file, or the value determined by running the *uname( )* function.

*$qualify_domain*

This variable holds the value set for this option in the configuration file.

*$qualify_recipient*

This variable holds the value set for this option in the configuration file, or if not set, the value of *$qualify_domain*.

*$rcpt_count*

When a message is being received by SMTP, this variable contains the number of *RCPT* commands received, and may be used in an ACL. At other times, its value is undefined.

*$received_for*

If there is only a single recipient address in an incoming message when the *Received:* header line is being built, this variable contains that address.

*$received_protocol*

When a message is being processed, this variable contains the name of the protocol by which it was received.

*$recipients*

This variable contains a list of envelope recipients for a message, but is recognized only in the system filter file, to prevent exposure of *bcc:* recipients to ordinary users. A comma and a space separate the addresses in the replacement text.

*$recipients_count*

When a message is being processed for delivery, this variable contains the number of envelope recipients that came with the message. Duplicates are not excluded from the count.

While a message is being received over SMTP, the number increases for each accepted recipient. It can be referenced in an ACL.

*$reply_address*

When a message is being processed, this variable contains the contents of the *Reply-To:* header if one exists, or otherwise the contents of the *From:* header.

*$return_path*

When a message is being delivered, this variable contains the return path (that is, the sender field that will be sent as part of the envelope). It is not enclosed in angle brackets. In many cases, *$return_path* has the same value as *$sender_address*, but if, for example, an incoming message to a mailing list has been expanded by a router that specifies a different address for bounce messages, *$return_path* contains the new error address, while *$sender_address* contains the original sender address that was received with the message.

*$return_size_limit*

This contains the value set in the `return_size_limit` option, rounded up to a multiple of 1000.

*$self_hostname*

When an address is routed to a supposedly remote host that turns out to be the local host, what happens is controlled by the `self` generic router option. One of its values causes the address to be passed to another router. When this happens, *$self_hostname* is set to the name of the local host that the original router encountered. In other circumstances its contents are null.

*$sender_address*

When a message is being processed, this variable contains the sender's address that was received in the message's envelope. For bounce messages, the value of this variable is the empty string.

*$sender_address_domain*

This variable holds the domain portion of *$sender_address*.

*$sender_address_local_part*

This variable holds the local part portion of *$sender_address.*

*$sender_fullhost*

When a message has been received from a remote host, this variable contains the host name and IP address in a single string, which always ends with the IP address in square brackets. The format of the rest of the string depends on whether the host issued a HELO or EHLO SMTP command, and whether the host name was verified by looking up its IP address. (Looking up the IP address can be forced by the host_lookup option, independent of verification.) A plain host name at the start of the string is a verified host name; if this is not present, verification either failed or was not requested. A host name in parentheses is the argument of a HELO or EHLO command. This is omitted if it is identical to the verified host name or to the host's IP address in square brackets.

*$sender_helo_name*

When a message has been received from a remote host that has issued a HELO or EHLO command, the first item in the argument of that command is placed in this variable. It is also set if HELO or EHLO is used when a message is received using SMTP locally via the -bs or -bS options.

*$sender_host_address*

When a message has been received from a remote host, this variable contains the host's IP address. For messages submitted locally, it is empty.

*$sender_host_authenticated*

During message delivery, this variable contains the name (not the public name) of the authenticator driver that successfully authenticated the client from which the message was received. It is empty if there was no successful authentication.

*$sender_host_name*

For a message received from a remote host, this variable contains the host's name as obtained by looking up its IP address. If lookup failed or was not requested, this variable contains the empty string.

*$sender_host_port*

For a message received from a remote host, this variable contains the port number that was used on the remote host.

*$sender_ident*

> For a message received from a remote host, this variable contains the identification received in response to an RFC 1413 request. For a locally submitted message, this variable contains the login name of the user that called Exim.

*$sender_rcvhost*

> This variable is provided specifically for use in *Received:* header lines. It starts with either the verified host name (as obtained from a reverse DNS lookup), or, if there is no verified host name, the IP address in square brackets. After that there may be text in parentheses. When the first item is a verified host name, the first thing in the parentheses is the IP address in square brackets. There may also be items of the form helo=*xxxx* if HELO or EHLO was used and its argument was not identical to the real host name or IP address, and ident=*xxxx* if an RFC 1413 ident string is available. If all three items are present in the parentheses, a newline and tab are inserted into the string to improve the formatting of the *Received:* header.

*$smtp_command_argument*

> While an ACL is running to check an *AUTH*, *EXPN*, *ETRN*, or *VRFY* command, this variable contains the argument for the SMTP command.

*$sn0* to *$sn9*

> These variables are copies of the values of the *$n0* to *$n9* accumulators that were current at the end of the system filter file. This allows a system filter file to set values that can be tested in users' filter files. For example, a system filter could set a value indicating how likely it is that a message is junk mail.

*$spool_directory*

> This variable holds the name of Exim's spool directory.

*$thisaddress*

> This variable is set only during the processing of the *foranyaddress* command in a filter file (☞ 10.15.7).

*$tls_cipher*

> For a message received from a remote host over an encrypted SMTP connection, this variable is set to the cipher that was negotiated. Otherwise, it is empty.

*$tls_peerdn*

> When a message is received from a remote host over an encrypted SMTP connection, and Exim is configured to request a certificate from the client, this variable is set to the value of the Distinguished Name of the certificate.

*$tod_bsdinbox*

This variable holds the date and time of day, in the format required for BSD-style mailbox files (for example, `Thu Oct 17 17:14:09 1995`).

*$tod_epoch*

The time and date as a number of seconds since the start of the Unix epoch.

*$tod_full*

This variable holds a full version of the date and time (for example, `Wed, 16 Oct 1995 09:51:40 +0100`). The time zone is always given as a numerical offset from GMT/UTC.

*$tod_log*

This variable holds the date and time in the format used for writing Exim's log files (for example, `1995-10-12 15:32:29`).

*$value*

This variable contains the result of an expansion lookup, extraction operation, or external command.

*$version_number*

This variable holds the version number of Exim.

*$warn_message_delay*

This variable is set only during the creation of a message warning about a delivery delay (☞ 19.8.5).

*$warn_message_recipients*

This variable is set only during the creation of a message warning about a delivery delay (☞ 19.8.5).

# Appendix B
# Regular expressions

Regular expression support in Exim is provided by the PCRE library, which implements regular expressions whose syntax and semantics are the same as those in Perl.[1] The description here is taken from the PCRE documentation, and is intended as reference material. For an introduction to regular expressions, see *Mastering Regular Expressions* by Jeffrey Friedl (O'Reilly).

When you use a regular expression in an Exim configuration, you have to be a little careful about backslash, dollar, and brace characters, which quite often appear in regular expressions, because these characters are also interpreted specially by Exim. Backslash is special inside quoted strings, and all four characters are special in a string that is expanded. One way of setting up such configuration items is as follows:

- First of all, create your regular expression according to the description in this appendix. In other words, find the character string that you ultimately want to pass to the regular expression matcher.

- If the Exim string will be expanded (this is the case for most configuration items where regular expressions can be used), put \N at the beginning and at the end of your expression, to stop the expander interpreting the special characters within it. An alternative is to go through your expression and insert a backslash before every backslash, dollar, and brace character.

- If the Exim option is a string inside double quotes, go through the expression and insert a second backslash before every backslash. You only need to use double quotes for Exim option settings if you specifically need to use escape sequences in the string, so this case should be rare.

For example, suppose you want to recognize domains whose first component consists of letters followed by three digits within some enclosing domain. A regular expression that matches the required domains is:

```
^(?>[a-z]+)\d{3}\.enc\.example$
```

If you want to use this pattern in a `domains` option in a router, you would have to set it as:

```
domains = \N^(?>[a-z]+)\d{3}\.enc\.example$\N
```

---

[1] PCRE was implemented and is maintained by the same author as Exim. Although originally written in support of Exim, it is a freestanding library that is now used in many other programs. However, the version that is incorporated in the Exim source is minimal. If you want to use PCRE in other programs, you should obtain and install the full distribution from *ftp://ftp.csx.cam.ac.uk/pub/software /programming/pcre*.

or

```
domains = ^(?>[a-z]+)\\d\{3\}\\.enc\\.example\$
```

because the option is expanded before it is used.

# B.1 Testing regular expressions

The PCRE library comes with a program called *pcretest* that can be used to test regular expressions, though it was originally written to test the library itself. The Exim distribution includes *pcretest*, but it does not install it automatically. If you have built Exim from source, you will find *pcretest* in the build directory.

When you run *pcretest*, it prompts for a regular expression, which must be supplied between delimiters and can be followed by flags. Then it prompts for a succession of data lines to be matched; for each one, the results of the match are output. For example:

```
$ pcretest
PCRE version 3.9 02-Jan-2002

  re> /^abc(\d+)/i
data> aBc123xyz
 0: aBc123
 1: 123
data> xyz
No match
```

After a successful match, string 0 is what the entire pattern matched, and strings 1, 2, and so on are the contents of the captured substrings. For more details of *pcretest*, take a look at its specfication, which is supplied in the file *doc/pcretest.txt* in the Exim distribution.

# B.2 Metacharacters

A regular expression is a pattern that is matched against a subject string from left to right. Most characters stand for themselves in a pattern, and match the corresponding characters in the subject. As a trivial example, the pattern:

```
The quick brown fox
```

matches a portion of a subject string that is identical to itself. The power of regular expressions comes from the ability to include alternatives and repetitions in the pattern. These are encoded in the pattern by the use of *metacharacters*, which do not stand for themselves, but instead are interpreted in some special way. When a pattern matches, it is possible to arrange for portions of the subject string that matched particular parts of the pattern to be identified. These are called *captured substrings*.

There are two different sets of metacharacters: those that are recognized anywhere in the pattern except within square brackets, and those that are recognized in square brackets. Outside square brackets, the metacharacters are as follows:

\  General escape character with several uses
^  Assert start of subject (or line, in multiline mode)
$  Assert end of subject (or line, in multiline mode)
.  Match any character except newline (by default)
[  Start character class definition
|  Start of alternative branch
(  Start subpattern
)  End subpattern
?  Extends the meaning of (
     also 0 or 1 quantifier
     also quantifier minimizer
*  0 or more quantifier
+  1 or more quantifier
{  Start minimum/maximum quantifier

Part of a pattern that is in square brackets is called a *character class*. In a character class, the only metacharacters are as follows:

\  General escape character
^  Negate the class, if the first character
-  Indicates character range
]  Terminates the character class

The following sections describe the use of each of the metacharacters.

# B.3 Backslash

The backslash character has several uses. First, if it is followed by a non-alphanumeric character, it takes away any special meaning that character may have. This use of backslash as an escape character applies both inside and outside character classes.

For example, if you want to match a * character, write \* in the pattern. The effect of backslash applies whether or not the following character would otherwise be interpreted as a metacharacter, so it is always safe to precede a non-alphanumeric with a backslash to specify that it stands for itself. In particular, if you want to match a backslash, write \\.

If a pattern contains the (?x) option (see later in this appendix), whitespace in the pattern (other than in a character class) and characters between a # outside a character class and the next newline character are ignored. An escaping backslash can be used to include whitespace or a # character as part of the pattern in this circumstance.

A second use of backslash provides a way of encoding non-printing characters in patterns in a visible manner. There is no restriction on the appearance of non-printing characters, apart from the binary zero that terminates a pattern, but when a pattern is being prepared by text editing, it is usually easier to use one of the following escape sequences than the binary character it represents:

| | |
|---|---|
| \a | Alarm, that is, the BEL character (character 7) |
| \cx | "Control-x", where x is any character |
| \e | Escape (character 27) |
| \f | Formfeed (character 12) |
| \n | Newline or linefeed (character 10) |
| \r | Carriage return (character 13) |
| \t | Tab (character 9) |
| \xhh | Character with hex code *<hh>* |
| \ddd | Character with octal code *<ddd>*, |
| | or a backreference (see later in this appendix) |

The precise effect of \cx is as follows: if x is a lower-case letter, it is converted to upper case. Then bit 6 of the character (hex 40) is inverted. Thus, \cz becomes hex 1A, but \c{ becomes hex 3B, and \c; becomes hex 7B.

After \x, up to two hexadecimal digits are read (letters can be in upper or lower case).

After \0, up to two further octal digits are read. In both cases, if there are fewer than two digits, just those that are present are used. Thus, the sequence \0\x\07 specifies two binary zeros followed by a BEL character. Make sure you supply two digits after the initial zero if the character that follows is itself an octal digit.

The handling of a backslash followed by a digit other than 0 is complicated. Outside a character class, PCRE reads it and any following digits as a decimal number. If the number is less than 10, or if there have been at least that many previous capturing left parentheses in the expression, the entire sequence is taken as a *back reference* (☞ B.12).

Inside a character class, or if the decimal number is greater than 9 and there have not been that many capturing subpatterns, PCRE rereads up to three octal digits following the backslash, and generates a single byte from the least significant 8 bits of the value. Any subsequent digits stand for themselves.

Here are some examples of the different ways a number can be interpreted:

\040   Another way of writing a space

\40    The same, provided there are fewer than 40 previous
       capturing subpatterns

\7     Always a back reference

\11    Might be a back reference, or another way of writing a tab

\011   Always a tab

\0113  A tab followed by the character 3

\113   The character with octal code 113 (since there can be
       no more than 99 back references)

\377   A byte with every bit set to 1

\81    Either a back reference, or a binary zero followed
       by the two characters 8 and 1

Note that octal values of 100 or greater must not be introduced by a leading zero, because no more than three octal digits are ever read.

All the sequences that define a single byte value can be used both inside and outside character classes. In addition, inside a character class, the sequence \b is interpreted as the backspace character (character 8). Outside a character class, it has a different meaning (see later in this appendix).

The third use of backslash is for specifying generic character types:

\d  Any decimal digit

\D  Any character that is not a decimal digit

\s  Any whitespace character

\S  Any character that is not a whitespace character

\w  Any "word" character

\W  Any "non-word" character

Each pair of escape sequences partitions the complete set of characters into two disjoint sets. Any given character matches one, and only one, of each pair.

A "word" character is any letter or digit or the underscore character (that is, any character which can be part of a Perl "word").

These character type sequences can appear both inside and outside character classes. They each match one character of the appropriate type. If the current matching point is at the end of the subject string, all of them fail, because there is no character to match.

The fourth use of backslash is for certain simple assertions. An assertion specifies a condition that has to be met at a particular point in a match, without consuming any characters from the subject string. The use of subpatterns for more complicated assertions is described later (☞ B.13). The backslashed assertions are as follows:

\b  Word boundary

\B  Not a word boundary

\A  Start of subject (independent of multiline mode)

\Z  End of subject or newline at end (independent of multiline mode)

\z  End of subject (independent of multiline mode)

These assertions may not appear in character classes (but note that \b has a different meaning, namely the backspace character, inside a character class).

A word boundary is a position in the subject string where the current character and the previous character do not both match \w or \W (that is, one matches \w and the other matches \W), or the start or end of the string if the first or last character matches \w, respectively.

The \A, \Z, and \z assertions differ from the traditional circumflex and dollar (☞ B.5) in that they only ever match at the very start and end of the subject string, whatever options are set. The difference between \Z and \z is that \Z matches before a newline that is the last character of the string as well as at the end of the string, whereas \z matches only at the end.

# B.4 Changing matching options

Some details of the matching process are controlled by options that can be changed from within the pattern itself. The syntax is a sequence of Perl option letters enclosed between (? and ). The option letters are as follows:

i  Case-independent matching

m  "Multiline" matching (☞ B.5)

s  "Single-line" matching (☞ B.6)

x  Ignore literal whitespace in the pattern

For example, (?im) sets caseless, multiline matching. It is also possible to unset these options by preceding the letter with a hyphen; a combined setting and unsetting such as (?im-sx) is also permitted. If a letter appears both before and after the hyphen, the option is unset.

The scope of these option changes depends on where in the pattern the setting occurs. For settings that are outside any parenthesized subpattern (defined later in this appendix), the effect lasts until the end of the pattern or until the option is changed explicitly.[1] For example:

    a(?i)bc

matches abc, aBc, aBC, and abC, whereas:

    a(?i)b(?-i)c

matches only abc and aBc. If the pattern contains several alternatives, changes of option that are made in one alternative do carry on into subsequent branches. For example:

    a(?i)b|c

matches ab, aB, c, and C, even though when matching C, the first branch is abandoned before the option setting. This is because the effects of option settings happen at compile time. There would be some very weird behaviour otherwise.

If an option change occurs inside a subpattern, the change is confined to that subpattern. For example:

    (a(?i)b)c

matches abc and aBc and no other strings.

In addition to the standard Perl options, PCRE has some extra ones of its own. These are as follows:

    U  Invert greedy/ungreedy matching (☞ B.11)
    R  Recursive matching (☞ B.17)

# B.5 Circumflex and dollar

Outside a character class, in the default matching mode, the circumflex character is an assertion that is true only if the current matching point is at the start of the subject string. Inside a character class, circumflex has an entirely different meaning (☞ B.7).

Circumflex is used in Exim configuration files to indicate that the string it introduces is a regular expression rather than a literal string, and it is interpreted as part of that

---

[1]  This behaviour agrees with Perl 5.8, and was changed in release 4.0 of the PCRE regular expression library. In earlier versions, a "top level" change applies to the whole pattern, independently of where it occurs in the pattern.

expression. However, when a string can only be a regular expression (for example, as part of the `matches` condition in a string expansion), a leading circumflex is not necessary.

If all possible alternatives start with a circumflex (that is, if the pattern is constrained to match only at the start of the subject), it is said to be an "anchored" pattern. (There are also other constructs that can cause a pattern to be anchored.)

A dollar character is an assertion that is true only if the current matching point is at the end of the subject string, or immediately before a newline character that is the last character in the string (by default). Dollar need not be the last character of the pattern if a number of alternatives are involved, but it should be the last item in any branch in which it appears. Dollar has no special meaning in a character class.

The meanings of the circumflex and dollar characters are changed if the (?m) option is set. This is referred to in Perl as the "multiline" option. When this is the case, circumflex and dollar match immediately after and immediately before an internal newline character, respectively, in addition to matching at the start and end of the subject string. For example, the pattern `^abc$` matches the subject string `def\nabc` (where `\n` represents a newline) in multiline mode, but not otherwise. Consequently, patterns that are anchored in single-line mode because all branches start with `^` are not anchored in multiline mode.

Note that the sequences `\A`, `\Z`, and `\z` can be used to match the start and end of the subject in both modes, and if all branches of a pattern start with `\A`, the pattern is always anchored.

# B.6 Dot (period, full stop)

Outside a character class, a dot in the pattern matches any one character in the subject, including a non-printing character, but not (by default) newline. If the (?s) option is set, a dot matches a newline as well. (In Perl, this is referred to as the "single-line" option.) The handling of dot is entirely independent of the handling of circumflex and dollar, the only relationship being that they both involve newline characters. Dot has no special meaning in a character class.

# B.7 Square brackets

An opening square bracket introduces a character class, terminated by a closing square bracket. A closing square bracket on its own is not special. If a closing square bracket is required as a member of the class, it should be the first data character in the class (after an initial circumflex, if present) or be escaped with a backslash.

A character class matches a single character in the subject; the character must be in the set of characters defined by the class, unless the first character in the class is a circumflex, in which case the subject character must not be in the set defined by the class. If a circumflex is actually required as a member of the class, ensure it is not the first character, or escape it with a backslash.

For example, the character class [aeiou] matches any lower-case vowel, while [^aeiou] matches any character that is not a lower-case vowel. This use of circumflex is just a convenient notation for specifying the characters that are in the class by enumerating those that are not. A character class that starts with a circumflex is not an assertion: it still consumes a character from the subject string, and fails if the current pointer is at the end of the string.

When caseless matching is set, any letters in a class represent both their upper and lower case versions, so for example, a caseless [aeiou] matches U as well as u, and a caseless [^aeiou] does not match U, whereas a caseful version would.

The newline character is never treated in any special way in character classes, whatever the setting of the (?s) or (?m) options is. A class such as [^a] always matches a newline.

The hyphen (minus) character can be used to specify a range of characters in a character class. For example, [d-m] matches any letter between d and m, inclusive. If a hyphen is required in a class, it must be escaped with a backslash, or appear in a position where it cannot be interpreted as indicating a range, typically as the first or last character in the class.

It is not possible to have the literal character ] as the end character of a range. A pattern such as [W-]46] is interpreted as a class of two characters (W and -) followed by a literal string 46], so it would match W46] or -46]. However, if the ] is escaped with a backslash, it is interpreted as the end of range, so [W-\]46] is interpreted as a single class containing a range followed by two separate characters. The octal or hexadecimal representation of ] can also be used to end a range.

Ranges operate in ASCII collating sequence. They can also be used for characters specified numerically (for example [\000-\037]). If a range that includes letters is used when caseless matching is set, it matches the letters in either case. For example, [W-c] is equivalent to [] [\^_`wxyzabc], matched caselessly.

The character types \d, \D, \s, \S, \w, and \W may also appear in a character class, and add the characters that they match to the class. For example, [\dABCDEF] matches any hexadecimal digit.

The interpretation of a non-negated class can be understood by reading it with the word "or" between each item, whereas for a negated class, "and not" is implied. For example, [ANZ] matches a character that is "A or N or Z", whereas [^ANZ] matches a character that is "not A and not N and not Z". This means that a negated class can conveniently be used with the upper-case character types to specify a more restricted set of characters than the matching lower-case type. For example, the class [^\W_] matches any letter or digit, but not underscore, because it matches a character that is not a non-word character (that is, it *is* a word character), and not an underscore.

All non-alphanumeric characters other than \, -, ^ (at the start) and the terminating ] are non-special in character classes, but it does no harm if they are escaped.

# B.8 POSIX character classes

Current versions of Perl support POSIX notation for character classes, which uses names enclosed by [: and :] within the enclosing square brackets. PCRE supports this notation. For example:

```
[01[:alpha:]%]
```

matches 0, 1, any alphabetic character, or %. The supported class names are:

| | |
|---|---|
| alnum | Letters and digits |
| alpha | Letters |
| ascii | Character codes 0–127 |
| cntrl | Control characters |
| digit | Decimal digits (same as \d) |
| graph | Printing characters, excluding space |
| lower | Lower case letters |
| print | Printing characters, including space |
| punct | Printing characters, excluding letters and digits |
| space | Whitespace (same as \s) |
| upper | Upper case letters |
| word | "Word" characters (same as \w) |
| xdigit | Hexadecimal digits |

The names ascii and word are Perl extensions. Another Perl extension is negation, which is indicated by a ^ character after the colon. For example:

```
[12[:^digit:]]
```

matches 1, 2, or any non-digit. PCRE also recognizes the POSIX syntax [.ch.] and [=ch=] where "ch" is a "collating element", but these are not supported, and an error is given if they are encountered.

# B.9 Vertical bar

Vertical bar characters are used to separate alternative patterns. For example, the following pattern:

```
gilbert|sullivan
```

matches either `gilbert` or `sullivan`. Any number of alternatives may appear, and an empty alternative is permitted (matching the empty string). The matching process tries each alternative in turn, from left to right, and the first one that succeeds is used. If the alternatives are within a subpattern (defined in the next section), "succeeds" means matching the rest of the main pattern as well as the alternative in the subpattern.

# B.10 Subpatterns

Subpatterns are delimited by parentheses (round brackets), which can be nested. Marking part of a pattern as a subpattern does two things:

- It localizes a set of alternatives. For example, the pattern:

  ```
  cat(aract|erpillar|)
  ```

  matches one of the words `cat`, `cataract`, or `caterpillar`. Without the parentheses, it would match `cataract`, `erpillar`, or the empty string.

- It sets up the subpattern as a capturing subpattern. When the whole pattern matches, that portion of the subject string that matched the subpattern is passed back to the caller, and in Exim, such values are made available in the numerical variables $1, $2, and so on. Opening parentheses are counted from left to right (starting from 1) to obtain the numbers of the capturing subpatterns.

For example, if the string `the red king` is matched against the following pattern:

```
the ((red|white) (king|queen))
```

the captured substrings are `red king`, `red`, and `king`, and are numbered 1, 2, and 3, respectively.

The fact that plain parentheses fulfil two functions is not always helpful. There are often times when a grouping subpattern is required without a capturing requirement. If an opening parenthesis is followed by ?:, the subpattern does not do any capturing, and is not counted when computing the number of any subsequent capturing subpatterns. For example, if the string "the white queen" is matched against the pattern:

```
the ((?:red|white) (king|queen))
```

the captured substrings are white queen and queen, and are numbered 1 and 2. The maximum number of capturing subpatterns is 65 535; there is no limit to the number of non-capturing subpatterns, but the maximum depth of nesting of all kinds of parenthesized subpattern, including capturing subpatterns, assertions, and other types of subpattern, is 200.

As a convenient shorthand, if any option settings are required at the start of a non-capturing subpattern, the option letters may appear between the ? and the :. Thus, the two patterns:

```
(?i:saturday|sunday)
(?:(?i)saturday|sunday)
```

match exactly the same set of strings. Because alternative branches are tried from left to right, and options are not reset until the end of the subpattern is reached, an option setting in one branch does affect subsequent branches, so these patterns match SUNDAY and Saturday as well as any other case variants.

# B.11 Repetition

Repetition is specified by quantifiers, which can follow any of the following items:

- A single character, possibly escaped

- The . metacharacter

- A character class

- A back reference (see the next section)

- A parenthesized subpattern (unless it is an assertion; see later in this appendix)

The general repetition quantifier specifies a minimum and maximum number of permitted matches, by giving the two numbers in curly brackets (braces), separated by a comma. The numbers must be less than 65 536, and the first must be less than or equal to the second. For example:

```
z{2,4}
```

matches zz, zzz, or zzzz. A closing brace on its own is not a special character. If the second number is omitted, but the comma is present, there is no upper limit; if the second number and the comma are both omitted, the quantifier specifies an exact number of required matches. Thus:

```
[aeiou]{3,}
```

matches at least three successive vowels, but may match many more, whereas:

```
\d{8}
```

matches exactly eight digits. An opening curly bracket that appears in a position where a quantifier is not allowed, or one that does not match the syntax of a quantifier, is taken as a literal character. For example, {,6} is not a quantifier, but a literal string of four characters.

The quantifier {0} is permitted, causing the expression to behave as if the previous item and the quantifier were not present.

For convenience (and historical compatibility), the three most common quantifiers have single-character abbreviations:

* Equivalent to {0,}
+ Equivalent to {1,}
? Equivalent to {0,1}

It is possible to construct infinite loops by following a subpattern that can match no characters with a quantifier that has no upper limit, for example:

```
(a?)*
```

Earlier versions of Perl and PCRE used to give an error at compile time for such patterns. However, because there are cases where this can be useful, such patterns are now accepted, but if any repetition of the subpattern does, in fact, match no characters, the loop is forcibly broken.

By default, the quantifiers are "greedy". They match as much as possible up to the maximum number of permitted times without causing the rest of the pattern to fail. The classic example of where this gives problems is in trying to match comments in C programs. These appear between the sequences /* and */, and within a comment, individual * and / characters may appear. An attempt to match C comments by applying the following pattern:

```
/\*.*\*/
```

to the following string:

```
/* first comment */  not comment  /* second comment */
```

fails, because it matches the entire string owing to the greediness of the .* item. However, if a quantifier is followed by a question mark, it ceases to be greedy, and instead matches the minimum number of times possible, so the pattern:

```
/\*.*?\*/
```

does the right thing with the C comments. The meanings of the various quantifiers are not otherwise changed, just the preferred number of matches. Do not confuse this use of question mark with its use as a quantifier in its own right. Because it has two uses, it can sometimes appear doubled, as in the following example:

```
\d??\d
```

which matches one digit by preference, but can match two if that is the only way the rest of the pattern can be matched.

If the (?U) option is set (an option that is not available in Perl), the quantifiers are not greedy by default, but individual ones can be made greedy by following them with a question mark. In other words, it inverts the default behaviour.

When a parenthesized subpattern is quantified with a minimum repeat count that is greater than 1, or with a limited maximum, more store is required for the compiled pattern, in proportion to the size of the minimum or maximum.

If a pattern starts with .* (or .{0,}) and the (?s) option is set, thus allowing the dot to match newlines, the pattern is implicitly anchored, because whatever follows will be tried against every character position in the subject string. At first, the .* item consumes the entire subject string, but if the rest of the pattern does not match, it "gives up" characters one by one until either the whole pattern does match, or the start of the string is reached (when .* matches no characters). If .*? is used instead of .*, the same thing happens, but in the opposite order.

For such patterns, therefore, there is no point in retrying the overall match at any position after the first. PCRE treats such a pattern as though it were preceded by \A. In cases where it is known that the subject string contains no newlines, it is worth setting (?s) when the pattern begins with .* in order to obtain this optimization, or alternatively using ^ to indicate anchoring explicitly.

When a capturing subpattern is repeated, the value captured is the substring that matches the final iteration. For example, after the following:

```
(tweedle[dume]{3}\s*)+
```

has matched `tweedledum tweedledee`, the value of the captured substring is `tweedledee`. However, if there are nested capturing subpatterns, the corresponding captured values may have been set in previous iterations, and they retain the last values that were set. For example, after the following:

```
/(a|(b))+/
```

has matched `aba`, the value of the second captured substring is `b`.

# B.12 Back references

Outside a character class, a backslash followed by a digit greater than 0 (and possibly further digits) is a back reference to a capturing subpattern earlier (that is, to its left) in the pattern, provided there have been that many previous capturing left parentheses.

However, if the decimal number following the backslash is less than 10, it is always taken as a back reference, and causes an error only if there are not that many capturing left parentheses in the entire pattern. In other words, the parentheses that are referenced need not be to the left of the reference for numbers less than 10. The overall handling of digits following a backslash was discussed earlier (☞ B.3).

A back reference matches whatever actually matched the capturing subpattern in the current subject string, rather than anything matching the subpattern itself. So the pattern:

```
(sens|respons)e and \1ibility
```

matches `sense and sensibility` and `response and responsibility`, but not `sense and responsibility`. If caseful matching is in force at the time of the back reference, the case of letters is relevant. For example:

```
((?i)rah)\s+\1
```

matches `rah  rah` and `RAH  RAH`, but not `RAH  rah`, even though the original capturing subpattern is matched caselessly.

There may be more than one back reference to the same subpattern. If a subpattern has not actually been used in a particular match, any back references to it always fail. For instance, the pattern:

```
(a|(bc))\2
```

always fails if it starts to match `a` rather than `bc`.

All digits following a backslash are taken as part of a potential back reference number. If the pattern continues with a digit character, some delimiter must be used to terminate the back reference. If the `(?x)` option is set, this can be whitespace. Otherwise an empty comment can be used.

A back reference that occurs inside the parentheses to which it refers fails when the subpattern is first used, so, for example, `(a\1)` never matches. However, such references can be useful inside repeated subpatterns. For example, the pattern:

```
(a|b\1)+
```

matches any number of `a`s and also `aba`, `ababbaa` and so on. At each iteration of the subpattern, the back reference matches the character string corresponding to the previous iteration. In order for this to work, the pattern must be such that the first iteration does not need to match the back reference. This can be done using alternation, as in this example, or by a quantifier with a minimum of zero.

# B.13 Assertions

An assertion is a test on the characters following or preceding the current matching point that does not actually consume any characters. The simple assertions coded as \b, \B, \A, \Z, \z, ^, and $ are described in section B.3. More complicated assertions are coded as subpatterns. There are two kinds: those that look ahead of the current position in the subject string, and those that look behind it.

An assertion subpattern is matched in the normal way, except that it does not cause the current matching position to be changed. Lookahead assertions start with (?= for positive assertions and (?! for negative assertions. For example:

```
\w+(?=;)
```

matches a word followed by a semicolon, but does not include the semicolon in the match, and the following:

```
foo(?!bar)
```

matches any occurrence of foo that is not followed by bar. Note that the apparently similar pattern:

```
(?!foo)bar
```

does not find an occurrence of bar that is preceded by something other than foo; it finds any occurrence of bar whatsoever, because the assertion (?!foo) is always true when the next three characters are bar. A lookbehind assertion is needed to achieve the other effect.

Lookbehind assertions start with (?<= for positive assertions and (?<! for negative assertions. For example:

```
(?<!foo)bar
```

does find an occurrence of bar that is not preceded by foo. The contents of a lookbehind assertion are restricted such that all the strings it matches must have a fixed length. The only permitted repetition is a quantifier with a fixed value (for example, a{4}); unlimited repeats are forbidden. However, if there are several alternatives in a lookbehind assertion, they do not all have to have the same fixed length. Thus:

```
(?<=bullock|donkey)
```

is permitted, but:

```
(?<!dogs?|cats?)
```

causes an error at compile time. Branches that match different length strings are permitted only at the top level of a lookbehind assertion. This is an extension compared with Perl 5.6, which requires all branches to match the same length of string. An assertion such as:

```
(?<=ab(c|de))
```

is not permitted, because its single top-level branch can match two different lengths, but it is acceptable if rewritten to use two top-level branches:

```
(?<=abc|abde)
```

Similarly, the previous example could be rewritten as:

```
(?<!dog|cat|dogs|cats)
```

The implementation of lookbehind assertions is, for each alternative, to temporarily move the current position back by the fixed number of characters, and then try to match. If there are insufficient characters before the current position, the match fails. Lookbehinds in conjunction with once-only subpatterns can be particularly useful for matching at the ends of strings; an example is given at the end of the section on once-only subpatterns.

Several assertions (of any sort) may occur in succession. For example:

```
(?<=\d{3})(?<!999)foo
```

matches `foo` preceded by three digits that are not `999`. Notice that each of the assertions is applied independently at the same point in the subject string. First, there is a check that the previous three characters are all digits, then there is a check that the same three characters are not `999`. This pattern does *not* match `foo` preceded by six characters, the first of which are digits and the last three of which are not `999`. For example, it does not match `123abcfoo`. A pattern to do that is as follows:

```
(?<=\d{3}...)(?<!999)foo
```

This time, the first assertion looks at the preceding six characters, checking that the first three are digits. Then the second assertion checks that the preceding three characters are not `999`.

Assertions can be nested in any combination. For example:

```
(?<=(?<!foo)bar)baz
```

matches an occurrence of `baz` that is preceded by `bar`, which, in turn, is not preceded by `foo`, while the following:

```
(?<=\d{3}(?!999)...)foo
```

is another pattern that matches `foo` preceded by three digits and any three characters that are not `999`.

Assertion subpatterns are not capturing subpatterns, and may not be repeated, because it makes no sense to assert the same thing several times. If any kind of assertion contains capturing subpatterns within it, these are counted for the purposes of numbering the capturing subpatterns in the whole pattern. However, substring capturing is carried out only for positive assertions, because it does not make sense for negative assertions.

Assertions count towards the maximum of 200 nested parenthesized subpatterns.

# B.14 Once-only subpatterns

With both maximizing and minimizing repetition, failure of what follows normally causes the repeated item to be re-evaluated to see if a different number of repeats allows the rest of the pattern to match. Sometimes it is useful to prevent this, either to change the nature of the match, or to cause it to fail earlier than it otherwise might, when the author of the pattern knows there is no point in carrying on.

Consider, for example, the pattern \d+foo when applied to the following subject line:

```
123456bar
```

After matching all six digits and then failing to match foo, the normal action of the matcher is to try again with only five digits matching the \d+ item, and then with four, and so on, before ultimately failing. Once-only subpatterns provide the means for specifying that once a portion of the pattern has matched, it is not to be re-evaluated in this way, so the matcher would give up immediately on failing to match foo the first time. The notation is another kind of special parenthesis, starting with (?> as in this example:

```
(?>\d+)bar
```

This kind of parenthesis "locks up" the part of the pattern it contains once it has matched, and a failure further into the pattern is prevented from backtracking into it. Backtracking past it to previous items, however, works as normal.

An alternative description is that a subpattern of this type matches the string of characters that an identical standalone pattern would match, if anchored at the current point in the subject string.

Once-only subpatterns are not capturing subpatterns. Simple cases such as the previous example can be thought of as a maximizing repeat that must swallow everything it can. So, while both \d+ and \d+? are prepared to adjust the number of digits they match in order to make the rest of the pattern match, (?>\d+) can only match an entire sequence of digits.

This construction can of course contain arbitrarily complicated subpatterns, and it can be nested.

Once-only subpatterns can be used in conjunction with lookbehind assertions to specify efficient matching at the end of the subject string. Consider a simple pattern such as the following:

```
xyz$
```

Suppose it is applied to a string that does not match. Because matching proceeds from left to right, PCRE will look for each x in the subject and then see if what follows matches the rest of the pattern. Now suppose the pattern is specified as follows:

```
^.*xyz$
```

The initial .* matches the entire string at first, but when this fails (because there is no following x), it backtracks to match all but the last character, then all but the last two characters, and so on. Once again, the search for x covers the entire string, from right to left, so we are no better off. However, if the pattern is written as:

```
^(?>.*)(?<=xyz)
```

there can be no backtracking for the .* item; it can match only the entire string. The subsequent lookbehind assertion does a single test on the last three characters. If it fails, the match fails immediately. For long strings, this approach makes a significant difference to the processing time.

When a pattern contains an unlimited repeat inside a subpattern that can itself be repeated an unlimited number of times, the use of a once-only subpattern is the only way to avoid some failing matches taking a very long time indeed. The following pattern:

```
(\D+|<\d+>)*[!?]
```

matches an unlimited number of substrings that either consist of non-digits, or digits enclosed in <>, followed by either ! or ?. When it matches, it runs quickly. However, if it is applied to the following:

```
aaaaaaaaaaaaaaaaaaaaaaaaaaaaaaaaaaaaaaaaaaaaaaaaaaaaa
```

it takes a long time before reporting failure. This is because the string can be divided between the two repeats in a large number of ways, and all have to be tried.[1] If the pattern is changed to the following:

```
((?>\D+)|<\d+>)*[!?]
```

---

[1]   The example used [!?] rather than a single character at the end, because both PCRE and Perl have an optimization that allows for fast failure when a single character is used. They remember the last single character that is required for a match, and fail early if it is not present in the string.

sequences of non-digits cannot be broken, and failure happens quickly.

# B.15 Conditional subpatterns

It is possible to cause the matching process to obey a subpattern conditionally or to choose between two alternative subpatterns, depending on the result of an assertion or whether a previous capturing subpattern matched or not. The two possible forms of conditional subpattern are:

```
(?(condition)<yes-pattern>)
(?(condition)<yes-pattern>|<no-pattern>)
```

If the condition is satisfied, the yes-pattern is used; otherwise the no-pattern (if present) is used. If there are more than two alternatives in the subpattern, a compile-time error occurs.

There are two kinds of condition. If the text between the parentheses consists of a sequence of digits, the condition is satisfied if the capturing subpattern of that number has previously matched. Consider the following pattern, which contains non-significant whitespace to make it more readable (assume the `(?x)` option) and is divided into three parts for ease of discussion:

```
( \( )?    [^()]+    (?(1) \) )
```

The first part matches an optional opening parenthesis, and if that character is present, sets it as the first captured substring. The second part matches one or more characters that are not parentheses. The third part is a conditional subpattern that tests whether the first set of parentheses matched or not. If they did (that is, if the subject started with an opening parenthesis), the condition is true, and so the yes-pattern is executed and a closing parenthesis is required. Otherwise, since the no-pattern is not present, the subpattern matches nothing. In other words, this pattern matches a sequence of non-parentheses, optionally enclosed in parentheses.

If the condition is not a sequence of digits, it must be an assertion. This may be a positive or negative lookahead or lookbehind assertion. Consider this pattern, again containing non-significant whitespace:

```
(?(?=[^a-z]*[a-z])  \d{2}-[a-z]{3}-\d{2}  |  \d{2}-\d{2}-\d{2} )
```

The condition is a positive lookahead assertion that matches an optional sequence of non-letters followed by a letter. In other words, it tests for the presence of at least one letter in the subject. If a letter is found, the subject is matched against the first alternative; otherwise, it is matched against the second. This pattern matches strings in one of the two forms *<dd-aaa-dd>* or *<dd-dd-dd>*, where *<aaa>* are letters and *<dd>* are digits.

# B.16 Comments

The sequence (?# marks the start of a comment that continues up to the next closing parenthesis. Nested parentheses are not permitted. The characters that make up a comment play no part in the pattern matching at all.

If the (?x) option is set, an unescaped # character outside a character class introduces a comment that continues up to the next newline character in the pattern.

# B.17 Recursive patterns

Consider the problem of matching a string in parentheses, allowing for unlimited nested parentheses. Without the use of recursion, the best that can be done is to use a pattern that matches up to some fixed depth of nesting. It is not possible to handle an arbitrary nesting depth. Perl provides a facility that allows regular expressions to recurse (among other things). It does this by interpolating Perl code in the expression at runtime, and the code can refer to the expression itself. A Perl pattern to solve the parentheses problem can be created in the following manner:

```
$re = qr{\( (?: (?>[^()]+) | (?p{$re}) )* \)}x;
```

The (?p{...}) item interpolates Perl code at runtime, and, in this case, refers recursively to the pattern in which it appears. Obviously, PCRE cannot support the interpolation of Perl code. Instead, the special item (?R) is provided for the specific case of recursion. The following PCRE pattern solves the parentheses problem (assume the (?x) option is set so that whitespace is ignored):

```
\( ( (?>[^()]+) | (?R) )* \)
```

First, it matches an opening parenthesis. Then, it matches any number of substrings, which can either be a sequence of non-parentheses, or a recursive match of the pattern itself (that is, a correctly parenthesized substring). Finally, there is a closing parenthesis.

This particular example pattern contains nested unlimited repeats, and so the use of a once-only subpattern for matching strings of non-parentheses is important when applying the pattern to strings that do not match. For example, when it is applied to the following:

```
(aaaaaaaaaaaaaaaaaaaaaaaaaaaaaaaaaaaaaaaaaaaaaaaaaaaaaaaaa()
```

it yields "no match" quickly. However, if a once-only subpattern is not used, the match runs for a very long time indeed because there are so many different ways the + and * repeats can carve up the subject, and all have to be tested before failure can be reported.

The values set for any capturing subpatterns are those from the outermost level of the recursion at which the subpattern value is set. If the previous pattern is matched against the following:

```
(ab(cd)ef)
```

the value for the capturing parentheses is ef, which is the last value taken on at the top level. If additional parentheses are added, giving the following:

```
\( ( ( (?>[^()]+) | (?R) )* ) \)
```

the string they capture is ab(cd)ef, the contents of the top level parentheses. If there are more than 15 capturing parentheses in a pattern, PCRE has to obtain extra memory to store data during a recursion. If no memory can be obtained, it saves data for the first 15 capturing parentheses only, as there is no way to give an out-of-memory error from within a recursion.

# B.18 Performance

Certain items that may appear in patterns are more efficient than others. It is more efficient to use a character class like [aeiou] than a set of alternatives such as (a|e|i|o|u). In general, the simplest construction that provides the required behaviour is usually the most efficient.

When a pattern begins with .* and the (?s) option is set, the pattern is implicitly anchored by PCRE, since it can match only at the start of a subject string. However, if (?s) is not set, PCRE cannot make this optimization, because the . metacharacter does not then match a newline, and if the subject string contains newlines, the pattern may match from the character immediately following one of them, instead of from the very start. For example, the pattern:

```
(.*) second
```

matches the subject first\nand second (where \n stands for a newline character) with the first captured substring being and. In order to do this, PCRE may have to try the match several time, starting after every newline in the subject as well as at the start.

If you are using such a pattern with subject strings that do not contain newlines, the best performance is obtained by setting (?s), or starting the pattern with ^.* to indicate explicit anchoring. That saves PCRE from having to scan along the subject looking for a newline to restart at.

Beware of patterns that contain nested indefinite repeats. These can take a long time to run when applied to a string that does not match. Consider the following pattern fragment:

```
(a+)*
```

This can match `aaaa` in 33 different ways,[1] and this number increases very rapidly as the string becomes longer. When the remainder of the pattern is such that the entire match is going to fail, PCRE has, in principle, to try every possible variation, and this can take an extremely long time.

An optimization catches some of the more simple cases such as:

    (x+)*y

where a literal character follows. Before embarking on the standard matching procedure, PCRE checks that there is a `y` later in the subject string, and if there is not, it fails the match immediately. However, when there is no following literal, this optimization cannot be used. You can see the difference by comparing the behaviour of:

    (x+)*\d

with the previous pattern. The former gives a failure almost instantly when applied to a whole line of x characters, whereas the latter takes an appreciable time with strings longer than about 20 characters.

---

[1]  The `*` repeat can match 0, 1, 2, 3, or 4 times, and for each of those cases other than 0, the `+` repeat can match different numbers of times.

# Index

Index entries for Exim variables such as *$local_part*, command line options such as -bp, and other configuration items that start with a non-alphabetic character (such as +include_unknown and :include:), are sorted without their leading special character. All options are indexed directly under their own names, but string expansion operators are placed under *expansion*. I have not indexed Appendix A, because the expansion items and variables appear there in alphabetical order.

# About the author

Philip Hazel has a Ph.D. in applied mathematics, but has spent the last 30 years writing general-purpose software for the Computing Service at the University of Cambridge in England. Since moving from an IBM mainframe to Unix in the early 1990s, Philip has become more and more involved with email. He started developing Exim in 1995 and PCRE (the regular expression library) in 1997. Since then, most of his working time has been spent maintaining and extending Exim.

# Colophon

This book was created on a Sun workstation running Solaris, mostly using applications software written by Philip Hazel. The original source was written using the NE text editor to create a marked-up file for processing by the SGCAL text formatting program. The figures were created in the Aspic drawing language that is integrated with SGCAL. The main output of SGCAL was converted into PostScript, at which point the EPSF screenshots were incorporated. The auxiliary output for the index and the table of contents was processed by Perl scripts to make further input that was re-processed by SGCAL. Finally, a Perl script joined the separate PostScript files together to form the complete book.

The main text of the book is set in Times fonts. The headings are set in Helvetica; the examples use Courier.

# Sponsors

The production of this book was sponsored by the following organizations:

SWITCH – The Swiss Education and Research Network
Linpro AS, Norway
Multithread Consultants Ltd, UK
Nova Web Hosting Ltd, UK

The author and publisher are grateful for this support from the Exim community. In the following pages you can read more about the sponsors and what they do.

# SWITCH

The Swiss Education & Research Network

For 15 years, the **SWITCH** Foundation has been operating the Swiss science network which guarantees the universities access to the information society. The high-performance network links users in Switzerland with each other, with Europe and with countries overseas. Operating the science network laid the foundation for SWITCH to establish the necessary know-how and the technological basis for the operation of the registration office for .ch and .li domain names.

With the science network as a foundation, the next step is to make e-Academia become reality where it is possible to work on the knowledge available in Switzerland at any time and from any location. When we speak of e-Academia we mean the community of students, researchers and lecturers who are carrying the free flow of ideas, the pooling of discoveries and the scientific debate into the new digital arena.

SWITCH's projects and services are making e-Academia a reality. Our high-performance network is its essential foundation. The other components are built on that: the authentication and authorization infrastructure, SWITCHaai, for secure and mutually compatible access to resources at different locations. Then SWITCHmobile, which allows all individual users to work with their own personal computer environment, regardless of which university that happen to be at in Switzerland. And finally, SWITCHvconf, the powerful video-conferencing infrastructure, which greatly simplifies working together in teams spread over several locations.

Since the introduction of the Internet in Switzerland, SWITCH has been registering domain names ending in .ch and .li. SWITCH thus has many years of experience and with its specialist expertise it is able to offer various tailor made services relating to the registration of domain names.

All standard processes on the internet are fully automated and are embedded in sophisticated technical and security concepts. Domain names ending in .ch and .li can be registered online at any time. It is a main concern for SWITCH to account for the language diversity in Switzerland. This is why all services related to domain names are available in German, French, Italian and English.

For many years Exim has played a key role for SWITCH. It enables a hassle free, cost effective and secure working environment. We wish to express our thanks to the community for Exim and want to encourage you to continue developing such sophisticated software in the future.

For more information about SWITCH and its services please contact:

SWITCH
P.O. Box
CH-8021 Zurich
Switzerland

Phone: +41 1 268 15 15
Fax: +41 1 268 15 68
e-mail: info@switch.ch
www.switch.ch

# Linpro's pocket guide to tuning Exim 4

## #1 Avoid external lookups

Contacting another server to acquire information adds complexity and decreases performance. Using a database or an LDAP catalogue as an information source is probably a good idea, but you should dump the relevant information to CDB files (or something similar) locally on the servers running Exim.

## #2 Optimize your backends

Building up connections is expensive. If you must use a backend server, be sure to optimize it as much as possible. MySQL can be configured to recycle its threads to reduce connection times. Be sure to choose the appropriate table type and tune well. If you use OpenLDAP as your backend enable the appropriate indexes.

## #3 Make sure your storage is fast

Especially on synchronous activity. A battery powered write-back cache will speed up the *fsync()* calls without having your Exim violate RFC 2821. SCSI is always faster than IDE.

## #4 Keep your queues small

The larger the queues, the slower Exim. If you're load balancing, use queue size as the key for weighting. We've written a tool with this purpose in mind, freely available from *http://www.linpro.no/projects/lvs-kiss/*. You should also consider using different servers for incoming and outgoing mail, delivering the former is usually much easier and faster than the latter.

## #5 Avoid bouncing

Strive to be as certain as possible that you can deliver the message before accepting it in the SMTP dialogue. Attempting to deliver a bounce is very expensive – undeliverable bounces will often do nothing but clog your queue. If you're doing content filtering, such as virus scanning, do so using Exim's ingenious *local_scan()* interface.

## #6 Avoid "verify = recipient"

Though using this in your RCPT ACL seems like a quick and easy way to determine whether or not you accept mail for the recipient, be aware of the fact that Exim routes mail to the very end when verifying the recipient. This includes reading the user's *.forward* file, possibly residing on a remote server. Instead, verification should be done locally and preferably independent of other servers in the solution.

Still too slow? Hire assistance from us. We really know how to work Exim and can also offer excellent programmers, system administrators/integrators and courses.

Linpro AS, Norway
*info@linpro.no*
*http://www.linpro.no/*

# MultiThread Consultants Limited

MultiThread Consultants (*http://www.multithread.co.uk*) provides Exim expertise to many clients ranging from the SME to global multinationals on both Linux and Solaris platforms. With extensive practical experience in building, securing and running Exim servers 24×7 we know that it provides our customers with a flexible, stable, low cost mail platform. MultiThread provides custom configurations incorporating antivirus and tools for performance monitoring, and also provides practical advice on scalability. In sponsoring Philip's book we are happy to put something back into the development of a fine Open Source product.

---

# Nova Web Hosting Limited

NovaWeb has carved a niche in the web hosting market by creating a secure, stable, modern and high performance web hosting platform while maintaining an affordable and flexible pricing structure. The platform is based on our custom developed Nova Internet Cluster Architecture which is based on enterprise class SUN servers running best of breed opensource software. All of our systems have been designed with no single point of failure including features such as dual diversely routed network connections, load balancers, hot spare servers and clustered web, email and database servers. In an effort to better fit our customer's requirements, all our packages are composed of a number of flexible options which can be customised further even after the signup process is complete.

As part of our philosophy of using best of breed opensource software we have selected Exim for all of our email requirements. Exim is running in a clustered environment and all routing and email delivery is achieved via dynamically created maps from our replicated MySQL backend.

Further information is available on *http://www.novawebhosting.net*.

---

# About UIT Cambridge

UIT Cambridge was established in 1992.

In parallel with our publication of specialist computer books, UIT is a networking and Internet security company, specializing in firewalls and e-mail systems. We supply both products and technical services. Our flagship project has been the introduction and development of Internet and Web services for a well-known international financial newspaper, and designing their very-high-performance, high-reliability mail system. For more information see our Web page: *http://www.uit.co.uk*.

- Our Product Division supplies the latest tools and applications for building and maintaining corporate networks, including a full range of firewall appliances, server software and virus scanners.

- Our Services Division offers installation and configuration of firewalls, virus scanning, e-mail, and server software.

- We offer a range of specialist technical training courses, delivered on-site at your premises. See: *http://www.uit.co.uk/services/index.htm#2*.

---

# So you want to write?

Do you have a book in you? Have you knowledge and experience of computer technology that you want to share with others? If so, please contact us at *editor@uit.co.uk*.

Your initial idea doesn't have to be very detailed – just an outline of what the book is about, who you think will want to read it, and why you are the right person to write it. All our editorial people have previously worked as network or system managers, or developers, so they are ideally placed to help you refine your idea and provide the editorial guidance and support that you need.

We are also keen to hear from experts in a topic or a technology who are interested in reviewing manuscripts for technical accuracy and relevance.

---